KEYNES AND ECONOMIC POLICY

Keynes and Economic Policy

The Relevance of *The General Theory* after Fifty Years

Edited by
Walter Eltis
and
Peter Sinclair

Introduced by The Rt Hon Nigel Lawson, MP

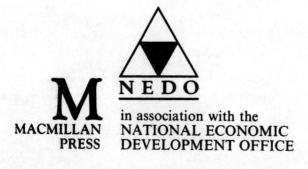

MACMILLAN PRESS

NEDO
in association with the
NATIONAL ECONOMIC
DEVELOPMENT OFFICE

© National Economic Development Office 1988

First edition 1988
Reprinted 1990

Published by
THE MACMILLAN PRESS LTD
Houndmills, Basingstoke, Hampshire RG21 2XS
and London
Companies and representatives
throughout the world

Typeset by Latimer Trend & Company Ltd
Plymouth
Printed and bound in Great Britain by
Antony Rowe Ltd
Chippenham, Wiltshire

British Library Cataloguing in Publication Data

Keynes and economic policy: the relevance
of the General theory after fifty years.
1. Economics, Keynes, John Maynard, 1883-
1946. General theory of employment interest
and money—Critical studies
I. Eltis, W.A. (Walter Alfred), 1933-
II. Sinclair, P.J.N. (Peter J.N.)
330.15'6

ISBN 0-333-46997-6

Contents

Contents

Preface

John Maynard Keynes published *The General Theory of Employment, Interest and Money* in February 1936, when UK unemployment was considerably in excess of 10 per cent. With unemployment again close to 10 per cent fifty years later, we thought it would be interesting and useful to invite an expert group of economists to examine how far the arguments which Keynes presented in 1936 are still central to the explanation of our failure to achieve high employment. We are delighted that so many very distinguished economists from government and academic life agreed that this question is worthy of close attention. The Chancellor of the Exchequer's 'Introduction' to the Conference which opens this volume underlines the directness of its subject to the concerns of government.

The National Economic Development Office's close links with government and the universities mean that we are uniquely placed to provide a forum where experts drawn from both these worlds can meet to discuss economic questions of national importance. When we sent our invitations to potential participants in December 1986 we outlined the questions we wished them to address in the following terms.

We regard it as vitally important to those responsible for the management of economics to know which elements of Keynes's seminal contribution are still relevant to the formulation of economic policy. Some of his central propositions have been superseded by more recent theoretical work, while others have been discredited by events in the 1970s and the 1980s. At the same time there may well be theoretical and empirical support for the continuing relevance and practical applicability of several of the propositions of the General Theory. It is crucial to know which propositions ought now to be discarded and which still stand, albeit in modified form.

We suggested that discussion should focus on the following questions:

The adequacy of market forces for the achievement of high employment. Did Keynes underrate market economies' powers of self-correction, or is there justification for his belief that there is a general case for government macroeconomic intervention?

Money wages and employment. Keynes insisted that even large falls in money wages would not necessarily raise employment. Does it now appear that money and real wage movements matter more than he supposed?

The effect of fiscal reflation upon employment. Keynes argued that when labour was in excess supply fiscal reflation would always raise effective demand and reduce unemployment, but how much of his belief in the efficacy of fiscal reflation still stands?

The inflationary impact of expansionary fiscal policy. Was Keynes right to believe that expansionary fiscal policy would not significantly raise the inflation rate when unemployment was high?

The significance of public sector borrowing. How far do the adverse long-term effects of persistent government borrowing undermine the short-term case for deficit financed expansion?

Policy to reduce interest rates. Is there still support for the view that monetary expansion will generally reduce interest rates?

Should reflationary fiscal policy have priority over monetary policy? Does the experience of the 1960s, and 1970s and the 1980s support the widely held Keynesian view that reflationary fiscal policy should have priority over monetary policy?

The international dimension. Countries which pursue Keynesian policies in isolation often experience deteriorating trade which forces their reversal: is it practical for countries to co-operate internationally to implement Keynesian expansion?

History. How well do Keynesian explanations of high unemployment in the 1950s and the 1960s, and the rise in unemployment in the 1970s and the 1980s stand up?

The contributors who accepted our invitation each addressed their attention to one of these topics. They presented earlier versions of their papers when we met in London on 15–18 September 1987 to discuss these questions, and the final versions which appear in this volume have benefited greatly from the opportunity for debate and discussion that this offered.

The major parties represented on the National Economic Development Council are HM Government, the Trades Union Congress and the Confederation of British Industry. Since these have differing political priorities, it is incumbent on us to approach all questions from a politically neutral standpoint where our sole interest is the elucidation and clarification of the principal issues that need to be resolved. Needless to say, we are aware that academic economists have a variety of approaches to practical questions which often have strong political implications. We therefore considered it important that each of these central questions should be addressed by two economists, where one could be expected to be sympathetic to a Keynesian approach while the other would be likely to argue that this has been superseded by more recent work. The distinguished economists who accepted our invitation have not all written along the lines we predicted, but the overall balance of the book is about as we expected.

A seminal event in the history of the UK economic profession was a letter which 364 economists addressed to *The Times* in March 1981 which was strongly critical of the economic policies of Mrs Thatcher's government. Of the UK contributors to this volume who hold university teaching posts in economics, five signed that letter, while six did not, which suggests that we have approximately equal representation of potential supporters and critics. Our authors also include the most senior economists in HM Treasury, the Bank of England and the Trades Union Congress, and a number who hold posts overseas. We are grateful to the participants for the very great trouble they have taken to produce articles which are undoubtedly of very high quality.

The originator of the project which has led to this book and the prime mover in seeing it through every stage to its fruition has been Walter Eltis, the Economic Director of the National Economic Development Office from 1986–1988. He has edited the articles in collaboration with his Oxford colleague, Peter Sinclair, who looked after the more technical aspects, and in the final chapter he writes of some of the conclusions that emerge. The administration of the Conference and presentation of the articles for publication has been handled by Inge Mann. I hope that the book and the conclusions to be drawn from it will receive close attention from those who are concerned with the theory and practice of economic management and will assist debate on the best practicable methods of returning to high employment.

JOHN CASSELS
Director General
National Economic Development Office

List of the Contributors

Michael J. Artis   Professor of Economics, University of Manchester

Alex Bowen   Economic Adviser, National Economic Development Office

Francis Breedon   Research Officer, London Business School

Alan Budd   Professor of Economics and Director, Centre for Economic Forecasting, London Business School

Sir Terence Burns   Chief Economic Adviser, HM Treasury and Head of the Government Economic Service

Bill Callaghan   Head of Economic Research, Trades Union Congress

W. Max Corden   Senior Adviser, Research Department, International Monetary Fund, Washington and Professor of Economics, Australian National University, Canberra

David Currie   Professor of Economics, Queen Mary College, London

Nicholas H. Dimsdale   Fellow of The Queen's College, Oxford

Walter Eltis   Economic Director, National Economic Development Office, and Fellow of Exeter College, Oxford

John S. Flemming   Chief Economist, Bank of England

Giampaolo Galli   Economist, Central Economic Research, Banca d'Italia, Rome

Ernst Helmstädter   Member of German Council of Economic Experts: Professor of Economics and Director of Institute of Economic Research, University of Munster

The Rt Hon Nigel Lawson MP   Chancellor of the Exchequer

Paul Levine   Senior Research Fellow, London Business School

Bennett T. McCallum   Professor of Economics, Carnegie-Mellon University, Pittsburgh

Rainer S. Masera   Director of Central Economic Research, Banca d'Italia, Rome

Robin C. O. Matthews   Master of Clare College, and Professor of Political Economy, University of Cambridge, and Chairman of Bank of England Academic Panel

Marcus Miller   Professor of Economics, University of Warwick

Terence C. Mills Lecturer in Econometrics, School of Economic Studies, University of Leeds

Patrick Minford Professor of Economics, University of Liverpool

Stephen Nickell Professor of Economics and Director of Institute of Economics and Statistics, Oxford University

Lord (Maurice) Peston Professor of Economics, Queen Mary College, London

Peter Sinclair Fellow of Brasenose College, Oxford

Peter Smith Research Fellow, London Business School

Alan Sutherland Research Associate, Parliamentary Unit, Department of Economics, University of Warwick

Christopher Taylor Head of Economic Research, Bank of England

Sir Alan Walters Professor of Political Economy, Johns Hopkins University and Personal Economic Adviser to the Prime Minister, 1981–3, and part-time since then

Geoffrey E. Wood Professor of Economics, City University Business School, London

Introduction

The Chancellor opened the Conference on 15 September 1987 with these reflections on the relevance of Keynes to UK economic policy in the 1980s:

'The difficulty', wrote Keynes in his Preface to the *General Theory*, 'lies, not in the new ideas, but in escaping from the old ones, which ramify, for those brought up as most of us have been, into every corner of our minds.'

For most of those attending this conference, I suspect, the ideas with which we were brought up were Keynesian ideas. Certainly that is true in my case, having read Politics, Philosophy and Economics at Oxford in the early fifties, with the endearingly eccentric Roy Harrod, Keynes's pupil and biographer, as my economics tutor.

Of course, practical Keynesianism – and I was always more interested in the practical application of economics to policy: my taste for theory was satisfied by philosophy – was rather different in those days from what it was subsequently to become.

The first text I was given to read was the 1944 Employment Policy White Paper (*Employment Policy*, CMD 6527, HMSO, May 1944): then seven years old and the *locus classicus* of the application of Keynesian theory to practical policy. A few quotations convey the flavour:

> Action taken by the Government to maintain expenditure will be fruitless unless wages and prices are kept reasonably stable. This is of vital importance to any employment policy, and must be clearly understood by all sections of the public. (Para 49)

Again,

> It would be a disaster if the intention of the Government to maintain total expenditure were interpreted as exonerating the citizen from the duty of fending for himself and resulted in a weakening of personal enterprise. For if an expansion of total expenditure were applied to cure unemployment of a type due, not to absence of jobs, but to failure of workers to move to places and occupations where they were needed, the policy of the Government would be frustrated and a dangerous rise in prices might follow. (Para 56)

And again,

> None of the main proposals contained in this Paper involves deliberate planning for a deficit in the National Budget in years of sub-normal trade activity ... (Para 74)

to the extent that the policies proposed in this Paper affect the balancing of the Budget in a particular year, they certainly do not contemplate any departure from the principle that the budget must be balanced over a longer period. (Para 77)

And so on.

It was subsequent degeneration of so-called Keynesian policy that led to the appalling and deeply damaging holocaust of inflation in the 1970s – something which Keynes himself, the author of *A Treatise on Money*, would have regarded with horror. Nevertheless it is hard to deny that there is inflationary bias at the heart of the *General Theory*.

If it took some time for the overriding need for macroeconomic policy to be directed towards the suppression of inflation to dawn on me, I can only plead the fact that, in those days, the inflationary danger was less obvious. During the first 10 years after I went down from Oxford, for example, inflation in Britain oscillated about an average of barely 3 per cent, with no sign of any acceleration.

Instead, my growing disenchantment began with, on the one hand, distaste for the increasing tendency for Government intervention in the micro-economy, of which incomes policy, of which I was publicly critical right from the start, was perhaps the prime but by no means the only example; and, on the other hand, disappointment with Britain's overall economic performance compared with our major competitors – although here I was perhaps slow to spot that our most successful competitors were those whose policies were least influenced by Keynesianism.

Unlike most of the Keynesians, Keynes himself was of course a free-market man through and through. Indeed, one of the purposes of the *General Theory* was to demonstrate that unemployment could be conquered in the context of a free economy – something which many in the 1930s had come to doubt, just as many in the 1970s had come to doubt that inflation could be conquered in a free democracy.

But the turning point, for me as no doubt for many (though clearly not all) others, was when inflation began to take off in the late sixties. It then became clearly the pre-eminent economic challenge, as it has remained ever since.

I suppose the views I finally arrived at can be summarised in terms of two interconnected reversals of the post-war conventional wisdom. The first is the conviction that the recipe for economic success is the greatest practicable market freedom within an overall framework of firm financial discipline – precisely how that financial discipline is best applied being essentially a second-order question, though clearly one of considerable practical and operational importance. This contrasts with the approach that culminated in the débâcle of the 1970s, in which ever-increasing erosion of market freedom was accompanied by the progressive abandonment of financial discipline.

The second reversal is that which I set out in my Mais lecture in 1984. That is to say, instead of seeking to use macroeconomic policy to promote growth and microeconomic policy to suppress inflation – or the symptoms of inflation – we must direct macroeconomic policy to the suppression of inflation and rely on microeconomic (or supply-side) policy to provide the conditions conducive to improved performance in terms of growth and employment.

I believe that any dispassionate observer must concede that, despite the problems that undoubtedly remain, the experience of the past eight years, and in particular the past five years, has vindicated this new (though in historical terms old) approach.

The budget deficit, even without the benefit of privatisation proceeds, has been more than halved, and real interest rates have consistently been historically high, while a succession of supply-side reforms designed to allow the market to work better have been introduced.

The result has not merely been five years of low inflation – though it needs to be lower still – but a sustained period of growth at some 3 per cent a year that is almost unprecedented in British economic history and during which we have out-performed most of our principal competitors.

I mentioned earlier my concern that the *General Theory*, despite the fact that it is unquestionably a work of considerable substance which has profoundly influenced economic thinking throughout the world, and indeed despite Keynes's earlier works, embodies a somewhat cavalier attitude towards inflation. This is seen, for example, in the notion, implicit in the *General Theory*, that inflation is a useful way of curing unemployment by reducing real wages. This attitude was no doubt a product of the circumstances of the great slump in which the book was written. But it is shared, with no similar excuse, by those who advocate so-called Keynesian policies today.

It is not shared by this Government. Nor, indeed, is it shared by the British people – otherwise I do not for a moment believe we would have been so convincingly re-elected to a third term of office. People know in their bones, now, not merely the immense economic and social harm that accelerating inflation is likely to inflict, but also how difficult and painful it is to bring it under control once it has been allowed to take off. Moreover, looking back, it must surely be clear that the success of so-called Keynesian policies in the fifties was not something that can now be repeated.

It is true the exchange rate regime of Bretton Woods imposed a degree of financial discipline which prevented the excesses that were later to occur. But it is also, I believe, the case that for many years after the war we were living in a transitional phase: not only did money illusion persist for a considerable time, but even though financial discipline was gradually being eroded, people for some time behaved as if it were still in place – just as for some years after the restoration of financial discipline by the present Government, people behaved as if it were *not* there: hence to a considerable extent the high level of unemployment we have sadly experienced.

The papers presented at the conference, and which are published in this book, deal with this and other key questions which are of continuing practical importance to all of us engaged in determining and executing economic policy.

Rt Hon Nigel Lawson MP
Chancellor of the Exchequer

Part I

The Adequacy of Market Forces for the Achievement of High Employment

1 Are Market Forces Adequate to Maintain Full Employment? If Not, Can Demand Management Policies be Relied Upon to Fill the Gap?

Michael J. Artis[1]

1.1 INTRODUCTION

Whatever the definition of Keynesian economics and whatever its differentiation from the 'economics of Keynes', it will be generally agreed that Keynes and the Keynesians both give a negative answer to the first of the questions in the title of this chapter and a positive one to the second. When the chips are down, this is what makes a Keynes(ian).

In this chapter, I first take a fresh look at what Keynes said on this subject, and then at the presumptions of mainstream Keynesian macroeconomics. This paves the way for a review of more recent contributions which, under the prodding of the new classical macroeconomics, have sought to identify sound microfoundations for market failure. In subsequent sections, we try to gather up these threads in order to see what basis now exists for Keynesian answers to the questions posed in the title and with what confidence these answers can be given.

1.2 THE GENERAL THEORY

What Keynes said in the *General Theory* and in later writings, notably in his 1939 *Economic Journal* paper 'Relative movements of real wages and output',[2] naturally provides the focus of much later attention. A summary of the salient points runs as follows:

(1) As a matter of fact, money wages are sticky downwards.

3

(2) The reason for this is that money wage rates are set asynchronously, so that any reduction in fact would represent a cut in *relative* pay for the group affected and would be resisted for this reason.

(3) Conditional on an assumption of diminishing returns, real wages and employment must be inversely correlated; it follows that a necessary condition for employment to rise is that real wages should fall.

(4) Because of (1), the required fall in real wages which might be brought about by money wage declines will not eventuate.

(5) *Further*, even if (1) did not apply,
   (a) the process of money and real wage declines would at best be very painful and protracted *and*
   (b) cannot be guaranteed to produce eventual full employment equilibrium. This is because, in a closed economy, the restorative adjustment process is *not* that lower real wages lead directly to more employment; rather, it is that lower money wages raise the real (wage unit-deflated) money supply, reduce interest rates and raise investment demand. But the liquidity trap represents a possible obstacle to the required decline in the interest rate.

(6) Monetary policy represents a complete alternative to a process of money wage declines and is preferable to it. It is subject to the same limitation from the liquidity trap obstacle, however. Public works programmes are not in principle subject to this limitation.

This summary shows the several facets of Keynes's argument. Given the assumption of diminishing returns, real wage declines are required to restore full employment, but these will be difficult to achieve through money wage adjustment for money wages are sticky for a good reason. In any case, *money wage declines are required* in order to raise demand through the real money supply-investment mechanism, another link, which may fail if there is an obstacle to the required fall in the interest rate. If the link does fail, public works policies are needed. If it does not fail, monetary policy is a superior alternative to money wage adjustment. The key role played in the argument by the assumption of diminishing returns deserves stress because, as Corry (1984) has emphasised, Keynes adopted this assumption as a 'stylised fact' and treated the inverse correlation of real wages and employment as a condition to be satisfied, not as an article of principled belief. When confronted with contrary evidence in papers by Tarshis and Dunlop, Keynes took the opportunity to state that if this contrary stylised fact could be adopted, 'it would be possible to simplify considerably the more complicated version of my fundamental explanation which I have expounded in my *General Theory*'.[3] Earlier in the same paragraph he contrasted his 'effective demand' explanation of the effects of public works with that of 'Professor Pigou, on the other hand, and many other economists . . . who explained the observed result by the reduction in real wages covertly effected by the rise in prices which ensued on the increase in effective demand. It was held that public investment policies . . . produced their effect by deceiving, so to speak, the working classes into accepting a lower real wage . . .'.[4] The paradox here, of course, is that it is precisely such a view of the *modus operandi* of public works to which Keynes's assumption of diminishing returns and the corresponding inverse correlation of real wages and employment appears to commit him.

Yet, in distancing himself from this explanation of the process Keynes was laying claim to having discovered, in the concept of effective demand, a more efficient tool for the analysis of the problem. Clearly, if Keynes had not felt obliged to accept as a datum the short-run inverse correlation of real wages and employment, he might have been able to demonstrate clearly how effective demand variations could lead to employment variations independently of their effects on real wages. But he did not take this route and it has been left to later writers to clarify the possibilities.

The other part of Keynes's argument was that monetary policy (or, equivalently flexible wages and prices) might encounter an obstacle preventing equilibration of the system in the form of a floor to the rate of interest (or 'liquidity trap'). Pigou's revelation of the real balance effect, however, put paid to this; with wage-price flexibility a recession would produce price declines which would not only increase the real value of the money supply, an effect Keynes already recognised, but would also raise effective demand directly, by making people feel wealthier as their real money balances rose and thus encouraging more spending.[5] For most of the profession, the demonstration of the real balance effect refocuses attention on the stickiness of the wage as the 'fundamental' problem, as in Modigliani's influential (1944) paper.

Thus, whilst in the *General Theory*, two markets are deficient – the labour market and the capital market – for the post-Keynesian neoclassical synthesis it was the labour market alone which was deficient, although 'practical' Keynesians added the product market too.

1.3 THE NEOCLASSICAL SYNTHESIS

Leijonhufvud (1986) articulated the curious divide in the development of macroeconomics which came to manifest itself in the post-war decades. On the one hand, the analytical appraisal of Keynes's contribution reduced it to the assumption of rigidity in money wages, itself often pejoratively portrayed as 'the assumption of money illusion' (this was unfair because, as we have already seen, Keynes articulated a good reason for downward wage rigidity). The import of this view, at any rate, was that Keynes's contribution as a theorist was trivial. By contrast, 'practical' macroeconomics 'got on with the job' with considerable vigour and éclat. For more than one generation of applied econometricians the Keynesian relationships provided the natural focus for the application of econometric method and this intellectual impulse was paralleled by the conversion of governments and international organisations around the world to economic policies of 'demand management'.

Practical macroeconomics first routinely assumed wage-price fixity, or more accurately the exogeneity of wages and prices to adjustments in output comprehended by the model, then conceded the Phillips curve as providing an endogeneity of prices (at one derivative up), yielding a smoothing of the inverse L-shaped aggregate supply schedule otherwise implied. Harry Johnson styled the Phillips curve as 'the only significant contribution to emerge from post-Keynesian theorizing' (Johnson, 1970); it filled a missing box in the Keynesian kit, providing an endogenous determination of money wages and thus an alternative to the view, adopted by some Keynesians that – given the commitment to full employment – the determination of money wages was essentially a 'political' matter exogenous to the short-run development of the economy. This latter view, set out by economists like Worswick (1944) and Kalecki (1944), had been adumbrated earlier by Robinson (1937). It can now be seen as correct in the essential respect that, in a game played between the authorities and the unions, for the authorities to commit themselves to maintaining a state of full employment is to underwrite and accommodate the wage demands emerging from inter-union rivalry.

Another aspect of the practical macroeconomics of this time which is worth stressing as it shapes contemporary concerns is that a good deal of work was done on the determination of prices. For a typical developed economy, this would mean consumer prices or the prices of domestically produced goods. The general verdict to emerge was that such prices were very sensitive to costs (usually 'normal' costs, a cycle-averaged measure), among which would be wages and various costs of imported goods, and invariably highly insensitive, given these costs, to demand factors.[6] Of course, demand factors could still be significant through their effect on wages or on 'flex-price' commodities imported from the rest of the world, when substituted into the final price equation. But subject to this caveat, these findings served to complement the suggestions of the Hall and Hitch (1939) full cost-pricing hypothesis, the Sweezy (1939) and Hall and Hitch (1939) kinked oligopoly demand curve and the 'administered price' approach, to the effect that prices are 'sticky'.

At an elementary level wage and price stickiness lend powerful support to the potential need and efficacy of the economic policy conclusions that were immediately derived from the *General Theory*. It will emerge below that in the post-war reapprasial of Keynesian theory it has also been discovered that wage and price rigidities have further subtle and fundamental implications. Before these can be set out, the existence of wage and price rigidities and their microeconomic underpinning needs to be explained.

1.4 MICROFOUNDATIONS

Keynesian macroeconomics can be thought of as the macroeconomic implications of fixed wages and prices. This way of looking at it, though, leaves open two questions.

First, it treats the issues of the microfoundations of wage-price rigidity as separable from the macro implications, so that the latter can be explored conditional on the first. But this could be misleading. It could be that the rationale underlying the fixity which is an inspired 'stylised fact' of the world is inconsistent with the macro outcomes modelled, conditional on this assumption. This appears to be true, for example, of the implicit contracts literature, as discussed below. Second, whether or not the methodological assumption is correct, it is important to find the reasons for wage-price rigidity; neither 'rigidity' nor 'unemployment' are unambiguously measureable concepts. Actually measured changes in unemployment, for example, might have an explanation which renders them fully explicable in terms of the equilibrium movement in unemployment. Rigidity is in any case relative: if the movements of unemployment are equilibrium movements, the fact that wages and prices do not respond to restore an earlier equilibrium should not be surprising. Some economists, confronted with statistical evidence of the stickiness of prices, will respond by saying that official price data fail to take adequate account of discounting, special deals and so on. Without a better understanding of how wage-price stickiness can arise, this kind of disagreement about (what *should* be) 'the facts of the matter' will continue. In any case, the prompting provided by adherents of the new classical macroeconomics to locate the microfoundations of market failure and thus to motivate a starting point for macroeconomics has been insistent and keenly felt.[7] Accordingly, there is much modern work exploring the microfoundations of rigid wages and prices, additionally providing some suggestion that credit and capital markets may, after all, be an important example of market failure of a certain type.

In what follows, we refer to this work in sequence, starting with explorations of the phenomenon of price rigidity.

1.4.1 Price stickiness

As already noted above, a large, empirically-based literature had appeared in the 1960s and early 1970s to support the practice of assuming fixity of prices, testifying to their inflexibility (or the inflexibility of the price-cost mark-up) with respect to demand, in contrast to their considerable flexibility with respect to costs. Rather little by way of theoretical justification was offered for what was essentially an empirical observation; full cost pricing and administered pricing 'theory' both seem more like redescriptions of the empirical observations than genuine theoretical support. The kinked oligopoly demand curve is a somewhat different case, but still seems a special one, applicable to small-group situations and resting on rather specific assumptions about rivals' reactions, perhaps rather difficult to generalise.[8]

More recent attempts to provide a rationale for price stickiness also, and necessarily, involve a departure from the assumption of the perfectly competitive – i.e. price-taking firm – but without implying that the industrial structure is necessarily oligopolistic. Barro (1972) analysed the case of a firm facing a downward-sloping demand curve and lump sum costs of changing prices. As is intuitively obvious in such a case, the fact that changing prices is itself costly imparts a stickiness to the price level in a way that depends critically on the magnitude and expected duration of shocks.

Although the costs of price change may include some components which are independent of the direction of change, it seems likely that a good part of the cost of a price change is the effect that the change will have on current and future prospective custom and this is not going to be independent of the direction of change. Contributions exploiting this perception in a search-theoretic framework include those due to Stiglitz (1979) and Okun (1981) among others. Okun pioneered the classic distinction between auction markets and customer markets, stressing that in the latter the existence of shopping costs necessarily provides the seller with an element of monopoly power. The kinked demand curve makes a fresh appearance in Okun, as it does in Stiglitz, but for different reasons from those introduced by the oligopoly theorists. The kink now reflects the existence of shopping costs. Because of these costs, customers will spend a period of time in search, locating a supplier with whom they believe they will afterwards be content to deal. There is an initial investment in locating a supplier. Henceforth, customers' knowledge – except for those still in the search phase – is localised. The customers know about the prices offered by the firm with which they customarily shop, but not about other prices. A reduction in the price will attract the business only of those individuals who are still searching and otherwise will simply reduce the profit on existing sales. As little price discrimination is possible, the firm thus views the price cut option very warily. A rise in its price, on the other hand, may induce existing regular customers to begin searching again. Perceiving this, the firm is inclined to refrain from raising its price. Thus, the price is sticky and the perceived demand curve kinked at its current level. Okun draws attention to the fact that it is widely considered 'reasonable' and 'fair' to raise prices when costs rise and attributes the prevalence of cost-oriented pricing to this attitude; this is another way of saying that if a supplier can succeed in convincing his customers that his price increase is cost-based he has already convinced them that search would merely confirm that all suppliers are indeed raising their prices based on common cost increases. Thus cost-based schemes relieve firms of the inhibition which would otherwise prevent them from raising prices.

The kinked demand curve, in a rather obvious way, introduces a rationale for sticky prices which makes possible macroeconomic equilibria which are very 'Keynesian': an early contribution in this vein is by Negishi (1976); later ones are by Woglom (1982) and Rowe (1987). In particular, such equilibria possess properties like monetary non-neutrality and bootstrapping, arising from the free-rider problem presented by the interdependence of pricing decisions through the kink in the firm's demand curve. In a recession, it may appear to no firm to be in its interest unilaterally to cut prices for the sorts of reasons given above; yet if all prices were cut, demand and output would be higher. The free rider aspect of the argument arises from the fact that whilst it is in no single firm's interest to initiate a process of price reduction that would lead, hypothetically, to a rise in demand it is in the collective interest that such a rise in demand should be initiated. In an obvious way, the government, as an external actor, can bring this about by demand management. The free rider aspect of the problem thus skirts the Lucas criterion that there are 'no $500 bills lying on the sidewalk'. There are such bills, but it requires collective action (through the government's management of demand) for them to be picked up. Individual agents pursuing their own self-interest cannot provide the correction needed.

The Stiglitz imperfect information approach and Hahn's conjectural equilibria analysis (Hahn, 1978) are similar in spirit, serving to pin price stickiness on the firm's pessimistic assessment of the return to price flexibility.

A potentially complementary analysis, which does not invoke the asymmetrical demand pessimism characteristic of a kinked demand curve approach highlights the presence of marketing costs. Howitt's (1985) contribution is in this vein; here prices are completely flexible, but as firms incur a transaction cost in marketing, the per unit size of which depends on aggregate demand, firms' perceptions of total aggregate demand are relevant to their pricing and output plans. In this analysis price flexibility[9] and quantity adjustments are not substitutes, but complementary.

1.4.2 Wage stickiness

Keynes contrasted nominal wage stickiness with real wage flexibility, and emphasised the importance of the asynchronous nature of wage contracting and the significance of interpersonal comparison, leading in such a context to downward money wage rigidity. The definition of involuntary unemployment associated with all of this derives directly from his assumption of diminishing returns and product market clearing. Involuntary unemployment arises when, in the event of a small fall in the real wage, both the demand for and actual stock of labour employed rise. Before contemplating some of the rationales offered for wage stickiness in more contemporary writing, a few comments on each of the elements in Keynes's approach to the question are in order.

Involuntary unemployment: of all Keynes's concepts, that of involuntary unemployment seems often the most dispensable. As stated, it is derived from his acceptance of the classical stylised facts about real wages and unemployment which appear to have been for Keynes an assumption inessential to his basic message. This already gives us some licence to depart from the requirement that unemployment be involuntary in this sense to be 'Keynesian'. But even in the case where the classical assumption holds, a demonstration of wage stickiness may be convincing only for one sector, albeit the larger part of the economy – the 'formal' or 'primary' sector. Alongside this sector, an informal or secondary sector may need to be admitted, for which it may be implausible to pose the same wage stickiness property. If so, a demand shock leading to redundancies in the formal sector produces potential employees in the informal clearing market. If these potential employees refuse to accept the lower wage offered in the informal market and join the dole queue, there is a clear sense in which this is 'voluntary' unemployment: i.e. *given the redundancy*, the worker chooses the dole queue in preference to the low wage available in the informal market. Even if the unemployment benefit is lower than the wage this may be a wholly rational choice.[10] Nevertheless, demand management could raise employment and output in the formal sector, reduce the dole queue and unambiguously improve utilities. There is, therefore, a clear sense in which such unemployment is Keynesian; i.e. it can be cured by Keynesian techniques. For a range of cases this is more important than whether, conditional on some forcing condition, unemployment is 'voluntarily' chosen.

Real or nominal wage stickiness: Keynes's argument for the existence of nominal wage stickiness appeals to a notion of fairness which Hicks later (in his *Crisis in Keynesian Economics*) deployed as an underpinning for 'real wage resistance', arguing that it had come to be seen as 'unfair' for a group of workers to accept a decline in real wages. This is quite important because in an inflationary environment an appropriate downward adjustment of real wages might not require nominal wage *cuts* and nominal wage resistance may appear irrelevant; all that is required is the acceptance of rates of nominal wage increase appropriately less than the inflation rate. This makes it seem as if in these conditions the necessary adjustments to maintain full employment might actually be easier to bring about. But 'real wage resistance' implies that this 'easy way out' is not in fact available. In the 1970s, many wage contracts *explicitly* incorporated cost-of-living escalator clauses and it might well seem that a form of Lucas critique applies: when experienced inflation is negligibly low, the real wage losses implied by nominal wage stickiness are low; when inflation is not negligible and is expected to characterise the environment, real wage resistance has to be made explicit.

At any rate, in the late 1960s and early 1970s empirical wage equation estimation took on board the notion of real wage resistance in one form or other: in the UK, the 'political economy' approach (e.g. Henry, Sawyer and Smith, 1976) coalesced with the technically inspired error correction model approach of Sargan (Sargan, 1971) to produce wage inflation estimates which incorporated real wages and static and dynamic homogeneity of wages in prices. The augmented Phillips curve similarly introduced the notion of dynamic homogeneity.

Fairness and staggering: the asynchronous nature of the wage bargaining process is vital to Keynes's account of the wage stickiness problem and those contemporary analyses which deploy a foundation of staggered wage contracts are well-called 'new Keynesian' in this respect.[12] They also have the property of ensuring that, even under rational expectations, a role for stabilisation policy exists as, in effect, part of the workforce at any time is bound by a precommitted wage and the authorities can make good this restriction on its opportunity set if they are able to engage in demand management policy. The fairness concept with which Keynes associated wage stickiness is not infrequently referred to in more contemporary analyses as a justification for practices associated with wage stickiness (see, especially, Okun, 1981). Clearly, fairness is a historically determined concept and some might want to argue that appeals to it as a motivation for wage stickiness do not go deep enough and even risk being vacuous and circular. Yet what can be deeper than a culturally determined attitude?

Microfoundations: contemporary analysis of the microfoundations of wage stickiness reveal a multiplicity of approaches without any single comprehensive framework being as yet dominant. Starting from the idea of wages being set in a contract, explicit or implicit, immediately establishes the idea of a social relationship being involved and admits the likelihood that notions of fairness will be relevant. In Okun (1981), the central idea is that wage contracting and personnel management contribute towards the goal of reducing turnover costs. A firm with a footloose labour force faces the prospect of repeated hiring and firing costs and forced reinvestments in training which make it profitable to consider ways of inducing employee loyalty. 'The development of rules and conventions for fair play becomes an essential element in the pursuit of efficiency' (Okun, 1981, pp. 84–5). An element of wage stickiness is a part of the resultant implicit contract. Okun develops the model initially without reference to unions, many of whose activities, however, 'can be viewed as formalizing and institutionalizing the conventions of the non-union career labour market'. These activities may in fact promote the reputation of the company's promises and enhance employee confidence in the employer – Okun concludes ... 'Thus collective bargaining can raise efficiency' (ibid., p. 123). Layoffs are a potential difficulty for this approach, to the extent that they represent a consequence of the sticky wage. Okun argues, however, that layoffs are a convincing demonstration that times are bad, whereas wage cuts would be seen as a breach of the implicit contract between employee and firm, the firm 'merely taking advantage of a weak labour market to enlarge its share of the bilateral surplus'. The suspicion that the wage cut might not in fact be necessary to maintain employment would sour relationships and so reduce effective future labour supply, thus always making it an unattractive option. On this basis, Okun argues that 'temporary downward adjustments of wage rates to save employment cutbacks may be viable only if they can be agreed upon by the firm and its workers' (ibid., p. 114). This prediction seems extensively confirmed, interestingly enough, in the sample of recent wage cuts in the UK cited by Carruth and Oswald (1986).

The turnover cost minimisation underlying Okun's argument seems a substantially more successful motivation than the implicit-contract-as-insurance-against-risk motivation that informed an important strand of the more formal contracts literature. In this literature (real) wage fixity emerges as a result of a Pareto-improving bargain in which risk-averse workers trade with risk-neutral firms. This asymmetry in attitudes towards risk allows a bargain to be struck in which workers receive a fixed (real) wage the certainty-equivalent value of which is less than that of their expected, stochastically variable, marginal product.[13] In effect, real (product) wages fall below the marginal product of labour in good states of the world by the amount of a premium paid by the workers to the firm, and exceed the marginal product in poor states of the world by the amount of an insurance payout paid by the firm to the workers. Layoffs may occur, but if they do they are *ex ante* actuarially agreed, and it is not easy to argue that they are involuntary at least, 'on average' (but individual employees might not have participated in the procedures leading to the contract and the membership of the union or negotiating body is unlikely to be homogenous). Taylor (1987a) following Akerlof and Miyazaki (1980) shows that actual unemployment, moreover, is actually stabilised in the sense of being less than would occur in a Walrasian spot auction market.

However, if firms are risk averse and also possess better information than workers, it is possible that unemployment will be higher under insurance-providing contracts, then under Walrasian spot auction markets (e.g. Taylor, 1987b); the argument – already rehearsed above – is that under such conditions, the contract wage will be state-contingent and in order to convince workers that the state of the world is bad enough to warrant a cut in the wage the firm may have to demonstrate a *reduction* in employment as well as a cut in the wage.

This hardly qualifies the unemployment as unambiguously involuntary, however. Once again, *ex ante* the contingency is provided for as part of the contract package, and whilst it is true that the promise of systematic demand management (assuming the authorities to possess superior information about the timing of shocks impinging on the system) can alter the prospects governing the bargain, it could also alter the outcome of a Walrasian spot auction market exchange process in the same circumstances; its differential effectiveness is not obvious, even if its practice is assumed to be costless.

As an underpinning for the staggered nominal wage contracts characteristic of new Keynesian theory, or more generally for Keynesian phenomena, the insurance-based contract approach does not seem, therefore, as promising as it once appeared. The theory motivates real, not nominal wage stickiness, gives no foundation for staggering as such and generates unemployment which is more accurately described as voluntary than Keynesian under either the traditional or alternative definitions. This is not to say that the approach does not produce some valuable insights and that it might not with suitable supplementation form a better foundation (for example, it is tempting to speculate that 'insider-outsider' theory can add involuntary unemployment, whilst real wage rigidity is certainly not foreign to Keynesian theorising).

An alternative approach to wage stickiness is provided by the *efficiency wage* concept. The key to the efficiency wage approach is the idea that direct control of work effort is prohibitively costly in many situations; if effort is positively related to the wage paid then the wage payment itself is an instrument that may be used to encourage productivity. More to the point, a reduction in the wage may cause such a reduction in work effort that it does not pay the employer to undertake the wage cut. In one version the negative impact of the wage cut is mediated through a damaging effect on 'morale'. A similar result, though, can be contained by appeal to turnover costs, as in Okun, or through adverse selection effects. Thus, if a wage cut induces quits and raises turnover costs, it may not be efficient to make the cut; if 'reservation' wages (the minimum wages that employees will accept) are positively correlated with ability, wage-cutting may produce a poor workforce. These and other ideas are spelt out in the introduction by Akerlof and Yellen to their book which collects together a number of important papers on the subject (Akerlof and Yellen, 1986). All these ideas are suggestive and prima facie plausible; they can produce predictions of equilibrium unemployment[14] as well as an aversion to wage-cutting.

However, they are also vulnerable to the suggestion that more complicated contracts, better screening or discrimination can reduce their plausibility. In particular, it is assumed that discrimination against new hires is not possible or practicable; because all must be paid the same wage, wage cutting at the margin of new hires is not possible and wage cuts across the board evoke bad morale, shirking, quits and other costly responses. Some current practices in the labour market both in the US and in the UK do suggest that discrimination against new hires is becoming more acceptable – though the extent to which, in the UK at least, this takes place in 'disguised' form[15] and its still comparative infrequency, even in the United States – is simultaneously testimony to the strength of traditional non-discriminating practices.

Some of the loose ends of contract theory and the efficiency wages approach can, it seems, be tied up by insider-outsider theory. According to this approach, with which much of Okun's sensitive discussion of the characteristics of 'career labour markets' is sympathetic, the pace in wage negotiation is set by an established core of workers, the insiders. For the kinds of reasons and in the kinds of ways established by Okun, firms are happy to attract the loyalty of their workers, with the result that the terms of wage contracts may make little concession to labour market conditions generally – unless these impinge, as in a deep recession, on the core workforce. In particular, across-the-board wage cuts will be resisted, though the theory would indicate some tolerance of two-tier wage contracts or disguised forms of them. The theory makes sense of empirical findings that the long-term unemployed do not 'count' in wage equation estimation, since, in effect, those who join the ranks of the long-term unemployed become 'outsiders', leaving the insiders as comprising the employed and the newly (short-term) unemployed. This line of argument suggests that the equilibrium or natural rate of overall unemployment will be subject to 'hysteresis', tending to rise (or fall) as actual unemployment rises (or falls).[16] Thus, as a recession begins and unemployment rises it is the ranks of the short-term unemployed which are particularly affected. After a time, the unemployment stops rising, and the short-term proportion falls as the long-term proportion rises. Wage inflation, which is first of all cut, now recovers: if hysteresis is complete, inflation will, *ceteris paribus* resume its old rate even whilst the *level* of unemployment has risen. The theory then implies that demand management may very well have long-term real effects, not merely short-term impacts. Insider-outsider theory applies most obviously, though not exclusively, to highly unionised employment; its 'loose end' is thus the casual labour market.

The literature is thus replete with a number of different approaches seeking to explain wage stickiness, real or nominal. None of these commands a consensus at the present time. Not all of them lend themselves to adoption as underpinning by neo-Keynesian macroeconomics. To admit this is clearly not to suggest that the phenomenon of wage stickiness does not exist, only that attempts to explain it are less than fully satisfactory. By the same token, it does not follow that demand management is mistaken or ineffective. Wage cuts *do* occur, but the evidence is overwhelming that they are rare even in situations of chronic depression and crisis; ' . . . something did happen to the British economy in the exceptional period of 1980–82. Real wages did not crash, but they trembled.' This is the verdict of Carruth and Oswald (1986). The point is that real wages *only* trembled.

1.4.3 Capital market imperfections

For completeness we should mention that imperfections in the capital market – not of the kind discussed by Keynes – have been invoked as an underpinning for Keynesian style policy by some writers, notably Stiglitz. Greenwald and Stiglitz (1987), it seems fair to say, give pride of place to capital and credit market imperfections in their account. In some respects the emphasis seems odd. We live in a period of unparalleled financial innovation and sophistication. Yet the proof of the necessary imperfection of credit markets is unexceptionable (Stiglitz and Weiss, 1981) and to this has been added the notion of the necessary failure of equity markets (Greenwald, Stiglitz and Weiss, 1984). The general point is that making loans (and borrowing money) is not like selling (buying) a can of beans. From the lenders' point of view, some appraisal of the customers' credit-worthiness is required. Information is less than perfect; a customer who offered to repay at a very high rate of interest would arouse the suspicion that he was not intending to make the onerous payments in any case (this is why he can afford to make the offer), so we cannot expect a 'free market' supply and demand solution. The response is to settle for uniformity of rates with collateral requirements and credit-rationing. Nor is the problem avoided in the equity market where, once again, the offer of a particularly attractive rate of return must arouse suspicion and information is inescapably imperfect.

1.5 REINTERPRETATIONS

The dependence of Keynesian macroeconomic conclusions on a starting point of wage price stickiness, which is obvious in a general way, is made explicit in the new formalisation of macroeconomics that appears in the writings of the 'disequilibrium macroeconomics' school, e.g. Barro and Grossman (1976) and Malinvaud (1977). The impetus for this new formalisation was provided by the 'reinterpretation' of Keynes which emerged in the late 1960s, exemplified in the work of Leijonhufvud (1968).

The outcome of the new formalisation is a framework for analysis which includes as special cases, the Walrasian equilibrium, Keynesian unemployment, classical unemployment, and Keynes's unemployment. Each of these, as discussed below, is seen as a possible temporary *equilibrium* position, dependent on the policy set and wage-price vector characterising the economy.

Actually, this outcome was a little way distant from Leijonhufvud's original reinterpretation. Leijonhufvud argued, particularly, that Keynes's use of the term 'equilibrium' and his preoccupation with comparative statics was essentially a use of a mode of language best suited to converting economists of the day. In fact, in Leijonhufvud's view, Keynes's analysis was to be understood as a disequilibrium analysis, one illustrating the hazards and difficulties of adjustment; in this respect Leijonhufvud particularly stressed the role of inelastic expectations in blocking the adjustment of asset prices.[17] In the development of his analysis Leijonhufvud invoked standard neoclassical general equilibrium analysis as a starting point for illuminating the Keynesian case. A key factor stressed in this is that whereas in the general equilibrium 'fable' an auctioneer 'solves' all the excess demand and supply equations before trading starts, in a 'real world' counterpart with no auctioneer, the solution cannot be assumed to be imposed from the start. Even if wages and prices are flexible the absence of the auctioneer means that trading will occur at prices different from their equilibrium values. In trading at these false prices, realised incomes will turn out differently from their equilibrium values and as they do so will further constrain the demands that agents can express for goods. In this way, given any initial disturbances from equilibrium, the realised income constraint on household purchases and the realised sales constraint on firms' employment decisions will produce an amplification. The analysis self-consciously emphasised the relevance of current income to expenditure and employment decisions and the notion of the multiplier as a deviation-amplifying phenomenon arising from the current or realised income constraint. This contribution complemented important insights by Clower (1965) and Patinkin (1965) and paved the way for the new formalisation of macroeconomics.

In this development the absence of an auctioneer was taken to justify an assumption of complete wage-price fixity. With this assumption, these analyses formally derived the multiplier (differing in detail from the conventional multiplier only in respect of special assumptions made about distribution), demonstrated the efficacy of demand management policy in certain regimes and the boundaries to its applicability. The taxonomy of regimes characteristic of this literature stresses the importance of a *combination* of absolute values of wages and prices (given nominal money stocks) and their *relative* value (real wages).

Both have to be right for Walrasian equilibrium to prevail. Keynesian unemployment arises when absolute prices and wages are too high, relative to the nominal money supply, to generate sufficient demand; real wages might be above, below, or by chance at their Walrasian value consistently with such a demand deficiency and neither the goods nor the labour market clears. Classical unemployment, by contrast, is characterised by too high a real wage: output and employment are not constrained by lack of demand, but by profit maximising employers' calculations that real wage costs make it unprofitable to expand output to extinguish the excess demand for goods. 'Keynes' unemployment then arises as a special case of classical unemployment where good prices happen to be at just that level which eliminates the excess demand for goods, though unemployment still reflects an excessively high real wage. The label derives from a reading of Chapter 2 of the *General*

Theory where Keynes adopts the convention of decreasing returns, and, making no claim that prices (as distinct from nominal wages) are sticky, appears to assume that they are fully flexible.

Because unemployment in the Keynesian region can be reduced and in some cases eliminated in principle without a *fall* in the real wage, on Keynes's own definition of it, which required that in the event of a small fall in the real wage both the demand for labour and the amount of labour actually forthcoming should rise, involuntary unemployment does not necessarily exist. Drazen (1980) reasonably proposes a new definition to cope with the point.[18] The analysis clearly achieves what escaped Keynes, namely a clear separation of the contribution of real wages and effective demand to the achievement of full employment, and does so without abandoning the assumption that technical conditions exhibit diminishing returns. Here, however, because effective demand may be the constraint on production the inverse correlation of wages and prices is not implied.

The success of the achievement is not unalloyed, however. The analysis is not dynamic; the outcomes described are those of equilibrium, temporary only in the light of an off-model assumption that between the periods analysed in the model wages and prices might gravitate towards some other values. It dispenses with a capital market and incurs a notable criticism in this respect, as outlined by Flemming (1973). If there *is* a process of adjustment of wages and prices in the 'Walrasian' direction, the existence of a perfect capital market, assuming that agents understand the direction of the adjustment, would allow agents to escape the current income constraint. The adjustment would not be blocked or confused by this constraint. Leijonhuf-vud, in a later paper (Leijonhufvud, 1981, Ch. 6) based his notion of the 'corridor' on this idea, arguing that the degree to which agents are able to base their current actions on 'permanent' rather than current income defines the width of a corridor within which the economy's self-righting properties can be trusted to work. Large or persistent shocks, however, may push the economy outside the corridor, straining the capacity of the market to buffer the multiplier effects. This establishes the relevance of the capital market to the questions at hand, in a different way from that stressed by Keynes.

1.6 THE OPEN ECONOMY

The *General Theory* is about a closed economy and it is natural to enquire whether openness makes a difference to the negative verdict in that volume on the adequacy of market forces to maintain full employment. On one view of the problem, openness does indeed make a difference, a crucial one, to the likelihood of the incidence of Keynesian market failure. Following the customary definition of the small open economy, Dixit (1978) argued that in such an economy the Keynesian regime, in the sense of Malinvaud, could not exist. The reasoning is that in such an economy the goods market by definition can always clear; firms can always sell overseas if they find it profitable to do so and cannot be constrained by a lack of demand. By the same token households can always avoid rationing by buying overseas which means that Malinvaud's category of classical unemployment in the full sense cannot apply. The labour market, however, need not be in equilibrium. In a traded-good economy this allows only observations of 'Keynes'-type classical unemployment to exist in the absence of equilibrium. On the same assumptions, Keynesian and full classical unemployment (in the sense of Malinvaud) can be restored as applicable categories either by introducing non-traded goods (e.g. Neary, 1980) or by breaking with the customary definition of the 'small open economy' as has been done in a number of subsequent papers in this area. Whether the exchange rate is fixed or floating is essentially immaterial to this result unless floating allows deviations of the real wage from equilibrium to be automatically eliminated. McKinnon's (1976) model of fiscal policy in a small open economy reflects the same set of considerations, though set out in terms of a conventional aggregate demand/aggregate supply framework. We *might* conclude from this that increased openness, such as is evident in the past fifty years has helped to eliminate the incidence of Keynesian afflictions.

But there is obviously more to be said. In some sense the invocation of the 'small open economy' assumption is misleading. It leads, as we have seen, to the assertion that no small open economy can suffer from Keynesian market failure problems (except in the non-traded goods sector) and reduces the demand management role of fiscal policy to that of hiring and firing civil servants (the paradigm non-traded service); but in a world of small open traded good economies this would appear to imply the logical non-existence of Keynesian phenomena. This seems simply inconsistent with the possibility of such phenomena existing in a closed economy of small competitive firms, the Malinvaud world, and it is. If we are prepared to abandon the assumption that no firm faces a demand constraint in the Malinvaud closed economy world, logic suggests that we should do the same for an open economy, that we should permit the same waiver of the 'no demand constraint' implication in the one as in the other. There seems in fact no reason not to do this. The implication is that in the model firms may be numerous and competitive, yet not perfectly competitive in that they may conjecture a sales constraint and prices may suffer from some stickiness for the sorts of reasons already discussed.

Still, openness obviously implies an alternative source of demand. This may be stabilising, and reduce the incidence of demand failure. But it may not. An open economy is exposed to world demand failure and may lose some freedom of policy action by reason of being part of a trading world. Conventional policy co-ordination models show that non-cooperative equilibria may very well reinforce Keynesian problems (e.g. Johansen, 1982).

For example, in a world of fixed exchange rates, balance-of-payments targets may inhibit individual action even though all countries could expand together without provoking a balance-of-payments problem anywhere. It is possible to go further. Granted the existence of Keynesian phenomena, it is desirable to have policies to deal with them. At the level of the nation-state, historical and political developments leave little doubt that the means to implement such policies exist. As openness increases, there is an increasing need to match these with forms of international policy co-ordination. The means, or the willingness, to provide these is conspicuously lacking. The Keynesian problem may become more deeply entrenched with openness.

1.7 OVERVIEW

1.7.1 Market forces fifty years on

Fifty years on, it seems unlikely that market failure of the Keynesian type has become any less common. In fact, the contrary is almost certainly the case.

Consider, first, the matter of wage stickiness. Keynes wrote the *General Theory* in the aftermath of the quite widespread wage cuts of the 1920s, of which the American experience has been recently reviewed by Mitchell (1986), who has no hesitation in concluding that 'wages were once more flexible than is currently the case'.[19] Indeed we know that in the heyday of the post-war Keynesian consensus it became increasingly common to insert cost of living escalation clauses in wage contracts (though it is true that in the counter-inflation episode of the 1980s, many of them were withdrawn). Mitchell argues that the degree of wage flexibility reflects to a degree the rigidity of the economy itself, and thus in turn could of course be traced to any of a number (or a combination) of factors: greater buffering of shocks by more developed capital markets, heavily reduced multiplier values due to built-in stabilising features and perhaps the fact and expectation of stabilising government policy. Some of the decline in wage flexibility, therefore, may reflect innocuously a decline in the need for it, but we can hardly be confident that this is the whole story.

Then there is price stickiness, a phenomenon not even contemplated by Keynes. Again, there seems every indication that the scope of customer markets has grown, not diminished and that the plausibility of price stickiness as a working assumption has, therefore, increased, not diminished.

Finally, capital markets. Here it seems that – Stiglitz notwithstanding – the boot may very well be on the other foot. The popularity of the 'permanent income' theory of consumption is a reminder of the extent to which we have become accustomed to supposing that current income constraints are not universally binding. In the fifty years since the *General Theory*, there has been a great development in capital markets and wealth/income ratios have increased. Moreover, our perceptions of the extent to which permanent income itself reflects current income have been shaken by the rational expectations revolution. Still, one cannot go too far. The second best theorem affords a reminder that what seems like a movement towards greater efficiency in one market need not make for a more efficient outcome overall. In any case, even in the United States, studies of saving and consumption continue to give significant weight to liquidity (current income) constraints and the capital markets remain especially imperfect for those most likely to suffer from spells of unemployment.

All this implies that demand management policies continue to have a role to play. It is not necessary to seek proof of actually rigid wages (and/or prices); some stickiness will do. There is no call to fault Keynes on his proposition that in comparing the dynamics of adjustment with and without the existence of policy, the pure market system scores badly (cf. also Hahn and Solow, 1986).

1.7.2 Problems with policy

The real problems with demand management policy arise at a different level. In principle, demand management policy can be crippled by weaknesses in the ability to forecast the future, given that policy takes time to have effect. This was the traditional monetarist criticism, put forward by Friedman. But this does not seem to be the main problem.

More to the point, typical system shocks may not be demand shocks of a type which are appropriately and completely amenable to treatment by demand management policies: there is surely a great deal in this point for the 1970s. But it does not seem that demand management policies are either ineffective or unnecessary: supply shocks usually have a 'demand' dimension, and demand management policies are a necessary – but not sufficient – part of the response. Again, it may be argued that the trade-offs are hostile to the use of demand management policies alone. This is with respect to inflation, in recent times (if not in 1988), largely true, yet hardly inconsistent with one of the key propositions of economic policy, the necessary matching of the number of targets and instruments. Finally, demand management might be hobbled by lack of technique or instruments; for national economies considered as closed systems this is largely untrue. For economies located in a world of free trade and free capital movements, the position is somewhat different. For in such a world, the means of co-ordinating the use of policy instruments which exist in the component economies has not yet been worked out. Undoubtedly, this weakens the relevance of demand management until such time as the means for an international co-ordination are worked out.

In sum: the markets cannot be relied upon to perform efficient equilibration and a role for demand management policies along traditional lines seems apparent in this fact. This does not imply either that demand management policies are sufficient, nor that in a closely integrated world their implementation can always be guaranteed.

Notes

1. A conversation with George Bulkeley in Copenhagen was very helpful in the writing of this chapter, though he can hardly be held responsible for the opinions expressed in it.
2. This paper is reprinted in the Royal Economic Society's *Collected Writings of John Maynard Keynes* as an Appendix to the *General Theory* (Vol. VII of the series) and is described in the editorial introduction as dealing with an error in the exposition of Chapter 2 of that book.
3. J. M. Keynes, *Collected Works*, vol. VII, p. 401.
4. Ibid., pp. 400–401.
5. Keynes does not appear to have fully grasped the analytics of the real balance effect (in contrast to Kalecki) or its ultimate significance (cf. Patinkin (1982), pp. 102–3 where correspondence between Kalecki and Keynes on the issue is published).
6. The study of the normal cost hypothesis is perhaps best exemplified in the paper by Godley and Nordhaus (1972). Despite the fact that this paper appears to be a quite exhaustive exploration of the hypothesis, however, Smith (1982) was able to detect some unexhausted and relevant estimation options which led him to a more sceptical conclusion about its relevance.
7. Their point is graphically illustrated by Lucas's injunction that the analysis should *not* imply '\$500 bills lying on the sidewalk' – i.e. opportunities for improvements which would automatically be taken up by private sector agents pursuing their own self-interest.
8. As Negishi (1979) points out, however, if demand falls short of supply even a competitive firm must be considered to face a kink in its demand curve at the current price.
9. Wages are flexible too, and the 'involuntariness' of unemployment again follows from a different definition from that employed by Keynes. The essential point is that household utility unambiguously rises with employment, as between equilibria. (But see Howitt (1985) for a fuller discussion).
10. For example, the employee may (correctly) believe that a future employer will use his current wage as an index of quality and he may also believe that search will be easier on the dole than on the job.
11. The 'easy way out' is, equally, denied by a one-derivative-up version of nominal wage stickiness. If wage bargains are struck asynchronously and each group jealously resists accepting a lower rate of money wage increase than the groups setting immediately before, inflation will not easily be wound down (cf. Weizacker's (1977) characterisation of wage restraint as a 'public good'), and real wages will not be flexible.
12. Fischer (1977) and Taylor (1980) are the best known of these.
13. The asymmetry can reasonably be motivated by an appeal to self-selection effects or to the relative wealth of workers and entrepreneurs (or shareholders) while the fact that the firm, not an insurance company, provides the insurance cover can be motivated in terms of the superior information base of the firm in respect of its employees.

14.   Thus, if quit rates depend negatively on wages and unemployment, an equilibrium can exist with high wages and unemployment as a 'worker discipline'. Clearly this unemployment in itself is not the product of Keynesian forces and the influence of demand shocks on the unemployment level must be mediated through stickiness in the wage.

15.   For example, through the introduction of quasi-permanent 'temporary' appointments, and the more extensive use of part-time and casual by-the-hour hires where effective (fringe benefit inclusive) per-hour employee compensation is less than that prevailing in 'regular' full-time employment, even if straight wage per hour payment is not.

16.   Whilst insider-outsider theory appears to predict hysteresis in the overall unemployment rate, hysteresis may equally be predicted from other considerations and is not dependent on the validity of insider-outsider theory.

17.   He notes (Leijonhufvud, 1986, pp. 95–6) explicitly that Keynes could have relied on a similar argument for the stickiness of money wage adjustment, but chose not to.

18.   As already observed, this is not the only instance in which contemporary reworking of Keynesian theories reveals unemployment that is Keynesian in the sense that it can be removed by demand management policy but does not accord with Keynes's definition of involuntary unemployment.

19.   Brown (1988) provides a wide-ranging historical survey of wage-price behaviour in major depressions since the 1870s.

References

AKERLOF, G. A. and J. L. YELLEN (eds) (1986) *Efficiency Wage Models of the Labour Market* (Cambridge University Press).

AKERLOF, G. and H. MIYAZAKI (1980) 'The Implicit Contract Theory of Unemployment Meets the Wage Bill Argument', *Review of Economic Studies*, vol. 47, pp. 109–28.

BARRO, R. (1972) 'A Theory of Monopolistic Price Adjustment', *Review of Economic Studies*, vol. 39, January.

BARRO, R. and H. GROSSMAN (1976) *Money, Employment and Inflation* (Cambridge University Press).

BROWN, A. J. (1988) 'World Depression and the Price Level', *National Institute Economic Review*, February.

CARRUTH, A. A. and A. J. OSWALD (1986) 'Wage Inflexibility in Britain', Centre for Labour Economics, LSE, Discussion Paper No 258.

CLOWER, R. W. (1965) 'The Keynesian Counter-Revolution: a Theoretical Appraisal', in F. H. Hahn and F. P. R. Brechling (eds), *The Theory of Interest Rates* (Macmillan).

CORRY, A. B. (1984) 'Keynes, Real Wages and Employment' (Mimeo).

DIXIT, A. K. (1978). 'The Balance of Trade in a Model of Temporary Equilibrium with Rationing', *Review of Economic Studies*, vol. 45, pp. 393–404.

DRAZEN, A. (1980) 'Recent Developments in Macroeconomic Disequilibrium Theory', *Econometrica*, vol. 48, pp. 283–306.

FISCHER, S. (1977) 'Long Term Contracts, Rational Expectations and the Optimal Money Supply', *Journal of Political Economy*, vol. 85.

FLEMMING, J. S. (1973) 'The Consumption Function When Capital Markets are Imperfect: The Permanent Income Hypothesis Reconsidered', *Oxford Economic Papers*, vol. 25, pp. 160–72.

GODLEY, W. A. H. and W. D. NORDHAUS (1972) 'Pricing in the Trade Cycle', *Economic Journal*, vol. 82 (September) pp. 853–82.

GREENWALD, B., STIGLITZ, J. E. and A. M. WEISS (1984) 'Informational Imperfections and Macroeconomic Fluctuations', *American Economic Association, Papers and Proceedings*, vol. 74, pp. 194–9.

GREENWALD, B. and J. E. STIGLITZ (1987) 'Keynesian, New Keynesian and New Classical Economics', *Oxford Economic Papers*, vol. 39, pp. 119–32.

HAHN, F. H. (1978) 'On Non-Walrasian Equilibria', *Review of Economic Studies*, February.

HAHN, F. H. and R. M. SOLOW (1986) 'Is Wage Flexibility A Good Thing?', in W. Beckerman (ed.), *Wage Rigidity and Unemployment* (Duckworth).

HALL, R. L. and C. J. HITCH (1939) 'Price Theory and Business Behaviour', *Oxford Economic Papers*, May.

HENRY, S. G. B., SAWYER, M. C. and P. SMITH (1976) 'Models of Inflation in the United Kingdom: An Evaluation', *National Institute Economic Review*, vol. 77.

HICKS, J. R. (1974) *The Crisis in Keynesian Economics* (Blackwell).

HOWITT, P. (1985) 'Transactions Costs in the Theory of Unemployment', *American Economic Review*, vol. 75, March, pp. 88–100.

JOHANSEN, L. (1982) 'A Note on the Possibility of an International Equilibrium with Low Levels of Activity', *Journal of International Economics*, pp. 257–65.

JOHNSON, H. G. (1970) 'Recent Developments in Monetary Theory', in H. G. Johnson and D. R. Croome (eds), *Money in Britain 1959–1969* (Oxford University Press).

KALECKI, M. (1944) 'Three Ways to Full Employment', in Oxford University Institute of Statistics: *The Economics of Full Employment* (Basil Blackwell).

LEIJONHUFVUD, A. (1968) *On Keynesian Economics and the Economics of Keynes* (Oxford University Press).

LEIJONHUFVUD, A. (1981) *Information and Coordination* (Oxford University Press).

MALINVAUD, E. (1977) *The Theory of Unemployment Reconsidered* (Basil Blackwell).

MCKINNON, R. I. (1976) 'The Limited Role of Fiscal Policy in an Open Economy', *Quarterly Review of the Banca Nazionale del Lavoro*, June.

MITCHELL, D. B. (1986) 'Explanations of Wage Inflexibility: Institutions and Incentives', in W. Beckerman (ed.), *Wage Rigidity and Unemployment* (Duckworth).

MODIGLIANI, F. (1944) 'Liquidity preference and the theory of interest and money', *Econometrica*, vol 12, January.

NEARY, P. J. (1980) 'Non-traded goods and the Balance of Trade in a Neo-Keynesian Temporary Equilibrium', *Quarterly Journal of Economics*, November, pp. 403–429.

NEGISHI, T. (1976) 'Unemployment, Inflation and the Microfoundations of Macroeconomics', in M. J. Artis and A. R. Nobay (eds), *Essays in Economic Analysis* (Cambridge University Press).

NEGISHI, T. (1979) *Microeconomic Foundations of Keynesian Macroeconomics* (North-Holland).

OKUN, A. M. (1981:) *Prices and Quantities* (Basil Blackwell).

PATINKIN, D. (1965) *Money, Interest and Prices* (Harper & Row).

PATINKIN, D. (1982) *Anticipations of the General Theory?* (Oxford: Basil Blackwell).

ROBINSON, J. (1937) *Essays in the Theory of Employment* (Macmillan).

ROWE, N. (1987) 'An Extreme Keynesian Macroeconomic Model with Microeconomic Foundations', *Canadian Journal of Economics*, vol. 20, May.

SARGAN, J. D. (1971) 'A Study of Wages and Prices in the United Kingdom', in H. G. Johnson and A. R. Nobay (eds), *The Current Inflation* (Macmillan).

SMITH, G. W. (1982) 'The Normal Cost Hypothesis: A Reappraisal', in M. J. Artis, D. Leslie and G. W. Smith (eds), *Demand Management, Supply Constraints and Inflation* (Manchester University Press).

STIGLITZ, J. E. (1979) 'Equilibrium in Product Markets With Imperfect Information', *American Economic Review*, vol. 69, May, pp. 339–45.

STIGLITZ, J. E. and A. M. WEISS (1981) 'Credit Rationing in Markets with Imperfect Information', *American Economic Review*, vol. 71, pp. 393–410.

SWEEZY, P. M. (1939) 'Demand Under Conditions of Oligopoly', *Journal of Political Economy*, vol. 47, pp. 339–45.

TAYLOR, J. B. (1980) 'Aggregate Dynamics and Staggered Contracts', *Journal of Political Economy*, vol. 88.

TAYLOR, M. P. (1987a) 'The Simple Analytics of Implicit Labour Contracts', in J. D. Hey and P. J. Lambert (eds), *Surveys in the Economics of Uncertainty* (Blackwell).

TAYLOR, M. P. (1987b) 'Further Developments in the Theory of Implicit Labour Contracts', in J. D. Hey and P. J. Lambert (eds), *Surveys in the Economics of Uncertainty* (Blackwell).

WEIZACKER, C. C. von (1977) 'The Employment Problem: a Systems Approach' (Mimeo).

WORSWICK, G. D. N. (1944) 'The Stability and Flexibility of Full Employment', in Oxford University Institute of Statistics, *The Economics of Full Employment* (Basil Blackwell).

WOGLOM, G. (1982) 'Underemployment Equilibria with Rational Expectations', *Quarterly Journal of Economics*, vol. 97, February, pp. 89–107.

2 The Role of Demand Management in the Maintenance of Full Employment

Bennett T. McCallum

2.1 INTRODUCTION

In his *General Theory*, Keynes (1936) put forth the radical proposition that competitive market economies have no automatic mechanism that tends, in the absence of governmental policy guidance, to eliminate or prevent unemployment. After a lengthy period of debate that was often confused, in part because of Keynes's reliance on non-traditional concepts and terminology, it came to be widely agreed that this proposition was false as a matter of pure economic theory.[1] But it also came to be widely agreed that the economy's self-correcting forces work slowly, so that well-designed demand management policy actions can be helpful in reducing the magnitude and duration of departures of employment and output from their full equilibrium levels. An influential expression of this point of view – the activist demand-management position – was provided by Patinkin (1951).

But, as all readers are well aware, a number of challenges to this position have arisen in the past twenty years. Arguments by influential analysts including Friedman (1968), Lucas (1972), Sargent and Wallace (1975), and Barro (1979) have claimed that the intellectual foundations of the activist position are seriously flawed, and have suggested that activist policies are apt to be counterproductive. Several weaknesses in these arguments have been detected,[2] however, and there has recently been something of a resurgence of Keynesian sentiment among macroeconomic researchers.[3] At present, consequently, there exists substantial disagreement among leading scholars concerning the nature of macroeconomic phenomena and the kind of policy that should be pursued.

The present chapter begins by identifying nominal price stickiness as the logical basis for the Keynesian or activist point of view concerning demand policy. It then characterises two alternative approaches to policy analysis that have been adopted by adherents of the Keynesian position, the 'disequilibrium' and 'Phillips curve' approaches. The former is inherently defective, it is argued, while the latter has yet to be satisfactorily implemented. Indeed, implementation that is not open to Lucas-critique weaknesses is not in sight. In response to the implied dilemma for policy makers, the chapter proposes a rule for the conduct of monetary policy that relies upon minimal understanding of price-adjustment dynamics and which should be robust to regulatory and technological change in the economy's financial and payments institutions. A bit of evidence is presented to suggest that the rule would, if adopted, lead to approximately zero inflation (on average) and to output/employment fluctuations that are small by historical standards. Possible criticisms relating to recent European experience and to recent theoretical developments are considered.

2.2 DISEQUILIBRIUM ANALYSIS

It is widely agreed that the Keynesian rationale for activist demand-management policy is based on a presumption that there exists a significant extent of nominal price stickiness somewhere in the macroeconomic system. This stickiness may pertain to product prices or wages or both, but some type is necessary for the Keynesian diagnosis and remedy to be applicable. For without any price stickiness, real demands and supplies for commodities including labour will be equated in a fashion that leaves no clear-cut role for demand management. And since demand-management actions are effected by way of nominal instrument variables, policy manipulation of real aggregate demand is itself dependent upon a significant degree of nominal stickiness.[4] It is *nominal* aggregate demand that is generally open to manipulation and with which demand-management policy is properly concerned.

The crucial status of price stickiness in the context of demand-management analysis leads directly to a significant issue: how is the concept of 'price stickiness' to be represented analytically? The concept is evidently one that is inherently dynamic in nature but, as we all know, the formal analysis of Keynes (1936) and of those writers[5] who clarified the message of the *General Theory* was conducted in a comparative-static framework. Accordingly, some means had to be found for representing a dynamic concept in a static setting. The device adopted by Keynes and the other early contributors was that of *conditional* equilibrium analysis – comparative statics in which the economy's slowly-adjusting prices are treated as if they were fixed quantities. Policy experiments conducted under this approach are comparative-static exercises carried out conditional upon 'given' values of the prices that are hypothesised to adjust slowly. For some given value of the nominal wage rate, for example, the analyst could compare values of endogenous variables that would obtain under alternative hypothetical magnitudes of the money stock or government purchases and use this comparison as the basis for analysis of an economy in which the nominal wage adjusts slowly.

But of course actual economies are not static entities, but ongoing dynamic systems. So the question remains of how to relate these conditional comparative-static exercises to actual problems of demand management. One conceivable approach would be simply to pretend that static analysis provides a satisfactory approximation. According to that approach, the analyst would use the model in choosing policy actions at time t by treating the current value of the sticky price (e.g. W_t) as historically given and ignoring the future (which can perhaps be attended to when it becomes the present). Then later in period $t+1$ the new value W_{t+1} could be treated as historically given and new policy actions selected conditional upon that value. By proceeding period after period in this fashion, it would be possible for the analyst to use the static model in practice without ever developing any explanation for the W_{t+j} values that are 'given' in the successive periods.

It would seem to be indisputable, however, that such a way of proceeding is highly suboptimal. For even if W_t were actually a given magnitude in t, in the sense of being unresponsive to current policy actions, its current value would certainly have been influenced by economic conditions and policy actions of the past. Any (temporarily) fixed price should be classified as a predetermined variable, not as one that is literally exogenous. Policy actions taken in t will accordingly have effects on future prices – on W_{t+1}, W_{t+2}, etc. – and these effects are ignored in the procedure under discussion. That procedure is consequently bound to be suboptimal.

As well as I can determine, this suboptimal approach to policy analysis is implicitly recommended in most of the literature that has passed under the title of 'disequilibrium' or 'fixed-price' macroeconomics.[6] The technically sophisticated contributors to that literature might deny any intention that their work be used in such a manner, but it is unclear that there is any other way to proceed with a model that provides no explanation for the evolution over time of the system's sticky prices. The primary objection to these models, according to my argument, is not that they treat prices as temporarily rigid, but that they include no explanation of price adjustment between periods. From a practical policy perspective, these models are crucially incomplete.[7]

A rather vivid illustration of the potentially misleading nature of policy analysis conducted with an incomplete, fixed-price model was provided by an example developed in McCallum (1980). In the model used for this example, real aggregate demand y_t^d is assumed to be dependent upon real money balances, real government purchases, and a stochastic shock term while (for simplicity) aggregate supply is taken to be a constant, $y_t^s = \bar{y}$. Prices are set at the beginning of each period and are unresponsive to developments occurring within the period, i.e., to shock realisations. Consequently, y_t^d and y_t^s will typically fail to coincide in which case the quantity actually transacted – the output forthcoming – is determined as in the disequilibrium literature as the smaller of the two: $y_t = \min(y_t^d, \bar{y})$. When there is a negative shock to demand, there will be a tendency for $y_t^s = \bar{y}$ to exceed y_t^d implying Keynesian unemployment proportional to $\bar{y} - y_t^d$.

Clearly this model is such that within any period in which $y_t < \bar{y}$, it is the case that if the money stock or government purchases were larger in magnitude, then y_t^d would be greater and $\bar{y} - y_t$ would be smaller – perhaps zero. So from the perspective of conditional comparative statics the model seems to be supportive of the idea that activist demand management can be effective in terms of preventing unemployment.

But in order to discuss the average effects over time of a sustained policy strategy, one needs to complete the model by specifying how prices adjust between periods and adding policy rules that determine policy instrument settings. In the example under discussion, the price adjustment specification is an augmented Phillips relation in which the proportionate price change is determined by the previous period's excess supply $\bar{y} - y_{t-1}$ and the expected proportionate change of the market-clearing price level.[8] The policy instruments, finally, are set by feedback rules that take account of all relevant variables realised in the past. Current magnitudes are assumed unknown, however, to the policy authorities.

In this setting, to come to the point, it is demonstrated that if expectations are rational the famous (or infamous) policy-ineffectiveness proposition obtains. That is, the evolution of y_t (and thus $y_t - \bar{y}$) is independent of the coefficients of the policy feedback rules: whether the instrument settings feature strong responses or none at all to (e.g.) past excess supply values makes no difference whatsoever in the time series behaviour of y_t or $y_t - \bar{y}$.

The purpose of citing this example is *not*, it should be emphasised, to suggest that the policy ineffectiveness proposition is applicable to actual economies. It is, rather, to illustrate the potentially misleading nature of conditional comparative-static policy analysis with incomplete fixed-price models. Such analysis is prone to overstate the potential effectiveness of demand management policy by failing to take account of dynamic considerations concerning the manner in which currently 'given' prices reflect previous responses to past economic conditions.

2.3 PRICE ADJUSTMENT MODELS

Many practical Keynesian analysts – especially those working with quantitative models – have recognised the point of the previous section, of course, and have adopted instead a second approach. Instead of treating the model's sticky price or prices as if they came out of the blue, this second approach adds[9] to the static Keynesian model another equation or set of equations – a

'Phillips curve' or a 'wage-price sector' – designed to explain movements over time in the slowly-adjusting price or prices. This step converts the model into one that is dynamic and complete, and renders it usable for policy analysis that avoids the particular source of suboptimality described above.

But while the inclusion of price-adjustment equations makes the second approach more suitable than the first, as a method of adapting Keynesian models to demand management purposes, the price adjustment equations that have been used in practice are open to a number of objections. At the most sympathetic level, one objection is that most of the utilised specifications fail to satisfy the *natural rate hypothesis*, i.e., the hypothesis that there is no path of price level or nominal demand values that will keep unemployment *permanently* below its natural-rate value.[10] This hypothesis, which expresses the notion that it is not possible for a society to permanently enrich itself in real terms by monetary means, is generally accepted by neoclassical theorists and is paid lip service by most Keynesian writers, but is violated by many econometric specifications. Models incorporating the concept of a non-accelerating-inflation-rate-of-unemployment (NAIRU), for example, do not satisfy the natural rate hypothesis. For if there is a stable relationship between the unemployment rate and the inflation acceleration variable, then there are evidently price level time paths that represent an acceleration magnitude that would yield a permanently lowered unemployment rate.[11] Of course the builders of such models do not intend that they be applicable to 'impractical' conditions such as a maintained acceleration of inflation. But this type of disclaimer amounts to an admission that the relation in question is not *structural* – i.e., is not invariant to policy regimes.

A more fundamental criticism of existing price adjustment specifications is expressed by proponents of the *equilibrium* approach to business cycle analysis. All readers will be aware that this line of work began with Lucas's (1972) celebrated theory of a Phillips-type relationship between nominal and real variables that results from confusion due to information gaps, not from price stickiness *per se*. Most readers will also know that Lucas's theory has recently suffered a decline in popularity as a consequence of its reliance, for real effects of monetary shocks, on an implausible degree of ignorance concerning current monetary conditions on the part of rational private agents. Since information regarding various aggregate nominal magnitudes – price indices as well as money supply figures – is available both promptly and cheaply, the Lucas 'monetary misperceptions' model has come to be viewed as inapplicable to today's developed economies.[12]

Disenchantment with the misperceptions model has not, however, led to the demise of the equilibrium school of business cycle analysis. Indeed, an important group of researchers has in a sense retained the Lucas model[13] despite its failure to rationalise output and employment effects of monetary shocks. Specifically, this group has developed a *real business cycle* (RBC) approach which denies that there is in fact any significant effect of monetary policy actions (even if unanticipated) on output. The money-output correlations that appear in the data are attributed, by RBC proponents, to 'reverse causation', i.e., policy and/or banking sector responses to output fluctuations. These fluctuations, to complete the story, are brought about by real shocks, primarily exogenous shocks to technology.

The RBC approach – which stems from the work of Kydland and Prescott (1982), Long and Plosser (1983), and King and Plosser (1984) – has gained a considerable amount of support in part because of the elusiveness of a rigorous theoretical account of money-to-output influences, but also because of quantitative work supportive of the RBC hypothesis. The pioneering study in this regard is that of Kydland and Prescott (1982), which demonstrates that a surprisingly good quantitative match to actual business cycle facts[14] can be obtained (via simulations) with a quantitative equilibrium model in which a stochastic technology shock provides the *only* source of fluctuations. In particular, the RBC models imply procyclical fluctuations in labour productivity and real wages, an implication that is more consistent with actual data than those of many traditional models that attribute cycles to demand fluctuations. Also, the relative variability of consumption and investment expenditures is well explained, as well as the serial correlation in output and employment magnitudes. These implications require the assumption that technology shocks are highly persistent, but that is entirely plausible.

Other types of evidence have also been put forth as supportive of the RBC hypothesis. I have argued (McCallum, 1986) that much of this is inconclusive if not irrelevant, but it remains a striking fact that money stock and other demand-related variables have very little predictive content for output fluctuations, especially in data series that have been first-differenced.

Probably the most serious weakness of the RBC approach is the lack of a convincing description of the unobserved 'technology shocks' that it posits as the source of cyclical fluctuations. If the term is interpreted literally as referring to shifts in the state-of-knowledge physical frontier relationship between inputs and outputs,[15] then it would seem implausible that there could exist much variability at the *aggregate* level; specific technological improvements should impact on the production functions for only a few of the economy's many products. And independent shocks to different productive sectors would tend to average out, yielding a relatively small variance in the aggregate.

For this and other reasons, most macroeconomists have found the RBC hypothesis unconvincing. But the vitality of the research being conducted by the RBC school is a testimony to the attraction of the equilibrium approach and to the dissatisfaction of many economists with existing models of price stickiness. Let us then return to our main theme by reviewing the basic rationale for the equilibrium approach.

Existing equilibrium models are ones in which all prices are perfectly free

Bennett T. McCallum 31

to adjust within each period, but that is not the defining characteristic of the approach. The latter's basic requirement, rather, is that a model's behavioural relations should all be rationalised in terms of choices made by optimising agents – households and firms – in response to their own objectives and the constraints they face (Lucas, 1980). The motivation for this modelling strategy is the objective of producing a model that is well-designed for the guidance of economic policy. The presumption is that by focusing on agents' objectives and constraints, it might be possible to construct a model consisting entirely of relations that are truly structural. Relations derived in this way would, because of the autonomy of preferences and technology, stand a reasonable chance of being invariant to policy changes.

As stated above, this strategy does not necessarily rule out price stickiness. One can conceive of a model, for example, in which multiperiod nominal contracts are endogenously explained as the response of rational agents to adjustment, bargaining, or marketing costs – in which case the model could be of the equilibrium variety. But the approach does not permit the inclusion of relations describing sluggish price adjustments effected by 'the market' or by some fictitious 'auctioneer' with ill-defined or non-existent objectives. Being poorly understood – not based on well-posed choice problems – such relations would not be structural. They would not, in other words, provide the analyst with any basis for knowing whether they would remain in place or shift if policy were substantially altered. But such knowledge is clearly crucial for designing policy, as a shift would invalidate the model's predictions about the effects of a contemplated policy change. In summary, it is necessary, according to the equilibrium-approach viewpoint, to understand the nature of price-adjustment sluggishness to know if its quantitative characteristics will remain intact in the face of altered conditions.

The foregoing argument is of course an application of the 'Lucas critique' developed in Lucas (1976). In principle, its considerations are applicable to most components of a macroeconomic model. But because of the crucial role of expectational considerations in the price-adjustment sectors of these models, it is these sectors that would seem to be especially susceptible to the critique. Relations among variables all of one type, either nominal or real, would seem to be less likely to break down in response to demand-management policy changes.[16]

The foregoing discussion suggests that, in principle, the modelling strategy of the equilibrium approach could provide a satisfactory basis for demand-management policy analysis. In practice, however, it has proved to be extremely difficult to model sluggish price adjustments in the manner required. Tangible resource costs of making price changes seem to be negligibly small, while 'bargaining' and 'marketing' costs of price adjustment are poorly understood. Consequently, to the present time all equilibrium models have been ones with complete price flexibility and, therefore, no role for demand management. No model of sticky prices has been devised that combines empirical veracity with an adjustment specification that is clearly based on individuals' objectives and constraints.

As a result, a sizeable group of researchers has reacted against Lucas's suggestion that price stickiness needs to be explained along equilibrium-approach lines. In reality, these researchers contend, prices do not adjust promptly for a variety of complicated strategic and semi-institutional reasons that are not amenable to taste-and-technology analysis. Consequently it is better (according to their view) to use a poorly understood but empirically justifiable Phillips-type relation than to pretend – counterfactually – that all price adjustments take place promptly, as equilibrium analysts have assumed in practice. An econometric model based on this presumption will track data better than if it incorporated the hypothesis of perfectly flexible prices. And policy predictions provided by the model could be satisfactory if the adjustment relation did not shift sharply when policy changes were undertaken.

It is hard not to have considerable sympathy for this last suggestion. Yet, on the other hand, the logic of the Lucas critique is inescapable: how can one know that the adjustment relation will not shift sharply if he does not understand its nature? Finding a way out of the implied dilemma is perhaps the most crucial task confronting policy-oriented macroeconomists today.

2.4　A STRATEGY FOR MONETARY POLICY

In light of the policy dilemma just described, the appropriate response would seem to be one that is not excessively ambitious. My proposed approach begins by accepting the idea that the nature of price adjustment relations – and thus the connection between nominal and real variables – is poorly understood. There is no compelling basis for selecting any one of the numerous competing theories of this mechanism, and no good prospect for better understanding in the near future. But the proposed approach reflects optimism nevertheless, for it involves a strategy for monetary policy behaviour[17] that gives promise of being effective regardless of the nature of the mechanism.

The basic idea is that, in whatever way it is that monetary (or fiscal) actions affect output, they do so through an intermediate influence on nominal aggregate demand. Evidence suggests, furthermore, that cyclical fluctuations in real output and employment are strongly related to those in nominal demand. Real GNP growth is usually strong, that is, when nominal GNP growth is above average.[18] Consequently, there is some basis for belief that cyclical fluctuations in real output would be significantly dampened if nominal GNP were kept on a smooth and steady growth path.

Of course the last statement would be questioned by proponents of the

RBC hypothesis. But according to their theory, the behaviour of output is independent of nominal variables in any event, and the behaviour of nominal variables is of no concern – except to the extent that inflation imposes an inefficient tax on the holders of real money balances. Consequently, RBC proponents should have no objection to a policy strategy that yields a steady growth rate for nominal GNP,[19] provided that it is not inflationary.

At what rate should nominal GNP be made to grow? While a mild deflation in accordance with the 'Chicago Rule' of Friedman (1969) is perhaps preferable in principle, from a practical point of view there is much to be said for an average inflation rate of zero.[20] Taking that as a goal, then, I suggest that nominal GNP should be made to grow at a rate equal to the long-term average rate of real output growth for the economy in question – about 3 per cent per year, for example, for the United States.

My suggested approach does not, however, consist merely of the adoption of a target path for nominal GNP. Equally essential is the mechanism for achieving that path. In that regard three considerations are extremely important. First, the mechanism should involve a policy *rule* that dictates each period's setting of the policy instrument. It is important to have a rule, rather than relying on 'discretionary' period-by-period choices of the instrument setting, in order to avoid dynamic inconsistency of the type described by Kydland and Prescott (1977) and Barro and Gordon (1983). Those authors show that period-by-period attempts to optimise, by a monetary authority who seeks to avoid both inflation and unemployment, will lead to more inflation and no less unemployment (on average) than could be obtained by adherence to a rule. It is my opinion that this type of inconsistency offers the best available explanation for the unprecedented post-war inflationary experience of most developed countries, experience which has seen the CPI climb to 4.5 times its 1950 level in the US and nearly 11 times in the UK.[21]

Second, the rule needs to pertain to a directly controllable variable, rather than one such as the M1 money stock (or any broader measure). Otherwise, the rule will not be operationally specified. Third, the rule should be designed in a manner that does not rely upon the absence of regulatory change and technical innovation in the payments and financial industries. While these processes may not produce as much turmoil in the future as they have in the recent past, it would be unreasonable to presume that they will not be present again to a significant extent.

Following up on previous suggestions of mine (McCallum, 1984), I have recently developed in quantitative terms a rule for US monetary policy based on these considerations. This rule dictates quarterly settings for the monetary base that are designed to keep nominal GNP close to a 3 per cent growth path.[22] It does not rely on any specific model of the economy or any details regarding the financial system: all it presumes is that an increase in the growth rate of the monetary base tends to have a stimulative effect on nominal GNP. Defining b_t = log of monetary base (for quarter t), x_t = log of nominal GNP, and x_t^* = target-path value of x, the rule is as follows:

$$\Delta b_t = 0.00739 - (1/16)[x_{t-1} - x_{t-17} - b_{t-1} + b_{t-17}] + 0.25(x_{t-1}^* - x_{t-1}).$$

Here the constant term is simply a 3 per cent annual growth rate expressed in quarterly logarithmic units, while the second term subtracts from this the average growth rate of base velocity over the previous four years.[23] Finally, the third term adds a gentle adjustment in response to cyclical departures of GNP from its target path.

To determine whether this rule would indeed keep nominal GNP close to the desired growth path, one must experiment with the economy or with a model. The former possibility is too expensive and the latter suffers from the absence of any reliable model. But it is my conjecture that the proposed rule would perform well with a wide variety of models. Here I will briefly summarise results for three extremely simple models. The first is an atheoretic regression of Δx_t on Δb_t and Δx_{t-1}; for the sample period 1954–85 the estimates are as follows:

$$\Delta x_t = 0.00749 + 0.257\Delta x_{t-1} + 0.487\Delta b_t + e_t$$
$$\quad\;\; (0.002) \quad (0.079) \qquad\quad (0.121)$$

$$R^2 = 0.23 \qquad \sigma = 0.0010 \qquad DW = 2.11.$$

Generating b_t and x_t values from the proposed rule and this model, with residuals fed in each period to represent shocks, one estimates that the root-mean-square value of $x - x^*$ for 1954–85 would have been only 2.0 per cent had the rule been in effect. Actual historical policy, by contrast, yielded a 77.1 per cent root-mean-square error (RMSE) relative to the x_t^* target path[24] and a 8.5 per cent RMSE relative to a fitted linear trend. The second model differs from the first only in lagging Δb_t one quarter, to reduce the possibility of reverse causation in the estimated effects. The resulting coefficient estimates are not much different and the simulated RMSE for 1954–85 is 2.2 per cent. The third model explored to date is a four-variable vector autoregression system in which the variables are growth rates of the base, the price level, and real GNP, plus a nominal interest rate. With this system, the estimated RMSE value is again 2.2 per cent.

Of course each of these experiments is in principle subject to the Lucas critique. I would argue that the first two are less susceptible – for the reason sketched above – than if the models included both real and nominal variables. But my main line of defence in this regard is to be based on the robustness of the rule to widely different models.[25]

My contention is not only that the suggested policy rule would keep nominal GNP close to its target path and thereby eliminate inflation, but would also result in smaller cyclical fluctuations in real output and employment than the US economy has experienced in the post-war era. But we know that these fluctuations have been small relative to those of previous historical eras, and reasonably small in absolute terms. Thus the contention is that the proposed rule would, if utilised in a developed economy,[26] result in macroeconomic performance of a high standard.

2.5 TOPICAL ISSUES

Before concluding, it will be useful briefly to address a few topical issues concerning the proposed policy rule and, more generally, Keynesian views on the need for activist demand management. The first of these issues pertains to the unusually high unemployment rates experienced during recent years in many European nations, including the UK. While some economists have attributed this unemployment primarily to inadequate demand, our proposed policy rule would have dictated substantially less nominal demand growth than was actually experienced over the last decade or so. Should this be regarded as a mark against the rule?

To answer that question properly one would have to identify the source of the unusual unemployment. Clearly, such a task is beyond the scope of the remainder of the present chapter. Nevertheless, as a crude check on the notion that demand inadequacy bears the primary responsibility, let us conduct a cross-nation comparison. To that end, Figure 2.1 plots average unemployment rates for 1980–84 against nominal GDP growth over the decade 1975–85 for 19 OECD nations.[27] If relatively high unemployment were associated with relatively slow demand growth in this cross-section, the points would indicate a downward-sloping relationship. But a glance at Figure 2.1 shows that no such relationship is present. It is also the case that, for many of the individual countries considered, nominal GDP growth has been more rapid in the 1975–85 period than during the low-unemployment years of 1950–70. At this level of extremely simple comparisons, then, the evidence does not support the notion that demand inadequacy is the source of the problem.

The other issues to be considered relate to recent theoretical developments that have been interpreted as supportive of the hypothesis that activist demand management is both needed and feasible. In particular, the so-called 'efficiency wage' model has been touted as justifying this hypothesis, while the phenomenon of 'hysteresis' has been used to justify calls for demand expansion. Influential papers on the two subjects have been written by Yellen (1984) and Akerlof and Yellen (1985) and by Blanchard and Summers (1986), respectively, while both developments have been drawn upon in a recent argument by Buiter (1987).

Figure 2.1   Unemployment rates, 1980–84, and nominal GDP growth, measured as a ratio of 1985 to 1975 values, for 19 OECD countries.

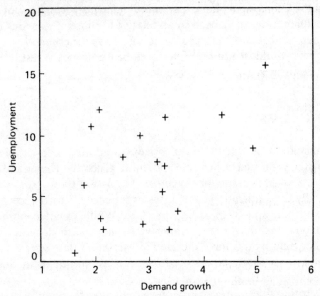

Sources: OECD *Economic Outlook* and IMF *International Financial Statistics.*

With regard to the efficiency wage idea, it is important to understand that this model does not itself rationalise any role for demand management. As Yellen (1984, p. 204) and Akerlof and Yellen (1985, p. 825) recognise but do not emphasise, the model is concerned with the configuration of equilibrium employment and output magnitudes in relation to their socially optimal levels. These equilibrium quantities are determined in a block of the macroeconomic system that is exogenous to nominal variables, just as in the textbook classical model. Changes in nominal aggregate demand therefore result in price level changes, with no effect on output or employment.

To illustrate that point, consider the following version of the static classical model, in which the symbols are y = output, n = employment, n^s = labour supply, w = real wage, r = interest rate, g = real government purchases, M = money supply, and P = price level:

$y = f(n)$	[Production function]	(2.1)
$f'(n) = w$	[MPL condition]	(2.2)
$n^s = h(w)$	[Labour supply]	(2.3)
$n = n^s$	[Market clearing]	(2.4)
$y = d(y,r) + g$	[IS function]	(2.5)
$M/P = L(y,r)$	[LM function]	(2.6)

With M and g set by policy, the first four equations in this system determine

w, y, n, and n^s with (2.5) and (2.6) then yielding r and P. Now the efficiency wage model alters this system by replacing (2.4) with the condition that labour cost per efficiency unit is minimised, which can be expressed as

$$\eta(w) = 1. \tag{2.4'}$$

Also, (2.1) and (2.2) are replaced with

$$y = f(\varphi(w)n) \tag{2.1'}$$

and

$$f'(\varphi(w)n)\varphi(w) = w. \tag{2.5'}$$

But with these changes, equations (2.1'), (2.2'), (2.3), (2.4') continue to determine w, y, n, and n^s. Changes in M or g then have effects only on r and P.[28]

In order to obtain an effect of M on n and y, Akerlof and Yellen (1985) replace w with W/P, divide firms into two types, and assume that one type does not change its nominal price and wage rates when M is altered.[29] This permits a fall in the *average* level of w, so has the effect of replacing (2.4') with a sticky-price condition. But of course an effect of M on w (and n) could have been obtained without the efficiency wage apparatus by directly adopting some sticky-price assumption in place of (2.4).[30] The principal role of the efficiency wage apparatus is to rationalise an assumption that the initial equilibrium is one with $n < n^s$. I find that suggestion dubious, but that is a topic for another paper.

Turning even more briefly to the topic of hysteresis, we find that a rather similar comment is applicable. In particular, acceptance or rejection of the hysteresis hypothesis – which suggests that the natural rate of unemployment adjusts upward or downward in response to past actual rates – has no bearing on whether aggregate demand policy can systematically influence the discrepancy between the two. In other words, if the specification of the wage-price sector is (is not) one that permits anticipated demand actions to affect the discrepancy in the absence of hysteresis, it will be one that does (does not) imply such effects in its presence.[31] Furthermore, it needs to be noted that the presence of hysteresis would not be sufficient, for the reason mentioned in note 10, to contradict the natural rate hypothesis. And it should be kept in mind that empirical models designed to represent the hysteresis phenomenon (e.g. Blanchard and Summers, 1986, pp. 50–55) are observationally equivalent to expectational Phillips relations in which lagged as well as current unemployment measures appear. For these reasons, it is unclear that the concept of hysteresis is a crucial one in the context of demand management issues.

2.6 CONCLUSION

It has been argued in this chapter that, despite fifty years of active research, leading scholars continue to disagree about the need for, and potential efficacy of, activist demand management policy. In my opinion, this situation does not result entirely from ideological predilictions or obstinacy on the part of either group of scholars; it is exceedingly difficult to acquire firm knowledge about the workings of a dynamic system as complex as an economy when experimentation is infeasible. But whatever the reason, while it is likely that some activist measures could be useful, this cannot be concluded with complete certainty. And even if the case were firmly established that activist policy can in principle be useful, it would remain true that its workings depend upon features of the economy that have not been modelled in a reliable fashion.

In these circumstances, the chapter suggests, a judicious way to conduct demand policy would be by adoption of a rule that promises to yield reasonably satisfactory results under a variety of assumptions regarding the nature of the economy's critical features. A particular rule designed in that spirit is here described – a semi-activist rule that would provide some stabilising adjustments but in an automatic manner that should do no harm if such adjustments were unnecessary.

Acknowledgements

The author is indebted to Michael Artis, Jean-Pierre Béguelin, Georg Rich and two anonymous referees for helpful comments.

Notes

1. Even if the liquidity trap was empirically relevant, the real-balance effect would (as prices fall) automatically stimulate aggregate demand as needed. Some writers have questioned this standard conclusion on the grounds that it neglects dynamic considerations involving expectations. In McCallum (1983) it is shown, however, that with rational expectations and flexible prices the standard conclusion obtains when expectational dynamics are taken into account.
2. Reviews have been provided by many writers. A recent version of my own account appears in McCallum (1987).
3. For one example of this resurgence, see Blanchard (1987).
4. Even if it were the case that the government directly controlled real government purchases – its actual instrument is *nominal* government purchases – it would not follow that real aggregate demand could be manipulated, as reference to the textbook model of a classical (i.e. flexible price) system indicates. A qualification to this statement, mentioned below in note 28, does not overturn the point.

5. In particular, Hicks (1937), Modigliani (1944), and Patinkin (1956).
6. Prominent examples are Barro and Grossman (1976) and Malinvaud (1977).
7. It should be said that price adjustment relations are discussed in various places by Barro and Grossman (1976). But this part of their work has not been adopted by subsequent contributors to the disequilibrium literature, which Barro and Grossman have abandoned.
8. Ironically, this is the form of price adjustment postulated by Barro and Grossman (1976) in their Chapter 4.
9. As in my 1980 example.
10. This statement does not require that the natural-rate value be a constant over time, nor that it be trend-stationary or even independent of past unemployment rates. Also, the phrasing in the next sentence of the text is not meant to deny that different maintained inflation rates have different welfare implications, such as those discussed by Friedman (1969).
11. For elaboration and some examples, see McCallum (1983, pp. 400–401).
12. It is possible, however, that misperceptions of the type featured in Lucas's theory were of greater significance in the years before the Second World War, when aggregate data were not readily available.
13. But with agents assumed to possess knowledge of current monetary aggregates.
14. For post-war US quarterly data, detrended by a specific smoothing filter.
15. If it is not, much of the impact and novelty of the RBC approach is lost.
16. Consider, for example, the effects of substantial but steady inflation on correlations between real variables as compared with correlations between one real and one nominal variable. More analysis is needed, however, to determine the extent to which the suggestion in the text is valid.
17. Implications for fiscal policy are briefly mentioned below.
18. In the seasonally-adjusted quarterly US data for 1954–85, the correlation is 0.81.
19. Here and elsewhere I refer to GNP rather than GDP as an American habit. The precise measure of nominal output/income to be used in the policy rule is an issue on which I mean to take no position. Gordon (1985) has suggested that nominal final sales would be better than GNP.
20. One reason is that it seems likely that official price indices overstate inflation to a small extent.
21. In the pre-Second World War era, monetary authorities were kept from this type of behaviour by the requirement of adherence to a commodity-money standard.
22. Or, to be more precise, a path growing at a rate equal to the economy's long-term average rate of output growth. Estimates of this rate could, if desired, be updated periodically in some specified manner. The monetary base, it might be mentioned, is a controllable variable since the central bank can read its value from its own balance sheet and make adjustments whenever required.
23. Note that

$$x_{t-1} - x_{t-17} - b_{t-1} + b_{t-17} = \sum_{j=1}^{17} (\Delta x_{t-j} - \Delta b_{t-j}).$$

This type of velocity correction was suggested by Meltzer (1987). The averaging period is set at four years since this term is not intended to pick up cyclical effects, but long periods would unduly slow the rule's response to non-cyclical institutional changes.
24. This huge RMSE value reflects average nominal GNP growth well in excess of 3 per cent, i.e., reflects the inflation that was experienced.

25. Since drafting this chapter, I have verified that the rule yields good results in four more VAR systems and in small 'structural' models representative of three different theories of cyclical fluctuations, namely, the RBC theory, the monetary misperceptions theory, and a version of Keynesian theory as expressed in the MPS quarterly econometric model. Details are reported in McCallum (1988).

26. Even for a highly open economy the appropriate objective for macroeconomic policy is to keep nominal demand growing at a non-inflationary rate. With regard to fiscal policy variables, one point is that the traditional automatic stabilisers provided by progressive tax schedules, etc., are helpful in promoting smooth growth of nominal GNP. Whether tax *rates* should be adjusted in response to deviations of x_t is debatable.

27. The GDP growth measure is the ratio of nominal GDP for 1985 to its value for 1975. That different periods are used for the two variables can be explained as follows. The 1980–84 period is used for unemployment rates so as to focus on the greatly increased levels of the 1980s, with 1984 the concluding year because comparable data are not available for all countries for more recent years. In the case of demand growth, earlier years were included to take account of the possibility that effects occur with a substantial lag. The choice of precise dates is clearly quite arbitrary; it is my belief that the basic finding is not sensitive to this choice.

28. This statement should be qualified as follows. There would be real effects of changes in g if the model were modified to permit direct government employment and production. In such a case, however, changes in g would not strictly represent 'demand management' actions.

29. They provide no justification for the assumption that these firms keep their *nominal* prices unchanged; one is attempted in McCallum (1986).

30. While his emphasis is very different, this conclusion is consistent with the analysis of Buiter (1987).

31. The 'core inflation' case presented by Buiter (1987) is one in which anticipated demand influences are effective. This case provides an example of a specification in which the natural rate hypothesis does not obtain: an accelerating inflation will keep unemployment (expectationally) below the natural rate permanently.

References

AKERLOF, G. A. and J. L. YELLEN (1985) 'A Near-Rational Model of the Business Cycle with Wage and Price Inertia', *QJE*, vol. 100 (Suppl.) pp. 823–38.

BARRO, R. J. (1979) 'Second Thoughts on Keynesian Economics', *AER*, vol. 69 (May) pp. 54–9.

BARRO, R. J. and H. I. GROSSMAN (1976) *Money, Employment, and Inflation* (Cambridge: Cambridge University Press).

BARRO, R. J. and D. B. GORDON (1983) 'A Positive Theory of Monetary Policy in a Natural Rate Model', *JPE*, vol. 91 (August) pp. 589–610.

BLANCHARD, O. J. (1987) 'Why Does Money Affect Output? A Survey', NBER Working Paper No. 2285, June.

BLANCHARD, O. J. and L. H. SUMMERS (1986) 'Hysteresis and the European Unemployment Problem', in *NBER Macroeconomics Annual 1986*, S. Fischer (ed.) (Cambridge, MA: The MIT Press).

BUITER, W. H. (1987) 'The Right Combination of Demand and Supply Policies: The Case for a Two-Handed Approach', NBER Working Paper No. 2333, August.

FRIEDMAN, M. (1968) 'The Role of Monetary Policy', *AER*, vol. 58 (May) pp. 1–17.

FRIEDMAN, M. (1969) *The Optimum Quantity of Money and Other Essays* (Chicago: Aldine).

GORDON, R. J. (1985) 'The Conduct of Domestic Monetary Policy', in A. Ando, H. Eguchi, R. Farmer and Y. Suzuki (eds), *Monetary Policy in Our Times* (Cambridge, MA: The MIT Press).

HICKS, J. R. (1937) 'Mr. Keynes and the "Classics": A Suggested Interpretation', *Econometrica*, vol. 5 (April) pp. 147–59.

KEYNES, J. M. (1936) *The General Theory of Employment, Interest, and Money* (London: Macmillan).

KING, R. G. and C. I. PLOSSER (1984) 'Money, Credit, and Prices in a Real Business Cycle', *AER*, vol. 74 (June) pp. 363–80.

KYDLAND, F. E. and E. C. PRESCOTT (1977) 'Rules Rather than Discretion: the Inconsistency of Optimal Plans', *JPE*, vol. 85 (June) pp. 473–91.

KYDLAND, F. E. and E. C. PRESCOTT (1982) 'Time to Build and Aggregate Fluctuations', *Econometrica*, vol. 50 (November) pp. 1345–70.

LONG, J. B. and C. I. PLOSSER (1983) 'Real Business Cycles', *JPE*, vol. 91 (February) pp. 39–69.

LUCAS, R. E., Jr. (1972) 'Expectations and the Neutrality of Money', *JET*, vol. 4 (April) pp. 103–124.

LUCAS, R. E., Jr. (1976) 'Econometric Policy Evaluation: A Critique', *Carnegie-Rochester Conference Series on Public Policy*, vol. 1, pp. 19–46.

LUCAS, R. E., Jr. (1980) 'Methods and Problems in Business Cycle Theory', *JMCB*, vol. 12 (November Pt. 2) pp. 696–715.

MALINVAUD, E. (1977) *The Theory of Unemployment Reconsidered* (Oxford: Basil Blackwell).

McCALLUM, B. T. (1980) 'Hahn's Theoretical Viewpoint on Unemployment: A Comment', *Economica*, vol. 47 (August) pp. 299–303.

McCALLUM, B. T. (1983) 'The Liquidity Trap and the Pigou Effect: A Dynamic Analysis with Rational Expectations', *Economica*, vol. 50 (November) pp. 395–405.

McCALLUM, B. T. (1984) 'Monetarist Rules in the Light of Recent Experience', *AER*, vol. 74 (May) pp. 388–91.

McCALLUM, B. T. (1986) 'On "Real" and "Sticky-Price" Theories of the Business Cycle', *JMCB*, vol. 18 (November) pp. 397–414.

McCALLUM, B. T. (1987) 'Inflation: Theory and Evidence', NBER Working Paper No. 2313, July. Forthcoming in *Handbook of Monetary Economics*, B. M. Friedman and F. Hahn (eds).

McCALLUM, B. T. (1988) 'Robustness Properties of a Rule for Monetary Policy', *Carnegie-Rochester Conference Series on Public Policy* 29 (Autumn), forthcoming.

MELTZER, A. H. (1987) 'Limits of Short-Run Stabilization Policy', *Economic Inquiry*, vol. 25 (January) pp. 1–14.

MODIGLIANI, F. (1944) 'Liquidity Preference and the Theory of Interest and Money', *Econometrica*, vol. 12 (January) pp. 45–88.

PATINKIN, D. (1951) 'Price Flexibility and Full Employment', in F. A. Lutz and L. W. Mints (eds), *Readings in Monetary Theory* (Philadelphia: Irwin).

PATINKIN, D. (1956) *Money, Interest, and Prices* (New York: Harper & Row).

SARGENT, T. J. and N. WALLACE (1975) 'Rational Expectations, the Optimal Monetary Instrument, and the Optimal Money Supply Rule', *JPE*, vol. 83 (April) pp. 241–54.

YELLEN, J. L. (1984) 'Efficiency Wage Models of Unemployment', *AER*, vol. 74 (May) pp. 200–205.

Part II

Money Wages and Employment

3 Wages and Unemployment Half a Century On

Patrick Minford

The normal modern interpretation – e.g. Parkin and Bade (1982) – of Keynes (1936) follows Hicks (1937) in postulating rigidity of money wages; variations in output, employment, and unemployment then occur as changing demand alters the price level and so the real wage. Firms hire labour and produce, with given capital, to the point where the real wage equals the marginal product. Changes in the stock of capital are driven primarily by 'animal spirits', though these are also suggested to be influenced by current demand conditions. There is no natural rate of unemployment; rather, unemployment will settle wherever demand settles.

I am not qualified in the arcana of Keynes's interpretation and so cannot say whether this is a truly accurate account of the great man's thought. But let me take this interpretation as a starting point.

There are a number of interesting points about it.

First, there is rigidity of *money* wages, absolutely central to the Keynesian result in this interpretation. Why this particular rigidity? Keynes, when challenged about it in a radio interview, stated that the fixing of benefits in nominal terms was a natural justification – Keynes (1930). As a good liberal intellectual, he accepted this as a part of the natural order of things and proceeded to spell out the implications for (money) demand policy, which operates implicitly by *reducing the real value of unemployment benefits*.

Second, there is after all a (sort of) natural rate in the model. We have, on the one hand, the *minimum* rate of unemployment, to be obtained once money demand has been expanded to the point at which nominal wages start to rise, namely when real benefits have fallen so much that they no longer are attractive as an alternative to work and all those who, in the absence of benefits, would wish to work are therefore doing so. Keynes's main policy prescription was that money demand should be expanded to and kept at this point. Nevertheless, in the absence of such an expansion in money demand, which would reduce real benefits, the unemployment resulting can be legitimately considered a natural rate *conditional on the real value of benefits*.

This is a strictly classical interpretation of Keynes's *General Theory* under the given institutional assumption of exogenous *money* benefits. That this assumption was valid seems clear from the astonishing changes in real benefits over the 1920s and 1930s – they (a weighted average) rose some 190 per cent between 1920 and 1931 as prices collapsed and nominal benefits were extended and raised, while during the 1930s they rose only slightly. The only policy-dictated cut in money benefits was in late 1931 when Ramsey MacDonald cut them by 10 per cent to reduce the large budget deficit. Following Benjamin and Kochin's seminal (1979) work, Matthews (1986) exhaustively examines this period and fits *this* 'Keynesian' model to the data from it; he shows that it was entirely valid and solid in its microfoundations and that it justified all Keynes's policy prescriptions. (Lloyd George could have done it and so forth.)

Keynes had a traditionally British (also continental) curiosity about and involvement in policy issues of his time. I daresay that he would have cared little that the *mechanism* he was deploying to underpin his policy recommendations was essentially classical; his insight, that classical *policy* conclusions would be ineffective under this version of the classical model – the one with a crucial nominal rigidity – remained secure, and revolutionary enough.

If this is all so, then there is a basic continuity of thinking about the determinants of unemployment in the short and long term evident running from the classical economists (Pigou, 1927, being a notable example) through Keynes and right up to the present time. What has changed during this time has not been the basic thinking so much as the institutional environment. Before the First World War, benefits were not significant at all. In Keynes's day, crucial policy variables such as benefits were set in nominal terms; voters and special interest groups were unable to obtain leverage over real payments received (or perhaps more to the point when these went *up* interest groups kept quiet and ordinary voters did not realise). Nowadays, the political market place discusses receipts and payments in real terms, having been too often duped by the inflationary process since the Second World War. Of course, there is a parallel story to be told about this institutional evolution and its roots no doubt in the inflationary 'Keynesian' policy making after the Second World War. But this would take me from my main theme which is to bring the account of the *wage/unemployment mechanism* up to date, especially as it concerns today's high unemployment in Europe.

There is now a growing chorus of economists saying that in Europe the equilibrium or 'natural' rate of unemployment has risen in the past decade.[1] The contrasting cases of the US, where the natural rate appears to have been fairly static in the region of 5–6 per cent, and Japan, where unemployment is negligible, are striking, and beg to be explained by a common theory. The theory that has emerged has centred around 'supply-side' explanations of the behaviour of real wage costs. In this chapter, I wish to try to integrate the perceptions in this growing 'natural rate' literature into a common framework. I shall stress similarities of approach and abstract from the many differences of emphasis that have arisen as individual researchers have ploughed their own furrows and differentiated their products.

This literature draws its original antecedents from three main strands of previous work. First, there is the accelerationist, expectations-augmented version of the Phillips curve due to Friedman (1968) and Phelps (1970); the non-accelerating-inflation rate of unempoyment, or Nairu, is the natural rate of unemployment in another guise, as ground out by micro-markets (Walrasian or not) with all their distortions. Second, and not to be forgotten merely because of its weak theoretical underpinnings at the time, is the 'cost-push' literature of which Hines (1964) was a prime example in its stress on the role of union power in pushing up wage costs. A third major strand is the work on unemployment benefits and their role in prolonging job search; this was a component of the UK 'Treasury View' in the 1930s and it influenced Keynes in postulating rigid wages. In the post-war period Grubel and his students explored its relevance more rigorously in a number of countries, e.g. for the UK (Maki and Spindler, 1975). But it was Benjamin and Kochin's later (1979) but seminal investigation of interwar UK unemployment that was probably most influential in focusing on benefits as a major explanatory mechanism; for they showed – in a way subsequently largely vindicated – that in that most demand-affected macro episode of all, the Great Depression, unemployment was to a large extent due to benefits in at least one major economy.

3.1 THEORY OF THE NATURAL RATE

The theory we now have can be illustrated by a four-quadrant diagram (Figure 3.1) adapted from Parkin and Bade (1982) for an open economy.

Starting from the bottom right-hand quadrant, the FF curve shows the relation between the real exchange rate, e, and the level of UK demand, y, required to give current account balance (assumed to be an equilibrium requirement). If the FF shifts (because world market conditions for UK products improve) raising e, this raises the *product* real wage facing firms for any given *consumption* real wage enjoyed by workers. Thus moving to the lower left-hand quadrant, we see the demand for labour curve (relating w, real wages, to L, employment, according to the marginal productivity condition) shift rightwards; the supply of labour slopes upward conventionally. The rightward shift along the supply curve thus translates into a rise in employment and through the production function (shown in the top left-hand quadrant) into a rise in output. The SS curve in the bottom right-hand quadrant traces out how such a rise in the supply of output results from a rise in the real exchange rate; it is therefore the economy's overall supply curve of output.

The focus of this chapter is on the two groups of variables affecting the supply of labour and the production function; we now turn to a more detailed consideration.

The upshot of the whole framework is to be seen in the fourth quadrant

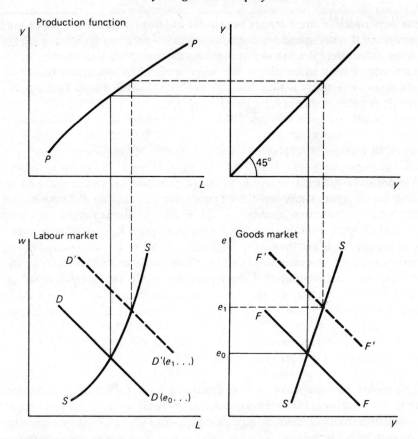

Figure 3.1 Equilibrium combination of output, employment, real wages and real exchange rate.

relating *e* and *y*. On the one hand we have a supply curve which slopes upward (because as the real exchange rate rises real consumer wages rise relative to real product wages) and is shifted to the right by unanticipated inflation (the 'Phillips curve' effect). On the other hand we have a 'demand curve', given by the condition of external balance, which slopes downward because as domestic expenditure expands, raising output, more of it must be 'switched' by a fall in *e* into domestic output in order to maintain external balance at the higher output level. The intersection of the two curves gives the 'natural rates' of *e* and *y*; working back through the other quadrants yields natural rates of real wages, unemployment, employment, and productivity.

'Macro-economic' effects – i.e. the 'cyclical' fluctuations – come when dynamics are added; these arise from adjustment costs, expectations, stock-flow interactions and nominal contracts. Without wishing in any way to denigrate the importance of these aspects, which are the staple fare of macroeconomic modelling, I shall spend little further space on them and assume in what follows that there is a fair degree of common ground in analysing them. In particular I shall assume that the effects of a cyclical shock tend to get eliminated effectively within three to five years, so that in accounting for trends in unemployment it makes sense to focus on the natural rate.

3.2 NATURAL RATE ANALYSIS IN PRACTICE

The natural rate literature requires above all a reason for an upward-sloping, even flat, long-run supply curve of labour. This is so because if for example the supply curve were perfectly inelastic, real wages would be perfectly flexible and whatever distortions entered the labour market, provided they did not directly affect the supply of labour, their effect would be entirely on real wages and not on employment or unemployment. Tax 'wedges', union-driven wage rises, regulatory restrictions, employer-financed social costs, are all included in the list of such employment-invariant distortions. Indeed, it seems to have been with such a framework in mind (familiar enough in international trade theory and espoused in Friedman (1982), p. 124) that Milton Friedman has rejected in media comment the idea that unions had a role in explaining Britain's rising unemployment.

A flat-rate unemployment benefit entitlement, which continues more or less indefinitely when its recipient remains unemployed, is an ideal candidate to generate an increase in long-run labour supply elasticity.[2] For as long as the average real wage falls, relative to this benefit, people will withdraw from labour supply – indefinitely, until the wage picks up again – substituting their time into better-rewarded leisure (or 'black-economy') activities. Notice that a benefit system giving a fixed *ratio* of benefits to previous earnings for a *limited* duration will not increase labour supply elasticity, but will only displace the supply curve leftwards as the unemployed search longer (but ultimately take a job at lower wages when benefits run out). A benefit system giving a fixed ratio *indefinitely*, however, would increase supply elasticity because as wages fell some people would withdraw from (or not return to) work, attracted by the benefit related to their *previous* wage, knowing that any future wage would be lower and with it any future benefit.

Once the supply curve has been rendered elastic by the benefit system, other distortions come into their own; in principle any distortion will now effect employment and unemployment. The analysis of unemployment, given such a benefit system, can literally involve looking at every permanent shock to the economy. It is for this reason that ordinary people and the press who talk endlessly about particular 'reasons' for unemployment (new technology, foreign competition, etc.) are correct to do so at one level. However, the economist can insist on two points. First, that the basic cause – in the sense that it is *the* (only relevant) necessary condition, if not a sufficient one – of unemployment lies in the benefit system; it is this (like grit in the oyster) that produces the crucial positive elasticity of supply. Second, that quantitative attribution of the rise in unemployment (*given* that benefit system) to the variation in relevant exogenous 'causes' is a complex task, requiring more than a commonsense and casual observation; and incidentally, variation in benefits may be quite a small 'cause' quantitatively without diminishing in any way its essential causal role.

3.3   NATURAL RATE ANALYSIS AND EUROPE: IS THERE A EUROPEAN DISEASE?

In many European countries unemployment has risen and stayed high during the 1980s. To name a few: Belgium, Holland, UK, France, Germany and Italy. Can this common model be applied to them, defining a European disease (or, as Giersch, 1985, has coined the term, 'Eurosclerosis')?

There are not yet convincing studies of all these countries. However, there is now quite a body of work for the UK, Germany and Belgium.

Work on the UK by Layard and Nickell (1985) and my own work (Minford, 1983) has identified significant effects on real wage costs of union power and taxes on employers. Whether the variation in benefit and income tax rates has significantly contributed to real wages has been a matter of controversy. The empirical debate turns on whether actual productivity should be included in the wage equation; if it is, it tends to make these variables insignificant in annual (though not necessarily in quarterly) data, otherwise they are significant. Inclusion of such a term in a labour *supply* function is however clearly wrong; though it could affect the union mark up, in the Layard–Nickell work this is included directly as an argument, so its determinants are redundant. In my work, the unionisation rate is used as a proxy for the mark-up with which it is in fact highly correlated. But in any case, Layard and Nickell, while querying this effect, do concede that the benefit *regime* must be largely responsible for permitting the widening gap between unemployment and vacancies, which they use as a proxy for factors inducing 'increased incentives to search'. Table 3.1 reveals the similarities in this work; it compares the Layard–Nickell and my own (Minford, 1983) estimates of the natural rate.

Detailed quantitative work on Germany was carried out by Davis and myself (1986), drawing on data for employer costs and state supplementary benefits trends provided by national experts. This work estimates the natural rate in Germany at 1.2 million (about 5 per cent) in 1980; with significant contributions from employer costs, union power and unemployment benefits (Figure 3.2). It seems that the social support system was materially changed by the SPD during the second half of the 1970s; supplementary and housing

Table 3.1   Comparison of Layard/Nickell and Minford NAIRU estimates –
% rise over period

	Layard and Nickell (males u/e)		Minford all u/e (1955–79)
	Model 1 (1955–83)	Model 2	
Taxes/benefits (model 1)	3.7	—	4.5
Unemployment/Vacancies (model 2)	—	4.8	—
Union mark-up	3.8	2.7	3.3
Other (especially mismatch)	1.5	1.7	—
	9.0	9.2	7.9

Sources: R. Layard and S. Nickell, 'The Causes of British Unemployment', *National Institute Economic Review*, vol. III (1985), P. Minford, 'Labour Market Equilibrium in an Open Economy', *Oxford Economic Papers*, vol. 35 (Supp.) (1983).

benefit (*Sozialhilfe* and *Wohngeld*) became more generous and were standardised nationwide (previously the key unemployment benefit was a ratio to earnings which declined over time) and employers were charged with increasing 'social' duties to their workers. A detailed account of these changes is contained in Soltwedel and Trapp (1987).

In Belgium, de Grauwe, Fratianni and Nabli (1985) have found that the 'tax wedge' (i.e. the sum of the tax rate on wages paid by employer and employee) significantly affects employment. Minford *et al.* (1983) estimate employment and wage functions similar in many ways to those for the UK; the Belgian natural rate is estimated at 340 000, around 8 per cent, and close to the actual rate for 1980. Tax rates (employer and employee as in De Grauwe, Fratianni and Nabli), union power and benefits are all significant (Figure 3.3).

A broad brush treatment of all European countries by Bean, Layard and Nickell (1987) has recently been attempted, using the unemployment/ vacancies (U/V) ratio as the benefit proxy variable in the wage equation. The results are encouraging for the theory in a broad way but, because (necessarily in such a uniform time-constrained treatment of all countries) not enough attention is given to the institutional peculiarities of state intervention in each country, they are not entirely convincing country by country and the use of the U/V ratio is an unsatisfactory indirect measure of the factors involved. For example, in Germany they attributed the rise in the natural rate of 3.5 per cent entirely to the U/V ratio. Italy – a country where they find little rise in the natural rate – is an institutional minefield; not only does the state subsidise employers who avoid laying off workers but keep them (idle) on their books, but there is also the large black economy (recently officially estimated by the Italian statistical office in the addition of 15 per cent to its GDP estimate) in which many 'unemployed' pursue full-time jobs.

Moving away from 'hard' studies of these countries, we can use the picture

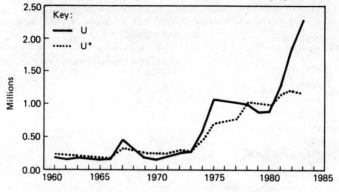

West Germany: Unemployment (U) and equilibrium unemployment (U*)

Logarithm of real unemployment benefits, including Sozialhilfe

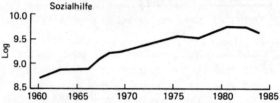

Unionisation rate. Percentage of employees in unions

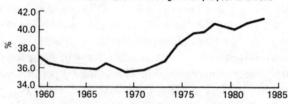

Employers' National Insurance contributions and non-wage costs. Indirect costs as a proportion of gross wages

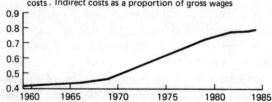

Employees' direct tax and National Insurance contributions as a percentage of employees' gross income

Figure 3.2   West Germany

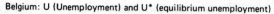

Belgium: U (Unemployment) and U* (equilibrium unemployment)

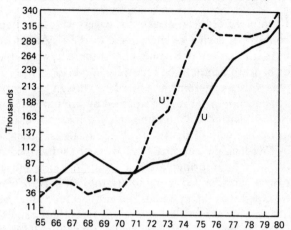

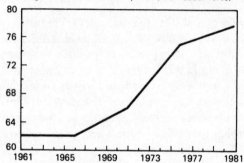

Belgium: Union membership rate (% of labour force)

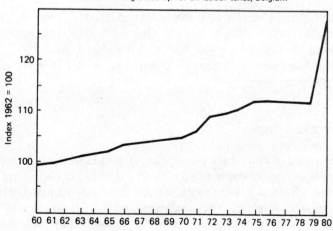

Real benefits grossed up for all labour taxes, Belgium

Figure 3.3   Belgium

building up from them of a European disease to suggest why some countries have avoided catching it. Clearly, we must look to their systems of state intervention in the labour market. We would expect those in which the state does not set a floor beneath wages to be relatively immune.

Two interesting cases are Switzerland and Sweden. Though both providing generous unemployment support, it is accompanied by strict monitoring and it is limited in time. In Switzerland, the unemployed have to report twice weekly to the benefit office with evidence of job applications; benefit ceases after 8 months. In Sweden, the support fund is partly subscribed by the unions, who assist with monitoring; after a year, the unemployed are automatically put on a state-funded 'community job' – a sort of workfare system. It should be noted that this system is not entirely successful: because presumably the rates paid are above market-clearing rates for the skills of the workfare workers, the system has increased public spending and created a pool of long-term *state* employed, a form of hidden long-term unemployment (Burton, 1987).

Outside Europe, Japan and the US are other countries where state unemployment support is strictly limited in both scale and duration. In both, the family and the individual is expected to provide long-term support.[3] 'Lifetime employment' in big Japanese firms applies to less that 40 per cent of Japanese employees; it is not a form of social security so much as a way of hiring and retaining a core of key employees. The secondary labour market provides flexible terms for subcontracted operations; also of course lifetime employment carries with it the obligation to accept profit-related pay (cuts if necessary).

3.4 TANGENTIAL ISSUES

A number of issues have arisen, as this literature has developed, that have a bearing on the interpretation of these results. First, what is the appropriate union model? Second, what is the role of demand and 'hysteresis'? Third, what is the extent and role of nominal and real wage rigidity? Fourth, is the extent of corporatism relevant?

3.4.1 Union behaviour

The simple model of union behaviour underlying most of the work reported above has the union monopoly fixing a wage and firms then being free to set employment. Rational intertemporal optimisation by such a union will introduce lagged adjustment and reaction to expected future trends before they occur, and universal wage contracts can be justified by such a union's transactions costs in policing its members. Implicitly, firms have little labour market power, which implies that the union will typically be multi-industry.

One or two authors (e.g. Layard and Nickell, 1985) have allowed for bargaining betwen union and groups of firms or employer associations in fixing the wage. This introduces possible indeterminacy but the arguments of the unionised wage function remain essentially unchanged.

In a recent paper, Beenstock (1987) has argued that unions will pursue 'salami' tactics. They maximise the expected utility of members currently in work, a majority of whom knowing that there is a social security safety net gamble that they will not lose their jobs when wages are pushed up; however, this gamble will be repeated by the workforce surviving from the first gamble – now again a majority will gamble on not being the ones to lose their jobs if wages go up another notch. In principle repetition can be indefinite until closure looms. Similar ideas have been advanced by Blanchard and Summers (1987). It is clearly a particularly ruthless and unattractive picture of 'union insider' behaviour. (As will be discussed below, it gives rise to unemployment developments that closely resemble 'hysteresis'.)

However, there is a difficulty in the theory which could well limit its applicability to a few accidental cases. Suppose, for argument's sake, it were true. Then the initial groups of employed union members would, if they are rational, be aware of what subsequent survivors will do. They will then compute the outcome of the chain of gambles their current gamble will unleash; and they will clearly vote against it, since a majority of them will ultimately lose their job as the chain proceeds. There is a sort of time-inconsistency here; the first group would only agree to gamble if all *promised* not to gamble again, yet of course once the gamble has occurred it no longer suits the survivors to carry out their promise. (There are parallels with the butchery of the French Revolution – a particularly nasty 'accident' for most participating revolutionaries.) We can go further: the first group will *expect* the survivors to renege unless there is some binding agreement for them to be punished for reneging. If there are no such arrangements, then the first group will vote on the assumption that any survivors will gamble again, and so as argued earlier, vote against.

In the standard monopoly union model, the current members vote for a *one-off* time-inconsistent plan to raise their collective welfare by sacrificing the jobs of a few for the higher living standards of the many. Why do they vote for it, then, if it is time-inconsistent and the survivors could do it again? Implicit in the model is some unstated union constitutional clause outlawing such repeat gambles; there must be of course or the plan could never attract a majority.

A rival union model, that of the 'efficiently bargaining' bilateral mono-poly, has been revived by Hall and Lilien (1979) and tested for the US by Pencavel and others (e.g. MaCurdy and Pencavel, 1985). In this model, union and firm (or employers' association) both have market power – and in particular the firm has monopoly power in the goods market, so that if its labour costs rise it has some monopoly profit it may cede to the union. They maximise their joint gains at the expense of the firm's consumers, and divide these gains via 'wages' according to their relative bargaining strength. The implication is that employment and output are invariant to the division of the gains, i.e. to wages. Consequently one will observe 'feather bedding' where unions are strong; their share of the gains will show up as high real wages and employment 'excessive' in relation to what a non-unionised employer would hire if faced with these wages.

Such a model clearly could not explain a rise in the natural rate of unemployment, since increased union power would not reduce employment. It is a model that casts the union in a potentially benevolent role – as argued by Freeman and Medoff (1979). Without damaging employment, they may force firms to be efficient in exploiting technological and market possibilities for profits, for distribution to workers and shareholders.

There is evidence of 'efficient bargaining' in certain US unionised sectors (e.g. MaCurdy and Pencavel, 1985); the evidence of actual union benevolence is on the other hand rather weak and there is some to the contrary (Addison and Burton, 1984; Hirsch and Addison, 1986). What is, however, relevant for our purposes is that the evidence strongly rejects such a model in Europe; rising union power *has* lowered employment and raised unemployment with rising real wages. Institutionally, it is unlikely that multi-industry unions such as found in Europe could negotiate efficient bargains with all the firms and industries they are dealing with; transactions and policing costs would no doubt be prohibitive. Observation by institutional labour market specialists clearly confirms that European unions do not behave in this way. We seem therefore to be on reasonably solid ground with the union model most widely used in this natural rate literature.

3.4.2　The role of demand and 'hysteresis'

It is obvious that 'demand' (in the sense of *domestic* expenditure,[4] potentially stimulated by fiscal and monetary policy) cannot affect the natural rate of unemployment. This is so because demand is endogenous to such a model.

There has been some confusion on this point because sub-models of the labour market will usually of necessity have some variable proxying demand from the wider model of the economy. Within the sub-model, it is then possible to allocate some variations in real wages and unemployment to 'demand' – this is done for example in Layard and Nickell (1985). But they are at pains to point out that when the sub-model is solved together with essential equations from the wider model, this variation has to be reallocated to the exogenous labour and other market factors identified earlier in this chapter as setting the natural rate.

More recently – if we accept that this route is closed – those impressed by the long-term importance of demand have sought to open up a new channel of influence from demand to the natural rate. This is 'hysteresis', a view perhaps inspired by the tendencies for the natural rate estimates to gravitate towards the actual unemployment rate. In theory, some mechanism is appealed to whereby a rise in actual unemployment, from whatever cause, precipitates an irreversible (or, in a weaker form, only very slowly reversible) change in the environment which raises the natural rate. Symmetry need not follow: a *fall* in actual unemployment does not necessarily precipitate an opposite change in the environment which lowers the natural rate – that will depend on the mechanism involved.

Some have been tempted to 'test' such a theory by fitting time series models to unemployment and searching for unit roots; the presence of such roots implies that a temporary shock will have a permanent effect, a result consistent with hysteresis. Occasionally they 'find' them; but this is not very convincing. First, unit roots are not readily distinguishable from roots that are large and could be associated with ordinary adjustment costs; *a fortiori*, if roots 'close' to unity are accepted (for 'weak' hysteresis), the same applies. Second, the time series representation of a natural rate model, in which the exogenous forcing variables are omitted, will have unit roots (and large ones close to unity) because these forcing variables frequently follow random walks or slow autoregressions. Convincing evidence of hysteresis from a *structural* model in which rival determinants of the actual rate are taken seriously is not forthcoming to my knowledge; once these determinants are included, unit roots disappear. True, there is strong evidence of large roots, particularly first order; but this could also be interpreted as adjustment. Layard and Nickell (1987) attributed dynamics of this type to hysteresis; but the attribution can readily be questioned.

We may go back to the theory to consider candidates for the hysteresis mechanism. One we have already rejected: that of union 'salami tactics' – the salami will not play. Some others suggested include: the experience of unemployment (a) reduces human capital (b) causes discouragement and passivity in 'search' (c) is conducive to disease and social malaise, including crime (d) stigmatises those involved from an employer's viewpoint (e) familiarises the unemployed with the system of benefits and the black economy.

There is no need to dismiss any of these ideas, all of which strike some chord of plausibility. The issue is rather precisely what relation do such mechanisms hold to the main determinants of the natural rate we have identified. It is after all rather striking that such mechanisms do *not* (significantly) it would seem operate in other countries, such as the US and Japan, where these determinants are *not* present.

In a system of state support that does not subsidise long-term unemployment, it is unlikely that any of (a) through (e) would apply. For *short-term* unemployment would not cause decay in human capital (one might expect at least some people to treat it rather as an opportunity to upgrade capital). It would not discourage active search – rather the opposite: the mind would be concentrated by the knowledge that support runs out quickly. This activity would hardly encourage disease or malaise; nor would it cause any stigma for many could be expected for a variety of reasons to have spells of short-term unemployment. As for learning about the system of support and the black economy, there would be nothing to learn about – of relevance to *long-term* unemployment, that is (the black economy participation of the *employed* would be another matter of no relevance here).

3.4.3 Wage rigidity, nominal and real

The idea of 'rigidity' in wages is an old one, especially in Europe, originally linked to the notion of cost push. Keynes regarded *nominal* wages as largely exogenous, fixed by cost push factors. More recently, Keynesian disequilibrium theory has treated *real* wages in the same way, with indexation or quite frequent re-contracting undermining nominal rigidity. As pointed out earlier, the literature discussed here has taken over and elaborated on the idea of *real* wage rigidity. It has in fact nothing to say about nominal rigidity, which is irrelevant to the *natural* rate of unemployment but relates to the Phillips curve and macroeconomics of the usual sort; the greater nominal rigidity, the shallower the slope of the Phillips curve, the greater the effect of monetary or other shocks.

There is a further distinction one might make between short-run and long-run real wage rigidity. In the long run, the European system makes labour supply more elastic (real wages more rigid); one would expect less elasticity (less real wage rigidity) in the US or Japan. But this greater elasticity produces higher numbers of people choosing to remain long-term unemployed; and it by no means follows that, if there is a short-run movement in labour demand, such people will be quickly and easily absorbed into work with a small change in real wages – *short*-run real wage rigidity (high supply elasticity). It is in fact more likely that having taken a long-term decision to withdraw, they cannot be easily induced to come back into the labour market in response to temporary changes in real wages.

The regressions run up to now suggest the following:

(1) Europe has much *less* nominal rigidity than the US. This is associated with a history of high and variable inflation in Europe which has produced widespread indexation and a reduction in contract lengths – much as predicted in Lucas (1973).

(2) Europe has *more long-run* real wage rigidity than the US – as evidenced by the literature we have been examining.

(3) In the short run Europe's real wage rigidity relative to the US is disputed. Three studies find *less* in Europe than in the US (Grubb,

Jackman and Layard, 1982; Minford *et al.*, 1983; Bean, Layard and Nickell, 1987), but Gordon (1987) finds no difference. He attributes his alternative view to his wage series which apply to the whole economy whereas earlier series are a mixture, mainly relating to manufacturing. This is not clear – it is also possible that his specification which for example uses inflation lagged one and two *years* (in a quarterly wage equation) to proxy expected inflation is the culprit.

This discussion suggests that there is nothing in the voluminous literature of wage equations, their nominal and real rigidity, that cannot be broadly reconciled with the natural rate literature we are here examining.

3.4.4 Efficiency Wages

Another reason that has been suggested for real wages to be raised above the competitive equilibrium is that of 'efficiency' wages. Suppose for purposes of argument the existence of a competitive non-union market and that workers have some reservation wage producing a positive supply elasticity. A variety of factors may lead employers to offer more than the competitive wage to their employees. The following list is not exhaustive.

Regulations limiting or penalising dismissal which make labour turnover costly may cause an employer to pay more to its incumbent employees to discourage them from leaving. This is not the optimal way to achieve this; seniority-related rewards produce longer tenure without raising the cost of hiring new employees. Nevertheless, the *average* labour cost will be raised by regulation even if the statutory wage is not, and this will depress employment.

The threat of unionisation may make non-union employers pay a premium to their workers to discourage union recruitment. The extent of this factor will depend on the freedom employers have under the law to hire new non-union workers, and fire the unionised, if unions enter the plant. But again here the existence of union powers under the law would raise non-union wages for certain threatened types of employers above the competitive level. This too will raise average wages and depress employment.

Asymmetrical information on the part of some employers about the quality of the labour they hire may lead them to pay more than the competitive rate because they wish to attract the better workers. Rather as I, lacking information about jewellery, may be willing to pay a higher price than the going rate in the bazaar, so ensuring that I will get a good quality piece. This argument presupposes both that there are significant costs of firing workers who are unsatisfactory (just as it is hard to resell jewellery) and that it is costly to obtain good information. The former may be true if regulations impose costs. The latter seems appropriate to infrequent transactions but regular hiring would presumably produce a market in information and screening devices; given such screening, it is not clear that an employer protects himself against deceptive employees by paying more than the going rate for any particular (screened) type of labour. (He may even attract the *more* deceptive employees who perceive a better pay off!) Again, however, a combination of regulation and high screening costs could produce higher wages in parts of the labour market, with effects on unemployment.

How important these effects may be is an empirical matter on which little evidence is yet available. But do we have here in any case anything more than a twist on the basic story? *Given* some factor inducing a significant positive supply elasticity of labour (this here being the 'reservation wage'), distortions such as those here under discussion (regulation, union laws, high information costs) will generate an employment, and not really a wage differential, effect. *Absent the supply elasticity*, non-union wages would simply drop to absorb the redundant workers.

3.4.5   Does corporatism affect the natural rate?

It has been argued – e.g. Jackman and Layard (1987) – that corporatism can bring down the natural rate. Sweden is held up as one example by these authors: there strong unions participate with government and industry in setting overall norms for real wage growth (incomes policy). This has contributed to holding unemployment down.

Bean, Layard and Nickell (1987) produce evidence that corporatism does affect the working of the labour market: real wages are less rigid (especially in the short run), they respond less to tax and terms of trade cost push pressures, and they adjust faster (as does employment). This is consistent with the idea that central consensus planning would force unions to pursue aims more in tune with national interests. Unions would cooperate with this if they gain rewards from the consensus.

There are a number of points to be made, before we rush off to embrace corporatism. First, corporatism tends in a cross-country comparison to lower the natural rate somewhat, *cet. par.* But corporatism is itself correlated with important factors raising the natural rate, notably union power and social welfare provision. There are two reasons for this: that unions require power and social welfare as the rewards for cooperation and that unions have to be large relative to the economy to reap *direct* gains from cooperation (small unions have a strong incentive to renege, free riding on the incomes policy, and so making it ultimately fail). So we find that the second and third most corporatist economies, Germany and the Netherlands respectively, had in 1987 high unemployment rates (8.9 per cent and 14.0 per cent) while the least corporatist, the USA, had only 6.1 per cent and has kept its natural rate of unemployment from rising much if at all.

Second, corporatism – with power given to large producer interests – reduces competition and so also innovation. This problem has recently been highlighted in the most corporatist economy, Austria; increasing deficits have paralysed the large nationalised sector, leaders in consensus creation, and the economy's performance has deteriorated.

Finally, of course, corporatism reduces economic and political freedom; this makes it controversial from a political viewpoint. It is far from a value-free proposal to raise the efficiency of the labour market.

Corporatism is therefore a double-edged sword; its introduction, supposing it could be engineered, may raise the natural rate if accompanied by other institutional changes (e.g. to benefits and union power) as the price of consensus. Its loss similarly may lower it, if it makes possible the removal of such concessions. Its other costs – in competition, innovation and freedom – must also be weighed.

3.5 SOME CONCLUDING REMARKS

I have argued that a growing literature has identified a European disease in which state intervention has reduced the long-run elasticity of labour supply, and, together with other exogenous factors thus able to have an effect on wages, pushed up its supply price, so raising the natural rate of unemployment. A detailed discussion of policy responses to the European disease would not be helpful; it would have to be voluminous and country by country since a reform strategy must be tailored to the political marketplace of the country. Experience since 1979 in Britain has shown at least that reform of a certain type, mainly in the direction of less state intervention, is possible; it is too early to pronounce it successful in limiting the natural rate though it has succeeded in sharply raising productivity growth (Matthews and Minford, 1987). Diverse set-ups in countries with low unemployment show that unemployment can be tackled in other ways. Some of these solutions may be costly – for example, the Swedish job guarantee is expensive to the tax-payer, and Austrian corporatism appears to have damaged the economy's dynamism. The mechanism identified in this chapter points to a first best solution of labour market competition for political entrepreneurs to achieve the gains of labour market efficiency while still meeting the social and other demands made by their fellow countrymen.

Finally, let me revert to Keynes. I have argued that today's thinking, classical in spirit as it most assuredly is, goes back to the classics in an unbroken line through Keynes himself. What has changed is the institutional constraints; as these constraints have changed, policy recommendations have necessarily changed with them. Keynes himself can surely not be blamed for the monetary excesses of post-war governments carried out in his name; they failed to see through the policy recommendations of the 1930s to the basic mechanism beneath. The final message is that macroeconomists, dead and alive, do not disagree about the essential mechanisms at work quite as much as is supposed.

Notes

1. Examples include, chronologically, Minford, 1983; De Grauwe, Fratianni and Nabli, 1985; Sachs and Wyplosz, 1986; Layard and Nickell, 1985, 1987; Blanchard and Summers, 1987; Davis and Minford, 1986. Bean, Layard and Nickell (1987) contains some more applications.
2. Other reasons are possible but unlikely. In the long run intertemporal substitution is irrelevant; and income and substitution effects otherwise found empirically are insufficient for the purpose here.
3. The exception is the notorious Aid for Families with Dependent Children (AFDC) which has caused severe labour market distortions for very low productivity workers and for blacks in particular (Murray, 1985; Swan and Bernstam, 1986).
4. Not of course *foreign* expenditure or the world terms of trade which enter the overseas budget constraint faced by an open economy.

References

ADDISON, J. T. and J. BURTON (1984) *Trade Unions and Society* (The Fraser Institute, Vancouver, British Columbia).

BEAN, C., R. LAYARD and S. NICKELL (eds) (1987) 'The Rise in Unemployment: a Multi-Country Study', in *The Rise in Unemployment* (Blackwell), pp. 1–22.

BEENSTOCK, M. (1987) 'Regret and Jubilation in Union Wage Bargaining', mimeo, Hebrew University of Jerusalem, forthcoming *Oxford Economic Papers*.

BENJAMIN, D. and L. KOCHIN (1979) 'Searching for an Explanation of Unemployment in Interwar Britain', *Journal of Political Economy*, vol. 87, pp. 441–70.

BLANCHARD, O. and L. SUMMERS (1987) 'Fiscal Increasing Returns, Hysteresis, Real Wages and Unemployment', *European Economic Review*, vol. 31, April, pp. 543–60.

BURTON, J. (1987) *Workfare* (Employment Research Institute, University of Buckingham).

DAVIS, J. and P. MINFORD (1986) 'Germany and the European Disease', *Recherches Economiques de Louvain*, vol. 52, pp. 373–98. (Symposium on Unemployment in Europe), J. Muysken and C. de Neubourg (eds).

DE GRAUWE, P., M. FRATIANNI and M. K. NABLI (1985) *Exchange Rates, Money and Output – the European Experience*, (Macmillan).

FREEMAN, R. B. and J. L. MEDOFF (1979) 'The Two Faces of Unionism', *Public Interest*, vol. 57 (Fall) pp. 69–93.

FRIEDMAN, M. (1968) 'The Role of Monetary Policy', *American Economic Review*, vol. 58, pp. 1–17.

FRIEDMAN, M. (1982) *Capitalism and Freedom*, 1982 reissue in paperback (University of Chicago Press).

GIERSCH, H. (1985) 'Euro-sclerosis: the Malaise that Flatters Prosperity', *Financial Times*, 2 January.

GORDON, R. J. (1987) 'Wage Gaps vs. Output Gaps: is There a Common Story for all of Europe?' in H. Giersch (ed.), *Macro and Micro policies for More Growth and Employment*, Symposium 1987 (Tübingen: Mohr, forthcoming).

GRUBB, D., R. JACKMAN and R. LAYARD (1982) 'Causes of the Current Stagflation', *Review of Economic Studies*, vol. 49, pp. 707–30, reprinted in *The Causes of Unemployment*, C. A. Greenhalgh, R. Layard and A. Oswald (eds), (OUP).

HALL, R. E. and D. M. LILIEN (1979) 'Efficient Wage Bargains under Uncertain Supply and Demand', *American Economic Review*, vol. 69, pp. 868–79.

HICKS, J. (1937) 'Mr. Keynes and the Classics; a Suggested Interpretation', *Economics*, vol. 5, pp. 147–59.

HINES, A. G. (1964) 'Trade Unions and Wage Inflation in the United Kingdom, 1893–1961', *Review of Economic Studies*, vol. 31, pp. 221–52.

HIRSCH, B. T. and J. T. ADDISON (1986) *The Economic Analysis of Trade Unions* (London: Allen and Unwin)

JACKMAN, R. and R. LAYARD (1987) 'Innovative Policies for the Reduction of Unemployment', forthcoming in *Monetarism and Macroeconomics*, P. Minford (ed.) (Readings 26, Institute of Economic Affairs, London).

KEYNES, J. M. (1930) in *Collected Writings* Volume xx (ed. D. Moggridge, 1981), pp. 318–19. (Original radio interview with Sir Josiah Stamp, transcript in *The Listener*, 26 Feb. 1930).

KEYNES, J. M. (1936) *The General Theory of Employment, Interest and Money* (Macmillan).

LAYARD, R. and S. NICKELL (1985) 'The Causes of British Unemployment', *National Institute Economic Review*, vol. III (February) pp. 62–85.

LAYARD, R. and S. NICKELL (1987) 'The Labour Market', in *The Performance of the British Economy*, R. Dombusch and R. Layard (eds.), (Oxford: UP).

LUCAS, R. E. Jnr (1973) 'Some International Evidence on Output in Inflation Trade-offs', *American Economic Review*, vol. 68, pp. 326–34.

MACURDY, T. E. and J. PENCAVEL (1985) 'Testing between Competing Models of Wage and Employment Determination in Unionised Markets', *Journal of Political Economy*.

MAKI, D. and A. SPINDLER (1975) 'The Effect of Unemployment Compensation on the Rate of Unemployment in Great Britain', *Oxford Economic Papers*, vol. 27, pp. 440–54.

MATTHEWS, K. G. P. (1986) *The Interwar Economy* (Gower).

MATTHEWS, K. and P. MINFORD (1987) 'Mrs. Thatcher's Economic Policies 1979–86', *Economic Policy*, autumn special issue on *The New Conservative Revolution*.

MINFORD, P. (1983) 'Labour Market Equilibrium in an Open Economy', *Oxford Economic Papers*, vol. 35 (Supp.), pp. 207–44.

MINFORD, P., D. DAVIES, M. PEEL and A. SPRAGUE (1983) *Unemployment – Cause and Cure*, 1st ed (Martin Robertson (now Basil Blackwell)).

MINFORD, P., P-R AGENOR and E. NOWELL (1986) 'A New Classical Econometric Model of the World Economy', *Economic Modelling*, vol. 3, pp. 154–74.

MURRAY, C. (1985) *Losing Ground* (Manhattan Institute).

PARKIN, M. and R. BADE (1982) *Modern Macroeconomics* British ed (Philip Allan).

PHELPS, E. S. (1970) 'The New Microeconomics in Employment and Inflation Theory', in *Microeconomic Foundations of Employment and Inflation Theory*, E. S. Phelps (ed.) (Norton, N.Y.), pp. 1–27.

PIGOU, A. C. (1927) 'Wage Policy and Unemployment', *Economic Journal*.

SACHS, J. and C. WYPLOSZ (1986) 'The Economic Consequences of President Mitterrand', *Economic Policy*, vol. 2, pp. 261–322.

SOLTWEDEL, R. and P. TRAPP (1987) 'Labour Market Barriers to More Employment: Causes for an Increase of the Natural Rate? The Case of West Germany', in H. Giersch (ed.), *Macro and Micro policies for more growth and Employment*, Symposium 1987 (Tübingen: Mohr, forthcoming).

SWAN, PETER L. and M. S. BERNSTAM (1986) 'The State as Marriage Partner of Last Resort: a Labour Market Approach to Illegitimacy in the United States, 1960–1980', Working Paper 86-029, October 1986, mimeo, Graduate School of Business, University of New South Wales.

4 Wages and Economic Activity

Stephen Nickell

The role of wages in economic fluctuations is a rather fraught topic, having been the subject of bitter controversy for many years. Like most such arguments, the fundamental issue is how well a decentralised market economy works and, when it patently does not work in practice, whose fault it is. Our purpose in what follows is to discuss how the economy responds to various kinds of shocks from both the demand and the supply side and to highlight the role of wages in particular and the labour market in general. In order to do this we set up a very simple closed economy model and study its response to shocks. Specific topics on which we focus include nominal inertia, real and nominal wage movements, price setting behaviour and hysteresis.

4.1 A SIMPLE AGGREGATE MODEL

Our analysis will be based on the following simple log-linear model

Demand:	$y = \alpha_0 + \alpha_1(m-p) + \alpha_2 x^d$	(4.1)
Price setting:	$p - w = \beta_0 - \beta_1[p-p^e] + \beta_2 y$	(4.2)
Wage setting:	$w - p = \gamma_0 - \gamma_1[p-p^e] + \gamma_2 y + z$	(4.3)

y = output, m = money stock, p = price of output, x^d = factors influencing real demand, w = wage, z = exogenous factors influencing wage determination. All parameters are non-negative with the possible exception of the constant terms.

The demand function represents the reduced form of an IS–LM system where x^d includes all the real factors affecting aggregate demand (e.g. fiscal stance). The size of the parameter α_1 is of some importance in what follows and depends on the interest elasticity of the demand for money and the impact of interest rates and real wealth on the level of expenditure. Prices are set as a mark-up on costs, the mark-up being influenced by the level of activity, y, and by nominal inertia, $(p-p^e)$. The latter effect arises from the fact that when prices are set individual firms must form expectations concerning their competitors' prices. If they underestimate these, prices will turn out higher than expected and the mark-up on costs will be 'too low'. Nominal inertia in price setting can also, of course, arise from firms' inability to forecast accurately changes in wage costs. We have ignored this possibility in order to keep the analysis simple. Nothing fundamental is lost by so doing.

This price setting equation, although simple, encompasses a wide variety of possible market structures. If firms are price-takers and the goods market is competitive, nominal inertia is not an issue because firms take prices as given at every point in time. So $\beta_1 = 0$. Furthermore given decreasing returns, β_2 must be positive. On the other hand, if firms are price setters, clearly nominal inertia may be important and the role of activity can easily be attenuated. Indeed, if prices are set solely on a normal cost basis, β_2 is zero. The micro foundations of this last possibility have exercised economists for many years from Kalecki (1938) to Stiglitz (1984) and Rotemberg and Saloner (1986). One of the reasons why this issue has excited such attention is that price setting behaviour is crucial to the behaviour of real wages in response to shocks. Thus, for example, in the *General Theory* Keynes (1973) assumed competitive pricing behaviour. However, when forced to confront a few relevant facts on real wage behaviour by Dunlop (1938) and Tarshis (1939), he readily admits, in Keynes (1939), that a method of price determination akin to mark-up pricing may well be more relevant. We shall return to this issue below.

Wage setting is also influenced by nominal inertia and the level of activity in the standard fashion. The latter effect is typically captured by unemployment, but it is convenient here to utilise the production function in order to translate this into an output based measure of activity. Although the wage equation is written in real wage form, it is important to be clear that wage setting behaviour is concerned with nominal wages. In fact (4.3) is simply a rewrite of the equation

$$\Delta w = \gamma_0 + [(\gamma_1 p^e + (1 - \gamma_1)p) - p_{-1}] - (w - p)_{-1} + \gamma_2 y + z \qquad (4.4)$$

When wages are set, a proportion γ_1 of agents do not know the aggregate price level and so the term in square brackets reflects the relevant expected inflation rate. The higher is γ_1, the larger the extent of nominal inertia. The lagged real wage term simply captures the fact that if last period's real wages are high, wage rises will be lower and vice versa.[1] The z variables capture all the exogenous factors influencing the nominal wage bargain, unemployment benefits or union power, for example. These are the source of the supply shocks in the economy.[2]

Taking the model as a whole, the no-surprise equilibrium is obtained by setting $p = p^e$. Using * values for equilibrium, we obtain

$$y^* = [-(\beta_0 + \gamma_0) - z]/(\beta_2 + \gamma_2) \qquad (4.5)$$

$$w^* - p^* = [(\beta_2\gamma_0 - \gamma_2\beta_0) + \beta_2 z]/(\beta_2 + \gamma_2) \tag{4.6}$$

$$p^* = m + \frac{\alpha_0 + \alpha_2 x^d - y^*}{\alpha_1} \tag{4.7}$$

So, for given levels of m, x^d, z, the model determines the level of activity, y^*, the real wage, $w^* - p^*$, and the price level, p^*. Note that demand-side factors have no impact on the real side of the economy in equilibrium and the equilibrium price level is proportional to the money stock. So the model has the standard natural rate properties despite the absence of competitive markets. Finally, note that $(\beta_2 + \gamma_2)$ must be positive if a stable equilibrium is to exist. So no problems are caused if one or other of these parameters is zero or negative so long as their sum is positive.

4.2   DEMAND SHOCKS

In this section, we consider the impact of demand shocks and the role of wages in their transmission. We begin with nominal demand shocks and consider a simple version of the model where $p^e = p_{-1}$. This is appropriate in a world in which nominal variables are stable rather than growing at a stable rate. We make this assumption purely for expositional simplicity. As we shall see, we obtain precisely the same kind of results under rational expectations and, as a consequence, there is no essential loss of generality involved.

Under these circumstances, equations (4.2) and (4.3) become

$$p - w = \beta_0 - \beta_1\Delta p + \beta_2 y \tag{4.2'}$$

$$w - p = \gamma_0 - \gamma_1\Delta p + \gamma_2 y + z \tag{4.3'}$$

and the equilibrium described in (4.5), (4.6) and (4.7) is that for stable prices. Suppose we start from this equilibrium and introduce our demand shock at time zero. For all $t \geqslant 0$, we can write our model in terms of deviations from the initial position. So if $\tilde{x}_t$ represents the deviation from the initial equilibrium state for any variable x, we have

$$\tilde{y}_t = \alpha_1(\tilde{m}_t - \tilde{p}_t) + \alpha_2 \tilde{x}_t^d \tag{4.8}$$

$$\tilde{p}_t - \tilde{w}_t = -\beta_1\Delta\tilde{p}_t + \beta_2\tilde{y}_t \tag{4.9}$$

$$\tilde{w}_t - \tilde{p}_t = -\gamma_1\Delta\tilde{p}_t + \gamma_2\tilde{y}_t + \tilde{z}_t \tag{4.10}$$

Our first experiment consists of a once-for-all reduction in the money stock at time zero.

Experiment 1 $\tilde{m}_t = m_1 < 0, \tilde{x}_t^d = \tilde{z}_t = 0$

In this case it is easy to demonstrate from (4.8), (4.9), (4.10) that for all $t \geqslant 1$ we have[3]

$$\tilde{p}_t = (1 - \omega^t)m_1 \tag{4.11}$$

$$\tilde{w}_t - \tilde{p}_t = \frac{(\gamma_2\beta_1 - \beta_2\gamma_1)}{(\beta_1 + \gamma_1)}\alpha_1\omega^t m_1 \tag{4.12}$$

$$\tilde{y}_t = \alpha_1\omega^t m_1 \tag{4.13}$$

$$\omega = [(\beta_1 + \gamma_1)/[(\beta_1 + \gamma_1)] + \alpha_1(\beta_2 + \gamma_2)] \tag{4.14}$$

$$0 \leqslant \omega < 1.$$

As we might expect, as $t \to \infty$, $\tilde{p}_t \to m_1$, $\tilde{w}_t - \tilde{p}_t \to 0$, $\tilde{y}_t \to 0$. So, in the long run, prices fall in proportion to the money stock and the real economy returns to equilibrium. In order to regain this equilibrium, both wages and prices fall throughout and we shall have more to say on the implications of this when we consider real demand shocks. The real recession arising from this nominal shock reaches its trough in the initial period and since $\tilde{y}_1 = \alpha_1\omega m_1$, the depth of the recession is determined by ω (and α_1). The key factors here are the full extent of nominal inertia $(\beta_1 + \gamma_1)$ and the impact of the level of economic activity on both wage and price setting $(\gamma_2 + \beta_2)$. The former factor makes the recession more severe whereas the latter acts in the other direction, both well known general results. So both price and wage stickiness accentuate economic fluctuations, but what of real wage movements?

Real wages will tend to be above equilibrium throughout the recession if $\gamma_2\beta_1 < \gamma_1\beta_2$ (remember $m_1 < 0$). This will occur if nominal inertia in price setting is low relative to that in wage setting and if the impact of the economic activity on prices is high relative to that on wages. This inequality is certain to hold if product markets are competitive $(\beta_1 = 0, \beta_2$ large) and we then obtain the standard story. An adverse nominal shock causes prices to fall below those expected, real wages then rise and output and employment fall. On the other hand, if prices are set on a normal cost basis and nominal inertia in price setting is high $(\beta_1$ large, $\beta_2 = 0)$, the inequality goes the other way and real wages fall as a consequence of the adverse nominal shock. In this story, firms are obviously price setters and because prices turn out lower than expected, they set prices 'too high' for the level of nominal demand. Output, employment and real wages all then fall together.

Perhaps the most interesting fact that emerges from this analysis is that there is no necessary relation between the depth of the recession induced by any given adverse shock and the movement of real wages. For example, we may observe real wages above equilibrium with a shallow recession ($\beta_1 = 0$, γ_1 small, β_2, γ_2 large) and real wages below equilibrium with a very deep recession (β_1 large, γ_1, β_2, γ_2 small). This is an important result for it tells us that, when the economy is subject to adverse demand shocks, examining the fluctuations in real wages is an entirely fruitless activity if one is looking for evidence on the causes of the severity of the recession. Only if the product market is competitive will we observe real wages and economic activity moving in opposite directions and once we get away from this demonstrably false assumption, then we may expect to observe no coherent patterns in the data.

These results are quite general and do not depend in any way on the special form of expectations generating mechanism we have assumed. For example, suppose that expectations are rational so that (4.9), (4.10) become

$$\tilde{p}_t - \tilde{w}_t = -\beta_1(\tilde{p}_t - \tilde{p}_t^e) + \beta_2 \tilde{y}_t \tag{4.9'}$$

$$\tilde{w}_t - \tilde{p}_t = -\gamma_1(\tilde{p}_t - \tilde{p}_t^e) + \gamma_2 \tilde{y}_t + \tilde{z}_t \tag{4.10'}$$

Suppose now that the money supply follows the rule

$$\tilde{m}_t = \tilde{m}_{t-1} + m_{1t}, \quad m_{1t} \text{ white noise}$$

Then it is easy to show that

$$\tilde{p}_t = \tilde{m}_{t-1} + (1 - \omega)m_{1t} \tag{4.11'}$$

$$\tilde{w}_t - \tilde{p}_t = \frac{(\gamma_2\beta_1 - \gamma_1\beta_2)}{(\beta_1 + \gamma_1)}\alpha_1\omega m_{1t} \tag{4.12'}$$

$$\tilde{y}_t = \alpha_1\omega m_{1t} \tag{4.13'}$$

The results are, therefore, fundamentally the same as in the previous case although now each shock only lasts for one period as we might expect in the rational expectations context.[4] In order to generate persistence in this case we need some element of hysteresis as we shall see later. So, aside from the issue of persistence, the assumptions we make about the precise form of the expectations generating mechanism are of little consequence. In the light of this we shall persevere with our assumption of static expectations because of its analytical convenience, and consider next the consequences of a real demand shock.

Experiment 2 $\tilde{x}_t^d = x_1^d < 0$, $\tilde{m}_t = \tilde{z}_t = 0$

The implications of an adverse real shock are, in a formal sense, the same as for an adverse nominal shock. In this case we have

$$\tilde{p}_t = (1 - \omega') \frac{\alpha_2 x - x_1^d}{\alpha_1} \tag{4.15}$$

$$\tilde{w}_t - \tilde{p}_t = \frac{(\gamma_2\beta_1 - \gamma_1\beta_2)}{(\beta_1 + \gamma_1)} \alpha_2 \omega' x_1^d \tag{4.16}$$

$$\tilde{y}_t = \alpha_2 \omega' x_1^d \tag{4.17}$$

Given the similarity of these results to those generated by the adverse nominal shock, we shall focus here on the nominal shifts required to regain the real equilibrium. The key point to note is that if α_1 is very small, both prices and wages must fall a very long way. In chapter 19 of the *General Theory*, entitled 'Changes in Money-Wages', Keynes makes two fundamental points. The first is that, for a variety of well known reasons, α_1 is likely to be very small (liquidity trap, trivial real balance effects, interest inelastic expenditure). The second is that if wages and prices are falling rapidly, the stability of the model is called into question. For example, the postponement of expenditure in this situation may simply take one further and further away from the equilibrium and cause significant disruptions in the economy. (Thus bankruptcies may become commonplace, a point emphasised in Hahn (1965).) The nub of Keynes's argument is that relying on the fixed money stock to restore equilibrium under such circumstances is a foolish policy response and that it is far better to offset the adverse real shock by making direct use of the available monetary and fiscal policy instruments.

A second aspect to Keynes's arguments concerns the practical difficulties involved in generating falls in nominal wages. It is clear in the above context that, if nominal wages cannot fall, then equilibrium will not be restored without either a rise in the money stock or a reversal of the real shock. Keynes, in fact, was concerned to argue that the practical difficulties in obtaining nominal wage cuts were not the crucial issue because, even if nominal wages were very flexible, the forces tending to restore equilibrium would be very weak. In other words, blaming the workings of the labour market under such circumstances was a pointless activity. It is important to recognise that Keynes's arguments are very specific to the particular situation where equilibrium is to be restored by large falls in wages and prices. In this context, Keynes's arguments appear perfectly sensible and he was under no illusions as to the inflationary consequences of a positive demand shock when starting out from a position of equilibrium.

4.3 SUPPLY SHOCKS

It is clear from the equilibrium of our model that it is supply shocks which can be expected to have long-run real effects. In order to see how these come about, we consider next the consequences of a once-for-all adverse supply shock.

Experiment 3 $\tilde{z}_t = z_1 > 0$, $\tilde{m}_t = \tilde{x}_t^d = 0$

In this case we obtain

$$\tilde{p}_t = \frac{(1-\omega')z_1}{(\beta_2 + \gamma_2)\alpha_1} \tag{4.19}$$

$$\tilde{w}_t - \tilde{p}_t = \left[1 - \frac{\gamma_2}{(\gamma_2 + \beta_2)}(1-\omega') - \frac{\gamma_1}{(\gamma_1 + \beta_1)}\omega' \right] z_1 \tag{4.20}$$

$$\tilde{y}_t = -\frac{(1-\omega')z_1}{(\gamma_2 + \beta_2)} \tag{4.21}$$

Equations (4.19) and (4.21) immediately reveal the classic stagflation response of the economy to the supply shock with rising prices and falling output. Furthermore, it is clear that the adverse consequences on the level of activity can only be offset by expansionary monetary and fiscal policy at the expense of yet further inflationary pressure. The extent to which the increased pressure on nominal wages, arising from the supply shock, is translated into real wage gains depends crucially on price setting behaviour. Real wages always rise in the first period unless $\beta_1 = \beta_2 = 0$ when they are held completely rigid by the pricing policies of firms. Subsequently real wages will continue to rise if

$$\frac{\gamma_1}{\gamma_1 + \beta_1} > \frac{\gamma_2}{\gamma_2 + \beta_2} \tag{4.22}$$

If this inequality is reversed, they will subsequently fall. In particular, if $\beta_2 = 0$ and we have normal cost pricing, real wages will fall back to their original level and the rise in pressure on nominal wages is wholly unsuccessful in terms of achieving long-run real wage gains.

Again we see that studying real wage movements will not, in general, reveal anything about the real consequences of adverse supply shocks even though the shocks themselves originate from the labour market. Thus, for example, the use of the so-called 'real wage gap',[5] popularised by Bruno and

Sachs (1985) cannot be recommended. Only in the case where we have competitive product markets ($\beta_1 = 0$, β_2 large) will real wages correlate well with the falls in activity, for then

$$\tilde{w}_t - \tilde{p}_t = \frac{\beta_2}{(\gamma_2 + \beta_2)}(1 - \omega')z_1 \tag{4.23}$$

If, on the other hand, there is normal cost pricing and considerable nominal inertia in price setting, real wages are

$$\tilde{\omega}_t - \tilde{p}_t = \frac{\beta_1}{(\gamma_1 + \beta_1)}\omega'z_1 \tag{4.24}$$

and for most of the time real wages will be falling as activity falls. The downward movements in European real wage gaps in the 1980s alongside the continuing rise in unemployment accord well with this particular parameter configuration.

4.4   THE ROLE OF HYSTERESIS

The notion of hysteresis was first popularised in the context of unemployment by Phelps (1972). However, it has rather wider applications as we shall see. In the context of our framework, we shall wish to consider hysteresis in both price and wage setting. On the price side, hysteresis describes the following phenomenon. If there is an adverse shock, activity falls and so does capacity utilisation. If the activity level remains low, investment declines, capacity falls and capacity utilisation then starts rising again. If the impact of activity on price setting behaviour operates, at least in part, via capacity utilisation then prices will start to rise even though activity remains at a lower level. The implication of this is that prices will respond more sharply to changes in the level of activity in the short run than they do in the long run.

Hysteresis on the wages side describes a precisely parallel process. A fall in labour market activity reduces wage pressure because of the increase in the number of unemployed individuals competing for a smaller number of vacancies. As time passes, the downward pressure exerted by the unemployment pool starts to wane as the unemployed become discouraged, their skills deteriorate and their desirability to prospective employers declines. Again we have a situation where the short-run impact of a change in labour market activity is larger than its long-run effect.

In terms of our basic model, the addition of such hysteresis effects leads to the price and wage setting equations being augmented by change terms. So (4.2) and (4.3) become

$$p - w = \beta_0 - \beta_1(p - p^e) + \beta_2 y + \beta_{21}\Delta y \tag{4.25}$$

$$w - p = \gamma_0 - \gamma_2(p - p^e) + \gamma_2 y + \gamma_{21}\Delta y + z \tag{4.26}$$

As an example of their implications, consider the consequences of a money supply reduction. Here, we repeat experiment 1, $(\tilde{m}_t = m_1 < 0,\ \tilde{x}_t^d = \tilde{z}_t = 0)$ again assuming that $p^e = p_{-1}$. The results for prices and output are

$$\tilde{p}_t = (1 - \omega_2'^{-1}\omega_1)m_1 \tag{4.11''}$$

$$\tilde{y}_t = a_1\omega_2'^{-1}\omega_1 m_1 \tag{4.13''}$$

$$\omega_1 = [(\beta_1 + \gamma_1)/(\beta_1 + \gamma_1 + (\beta_2 + \gamma_2 + \beta_{21} + \gamma_{21})a_1] < \omega$$

$$\omega_2 = [(\beta_1 + \gamma_1) + (\beta_{21} + \gamma_{21})a_1]/[\beta_1 + \gamma_1 + (\beta_2 + \gamma_2 + \beta_{21} + \gamma_{21})a_1] > \omega$$

So, although the long-run solution of the model is the same, the addition of the hysteresis terms reduces the depth of the recession induced by the adverse shock (since $\omega_1 < \omega$) but tends to slow down the speed of the return to equilibrium (since $\omega_2 > \omega$). This latter is a completely general implication of hysteresis. That is, it will always tend to weaken the equilibrating forces in the economy. This applies equally as much under rational expectations as under any other form of expectations formation. Indeed if hysteresis effects on wage and price setting are very large relative to long-run effects, $(\beta_{21} + \gamma_{21}) \gg (\beta_2 + \gamma_2)$, the economy will drift away from equilibrium for very long periods in response to shocks, whether or not expectations are rational. Overall, therefore, such effects may have a profound impact on the efficient operation of a decentralised economic system.

4.5 SUMMARY AND CONCLUSIONS

We have studied the relationship between wage movements and economic activity as the economy responds to a variety of shocks. Our main conclusions are as follows. First, real wage movements are, in general, not related in any systematic way to movements in activity as a result of either demand or supply shocks. Their behaviour depends crucially on how prices are set. Second, in an era of relatively stable wages and prices, adverse demand shocks generate a tendency for wages and prices to fall whereas adverse supply shocks produce the opposite tendency. If the reduced form impact of real money balances on aggregate demand is small, then adverse real demand shocks require large downward shifts in wages and prices to equilibrate the economy. As Keynes argued, it is doubtful whether such an equilibrating mechanism would be very effective in practice. Third, hysteresis effects in either price or wage setting tend to weaken the equilibrating forces in the economy. If these effects are large, the economy can drift for long periods well away from equilibrium even under rational expectations.

None of these conclusions is new, indeed the second is only included for the sake of completeness. The first and third are, however, not always fully appreciated as the endless statements concerning real wages being 'too high' so clearly testify.

Acknowledgements

I am most grateful to the Economic and Social Research Council for financial assistance (Project no B00 23 2174, Wages, Prices and Employment in Interwar Britain) and to Peter Sinclair and other participants at the conference for helpful comments on an earlier draft.

Notes

1. This is the standard error correction effect. In a growing economy, the relevant effect is, of course, the deviation of last period's real wage from trend productivity.
2. In an open economy one should also include terms of trade shifts. In fact, most of what is discussed in this chapter can be applied to an open economy so long as prices are defined as the GDP deflator.
3. Note that adding (4.9), (4.10) and using (4.8) to eliminate $\tilde{y}_t$ yields

$$0 = -(\beta_1 + \gamma_1)(\tilde{p}_t - \tilde{p}_{t-1}) + (\beta_2 + \gamma_2)\alpha_1(m_1 - \tilde{p}_t)$$

or

$$\tilde{p}_t = \omega\tilde{p}_{t-1} + (1 - \omega)m_1$$

Backward substitution now yields

$$\tilde{p}_t = (1 - \omega)(1 + \omega + \ldots + \omega^{t-1})m_1$$

$$= (1 - \omega^t)m_1$$

4. In other respects, of course, the assumption of rational expectations makes a great deal of difference. For example, only unanticipated exogenous demand shifts have real effects. For our present purpose, however, the assumption we make about expectations formation is entirely irrelevant. The determinants of the size of the real effects of nominal shocks and of the direction of real wage movements are unaffected by the expectations formation mechanism.
5. The real wage gap is the difference between the actual real wage and the real wage consistent with full employment. It only makes sense when product markets are perfectly competitive.

References

BRUNO, M. and G. SACHS (1985) *Economics of Worldwide Stagflation* (Oxford: Blackwells).

DUNLOP, J. G. (1938) 'The Movement of Real and Money Wage Rates', *Economic Journal*, September, pp. 413–34.

HAHN, F. H. (1965) 'On Some Problems of Proving the Existence of an Equilibrium in a Monetary Economy', in F. H. Hahn and F. Brechling (eds), *The Theory of Interest Rates* (London: Macmillan).

KALECKI, M. (1938) 'The Determinants of Distribution of the National Income', *Econometrica*, April, p. 102.

KEYNES, J. M. (1939) 'Relative Movements of Real Wages and Output', *Economic Journal*, March, pp. 34–51.

KEYNES, J. M. (1973) *The General Theory of Employment, Interest and Money* (Macmillan for the Royal Economic Society).

PHELPS, E. S. (1972) *Inflation Policy and Unemployment Theory* (London: Macmillan).

ROTEMBERG, J. J. and G. SALONER (1986) 'A Supergame-Theoretic Model of Price Wars during Booms', *American Economic Review*, June.

STIGLITZ, J. E. (1984) 'Price Rigidities and Market Structure', *American Economic Review, Papers and Proceedings*, May, pp. 305–355.

TARSHIS, L. (1939) 'Changes in Real and Money Wages', *Economic Journal*, March, pp. 150–54.

Part III

The Effect of Fiscal Reflation Upon Employment

5 The Effect of Fiscal Reflation Upon Employment

Francis Breedon, Alan Budd, Paul Levine and Peter Smith

The first part of the chapter discusses Keynes's theory of prolonged involuntary unemployment and the role of fiscal policy in cutting it. The second part describes the labour market sector of the LBS model and compares it with the Keynesian approach. The third part uses the LBS model to explore the effects on unemployment of types of fiscal expansion.

5.1. KEYNES AND UNEMPLOYMENT

Since all the papers at this conference are concerned with aspects of the *General Theory* we limit our discussion to those parts of it which are relevant to the task we have been set. We take the main relevant elements of the *General Theory* to be as follows:

(i) The distinction between voluntary and involuntary unemployment.
(ii) The relative rigidity of money wages compared with real wages.
(iii) The possibility of prolonged involuntary unemployment because of inadequate aggregate demand.

It is important to note that points (ii) and (iii) were logically distinct for Keynes. Even if money wages were flexible, such flexibility could not ensure full employment since there was no guarantee that a fall in money wages would produce a fall in real wages. Keynes believed that the necessary process consisted of an increase in aggregate demand which simultaneously increased output and reduced real wages. (It is well recognised that Keynes assumed in the *General Theory* that a fall in real wages was necessary.)

Keynes distinguished between three types of unemployment: 'frictional', 'voluntary' and 'involuntary'. Frictional unemployment allows for

various inexactnesses of adjustment which stand in the way of continuous full employment; for example, unemployment due to a temporary want of

balance between the relative quantities of specialised resources as a result
of miscalculation or intermittent demand; or to time-lags consequent on
unforeseen changes; or to the fact that the change-over from one employment to another cannot be effected without a certain delay, so that there
will always exist in non-static society a proportion of resources unemployed 'between jobs'. (Keynes, 1936, p. 6)

Keynes regarded frictional unemployment as part of classical unemployment. The second type of classical unemployment was 'voluntary'.

due to the refusal or inability of a unit of labour, as a result of legislation or
social practices or of combination for collective bargaining or a slow
response to change or of mere human obstinacy, to accept a reward
corresponding to the value of the product attributable to its marginal
productivity. (Keynes, 1936, p. 6)

Keynes's definition of involuntary unemployment was as follows:

Men are involuntarily unemployed if, in the event of a small rise in the
price of wage-goods relatively to the money-wage, both the aggregate
supply of labour willing to work for the current money-wage and the
aggregate demand for it at that wage would be greater than the existing
volume of employment. (Keynes, 1936, p. 15)

The firms employing these workers were assumed to operate in a perfectly
competitive goods market. This is clear from the first classical postulate.

I. The wage is equal to the marginal product of labour
That is to say, the wage of an employed person is equal to the value which
would be lost if employment were to be reduced by one unit (after
deducting any other costs which this reduction of output would avoid);
subject, however, to the qualification that the equality may be disturbed, in
accordance with certain principles, if competition and markets are imperfect. (Keynes, 1936, p. 5)

Keynes uses this later.

In emphasising our point of departure from the classical system, we must
not overlook an important point of agreement. For we shall maintain the
first postulate as heretofore, subject only to the same qualifications as in
the classical theory; and we must pause, for a moment, to consider what
this involves.
   It means that, with a given organisation, equipment and technique, real
wages and the volume of output (and hence of employment) are uniquely

correlated, so that, in general, an increase in employment can only occur to the accompaniment of a decline in the rate of real wages. (Keynes, 1936, p. 17)

This rules out one direct route for demand to affect employment which comes from imperfect competition in the goods market as we discuss below.

Keynes discusses wage-setting behaviour at some length in Chapter 2 of the *General Theory* and then does not return to the topic until Chapter 19. The reason for that is that he uses the intervening chapters to describe his theory of aggregate demand. In Chapter 2 he concludes that the resistance to cuts in money wages represents a reasonable concern about relative pay:

In other words, the struggle about money-wages primarily affects the *distribution* of the aggregate real wage between different labour-groups, and not its average amount per unit of employment, which depends, as we shall see, on a different set of forces. The effect of combination on the part of a group of workers is to protect their *relative* real wage. The *general* level of real wages depends on the other forces of the economic system. (Keynes, 1936, p. 14)

Most of the *General Theory* is concerned with explaining 'the other forces of the economic system'. The broad conclusion is that fluctuations in aggregate demand can alter the level of involuntary unemployment by altering the real wage. Such changes affect the demand for labour but not its supply. As Keynes argues:

Every trade union will put up some resistance to a cut in money wages, however small. But since no trade union would dream of striking on every occasion of a rise in the cost of living, they do not raise the obstacle to any increase in aggregate employment which is attributed to them by the classical school. (Keynes, 1936, p. 15)

The *General Theory* was concerned with explanation rather than prescription. In discussing aggregate demand, Keynes's emphasis was on the role of investment and he believed that policy should be directed towards ensuring that investment should equal the full employment level of savings. He did not believe that the market system (including the financial system) could achieve this outcome unassisted. His general policy conclusions, stated in the final chapter 'Concluding Notes' are, perhaps, worth quoting at length.

In some respects the foregoing theory is moderately conservative in its implications. For whilst it indicates the vital importance of establishing certain central controls in matters which are now left in the main to individual initiative, there are wide fields of activity which are unaffected.

The State will have to exercise a guiding influence on the propensity to consume partly through its scheme of taxation, partly by fixing the rate of interest, and partly, perhaps, in other ways. Furthermore, it seems unlikely that the influence of banking policy on the rate of interest will be sufficient by itself to determine an optimum rate of investment. I conceive, therefore, that a somewhat comprehensive socialisation of investment will prove the only means of securing an approximation to full employment; though this need not exclude all manner of compromises and of devices by which public authority will cooperate with private initiative. (Keynes, 1936, p. 377)

It is hard to find in that section (or anywhere else in the *General Theory*) the idea that deficit financing would play a major role in establishing full employment. Keynes, as it happened, was not simply interested in investment as a means of ensuring full employment, he also wanted to end the scarcity of capital because he believed that such a step would have the desirable effect of ending rentier captialism. He recognised that it was possible that that objective might require a budget surplus at full employment:

But while there may be intrinsic reasons for the scarcity of land, there are no intrinsic reasons for the scarcity of capital. An intrinsic reason for such scarcity, in the sense of a genuine sacrifice which could only be called forth by the offer of a reward in the shape of interest would not exist, in the long run, except in the event of the individual propensity to consume proving to be of such a character that net saving in conditions of full employment comes to an end before capital has become sufficiently abundant. But even so, it will still be possible for communal saving through the agency of the State to be maintained at a level which will allow the growth of capital up to the point where it ceases to be scarce. (Keynes, 1936, p. 376)

There are only two references to the Budgetary deficit in the index to the *General Theory*. The first is in effect a reference to built-in stabilisers. The second involves Keynes's (ironic) proposal that the Treasury should fill old bottles with bank-notes and bury them in disused coal mines. As he said,

It would, indeed, be more sensible to build houses and the like, but if there are political and practical difficulties in the way of this, the above would be better than nothing. (Keynes, 1936, p. 129)

If Keynes did not discuss budget deficits in the *General Theory* at any length, his support for public spending as a means of cutting unemployment was obvious from his other writings, most notably those in support of Lloyd George's 1929 Election proposals. In *Can Lloyd George Do It?* Keynes was concerned with cures rather than causes. The cure to unemployment lay in the expansion of demand. He scorned those who doubted that such policies would work:

> The Conservative belief that there is some law of nature which prevents them from being employed, that it is 'rash' to employ men, and that it is financially 'sound' to maintain a tenth of the population in idleness for an indefinite period, is crazily improbable – the sort of thing which no man could believe who had not had his head fuddled with nonsense for years and years. (Keynes, 1929, p. 90)

Keynes opposed the Treasury view that any money raised by the state to finance capital spending must reduce pound for pound the supply of funds available for industry. He also rejected the idea that increased capital spending would cause inflation:

> The suggestion that a policy of capital expenditure, if it does not take capital away from ordinary industry, will spell inflation, would be true enough if we were dealing with boom conditions. And it would become true if the policy of capital expenditure were pushed unduly fast, so that the demand for savings began to exceed the supply. But we are far, indeed, from such a position at the present time. To bring up the bogy of inflation as an objection to capital expenditure at the present time is like warning a patient who is wasting away from emaciation of the dangers of excessive corpulence. (Keynes, 1929, p. 117)

Keynes's polemical writings together with the *General Theory* suggest that the solution to involuntary unemployment is to expand aggregate demand, possibly through a programme of deficit-financed public spending. Such an expansion of aggregate demand would create higher employment by cutting real wages.

In this chapter we are concerned with discussing the effects of fiscal policy on unemployment in relation to the LBS model. However, it is perhaps worth providing some general remarks about the development of such models in the UK. The models described in such volumes as Hilton and Heathfield (1970) and Renton (1975) may have differed in details but they commonly embodied what were known as 'Keynesian' properties. Fiscal expansion increased aggregate demand and thereby raised output. Employment was linked to output by some version of a simple inverted production function which did not involve prices of factors of production. Output could be expanded (and unemployment reduced) apparently without limit. The models might include a version of the Phillips curve so that wage inflation increased as unemployment fell. But this did not bring the process of expansion to an end. On the contrary it might assist it since wages could rise more rapidly than prices thereby further increasing aggregate demand.

We can now recognise that such models were far cruder in their analysis of aggregate supply than was Keynes in the *General Theory*. However, doubts about their validity were triggered not so much by a re-reading of Keynes as by the policy débâcle of 1972–3 with its aftermath, in 1975, of simultaneous record inflation and (at that time) record post-war unemployment. It was also noted that the disasters were forecast by monetarist economists (without benefit of macro-econometric models).

In response to those events the existing models underwent changes and new models, such as those at Liverpool and the City University Business School were constructed which placed greater emphasis on supply conditions and on the role of money.

A version of the LBS model, described in Ball, Burns and Warburton (1979) produced 'monetarist properties' without an explicit supply side. A fiscal expansion accompanied by a monetary expansion generated only a brief expansion of output. The crowding out process was contained in a rapid response of inflation to monetary expansion (via the exchange rate) accompanied by a tendency for the personal sector's savings ratio to rise in response to that inflation. Subsequent versions of the LBS model have implied sustained multiplier effects so that fiscal expansion has a prolonged effect on unemployment. The question we ask is why this is so, if we now recognise, in theory at least, the potential supply constraints which were described by Keynes, quite apart from the stronger constraints implied by some macro-economic models.

We should hardly need to add that we are concerned to understand the world, and that understanding the LBS model is a means to that end, not an end in itself. We concentrate on the operation of the labour market.

5.2   THE LABOUR MARKET IN THE LBS MODEL

It would be intellectually satisfying to demonstrate the counterparts of Keynes's three types of unemployment in the LBS model; but we need not be too apologetic if such a matching is not possible since economics has moved on since 1936. What we find is that only some elements of the Keynesian analysis can be applied. The important differences are that neither the conditions of the supply of nor the demand for labour correspond precisely to Keynes's formulation and that firms operate in imperfect (oligopolistic) markets. It remains true, however, that part of the mechanism by which unemployment can be reduced by a fiscal expansion is through a cut in real wages. But that is not a necessary part of the solution; an important part of the process is a shift in the demand for labour brought about by an expansion of aggregate demand.

The labour market in the LBS model has been described in Smith and Holly (1985) and in Budd, Levine and Smith (1987). The basic model uses the idea of wage-bargaining, with real wages set in a bargain between unions and employers. Employers set employment in order to maximise profits at the given expected real wage. Thus bargaining is subject to the firm's demand curve for labour.

In the current version of the model there are separate bargains in the manufacturing sector and in the non-public, non-manufacturing sector although unions take account of wages and benefit payments outside their sector. It is assumed that the public sector's level of employment is set by the government, while the level of public sector wages moves in line with wages in the private sector.

In contrast to Keynes's discussion of wage-bargaining, the model suggests that unions do bargain for expected real wages and evaluate changes in money wages in terms of their effect on real wages rather than in terms of their effect on relative pay except to the extent that outside pay determines a fall-back position for the union in any sector. (The level of aggregation in the LBS model hardly allows us to take changes in relativities into account.) Again, in contrast to Keynes, the LBS model implies that firms operate in imperfectly competitive conditions and there is a downward sloping demand curve for goods.

Each firm in each private sector is assumed to produce a differentiated good and to choose employment, output and the price of its output on the basis of profit-maximisation. We can write the production function as

$$Y_i = f_i(L_i, K_i, M_i) \qquad f_{i1}, f_{i2}, f_{i3} > 0 \tag{5.1}$$

for the representative firm i where Y_i is output and L_i, K_i and M_i denote quantities of labour, capital and raw materials (including fuel) respectively.

For simplicity we ignore the distinction between domestic and foreign markets and any effect of relative prices between sectors on demand. Then we may write the demand function for the output of firm i as

$$Y_i = D_i(P_i/P, \sigma) \qquad D_{i1} < 0, \ D_{i2} > 0 \tag{5.2}$$

where P_i is the price of the firm's output, P is the aggregate price level and σ is demand.

We adopt the conventional assumption that output, employment and price are chosen for a given nominal wage net of employment taxes (W) and capital stock. We also assume that the remaining factors M_i and L_i are consumed in fixed proportions with $M_i = \alpha_i L_i$. Then maximising profits,

$$L_i = \ell_i(W/P_i, P_i^{rm}/P_i, e_i, K_i) \qquad \ell_{i1}, \ell_{i2} < 0, \ \ell_{i3}, \ell_{i4} > 0 \tag{5.3}$$

where P_i^{rm} is the price of raw materials and

$$e_i = -\frac{P_i}{Y_i}\frac{\partial Y_i}{\partial P_i}$$

is the elasticity of demand.

Under conditions of perfect competition in the goods market the argument e_i in (5.3) is absent so that the demand for labour can only increase if, conditionally, the real product wage W/P_i falls and/or the real user cost of raw materials P_i^{rm}/P_i falls and/or the firm chooses to increase the capital stock K_i. Under conditions of imperfect competition an alternative mechanism emerges. A standard result from industrial economics is that the mark-up of price over marginal cost decreases in a boom (see Domberger, 1979, for example). This implies that e_i increases in a boom or in other words $e_i = e_i(\sigma)$, $e_{i1} > 0$. Thus the demand for labour schedule (5.3) shifts outwards as aggregate demand increases.

Turning to wage determination, nominal wages in the private sector are assumed to be determined by a bargaining process over expected real wages. Then public sector earnings adjust to those in the private sector.

The real wage bargain results in an outcome on the demand for labour curve on the assumption that the union has no direct means of affecting the firm's choice of employment level. The wage outcome from this process depends on the relative bargaining strength of the two parties. The level of unemployment is a key determinant of the wage outcome. The union's bargaining strength varies inversely with the probability of its members losing their jobs. This probability can be assumed to rise with unemployment. Thus we expect the implicit supply curve for labour to be upward sloping in employment – real wage space. A number of other factors also determine the position of the curve. Wages in all sectors can be expected to be positively correlated if unions use outside wage growth as a fall-back position in the bargaining process. The level of unemployment benefit is one of these alternatives. The real wage equation that describes the outcome of the bargaining process should therefore, in principle, contain all the determinants of the firms' and unions' bargaining positions.

The real wage equation for the private sector then takes the general form

$$W/PC^e = f(U, R, W^o/PC^e, X) \qquad f_1 < 0, f_2, f_3 > 0 \tag{5.4}$$

where W is the nominal wage rate, PC^e is the expected consumer price index, U is the unemployment rate and W^o is the nominal wage rate in the other sector. There are a large number of possible variables for the exogenous variables X. Possible candidates are replacement ratios, tax rates affecting both employers and employees, mismatch indices, an incomes policy dummy and trade union membership. An innovative feature of (5.4) is the inclusion of the ratio of long-term to total unemployment, R, which captures the view that the long-term unemployed exert less downward pressure on wages than the short-term unemployed. In terms of the bargaining model this implies that the union members consider the probability of losing their job to be lower when the ratio is high (see, for example, Layard, 1986).

In our estimate of (5.4), in common with many other studies, we were unable to find any role for direct taxes in either the manufacturing or non-manufacturing sector. The real wage equation (5.4) may be thought of as a trade union or bargaining supply curve for labour. Individual labour supply, which determines the total labour force $N = L + U$ is modelled in terms of the differential labour force participation decisions of males and females. Male labour force growth is assumed to follow the male population of working age.

The female labour force participation function takes the form

$$\frac{N^f}{POP^f} = f\left[U, \frac{W(1-\tau)}{P}, X\right] \qquad (f_1 \gtrless 0, f_2 > 0) \tag{5.5}$$

where POP is the total population of working age. The f superscript refers to females, W is now the average nominal wage throughout the economy and τ is the direct tax rate. The female participation decision depends on unemployment and the average after-tax level of the real wage. The effect of unemployment on labour supply is ambiguous. High unemployment may discourage women from registering as it reduces the expected probability of finding a job, but the effect of unemployment on household incomes could have the opposite effect. We find that the discouragement effect dominates empirically. Included in exogenous variables is the relative earnings of females to males, which picks up the effect of equal pay legislation.

The labour market is then completed with an equation that determines long-term unemployment in terms of lags in unemployment and vacancies and an unemployment–vacancies relationship (see Budd, Levine and Smith, 1985). The estimated equations are shown in the Appendix.

5.3 KEYNESIAN ECONOMICS AND THE LBS MODEL

Having described the labour model at some length we can examine in more detail its relation to the ideas presented in the *General Theory*. In particular we are interested in the question of whether we can usefully distinguish between voluntary and involuntary unemployment, whether there can be prolonged involuntary unemployment and whether it can be cut by fiscal policy.

The distinction between voluntary and involuntary unemployment is possible, but it is not obviously useful. Since the model implies that the bargain is about real wages, it will not be possible to increase the equilibrium *supply* of labour (with an unchanged structure of tax rates, social security payments, etc.) unless real wages rise. Persistent unemployment will, in the LBS model, reflect the unions' utility function. Keynes specifically mentioned 'combination for collective bargaining' as a possible source of voluntary unemployment. But that may be thought to stretch the meaning of 'voluntary'. Not everybody belongs to a union (although we assume that unions set the bargain for everybody) and workers who become unemployed may strongly disagree with the unions' implied welfare functions even if they are members. As an illustration of the unhelpfulness of the term 'voluntary', the model suggests that a demand shock will affect employment rather than real wages. Thus, after a fall in aggregate demand, the new bargain will apparently involve considerably higher unemployment and only slightly lower real wages initially and higher real wages in the medium term. That may conform with experience but it does not conform with the popular definition of 'voluntary'.

Although we may describe union-induced unemployment as voluntary, it will, according to the LBS model, respond to Keynesian remedies of demand expansion. Thus it seems possible to cut voluntary unemployment, which is not what Keynes implied. Finally there can be involuntary unemployment, in Keynes's sense, in the period of adjustment from one equilibrium to another. In the LBS model the adjustment of real wages takes time. One can define the temporary raising of unemployment above its new equilibrium level as 'involuntary' but it is difficult to measure it in practice.

Now consider whether unemployment can be cut by fiscal policy and, in particular, whether cuts can be permanent. The first point to be made, regarding the LBS model, is that there is considerable inertia in price and real wage behaviour. This means that in the simulations, reported in detail in the next section, the model has not reached a steady state in all variables at the end of the eight-year simulation periods. (This it should be noted is in response to permanent policy changes; if changes are transitory or even merely persistent the steady state is reached sooner.)

The complexity of our large-scale model means that its steady-state properties cannot be obtained analytically. The description of the labour market in the previous section, however, permits a qualitative assessment of the effects of fiscal expansion in both the short run and long run. A quantitative approximation of the long-run characteristics (i.e. beyond eight years) requires us to extrapolate beyond the simulations.

Consider a fiscal expansion involving both an increase in public sector employment and various forms of purchases from the private sector. Public employment has an immediate impact on GDP (by definition). The procurement component of the public expenditure increase can only increase GDP if private sector output increases. This can take place through one or more of the following mechanisms:

(i) The real product wage decreases.
(ii) The demand for labour curve shifts outwards.

(iii) The labour supply curve shifts outwards.

In manufacturing (i) can occur through the depreciation of the exchange rate which drives a wedge between manufacturing prices and the GDP deflator. However, this open-economy effect is cancelled out in the longer term by an opposite effect in non-manufacturing. For the economy as a whole this leaves the possibility of surprise inflation bringing about a fall in the real product wage, with nominal wages reacting slowly to price increases.

The possibility that under conditions of imperfect competition the demand for labour curve shifts outwards is discussed in detail in the previous section. As with surprise inflation we do not expect this to be a long-term phenomenon. Finally from (5.4) and (5.5) the labour supply curve can shift outwards if direct taxes and unemployment benefits decrease. However, from the Appendix we can see that these latter effects are not strong.

In the short run the effect (ii) dominates and higher private sector employment occurs without a drop in the real product wage for the economy as a whole. In the longer run 'crowding out' is experienced by the following means. The real product wage increases as a fall in unemployment brings about a rise in the real consumption wage. If fiscal expansion is accompanied by tax increases, the labour supply curve shifts inwards. Finally the demand for labour curve shifts back reflecting the cyclical character of the aggregate demand effect on the demand for labour.

Neither the effect of unemployment on real wages nor the tax effect on the supply of labour are strong in the LBS model. Households do seem to absorb most of any increase in direct taxes. Extrapolation beyond the eight-year simulation period suggests that the drop in private sector output in the steady state is only small. The effect of this is that most of the public sector employment contribution to GDP is not crowded out.

The final 'equilibrium' which is suggested by the simulations of the next section is that fiscal expansion leads to GDP increasing by an amount slightly lower than the contribution of public sector employment. Those initially in work absorb the tax increases which finance the increase in consumption of the newly employed. The average 'social wage' rises but at the expense of average disposable income of those employed.

5.4 POLICY SIMULATIONS

We report the results of four policy simulations. Two involve increases in public spending and two involve tax cuts. For each type of fiscal stimulus we distinguish between the case in which real interest rates are kept constant and the case in which nominal interest rates are kept constant. The first pair of simulations consists of a sustained, previously unanticipated, increase in government spending of £1 bn per annum in 1980 prices. The extra expenditure is split equally between procurement and employment expenditure. The second pair of simulations consists of a sustained previously unanticipated reduction in the standard rate of income tax of 1.5 pence. This is equivalent to £1 bn per annum at 1980 prices. In each case the simulations start in 1987 quarter 3 and run for eight years.

The relative effects of the two forms of fiscal expansion can be compared but the absolute figures should be regarded as illustrative rather than definitive. Comparisons of absolute figures need to take into account the effects on the inflation – and cyclically – adjusted fiscal deficit which is outside the remit of this chapter.

The financing of fiscal policy changes has proved to be one of the more controversial areas of post-Keynesian economics. We consider two possible assumptions concerning financing. The first is akin to the pure money finance case. We assume that the government issues sufficient money and other short-term instruments to keep the current value of the nominal short interest rate constant throughout the simulation. The reallocation of portfolios by agents in financial markets following a fiscal change requires the authorities to issue a certain number of treasury bills as well as cash. The second assumption is that the authorities aim to keep the real interest rate constant. This is akin to bond finance although again a number of extra shorter-term instruments have also to be issued. These two regimes are intended as characterisations of the standard textbook financing assumptions.

Tables 5.1 and 5.2 show the effects of the increase in public expenditure and the cut in income tax with nominal interest rates held fixed. In Table 5.1 it can be seen that after four years unemployment is cut by 118 000. After eight years the effect on unemployment is slightly smaller and prices are 3.1 per cent higher. The short-run effect on unemployment is smaller when the simulation consists of income tax cuts. After eight years the cut in unemployment is close to the public expenditure case; but prices are 6.9 per cent higher than in the base run. The income tax case also produces a larger deterioration of the balance of payments.

The main mechanisms through which the rise in employment comes about are as follows. Increased domestic demand shifts the demand curve for labour according to our model of the labour market. As described earlier, this effect is independent of a reduction in unemployment due to a reduction in the own product real wage. In addition, in the manufacturing sector the immediate depreciation of the exchange rate causes a gain in competitiveness which increases export demand from abroad and thus provides a further source of demand for traded goods. It also results in a wedge between producer and consumer prices as outlined above. Price adjustment in the manufacturing sector is relatively rapid in both simulations. The depreciation of the exchange rate which leads to increased costs of raw material inputs also puts firms in manufacturing in a position where they are more competitive on a cost and price basis. Firms are assumed to raise output

Table 5.1 Simulation 1: Government procurement and employment spending up by £1 bn. Nominal interest rates fixed (1980 prices)

	1989	1991	1995
GDP (%)	0.66	0.66	0.51
Price level (%)	0.77	1.52	3.07
(Consumer Price index)			
Unemployment (000s)	−104	−118	−113
Exchange rate (%)	−2.9	−3.6	−5.1
Private investment (%)	0.46	0.62	0.27
Consumption (%)	0.13	0.25	0.10
Current BOP (£m)	−383	−947	−1382
Labour cost competitiveness (%)	−2.37	−1.99	−1.77
Producer price competitiveness (%)	−1.70	−1.56	−1.54
Export volume (%)	0.67	0.70	0.56
Import volume (%)	0.33	0.65	0.47
PSBR (£m, financial year)	446	5	−279
Employment (%)			
(i) Manufacturing	0.52	0.90	1.09
(ii) Non-manufacturing	0.28	0.36	0.29
Real consumption wage (%)			
(i) Manufacturing	0.22	0.26	0.28
(ii) Non-manufacturing	0.16	0.22	0.24
Real product wage (%)			
(i) Manufacturing	−0.31	−0.42	−0.48
(ii) Non-manufacturing	0.21	0.15	0.17
Working population (%)	0.14	0.20	0.23

prices rather faster than the increases in input prices in an attempt to increase profits as demand expands. Final consumer prices, which affect wage bargaining, follow rather more sluggishly. The effect is therefore that real manufacturing producer wages fall while real consumption wages rise. Simulation 1 shows that the proportional increase in employment is larger in the manufacturing sector than in private non-manufacturing; this is partly because the non-manufacturing sector produces less traded output. The same is true in Simulation 2, where there is a larger fall in the own product real wage in both sectors and a greater improvement in competitiveness. (The larger fall in unemployment in the public spending case is explained by the increase in public sector employment. As can be seen, the income tax case produces a larger rise in private sector employment.)

The distributed lags in the adjustment of the overall price level make the wedge between producers' and consumer price real wages rather larger in the early part of the simulation. This is consistent with rather faster employment growth in this period. Comparison of the paths of manufacturing and non-manufacturing employment growth shows that the wedge is rather smaller for non-manufacturing. The residual sector in this analysis is the government

Table 5.2   Simulation 2: 1.5 per cent off basic personal income tax rate. Nominal interest rates fixed

	1989	1991	1995
GDP (%)	0.79	0.89	0.70
Price level (%)	1.51	3.14	6.90
(Consumer Price index)			
Unemployment (000s)	− 57	− 103	− 112
Exchange rate (%)	− 5.49	− 7.01	− 10.53
Private investment (%)	0.58	1.00	0.43
Consumption (%)	0.64	0.98	0.75
Current BOP (£m)	− 594	− 1660	− 2647
Labour cost competitiveness (%)	− 4.65	− 3.96	3.69
Producer price competitiveness (%)	− 3.34	− 3.08	− 3.30
Export volume (%)	1.18	1.34	1.11
Import volume (%)	0.38	1.14	0.91
PSBR (£m, financial year)	905	562	− 132
Employment (%)			
(i) Manufacturing	0.85	1.60	1.97
(ii) Non-manufacturing	0.43	0.74	0.76
Real consumption wage (%)			
(i) Manufacturing	− 0.06	0.15	0.31
(ii) Non-manufacturing	0.11	0.26	0.31
Real product wage (%)			
(i) Manufacturing	− 0.83	− 0.94	− 0.88
(ii) Non-manufacturing	0.60	0.53	0.56
Working population (%)	0.14	0.25	0.31

sector which only produces non-traded value added, by assumption. The fall in unemployment which results from increased employment has a direct effect on wage outcomes and following the bargaining approach has a Phillips curve type effect on real consumption wage outcomes in both private sectors. The result is that, following the analysis in Section 5.3, the level of employment rises in both private sectors. Real producer wages are bid up a little through the effect of reduced unemployment as employment rises. Real consumer wages rise rather more than real producer wages. Unemployment, however, does not fall by as much as the increase in employment due to a rise in the working population.

This labour supply response is due to greater participation in the work-force by women. In both forms of fiscal expansion this apparent supply-side effect is contingent on employment creation as reduced unemployment has an encouraged-worker effect on female labour force participation. In the case of tax cuts this is further enhanced by increased after-tax real wages which induce further female participation. This effect serves to offset the effect on unemployment of tax cuts rather more than in the case of increased spending.

The dynamics of wage and employment adjustment are affected by the process determining the proportion of the long-term unemployed in the total.

Fiscal expansion, however realised, results in an initial rise in the ratio as leavers are concentrated among the short-term unemployed. Over time an overall reduction in unemployment reduces the ratio. Over the transition path the result is that wage growth is slower in the simulations than if unemployment of all durations had the same effect on real wage adjustment.

It may be suggested that a simulation in which nominal interest rates are kept constant despite a rise in inflation is inconsistent. It is true of the LBS model that attempts to maintain nominal rates under such conditions can destabilise financial markets, but this is not so over the ranges involved in these simulations.

In Simulations 3 and 4 we repeat the first two simulations with real short-term interest rates fixed. The main impact on the simulations of the alternative financing assumptions is through the exchange rate. The expenditure increase simulation shows that in the case of fixed nominal interest rates the real rate is lower by some 0.5 annual percentage points throughout the simulation period. The real exchange rate in price terms falls by 2.4 per cent on impact and appreciates thereafter. When the real interest rate is fixed Table 5.3 shows that the exchange rate is lower by 2.19 per cent after two

Table 5.3   Simulation 3: Government procurement and employment spending up by £1 bn. Real interest rates fixed

	1989	1991	1995
GDP (%)	0.47	0.54	0.52
Price level (%)	0.51	1.07	2.32
(Consumer Price index)			
Unemployment (000s)	−81	−92	−103
Exchange rate (%)	−2.19	−3.04	−4.41
Private investment (%)	0.01	0.25	0.19
Consumption (%)	−0.07	−0.08	0.16
Current BOP (£m)	−75	−466	−892
Labour cost competitiveness (%)	−1.75	−1.87	−1.63
Producer price competitiveness (%)	−1.30	−1.41	1.37
Export volume (%)	0.46	0.56	0.56
Import volume (%)	0.02	0.30	0.39
PSBR (£m, financial year)	808	983	963
Employment (%)			
(i) Manufacturing	0.32	0.64	1.04
(ii) Non-manufacturing	0.10	0.14	0.18
Real consumption wage (%)			
(i) Manufacturing	−0.20	0.20	0.28
(ii) Non-manufacturing	0.14	0.16	0.21
Real product wage (%)			
(i) Manufacturing	0.20	−0.40	−0.58
(ii) Non-manufacturing	0.18	0.15	0.16
Working population (%)	0.11	0.15	0.21

Table 5.4   Simulation 4: 1.5 per cent basic personal income tax rate. Real interest
rate fixed

	1989	1991	1995
GDP (%)	0.41	0.66	0.72
Price level (%)	1.00	2.18	5.16
(Consumer Price index)			
Unemployment (000s)	− 12	− 48	− 89
Exchange rate (%)	− 3.94	− 5.70	− 8.90
Private investment (%)	− 0.30	0.28	0.21
Current BOP (£m)	64	− 689	− 1846
Labour cost competitiveness (%)	− 3.38	− 3.74	− 3.57
Producer price competitiveness (%)	− 2.50	− 2.80	− 2.29
Export volume (%)	0.75	1.07	1.13
Import volume (%)	− 0.21	0.43	0.76
PSBR (£m, financial year)	2244	2563	2901
Employment (%)			
(i) Manufacturing	0.44	1.04	1.73
(ii) Non-manufacturing	0.09	0.30	0.57
Real consumption wage (%)			
(i) Manufacturing	− 0.08	0.04	0.30
(ii) Non-manufacturing	0.08	0.16	0.27
Real product wage (%)			
(i) Manufacturing	− 0.58	− 0.86	− 1.03
(ii) Non-manufacturing	0.53	0.53	0.55
Working population (%)	0.08	0.15	0.26

years. The impact depreciation in the real rate is 1.6 per cent and the
appreciation thereafter leaves it at a higher rate than in the case of the fixed
nominal interest rate. This is due to the fact that the integral balance-of-
payments deficits is rather smaller in the case of fixed real interest rates. The
real trade surplus required to finance interest payments on the stock of net
foreign debts created is consequently smaller requiring a lower long-run real
depreciation. In the labour market, reduced depreciation results in lower
inflation and less growth of output in the short run. The reduction in real
product wages in manufacturing is smaller and thus employment increases
are somewhat lower. Part of the additional demand created by lower real
interest rates is lost in this case. Investment and consumption of durables are
significantly reduced as a result of relatively higher interest costs. Output
growth in the longer run is greater when real rates are fixed and rather more
bonds and less money are issued to finance both the expenditure increase and
the tax cut. Wealth effects of personal sector holdings of government issued
debt increase consumption expenditure relatively more in these cases,
although the effects take some years to accumulate.

Finally, we return to the issue of the position of the aggregate supply curve
in the LBS model and the extent to which fiscal expansion can raise output.

As we have noted above, there is some difficulty in identifying the extent of demand versus supply schedule shifts in outcomes in the labour market. In the model as a whole we can trace out short- and long-run supply curves by varying the size of the fiscal expansion and thus the shift in the aggregate demand curve. In Figure 5.1 the results of this exercise are shown for both the expenditure increase and tax reduction cases. Both are for cases of fixed nominal interest rates. In each case the short-run curve is for results after three years of simulations and the long-run curve for results after eight years. In cases of both expenditure increases and tax reductions the long-run curve is steeper than the short-run curve. There is more inflation than in the short run when we can expect price stickiness to lead to strong output effects. In the long run, something close to full adjustment in prices results. The relative slopes of the long-run curves give some indication of the relative effectiveness of expenditure increases versus direct tax reductions. As in the short run the trade-off is steeper in the case of tax reductions. It may be that points on the curves may be compared on a pure expenditure or an adjusted PSBR cost basis. However, the slopes of the curves make clear that a long-run trade-off does exist in the LBS model and that in the region of solution values we examine there is evidence for the effectiveness of expansionary fiscal policy.

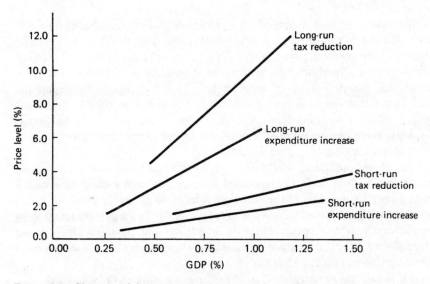

Figure 5.1   Short- and long-run supply curves for LBS model. Constructed by simulation of increasing expenditure increases and income tax reductions. Short run is after three years and long run after eight years of the simulation.

5.5   CONCLUSIONS

A fiscal stimulation, according to the current version of the LBS model will produce a sustained fall in unemployment. An expansion of public spending is more effective than a cut in income tax. The fall in unemployment is associated with a rise in inflation.

Those results would have seemed perfectly conventional when the LBS model was first constructed, in the Keynesian tradition, more than twenty years ago. But since then we have seen the disenchantment with Keynesian policy (at least in the form practised by the Heath–Barber administration of 1970–74) and developments in macroeconomic theory which include: the natural rate of unemployment, the rational expectations revolution and the switch in emphasis to supply-side considerations. But we have also seen, particularly in Europe, a dramatic rise in unemployment accompanying the attempts, since about 1980, to cut inflation. That development has been accompanied in turn by the theory of insiders and outsiders in the labour market and by the idea of hysteresis.

Given those events it is perhaps not completely surprising that we have ended fairly close to where we began. The important difference is that we now feel constrained to understand the micro-foundations of our macroeconomic results.

We have identified a number of mechanisms which could allow a fiscal expansion to have a prolonged effect on unemployment. As it happens, the mechanism proposed in the *General Theory*, namely a cut in the own product real wage brought about by a general cut in real wages, does not seem to be important, except in the short term. In the LBS model, unions do bargain for real wages, thus they will not be fooled by a rise in prices relative to nominal wages in the long run. However, since price expectations are backward looking, there can be some temporary cut in real wages accompanied by a shift along the demand curve for labour.

The more important effects are shifts in the demand curve for labour associated with imperfect competition and open economy effects associated with a real depreciation of the exchange rate. How plausible are these effects in producing sustained cuts in unemployment? We might reasonably be cautious about attributing long-run effects to the outward shift in the demand curve for labour since the change in the mark-up has previously been identified as a cyclical phenomenon.

It is important to recognise that the effects described in the simulations are persistent over the period examined but that does not imply that they operate indefinitely. Mainly they operate because the model suggests that the economy takes a very long time to reach a full equilibrium steady state. As we have argued, the simulations suggest that in the long run, the effects are largely crowded out, but we all know what Keynes said about the long run.

Acknowledgements

The authors are grateful for the comments of their colleagues. The research was carried out under ESRC grant number B01250012.

References

BALL, J., T. BURNS and P. WARBURTON (1979) 'The London Business School Model of the UK Economy: an Exercise in International Monetarism', in P. Ormerod (ed.), *Economic Modelling* (Heinemann).

BUDD, A. P., P. L. LEVINE and P. N. SMITH (1988) 'Unemployment, Vacancies and the Long-Term Unemployed', Centre for Economic Forecasting, London Business School, Discussion Paper No. 154 (revised) and forthcoming in the *Economic Journal*.

BUDD, A. P., P. L. LEVINE and P. N. SMITH (1987) 'Real Wage Adjustment and Long-term Unemployment', in R. Cross *et al.* (eds), *Unemployment, Hysteresis and the Natural Rate Hypothesis* (Oxford: Basil Blackwell).

DOMBERGER, S. (1979) 'Price Adjustment and Market Structure', *Economic Journal*, 89.

HILTON, K. and D. F. HEATHFIELD (eds) (1970) *The Econometric Study of the United Kingdom* (Macmillan).

KEYNES, J. M. (1929) 'Can Lloyd George Do It?', *Collected Writings*, vol. IX.

KEYNES, J. M. (1936) *The General Theory of Employment, Interest and Money* (Macmillan).

LAYARD R. (1986) *How to Beat Unemployment* (Oxford University Press).

RENTON, G. A. (ed.) (1975) *Modelling the Economy* (Heinemann).

SMITH, P. N. and S. HOLLY (1985) 'Employment and Wage Determination in the UK', Centre for Economic Forecasting, London Business School, Discussion Paper No. 137 (revised).

APPENDIX

The equations that constitute the labour market in the LBS model are given in this appendix. The definitions and sources of the data used in their estimation are given in the data appendix which follows.

Long-term unemployment equation

	$\log S_t$
$\log S_{t-1}$	0.8432
	(9.41)[a]
$\log S_{t-3}$	-0.4705
	(3.36)
$\log S_{t-4}$	0.4900
	(4.24)
$\log (u/v)_{t-3}$	-0.06094
	(2.27)
$\log R_{t-1}$	0.4218
	(5.05)

$\log R_{t-3}$	-0.4392
	(4.78)
constant	-0.2541
	(1.68)

Test statistics

$\bar{R}^2$	0.955
se	6.16%
DW	2.02
$LM(5)^b$	11.52
$Z_1(4)^c$	0.161

Steady-state coefficients

$\log(u/v)$	0.444
$\log R$	0.127
constant	-1.851

Variables

S: average probability of unemployed at $t-4$ finding a job between $t-4$ and t; ($S = U^{LT}/U_{t-4}$), U: unemployment level, u: unemployment rate $= U/V$, N: total labour force, V: vacancy level, v: vacancy rate $= V/L$, L: total employment, U^{LT}: long-term unemployment, R: ratio of long-term unemployment to total. ($R = U^{LT}/U$)

Notes

(a) *t*-statistics in parentheses.
(b) LM(5): Lagrange multiplier test for up to 5th order autocorrelation.
(c) $Z_1(4)$: Chow test of within sample parameter stability.

Estimation period: 1972q1–1985q4   *Method:* OLS

U–V curve

	$\log u_t$
$\log u_{t-1}$	1.108
	(30.66)
$\log u_{t-4}$	-0.3103
	(9.30)
$\log v_t$	-0.1434
	(5.98)
$\log R_{t-2}$	0.2427
	(8.48)
$1/\text{time}^2$	-729.71
	(3.52)
constant	0.7165
	(12.92)

Test statistics

$\bar{R}^2$	0.99
se	2.52%
DW	2.02
LM(5)	12.17
$Z_1(4)$	0.410
$Z_2(7)^a$	1.15

Steady-state coefficients

$\log v_t$	-0.7088
$\log R_t$	1.1997
constant	3.5418

Note

(a) $Z_2(n)$ is a test for the validity of the n instruments used, additional instruments are $\log v_{t-1}$, $\log v_{t-2}$, $\log v_{t-3}$.

Estimation period: 1972q1–1985q4   *Method:* Instrumental variables

Real wage equations

	Manufacturing $\log(W^m/PC^e)_t$	Non-manufacturing $\log(W^n/PC^e)_t$
$\log(W/PC)_{t-1}$	0.9431	0.3761
	(13.75)	(2.97)
$\log(W/PC)_{t-2}$		0.1444
		(1.10)
$\log(W/PC)_{t-3}$	−0.1897	−0.3433
	(2.90)	(2.94)
$\log[W^{m*}(1-TAX)/PC]_{t-1}$		0 1343
		(1.82)
$\log u_{t-1}$	−0.1002	−0.1135
	(3.53)	(2.33)
$\log u_{t-2}$	0.1365	0.2004
	(3.68)	(2.34)
$\log u_{t-3}$		0.1319
		(2.73)
$\log u_{t-4}$	−0.06136	
	(3.75)	
$\log(UBEN/PC)_{t-1}$		0.07386
		(1.67)
$\log R_{t-4}$	0.0219	
	(2.09)	
$\log(1+TAX3)_t$	−0.4475	
	(1.91)	
$\log(1+TAX3)_{t-2}$	0.5321	
	(2.18)	
IPOL	−0.00763	−0.0049
	(1.68)	(0.70)
time	0.001454	0.00359
	(2.97)	(4.43)

Test statistics

$\bar{R}^2$	0.997	0.982
se	0.83%	1.77%
DW	1.96	2.06
LM(5)	11.03	7.13
$Z_3(8)$	3.71	5.16

Steady-state coefficients

$\log[W^m(1-TAX2)/PC]$		0.163
$\log u$	−0.102	−0.0547
$\log R$	0.0886	
$\log(UBEN/PC)$		0.0898
$\log(1+TAX3)$	1.710	
IPOL	−0.0309	−0.00605
time	0.00590	0.00437

Notes
Variables used in addition to above:
W^m: wages in manufacturing, W^n: wages in non-manufacturing, PC: consumption deflator, PC^e: expected consumption price deflator, $TAX2$: direct tax index, $TAX3$: indirect tax index, $UBEN$: unemployment benefit index, $IPOL$: incomes policy dummy, $Z_3(4)$: test of the outside sample parameter stability.

Estimation period: 1965q2–1985q4   *Method:* OLS

Employment equations

	Manufacturing $\log L_t^m$	Non-manufacturing $\log L_t^n$
$\log L_{t-1}$	1.1799 (8.72)	1.349 (3.29)
$\log L_{t-2}$	−0.2603 (2.10)	−0.414 (3.29)
$\log Y_t$	0.08265 (5.06)	0.1827 (3.40)
$\log Y_{t-1}$		−0.248 (3.28)
$\log [W(1 + TAX1)/P]_t$	−0.1742 (3.56)	−0.0709 (2.93)
$\log [W(1 + TAX1)/P]_{t-1}$	0.1052 (2.10)	
$\log [W(1 + TAX1)/P]_{t-2}$		
$\log (P^{rm}/P)_t$	0.04866 (2.57)	
$\log (P^{rm}/P)_{t-1}$	−0.05163 (3.06)	

Test statistics		
$\bar{R}^2$	0.99	0.534
se	0.3%	0.476%
DW	1.83	2.22
LM(5)	0.027	9.06
$Z_3(8)$	0.75	7.34
$Z_2(12)$	7.10	8.96

Steady-state coefficients		
$\ln [(W/P)(1 + TAX1)]$	−0.859	−1.086
$\ln Y$	1.028	1.0
$\ln (P^m/P)$	−0.0369	0

Variables (in addition to above)
L^m: employment in manufacturing, L^n: employment in non-manufacturing, Y^m: output in manufacturing, Y^n: output in non-manufacturing, $TAX1$: employers' national insurance contributions rate, P^{rm}: price of raw materials in manufacturing.

Notes
Additional instruments used: current values and lags of world GNP, money supply, real world price of raw materials.

Estimation period: 1965q2–1984q4   *Method:* Instrumental variables

Female participation rate equation

	$\Delta \log N_t^f$
$\Delta \log N_{t-1}^f$	−0.172
	(1.29)
$\Delta \log N_{t-2}^f$	−0.423
	(2.59)
$\log (N_{t-3}^f/P_{t-1}^f)$	−0.599
	(4.49)
$\log u_t$	−0.0801
	(2.76)
$\log u_{t-1}$	0.0710
	(1.65)
$\log u_{t-2}$	−0.0507
	(2.07)
$\log [WSI^*(1 - TAX2)/PC]_t$	0.00696
	(1.92)
$\log [WSI^*(1 - TAX2)/PC]_{t-3}$	0.0914
	(1.73)
$\log (W^f/W^m)_{t-1}$	0.216
	(1.88)
$\log (W^f/W^m)_{t-3}$	0.0873
	(0.71)
time	0.0017
	(3.19)

Test statistics

$\bar{R}^2$	0.559
se	0.555%
DW	1.99
LM(5)	16.93
$Z_3(8)$	0.136

Steady-state coefficients

$\log p^f$	1.0
$\log u$	−0.100
$\log [WSI^*(1 - TAX2)/PC]$	0.164
$\log (W^f/W^m)$	0.507
time	0.00286

Variables (in addition to above)
N^f: female working population, P^f: female population of working age, WSI: wage and salary index, W^f/W^m: relative female to male wage rates

Estimation period: 1965q2–1984q4   *Method:* OLS

6 Aspects of the Theory of Fiscal Policy

Maurice Peston

6.1 INTRODUCTION

The purpose of this chapter is to re-examine the standard theory of fiscal policy with a view to seeing where we are at the present time. It is apparent that much of the theoretical literature contradicts certain widely accepted beliefs, held more, perhaps, by market practitioners than by professional economists. It is also the case that existing theory has certain limitations which have not been at all easy to overcome. In particular, it is nearly as true as it was fifty years ago that except in very simple cases it has not been possible to incorporate stock theories and flow theories within a unified framework.

It is now generally accepted that there are many possible forms of government intervention which may be classified under the heading of fiscal policy. What they have in common is some connection with government expenditure and taxation, but that is all. The range between fine tuning in the optimal stochastic control sense and occasional strong moves to deal with a slump or a hyper-inflation is immense. Indeed, the differences are so large it is not at all clear that there is much to gain by lumping them all together.

Well before the publication of the *General Theory* there was a long debate on the question of public works. Economists were strongly divided on their effectiveness. They were favoured by Keynes and Pigou, and opposed by many others.[1] Curiously enough, as the oral evidence placed before the Macmillan Committee shows, the discussion revolved around the rate of return on public investment.[2] It was agreed there were underutilised resources. If the private sector did not consider it worth while to use them, did this not mean that it was inadvisable for the public sector to do so? Some economists argued that the private sector required too high a rate of return; therefore, public works with a lower rate of return could be justified. Others disagreed, and concentrated on the hypothesis of a constant flow of savings and traditional crowding out. There were few, if any, advocates of employment subsidies based on the proposition that the shadow price of unemployed labour is below the money wage rate.[3] It follows that they failed to comprehend the notion of policy as creating an external economy or public good.

The origin of the scientific analysis of fiscal policy as a means of directly raising aggregate demand is rather obscure. Contrary to common belief, the idea is not fully articulated in the *General Theory*, but it is apparent that Keynes fully understood the basic principles when he came to write *How to Pay for the War*. It is claimed that Lindahl antedated Keynes in his approach to the problem. Certainly, there were several US economists and policy advisers who rapidly appreciated the significance of the *General Theory* as an analytical basis for macroeconomic intervention.[4]

All that is in the sense of appreciating how it was possible to manipulate aggregate demand. It led inexorably to the balanced budget multiplier and the literature to do with the 'unity' theorem.[5] What is less apparent is when the idea of contracyclical policy emerged, and who was its originator. Lerner has a great claim to originality here, and possibly Alvin Hansen as well.[6] In deciding all that, it is worth reiterating that there is a significant intellectual jump from the proposition that the government might on rare occasions deal with a major depression by raising public expenditure to the notion that it would intervene regularly to stabilise the economy at full employment.

A last point worth noting here is that Lerner was the first to take cognisance of the monetary consequences of a budget deficit, and to state that there were later round effects of the endogenous rise in the money supply. He did not, however, derive the corresponding long-run multiplier theorem.

These aspects of the history of thought are worthy of further exploration, especially as they relate to the perennial question of what was original about the *General Theory*. But they are not germane to the principal theme of this chapter, except as a reminder that the debate on the efficacy of fiscal policy goes back a very long way.

6.2 IS/LM ANALYSIS

I shall now present briefly the main results of the theory of fiscal policy as it is set out within the standard IS/LM model. It is customary to distinguish four cases depending on whether there is a fixed or floating exchange rate, and whether or not there is international capital mobility. In discussing these cases several fundamental problems arise common to all of them. It will not be necessary, therefore, to repeat the relevant discussion four times.

The main results are set out formally in Appendix I. It is worth reminding ourselves that the IS curve defines goods marked equilibrium, the LM curve money market equilibrium, and the *BK* balance-of-payments equilibrium; all in interest-income space. The curves are treated as if they are independent, but are obviously not so once sector financial balance considerations are brought into play.[7]

The basic equations are

$$Y = F\{Y(1-t), r\} + G + B \tag{6.1}$$

where

Y = national income
r = rate of interest
F = private expenditure
G = government expenditure
t = tax rate
B = balance of trade

Make the usual assumptions:

$$0 < F_y < 1$$
$$F_r < 0$$

$$M = M(Y, r) \tag{6.2}$$

where M = quantity of money

$$M_y > 0$$
$$M_r < 0$$

$$B = B(Y, E) \tag{6.3}$$

where E = exchange rate

$$B_y < 0$$
$$B_E > 0$$

If the exchange rate is left to float freely,

$$B = 0 \tag{6.3'}$$

For any given exchange rate this will define a unique level of income.

6.2.1 Fixed exchange rate and no capital mobility

An increase in public expenditure shifts the IS curve to the right to an extent depending on the size of the multiplier. That itself is determined by net leakages into imports and taxes. The extent of the initial increase in output will then depend on the slope of the LM curve. If that curve is steep, indicating a high income and a low interest elasticity of demand for money, fiscal policy is less effective, but can be strongly assisted by monetary expansion.

Starting from initial balance, the current account will move into deficit, as will the government budget.

All that is for a given price level. More generally, the aggregate demand curve moves to the right, and the ultimate rises in output and price level depend on the slope of the aggregate supply curve. (This is discussed further below.)

It is also helpful to consider the following equation

$$\Delta(I-S)+\Delta D+\Delta B=0 \tag{6.4}$$

where

I = investment
S = saving
D = budget deficit
B = current account

As output and the rate of interest rise, it normally follows that, starting from balance, $(I-S)$ becomes negative.[8] It follows that $D+B$ becomes positive. If the government does not pursue a policy of sterilisation, the money supply will increase. The LM curve shifts to the right, the interest rate falls, and output rises further until $I-S$ is zero again. At that point $D+B$ is also zero. Since output is larger than in the initial position, B must be negative and D positive. And since S is larger than in the initial position, so is I; therefore, the rate of interest is lower. The government is losing reserves. If this position is not sustainable indefinitely, policy must be adjusted to make B zero again. For the given exchange rate that means returning output to its initial position. Alternatively, the real exchange rate must be devalued. Another way of putting all this is to say that the fixed real exchange rate must be that which is compatible with full employment, and the role of fiscal policy is to adjust aggregate demand to equal full employment aggregate supply.

6.2.2 Fixed exchange rate and capital mobility

The simplest way of examining this case is to postulate that capital flows are positively related to the domestic rate of interest.

$$K=K(r) \tag{6.5}$$

where K = inward capital flows

$$K_r>0$$

If the exchange rate floats

$$B(Y, E) + K(r) = 0 \tag{6.6}$$

The IS and LM curves remain unchanged. But it is necessary to consider in interest rate-income space the combinations of r and Y that leave the overall balance of payments in balance for the given exchange rate. A rise in Y worsens the current account. This may be offset by a rise in r improving the capital account. There will be a positive relationship between r and Y compatible with overall balance for the given E. Call this the BK line. It should be noted that the more mobile is capital, the less r has to rise to offset the increase in Y, i.e. the flatter will be the BK line.

Once again when government expenditure rises, there will be a new equilibrium with higher income and interest rate. The result is that the current account moves into deficit and the capital account to surplus. The overall external account may move in either direction or stay in balance. The flatter the BK line, i.e. the more mobile are international capital flows, the more likely it is that the overall external account will move into surplus. As far as impact effects are concerned, what capital mobility does for fiscal policy is to finance the current account deficit. The more mobile is capital internationally, the more easily is the deficit financed, and the less likely it is that reserves will be used. Of course, the flow of capital can be regarded as borrowed reserves.[9]

It continues to be the case that $I - S$ becomes negative and $D + B + K$ positive. Thus, yet again the money supply increases, the LM curve moves to the right, and output rises more still (unless there is neutralisation by the Central Bank).[10]

What more can be said of the new equilibrium? With output higher, S will be higher. If I is to increase, r must be lower than in the initial equilibrium. It follows that both B and K must become negative if they were zero to begin with. Thus, the government budget goes permanently into deficit. It could be argued as before that the current account cannot remain in deficit indefinitely, especially if at the same time there are capital outflows. In that case once again we return to the proposition that there can be no move from the status quo or that the currency must be devalued.

There are some additional comments to be made that highlight the less than satisfactory nature of this formulation. One concerns the sustainable level of reserve flows. It is said that $B + K$ cannot be negative indefinitely. A country cannot be a permanent loser of reserves. (I ignore the large country problem, and the provision of international reserves.) Some economists certainly believe that $B + K$ can be permanently positive. It is a triviality that the two positions are contradictory, since a positive sign for one country implies a negative one for at least one other. More generally, what is sustainable depends on the desired composition of portfolios, and the nature of borrowing and lending that a country wishes to engage in. It is difficult to lay down an equilibrium condition *a priori*. It is by no means obvious that the correct condition is $B + K$ equal to zero or B equal to zero.

Having said that, it must be recognised that the flow equilibrium characteristic of IS/LM may be as seriously misleading for the international capital account as it is for the domestic one. K not being equal to zero implies an indefinitely large or an indefinitely small stock of overseas assets. Is this meaningful within a static framework? The answer has to be the usual one that the flow equilibrium is only a temporary one, and that IS/LM needs to be replaced by a more sophisticated long-run theory.

A final comment that must be made is that it is wrong to treat the current and capital accounts as independent. A capital outflow in this period implies a subsequent interest and profit inflow which is added to the current account. If K is negative and is not wasted, eventually B must become positive.[11]

6.2.3   Floating exchange rate and no capital mobility

A floating exchange rate has two principal effects. There are no changes in the reserves, and, therefore, no later round monetary effects from that source. In addition, the IS curve is flatter than in the fixed exchange rate case. The reason is the obvious one that, starting from a goods market equilibrium, a fall in the interest rate raises output more because none of the extra demand leaks into imports. It is then equally obvious that when government expenditure is increased, the IS curve shifts more to the right when the exchange rate is floating. Essentially, at the initial exchange rate the current account moves into deficit. In the floating case the exchange rate falls expanding exports, reducing imports, and increasing income more. For the given LM curve this also means that the interest rate rises more, and in turn $I - S$ and the budget deficit become more negative. The final equilibrium in which I equals S is also one with higher income. This is because there is no current account deficit; thus tax revenues have to rise fully to finance the higher level of public expenditure.

6.2.4   Floating exchange rate and capital mobility

The equilibrium condition is now that the combined current and capital accounts must balance, i.e. $B + K$ equals zero. The effect of capital mobility is to make the IS curve flatter still. Again the argument is simple. The fall in r and the rise in Y require a devaluation to offset the deterioration in the current account, and a further devaluation to offset the effects of a capital outflow. This by itself does not tell us whether a floating exchange rate makes fiscal policy more or less effective. It will be recalled that in the fixed exchange rate case fiscal expansion might have any effect on the overall balance of payments since the two accounts move in opposite directions. Only if the effect was an overall deterioration would the exchange rate be devalued, and income expand more. The more mobile capital is internationally the more capital inflows are likely to exceed the current account deficit. The exchange rate will then be revalued upwards, making fiscal policy less effective. In the limit with perfect capital mobility the IS curve becomes horizontal. It is a commonplace that when capital is perfectly mobile, the domestic interest rate in equilibrium equals the world interest rate, and monetary policy is effective and works via its influence on the exchange rate. (I ignore the additional complications of interest parity and overshooting which are not central to the present discussion.) It is equally obvious that, with perfect capital mobility and a horizontal IS curve, fiscal policy on its own is totally ineffective. A rise in government expenditure in those circumstances causes an appreciation of the exchange rate and full crowding out of net exports. The resulting current account deficit is automatically financed by capital inflows.

There is no need to add to the earlier criticisms of IS/LM except to remind ourselves that they apply in this case too. It is especially important to reflect on a correct approach to perfect capital mobility. In the present formulation a country, especially a small one, can borrow or lend limitless amounts at the going rate of interest. Before applying such ideas to the real world it is surely necessary to enquire whether something akin to borrowers' and lenders' risk ought to be introduced into the discussion. This is also relevant to the determination of which currencies are acceptable as international reserves, and how fiscal policy works in those countries.

6.3 THE EFFECTS OF SHOCKS TO THE CURRENT AND CAPITAL ACCOUNTS

It could be argued that the mainstream discussions which we have summarised are somewhat beside the point, and what really matters is how policy reacts to external shocks. Let us start with a shock to the current account caused say by a change in foreign income or propensity to import. Such shocks cause the IS curve to fluctuate if the exchange rate is fixed. (Assume monetary policy offsets the monetary effects of the external account, and the LM curve stays where it is.) If nothing is done to offset them, output and the interest rate fluctuate too. It is apparent that these current account shocks can be offset by corresponding movements in the level of government expenditure. Output and the interest rate are stabilised, but the current account and the reserves are not. Monetary policy could be used instead to stabilise output, but the interest rate would then fluctuate. Finally, the exchange rate could be left to float and fully insulate the economy from these international sources of difficulty. In sum, stabilisation of output in the presence of current account shocks involves destabilising public expenditure, the interest rate, or the exchange rate. It is, presumably, unnecessary to add that the extent to which stabilisation is possible also depends on the system's dynamics, and it is absurd to suggest that perfect control is possible. It should also be added, of course, that monetary policy is not a possibility if there is perfect capital mobility.

Consider next shocks originating in the capital account. If the exchange rate is fixed, the IS curve stays where it is. If as before monetary policy is used to keep the LM curve from moving, output and the interest rate are unaffected. The whole burden of external capital shocks is taken by the reserves. If the exchange rate is floating, it will appreciate or depreciate depending on whether capital flows in more or less rapidly. Thus the IS curve fluctuates with corresponding effects on output and the interest rate. Stabilisation of output can then be achieved by fiscal policy, or by monetary policy which would again cause the interest rate to vary. If there is perfect capital mobility, the fiscal policy option ceases to be available. Monetary policy, *per contra*, becomes most effective.

Consider further the case of perfect, or at least a high degree of, capital mobility. Fiscal policy ceases to be effective if the exchange rate is floating, and a fixed exchange rate is equally damaging to monetary policy. It follows that decisions on policy options cannot be taken independently of decisions on the exchange rate regime. To the extent that exchange rate policy must be decided by the likely source of the external shocks to the economy, the problem is even more complicated. The logic of the situation seems to suggest that the exchange rate is allowed to float between broad, and not necessarily fixed bands, that both fiscal and monetary instruments be used, and that the degree of fine tuning will depend on how exactly the source and scale of the shocks can be filtered out of the available signals. This is where the classic papers by Phillips and Friedman have led us to.[12]

6.4 THE RELEVANCE OF THE AGGREGATE SUPPLY CURVE

This topic can be dealt with separately because the shape and behaviour of the aggregate supply curve is relevant to the whole of macroeconomics, and not just to fiscal policy. In elementary economics and in a good deal of policy analysis the aggregate supply curve is assumed to be horizontal. This is not because most economists believed it to have that shape, but rather for analytical convenience. Indeed, as long as the curve is upward sloping (but not vertical) below full employment, nothing of theoretical interest is lost by concentrating on the horizontal case. None the less, it is worth noting that in the *General Theory* Keynes did seem to suggest in some passages that he believed that the price level would vary directly with the level of output.

The significance of an aggregate supply curve with a positive slope lies in practical policy making. Whatever the theoretical position, there is a world of difference between circumstances in which expansionary policy has little effect on the price level and those in which the effect is large. It is fallacious to identify the once for all change in the price level in the standard model with a rise in the rate of inflation. But, risking the pseudo-dynamics, it may safely be said that expansionary policies that raise the inflation rate a little need to be distinguished from, and are a good deal more attractive than, those that raise it a lot. This is so even though in formal terms all that is being said is that p is positive.

The determination of the slope of the aggregate supply curve is an important question. For a given money wage the price level may rise as output rises because of the law of diminishing returns. It may also be that the money wage varies directly with output.[13] The two cases must be distinguished because one implies that the real wage varies inversely with employment, and the other leaves that an open question. In addition, there may also be profit push at work as a source of price increases.

Quite separate from that, more recent work suggests that the slope of the aggregate supply curve may be directly policy dependent. The impact of indirect taxes (and some direct taxes) will be related to their incidence, and this will be revealed by what happens to the aggregate supply curve. The connection between the tax-mix and effective demand have been fully explored. The corresponding analysis for the supply side is much less complete.[14]

Policy may also influence the aggregate supply curve via the route of expectations of whether the authorities will validate cost push. This is an important matter, but too much tends to be made of it. It is used to explain why, whatever the state of the economy, it will tend to remain there. All attempts to raise demand will cause offsetting movements in the aggregate supply curve. Output and employment stay the same; only the price level rises. In some arguments the supply shift follows the demand, and there are temporary gains in outputs.[15] In others they are coincidental, and no output gains occur at all.

The difficulty with such approaches to the problem is that no explanation is forthcoming as to why the system is where it is. Sometimes there is recourse to the doctrine that the economy is always at full employment. But that is to trivialise the whole subject, for then policy intervention may not work, but nobody would see the need for using it, anyway. Even the most blinkered of economists have noticed that employment varies. They are obliged, therefore, either to take the position that all observed employment levels are full employment, or at the very least that the economy is always on its optimal adjustment path. The first is semantic. My fluctuations in unemployment are your fluctuations in full employment unemployment. The second proposition begs the question, and is an *ad hoc* generalisation of the *ad hoc* view that the economy is always at full employment.

The conclusions to be drawn from all this are as follows:

(a) The slope of the aggregate supply curve is not a problem which is uniquely difficult for fiscal policy. It applies as much to monetary policy or to an increased private propensity to spend. Moreover, the nature of the problem differs according to whether the curve is steep because of real forces or nominal ones. In the former case it might be argued that the economy is anyway close to full employment, and the issues are ones of technology and factor scarcity. In the latter case incomes and competition policy are relevant. It is worth emphasising that there are plenty of problems for which fiscal intervention is inappropriate. Another obvious one is where output varies because of supply forces. In that case fiscal intervention may be useless. But it is quite another matter to argue that those are the only cases worth considering, or even the most usual ones.

(b) The validation of cost push is of interest, but is decisive only if it is believed that its effect is to destroy the government's ability to raise real expenditure. That is theoretically possible, but on the whole seems rather far-fetched.

(c) It is pointless to discuss policy if assumptions are made about the supply side which amount to the view that there is no policy problem in the first place.

6.5 FURTHER CRITICISM OF IS/LM

All of this discussion has been in the context of standard IS/LM or AS/AD static theory. The power of such theory is undoubted, both in intellectual terms and with respect to its stamina. It seems to be implicit in nearly all mainstream economics, quite independent of the level of sophistication. None the less, it is widely agreed that the theory is unsatisfactory, and needs to be reformulated dynamically. The trouble is that no one has put forward a dynamic version which meets the criteria of being convincing, of covering all the relevant ground, and of being easily manipulable.

The chief worries about existing theories are these:

(a) The effects on aggregate demand of capital accumulation ($I > 0$) are ignored even though wealth and liquidity effects are taken into account via the government budget constraint.

(b) The effects of capital accumulation on aggregate supply are ignored.

(c) The explanation of unemployment in terms of sticky money wage levels is less easy to accept when it is transferred to a sticky rate of change of money wages. This is not to say that the explanation is wrong; only that it needs more justification than it has received so far.

Another way of putting this is to say that the neoclassical synthesis in its static form makes life too easy. The full employment levels of output, employment, and the real wage are known, or at least their expected values are. There will be random shocks which, when predictable, can be offset by the government, and, when not, have to be accepted. The internal dynamics of the system in response to shocks may be unattractive, but structural measures may be taken to improve the economy's stability. Above all, if sticky money wages are the source of the trouble, this failure of the price mechanism can be offset by fiscal and monetary means.

The policy problem in this approach involves optimal estimation, optimal forecasting, and optimal intervention. The system is guided to behave as well as possible on average, and possess minimum variance. Moreover, in the linear case it is possible to separate the prediction part from the intervention. Policy can then be described as using the latter to bring the forecast state of the economy as close to the desired state as possible.[16]

The question of knowledge of the macroeconomic equilibrium is touched on in the next section. This part may be concluded by a reminder of what has been done, and what further steps are needed. If the real equilibrium growth path of the economy is given, it is comparatively easy to reformulate the rules and theorems of policy analysis. The static results still hold in terms of bringing the economy to the equilibrium path by manipulating aggregate demand. The additional dynamic proposition concerns the means by which demand is made to grow at the same rate as supply. It is obvious that if aggregate demand increases faster than aggregate supply in nominal terms, the economy will move closer to the real growth path if it is not there already. How much of nominal demand is converted into real supply depends on the Phillips curve, which in turn depends on the degree of capacity utilisation. At full capacity utilisation the Phillips curve becomes vertical, and no further sustainable expansion above the underlying growth rate is possible. Lying behind the aggregate demand curve will still be an IS curve in which some spending decisions will depend on the real rate of interest. There will also be an LM curve, but here it is important to bear in mind that the nominal interest rate is important. It is now accepted that this means that the demand for real cash balances may vary inversely with the rate of inflation.

All this is straightforward. Complications arise when the question is asked whether it is reasonable to take the real supply side as given. Surely, it would be in the spirit of Keynes's theory to examine a direct connection between what is happening to demand, and the behaviour of capital accumulation and technical progress. In addition, on the financial side, is it not important to consider a broader range of financial assets, and the markets in which they are traded? Answering in the affirmative is a long way from having anything very positive to contribute!

6.5 THE SIGNIFICANCE OF EXPECTATIONS

The debate on policy effectiveness in recent years has revolved around the question of whether the expectation of policy itself influences the private sector decision-making process. The private sector is assumed not merely to react to circumstances as they change, or to base its decision making on a crude extrapolation of past experience. Instead it will be forward looking, and have a reasoned or interpretative quality.

It will be readily agreed that economists trained in the microeconomics of maximisation would expect something similar to show up at the level of the whole economy. This has little to do with aggregation theory, but a lot to do with the rational decision maker not making systematic errors when it is not profitable to do so. Some economists start from the proposition that households and firms base their behaviour on correct forecasts in the non-trivial senses of being unbiased and of minimum variance. Others have gone less far, and have suggested only that in due course, subject to exogenous stability, the system will converge to such behaviour. Yet others have made the smaller claim that only some people will behave in that way, but the larger one that it is sufficient to ensure that the economy operates as if everyone does.

Within some models two conclusions follow. Anticipation of policy means that there is neither scope nor need for policy. This refers to both monetary and fiscal policy. In addition the economy is at full employment on average, and fluctuations about that state are at a minimum. Policy does not work, but that is no cause for alarm for policy is not necessary.

There are, of course, other models in which different conclusions follow. In them anticipation of policy is helpful, especially if it is anticipated to be successful. Decision makers then respond less sensitively to exogenous shocks, and are less likely to move the economy away from full employment. But they behave this way because they take it for granted that policy works, and will be used if necessary. It is easy to construct paradoxes in which policy works if it is believed to do so, and does not work if there are widespread doubts about its effectiveness. In both cases the prophecy is self-fulfilling, but in neither case is there much to do.[17]

This kind of analysis has a sort of plausibility. The trouble with it is that it flies in the face of actual experience. It is impossible to see how anyone examining the way the British economy has behaved in the 1980s can continue to accept rational expectations theory in the way in which it is usually put forward. The point holds *a fortiori* when attention is paid to what allegedly expert forecasters have had to say.

Participants in economic controversy clearly believe that they are discussing fundamentals. If rational expectations theory in some of its forms is accepted, all disagreement, whether in theory, choices of model, or policy, is about random error. (I say nothing of the methodological problem of discussing rational expectations theory itself.)

My own view is that the significance of this sort of analysis is the reverse of what is sometimes supposed. It is not the demonstration of policy ineffectiveness that should draw our attention. Instead the examples cited should be used to criticise the theory of macroeconomic policy in a more direct way. The proponents of intervention should be obliged to answer the question, What is it that makes policy effective? The critics of interventionism and market failure theory are right to raise the questions they do. They are wrong to infer that, because they are not readily answered, markets work perfectly and policy, notably fiscal policy, is not needed.[18]

Keynes did not avoid these issues. He did try to explain sticky money wages as a form of market failure which could be rectified by enough unemployment, but which could be much more sensibly dealt with by fiscal, monetary, and exchange rate adjustment. His approach in these terms well antedates the *General Theory*. It must be remembered that he offered a theory of wage stickiness, which, correct or not, should have pointed economists at an important problem. Keynes should not be blamed because it took them twenty-five years to respond.

His approach to risk and uncertainty was also non-trivial. The probabilistic basis of rational expectations theory was not acceptable to him, and it is obvious he would have rejected its main conclusions. This is not to assert that other approaches have been more fruitful. We may be impressed by what Shackle has written, and acknowledge that the world is dominated by Knightian uncertainty. Unfortunately, too little or too much follows from that. In particular, it is hard to accept that nothing in the past predisposes the future to be one thing rather than another. We may be constantly taken by surprise, yet today hardly differs from yesterday. If rational action is then possible, it seems to follow that there is such a thing as an optimal forecast. It would then seem to follow that there should be no systematic differences between economists. That might be so in a world in which economics was in some sense complete. Even if that were logically possible, however, which I doubt, it can hardly be claimed that we are there now.

Having aired these methodological questions, I am in no position to answer them, but they are sufficient to cast doubt on what may be called the naive form of rational expectations. There are some further comments to be made which undermine that approach further. They are well known, but receive too little attention.

There is no reason to believe that in general government economists are technically better forecasters than those in the private sector. Indeed, if they do have better techniques, the government ought to sell them to the private sector, or better still, because a forecast has many of the characteristics of a public good, make them freely available. If it is the forecasters themselves who possess special talents, they can sell themselves to the highest bidder in a free market. In fact, on the public goods point, the government should be the highest bidder. In addition, the government knows more about its own behaviour than outsiders can. City firms and journalists do try and anticipate how the government will act, but their powers to do so are limited. Moreover, the government has earlier and better access to key statistics. It follows that one way of explaining policy effectiveness is to interpret it as a form of insider trading.

Another aspect of the public goods interpretation of the subject is to consider the old point that macroeconomic intervention may well be more effective than the corresponding microeconomic adjustments of the free market left to itself. That takes us back to Keynes and sticky money wages. To reiterate, Keynes did not deny that if money wages needed to fall in response to an external shock, eventually, through many trials and tribulations they would do so. His argument was that in, certain circumstances, it would be much more sensible to devalue the currency or increase the money supply. Incidentally, he did not see this as destroying the market mechanism, but allowing it to do the best job it can where it can. We are back again with public goods theory. The ability to operate on a sufficient scale with certain key instruments enables the government to create a public good, i.e. a large scale and coincident response of the whole economy. This is not to deny that a government might choose instead to create a public bad. It is simply to point out that there is a logical basis in economics to the claim that fiscal policy is effective.

6.6 FINANCING A DEFICIT

One way of analysing the problem of unemployment is to note that deficient aggregate demand means that full employment saving exceeds full employment investment. If the economy were at full employment, there would be a flow disequilibrium. It has been argued that the interest rate might fall to solve this problem, but the mainstream view after Keynes was that the interest rate's role is to maintain stock equilibrium in the asset market. This was often stated as the proposition that the interest rate caused the stock of money to be willingly held. It could be reformulated as the interest rate causing the stock of other assets to be willingly held. None the less, if an optimistic view were taken of the effects of open market operations and the interest sensitivity of investment, monetary policy on its own (in a closed economy) could guarantee full employment.

We have already stressed that the equilibrium at full employment, if it could be established, would be a temporary one. On the real side, with investment positive, the capital–income ratio, and the capital–labour ratio, would be rising without limit. On the nominal side, with saving positive, the financial asset–income ratio would also be rising without limit. That is why a dynamic theory is needed.

But there is an additional, and rather different, point to be made. Recall the fundamental proposition of a closed economy.

$$S = I + D \tag{6.7}$$

Saving finances private sector investment plus the government deficit. (Assume the deficit is defined to include public sector investment.) If also for simplicity the government deficit is defined to be the public sector borrowing requirement, another way of putting this is that the public sector borrowing requirement must equal the net private sector lending requirement.

Now the crucial proposition, which is implied in standard theory, but not always articulated, is that there is nothing more to be said. I is set by the interest rate and full employment output. D is adjusted so that aggregate demand equals aggregate supply at full employment. S is the corresponding level of saving. There is money stock equilibrium; therefore, no part of S is a demand for money. It must instead be a demand for bonds.

How then can a problem of financing the deficit arise? For simplicity assume that I is at a maximum, and tax revenues are given. The question can then be put most starkly as: Can there be a difficulty of financing public expenditure which can prevent the attainment of full employment?

It seems to be obvious that within a closed economy the answer must be no. At full employment the saving is there. It is not a demand for money. The investment is also there, and is already financed. The remaining saving can only be used to buy government bonds. If it is now argued that the saving is not there, it follows at once that extra private spending is. Government spending can now be lower while full employment is maintained, but there is still no financing problem.

The argument continues to hold if saving is made a function of the interest rate. Indeed, that is helpful, because anything that reduces saving out of full employment income raises private expenditure. A public sector deficit is then less necessary for achieving full employment. This is not to deny that governments can make things difficult for themselves by spending too much at full employment, and refusing to increase taxes. It is clearly possible for governments to generate an inflationary disequilibrium at full employment. But that state of affairs would happen by design and not necessity.

We have said that the government can behave stupidly. What happens if it is expected to behave stupidly? Suppose that in the recovery process savers come to believe that at full employment D will be excessive, and will be financed in an inflationary way. Inflationary expectations will become built into the system. It is also possible that the demand for equity will rise relative to bonds. While that may be a cause for alarm, it is not clear that it is wholly damaging to the recovery programme. On this argument, the more difficulty the government has in selling bonds, the more the flow of saving will switch to private borrowers, and the easier it will be to sell equities. That will make it easier for the private sector to spend, chiefly, it is to be hoped, on investment. The greater difficulty the government has in borrowing the less need it has to borrow.

There is one way of putting all of this which is surely decisive. It is not denied that the government can spend, tax, and create the deficit in the first place. It is also usually agreed, notably by the anti-interventionists, that the deficit can be financed by money creation. To finance the deficit by bond creation is equivalent to expanding it by money creation, and then engaging in open market operations. Thus, to take the position that the deficit cannot be financed satisfactorily is to say that open market operations are an impossibility.

How are matters changed if we go on to examine an open economy, with perfect or near perfect capital mobility? We have already accepted that fiscal policy will not work if exchange rates are floating, so we must concentrate on a fixed exchange rate (but one which corresponds to full employment equilibrium). The capital mobility assumption does not imply that home and overseas interest rates are exactly equal. The two may diverge somewhat to allow for bias towards domestic assets in portfolios, and a risk premium. None the less, the two rates will move in parallel, except possibly in the very short run.

Assume that the exchange rate is targeted to achieve a current account surplus equal to the desired rate of capital outflow at full employment. Starting from full employment equilibrium, let private sector investment fall, and let government investment rise by the same amount. Also to add to the difficulties suppose savers continue to want to hold private sector assets at the margin rather than government bonds. They will bid up the price of equities, and also send funds overseas. But the capital mobility assumption means that a small country cannot significantly upset the structure of rates of return on financial assets. All that will happen is the outflow of private sector saving will be replaced by an inflow of foreign lending to the government. Opening the economy makes policy easier, not harder, on the financial side.

It could be argued that the risk premium on government bonds will rise, but it is not clear why this should be so. The exchange rate remains in equilibrium so there should be no additional exchange risk. The UK government has not increased its propensity to default, if it ever had such a propensity in the first place. The fiscal intervention is merely to maintain full employment, and will be reversed if the private propensity to spend recovers; thus, nothing should be added to the inflation rate, actual or expected.

In sum, savers want bonds, public and private, domestic or foreign, equities, domestic or foreign, and money. Taking a given private sector propensity to spend, and with no shortage of foreign paper assets, a given international structure of financial returns means that the government can finance its borrowing. Of course, it may make mistakes and be stupid, but that is a general problem of policy making and is not connected with borrowing as such. The government's propensity to behave in this way may influence the terms on which it can borrow. But even then, it may be supposed that this is already allowed for. Difficulty will occur only if it is thought that its propensity to make a mess of things has risen. But the policies we have described are sensible ones, so that it is not clear why an intelligent world financial community would interpret them otherwise. It may be then that the problem revolves around whether that community is intelligent, but that takes us far beyond the present topic. My conclusion is that the government has many difficulties in trying to reach and maintain full employment. Financing a deficit should not be one of them.

6.7 CONCLUSIONS

We have summarised what we have had to say as we went along so that there is not a lot to add by way of conclusion. My main task in this chapter has been to re-establish the case for fiscal policy as an effective instrument of macroeconomic control. It has not been to say that fiscal policy always works or is always best. It has not been to claim that governments never act unintelligently or in an unprincipled way. But it is obvious that those who oppose intervention in general or fiscal policy in particular are supported neither by logic nor received economic theory. Even where they have a useful contribution to make, they ruin it by making assumptions which render the problem a trivial one. One final *curiosum* is that in the UK anti-interventionism did not last long, and there are few in practice who will admit that they ever had such views. The rhetoric has survived a little longer than the practice, but even that is now fast disappearing.

Notes

1. It is worth remarking that the concept of fiscal policy did change its meaning after the appearance of the *General Theory*. The earliest use of the term has a connotation of tax structure which would appeal to many present-day supply siders.
2. J. J. Keynes. *Collected Writings*, D. Moggridge (ed.), vols IX, XII. See also A. C. Pigou, *The Theory of Unemployment* (1933), p. 213. Reference may also be made to Keynes's 'Open Letter' to the *New York Times*, 1953.
3. The idea underlying this is that a condition for a desirable expansion of employment and output may be a fall in the money wage paid by the employer. If the money wage received by the employee cannot fall, a reduction in employment taxes or an increase in wage subsidies are called for. Of course, more sensible still would be a rise in the money supply. An important early

contribution was N. Kaldor, 'Wage Subsidies as a Remedy for Unemployment', *JPE*, December 1936.

4.   S. Slichter. 'The Economics of Public Works', *AER*, November 1934. J. M. Keynes, *How to Pay for the War*, Collected Writings, vol. IX. E. Cary Brown, 'Fiscal Policy in the Thirties: An Appraisal', *AER*, 1956. E. Lindahl, *Penningpolitikens Medel* (1930). What the *General Theory* did provide was the concept of aggregate demand without which none of the relevant interventions can be analysed sensibly.

5.   J. Gelting, 'Nogle Bemaerkinger om Finansimingen af offentlich Virksomhed', *Nationalokonomist Tiddskreft* (1941), no. 293–9. T. Haavelmo, 'Multiplier Effects of a Balanced Budget', *Econometrica* (1945), pp. 311–18.

6.   A. Hansen, *Fiscal Policy and Business Cycles* (1941). A. P. Lerner, 'Functional Finance and the Federal Debt', *Social Research* (1943). *The Economics of Control* (1946).

7.   D. Currie, 'Macroeconomic Policy and Government Financing', in M. Artis and A. Nobay, *Studies in Contemporary Economics* (1978) (London: Croome Helm).

8.   If investment is an increasing function of income, there is the theoretically possible, but typically unstable case, of *I–S* becoming positive to consider.

9.   This is all, of course, relevant to what may be called the middle phase of President Reagan's economic policy.

10. It should also be recalled that, if there is perfect capital mobility, monetary policy becomes impossible. An infinite quantity of reserves would flow out if an attempt were made to add to the money supply (or flow in if monetary policy were made more restrictive).

11. Another important topic which we ignore concerns the currencies in which international capital and interest flows are denominated. This is of considerable significance in determining the effects of a devaluation.

12. W. Phillips, 'Stabilisation Policy in a Closed Economy', *Economic Journal* (1954). M. Friedman, 'The Effects of a Full Employment Policy on Economic Stability', in *Essays in Positive Economics* (1953). Both of these papers emphasised how policy intervention (fiscal or monetary) could be destabilising if time lags or the magnitude of shocks were miscalculated. It is also recognised now that the source of the shocks is of great significance.

13. Both of these suggestions are to be found in the *General Theory*.

14. M. H. Peston, *Theory of Macroeconomic Policy*. 2nd edn (1982), ch. 8 (London: Philip Allan).

15. M. Friedman, *Unemployment Versus Inflation*, IEA Occasional Paper 44 (1975).

16. It is worth recalling that the policy approach underlying this goes back to the work of Theil, Holt and Phillips in the 1950s. Economists earlier than that may have had some intuitive notion of optimisation applied to macroeconomic problems and of a feedback rule; but they were unable to offer a rigorous formulation.

17. M. H. Peston, *Whatever Happened to Macroeconomics* (1980), ch. III (Manchester: University Press).

18. M. H. Peston, 'The Efficacy of Macroeconomic Policy', in *Public Choice, Public Finance, and Public Policy*, D. Greenaway and G. Shaw (eds) (1985) (Oxford: Blackwell).

APPENDIX I

From equations (6.1) and (6.2)

$$\begin{bmatrix} 1-F_y(1-t)-By-F_r \\ M_y & M_r \end{bmatrix} \begin{bmatrix} dY \\ dr \end{bmatrix} = \begin{bmatrix} dG \\ dM \end{bmatrix} \tag{6.8}$$

$$\begin{bmatrix} dY \\ dr \end{bmatrix} = 1/\Delta_f \begin{bmatrix} M_r & F_r \\ -M_y & 1-F_y(1-t)-B_y \end{bmatrix} \begin{bmatrix} dG \\ dM \end{bmatrix} \tag{6.9}$$

$$\Delta_f = M_r(1-F_y(1-t)-B_y)+F_rM_y > 0 \tag{6.10}$$

$$\therefore \ dY/dG > 0 \tag{6.11}$$

$$dY/dM > 0 \tag{6.12}$$

$$dr/dG > 0 \tag{6.13}$$

$$dr/dM < 0 \tag{6.14}$$

$$Y-F \equiv S-I \tag{6.15}$$

$$d(Y-F)/dY > 0 \tag{6.16}$$

$$\therefore \ d(G+B)/dY > 0 \tag{6.17}$$

Assume equation (6.4) holds

$$\begin{bmatrix} 1-F_y(1-t)-F_r \\ M_y & M_r \end{bmatrix} \begin{bmatrix} dY \\ dr \end{bmatrix} = \begin{bmatrix} dG \\ dM \end{bmatrix} \tag{6.18}$$

$$\begin{bmatrix} dY \end{bmatrix} = 1/\Delta_f \begin{bmatrix} M_r & F_r \\ -M_y & 1-F_y(1-t) \end{bmatrix} \begin{bmatrix} dG \\ dM \end{bmatrix} \tag{6.19}$$

$$\Delta_v = M_r(1-F_v)+F_rM_v < 0 \tag{6.20}$$

$$\Delta_f = \Delta_v - B_yM_r \tag{6.21}$$

$$|\Delta_f| > |\Delta_v| \tag{6.22}$$

$$\therefore \ dY/dG|_f < dY/dG|_v \tag{6.23}$$

$$dr/dG|_f < dr/dG|_v \tag{6.24}$$

$$dY/dM|_f < dY/dM|_v \tag{6.25}$$

$$dr/dM|_f = (1 - F_y(1 - t) - B_y)/\Delta_f \tag{6.26}$$

$$dr/dM|_v = (1 - F_y(1 - t)|\Delta_v \tag{6.27}$$

$$dr/dM|_f \gtrless dr/dM|_v \text{ iff } (1 - F_y(1 - t) - B_y)/(\Delta_v - B_y M_r) \gtrless (1 - F_y(1 - t))/\Delta_v \tag{6.28}$$

$$\text{i.e. } -\Delta_v By \gtrless -B_y M_r(1 - F_v) \tag{6.29}$$

$$\text{i.e. } \Delta_v \gtrless M_r(1 - F_v) \tag{6.30}$$

from equation (6.24) it is obvious that $<$ holds (6.31)

$$dr/dM|_f < dr/dM|_v \tag{6.32}$$

From equations (6.6) and (6.7).

$$\begin{bmatrix} 1 - F_y(1-t)K_r & -F_r \\ M_y & M_r \end{bmatrix} \begin{bmatrix} dY \\ dr \end{bmatrix} = \begin{bmatrix} dG \\ dM \end{bmatrix} \tag{6.33}$$

$$\begin{bmatrix} dY \\ dr \end{bmatrix} = 1/\Delta_{vk} \begin{bmatrix} M_r & F_r - K_r \\ -M_y & 1 - F_y(1-t) \end{bmatrix} \begin{bmatrix} dG \\ dM \end{bmatrix} \tag{6.34}$$

$$\Delta_{vk} = \Delta_v - M_y K_r \tag{6.35}$$

$$\Delta_{vk} < \Delta_v < 0. \tag{6.36}$$

It is clear that

$$dY/dG|_{vk} < dY/dG|_v \tag{6.37}$$

$$\text{and } dY/dG/_{vk} \to 0 \text{ as } K_r \to \infty \tag{6.38}$$

How do $dY/dG|_f$ and $dY/dG|_{vk}$ compare? From equations (6.19) and (6.25).

$$dY/dG|_f = M_r/(\Delta_v - B_y M_r) \tag{6.39}$$

and from equations (6.34) and (6.35)

$$dY/dG|_{vk} = M_r/(\Delta_v - K_r M_v) \tag{6.40}$$

If follows that

$$\mathrm{d}Y/\mathrm{d}G|_{\mathrm{f}} \gtrless \mathrm{d}Y/\mathrm{d}G|_{\mathrm{vk}} \text{ iff} \tag{6.41}$$

$$-B_y M_r \gtrless -K_r M_y \tag{6.42}$$

$$\text{i.e. } -M_y/M_r \gtrless -B_y/K_r \tag{6.43}$$

The first of these terms is the slope of the LM curve, the second the slope of the BK curve.

It is obvious that $>$ holds for K_r sufficiently large.

$$\mathrm{d}Y/\mathrm{d}H|_{\mathrm{vk}} = (F_r - K_r)(/\Delta_v - M_y K_r) \tag{6.44}$$

It is easy to see that this increase as K_r increases, and by a similar argument to that of equations (6.29) and (6.30)

$$\mathrm{d}Y/\mathrm{d}M|_{\mathrm{vk}} > \mathrm{d}Y/\mathrm{d}M_v \tag{6.45}$$

$$\mathrm{d}Y/\mathrm{d}M_{\mathrm{vk}} \to 1/My \text{ as } K_r \to \infty \tag{6.46}$$

$$\mathrm{d}r/\mathrm{d}G|_{\mathrm{vk}} = -M_y/\Delta_{\mathrm{vk}} > 0 \tag{6.47}$$

$$\mathrm{d}r/\mathrm{d}M|_{\mathrm{vk}} = (1 - F_y)\Delta_{\mathrm{vk}} < 0 \tag{6.48}$$

$$\mathrm{d}r/\mathrm{d}G|_{\mathrm{vk}} \to 0 \text{ as } K_r \to \infty \tag{6.49}$$

$$\mathrm{d}r/\mathrm{d}M|_{\mathrm{vk}} \to 0 \text{ as } K_r \to \infty \tag{6.50}$$

APPENDIX II

Fiscal stance and the PSBR

In order to simplify matters certain summary measures are sometimes used to ascertain the effects of fiscal policy in practice. In this appendix it is shown how such a measure may be misleading.

We consider a standard but more explicit version of the model in the main text.

$$Y = I + C + G + EX - IM \tag{6.51}$$

$$C = a(1 - t_i)(1 - t_d)Y \tag{6.52}$$

$$IM = m_I I + m_C C + m_G G \tag{6.53}$$

$$Y = [(1 - m_1)I + (1 - m_G)G + EX] \ [1 - a(1 - m_C)(1 - t_d)(1 - t_i)] \qquad (6.54)$$

where m_1 etc are the various marginal propensities to import, t_d is the direct tax rate, and t_i is the indirect tax rate. (The latter is set as a mark down from market prices, rather than a markup on factor cost.)

Total direct tax yield is given by

$$T_d = t_d Y \qquad (6.55)$$

Total indirect tax yield is given by

$$T_i = a t_i (1 - t_d) Y \qquad (6.56)$$

$$Y = [(1 - m_1)I + EX + (1 - m_G)G - aT_d - T_i] / [1 - a + am_c(1 - t_d)(1 - t_i)] \qquad (6.57)$$

We could define $(1 - m_G)G - aT_d - T_i$ as the weighted average fiscal deficit and a measure of fiscal stance.

It is also worth noting that the following balanced budget results hold:

$$dt_i/dt_d = -1/a(1 - t_d)^2 < 0 \qquad (6.58)$$

$$dY/dt_d = Y/(1 - t_d) > 0 \qquad (6.59)$$

What is more important to realise is that the formula in equation (6.57) is deceptive. The change in Y cannot be written simply as the change in fiscal stance as defined. This can be seem directly by noting that if, for example, t_d changes, that will affect not only the fiscal stance term in the numerator, but also the denominator. We have

$$d(aT_d + T_i) = a[Y(1 - t_i)dt_d + (t_d + (1 - t_d)t_i)dY] \qquad (6.60)$$

$$dY = -Ya(1 - m_c)(1 - t_i)dt_d / [1 - a(1 - m_c)(1 - t_d)(1 - t_i)] \qquad (6.61)$$

$$dY = [-d(aT_d + T_i) + am_c(1 - t_i)Ydt_d] / [1 - a + am_c(1 - t_d)(1 - t_i)] \qquad (6.62)$$

The point holds *a fortiori* if there is also a change in an exogenous variable such as I. Instead of the dY terms in the previous equations the following expression becomes relevant

$$dY - (1 - m_1)dI / [1 - a(1 - m_c)(1 - t_d)(1 - t_i)]$$

Part IV

The Inflationary Impact of Fiscal Policy

7 Inflation and Fiscal Expansion

Christopher Taylor

I

The various mechanisms by which it is nowadays thought that fiscal expansion may raise inflation are all ones that were familiar to Keynes. Basic among them was and still is the notion of rising supply price, i.e., that an economy at or near a full or high employment equilibrium typically has rising marginal costs in most of its markets for goods and services, so that in the general case output expansion implies higher prices.[1] The perception that labour itself has a rising supply price, reflecting various inelasticities with given working population, human capital, etc. is an element in this. Familiar too was and is the notion of 'mark-up' inflation: the view that sellers' margins or economic rents respond to the state of demand, not least the sellers of labour services.[2] We, like Keynes, would doubtless expect a degree of asymmetry in any such tendencies: margins, if flexible, are likely to be more flexible upwards than downwards. No less familiar were and are the financial routes to inflation particularly associated with fiscal expansion: the view that fiscal deficits may well in general be inflationary because they mean an accumulation of financial assets in private hands, not necessarily backed by physical assets. Keynes of course recognised this mechanism and, like us, saw methods of deficit-financing as having an important bearing on the result. Implicit in the *General Theory* is certainly that the mix of monetary and fiscal policy matters, although conceived there to operate in a more roundabout way – through interest rates and thence domestic expenditure – than we might think nowadays. At any rate Keynes would surely have agreed that in general money-financed deficits are more likely to be inflationary than bond-financed ones. His writings suggest that he held this view in relation to the financing of First World War deficits. And it was a view, perhaps inspired by Keynes, that influenced the financing policies of the UK authorities during the Second World War.

It is worth pausing to ask what is the special inflationary risk associated with fiscal deficits as distinct from deficits arising elsewhere in the economy. It is hard to accept that, pound for pound in similar circumstances, public sector deficits are necessarily more inflationary than private deficits. Their special inflationary feature presumably comes from the reasonable belief that on the whole governments are less constrained than firms or individuals from running deficits by immediate creditworthiness and prudential considerations; and that when governments monetise their deficits they generate high-powered money, whereas the money that banks create when they lend to the private sector is low-powered.

We put heavy emphasis on inflationary mechanisms that work via external linkages – more so at least than in the *General Theory*, which dealt mainly with closed economy problems. Nowadays it is the possible exchange rate consequences of fiscal action that seem at the forefront of most commentarors' minds, an emphasis that is echoed so far as I am aware in all the large econometric models of the UK economy. The view that persistent, unilateral, fiscal expansion sooner or later precipitates a balance of payments crisis (and abrupt policy reversal) became, not surprisingly in view of experience, an established part of thinking in the post-war era of fixed exchange rates. After the switch to floating by major currencies, the view shifted to one in which fiscal expansion sooner or later means exchange depreciation and thence higher inflation. This is perhaps still the major popular worry about fiscal expansion in the UK.

Several major developments have occurred in the past fifteen or so years which weaken the prospects for non-inflationary fiscal expansion. Principal among them is the process of international financial liberalisation and deregulation in which most of the major industrial countries have been involved to some extent or other. Despite its longer-term advantages, this process must have greatly increased the responsiveness of the major exchange rates, not least sterling, to domestic policy divergences. The abandonment of UK exchange control in 1979 was a major milestone in this as in other respects, together with the consequent internationalisation of the UK's main financial markets. Even with managed floating, sterling must now be a much more sensitive barometer of international differences in demand pressure than it was in the 1930s.

Secondly, the great proliferation of up-to-date (or relatively up-to-date) economic statistics and the more rapid dissemination of market information and opinion that occurs in today's world of electronic technology must have affected economic behaviour in important ways. One does not have to accept the more extreme implications of the Lucas Critique or the literal results of full-scale rational expectations models to see that policy-learning effects and systematic forward-looking expectations matter more than they used to. This development is likely to augment and accelerate the inflationary consequences of fiscal expansion, short-circuiting as it does the traditional mechanisms of private sector response, particularly among 'jump variables' like the exchange rate and other financial asset prices, which are potentially much more flexible than most real economy variables, and which have displayed in recent years a more pronounced tendency to overshoot than previously. The spread of rational-type expectations in this context has been accompanied by unfavourable generalised perceptions from experience in the past fifteen years, in which periods of high inflation in major countries have usually been associated with large (nominal) fiscal deficits. Rightly or wrongly the causality is generally perceived to flow mainly from the latter to the former, and faith in Keynesian-style economic management has diminished. The strongly-held conventional wisdom across most of the political spectrum nowadays is that high fiscal deficits are sooner or later inflationary.[3] Nor surprisingly the 'model' in market participants' minds has changed and this has conditioned financial market responses which have acquired increased influence in determining the consequences of fiscal and other policy actions.

The foregoing developments seem to me to point inexorably to greater pessimism about the consequences of fiscal expansion, especially if devised and carried out unilaterally, turning as they do on enhanced international linkages and feedbacks. Two other developments have also to be mentioned which matter as much, or particularly, in a multilateral context. One is the appearance on the scene of OPEC. Cartels are not of course new; they were an important part of the machinery of trade protection erected in the 1930s. But the impact that OPEC achieved on energy prices in the 1970s must surely be unprecedented. In the event OPEC has not been able to prevent real oil prices from falling a long way below their peak of the early 1980s – in part because of the inflation response and recession in the industrial world, and in part because alternative sources of supply have been developed. And admittedly prices in a cartelised market are unlikely to be more demand sensitive, *ceteris paribus*, than in a competitive one. Nevertheless where the cohesiveness of the cartel is itself as highly sensitive to the state of demand as OPEC's, energy and other commodity prices are likely to be more sensitive to concerted output expansion in the industrial countries than before. That must be bad news for fiscal optimists. For the time being, the UK is sheltered by its oil surplus from the adverse *income* effects of a hike in oil prices – but less so from the price effects.

A second development with gloomy implications for fiscal expansion in a multilateral as well as unilateral context is the apparent debilitation which has come upon labour markets in a number of major industrial countries in the past thirty or so years. I shall return to this theme after a short digression.

There is one rather limited consolation that friends of fiscal expansion might draw from the developments of the past few years. International financial liberalisation seems to have increased the leverage that monetary as well as fiscal policy can exert over exchange rates. The international financial markets are not perfect, but it seems that relatively moderate international interest rate differentials can establish and maintain large movements in exchange rates. In the context of fiscal policy this means that some (but perhaps not all) governments may be able to successfully counteract the inflationary effects of fiscal expansion through pursuing a non-accommodating monetary policy if they choose – at least for a period of years. This is one of the lessons of US experience between 1979 and 1985. Given the UK's history of inflation, there can be less confidence that the same policy mix would have similar results here. But assuming it would, such a policy combination would see fiscal expansion accompanied by high real interest rates and a high real exchange rate, which in most UK models would imply such substantial crowding-out of the output effects that the worthwhileness of the fiscal expansion might well be questioned anyway.

II

Nevertheless, the accepted view among many economists has been and probably still is that fiscal (or any other) expansion is unlikely to be inflationary when there are large amounts of unemployed resources. Keynes put it thus:

> It is probable that the general level of prices will not rise very much as output rises, so long as there are available efficient unemployed resources of every type. (*General Theory*, p. 300).

Although he immediately added:

> But as soon as output has increased sufficiently to begin to reach the 'bottlenecks', there is likely to be a sharp rise in the prices of certain commodities.

With the unemployment rate in the UK officially put still at some 10.5 per cent on the latest basis of measurement (some unofficial estimates put it higher), it might be thought that despite the underlying fall that has occurred since 1986 (the size of which is disputed) we are still well within the area where expansion could safely be undertaken. The rationale for such a view is clear, and need not be dwelt upon. It is basically that, with large unused plant and overhead capacity in industry, most industrial firms are producing at a point where their costs are falling rather than rising; and that most labour and commodities markets are operating at a point where supply is highly elastic, despite the cutbacks of the past few years.

And yet there are important doubts, in the UK and many similar countries. Here, although perhaps less so elsewhere, they stem largely from the persistence of relatively high domestic cost inflation in the face of what many take to be a still heavily underemployed economy. The question is thus largely seen as an empirical one; and economists have been hard at work trying to explain the new problem of stagflation. Understandably, much attention has been devoted to the labour market, widely seen as the root of the UK's economic problems. A good deal of this effort has been and is still going into estimating wage equations of some form or other, and particularly into the nature of the modern Phillips curve, if there is one, although the focus has shifted from the natural rate of unemployment associated with zero inflation in the long run to its latter-day counterpart, the NAIRU, associated with constant inflation.

What does this research tell us? What follows is a brief summary of some interesting recent findings.

The range of results is quite wide and in some respects there are conflicts; but there are at least some notable conclusions which seem quite widely supported. Pre-eminent among them to my mind is the conclusion that there has been a substantial rise in the NAIRU in the UK in the past thirty or so years. Estimates of its size differ somewhat, but not dramatically: for male unemployment (recently 12.25 per cent, equivalent to perhaps 14 per cent on the basis in use before the March/April 1986 changes) it is perhaps of the order of 8 or 9 percentage points, implying that whereas a sustainable rate of male unemployment might have been of the order of 2 per cent in the early 1960s, it rose to around 8 per cent in the late 1970s and is nowadays in the area of 9–11 per cent (on the old basis).[4] As Patrick Minford points out in Chapter 3, a similar phenomenon can be detected in a number of other European countries, but not in the USA or Japan. The reasons for the shift are not wholly clear or agreed, but they have been the subject of considerable debate in the profession, and I will therefore not go into them here.

I cannot, however, forbear from saying that it is a phenomenon about which sociologists may have as much to contribute as economists. I am mindful of a remark that John Goldthorpe made some years ago when he described the rise of wage inflation as a process in which workers have at last begun to 'punch their own weight'. It might be added that unemployed workers have not yet learned the trick of it; or perhaps it is that the unemployed simply do not have much weight, in pay bargaining at any rate.

A second fairly well established finding of recent labour market research is that variations of unemployment around the NAIRU do have a measurable impact on the rate of change of real and hence money wages: the Phillips curve survives. However, two other results seem fairly well supported: the relation appears to be non-linear, in that given absolute increases in unemployment lead to successively smaller increases in wages. That seems to be very much in the Phillips curve tradition; Phillips himself found that his curve was convex in U. Lipsey attributed this property of the curve to the aggregation effects of combining different wage-unemployment trade-offs in individual industries and markets. The other main result from recent work on the Phillips curve is less traditional, namely that the unemployment effect is relatively weak, especially at the levels seen recently. Estimates vary somewhat, but they seem to indicate an elasticity of between 0 and minus 0.15 at recent levels, with a central estimate of minus 0.1, meaning that a fall of half a percentage point in the unemployment rate (just under 150 000, or 5 per cent of the unemployed) is nowadays likely to increase real wages on its own by only 0.5 per cent in due course, implying a roughly corresponding rise in the nominal wage, the effects of which would tend to iterate through the wage and price system. The impact of a similar percentage change in unemployment ten years ago might have been twice as large. These two results, if right, are also important.

A further result, which has tended to gather support from recent work, is that changes in short-term unemployment (those out of work for up to 26 weeks) have more impact than those in medium or longer-term unemployment; some results suggest that *only* short-term unemployment matters. Such results are explained in terms of labour market hysteresis, operating partly through supply-side effects – individuals get discouraged and drift out of the labour force – and partly through demand-side ones – employers perceive that the human capital of the unemployed obsolesces, and decays from disuse.[5] Nickell takes the argument further by pointing out that the proportion of long term in total unemployment is positively related to the *level* of unemployment in the long run, but negatively related to the *change* in unemployment in the short run. In practical terms, this would imply that, although (male) unemployment is still well above the estimated NAIRU in the UK, even gradual reductions in the unemployment will raise wage inflation in the short run – because the relatively sharp upward pressure on wages coming from the reduction in short-term unemployment as 'employable' workers return to jobs more than offsets the modest downward pressure exerted by the excess of unemployment above the NAIRU (Nickell, 1987, pp. 124–6). If right, this is a gloomy result in the present context, although there may be a silver lining as we shall see later. Although the reasons given for rather pronounced hysteresis in the labour market seem fairly plausible, the issue is by no means settled. Minford puts some counter-arguments in Chapter 3; among them – why do not corresponding effects operate in the USA and Japan? (The answer may be that unemployment has not emerged there on a scale large enough to make such effects noticeable.) Moreover the econometric evidence, although suggestive, is not unanimous. Whereas several studies support the finding that the impact of short-term unemployment is better determined than that of total unemployment (Hall and Henry, 1987) others find that it is not (Carruth and Oswald, 1987). Recent work in the Bank comes down on the side of short-term unemployment as the significant unemployment variable (Mackie, 1987). This issue is obviously one that merits further investigation.

Other results from labour market research of particular relevance to the present theme are on the whole less conclusive but nevertheless interesting. There is support for the view that relevant tax rates have appreciable effects on wage bargaining. Hall and Henry (1987) for example find that both employers' and employees' labour taxes have significant positive effects on (pre-tax) real consumption earnings (earnings deflated by a consumer price index). The sign of the former effect is puzzling, since one would expect an increase in employers' labour taxes to reduce real wages, but the latter is consistent with the reasonable view that real wages are bargained in net of tax terms. Recent work in the Bank also suggests that existence of marked effects on nominal wages from both employers' and employees' taxes, both with expected signs, although the former effect only operates in the short run (Mackie, 1987). The effect from the employee's tax rate is quite strong, suggesting a coefficient from the retention ratio (of take-home to gross pay) of around minus 1. Phillips curve effects are also present in this new Bank work, although they are rather weak. As would be expected in nominal wage equations, the impact of inflation is strong, both via past inflation, where the pass-through from lagged nominal variables is strong although somewhat delayed (as each wage sector waits, in part, for other sectors to respond to price shocks), and via expectations of future inflation.

The combination of strong retention ratio effects and weak Phillips curve effects in these experimental new Bank equations produces some interesting results when they are incorporated into simulations using the Bank's large econometric model. The details can be found in David Mackie's 1987 paper. The essential picture is that income tax cuts create a sort of virtuous circle, reducing the rise in nominal earnings and prices, while small falls in the real (product) wage raise the demand for labour for given output, so that although GDP rises only marginally above base after ten years, total unemployment ends substantially below base.[6] These results contrast with those from a parallel simulation of a stimulus of the same *ex ante* size applied through increasing government current expenditure which, even with the exchange rate constrained to base levels, generates a (small) rise in inflation, and only a small fall in unemployment, partly because some of the modest increase in GDP above base is crowded-out by appreciation of the *real* exchange rate due to the rise in domestic costs (with the exchange rate constrained). These simulations, as all such exercises, need to be taken with a pinch of salt, but they are useful in illustrating that possible retention ratio effects are a factor to bear in mind in assessing the effects of fiscal expansion.

There is finally one aspect of recent research, particularly relevant to the present debate, where the results have proved surprisingly inconclusive, namely the role of profitability or employers' 'ability to pay'. On the whole, most research gives little support to any impact on wages from profitability, cash flow, or other measures of companies' financial position. This seems true of the work of Layard and Nickell, of the National Institute, and of Bank research. Such lack of success seems to fly in the face of much anecdotal evidence and casual empiricism, and of such survey evidence as there is; for example, a recent survey by Blanchflower and Oswald (1987), who in a nationally-representative questionnaire survey of nearly 1300 managers in UK private industry found that 'profitability and productivity' were the most commonly-cited influence on recent wage settlements. The econometric evidence is also at odds with the emphasis in the past few years on 'insider–outsider' theories of wage determination, which stress the internal situation and financial performance of individual firms, and downplay the role of the labour market in a broad sense, since those outside the bargaining relationship, especially the unemployed, cannot readily influence wage settlements. If the insider–outsider divergence is important it will lead to divergent patterns of behaviour across the economy, and may mean that research using aggregate data misses important effects, if, for example, there are asymmetrical effects divided between large numbers of moderately well-off firms and small numbers of firms in positions of extreme financial comfort or discomfort.

Investigation of individual wage settlements in the period when real wages fell in the UK between 1980 and 1982 shows that real wages actually fell sharply in the cases where firms or industries experienced serious financial pressure, whereas where there were smaller alterations in product demands or other individual circumstances, no squeeze on real wages was detectable (Carruth and Oswald, 1987). However, when the same researchers sought to find corroboration in econometric analysis of macro-data they were only partially successful, finding an effect from real profitability on real product earnings that few other researchers have found; but failing to find a similar influence on real consumption wages,[7] or any significant role in any of their equations for other 'internal pressure' variables like bankruptcies or inventory changes. Their overall conclusion is that real wages, while not entirely rigid, do not respond much to moderate variations in demand; but buoyant profits since 1984 may, perhaps, help to explain the persistence of rather high wage inflation in UK industry in the subsequent two years.

III

Where do these investigations leave us in the debate on fiscal expansion?

Labour market behaviour is not of course the only consideration; responses in product markets are important too. Indeed, industry's response to faster demand growth is both a crucial and an unpredictable factor, depending as it does on expectations and views about sustainability, which will depend somewhat in turn on the source of increased demand. In that respect, fiscally-induced expansion may meet with a smaller output response than demand emerging spontaneously, especially in export markets, even when there is perceived to be widespread excess capacity.

Keynes's relative optimism about non-inflationary expansion in an economy with excess capacity is strengthened if one believes that some firms would reduce or at least hold down prices through using the opportunity to spread fixed costs over larger outputs. Modern research has been less prolific on this question than on labour market issues, but the results seem to suggest that pressure of demand effects do not have strong effects on pricing behaviour – although they do have a very limited role, contrary to the wholly negative findings of some earlier studies [Godley's work with Nordhaus, (1972) and with Coutts, (1978)]. This at least is true of the price equations in the Bank model, and I think these are fairly typical of other large models of the UK economy. The manufacturing price equations there are consistent with pricing as a fairly constant mark-up on normal (or standard) historic costs, with only minor effects from pressure of demand variables. If this is still the prevalent pattern, the probable fact that many firms now face low or falling costs will have only a limited bearing on output price inflation. Recent pricing developments in UK manufacturing provide an unusually good demonstration of this point. In the year to the first quarter of 1987, manufacturing output rose strongly and with it output per head, enabling the rise in unit labour costs to be confined to just under 1 per cent despite average earnings growth of nearly 8 per cent; with a sharp fall in fuel prices and virtual stability in materials prices, there was little overall change in manufacturers' total unit costs. Yet, despite that, manufacturers' output prices continued to rise steadily at an annual rate of between 4 and 5 per cent as though nothing had happened, delivering a strong rise in current cost profits. Virtually the whole of the increase in manufacturing prices over this period was accounted for by the increase in unit gross trading profits. That is not in itself an undesirable development, since real manufacturing profitability needs to recover further. But it casts doubt on the view that falling mark-ups will compensate for any rising inflationary pressures (from bottlenecks etc.) when expansion occurs with large excess capacity.

The weight of evidence from product and labour markets therefore does not encourage optimism about the inflationary consequences of fiscal expansion, even starting from a low activity level. There is persuasive evidence that inflation in the UK has remained high despite high unemployment because powerful economic and social factors have reduced the level of activity at which the economy can operate without pushing up inflation; and the responsiveness of wages to unemployment is too weak to mean that high unemployment will, in itself, be much of a corrective force, except very gradually and over a long period of years. The tendency of the long-term unemployed to desert the active labour market, coupled with the fact that the long-term component of unemployment has risen in recent years, seems to have added to this problem. Unemployment is thus in present circumstances a weak medicine, although perhaps the only ultimately effective one known to economists. There is little indication here that the risks of fiscal or any other policy-applied stimulus would be small in present circumstances. The problems are evidently compounded by nominal inertia and 'smoothing' of input price changes in industrial pricing behaviour, and by the fact that the economy is experiencing a phase of rebuilding profitability and the financial position of companies which, however desirable for long-run reasons, is likely for the time being to encourage rather than contain upward wage pressure.

Fiscal optimists may possibly derive a glimmer of hope from two sources. There is some evidence that a fiscal expansion which concentrates on income tax cuts will have distinctly better consequences for wage inflation than policies that concentrate on increasing general expenditure, owing to retention ratio effects. And if variations in long-term unemployment have little or no effect on wages, as some recent work suggests, a fiscal expansion that is targeted closely on the long-term unemployed should have smaller inflationary consequences than one that impacts mainly on short-term unemployment. There are perhaps lessons here for the design and composition of fiscal measures, if not for the overall thrust of fiscal policy.

Even so, any sustained expansion of activity, from whatever source, is likely to be subject in present day circumstances to significant inflationary risks. As is well known, the UK economy has been expanding at a rate fast enough to produce rapid expansion in economic activity since mid 1986, for reasons that would make an interesting study in themselves. No one can be confident that the rate of expansion seen recently is sustainable without some re-emergence of inflationary pressure; the authorities signalled last month that they would prefer the pace to slow a little.

Some rise of activity is probably needed if unemployment is to fall. The evidence suggests that this can only happen without pushing up inflation if the NAIRU falls. We should not make the mistake of thinking that the UK is stuck with a high NAIRU for ever. The economist's instinct is to see remedies in terms of his own discipline: if markets do not work they should be made to, through appropriate institutional changes. That is no doubt part of the answer. Most of us would probably agree that reforms to make labour markets work better, ranging from the ending of restrictive practices to the beefing up of vocational and youth training schemes, are sensible and beneficial. (Other developments, less within our control, may help: for example, the fall in real energy prices in 1986–87 will have temporarily lowered the NAIRU – although the recent rise may be pushing it up again.) They are, however, probably not the whole of what needs to be done: attitudes and perceptions need to change too. Sociologists like Goldthorpe have in the past been impatient with economists for being too eager to see tackling inflation as purely an exercise in repairing a leak in the nation's economic plumbing. Keynes would have had sympathy with a multi-faceted approach to what is surely a very complex phenomenon.

Notes

1. 'Hence, in general, supply price will increase as output from a given equipment is increased. Thus increasing output will be associated with rising prices, apart from any change in wage unit.' (*General Theory*, p. 300).
2. The notion of cyclically-influenced mark-up inflation, or something close to it, was prominent in Keynes's writings, although variously expressed, even before the *General Theory*. See for example Book IV ('The Dynamics of the Price-Level') in the *Treatise on Money* (vol. I), where it is said that the expectation of higher business profits associated with a cyclical rise in money or credit induces entrepreneurs to bid more eagerly for the services of factors of production, hence causing prices to rise above costs of production. (In particular, pp. 264–9 and pp. 284–8.)
3. There is admittedly the seemingly perverse US case in the period 1979–85, when, with rational expectations and high international capital mobility, fiscal expansion was associated for several years with strong exchange rate *appreciation*. As will be argued below, this was a case in which US monetary policy was, initially at least, highly non-accommodating, and that may be part of the explanation. Since early 1985, the dollar's appreciation has been more than reversed.
4. Layard and Nickell (1985). These authors consider the male rate to be the most accurate available measure of the aggregate unemployment rate (including unregistered women).
5. The mechanics of changes in the maturity composition of unemployment and their implications for inflation are helpfully set out in LBS briefing papers by Budd, Levine and Smith (1986 and 1987).
6. These substantial effects come from the interaction of the wage equations (including a large retention ratio effect) with the manufacturing labour demand equation, which has a strong real wage effect.
7. Unlike Rowlatt (1986), whose identification of a profitability effect related to the real consumption wage.

References

BLANCHFLOWER, D. G. and A. J. OSWALD (1987) *Internal and External Influences upon Pay settlements: new Survey Evidence*, LSE Centre for Labour Economics, Discussion Paper 275 (March).

BUDD, A., P. LEVINE and P. SMITH (1986) 'The Problem of Long-term Unemployment', LBS *Economic Outlook* (February).

BUDD, A., P. LEVINE and P. SMITH (1987) 'Long-term Unemployment and the Labour Market: Some Further Results', LBS *Economic Outlook* (February).

CARRUTH, A. A. and A. J. OSWALD (1987) 'Wage Inflexibility in Britain', *Oxford Bulletin of Economics and Statistics*, vol. 49, p. 1.

COUTTS, K., W. A. H. GODLEY and W. D. NORDHAUS (1978) *Industrial Pricing in the United Kingdom*, University of Cambridge Department of Applied Economics Monograph 26 (Cambridge University Press).

GODLEY, W. A. H. and W. D. NORDHAUS (1972) 'Pricing in the Trade Cycle', *Economic Journal*, vol. 82 (September).

HALL, S. G. and S. G. B. HENRY (1987) 'Wage Models', *National Institute Economic Review* (February).

KEYNES, J. M. (1930) *A Treasure on Money* (London: Macmillan).

KEYNES, J. M. (1936) *The General Theory of Employment, Interest and Money* (London: Macmillan).

LAYARD, R. and S. NICKELL (1985) 'The Causes of British Unemployment', *National Institute Economic Review* (February).

MACKIE, D. J. (1987) *A Three Sector Model of Earnings Behaviour*, Bank of England Discussion Paper, Technical Series No. 16 (August).

NICKELL, S. (1987) 'Why is Wage Inflation in Britain So High?', *Oxford Bulletin of Economics and Statistics*, vol. 49, p. 1.

ROWLATT, P. A. (1986) *A Model of Wage Bargaining*, Government Economic Service Working Paper No. 91.

8 Is Fiscal Expansion Inflationary?

Peter Sinclair

8.1 INTRODUCTION

This chapter examines the effect of fiscal expansion on the price level. The short answer to the question 'Is fiscal expansion inflationary?' is this. There is a variety of reasons for thinking that it could be initially disinflationary. President Reagan's fiscal policies in the United States – the only large economy in the world to have reduced both inflation and unemployment since the early 1980s, and the only one to have witnessed major fiscal expansion – appear to furnish an important contemporary instance of this. But in the United Kingdom, at least, it seems that increased government expenditure exerts upward pressure on prices. This confirms what one would expect the longer run consequences of fiscal expansion to include.

Section 8.2 is devoted to definitional questions, and to analysing the views that Keynes himself had on how fiscal expansion might affect the price level. It is clear that Keynes thought that higher nominal demand would lead at once to a jump in prices. Five cases where fiscal expansion could be disinflationary are identified in Section 8.3, although such consequences, if they occur, may well be conditional and temporary, with a positive impetus to inflation often occurring later. Perhaps the most interesting of the cases involve the reactions of the exchange rate and the price of oil to fiscal news (Sections 8.3.4 and 8.3.5). Those two models provide some explanation for the apparent success the United States has enjoyed in the 1980s in reducing both inflation and unemployment under the impact of fiscal expansion with tight money (Section 8.4.1). Sections 8.4.2 and 8.4.3 turn to international and British evidence on the connection between inflation and fiscal variables. Recent international evidence suggests that they are completely uncorrelated (Section 8.4.2), but British time-series data point to some positive price level effect from fiscal expansion (Section 8.4.3). In particular, it appears that higher spending by the government leads to an increase in the relative cost of the goods and services it buys.

8.1.1 Some Preliminaries

'Fiscal expansion' may mean many things. The traditional Keynesian interpretation is a rise in spending or transfer payments by the government or a cut in tax rates: such measures are seen as ways of raising aggregate demand. The layman's definition is probably a rise in the budget deficit (which is incidentally what each of those changes would be likely to induce). Then there is the possibility of parallel increases in the government's disbursements and revenues, designed to leave the budgetary position unchanged: this is shown to raise aggregate demand on balance, given Keynesian assumptions, because higher taxes will be partly offset by lower savings.

One weakness of the 'rise in budget deficit' definition is that the budget deficit is not something that depends solely on the government's actions. Tax receipts are sensitive to the level and pattern of spending and incomes, for example. Partly for this reason, this chapter will concern itself largely with the inflation effects of the first and third definitions of fiscal expansion. But it is important to stress that any increase in the budget deficit, however caused, is likely to be inflationary if it is even partly monetised. In a simple case, where the income-velocity of circulation of money (v) increases linearly with the rate of inflation (π) – let $v = a_0 + a_1\pi$ – the link between inflation and the budget deficit as a proportion of national income (x) will be given by

$$\pi = (a_0\theta x - g)/(1 - a_1\theta x)$$

where g is the growth rate of real income, and θ the proportion of the budget deficit monetised. Clearly π rises with x if θ is positive.

If fiscal expansion, however defined, succeeds in lowering the rate of unemployment, pressure for higher money wage rises is obviously likely to result. That could be translated into increased price inflation, especially if monetary or exchange rate policy is accommodating. I am not seeking to deny that these consequences may ensue. The central argument of the chapter is that the two links between fiscal variables and the rate of inflation just considered (the deficit-monetisation effect and the Phillips curve effect) do not give an adequate account of the full story by themselves. Ultimately these two mechanisms reduce to only one. The nominal money supply and the money wage rate cannot both be exogenous. Sooner or later one of them must accommodate itself to the other. On the contrary, superimposed upon them lie a number of additional factors at work, some of which, at least, could exert *disinflationary* effects, particularly in the short run. From this it emerges that a policy of fiscal expansion, accompanied by tight money, could act to *postpone* inflation. Its initial effects may be disinflationary; in the longer run, the rate of inflation could increase. This feature of the policy may commend it to myopic governments anxious to achieve quick results for the

inflation-unemployment trade-off. Fiscal expansion is certainly not a permanent cure for inflation. But it might well be a tempting, temporary palliative.

8.2 KEYNES'S VIEWS

In the *General Theory*, Keynes did not specifically address the question of
how the price level was affected by fiscal reflation. But he did devote space to
examine the price level effects of increases in nominal demand. Much of
chapters 20 and 21 look at this issue. Indeed, we are fortunate that his
analysis at this point is both verbal and formal. This is really the only point in
the *General Theory* where a detailed mathematical presentation is offered. It
comes in two parts: pp. 280–6 in chapter 20, and pp. 304–6 in chapter 21.

In sharp contrast to the clarity of the verbal account given in these
chapters, the formal treatment is less than successful. Given Keynes's
hostility to 'pretentious and unhelpful symbols' (p. 298), it may be that it was
conducted with more speed than enthusiasm. There are a number of
infelicities. He looks at the employment, output and price level effects of
higher *nominal* demand (call this *pa*) rather than real demand conditional on
the price level. So the aggregate demand function $a(p)$ is treated as a
rectangular hyperbola, with unit elasticity imposed. In chapter 20, this
parameter, nominal demand, is defined 'in wage units' (i.e. deflated by the
money wage rate). In chapter 21, it is undeflated.

Keynes derives formulae for the elasticity of the price level to nominal
demand (e_p). In his notation,

$$e_p = 1 - e_o(1 - e_w)$$

on p. 285, while on p. 305 we find

$$e_p = 1 - e_e e_o(1 - e_w)$$

Here, e_o, e_e and e_w are the nominal demand elasticities of output, employment
and the money wage rate. These expressions are inconsistent unless e_e is
unitary.

Is e_e equal to unity? The discussion on pp. 306–7 shows that Keynes did
not think so. But, as a first-order approximation, unitary it must be, simply
because N (employment) will be given by

$$N = \frac{ap}{\alpha w}$$

where α is labour's share in the value of output. The elasticity of N to pa/w is necessarily unitary when α is a parameter in the limit. This reconciles the two seemingly discordant expressions for e_p quoted above.

Another difficulty is the definition of e_o. In chapter 20 this is given, quite properly, in terms of the properties of the production function for a particular industry, and hence, under appropriate aggregation conditions, for the macroeconomy. But in the next chapter, Keynes seems to be treating it as the elasticity of $\text{Min}(\psi(N^d), \psi(N^s))$. Even in its former guise, as a concept based on the demand for labour, it could usefully have been expressed in terms of the elasticity of substitution between labour and the fixed factor capital. Hicks had all but done this in his appendix to the *Theory of Wages* (1932), which Keynes himself had read in pre-publication draft. Hicks's formulae show that the real-wage elasticity of the demand for labour, when the price of the product is given and labour is the only variable factor of production, equals the ratio of the elasticity of substitution to the share of profits in output, given perfect competition. It is only a small step from that to derive the competitive price-elasticity of supply of output: this is the elasticity of substitution, multiplied by the wages:profits ratio, given that the money wage rate is given.[1]

Whatever the shortcomings of the technical discussion, Keynes's verbal account is lucid and unambiguous. Both treatments, mathematical and literary, point to the same result. Higher nominal demand will increase output *and* the price level, except in the 'classical' limiting case of full employment when only the price level responds. This is a recurrent theme in the *General Theory*:

> The increase in output will be accompanied by a rise in prices (in terms of the wage unit) owing to increasing cost in a short period. (p. 249)

> . . . in general, supply price will increase as output from a given equipment is increased. Thus increasing output will be associated with rising prices, apart from any change in the wage unit. (p. 300)

The increase in prices would be amplified, to some extent, by an induced jump in money wage rates:

> When there is a change in employment, money-wages tend to change in the same direction as, but not in great disproportion to, the change in employment; i.e. moderate changes in employment are not associated with very great changes in money-wages. (p. 251)

Keynes is quite clear that there is an upward-sloping supply curve of aggregate output, except under conditions of full employment when it becomes vertical. Keynes will have been familiar with the possibility of a downward-sloping relationship between output and the price level under imperfect competition: Harrod's (1930) paper stressing this was indeed edited by Keynes for the *Economic Journal*. But he chose to retain a Marshallian, short-period perfectly competitive framework, perhaps because this will have been better known to his readers, and perhaps also because the introduction of imperfect competition might have seemed to weaken his arguments about why unemployment occurs and limit the domain of their application. Peden (1980) shows that Keynes was very concerned that government rearmament expenditures in the later 1930s would exert an inflationary impact on the macroeconomy. This train of thinking is also dominant in his *How To Pay for the War* (1940).[2] Keynes saw that the massive rise in government spending that was required would necessarily entail inflation, unless elaborate steps were taken to squeeze private sector demand. Direct and indirect tax increases, rationing and controls to eliminate inessential private investment were advocated as methods of achieving this. It is a supreme irony that the first major application of Keynesian macroeconomics was in wartime Britain. The brilliant protagonist of fiscal reflation became the architect of sophisticated measures of fiscal restriction. It was largely due to such measures that Britain achieved rates of inflation and interest between 1941 and 1945 that were *lower* than in 1937–41, or any four-year period after 1945. This remarkable success is perhaps the greatest of Keynes's many monuments.

8.3 SOME CASES WHERE FISCAL REFLATION LOWERS THE PRICE LEVEL

8.3.1 An income tax cut in a simple Keynesian model

This part of the chapter investigates a number of odd cases where fiscal expansion can succeed in *reducing* the price level. I examine how this can happen in a partial equilibrium, oligopolistic setting; then in a Walrasian, two-sector model of a closed economy; then in a non-Walrasian, open economy; then back to a Walrasian economy in long-run growth with exhaustible resources and rational expectations. The section concludes with a brief survey of other cases where fiscal expansion can lower prices. But it begins by taking a very simple model close to the *General Theory* of Keynes.

The term 'fiscal expansion' can mean higher levels of government spending. But it also encompasses the case of tax cuts. Both types of measure affect aggregate demand. Let aggregate demand, A, depend on government spending, G; on the proportion of income that is disposable for spending, $1 - t$ (where t is an income tax rate); and on real balances of money (M/P). Write this in rate-of-change form, where lower case letters (except for t) represent logarithmic changes:

$$a = a_G g + a_t \frac{dt}{1-t} + a_M(m\text{-}p) \tag{8.1}$$

Here, a_G and a_M, the elasticities of aggregate demand to government spending and real balances, are both positive. That on the tax rate cannot be signed with perfect confidence, because a tax cut will not just stimulate private sector spending (displacing the IS curve to the right): it could lead to an increase in the demand for money[3] (pushing the LM curve to the left). On the supply side, there is an aggregate production function, just as in Keynes, where output (Q) is increasing and concave in labour (N):

$$q = zn \tag{8.2}$$

where z represents labour's competitive share in the value of output. Since the real wage rate equals the marginal product of labour, we have

$$w = p + (q-n)/\sigma = p - \frac{1-z}{\sigma}n = p - \frac{1-z}{\sigma z}q \tag{8.3}$$

where w and p are changes in the logs of the money wage rate and the price level, and σ is the elasticity of substitution between labour and the fixed factor of production (capital). Lastly, we depart from Keynes's views on money wage rates and allow them to vary in response to prices and the income tax rate:[4]

$$w = b_p p + b_t \frac{dt}{1-t} \tag{8.4}$$

The system can now be solved for the impact effects of changes in the three policy parameters (G, t and M) for the price level:

$$p(c(1-b_p) + a_M) = a_\sigma g + \frac{dt}{1-t}(cb_t - a_t) + a_M m \tag{8.5}$$

where c is the elasticity of aggregate supply ($= \sigma z/(1-z)$). Intuition suggests $> b_p \geqslant 0$, $b_t \geqslant 0$; if this is so, we can be sure that higher government spending or monetary expansion will lead to an increase in the price level, but it appears that reflation via income tax cuts could have the opposite effect. A reduction in the rate of income tax will tend to lower the pre-tax money wage rate for which labour stipulates, and provided that the aggregate demand effects are relatively weak (or, indeed, perverse), the reduction in labour costs facing firms will then be reflected in lower output prices. Although (8.4) provides the key to this possibility, in a somewhat unKeynesian fashion, it is worth stressing that this simple model of a (partly) sticky money wage rate and a flexible price of goods that adjusts to equate aggregate effective demand and supply in the goods market, corresponds closely to the *General Theory* model. Similar results would of course ensue from cuts in indirect tax rates, once the model was broadened to allow for them. The very crude, comparative static model sketched here can also be expanded to study the effects of fiscal policy on inflation trajectories. Buiter and Miller (1985) provide a detailed treatment along those lines, and emerge with the conclusion that indirect tax cuts – and possibly cuts in direct taxation, as well – are an indispensable ingredient in a policy of *optimal* disinflation.

So tax cuts lead, unsurprisingly, to price cuts. The same cannot be said for government spending rises, as (8.5) testifies. But as it stands, (8.5) gives us only the *impact* effects of changes in these fiscal parameters upon the price level. To explore the subsequent *dynamics* of prices, we must look elsewhere. An (increased) inflationary trend may emerge from two sources. A conventional Phillips curve would imply a faster rate of increase over time in money wages, as a result of any fall in unemployment; and any resulting increase in the budget deficit would generate additional inflation if it were monetised. Furthermore, under rational expectations, anticipations of faster inflation in the future could drive down the demand for real money in advance.

These results were obtained under Keynes's *General Theory* assumptions of perfect competition, and returns to labour that diminish in the short run because capital is fixed with the consequence that marginal costs slope up. Weitzman (1982) is one of many who argue that Keynesian conclusions emerge with greater coherence in an imperfectly competitive setting. What follows next is a brief demonstration of how higher government spending might lower prices in such a framework.

8.3.2 Government spending on the product of an oligopolistic industry

Consider an oligopoly of the simplest type. There are n firms, all with common costs. They sell an undifferentiated product at a common price in a market consisting of both private and public buyers. If each firm acts independently, setting output to maximise profit as in Cournot's theory and ignoring the repercussions that it will have on its rivals, the price will be given by

$$(p - c')/p = 1/\varepsilon n \tag{8.6}$$

where c' represents marginal cost, and ε (defined as a positive number) is the price-elasticity of total demand.

When the number of firms, n, is taken as given, the relationship between government demand and price depends on the slope of the marginal cost curves (c'') and on how ε is affected. The price could be independent of the level of government demand. This will be so if two conditions hold: if c'' vanishes (so that marginal cost is horizontal), and if public and private demand are equally price-elastic. If the state's demand has lower price-elasticity than private demand, or if marginal cost slopes up ($c'' > 0$), the price of the product will climb as government raises its demand.

A rather different result obtains if n, the number of firms, is endogenous. Suppose that entry into the industry occurs whenever each firm's profits, gross of any fixed cost, exceed a particular value. This allows for the possibility of free entry, when gross profit will tend to equality with fixed cost. It also covers the case of a less-than-perfectly contestable industry, where pure profits can survive at, but not above, some given positive value. Entry may be phased and slow. In that case the full impact of higher government demand on the price of the product is felt only in the long run when the process is complete.

This long-run effect of government demand on price will probably be negative. The essence of the story is that new firms come in when demand goes up, whatever the reason; and that in turn, under the Cournot–Nash assumptions about firm behaviour given above, means that the price comes closer to marginal cost.

These are the results obtained when one assumes Cournot–Nash behaviour among firms, and, in the long-run case, some entry mechanism that raises the number of firms as government demand increases. There are various reasons, however, for being sceptical about the practical likelihood of higher government demand leading to lower prices in the long run. Here are three.

One such reason stresses the fact that Cournot–Nash is not the only possible oligopolistic equilibrium. An obvious alternative is collusion. Stigler (1964) emphasised long ago that collusive equilibria are easier to sustain when the industry in question sells to a government monopsonist than to a purely private market. Secret bilateral deals with individual customers provide some incentive to cheat that the others will find hard to detect or prevent in the second case; but they become impossible in the first. A second reason for expecting government demand and price to be positively related turns on the well-known reluctance of government agencies to consider purchasing from foreign sources if domestic firms can produce the good in question. Import-penetration is much more pronounced, for example, in the British private car market than for military, police or public hospital vehicles. There can be few if any car-producing countries in which this is not true. A third factor militating against any negative association between s and p is the fact that government bureaucracies find it advantageous to build up long-term relationships with particular suppliers. This may be rationalised in agency-theoretic terms: multi-period contracts give less trouble when important informational asymmetries are present. Be this as it may, it is not going to be easy for a new firm – domestic or foreign – to break into an established public-sector market.[5]

Higher government spending *could* therefore lead to lower prices, at least in a partial equilibrium, imperfectly competitive framework. Could the same thing happen under competitive conditions, or in a more general model? The answer to this is affirmative. What follows will demonstrate the possibility that this could occur in a competitive, miniature general equilibrium model.

8.3.3 Fiscal activity and the price level in a simple general model

A change in the government's fiscal policy can alter the prices of factors of production, at least in a simple, competitive, closed economy. Suppose that it raises its spending on relatively labour-intensive goods, with a less-than-offsetting fall in private sector spending upon them. There will be upward pressure on real wage rates, and downward pressure on capital rentals, if factors are mobile between sectors. If there is just one wage rate and one real interest rate in the economy, the ratio of the former to the latter, w/r, will have to go up. The real interest rate (augmented by the rate of inflation) will capture the opportunity cost of holding money, while the wage rate will govern the value of the time savings that higher money balances can provide (money economises on the time that the household devotes to transactions). A rise in w/r should therefore raise real money demand. If the nominal money supply is given, an index of nominal goods prices will have to fall to re-equilibrate the money market. Fiscal expansion can therefore deliver a clear, once-only negative effect on the rate of inflation, by changing the composition of output, the structure of relative factor prices, and hence the demand for real money.

This section has concentrated on the possibility that higher government spending might lead to a *lower* rate of interest, in a closed economy where output is produced from labour and capital alone. The next two sections, by way of contrast, examine how higher government spending can again lead to downward pressure on the price level. But this time this arises because of positive, not negative pressure on interest rates; and the framework within which it does so is changed. In the next section, we investigate an open rather than a closed economy; in the section after that, a model where output depends on natural resources as well as the two familiar factors of capital and labour.

8.3.4 Fiscal reflation and the price level in a small open economy

It is now time to examine the significance of opening the economy to the issue of how fiscal activity affects the level of prices. If foreign exchange rates are fixed the question loses much of its interest, especially if nominal wage rates, and non-traded goods prices, are also frozen. What happens in a Walrasian set-up with fixed exchange rates can be sketched briefly. If the government increases its spending on non-traded goods, their nominal price, and that of labour, should increase, at least in the short run. This is what will occur, for example, in the Walrasian first part of Neary's powerful paper (Neary, 1980). But at the initial short-run equilibrium, the trade balance is very likely to have worsened. Higher product real wage rates, in terms of traded goods whose nominal price is given, will have risen, squeezing supply in that sector; and demand for traded goods should rise, assuming gross substitution, in the wake of the relative price change. So the next thing that happens is that the money supply is likely to fall, relative to trend, assuming that these balance-of-payments effects are not sterilised. This process will lead to continuing falls in the nominal wage rate to labour and price of non-traded goods, until full stock equilibrium is re-established. At this point, where monetary flows across the exchanges cease, it is likely that non-traded goods prices will be permanently higher than before. So the impact effect of higher state spending on non-traded goods is to raise their nominal price, while the transition to the new long-run equilibrium generates a less-than-offsetting and gradual decline. Had the state raised its expenditure on traded output, the only impact effect will be felt on the balance of payments, and hence on the money supply. The transition to the new long-run equilibrium will entail a gradual reduction in nominal non-traded goods prices, and probably also money wage rates.

So much for what is likely to happen to prices in a fixed exchange rate system. If we turn now to a floating regime, the analysis becomes more complex, since exchange rate changes have to be brought into the picture. To keep matters tractable, assume that the domestic country's output is now homogeneous – no division between traded and non-traded sectors – and that the feedback effects of trade and budget deficits on the supply of money or other variables can be safely ignored. It is a fairly straightforward matter to extend the sluggish prices-rational expectations-perfect international capital mobility model developed by Dornbusch (1976) and Buiter and Miller (1981) to the case of fiscal policy changes. Make aggregate demand, a, increase with international competitiveness (c) and liquidity (l), and also with government spending (g). Let it decrease in the income tax rate, t, and the real rate of interest (defined as the excess of the domestic nominal rate of interest, r, over the rate of 'core' inflation, $\dot{m}$). Hence, in linear form:

$$a = a_0 + a_1 c + a_2 g + a_3(1 - t) + a_4 l - a_5(r - \dot{m}) \qquad (8.7)$$

The variables a, c, g, l and also m, m_d, p, p^*, p', q and x are all defined in logs, while $\dot{m}$ is the proportionate growth of the level of the money supply. Competitiveness is defined as

$$c = p^* + x - p \qquad (8.8)$$

where p and p^* represent the domestic and foreign price levels, and x is the domestic price of foreign currency (a rise in x is a depreciation of home currency). Liquidity is the level of real balances, deflated by the domestic cost-of-living, p':

$$l = m - p' \tag{8.9}$$

$$p' = bp + (1 - b)(p^* + x) \tag{8.10}$$

The money supply, m, equals the demand for money, m_d, which increases in aggregate real demand, decreases in the home nominal rate of interest, and may also be affected by income tax:

$$m = m_d = p' + \gamma_0 + \gamma_1 a - \gamma_2 r + \gamma_3(1 - t) \tag{8.11}$$

The system is completed by a Phillips curve relating domestic output price increases to core inflation, and the deviation between aggregate demand and an assumedly given natural rate of output, q:

$$\dot{p} = \dot{m} + \delta(a - q) \tag{8.12}$$

Lastly, perfect international capital mobility ensures that the difference between the domestic and foreign rates of interest exactly matches the expected change in the exchange rate, which is itself correctly foreseen in the absence of future shocks

$$r - r^* = E(\dot{x}) \sim \dot{x} \tag{8.13}$$

All the elasticities and semi-elasticities in the system are non-negative, save γ_3 which may be positive or negative. It is assumed that real balance effects on aggregate demand are weak enough for $1 > \gamma_1 a_4$, unless specified to the contrary.

I follow Buiter and Miller (1981) in representing the behaviour of this system in competitiveness-liquidity space. Stationarity loci can be constructed for c and l. If the Phillips curve is steep enough for $\delta > \gamma_1/\gamma_2$, the $\dot{c} = 0$ locus slopes down. The reason for this is that maintaining constancy in competitiveness is now primarily a matter of keeping domestic output prices to trend. A rise in liquidity boosts aggregate demand and must be accompanied by a fall in competitiveness to keep aggregate demand balanced, and home output inflation steady. Reverse this inequality, so that the Phillips curve is now flat enough for $\delta < \gamma_1/\gamma_2$, and one finds that constancy in competitiveness has become chiefly a matter of constancy in the exchange rate relative to trend. Movements in the exchange rate over time are matched by the interest differential (from (8.13)). So domestic interest rates have to be kept steady. Now a rise in liquidity at home will push interest rates down: the

'LM curve' has moved to the right. Competitiveness must therefore increase to prevent the interest rate from falling, because this will amount to a rightward displacement in the 'IS curve' that neutralises the interest rate effect.

What of the stationarity locus for liquidity? This too can unfortunately slope either way. If the Phillips curve is sufficiently steep, so that δ exceeds φ ($\varphi \equiv ((\dot{1}-b)/b)(l-\gamma_1 a_4)/(a_4\gamma_2 + a_5)$), keeping liquidity steady really involves keeping aggregate demand close to natural output above all else. Equation (8.12) shows that when a and q are equal, liquidity will indeed be constant (defined in terms of *domestic* goods). If aggregate demand is boosted by higher liquidity, lower competitiveness is needed to offset it. So in this case, the $\dot{l}=0$ locus must slope down. But liquidity does not just depend on the movement of domestic prices. Especially if b is small, the exchange rate becomes very important. As we saw earlier, keeping the exchange rate steady means raising competitiveness at the same time as liquidity, so that there is no net pressure on the domestic rate of interest, and hence on the exchange rate path.

So there are four possible types of phase diagram.[6] All are illustrated in Figures 8.1–8.4. Fortunately, however, that is really where the differences cease. All four cases generate saddle paths approaching the unique long-run equilibrium from the southwest and the northeast. In every case, the effect of a once-and-for-all and unexpected jump in g is to push the long-run equilibrium southwards. There is no change in the long-run level of liquidity, and a guaranteed decline in long-run competitiveness. Imposing rational expectations means that the forward looking nominal exchange rate will jump at once, to push c and l onto the saddlepath that approaches the new long-run equilibrium. In each of the four cases, there is immediate appreciation in the nominal exchange rate, and immediate changes in liquidity and competitiveness. Competitiveness deteriorates – but not by as much as it will in the long run – and liquidity improves (but only temporarily). There is immediate downward pressure on the domestic nominal price index, then a

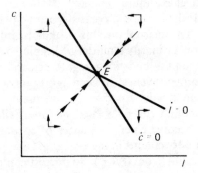

Figure 8.1   The dynamics of competitiveness and liquidity when $\delta > \mathrm{Max}[\varphi,(\gamma_1/\gamma_2)]$

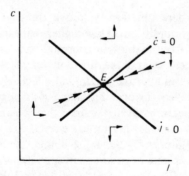

Figure 8.2   The dynamics of competitiveness and liquidity when $(\gamma_1/\gamma_2) > \delta > \varphi$

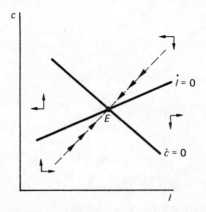

Figure 8.3   The dynamics of competitiveness and liquidity when $\varphi > \delta > (\gamma_1/\gamma_2)$

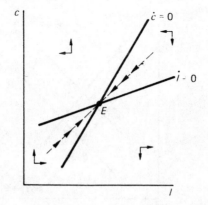

Figure 8.4   The dynamics of competitiveness and liquidity when $\delta < \text{Min}[\varphi, (\gamma_1/\gamma_2)]$

protracted phase where inflation is above trend. There is no enduring, permanent effect on liquidity, since the higher real exchange rate just cancels the increase in the cost of living that is brought about by the higher level of domestic output prices. A cut in the rate of income tax, again unexpected and permanent, will have qualitatively identical effects if γ_3 is zero. A negative value for this coefficient means that there will be a long-run decline in liquidity, as well as competitiveness, since the demand for money is cut; a positive value to γ_3 will mean that the new equilibrium lies to the right of, and not just below, the old one. Figures 8.5–8.8 illustrate the effects of once-and-for-all unexpected increases in government spending (or cuts in income tax, if γ_3 vanishes) in each of the four cases identified in Figures 8.1–8.4.

In each case, initial equilibrium is at E_0. An unexpected once-and-for-all increase in g establishes a new long-run equilibrium at E_1. The impact effect is

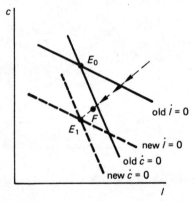

Figure 8.5   Permanently higher g when $\delta > \text{Max}[\varphi, \gamma_1/\gamma_2]$

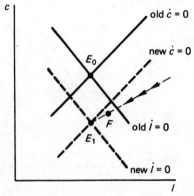

Figure 8.6   Permanently higher g when $\gamma_1/\gamma_2 > \delta > \varphi$

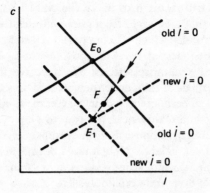

Figure 8.7 Permanently higher g when $\varphi > \delta > (\gamma_1/\gamma_2)$

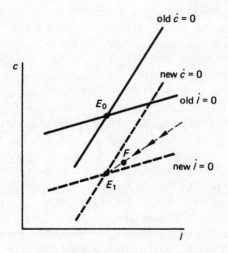

Figure 8.8 Permanently higher g when $\delta < $ Min $[\varphi, (\gamma_1/\gamma_2]$

from E_0 to F, from where the system gradually converges on E_1 along the saddle-path.

There are three remaining difficulties to be dealt with. One concerns the presence of *core* inflation, rather than *expected actual* inflation, in the aggregate demand equation (8.7). The problem here is one of potential global instability if it is actual expected inflation, rather than core inflation, that increases aggregate demand for a given nominal rate of interest. Suppose that aggregate demand increases. The Phillips curve equation (8.12) tells us that domestic inflation will increase, and rational expectations imply that agents' expectations of this will then serve to boost aggregate demand further. There is therefore a positive feedback effect at work. If the Phillips curve is steep (δ high), and aggregate demand is strongly sensitive to forecast inflation, the effect could be powerful enough to make the whole system unstable. This possibility arises in the Buiter and Miller (1981) model, too; it is absent from Dornbusch's (1976) model, which effectively stipulates that a_5 is zero as far as expected inflation is concerned.

The second difficulty is more serious. We have swept away issues concerned with the dynamics of the budget deficit, or balance of payments. The model predicts that a permanent rise in government spending leads to a permanent decline in competitiveness, in order to keep aggregate demand at the natural output level, q. Suppose that the current account of the balance of payments was initially in balance. Now it must be in deficit. That means that domestic residents are decumulating claims against the rest of the world. That cannot go on for ever; and even if it lasts for a while, net interest receipts from abroad will keep falling. This implies that sooner or later competitiveness will have to recover, to stem the haemorrhage of net overseas assets, to make good the loss of overseas interest income (or defray the costs of the new overseas debts), and to rebuild aggregate demand which will also be wilting for the same reason. As this happens, it will be upward, not downward, pressure on the domestic cost of living that is exerted. Furthermore, the government's intertemporal solvency constraints may imply that fiscal expansion today has to be paid for by additional fiscal squeezes at some date in the future. If and when that happens, all the effects examined so far swing into reverse, except for the fact that this time they may not occur as a surprise (several of these mechanisms are studied in detail in Buiter (1987b)).

The final issue concerns the type of wage sluggishness that has been assumed. We have taken *nominal* wage rates to evolve slowly, according to the Phillips curve (8.12). What happens if it is consumption real wage rates $(w - p')$ that are sluggish? As van der Ploeg (1987b) has shown, money now becomes neutral, and fiscal expansion has favourable supply-side effects on output and employment (if there is enough labour to meet increased demand). A rise in the real exchange rate narrows the gap between employers' and workers' perceptions of the real wage, permitting an increase in employment (this mechanism is also at work in Minford's contribution to this volume). But it remains true – and it is indeed central to this result – that fiscal expansion induces an exchange rate real appreciation (a competitiveness decline). This of course continues to imply negative direct impact on the cost of living, p'.

8.3.5 Fiscal expansion and the price level in the presence of exhaustible resources

Until the 1970s, the macroeconomic role of raw material prices was ignored. The conventional view had it that output depended on capital and labour alone. The price level was seen as governed exclusively by conditions in money and labour markets. The oil price shocks of recent years have taught us to reinsert primary commodities into the production function, and to add them to the list of factors that can help to explain inflation. Indeed, Beckerman and Jenkinson (1986) go so far as to claim that the course of inflation in the UK was dominated by changes in oil and other primary commodity prices, virtually to the exclusion of everything else.

An oil price jump squeezes aggregate supply. It raises the price level, and exerts downward pressure on output (at least in an oil-importing economy). So the oil price declines in the 1980s should have had pronounced disinflationary, and perhaps output-increasing, effects in the OECD economies. The 1970s were characterised by oil price jumps and negligible, even negative real rates of interest. The 1980s have witnessed weakening real oil prices and very high real interest rates. Many factors underlie the rise in real rates of interest. One of the culprits, surely, is the widespread fear that high levels of government spending in the United States are squeezing capital formation in that country and elsewhere. Rising real interest rates go hand in hand with falling ratios of capital to output.

Those lucky enough to own oil wells have to decide when to extract. Their portfolios can be in equilibrium only if marginal prospective yields on different assets are equal, after due allowance for risk and tax. As Hotelling (1931) first demonstrated, the higher the rate of interest, the faster oil prices must be expected to rise. Oil should give the same return above the ground as below it. Anything that causes interest rates to jump must lead one to expect oil prices to climb more quickly in the future.

If oil prices are suddenly expected to rise more quickly, because people expect future interest rates to be higher, and output to be more limited by greater scarcity of capital, oil prices must collapse now. Lower output in the future means a lower demand for oil in the future. So, in a forward-looking rational expectations model, where the current stock of known oil reserves is given, the price of oil must drop as soon as agents come to expect higher future interest rates. One possible trigger for such events is the sudden realisation that fiscal policy is cutting the long-run share of capital formation in national income.

There are numerous factors that underlie the fall in oil prices in the 1980s. In the wake of the 1970s oil price rises, production and transportation have gradually shifted to less oil-intensive techniques. Greater incentives to explore have led to new discoveries. OPEC's share of world production has fallen, reducing its influence on market prices. But it is not unthinkable that the changes in actual and expected real interest rates contributed as well, partly by the Hotelling effect noted above, and partly, also, by their tendency to dislodge a cartel from its cooperative equilibrium.[7] The elements in the story relevant to our purposes are:

(i)   The US government raises its perceived permanent level of government spending, in relation to national income;

(ii)   The evolution of future capital stocks is depressed by the interest rate effects of (i), and not only in the United States because of the international mobility of capital;

(iii) Higher prospective interest rates imply a steeper rate of ascent for oil prices in the future;

(iv)   Oil prices must fall now, in order to attain their saddle path to the new dynamic equilibrium.

The long-run effects of lower future capital stocks entail a permanent reduction in the growth rate and a permanent increase in the rate of oil extraction. Permanently slower growth in output implies faster long-run inflation, if the rate of monetary expansion can be taken as given. The new steady-state growth path, occasioned by the fall in the investment/income ratio, displays a higher real rate of interest, a faster rate of rise of oil prices, faster depletion of oil reserves, and a lower long-run growth rate.

The short-run effects are quite different. Cheaper oil raises oil consumption, and increases output for given stocks of capital. The lower oil price exerts negative pressure on indices of final output prices. If the money wage rate is given, the demand for labour will be unchanged if the adverse effect of a higher real wage rate cancels the favourable effect of higher output (this is exactly what happens if aggregate production is governed by a constant-returns, Cobb–Douglas production function depending on labour, capital and oil extraction; and if aggregate demand is inversely proportional to the price level). In this case, the impact effects of cheaper oil are independent of the slope of any Phillips curve that may be in operation. Put another way, higher real income and output raise the real demand for money, and money market equilibrium is preserved, for a given path for the nominal money supply, by a lower price level. This last effect may be qualified by the price-level-increasing effects of the higher rate of interest: an increased nominal interest rate should entail a lower demand for real money.

The appendix sketches out the formal analysis that underpins the argument of this section. The basis of this argument merits repetition here. The past fifteen years have witnessed a strong negative association between the level of real oil prices and real rates of interest. One way of accounting for this, given rational expectations, is the notion that increased real long-run interest rates imply a faster trend increase in expected oil prices, and require, all else equal, a fall in the price of oil as soon as the expectations of future interest rates are revised. Cheaper oil is temporarily disinflationary and output-increasing. In the longer run, oil prices have to go up more quickly; depletion rates are permanently increased; output grows permanently at a slower rate; and, for a given path of the nominal money supply, there will be a higher rate of inflation. One event that could set off all these effects would be a long-run change in fiscal policy that was expected to lower long-run levels of capital formation. A final point of note is the fact that the increase in the rate of interest, and fall in the rate of growth, both lower the chance that any given budget-deficit/national-income ratio is sustainable. So, even if the higher government spending is accompanied by matching rises in taxation, there may still be increased fears of future inflation.

We have investigated five sets of cases where some type of fiscal reflation may exert downward pressure on the price level in some sense. This does not exhaust the list of possibilities. Suppose that money demand is linked positively to current output, that the labour supply curve is backward bending and that the government simultaneously raises its spending and income tax rates so as to keep the budget in balance. With the nominal money supply given, and all prices flexible, the price level should decline. That is an example of an uninteresting, if clear-cut, static case. Now consider how a temporary income tax cut – again an instance of fiscal reflation – may affect the trajectories of output and employment in a simple New Classical set-up. Because the tax cut is temporary, there are no income effects to speak of. This leaves a set of pure substitution effects, out of current leisure and into current consumption and leisure in future periods (the relative opportunity cost of which has fallen). Employers and employees will rephase their production and employment plans. Current output increases, and all the more so in this case because the tax cut is perceived as temporary. Once again, if money demand increases in current output, there will be downward pressure on the current price level. Yet a further case where fiscal expansion or laxity may exert deflationary effects has been provided recently by Buiter (1987a). Buiter shows that fiscal indiscipline could generate hyperdeflation, rather than hyperinflation, in the Sargent–Wallace (1981) model – given that agents are allowed to form price expectations off the saddle path, on an ultimately unsustainable 'bubble' path.

Theory provides us, therefore, with numerous reasons for doubting the popular claim that government spending increases must be inflationary. The remainder of this chapter is concerned with what may be gleaned about the effect of fiscal expansion on inflation from empirical evidence. It begins by looking at the record of the United States in the 1980s, which suggests that a combination of fiscal expansion and tight money has delivered less inflation and less unemployment, at least for a while. But before turning to those issues, we may notice that the possibly disinflationary effects of fiscal expansion are apparent in the counterfactual demi-monde of simulation. A powerful recent paper by van der Ploeg (1987a) reveals that expansionary fiscal shocks can often exert disinflationary effects. Van der Ploeg's model is enriched by introducing political competition between parties, and uncertainty about the outcome of elections. His findings on the inflation effects of fiscal policy changes differ, however, from those of Sheen (1987), who identifies unambiguously positive inflation effects from fiscal expansion (although inflation will overshoot its long-run value with a conservative government, and undershoot it with a liberal one).

8.4   EVIDENCE ON FISCAL EXPANSION AND INFLATION

8.4.1   The Reagan experiment

No single event can have dominated economic discussion in the 1980s more than the growth of the federal budget deficit in the United States. Like F. D. Roosevelt nearly half a century before him, Ronald Reagan challenged an incumbent president, chastised him for fiscal irresponsibility, won, and then let the deficit climb still faster. As a share of national income, it has more than doubled; in nominal terms it may treble between 1980-1 and 1988-9. Income tax cuts and higher defence spending are the leading culprits.

Keen debate has centred on whether Reagan's Deficit has been good, bad or indifferent. It has been accompanied by a sharp jump in output. Some claim that this is supply-propelled, and evidence of tax-induced, New Classical intertemporal substitution. For others it is demand driven, a new classic case of a Keynesian boom. There may be those who maintain that output would have risen anyway. But what is remarkable about Reagan's Boom is that it has coincided with a sharp decline in inflation, from nearly 10 per cent in 1981 to about 4 per cent today. Put another way, the United States has succeeded – in marked contrast with most European economies – in lowering both inflation and unemployment.[8] Disinflation in Europe has gone hand in hand with rising or at best stagnating unemployment. In the United States, unemployment has fallen by more than two-fifths since its 1982 peak. For decades, macro policy-makers have seen their role as a precarious highwire act, teetering on a fragile tightrope between inflation and unemployment. Does the US experiment of fiscal expansion and tight money mean that all this is illusion? Or is the experiment itself just a conjuring trick?

The models presented in Sections 8.3.4 and 8.3.5 offer some interesting clues. Fiscal expansion in the US has indeed been accompanied by a sharp decline in the real price of oil, just as the model in Section 8.3.5 predicts. In accordance with the model of Section 8.3.4, it also coincided with a sharp appreciation of the dollar, which occurred between 1980 and 1985 (since wholly reversed). Cheaper oil and the dearer dollar combined to exert strong downward pressure on US price indices, in the latter case by perhaps 8 per cent.[9]

There are features unique to the US which make it hazardous to try to apply these lessons to fiscal expansion elsewhere. The US is still largely a closed economy. Real exchange rate appreciation will have damaged production, employment and profits in the traded goods industries, such as agriculture, cars and steel. But for industries that sell their wares within the national boundaries, and whose international contacts are chiefly limited to purchasing internationally traded inputs, exchange rate appreciation is favourable. There may be trouble in Detroit, Pittsburgh and the farm belt, but economic prospects in California and Massachusetts improve. The contrast with the smaller, open economies of Western Europe is stark. The real appreciation of sterling from 1979 to 1981 may have added five percentage points to UK unemployment. So much domestic output is sold abroad or impacted by imports that the adverse effects dominate in the aggregate. So if fiscal expansion causes the exchange rate to appreciate – which may itself be doubtful outside the US – its favourable effects on aggregate output and employment are much likelier to be blunted or neutralised in a more open economy.

Another difference between fiscal expansion in the United States and elsewhere is the effect on world interest rates. Simply by virtue of its great size, America can exert pressure on the international prices of primary commodities, and particularly natural resources such as oil, as a result of the impact of fiscal policy on world rates of interest. Higher government spending in a smaller country might cause domestic rates of interest to deviate further from world rates, but they will leave the latter unchanged. So the closed economy model of Section 8.3.5 may capture important features of the world economy when it is fiscal expansion in America that is considered. But budgetary reflation in a single West European country may be no more significant than higher public spending in a single US state.

A third difference centres on the relation between the fiscal and monetary variables. In the US, fiscal and monetary policies are set independently; at least this is the outward appearance. The financial markets have yet to perceive any serious threat that budget deficits could be monetised. The debt–income ratio is low enough, and the reputation of the monetary authorities high enough, for the Sargent–Wallace (1981) model of a government dancing on the edge of its credit line to seem wholly inapplicable. In Western Europe, it is different. News of growing budget deficits in the US raises the dollar; but news of a fiscal expansion programme in France, when the Socialists gained power in 1981, led to a giddy set of franc devaluations. Presumably the markets suspected that monetary growth would increase as a result. The notion that fiscal expansion causes exchange rate depreciation outside the US, but dollar appreciation when it is applied in America, has been christened 'Dr Gleske's Asymmetry' (Blanchard and Dornbusch, 1985). If true, it suggests that fiscal expansion in a small country can induce a powerful favourable reaction in output, but with highly adverse short-term effects on the rate of inflation.

So the United States seems uniquely placed to gain from both the disinflationary and output-enhancing effects of fiscal expansion. But how long lasting will these effects prove? The models of Sections 8.3.4 and 8.3.5 give plenty of cause for pessimism. In Section 8.3.4, the exchange rate jump that accompanies news of a fiscal expansion is typically followed by a backward slide. This second effect will eventually start to exert upward pressure on the price index. The decline in the dollar since 1985 has indeed already begun to raise the US rate of inflation. The oil price collapses in Section 8.3.5 because only this creates room for the steeper rate of climb in subsequent periods, by obedience to Hotelling's (1931) rule. Powerful negative pressure on inflation was imparted by the oil price falls of 1984–6 in the US and elsewhere, but this factor has now ceased to operate. Furthermore, the Keynesian camp in the US worry about the inhibiting demand effects of rising debt service costs, while New Classicals argue that if output and employment plans were boosted in the early and mid-1980s, this was chiefly because agents' activity plans have been rephased to allow for somewhat *lower* output and employment subsequently (especially if the rational political observer predicts that tax rates will have to rise). All in all, therefore, the United States may well come to experience rising inflation, rising unemployment and slower output growth, as the longer-term adverse effects of its fiscal expansion start to take effect. The sharp fall in the external value of the dollar which has already occurred since its peak in January 1985 may partly reflect the market's anticipation of such events. It may also make them likelier.

This section has discussed US evidence informally, and conjectured that the lessons might not generalise. It is appropriate to examine the links between fiscal variables and the price level in more detail. This is the purpose of the next sections, where some preliminary econometric results will be reported.

8.4.2   Some international cross-section evidence on the relation between fiscal policy and prices: correlations that aren't

What follows investigates the statistical association between inflation and fiscal policy in the twenty industrial countries for which comparable IFS data are available. Data are drawn from the 1987 International Financial Statistics Yearbook for the period 1972–85. The countries concerned are the US, Australia, Canada and New Zealand; and, in Europe, the EEC-10, plus Austria, Finland, Iceland, Norway, Spain, Sweden and Switzerland. In Canada, and all the European countries except France, the Netherlands and Sweden, the sample period is cut by a year or two, either because 1972 or 1973 data are not reported, or because the 1985 figures have yet to be released.

Inflation is measured by the percentage annual average rise in the GDP deflators for the twenty countries concerned. Inflation is labelled i. I present simple bivariate OLS regressions of this definition of inflation on two fiscal variables: central government expenditure plus lending net of repayments

(g_1) and the central government overall deficit (g_2). Both g_1 and g_2 are expressed as ratios to GDP, averaged over the sample period. Each regression enjoys a comfortable 18 degrees of freedom. Yet, despite this, it is noteworthy that the degree of fit is so poor that the $\bar{R}^2$ statistic is actually *negative* in both cases! The data presented in Table 8.1 give the following results:

$$i = 11.55 + 0.001 \ g_1 \qquad \bar{R}^2 = -0.055, \text{ s.e.} = 11.5$$
$$(1.1)$$
$$i = \ \ 9.97 + 0.408 \ g_2 \qquad \bar{R}^2 = -0.029, \text{ s.e.} = 11.3$$
$$(0.8)$$

The two coefficients on fiscal policy variables are both positive, but devoid

Table 8.1   Inflation, government spending and budget deficits in twenty industrial countries, 1972–85

Country	Average annual rise in GDP deflator	Central Government expenditure and lending minus repayments: average ratio to GDP	Central Government deficit: annual average in ratio to GDP
US	6.83	23.10	3.17
Australia	10.48	27.88	2.46
Canada*	8.55	22.50	3.98
New Zealand	12.72	39.47	6.38
Austria†	6.02	36.74	2.93
Belgium†	6.92	48.15	7.24
Denmark†	9.42	37.01	1.94
Finland†	11.19	29.24	0.94
France	9.74	40.13	1.56
Germany (West)†	4.52	29.37	1.61
Iceland†	43.94	31.46	2.92
Ireland†	13.96	47.08	11.17
Italy‡	17.12	47.80	12.60
Luxembourg¶	8.41	39.80	0.90
Netherlands	6.13	49.37	3.96
Norway¶	13.88	42.26	2.62
Spain¶	15.27	25.76	2.93
Sweden	9.43	43.36	5.40
Switzerland†	4.88	19.54	0.08
UK†	12.31	39.77	5.40

*1974–84; †1972–84; ‡1973–85; ¶1972–83

Source: Adapted from *International Financial Statistics Yearbook 1987*, International Monetary Fund.

of any significance. The bracketed numbers are standard errors. There are many reasons for interpreting these results with caution. The period could be atypical. Bivariate regressions may conceal a significant relationship because other variables, such as monetary growth, have been omitted. The short-term and long-term inflation effects of fiscal policy changes may work in opposite directions as at least two of the models explored in Section 8.3 have suggested; tests that smudge the dynamic pattern of possible effects may be highly unreliable. Then there is the fact that g_1 and g_2 omit the lower tiers of government. Above all, Iceland provides a dramatic outlier for inflation, and its exclusion leads to a considerable improvement in fit. The $\bar{R}^2$ statistics change sign once Iceland is excluded; but the fiscal variables still remain insignificant. Lastly, forward looking models, such as those in 8.3.4 and 8.3.5 above, cause exchange rate and oil price reactions at the date that the fiscal news becomes known, rather than the date at which the fiscal variables actually change. But these results should serve to throw doubt on the idea that there is a robust and simple link between fiscal variables and the rate of inflation.

8.4.3 Government spending and the relative price of public goods: the British case

International cross-section data cannot be said to furnish evidence that fiscal expansion raises or reduces the rate of inflation. But what does time-series evidence tell us? Could it be that government spending affects relative prices, rather than, or in addition to, any impact on the aggregate price level? This section is devoted to a brief empirical scrutiny designed to throw light on these questions.

The time-series evidence lends some support to the hypothesis that government spending is inflationary, at least in the British case. Consider, first, the relation between the GDP deflator and the ratio of general government final consumption to GDP (call this g_3). Between 1970 and 1980 there is quite a good fit between these variables in difference form. The later 1960s and early 1980s weaken the association. Sample regressions are:

$$1970\text{-}80 \quad \Delta i = -0.76 + 0.98\Delta g_3 \qquad \bar{R}^2 = 0.53, \text{ s.e.} = 4.4$$
$$\qquad\qquad\qquad (0.28)$$
$$1965\text{-}85 \quad \Delta i = -0.76 + 0.71\Delta g_3 \qquad \bar{R}^2 = 0.26, \text{ s.e.} = 4.5$$
$$\qquad\qquad\qquad (0.25)$$

The coefficients on g_3 are significantly positive. But the reasonably close fit, particularly in the shorter period, owes much to the coincidence that inflation peaked in years when GDP fell (1974–75 and 1980), so that the rising share of general government final consumption in GDP that occurred at these times may tell us little. Data employed in these tests were drawn from *National Income and Expenditure* (the Blue Books).

Perhaps the more interesting issue is the effect of government spending on the relative price of the goods the government buys. General government final consumption is devoted largely to wages. Some form of incomes policy was in force for much of the 1960s and 1970s. When applied rigorously, incomes policy will have frozen relative rates of pay in the public and private sectors. If this coincided with a period where government spending was rising, one would surmise that pressure for increases in the relative price of government goods would be stored up and released later when the policy was relaxed. The picture is further complicated by the fact that incomes policy varied in its nature and in the intensity with which it was applied.

Accordingly I constructed a set of weights to capture the ferocity of any incomes policy in force. When given its maximum weight of one, incomes policy was assumed to permit declines in the ratio of the GGFC deflator to the GDP deflator in responses to any fall in general government final consumption; but rises would be blocked. Such increase as would have occurred in the absence of policy is assumed to be deferred. Release of cumulated pressure for the relative GGFC deflator to increase depends on the incomes policy weight for the data in question.

The ratio of the general government final consumption deflator to the GDP deflator (y) was then regressed on the level of real general government final consumption (G), in first-difference form. To reflect the fact that incomes policy was anticipated, but barely in force, in 1974, I added a dummy variable to take the value of $+1$ in 1974, -1 in 1975 and zero in all other years. The G variable was adjusted to allow for the effects of incomes policy in the way outlined above. The resulting regression for the years 1965–85 was:

$$\Delta y/y = 0.09 + 0.87 \Delta G/G + 4.1D \qquad \bar{R}^2 = 0.55, \text{ s.e.} = 2.7$$
$$\quad\quad\quad (0.17) \qquad (1.1)$$

The coefficient on G is positive and highly significant. What it suggests is that approximately 45 per cent of any increase in government final consumption is 'wasted' in bidding up the relative price of the goods the government buys. If the government wishes to increase its volume of purchases in real terms by 1 per cent, it should budget for a real increase in outlay of approximately 1.8 per cent. The British government seems to face an upward sloping supply curve of the goods and services (chiefly labour) that it buys. This curve appears to have an elasticity of about unity or perhaps a little more. Strict incomes policy will enable the government to escape briefly from this uncomfortable fact, but if it has attempted to increase its real spending when such a policy is in force, the relative deflator for government spending will jump to compensate once the policy is relaxed.

This last finding is subject to qualification, however. I have yet to disaggregate general government final consumption into its separate parts (defence, health, education for example) and study the connexion between spending volume and relative prices in finer detail. There have been quite large swings between education and defence spending under Labour and Conservative governments. The incomes policy ferocity index is rather arbitrary, and my assumptions about how it operated may not have been valid. Public sector pay aggregates cloak changes in relative pay for different groups (such as men and women, and skilled and unskilled employees) which recent work by Elliott and Murphy (1987), for example, reveals to have been substantial, as well as changes in the composition of employment between such groups. Furthermore, the test is acutely sensitive to the way the *volume* of public spending is quantified. Independent measures of output or productivity are generally wanting. The statisticians have to resort to measuring output by input in many cases, which imparts an upward time-trend in the measured relative cost of government goods in a world where marketed sector labour productivity is advancing and pay differentials mark time. Lastly, US evidence appears to be very different. There is little association between y and G there. This is especially true for defence spending. Official US national income statistics imply that the relative cost of defence purchases fell between 1982 and 1985, a period of sharply increased military spending. This surprising, and frankly rather unbelievable,[10] development spoils what would otherwise be a weak positive association between changes in y and G, on the margin of significance.

8.5 CONCLUSION

The links between fiscal policy variables and the rate of inflation are complex. Fiscal expansion does not lead inevitably to faster inflation. This is especially so if the rate of monetary expansion remains unaffected. It is quite possible that there will be *initial*, temporary, disinflationary effects. There are a number of ways these might be brought about. Fiscal expansion may induce an appreciation of the real exchange rate; the cost of living will register a drop as the local currency price of foreign goods comes down. Current and expected future interest rates might go up, inducing a fall in primary product prices (particularly oil). Fiscal expansion could help to lower inflation and unemployment if it took the form of cuts in the tax wedge splitting employers' and employees' perceptions of the real wage. However, in each of these cases, there are grounds for thinking that *subsequent* inflation may rise. The exchange rate may have to depreciate later to compensate for the reduction in net interest income from overseas (the higher real exchange rate will have had adverse effects on the trade balance). In the oil case, output may grow more slowly in future, as a combined result of the squeeze on capital formation and the increasing scarcity of the exhaustible natural resource. In each of the cases, rates of monetary expansion may rise under the impact of higher budget deficits. Added to this is the possibility that prices may jump to reflect expectations of these future developments, and, of course, the likely impetus to higher pay settlements as and when unemployment falls.

The evidence on the issue is mixed. Cross section data fail to establish any association between budget deficits and government spending on the one side, and inflation on the other, for a group of twenty industrial countries in the period 1972–85. British time series evidence points to a positive association between inflation and the share of government spending in national income, which was quite marked at the time of the two oil shocks of the 1970s, but weaker before then and since. It also appears that the government faces an upward sloping supply curve for the goods it buys: in the UK at least, nearly half of any rise in government spending is apparently dissipated in bidding up their relative price, once the effects of incomes policy are allowed for.

In the past six years or so, the United States has reduced its rates of inflation and unemployment together. In many European countries, where fiscal policy has been less expansionary, disinflation has accompanied stagnating or even rising unemployment. The two sides of the Atlantic economy have displayed a marked difference in their relative economic performance. If fiscal expansion is really a method of postponing inflation, or unemployment, will the next six years see a reversal?

APPENDIX

Consider a closed economy where output, $Q(t)$, varies with capital, $K(t)$, labour, $N(t)$ and resource extraction, $R(t)$, in a constant returns, Cobb–Douglas fashion:

$$Q(t) = T(t)K(t)^{a_1}N(t)^{a_2}R(t)^{1-a_1-a_2} \tag{8.14}$$

In (8.16), $T(t)$ denotes a technology index for date t, and the elasticities of output to capital and labour, a_1 and a_2, are both positive and sum to less than one. Technology advances at a constant proportionate rate $\hat{T}$, and labour at n. There is perfect competition in its fullest sense, including perfect foresight. The absence of extraction costs, uncertainty and market imperfections allows us to impose Hotelling's rule, and equate the rate of interest, $r(t)$, with the proportionate rate of increase in the price of the natural resource. Writing $c(t)$ for the average product of capital, differentiation of (8.16) gives $r = a_1 c$, and linking this to the change over time in the marginal productivity of $R(t)$ yields

$$r(t) = a_1 c(t) = \hat{Q}(t) - \hat{R}(t) \tag{8.15}$$

Suppose that the government spends the fraction g of Q, and pays for it by lump sum taxes. Government spending is devoted solely to public consumption, let us say.

Households save a fixed fraction s of their after-tax income, $(1-g)Q$. The growth rate of the capital stock will therefore be

$$\frac{\dot{K}}{K}=sc(1-g) \qquad (8.16)$$

Now time-differentiate (8.14) and use (8.15) and (8.16) to eliminate terms in the growth of K and R. What results can be expressed as a law of motion for the average product of capital:

$$\dot{c}/c=(a_1+a_2)^{-1}(\hat{T}+a_2n-a_1c(t)(1-a_1-a_2\theta)) \qquad (8.17)$$

where $\theta=1-s(1-g)/a_1$. It is clear from (8.17) that c is self-stabilising.

The next thing to do is to find out how $R(t)$ behaves over time. This natural resource is fixed in total supply; extraction now must diminish the stock, $S(t)$, so that

$$R=-\dot{S} \qquad (8.18)$$

Define R/S as δ, so that

$$\dot{R}/R=\dot{\delta}/\delta-\delta \qquad (8.19)$$

(8.19) may now be combined with (8.14)–(8.16) to yield a law-of-motion for the natural resource depletion rate:

$$\dot{\delta}/\delta=\delta+(a_1+a_2)^{-1}(\hat{T}+a_2n-a_1c(1-s(1-g))) \qquad (8.20)$$

The dynamic behaviour of the depletion rate and the average product of capital is illustrated phase-diagramatically in Figure 8.9. There is a unique equilibrium at A, and a unique saddle path, shown by the dashed line, that approaches it from the southwest and the northeast. The long-run equilibrium values of δ and c at A are, respectively, $\theta(\hat{T}+a_2n)(1-a_1-a_2\theta)^{-1}$ and $(\hat{T}+a_2n)a_1(1-a_1-a_2\theta)^{-1}$.

We have now made it a simple matter to examine the effects of a once-and-for-all and unexpected rise in the ratio of government spending to national income, g. Equation (8.17) tells us that the stationarity locus for the average product of capital is displaced rightwards. This must happen, because savings will be squeezed and the capital stock will grow more slowly. We can also see from (8.20) that the stationarity locus for the depletion rate will be pushed upwards, and to the left. The reason here is that the greater scarcity of the capital stock will force up the rate of interest, and that in turn, by Hotelling's rule, means that the natural resource will have to be expected to appreciate faster. With a given stock, this implies an increased rate of depletion. So the new equilibrium, shown at point C in Figure 8.10, must lie somewhere to the northeast of A.

So much for the long-run equilibrium, at which a permanently higher share of public consumption in national income must mean increased long-run values of the depletion rate and the average product of capital. What happens in the short run? This is where the saddle path comes in. The depletion rate is the 'jump' variable; there will have to be an immediate increase in the depletion rate. What sets this going is a collapse in the spot price of the natural resource. By contrast, the capital stock is sluggish. Its average product can change in the short run, however, by virtue of changes in the rate of extraction of the natural resource. This means that the impact effect of the higher government spending is to push the economy at once from point A to somewhere such as B.

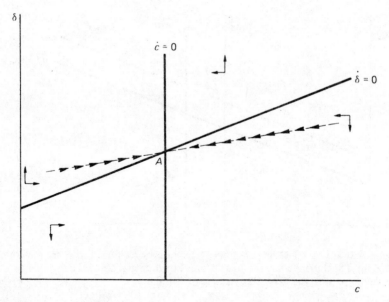

Figure 8.9   The dynamic adjustment of the depletion rate and the average product of capital: long-run equilibrium at *A*.

This model has so far been couched purely in real terms. But we may conjecture what will happen to the price of final output. Suppose that the nominal money supply is exogenous. Suppose that money demand at each date is simply a function of real output at that date. In that event, we would witness a spot *decline* in the price level at the same time as the sudden jump from *A* to *B* in Figure 8.10. The price level would have to fall, because nothing else would re-equilibrate the money market. There will be other effects on the price level, however, if the money demand function is enriched. Suppose that real money demand decreases in the rate of inflation, as well as increasing in output. If expectations of inflation are formed rationally, agents will observe that the long-run growth rate of output *decreases* in *g*: in balanced growth, where δ and *c* are stationary,

$$\dot{Q}/Q = (1 - \theta)(\hat{T} + a_2 n)/(1 - a_1 - a_2 \theta) \tag{8.21}$$

If the path of the nominal money supply is given, therefore, faster inflation will be expected in the steady state because output will be forecast to grow more slowly. Any increase in inflation expectations will serve to reduce the demand for money. It will oppose the price-reducing effect of higher output. A second factor may serve to weaken the price fall brought about by (initially) higher output. This is the fact that there will be upward pressure on the real rate of interest: and if money demand decreases in the nominal rate of interest, this will be important. The long-run rate of interest increases in line with *a*, because their ratio, the capital share in output, is constant in the Cobb–Douglas case. But there will also be some immediate increase in the rate of interest, if only because higher resource depletion will serve to raise the marginal product of capital the moment the economy is shocked from *A* to *B* in Figure 8.10.

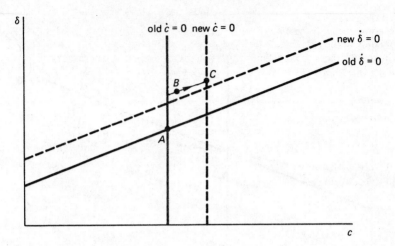

Figure 8.10 The effect of an unexpected, once-and-for-all rise in government spending. The impact effect is a jump from *A* to *B*, then a gradual convergence along the saddle path to the new steady state equilibrium at *C*.

In the longer run, higher government spending will be inflationary. This is because of the negative association, shown in (8.21), between g and the steady state growth rate. It is worth stressing how important natural resources are to deriving this result. If output had depended on output and capital alone, the long-run growth rate of output would be driven to equality with that of labour, scaled up for Harrod-neutral technical progress. Changes in government spending or savings would alter the long-run level of output per head, but leave no permanent effect on the growth rate. In this model with natural resources, on the other hand, alterations in s or g leave an indelible mark on the growth rate of the system. The fall in the long-run growth rate may have another, more subtle effect. It is a well-known result that a steady deficit is unsustainable if the rate of interest exceeds the growth rate. Note here that an increase in government spending raises the rate of interest and lowers the rate of growth, and that both effects are permanent. This suggests that higher government spending, even if accompanied by higher tax receipts, may increase the likelihood that any given deficit is unsustainable. In a context such as that proposed by Sargent and Wallace (1981), therefore, where it is fiscal variables that ultimately determine the rates of monetary expansion and inflation, even a tax-financed increase in government spending could be enough to provoke expectations of increased monetisation of any given deficit.

The model studied here has the feature that the demand and supply of labour are kept in continuous balance, by virtue of complete price flexibility. This is a highly restrictive assumption, at least for the short run. What difference would it make if one assumed instead that the money wage rate was temporarily frozen, and that employment was demand-determined? If real money demand is taken to be proportional to the level of current output, the answer is none whatever. The reason for this somewhat surprising finding is that a sudden drop in the price of oil (occasioned, in our case, by a permanent rise in government spending, and an increase in the expected real rate of interest that ensues from this) will have no effect on the equilibrium money wage rate at a given level of labour supply. The positive effect on labour demand from a higher level of output just cancels the fall that follows a rise in the real wage rate, given the parameter values assumed. So it would be quite wrong to think of the price level consequences of fiscal expansion in a world with oil that have been traced above, apply only to the case where the Phillips curve is vertical. Given the other restrictions of the model, they would extend equally to the case of a downward sloping short-run Phillips curve with any gradient!

Acknowledgements

I should like to thank Walter Eltis, other conference participants, Willem Buiter, Rudiger Dornbusch, Rick van der Ploeg and Mark Williams for valuable comments or discussions, and particularly Mark Griffiths for his detailed scrutiny of a previous draft.

Notes

1. One would therefore be tempted to modify Keynes's expression for e_p to:

$$\frac{d \log q}{d \log p} = \sigma \frac{\alpha}{1-\alpha} \left(\frac{\partial \log w}{\partial \log p} \right)$$

    given excess supply of labour, where α represents labour's share in income, σ is the elasticity of substitution and q the level of output.
2. We also find Keynes alarmed, *inter alia*, by the dangers of inflation at the outbreak of the First World War (Keynes, 1914), although on this occasion because of the consequences of lax monetary policy.
3. See Sinclair (1983, ch. 7) for more detailed discussion of this.
4. Sargan (1980) provides clear evidence that money wage rates respond one-to-one with the price level in the UK in a rather rapid fashion. The argument that marginal tax rates increase money wage rates can be found in Bacon and Eltis (1976), *inter alia*, and receives econometric support in Layard and Nickell (1986) and elsewhere.
5. The entry of a new firm is not necessarily an ideal thing for policy to aim at. In the somewhat different context of an oligopolistic industry producing solely for private demand, Cremer, Marchand and Thisse (1987) find that it is unambiguously better from a welfare standpoint for the government to *own* one of the firms, rather than establish a new one. This can enable the government to increase industry output, and lower its selling price, so as to maximise the sum of consumer and producer surplus, and at less cost than would be incurred by the creation of a new state-owned firm.
6. The fact that this is so can be established by investigating the gradients of the stationarity loci for competitiveness and liquidity. Respectively, they are

$$\frac{\dfrac{1-\gamma_1 a_4}{\gamma_2} + \delta \left(a_4 + \dfrac{a_5}{\gamma_2} \right)}{\sigma_1 \left(\dfrac{\delta_1}{\gamma_2} - \delta \right)} \quad \text{and} \quad \frac{b \left(a_4 + \dfrac{a_5}{\gamma_2} \right) (\delta - \varphi)}{a_1 \left(b\delta + (1-b)\dfrac{\gamma_1}{\gamma_2} \right)}$$

Given that $1 > \gamma_1 a_4$ by assumption, this tells us that $\dot{c} = 0$ cuts $\dot{l} = 0$ from below, if and only if the Phillips curve is flat enough for $\delta < \gamma_1/\gamma_2$.

7. For a member of OPEC, the discounted value of any reward from keeping to its monopoly-quota falls relative to the gain from infringing it.
8. The falls in inflation and unemployment have not been precisely synchronised; unemployment only began to fall after the end of the 1980–2 recession.
9. Dornbusch (1986, p. 22) puts the disinflationary effect of dollar appreciation at 2 per cent or more for each 10 per cent appreciation.
10. The biggest single US defence project undertaken in these years has been the recommissioning of the four Iowa class battleships. This appears to have cost over 20 times as many constant (GDP-deflator deflated) dollars as their construction four decades earlier. This example hardly strengthens one's confidence in the notion that we live in an era of falling relative cost of defence procurement.

References

BACON, R. W. and W. A. ELTIS (1976) *Britain's Economic Problem: Too Few Producers* (London).
BECKERMAN, W. and T. JENKINSON (1986) 'What Stopped the Inflation? Unemployment or Commodity Prices?', *Economic Journal*.
BLANCHARD, O. and R. DORNBUSCH (1985) 'U.S. Deficits, the Dollar and Europe', in O. Blanchard, R. Dornbusch and R. Layard (eds), *Restoring Europe's Prosperity* (Cambridge: Massachusetts).
BUITER, W. H. (1987a) 'A Fiscal Theory of Hyperdeflations? Some Surprising Monetarist Arithmetic', *Oxford Economic Papers*.
BUITER, W. H. (1987b) Does an Improvement in the Current Account or the Trade Balance at Full Employment Require a Depreciation of the Real Exchange Rate? mimeo (Yale and NBER).
BUITER, W. H. and M. H. MILLER (1981) 'Monetary Policy and International Competitiveness: the Problems of Adjustment', *Oxford Economic Papers*.
BUITER, W. H. and M. H. MILLER (1985) 'The Costs and Benefits of an Anti-Inflationary Policy: Questions and Answers', in V. Argy and J. Nevile (eds) *Inflation and Unemployment* (London).
CREMER, H., M. MARCHAND and J-F. THISSE (1987) 'The Public Firm as an Instrument for Regulating an Oligopolistic Market', *CORE Discussion Paper 8710* (Louvain-la-Neuve).
DORNBUSCH, R. (1976) 'Expectations and Exchange Rate Dynamics', *Journal of Political Economy*.
DORNBUSCH, R. (1986) *Dollars, Debts and Deficits* (Cambridge, Massachusetts).
ELLIOTT, R. F. and P. D. MURPHY (1987) 'The Relative Pay of Public and Private Sector Employees 1970–1984', *Cambridge Journal of Economics*.
HARROD, R. F. (1930) 'Notes on Supply', *Economic Journal*.
HICKS, J. R. (1932) *Theory of Wages* (London).
HOTELLING, H. (1931) 'The Economics of Exhaustible Resources', *Journal of Political Economy*.
KEYNES, J. M. (1914) 'The Prospects of Money', November 1914, *Economic Journal*.
KEYNES, J. M. (1936) *The General Theory of Employment, Interest and Money* (London).
KEYNES, J. M. (1940) *How to Pay for the War* (London).

LAYARD, P. R. G. and S. J. NICKELL (1986) 'Unemployment in Britain', *Economica*.

NEARY, J. P. (1980) 'Non Traded Goods and the Balance of Trade in a neo-Keynesian Temporary Equilibrium', *Quarterly Journal of Economics*.

PEDEN, G. C. (1980) 'Keynes, the Treasury and Unemployment in the Later Nineteen Thirties', *Oxford Economic Papers*.

SARGAN, J. D. (1980) 'A Model of Wage-Price Inflation', *Review of Economic Studies*.

SARGENT, T. A. and N. WALLACE (1981) 'Some Unpleasant Monetarist Arithmetic', *Federal Reserve Bank of Minneapolis Quarterly Review*.

SHEEN, J. (1987) 'Inflation Debt and Fiscal Policy Attitudes', *Oxford Economic Papers*.

SINCLAIR, P. J. N. (1983) *The Foundations of Macroeconomic and Monetary Theory* (Oxford).

STIGLER, J. (1964) 'A Theory of Oligopoly', *Journal of Political Economy*.

VAN DER PLOEG, F. (1987a) 'Optimal Government Policy in a Small Open Economy with Rational Expectations and Uncertain Election Outcomes', *International Economic Review*.

VAN DER PLOEG, F. (1987b) 'International Interdependence and Policy Coordination in Economies with Real and Nominal Wage Rigidity', mimeo (London School of Economics).

WEITZMAN, M. L. (1982) 'Increasing Returns and the Foundations of Unemployment Theory', *Economic Journal*, vol. 92, December.

Part V

The Significance of Public Sector Borrowing

9 Government Deficits and Debts. The Necessity and Cost of Adjustment: the Case of Italy

Giampaolo Galli and Rainer S. Masera

What a government spends the public pay for. There is no such thing as an uncovered deficit. But in some countries it seems possible to please and content the public, for a time at least, by giving them, in return for the taxes they pay, finely engraved acknowledgements on watermarked paper. The income-tax receipts, which we in England receive from the Surveyor, we throw into the wastepaper basket; in Germany they call them bank notes and put them into their pocket-books; in France they are termed *rentes* and are locked up in the family safe. (J. M. Keynes, *A Tract on Monetary Reform*, Macmillan, 1923)

If it is accepted, the above reasoning shows how 'wasteful' loan expenditure (the net borrowing of public authorities on all accounts, whether on capital account or to meet a budgetary deficit) may nevertheless enrich the community on balance. Pyramid-building, earthquakes, even wars may serve to increase wealth, if the education of our statesmen on the principles of the classical economics stands in the way of anything better. (J. M. Keynes, *The General Theory*, Macmillan, 1936)

9.1 SUMMARY AND INTRODUCTION

This chapter considers the issue of the sustainability of the public debt and the problems which arise in the medium term in connection with attempts to stabilise its growth with particular reference to the case of Italy.

The first part, which comprises Sections 9.2 and 9.3, is devoted to a formal examination of the problem. Section 9.2 collects analytical arguments pointing to the necessity of adjusting. In addition to the reasonably well understood problems of crowding out of domestic capital and of net foreign assets, a high and rapidly rising level of the debt may be a matter of concern because issues of credibility may arise. In this connection the relation between the rate of interest and the rate of growth of the economy is a critical one: however, even in the most favourable case (in which the latter exceeds the former at a particular date) the need for fiscal adjustment may arise because the market may rightfully take such variables as the level and the growth rate of the debt as indicators of whether the government will in fact be able to honour its obligations in the future.

Section 9.3 deals with the problems which arise when the stabilisation of the public debt is pursued by reducing real government consumption or increasing net taxes. In his review of English developments after the First World War, J. M. Keynes observed that tight fiscal policies (the budget was almost continuously in large surplus throughout the whole interwar period) did not succeed in reducing the debt/income ratio. While the pound value of the debt was stabilised, its ratio to GNP rose owing to falling real income and prices. According to Keynes, the latter were the consequences of the restrictive fiscal and monetary policies that were pursued with the goal of returning to the gold standard at the prewar parity. He concluded that 'it does not pay to be good' (Keynes, 1963). As well documented by Alesina (1987), this is an interesting contrast to the successful experience of the US after the Second World War. The budget turned to a surplus in the years immediately following the war and was close to balance throughout most of the 1950s; the debt/income ratio fell continuously from 1.3 in 1946 to 0.6 in 1960. Clearly, tight fiscal policy is only part of the medicine; the rest concerns its timing and dosage in relation to monetary and exchange rate policies. Nor can one overlook other domestic and foreign factors affecting prospects for economic stability and growth. From the perspective of a medium-term strategy, even if tight policies succeed in stabilising the debt, there is a problem concerning its possible costs in terms of Keynesian idle resources. These issues are analysed using an overlapping generations version of the classical Mundell–Fleming–Dornbusch model of an open economy.

The second part of the chapter is empirical in nature. In Section 9.4 the key relationship affecting the transversality condition – namely that between the rate of interest on the public debt and rate of growth of GNP – is examined in a long-term perspective in the case of the US, the UK and Italy. Section 9.5 is devoted to a quantitative assessment of debt trends and their interactions with the overall Italian economic system: a brief overview of developments in the 1970s and 1980s is presented pointing to the size of the imbalances in the public finances and which go well beyond those accountable for by inflation and cyclical factors. To substantiate this, the development of the debt/income ratio, in the absence of structural adjustment of the budget, is then projected up to the year 2000.

Finally, Section 9.6 contains some concluding comments and stresses the need for fiscal adjustment in Italy.

9.2   THE NECESSITY OF ADJUSTMENT

In several countries in the last few years questions have been raised as to whether existing trends in public finance could be sustained in the long run or whether action should be taken, by the fiscal and/or the monetary authorities, to invert such trends. Neither history nor economic theory provide definite answers to the questions of whether there exists a threshold for the national debt. History provides examples of countries that have been able to sustain public debts as large as two or three times national income (see Buiter, 1985). As to economic theory, it provides us with the statement that a crisis is generated at the moment in which investors are no longer sure that the government will honour its obligations. This is the essence of the solvency requirement according to which the present value of future expenses must be lower or equal to the present value of net taxes plus the initial debt (Blanchard, Dornbusch and Buiter, 1985; Buiter, 1985). For fixed values of the non-interest deficit as a ratio to income, this condition is generally satisfied if the rate of interest on the debt is lower than the growth rate of the economy. In this case, the demand for the debt grows at a rate which is higher than supply: hence the government can go on forever satisfying old creditors by creating new ones. In the opposite case, solvency imposes a constraint on future budgets: surpluses must sooner or later be generated in order to repay the debt.

All this is, of course, not much; indeed it is like telling a banker that he should lend to good borrowers. But who are the good borrowers? In the case of the government the question is particularly hard because one cannot look at a record of failures and defaults of the last 20 years, while looking at 100 years is hardly meaningful. One can look at the market performance: if the public is willing to buy the debt and even to buy it at a discount relative to, say, private debt, it obviously trusts the government. From the point of view of policy, however, the question is whether the market will still trust the government ten years from now, even if nothing is done to stop the growth of the debt. In extraordinary situations, such as wars, the public may rightfully believe that a fast growth of the debt is only a temporary phenomenon as should be the case under optimal time consistent strategies when non-distorting taxes are unavailable (as shown by Lucas and Stockey (1983); see also Lucas (1985) and Barro (1987)). In a normal situation, however, with no drastic changes expected for the near future, such variables as the growth of the debt, or the average level of the deficit, can be used by the market to evaluate the creditworthiness of the government. From this point of view the same level of debt may be a more serious problem in peacetime than during a war.

Consider the simple case in which, as in Domar (1944), the real rate of interest (r), the real rate of growth of the economy $(\hat{y})$, the ratio of the primary deficit to GNP (g), the growth of the money supply $(\hat{M})$ and its ratio to GNP (m) are all constant; in this case the dynamics of the interest yielding debt to GNP ratio (b) can be written as

$$\dot{b} = (r - \hat{y})b + g - m\hat{M} \tag{9.1}$$

If $r < \hat{y}$, b tends towards a finite value given by

$$\lim_{t \to \infty} b(t) = \frac{g - m\hat{M}}{\hat{y} - r} \tag{9.2}$$

If $g - m\hat{M}$ (primary deficit net of seignorage) is positive, the debt/income ratio tends towards a positive value. Technically the state is solvent although it always runs a deficit. If $r > \hat{y}$ and $g - m\hat{M} > 0$, the debt/income ratio rises without bounds. In this case the assumption that $g - m\hat{M}$ is constant cannot be maintained. At some point surpluses must be generated to cover interest payments, i.e.

$$g - m\hat{M} = -(r - \hat{y})b < 0 \tag{9.3}$$

Equation (9.3) may be satisfied by a primary surplus ($g < 0$) or by larger seignorage ($m\hat{M}$).

It is clear that in the unstable case, some action must be taken to stabilise the system. Should anything be done in the stable case? The answer is that there is no need to adjust if:

(a) r and $\hat{y}$ are in fact exogenous (as postulated in writing eqn (9.1));
(b) there is no uncertainty as to the fact that r will remain below $\hat{y}$ in the future.

If we drop assumption (b), we immediately have to consider that, should $r - \hat{y}$ turn positive in the future, the required adjustment of $g - m\hat{M}$ (from eqn (9.3)) increases with the inherited level of the debt. If, for instance, $g - m\hat{M}$ equals 0.1 and $\hat{y} - r$ equals 0.01, b will tend towards 10 times GNP. If, in such a steady state, $\hat{y} - r$ turns negative and, say, equal to -0.01, $g - m\hat{M}$ must be reduced by 20 percentage points of GNP, an action that most would consider unfeasible. The general point is that as long as there is a positive probability of r becoming larger than $\hat{y}$ and if there is a limit to the feasible adjustment of the budget, for large values of b, the market will stop trusting the government.

If we drop assumption (a), the possibility arises that the growth of debt will push up r and depress $\hat{y}$. r may rise owing to crowding out of the capital stock or because of portfolio considerations in models in which there is little substitutability between money and bonds; $\hat{y}$ may be reduced while the capital stock is being crowded out. In a variety of models (see Cividini *et al.* (1987) and Galli (1986)), $r - \hat{y}$ can be expressed as an increasing (possibly linear) function of b. Let

$$r - \hat{y} = -a_0 + a_1 b \qquad (9.4)$$

Substituting eqn (9.4) into (9.1), yields a quadratic expression. If the discriminant, $a_0^2 - 4a_1(g - m\hat{M})$, is negative the system is always unstable; regardless of the initial condition, $r - \hat{y}$ at some point becomes positive and b grows without bounds. If the discriminant is positive, the system is stable if the initial value of the debt is lower than the larger root of the equation, a condition that turns out to be more stringent than $r - \hat{y} = -a_0 + a_1 b < 0$.

In summary, the comparison between r and $\hat{y}$ is a critical issue; however, even if r is lower than $\hat{y}$ to start with, adjustment may be required. The problem is one of credibility: policies must be such as to reassure investors that the government will be solvent. In normal times the level and growth of the debt *matter* because they may rightfully be taken by the market as signals as to whether the government will in fact be able to honour its obligations in the future. In addition, as is well known, in models in which the 'Ricardian' equivalence does not hold,[1] even a perfectly credible debt may be a problem because of its effects on the capital stock (as in Modigliani (1961), and in Diamond (1965)) and on the accumulation of foreign debt.

9.3 THE COSTS OF ADJUSTING

This section deals with the problem that, as Keynes stressed, reducing deficits may depress aggregate demand and may even fail to stabilise the ratio of the debt to national income.

Two points deserve attention. First, while deficits are being reduced, the debt continues to grow; unless 'Ricardian' equivalence holds, there are in principle two conflicting influences on aggregate demand originating from a declining flow and a growing stock. It can therefore be asked whether there exists a strategy of gradual adjustment that stabilises the debt while keeping aggregate demand along a desired path.

The second point relates to the behaviour of monetary policy in the case in which flow effects dominate and fiscal policy puts downward pressure on aggregate demand. If effective controls on financial transactions with non-residents are in place, it should in principle be possible to manage money so as to crowd in private spending and keep unemployment unchanged. This course also eases the stabilisation of the debt/income ratio because the implied fall in the real rate of interest slows the growth of the numerator while avoiding reductions in the denominator. As far as inflation is concerned, no problems should be expected in models in which prices and wages depend on excess demand.

Unfortunately, the extension of this logic to the case of free capital mobility is not straightforward. Unless a strong Laursen–Metzler effect is at work, the main mechanism that can avoid unemployment while the public sector deficit is reduced is a depreciation of the exchange rate that crowds in net exports. Money can in principle be managed to achieve this goal. However, with a depreciating exchange rate there will probably be more inflation as well as welfare losses due to worsening of the terms of trade. Thus the stabilisation of the debt poses a difficult trade-off between unemployment on the one hand and inflation on the other. In turn, the choice that is made between these two outcomes feeds back on the dynamics of both the numerator and the denominator of the ratio between debt and national income.

These issues are studied here with the aid of an open economy model that has four key features.

First, debt policy matters because, as in Blanchard (1985), a finite probability of survival (with no bequest motive) causes agents to discount future net non-interest income at a rate which is higher than the market rate.

Second, the possibility of unemployment arises because of the Mundell–Fleming assumption that domestic goods are imperfect substitutes for foreign goods. Perfect substitutability is instead assumed between domestic and foreign assets.

Third, unemployment actually arises because wages are not assumed to clear the market instantaneously. In this respect this model shares some features with those of Van Wijnbergen (1985), Cuddington and Viñals (1986) and Viñals (1986). However, since we are interested in the dynamics of inflation, we do not use their assumption that there are two periods and the second one is expected to be in Walrasian equilibrium. Instead, we let wages respond to excess demand, in continuous time, according to the well-known accelerationist hypothesis of M. Friedman (1968): if unemployment falls short of the natural rate, nominal wages and prices *accelerate*. It is thus the second derivative of the (log of the) price level that responds to excess demand. Sufficient assumptions about policy rules are made to guarantee the existence of a stable long-run solution in which inflation is constant and all real variables are at their Walrasian equilibrium.

Finally, wage earners are assumed to care for the consumption price: this provides a direct link from the exchange rate to price–wage dynamics that considerably complicates the problem of finding a sensible, if not optimal, strategy, to slow down the growth of the public debt.

9.3.1 The model

Following Frenkel and Razin (1984) and Blanchard (1985), an individual agent (defined by his or her date of birth, s) maximises an additively time separable log–linear utility function:

$$u(t,s) = \int_t^\infty [\alpha\gamma \log c + \alpha(1-\gamma)\log c^* + (1-\alpha)\log m]\, e^{-(\theta+\pi)(t-v)}\, dv \qquad (9.5)$$

where c, c^* and m are domestic consumption, imports and real money (in terms of domestic goods). θ and π are the subjective discount rate and the instantaneous probability of death. The dynamic budget constraint of the s-consumer is

$$\dot{w} = (r+\pi)w + y - \tau - c - zc^* - (\dot{p}+r)m \tag{9.6}$$

w is non-human wealth in units of domestic goods, r is the domestic real rate of interest, y is income, τ is lump-sum taxes, z is the level of the real exchange rate (an increase being a depreciation), $\dot{p}$ is the rate of inflation (p being the log of the price level). The only existing assets are public debt and foreign bonds. Real wealth is hence defined as

$$w = d + zf \tag{9.7}$$

where d (= money plus short-term bonds in real terms) is the real public debt and f are foreign bonds in units of foreign goods.

Solving the maximisation problem and aggregating over consumers, as in Blanchard (1985), yields the following equations:

$$e = c + zc^* + (\dot{p}+r)m = (\theta+\pi)(h+w) \tag{9.8}$$

$$\dot{h} = (r+\pi)h - (y-\tau) \tag{9.9}$$

$$\dot{w} = rw + y - \tau - e \tag{9.10}$$

$$c = \alpha\gamma e \tag{9.11}$$

$$zc^* = \alpha(1-\gamma)e \tag{9.12}$$

$$(r+\dot{p})m = (1-\alpha)e \tag{9.13}$$

All the relevant variables are now interpreted as aggregates over all consumers. As in Barnett (1980), e can be thought of as total (real) expenditure on goods and money (whose 'price' or opportunity cost is the nominal rate of interest). As in Modigliani and Brumberg (1979), total expenditure is a constant fraction of life-time resources, i.e. assets (w) plus the discounted value of net non-interest income (h), whose dynamics are given by eqn (9.9). After aggregation, eqn (9.10) is a standard wealth accumulation. Equations (9.11) to (9.13) are usual constant share Cobb–Douglas demand functions. Note the unit elasticity of the demand for money with respect to the nominal interest rate; as in Spaventa (1987) this formulation eliminates any incentive for the government to use the inflation tax as a means to finance the deficit, because seignorage is independent of the rate of inflation.

We complete the description of the economy with the following equations

$$r = r^* + \hat{z} \qquad \text{open interest parity} \tag{9.14}$$

where r^* is the foreign real rate of interest; (9.14) is adopted here for analytical simplicity, although in the description of the Italian case contained in Section 9.5 imperfect capital mobility plays a role, largely as consequence of administrative controls.

$$y = c + g + xz^\sigma \qquad \text{goods market equilibrium} \tag{9.15}$$

where g is real public consumption (of domestic goods) and xz^σ is exports; the latter depend positively on the real exchange rate with an elasticity σ.

$$\dot{d} = rd + g - \tau - (\dot{p} + r)m \qquad \text{public sector deficit} \tag{9.16}$$

Substituting (9.7), (9.8), (9.14), (9.15) and (9.16) in (9.10), we get the foreign asset accumulation equation (which is consequently redundant)

$$\dot{f} = r^* f + xz^{\sigma-1} - c^* \tag{9.17}$$

As to the dynamics of prices, we write

$$\ddot{p} = \varphi(y - \bar{y}) + (1 - \gamma)\hat{z} \tag{9.18}$$

where $\bar{y}$ is the level of income corresponding to the NAIRU. The change in the rate of inflation of the GDP deflator is related to the excess demand in the labour market[2] and to the percentage change in the exchange rate. Equation (9.18) can be derived as follows. We postulate the following discrete time specification of the Phillips curve

$$\Delta p_{t+1} = \varphi(\cdot) + \Delta p_t^c \tag{9.19}$$

which states that the rate of change of the GDP deflator in the next period ($\Delta p_{t+1} = p_{t+1} - p_t$) equals $\varphi(\cdot)$ plus today's consumer price inflation. Equation (9.19) is consistent with the assumptions that wage earners care about the consumption wage and that the domestic price is a mark-up over labour costs, as would be predicted by monopolistic competition among a large number of identical firms.[3] Although eqn (9.19) is open to well-known criticisms (see also Chapter 2, Bennett McCallum's contribution to this volume), it is adopted here for lack of more convincing specifications allowing for activist demand policies. Letting p_t^* be the log of the domestic currency price of foreign goods, we have

$$p_t^c = \gamma p_t + (1 - \gamma)p_t^* \tag{9.20}$$

$$\log z_t = p_t^* - p_t \tag{9.21}$$

Substituting into (9.19), yields

$$\Delta p_{t+1} - \Delta p_t = \varphi(\cdot) + (1 - \gamma)\Delta \log z_t \tag{9.22}$$

which, in continuous time, corresponds to eqn (9.18).

The model defined by equations (9.8) to (9.18) can be used, without further additions, to analyse the effects of changes in the level of the debt in the steady state. The latter is defined as a situation in which inflation is constant (not necessarily zero) as are all real variables; it can be shown to exist (with positive consumption and positive net assets) if

$$\theta < r^* < \theta + \pi \tag{9.23}$$

The following results can easily be obtained (and will not be proved). When g is used to balance the budget (eqn (9.16) with $\dot{d}=0$), consumption and total assets are unaffected; the purchasing power of foreign assets in terms of domestic goods falls one to one with the increase in the debt; in terms of foreign goods it falls by more because the exchange rate depreciates. If, instead, taxes are used to balance the budget, the possibility arises that a higher debt should be matched by *lowering* taxes so as to increase consumption and the demand for monetary liabilities of the government. Neglecting this possibility (as Keynes probably would *not*) a rise in the debt depresses consumption and wealth, crowds out foreign assets (in terms of domestic units, by more than in the previous case) and again depreciates the exchange rate.

From the demand for money (eqn (9.13)), in steady-state domestic prices and money grow at the same rate. Constancy of the real exchange rate implies that the nominal exchange rate moves at the rate equal to the difference between domestic and foreign inflation.

9.3.2 Alternative stabilisation strategies

Our main concern is with alternative strategies to stabilise the debt. The general problem is the following. If, say, g is reduced to stabilise the debt (with τ fixed) and the real exchange rate is devalued to sustain employment, inflation cannot be kept constant. Alternatively g can be used to target employment (i.e. it is reduced at a rate which just offsets the expansionary effect of a growing debt); here again, the stabilisation of debt may require a depreciating exchange rate. Since the stabilisation of the debt is only an integral condition (i.e. there are infinite paths which satisfy the transversality condition), if one gives up either the employment or the inflation target there are infinite strategies which satisfy the remaining two targets (on this point, see Sheen, 1987). The issue of how to compare such different strategies is not addressed here: we rather concentrate on two relatively simple examples which illustrate the principles involved.

The two examples differ about their assumptions on the real exchange rate: in the first one the exchange rate is moved once and for all after a shock in order for the transversality requirement to be met under the condition that g is continuously moved to maintain employment at the NAIRU. Since, along the adjustment path, the real exchange rate is fixed, so is the rate of inflation; the inflationary cost of this strategy all shows up at the beginning, when the exchange rate undergoes a discrete upward jump.

In the second example, the exchange rate is adjusted continuously so as to maintain a balanced current account; when g is used to target either output ('liberal strategy') or inflation ('conservative strategy'), under certain additional conditions, the system tends towards a stable solution.

These two examples differ in many respects; both, however, illustrate the two basic points that generally:

(a) Gradual strategies of fiscal recovery exist which are consistent with fixed employment.
(b) Such strategies do have some costs in terms of inflation; unless other policy instruments are used (e.g. incomes policy) these costs may not be avoidable.

In substance, these points restate the well-known fact that by loosening money the stabilisation of the debt can be eased. The mechanism that is highlighted, however, is not the traditional one associated with the inflation tax, but the fact that a real depreciation, while creating inflation, sustains aggregate demand: this improves the cyclical budget (the Keynesian effect) and makes it politically feasible to reduce the structural deficit. Unless a policy of fiscal recovery accompanied by wage–price responsibility is implemented, the monetary authorities are confronted with the dilemma between the two conflicting objectives of disinflation and the easing of the process of debt stabilisation.

In the first example, since y is fixed ($y=\bar{y}$) and z only takes an initial discrete jump (hence expected depreciation is zero and in eqn (9.14) $r=r^*$), we can solve for a constant level of human wealth from eqn (9.9); substituting the resulting expression and eqn (9.11) in eqn (9.8), we can write the consumption function as

$$c = \alpha\gamma(\theta + \pi)\left(\frac{\bar{y}-\tau}{r^*+\pi} + w\right) \qquad (9.24)$$

Using again eqn (9.11) and eqn (9.24), to eliminate expenditure from the consumer budget constraint (eqn (9.10)), the dynamics of wealth becomes

$$\dot{w} = -(\theta + \pi - r^*)w + (\bar{y} - \tau)\frac{(r^* - \theta)}{(\pi + r^*)} \tag{9.25}$$

The phase diagram of the system represented by eqns (9.24) and (9.25) is shown in Figure 9.1. The vertical schedule is the locus along which $\dot{w} = 0$ from eqn (9.25); under the existence condition (eqn (9.23)), the root of this equation $(r^* - \pi - \theta)$ is negative. The upward sloping schedule (CC) is the consumption function (eqn (9.24)).

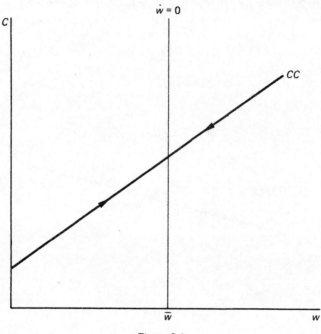

Figure 9.1

We are interested in studying the properties of the system on the left of steady-state wealth $(w < \bar{w})$, because, as is shown below, that is where public spending is reduced while the debt (along with total wealth and consumption) is rising.

Since consumption rises and exports are fixed, we know from eqn (9.15) (goods market equilibrium) that g declines at a rate which is just sufficient to keep income at the natural rate. As in Dornbusch (1986), the dynamics of g along the saddle path can be written as

$$\dot{g} = -v(g - \bar{g}) \qquad v = \alpha\gamma(\theta + \pi) \tag{9.26}$$

where $\bar{g}$ is the steady-state level of g. Not surprisingly the speed of adjustment of g is equal to the propensity to spend on domestic consumption out of total wealth (see eqn (9.24)).

That the public debt rises can be seen by substituting eqns (9.11), (9.13) and (9.15) in the public sector budget constraint (eqn (9.16)):

$$\dot{d} = r^*d + \bar{y} - \tau - xz^\sigma - \frac{1 - \alpha(1 - \gamma)}{\alpha\gamma} c \tag{9.27}$$

Further substituting eqn (9.24) in eqn (9.27), we have a differential equation in d and w, which, together with eqn (9.24), has the representation shown in Figure 9.2.

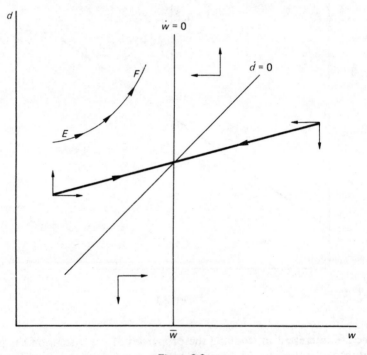

Figure 9.2

The $\dot{w} = 0$ schedule is the same as the one drawn in Figure 9.1. The $\dot{d} = 0$ schedule is upward sloping because higher wealth improves the budget (because it implies higher consumption and hence both higher seignorage and lower full employment spending) while higher debt worsens it through higher interest payments. The system is stable around the $\dot{w} = 0$ line and unstable (because of interest payments) around the $\dot{d} = 0$ line. The saddle path is hence upward sloping, as drawn.

To sum up, we are describing a situation in which the public debt is rising because of some, so far unspecified, inherited imbalance; the resulting increase in wealth pushes up consumption through life-cycle considerations; public spending is reduced in order to balance the budget, but at a rate which is no faster than is compatible with constant employment. Since the real exchange rate is fixed, we know from the Phillips curve (eqn (9.18)) that along the adjustment path inflation is constant ($\dot{p}=0$) at some inherited level.

Apparently things are fine. There is, however, a problem: there is no guarantee that the speed with which spending is reduced is sufficient to actually balance the budget; in other words the transversality condition for the public sector need not be satisfied. This is a critical point. Consumers are assumed to always make plans that satisfy their transversality condition; since the system is not growing this means that aggregate wealth tends to a constant. This is represented in Figure 9.1 where consumption is always assumed to be on the stable (saddle) path represented by eqn (9.24). However, the *fact that wealth is constant in steady state does not imply that the same holds for its composition between public debt and foreign assets*: indeed the debt may grow and foreign assets may fall without bounds. Figure 9.2 illustrates this point graphically: d is a predetermined variable and there is no reason why w should be such as to keep the system along the saddle path. The assumptions that we have made so far do not rule out a point like E in the figure in which the debt rises without bounds while wealth tends towards a stable value. If the initial situation is like in point E, either g must be reduced at a faster rate (hence the employment target abandoned) or the exchange rate must depreciate. *The latter crowds in net exports thus making it possible to maintain employment at the NAIRU with a lower level of* g.

To see how this works suppose, for the sake of simplicity, that at point E (where the system has just 'landed' after some exogenous shock) net foreign assets are zero, i.e. $d=w$. A depreciation of the real exchange rate (an increase in z) leaves wealth and consumption unaffected: it increases exports, which enter eqn (9.27) with a negative sign because, for given employment, they substitute public spending. The $\dot{d}=0$ line shifts upward; with the right change in the exchange rate the saddle path will pass through point E in Figure 9.2. If the authorities commit themselves to henceforth keep z constant the system will converge to a fixed level of the debt.

Three points should be made

(1) In the transition, the jump in the exchange rate causes a permanently higher rate of inflation, unless workers accept a permanently lower real wage (i.e. unless eqn (9.18) is temporarily suspended).
(2) There is no market mechanism that makes the exchange rate jump to its correct level. This is a task for the public authorities.
(3) The reason why we concentrate on a point like E (rather than, say, a

point like C where an appreciation may instead be called for) is that we are interested in shocks which tend to increase the debt. In other words, the problems that we are discussing arise because some shock has thrown the system out of equilibrium to a point at which, unless appropriate policies are pursued, there is an explosion of the debt.

Consider one such shock: an increase in the foreign rate of interest. It is easily seen that, regardless of the exchange rate, both schedules in Figure 9.1 shift to the right (see Figure 9.3).

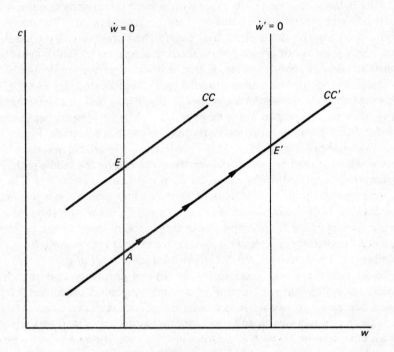

Figure 9.3

Consumption initially falls from E to A because the present value of non-interest income has fallen.[4] From A to E' the debt rises because of higher interest payments, thus pushing up wealth and consumption. The postulated logarithmic utility function ensures that the new steady-state consumption (point E') is higher than in the pre-shock equilibrium, but by less than the increase in wealth. Interestingly the increase in the rate of interest is initially deflationary; eventually, as the public debt piles up, consumption puts upward pressure on aggregate demand. Also the $\dot{d} = 0$ schedule shifts to the right because higher interest payments must be compensated by higher wealth (hence higher consumption and seignorage and lower spending). It also becomes flatter as shown in Figure 9.4 (dashed line $\dot{d}' = 0$).

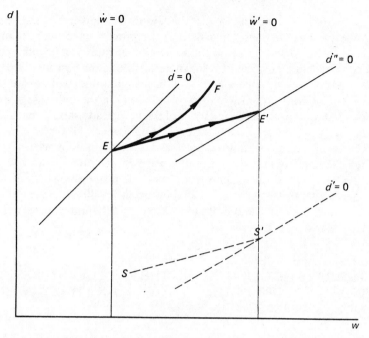

Figure 9.4

The corresponding saddle path (line SS') lies south of point E (see Appendix 9.1). Unless the authorities intervene, the system moves along the explosive path EF. Since agents are forward looking they know that both the public debt and the foreign debt will not be repaid: there would hence be an immediate collapse of the system (the risk premium required to hold the debt could jump to infinity and eqn (9.14) could break down). A real depreciation shifts upward the $\dot{d}' = 0$ line (to $\dot{d}'' = 0$) so that the new saddle path passes through point E leading the system to the stable solution E'.

In the second example, as an alternative to an initial depreciation, we consider a strategy in which the real exchange rate is continuously used to target the level of foreign assets. If it is again assumed that initial foreign assets are zero, the formal analysis of this case, contained in Appendix 9.2, is relatively manageable. This strategy is probably more realistic than the previous one since the authorities are not supposed to have perfect foresight about the whole future development of the economy and are allowed to adjust the exchange rate along the way. If foreign assets are continuously kept at a constant (zero) level, the question of the sustainability of the foreign debt does not arise. Since consumers are assumed to meet their obligations in all cases, also the sustainability of domestic debt is not an issue. There are, however, two further problems. The first one is technical: the stability of the system requires that the elasticity of the demand for exports be greater than one. The second one concerns the fact that along the adjustment path (after a shock like the one we considered before) the growth of the debt tends to crowd out foreign assets: to avoid this the exchange rate must be falling until the system reaches a position of rest. Therefore along the adjustment path g can be reduced at a rate which is either compatible with a constant employment or with a constant rate of inflation. In the first case ('liberal strategy') inflation rises continuously until the new steady state is reached; in the second one ('conservative strategy') employment is kept below the NAIRU during the transition. In both cases, the main difference with the previous examples is that the costs of fiscal recovery are spread over the whole period in which the economy adjusts to its new stable position.

From a substantive point of view, all these examples illustrate the trade-off between unemployment and inflation faced by a country with a large cumulated imbalance in public finance.

9.4   THE RATE OF GROWTH AND THE RATE OF INTEREST ON GOVERNMENT DEBT IN THE US, THE UK AND ITALY: A HISTORICAL PERSPECTIVE

As discussed in Section 9.2, one of the critical relations affecting the sustainability of the debt is that between the rate of growth of the economy and the rate of interest on the debt. In some recent theoretical literature the rate of interest is often *a priori* constrained to be higher than the rate of growth. In neoclassical models of growth this restriction may be justified on the ground that in the opposite case (a lower rate of interest than of growth) the system would be in the inefficient region relative to the golden rule, unless the rate of depreciation of the capital stock is sufficiently high to make up for the difference. A regime of *laissez faire*, in which agents have finite horizons, might lead to such a situation; if these conditions were to apply a public intervention would, however, discourage investment and produce an increase of the sustainable steady-state level of consumption.

In any event, the data reported in Figures 9.5–9.7 relative to the US, the UK and Italy indicate that most of the time, and on average, the rate of interest on the debt (gross of taxes) has been *lower* than the rate of growth. In the US in the period 1890–1985 the average growth of nominal GNP was slightly below 6 per cent while the interest rate on long-term public bonds was 4.84 per cent; dividing the flow of interest paid by the Federal Government (including those paid to the Federal Reserve) by the overall debt (again including debt held by the Fed), one obtains an average cost of the debt of 3.75 per cent (Figure 9.5). Similar conclusions are reached by Darby (1984) using the yields on US Treasury bills elaborated by Ibbotson and Sinquefield (1982) for the period 1926–81. There are exceptions, however: among the most relevant being the beginning of the 1920s and the years

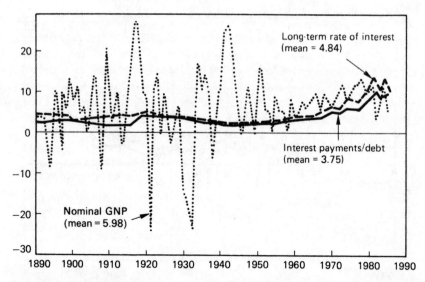

Figure 9.5   United States.
Sources: US Dept. of Commerce, 'Historical Statistics of the United States', USGPO; 'Economic Report of the President', Feb. 1986; 'Budget of the United States Government – Fiscal Year 1987'.
Note: The item 'interest payments/debt' includes interest received in the numerator and the debt held by the Central Bank in the denominator. It measures the average cost of the whole mix of interest-yielding liabilities of the government.

of the Great Depression. For the present analysis the most important exception is that of the 1980s, with the rate of interest rising to values that are unprecedented and well above the rate of growth.

For the UK, the evidence is less clear-cut. Between 1896 and 1985 the average growth of nominal GNP (5.08 per cent) exceeds the long-term rate of interest and the average cost of interest-yielding debt by about 70 basis points (Figure 9.6). This average result is heavily affected, however, by the observations covering the two wars and the first half of the 1950s. Both before the First World War and after it until the mid-1930s the rate of interest considerably exceeded the rate of growth. As in the US, the 1980s are a notable exception to the pattern prevailing after the Second World War: nominal interest rates are very high by historical standards and exceed the rate of the growth.

Figure 9.7 reports data which have recently been produced for Italy between 1915 and 1941. The pattern for this period is similar to that of the UK with the rate of interest exceeding the growth rate between 1926 and 1934. The 1980s are again a notable exception to the postwar pattern (not in the figure; see Section 9.5).

Note that in these three countries the movements of the GNP series largely

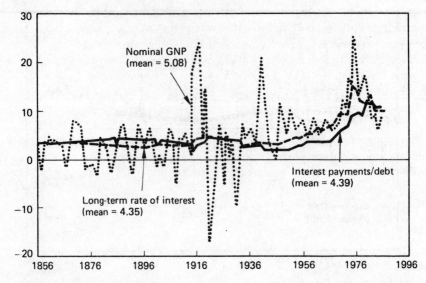

Figure 9.6   United Kingdom.

Sources: C. B. Feinstein, *National Income Expenditure and Output (1855–1965)* (Oxford: OUP, 1972); B. R. Mitchell, *Abstract of British Statistics* (Oxford: OUP, 1962); B. R. Mitchell and H. G. Jones, *Second Abstract of British Historical Statistics* (Oxford: OUP, 1971); Central Statistical Office, *Financial Statistics*.

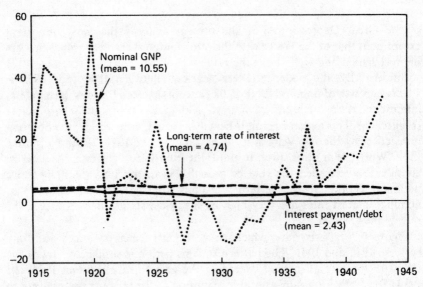

Figure 9.7   Italy.
Source: A. Confalonieri and E. Gatti, 'La politica del debito pubblico in Italia' (Cariplo-Laterza, 1986).

dominate those of the rates of interest. The latter appear as virtually constant, in spite of wide variations in nominal GNP. Only in the 1970s did they start to rise, first in line with inflation and then faster.

Overall, the data do not permit clear-cut general conclusions about the 'normal' relationship between growth and rates of interest: most of the time in the three countries that we have considered the latter falls short of the former. The opposite has none the less occurred for fairly long periods of time. Also, the unprecedented increase in interest rates of the 1970s and the 1980s appears to be more than a transient phenomenon and warrants concern about future developments of the relationship between debt and national income, unless adjustments are made to 'primary' balances.

9.5 THE ITALIAN EXPERIENCE

In Italy, the structure of the public finances changed very significantly between the 1960s and the 1970s. The continued growth in expenditure and in the deficit was accompanied in the past decade by monetisation of the public sector borrowing requirement and by reductions of the real value of the debt through inflation and exchange rate depreciation. During the 1980s, with a gradual tightening of monetary and exchange rate policies, inflation fell and real interest rates rose; the deficit was largely financed by direct acquisitions of government paper by the household sector. In 1985 it became evident that only a rigorous policy of fiscal recovery, centred on reducing the borrowing requirement net of interest payments to zero, would prevent problems of sustainability of the debt. A medium-term adjustment plan was adopted, which showed its effects in 1986, but was not pursued in 1987 – an election year – according to the objectives originally set.

The factors which led to Italy's growing budget deficit are shown in Tables 9.1 to 9.3 (on these points see also Spaventa (1984), Spaventa *et al.* (1984), Morcaldo and Salvemini (1984)).

Between 1960 and 1985 public sector revenues rose from 31 to 46 per cent of GDP,[5] largely because of increases in direct taxes and social security contributions. Expenditure, however, rose from 33 to 63 per cent, mainly because of rising transfer payments.[6] There was also a rise in financial transfers – with corresponding changes in public sector financial assets (on this point see Monti *et al.* (1983)). The divergence between revenue and expenditure trends widened progressively through the 1970s and has persisted in the 1980s; though it now owes more to the size of interest payments as a result of both higher real rates and the larger debt.

The current balance, which averaged a surplus of 1.7 per cent of GDP in the 1960s, recorded a deficit of between 7 and 8 per cent from 1981 to 1985. At the same time, net indebtedness rose from 2.7 to 14.2 per cent and the overall borrowing requirement from 3.6 to 17.5 per cent. The borrowing

Table 9.1 Public sector revenues (percentage of GDP)

	1960	1970	1980	1981	1982	1983	1984	1985	1986
Current revenues	31.2	32.1	38.1	39.9	42.7	45.7	44.8	45.5	46.3
direct taxes	5.5	5.6	11.1	12.8	14.3	15.8	15.2	15.5	15.3
indirect taxes	12.1	11.2	9.9	9.5	9.9	10.7	11.0	10.6	10.8
social security contributions	8.3	10.7	13.1	13.2	14.3	14.7	14.1	14.2	14.6
Capital account revenues	0.3	0.3	0.2	0.3	0.4	0.2	0.4	0.4	0.3
Total revenues	31.5	32.4	38.3	40.2	43.1	45.9	45.2	45.9	46.6

Table 9.2 Public sector expenditure (percentage of GDP)

	1960	1970	1980	1981	1982	1983	1984	1985	1986
Current expenditure	27.8	31.7	43.3	47.9	50.5	52.8	52.8	53.7	53.7
Operating costs	16.0	16.6	19.5	21.7	21.9	22.3	22.3	22.6	22.2
Interest payments	1.6	2.0	6.3	7.3	8.5	9.1	9.8	9.8	10.2
Transfer payments	10.2	13.1	17.4	18.9	20.1	21.5	20.7	21.3	21.4
Capital account expenditure	4.7	4.8	5.3	5.9	6.2	6.2	6.1	7.0	6.1
Total expenditure	32.5	36.5	48.6	53.8	56.7	59.0	58.0	60.7	59.9
Financial items*	0.7	0.6	2.3	0.7	2.6	4.2	2.2	1.9	0.7
Grand total	33.2	37.1	50.9	54.5	59.3	63.2	61.1	62.6	60.6
Health care†¶	3.1	4.7	6.0	5.8	6.1	6.3	6.1	6.3	6.1
Pensions‡¶	5.3	7.9	11.5	12.8	13.3	14.7	14.6	15.2	15.5

Source: Morcaldo and Zanchi (1984), and update.
† Total expenditure on current and capital account including the cost of administrative services.
‡ Including pensions (civil and war), payments to the blind, deaf-mutes and disabled persons.
¶ *Source*: ISTAT (1983).

Table 9.3 Public sector deficit (percentage of GDP)

	1960–69	1970–79	1980–86	1980	1981	1982	1983	1984	1985	1986
Deficit on current account	−1.7	4.2	7.4	5.2	8.0	7.8	7.1	8.0	8.2	7.4
Deficit	2.7	8.7	13.2	10.3	13.6	13.6	13.1	13.7	14.8	13.2
Overall borrowing requirement	3.6	11.0	15.1	11.1	13.4	16.3	16.8	16.6	17.5	14.4
Interest payments	1.6	3.9	8.7	6.3	7.3	8.5	9.1	9.8	9.8	10.2
Borrowing requirement less interest payments	2.0	7.1	6.4	4.8	6.1	7.8	7.7	6.8	7.7	4.2

Note: These and the following tables use old national accounts data. Revised figures are not yet available for the years preceding 1980.

requirement net of interest payments was less than 2 per cent in the 1960s, but averaged around 7 per cent in the following 15 years.

These developments concurred in 1985 to centre economic policy in fiscal rehabilitation. If the deficit, net of interest, had been held at the average values recorded in the years 1970–85 (about 7 per cent), even assuming that the real average rate of interest on the debt could be kept at levels of about 2.5 per cent, with output growing at an annual rate of 3 per cent, the theoretical equilibrium ceiling for the debt to income ratio would be 7%/ (3%–2.5%) = 14. It is evident that a ceiling of this level would have posed some of the problems discussed in Section 9.2 regarding credibility and concerns about the possibility of monetisation; the ensuing risk premium would have tilted the relationship between growth and interest rates.

As is well known, the nominal budget position does not represent an accurate measure of the thrust of fiscal policy. For this purpose, suitable adjustment must be made for inflation and the economic cycle.

The varying importance of monetary erosion from the early 1970s on is illustrated in Figure 9.8, which traces trends in the nominal public sector borrowing requirement and the corresponding change in real debt as a ratio to GDP. The note accompanying the figure explains that the area between the two lines represents monetary erosion, which increased from 1–2 per cent in the 1960s to 5–10 per cent in the 1970s and 1980s.

A similar picture emerges if reference is made to the 'inflation tax' – calculated as the algebraic sum of monetary erosion and nominal interest payments on the debt.[7] In the 1960s for the most part there were net transfers, albeit small ones, from the public sector to the rest of the economy. Average real interest rates were positive. The inflation tax reached its highest levels in 1974, 1976, 1979 and 1980, amounting to respectively 5.9, 6.6, 4.6 and 5.1 per cent of GDP. Thereafter the tax first shrank and then swung back into net positive transfers since 1983.

Having reviewed the figures for inflation correction in the Italian experience, let us now add some words of caution on their use. This approach is often wrongly used to derive one-sided indications about the strength and the sign of the fiscal impulses imparted by the nominal budget at a given moment. To look only at the budget figures corrected for inflation is to make the same mistake as those who consider only the growth rate of real monetary balances to assess monetary impulses. As we know, this kind of error has often led at the outset of hyperinflation to the conviction that monetary policy was actually playing a restrictive role!

That high inflation often significantly reduces the corrected budget deficit – or even turns it into a surplus – does not justify concluding that if there is a drop in inflation the budget will automatically return to balance. Apart from any other considerations, at least the trends that actually affect the items of the budget over a given period of time must be taken into account. An exercise along these lines has been undertaken to show the need for fiscal adjustment and will be presented below.

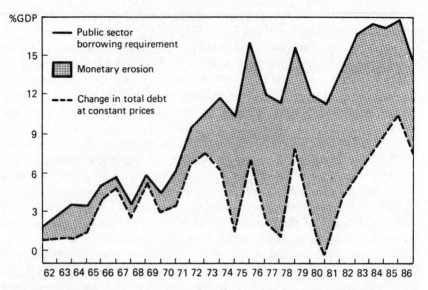

Figure 9.8   Public sector borrowing requirement (general government and autonomous agencies) and changes in total debt.
Note: The public sector borrowing requirement is broken down into two components for accounting purposes: the change in the corresponding gross debt at constant prices as a share of real GDP and the monetary erosion of the stock of debt at current prices at the beginning of the period as a ratio of nominal GDP.

$$\frac{FB}{Y} = \left(\frac{1}{y}\right) \Delta d + \left(\frac{1}{Y}\right) D_{-1}\pi$$

where $FB = D - D_{-1}$ is the gross nominal borrowing requirement, Y is the nominal GDP, y is the real GDP, d is the gross debt at constant prices, D is the gross debt at current prices, $\pi = (P - P_{-1})/P_{-1}$ is the inflation rate and $p =$ GDP deflator.

The definition of the structural budget surplus or deficit should also take cyclical fluctuations into account. Moreover, for an open economy, like Italy's, reference to the concept of sustainable potential income would have to take the external constraint explicitly into account. Since present methodology is largely based on the US economy, it does not give this element the consideration it requires.

Even if the nominal adjustments for both inflation and the cycle are made, and neglecting the caveats just formulated, the deficit of the Italian public sector remains exceedingly high.

We come now to a second set of considerations on the sustainability of budget deficits, hingeing on the analysis of the implications of the budget constraint for the creation of financial assets and monetary base (on this point see also Arcelli and Valiani, 1981).

Using a flow-of-funds approach at current prices, it is possible to identify the links between total flows of financial assets and the channels of creation, one of which is the borrowing requirement (ΔD).

$$\Delta AF = \Delta AFI + \Delta AFE \tag{9.28}$$

$$\Delta AFI = \Delta D + \Delta PFI + BP = \Delta CTI + BP \tag{9.29}$$

where AF is total financial assets, AFI is domestic financial assets, AFE is foreign financial assets, PFI is the domestic indebtedness of firms and households, BP is the balance of payments and CTI is total domestic credit.[8]

Equation (9.28) shows how the public sector borrowing requirement contributes to the creation of financial assets. This is detailed with reference to the Italian experience in Table 9.4, which shows the increasing importance of the fiscal deficit in the creation of domestic financial assets.[9]

In the 1960s, while average annual increases of 5.8 and 4 per cent were recorded in real GDP and consumer prices, domestic financial assets expanded by an average rate of 13.4 per cent. The public debt grew at a rate of 8.6 per cent, and accounted for only one-fifth of the total expansion of financial assets. In the succeeding decade, growth in real product almost halved, dropping to 3.3 per cent, while consumer prices rose at an average rate of about 13.5 per cent, almost four times higher; financial assets recorded a growth rate of 18.9 per cent, five points up on the 1960s rate. Deficits pushed up the public debt at an average rate of 23.6 per cent, and accounted for about half the overall creation of domestic financial assets.

In the six-year period from 1980 to 1985 domestic financial assets expanded at a rate slightly lower than that recorded in the 1970s, while the public debt grew marginally faster, at an annual rate of closer to 24 per cent. As a result of the latter and the growing share of public debt instruments in financial assets, the public deficit accounted for more than 70 per cent of the creation of domestic financial assets. A similar picture emerges from Table 9.5, where the calculations just described are repeated for total domestic credit and the state's share.

On average, between 1971 and 1980 the rapid growth of total financial assets was matched by corresponding increases in the adjusted monetary base and in nominal output. As a result, the ratio of the private sector's financial assets to GDP was roughly the same in the first and last years of the ten-year period.

At the turn of the 1970s, it gradually became obvious that the public had become aware of the inflation tax and was reacting to the rise in prices by substantially reducing its rate of financial saving. The rate of net financial saving appropriately corrected for inflation (see Lecaldano, Marotta and Masera, 1985) averaged 10.7 per cent during the 1970–72 period, i.e. before the inflationary wave. Between 1973 and 1978 the average rate was 2.5 per cent; in 1979 and 1980 it declined to -0.2 and -4.1 per cent respectively.

Table 9.4 Domestic financial assets: growth rate and share 'explained' by the state-sector debt

	1960–69	1970–79	1980–85	1980	1981	1982	1983	1984	1985	1986
			Average growth rate throughout the period							
Domestic financial assets	13.4	18.9	18.3	15.8	17.8	19.0	20.5	19.1	17.7	16.9
State-sector debt	8.6	23.6	23.9	20.9	22.9	28.0	27.1	22.8	21.8	17.6
Share* 'explained' by the state-sector debt	20.8	47.7	72.2	64.2	65.2	79.2	76.0	70.8	77.5	67.7
Memorandum items										
Real GDP	5.8	3.3	1.4	3.9	0.1	−0.5	−0.4	2.6	2.7	2.7
Nominal GDP	10.9	17.2	16.5	25.4	18.5	17.2	14.6	11.5	11.8	11.0
Consumer prices	4.0	13.5	15.0	21.2	17.8	16.5	14.7	10.8	9.2	5.9

* Proportion of change in domestic financial assets represented by the change in state-sector debt.

Table 9.5 Total domestic credit: growth rates and share 'explained' by the state-sector debt

	1960–69	1970–79	1980–85	1980	1981	1982	1983	1984	1985	1986
				Average growth rate throughout the period						
Total domestic credit	13.6	18.9	19.4	18.6	18.1	20.9	20.7	20.2	18.1	15.1
State-sector debt	8.6	23.6	23.9	20.9	22.9	28.0	27.1	22.8	21.8	17.6
Share* 'explained' by the state-sector debt	21.1	44.3	64.8	53.8	61.7	68.7	71.0	64.1	69.8	69.8

* Proportion of change in total domestic credit represented by the change in state-sector debt.

In these circumstances, it was only with a tightening of monetary policy that savers were enticed to return to financial saving, and notably to direct acquisitions of government bonds. The required portfolio shifts were accompanied by progressively rising real rates of interest.

Empirical evidence on Italy over the last decade, obtained by adjusting both the disposable income and the final savings of the household sector for purchasing power losses on financial assets, suggests that changes in the real rate of interest on financial assets exerted a noticeable effect on financial saving. This effect is partly due to a reallocation of existing wealth between financial and non-financial assets and partly to the change in the allocation of new savings (see Lecaldano, Marotta and Masera, 1985). In 1980, when the average real yield on the total financial assets held by the household sector was around − 8 per cent, the share of disposable income devoted to financial saving was around three percentage points below that required to maintain the purchasing power of the initial stock of financial assets. By contrast, in 1984–6, when the average yield climbed back to positive values in real terms, the share of income allocated to financial asset accumulation (notably government paper) was some 10 percentage points above that required to restore the initial purchasing power.

In the years 1973–4 some four-fifths of households' financial saving went into monetary (M2) assets. Ten years later, the proportion had fallen to less than two-fifths. Treasury and other medium- and long-term bonds, which ten years ago accounted for one-tenth of financial saving, now represent about one-half. The private sector's holdings of domestic financial assets rose as a ratio to GDP from 1.11 in 1981 to 1.40 in 1986.

Here again, however, it is evident that the situation is not a stable one. The portfolio distortions implicit in a situation where savers are called upon to hold an increasing proportion (a) of their wealth in financial assets, and (b) of their financial assets in government bonds do not appear sustainable beyond the medium term. Higher yields on a growing proportion of financial assets trigger the risks of dynamic instability already alluded to.

The Italian system provides the Treasury with direct access to the central bank, via its current account overdraft facility. The amount of this facility is fixed by law (a ceiling of 14 per cent of each year's original spending estimates and subsequent modifications). Obviously, this legislative provision could easily be circumvented if the Bank of Italy did not have full discretionary powers to decide on the amount of its purchases of government securities in order to keep the overall expansion of Treasury monetary base in line with targeted monetary and credit flows. In principle, the central bank can control the Treasury's overall creation of monetary base by its net purchases of government securities (at issue or on the open market). Until the 'divorce' in 1980, this control was, however, limited by the Bank of Italy's commitment to purchase all Treasury bills not sold at issue (see Capriglione (1987), especially on changes in the way Treasury bills have been issued).

Table 9.6 Monetary base: growth rates and share 'explained' by the Treasury

	1960–69	1970–79	1980–85	1980	1981	1982	1983	1984	1985	1986
			Average growth rate throughout the period							
Monetary base	9.1	17.1	14.7	13.8	13.3	14.1	15.0	14.4	17.3	7.1
Treasury monetary base	8.4	21.8	19.9	23.5	27.8	19.5	5.9	12.3	30.1	9.2
Memorandum										
Adjusted monetary base	10.2	16.2	13.0	13.0	11.7	12.7	13.3	12.5	14.6	5.8
Share* 'explained' by the Treasury	57.6	79.0	108.8	123.8	164.8	122.6	35.8	72.4	144.3	119.5

* Proportion of change in monetary base represented by the change in monetary base created by the Treasury.

The data of Table 9.6 show that, starting in the early 1970s, the Treasury has played a dominant role in the creation of monetary base; they also show that the central bank has enjoyed a significant degree of freedom since the 'divorce'.

Between 1960 and 1969, the average growth rate of the monetary base was 9 per cent (10 per cent when adjusted for changes in the compulsory reserve ratio) (see Zautzik (1982) on the adjustment of the monetary base in Italy). The Treasury component grew at a slightly lower rate, accounting for 60 per cent of the growth of the total aggregate. In the following decade the average growth rate reached 22 per cent: overall expansion was held below this rate by destroying monetary base through other channels. From 1980 to 1985, despite further increases in the budget deficit and the expansion of 24 per cent in the public debt, the rate of growth of the monetary base slowed to 13.0 per cent on an adjusted basis.

The ratio of the growth rate of the 'adjusted' base to the growth rate of government debt, as a component of *AFI*, can be taken to represent an indicator of monetary 'friction' in portfolio accumulation. In the 1960s the ratio on average was 1.1, declining to 0.68 in the 1970s and 0.5 in the period 1980–86.

Table 9.7 reports some projections of the debt to GDP ratio obtained using formula (9.1) of Section 9.2. The entries of the table are values of the ratio of the total debt of the central government to GDP (using again the old national accounts) in three selected years and, when relevant, in the steady

Table 9.7   Ratio of central government debt to GDP

$g - m\hat{M}$	Year	$\hat{y} - r$					
		-0.025	-0.015	-0.005	$+0.005$	$+0.015$	$+0.025$
0.02	1990	1.19	1.14	1.10	1.05	1.02	0.98
	1995	1.43	1.31	1.22	1.13	1.05	0.98
	2000	1.70	1.50	1.35	1.20	1.09	0.98
	Steady state	—	—	—	4.19	1.52	0.99
0.04	1990	1.29	1.24	1.20	1.15	1.11	1.07
	1995	1.65	1.53	1.43	1.33	1.24	1.16
	2000	2.06	1.84	1.66	1.50	1.35	1.23
	Steady state	—	—	—	8.19	2.85	1.79
0.06	1990	1.40	1.35	1.30	1.25	1.21	1.17
	1995	1.88	1.75	1.63	1.52	1.42	1.33
	2000	2.42	2.18	1.97	1.72	1.62	1.48
	Steady state	—	—	—	12.19	4.19	2.59

Note: These results are obtained using formula (9.1) of the text with initial condition equal to 0.957.

state. The state of the system at any date depends on the initial condition (set at 0.957, the 1986 debt to GDP ratio), on $g - m\hat{M}$, the primary deficit (g) net of seignorage ($m\hat{M}$) (which is allowed to vary from 0.02 to 0.06) and on $\hat{y} - r$, the excess of the rate of growth over the real rate of interest on the debt (from -0.025 to $+0.025$).

Debt developments are clearly very sensitive to assumptions about both variables. The most pessimistic case is $\hat{y} - r = -0.025$ and $g - m\hat{M} = 0.06$; the debt would reach 240 per cent of GDP by the year 2000.

The values of g (primary deficit) and m (ratio of Treasury monetary base to GDP) in 1986 were 0.056 and 0.17 respectively. A growth of the monetary base of, say, 9 per cent per year would imply $g - m\hat{M} = 0.04$. Looking at the middle row ($g - m\hat{M} = 0.04$) one finds values ranging from 1.2 to 2 in the year 2000 depending on $\hat{y} - r$. At present, the real rate of interest on long-term government paper is considerably in excess of the growth of income; even if the average rate on government debt could be kept in line with GDP growth, the debt would still grow and reach about 150 per cent of GDP by the end of the century.[10]

Setting g constant and equal to its 1986 value is in one sense overly pessimistic because reducing the deficit is a priority target of the government. It does, however, require significant structural adjustments to fiscal parameters. In particular, demographic trends are likely to produce in the next few years considerable further pressure on social security spending (see Franco and Morcaldo, 1986).

It is thus not a forecast, but a simple projection that indicates that, on current trends, the debt would hardly be below 150 per cent of GDP by the year 2000. Such projections largely accord with those of Morcaldo and Salvemini (1984), who use a formula similar to (9.1) with money a constant share of the deficit. They also accord with the results of Cividini, Galli and Masera (1987), who perform simulations with the econometric model of the Bank of Italy (vintage summer 1986); the latters' assumptions and main results are briefly summarised here.

In their 'base run', they assume:

(a) $g = 0.056$.
(b) Growth of world trade $= 3.5$ per cent per year.
(c) Foreign inflation $= 3$ per cent (same for finished goods and raw materials).
(d) World real rate of interest $= 4.5$ per cent.
(e) Fixed nominal exchange rate of the lira.

Under capital mobility, the assumed exchange rate rule fixes the domestic nominal rate of interest and the rate of growth and the monetary base.

With these assumptions, the debt to GDP ratio turns out to be 1.21, 1.57 and 1.91 in 1990, 1995 and 2000 respectively. It is equal, instead, to 1.15, 1.41 and 1.48 in those three years if assumption (e) above is replaced by a rule that keeps the real exchange rate fixed at its 1986 level. This rule accommodates any domestic wage–price pressure and results in inflation rising steadily and reaching 18 per cent at the end of the period (while it stays around 3.5 per cent in the base run). This fact and a moderately higher growth of GDP than in the base run (3.2 per cent on average against 2.7 in the base run) are responsible for the lower growth of the debt in the simulation in which the real rate of exchange is held constant.

The dilemma confronting the authorities may be in fact more acute than suggested by these projections, because of adverse shifts in the key relationship between interest rates and growth. If monetary growth is gradually restrained in line with the objective of disinflation and deceleration in nominal income expansion, the absorption of government securities in private portfolios may well require increasing real rates of interest, with adverse effects on investment and income growth; ultimately, this policy may indeed prove ineffectual in containing aggregate demand because of the working of the income effect on consumer spending. But even before that critical point is reached, the balance between growth and real interest rates on the debt may be tilted towards instability. On the other hand, monetary financing of the deficit would make it impossible to pursue the goal of non-inflationary growth. And, as has been pointed out, the risks implicit in monetisation are now much greater than during the 1970s.

We come to the conclusion that unless a policy of fiscal responsibility is pursued the economy runs the risk of being tossed in the short term between the Charybdis of stagnation and the Scylla of inflation; beyond that the situation of public finances would anyhow be unsustainable.

9.6 CONCLUSIONS

The debate on public debt and deficits is a time-honoured one in economics. Barro's equivalence theorem is, wrongly, associated with the position taken over a century ago by Ricardo. Fifty years ago Pigou on the one hand and Keynes and Hawtrey on the other – albeit with important differences in the latters' respective positions – were discussing broadly the same problems which are being analysed in this volume.

If the line is taken that the economic system is self-righting the role and significance of fiscal policy is necessarily reduced; in particular it is clear that public deficit spending ultimately crowds out corresponding private expenditure.

In this chapter we have not taken this line – which we do not regard as warranted – and instead have developed a simple theoretical model, which we believe to be capable of capturing some important features of the interactions between debt, deficits and economic activity in an open economy framework.

The question of sustainability of the public debt is a complex one in this approach. The short-term effects of deficits and debts on total demand are present and, in principle, are of a traditional nature. The lure of demand and exchange rate management must, however, be carefully weighted in the light of longer-term considerations: the debt/income ratio must be sustainable over time in a non-inflationary environment.

The crucial relationship in this respect is that between growth and debt interest rates. Following this approach, and coming to the experience in Italy, we show how the debt/income ratio evolved in the 1970s and in the 1980s. After a period when resort was made to monetary financing of the deficits and to the inflation tax, non-accommodating monetary policy has gradually brought to the fore the unsustainability of fiscal parameters.

The inherited imbalances are so large that they cannot be cured even if it proved possible to maintain a sustained rate of growth up to the end of the century with the real rate of interest on the debt constant at present levels. It is indicated, however, that such an assumption is clearly untenable: interest rates would tend to rise to permit the absorption of an ever-increasing share of government securities in private portfolios.

The chapter shows therefore that, under present Italian conditions, the primary concern of economic policy must be to redress the budget. This implies that the deficit net of interest should be brought to zero: this was in fact the objective set out by the Government in its 1985 three-year plan of fiscal adjustment. Care must be taken to avoid unleashing sharp deflationary forces, lest the dynamic relationship between growth and interest be adversely affected. From this point of view gradual adjustment is preferable with respect to a shock treatment. But any relaxation – and even worse reversal – of the adjustment effort might precipitate the system towards a crisis. As was recalled developments in 1987 are not in line with the 1985 plan. The financial bill for 1988 represents therefore a crucial test for the sustainability of debt along a non-inflationary path.

It must be stressed that monetary policy can hardly continue to sustain a process of disinflation in the absence of fiscal adjustment. Also as a result of the liberalisation of capital movements, increasing yields on domestic debt would become necessary to force the acquisition of government securities in private portfolios. Interest rates in real terms are already high in comparison with other industrial countries. Apart from the adverse impact this policy has on investment growth, it may prove ineffectual in containing aggregate demand in the medium term because of the income effect on consumption.

On the other hand, it would not be possible to reduce the short-term cost of the adjustment needed in the Italian economy by monetary accommodation of the deficits, i.e. by resorting to the inflation tax again. This might, of course, be a temptation because, as the experience of many countries shows, when inflation rises, real interest rates tend to decline, at least temporarily (see, for instance, Galli and Masera, 1983). Quite apart from any other considerations, the public debt has doubled, as a ratio to income to close on 100 per cent. Furthermore, nearly all government debt is now either short term or at variable rates of interest. Finally, savers have become extremely alert to the real return on the assets in their portfolios. A renewed acceleration of prices would push them away from financial assets into housing, consumer durables and foreign assets. The latter shift would be especially important as a result of the progressive liberalisation of capital movements. The experience of the 1970s would be repeated, with the risk of seeing the rate of price changes accelerate above the levels reached in that decade.

APPENDIX 9.1

To see that a depreciation is in fact required (i.e. the SS' line lies south of point E) we need to write the intertemporal budget constraints for consumers and for the whole economy (which, together, imply the intertemporal budget constraint of the government)

$$w(t_0) + \frac{\bar{y} - \tau}{r^*} = \frac{1}{\alpha\gamma} PV(t_0) \tag{A.1}$$

$$f(t_0)z + \frac{xz^\sigma}{r^*} = \frac{1-\gamma}{\gamma} PV(t_0) \tag{A.2}$$

where PV is the present value of domestic consumption.

Equation (A.1) states that initial wealth plus the present value of non-interest income must equal the present value of total consumer expenditure (including money); since $c = \alpha\gamma e$ (eqn (9.11)), the latter is simply equal to the present value of domestic consumption (c) divided by $\alpha\gamma$.

Equation (A.2) states that the initial value of foreign assets plus the present value of exports is equal to the present value of imports; since, from eqns (9.11) and (9.12), $zc^* = ((1-\gamma)/\gamma)c$, the latter is equal to the present value of domestic consumption multiplied by $(1-\gamma)/\gamma$. Solving for $PV(t_0)$ from (A.1), substituting in (A.2) and recalling $w = d + zf$, yields

$$zf(t_0)[1 - \alpha)(1-\gamma)] + \frac{xz^\sigma}{r^*} = (1-\gamma)\alpha \left[d(t_0) + \frac{\bar{y} - \tau}{r^*} \right] \tag{A.3}$$

(A.3) holds in any initial steady state. After a shock, however, it will generally not be satisfied unless z is at the right level; the latter can be found by differentiating with respect to r^* and z:

$$\frac{dz/z}{dr^*/r^*} = \frac{(1-\gamma)\alpha \, d(t_0) - zf(t_0)[1 - \alpha(1-\gamma)]}{zf(t_0)[1 - \alpha(1-\gamma)] + \sigma(xz^\sigma/r^*)} \tag{A.4}$$

Starting from a position of balanced trade (which implies $f(t_0) = 0$, as it has been assumed in the discussion so far) or close to it, dz/dr^* is positive; it follows that a depreciation is initially required. An appreciation may instead be required in some rather uninteresting cases which occur if the initial foreign position is very large relative to the domestic debt. If it is large and negative, the denominator of (A.4) becomes negative; a necessary condition for this to occur is that the extended Marshall–Lerner condition fails (i.e. depreciation, though improving the trade balance, worsens the current account through the effect on the valuation of foreign debt). In this case an appreciation is the way to increase wealth and therefore consumption and the net surplus of the public sector.

If the foreign position is large and positive, the numerator of (A.4) is negative. Recalling that $zc^* = \alpha(1-\gamma)e$ (eqn (9.12)), the condition that the numerator be negative can be expressed as $w/e < f/c^*$, i.e. the ratio of wealth to expenditure is smaller than the ratio between foreign assets and imports; this circumstance is unlikely to occur in practice but cannot be ruled out on purely mathematical grounds. In this case the increase in the rate of interest does not significantly worsen the public sector budget (because the debt is relatively small) which instead benefits (in present value sense) from the increase in future consumption.

APPENDIX 9.2

In order to solve the model of the second example in Section 9.3.2, we start by noting that with zero initial foreign assets, the zero current account assumption implies

$$xz^\sigma = \frac{(1-\gamma)}{\gamma}c \tag{A.5}$$

Substituting eqn (A.5) in eqn (9.15), we have

$$y = \frac{c}{\gamma} + g \tag{A.6}$$

Along eqn (A.6) the goods market is in equilibrium and the current account is equal to zero.

Substituting eqn (A.5), log differentiated with respect to time, and eqn (A.6) in the price dynamics eqn (9.18), yields

$$\ddot{p} = \varphi(y - \bar{y}) + (1-\gamma)\hat{z} = \varphi\left(\frac{c}{\gamma} + g - \bar{y}\right) + (1-\gamma)\frac{\hat{c}}{\sigma} \tag{A.7}$$

Solving for g and using a dummy variable β, which can be either 0 or 1, we write

$$g = \bar{y} - \frac{c}{\gamma} + \frac{\beta}{\varphi}\left[\ddot{p} - (1-\gamma)\frac{\hat{c}}{\sigma}\right] \tag{A.8}$$

If $\beta = 0$, g will always be such as to maintain $y = \bar{y}$. If it is equal to 1, g is used to target $\ddot{p}$. The latter variable will always be zero in the steady state, but may transitorily be positive or negative. The particular parametrisation of (9.28) allows consideration of fixed employment ('liberal') and fixed inflation ('conservative') strategies.

The model can be solved as follows. From eqns (9.11) and (9.13), we get

$$(r + \ddot{p})m = \frac{1-\alpha}{\alpha\gamma}c \tag{A.9}$$

Let $\delta = (d/c)(=(w/c))$; differentiating (9.8), using (9.9), (9.10) and (A.9), the dynamics of consumption can be written as

$$\hat{c} = (r - \theta) - \alpha\gamma\pi(\theta + \pi)\delta \tag{A.10}$$

From (9.14) and (A.5), we get

$$r = r^* + \hat{z} = r^* + \frac{\hat{c}}{\sigma} \tag{A.11}$$

Substituting (A.11) in (A.20) yields the basic differential equation for consumption

$$\hat{c} = \frac{\sigma}{\sigma - 1} [(r^* - \theta) - \alpha\gamma\pi(\theta + \pi)\delta] \tag{A.12}$$

Substituting (A.8) and (A.11) into the public sector budget constraint (eqn (9.16)), using expression (A.12) for $\hat{c}$ and expressing the result in terms of δ, yields the basic dynamic equation for the debt to consumption ratio.

$$\dot{\delta} = \theta\delta + \alpha\gamma\pi(\theta + \pi)\delta^2 \quad + \frac{1}{c}\left[\bar{y} - \tau + \frac{\beta\ddot{p}}{\varphi} - \frac{(r^* - \theta)(1 - \gamma)\beta}{\varphi(\sigma - 1)}\right]$$

$$+ \frac{\delta}{c}\left[\frac{\beta(1 - \gamma)\alpha\gamma\pi(\theta + \pi)}{\varphi(\sigma - 1)}\right] - \frac{1}{\alpha\gamma}$$

The $\dot{\delta} = 0$ locus is

$$c = \frac{\bar{y} - \tau + \beta\left[\dfrac{\ddot{p}}{\varphi} - \dfrac{(r^* - \theta)(1 - \gamma)}{\varphi(\sigma - 1)}\right] + \delta\dfrac{\alpha\gamma\pi(\theta + \pi)(1 - \gamma)\beta}{\varphi(\sigma - 1)}}{\dfrac{1}{\alpha\gamma} - \theta\delta - \alpha\gamma\pi(\theta + \pi)\delta^2} \tag{A.14}$$

From eqn (A.12), the $\hat{c} = 0$ locus is

$$\delta = \frac{r^* - \theta}{\alpha\gamma\pi(\theta + \pi)} \tag{A.15}$$

With $\ddot{p} = 0$, the phase diagram of the system is as shown in Figure A.1. The $\hat{c} = 0$ locus is vertical. With $\sigma > 1$ to its left consumption rises and vice versa. Regardless of the value of β, the $\delta = 0$ locus is upward sloping with a positive second derivative and a vertical asymptote at $\delta = \delta^+ = 1/\alpha\gamma(\theta + \pi)$, where δ^+ is the (unique) positive root of the denominator of eqn (A.10). Using (A.15) and (A.14) yields the steady-state level of consumption (independently of β)

$$\bar{c} = (\bar{y} - \tau)\frac{\alpha\gamma\pi(\theta + \pi)}{(\pi + r^*)(\theta + \pi - r^*)} \tag{A.16}$$

From (A.15) and (A.16) $\bar{c}$ and $\bar{\delta}$ positive require condition (9.23), which also ensures $\bar{\delta} < \delta^+$. The direction of motion is unstable around both $\delta = 0$ loci. Under condition (9.23) equilibrium exists and is unique; with $\sigma > 1$, it is (saddle) stable. When $\beta = 1$, the

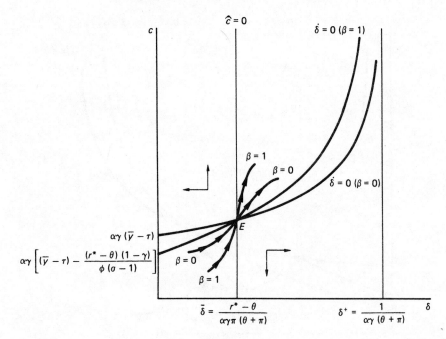

Figure A.1

$\delta = 0$ locus has a smaller intercept, is steeper and determines a correspondingly steeper saddle path than when $\beta = 0$.

Consider the effects of an increase in the foreign real rate of interest r^* (Figure A.2). The $\hat{c} = 0$ locus shifts to the right ($\hat{c}' = 0$). The $\delta = 0$ locus with $\beta = 0$ is unaffected. Equilibrium hence shifts from E to E' where both c and δ are higher. The $\delta = 0$ locus with $\beta = 1$ shifts down at the intercept and crosses the $\hat{c}' = 0$ locus at E'.

Consider first the $\beta = 0$ strategy. Initially consumption falls from E to A along an equilateral hyperbolis defined by $c = d/\delta$ (because the debt, not its ratio to consumption, is the predetermined variable of the system). The reason is that labour income is discounted at a higher rate (h falls in eqn (9.8)). Since, by assumption $\bar{y} = y = (c/\gamma) + g$, as c falls g rises. The deficit turns positive because of higher interest payments, lower money demand and also because, to avoid a fall in employment, 'liberal' authorities increase spending. The exchange rate appreciates.

The adjustment from A to E' can be described as follows.

Deficits increase non-human wealth and life-cycle consumption (see eqn (9.8) again). At the new level of the exchange rate, if g did not fall, the rise in the domestic debt would spill over into an increase in foreign debt. The fiscal authorities are then under pressure to reduce the deficit while the monetary authorities to devalue. If the whole burden of the external adjustment fell on fiscal policy, aggregate demand would decline and the monetary authorities would again be under pressure to devalue in order to crowd in net exports.

If, however, the right mix between the two policies is hit, employment remains constant. Along the adjustment path inflation increases since $y = \bar{y}$ and $\hat{z} > 0$.

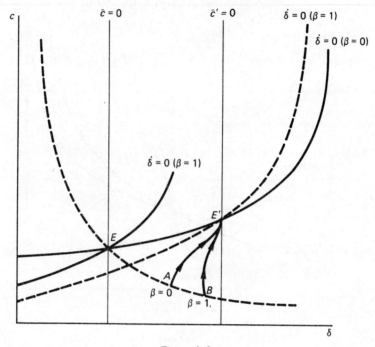

Figure A.2

Under a conservative strategy instead, the authorities initially let aggregate demand fall along with (although not necessarily as much as) consumption. At point *B* consumption is lower than at point *A* because of lower expected non-interest income: in other words there is a Keynesian multiplier effect. From *B* to *E'* the deficit is reduced, consumption and employment rise, the exchange rate depreciates and inflation is fixed.

Across steady states a higher real rate of interest pushes up the domestic debt. There is no need to reduce the deficit to the extent of keeping the debt constant, because, at the higher interest rate, consumers are willing to absorb a larger amount of financial wealth. The debt consequently rises, while foreign assets are kept at their target level.

Acknowledgements

We thank William Branson and an anonymous referee for helpful comments.

Notes

1. The extremely rarefied set of assumptions which have to be satisfied for the equivalence proposition to hold have been spelt out in detail to show its limited practical relevance by Buiter (1985).
2. The implicit assumption is that *y* is produced by labour with constant returns to scale.

3. Suppose that workers and firms negotiate over expected real wages, i.e.

$$\Delta\omega_{t+1} - {}_t\Delta p^c_{t+1} = \varphi(\cdot)$$

where ω_t is the nominal wage and ${}_t\Delta p^c_{t+1}$ the rate of *CPI* inflation expected at t for the period between t and $t+1$. Equation (9.19) is immediately derived under the assumptions of static expectations about the rate of inflation (${}_t\Delta p^c_{t+1} = \Delta p^c_t$) and mark-up pricing.

4. If net foreign assets are non-zero the initial level of wealth will change with the exchange rate so that the system may jump to a different point on the *AE'* line.

5. Reference is made in this study to the 'old' national accounts. In 1987 Italian GDP was substantially revised with respect to the old series. Consistent data going back to the 1970s are not yet available.

6. By aggregating current contributions to production, payments to the Wage Supplementation Fund, state assumption of certain employer social security contributions, capital account transfers to state-controlled companies and net financing to the non-state sector, we get the expenditure for private and public enterprises (see Alvaro, 1984). This increased from 2980 billion lire in 1964 to 45 900 billion in 1983, and from 2.7 per cent to 9.7 per cent of GDP.

7. Keynes (1923, ch. 2) was the first to make a complete investigation of inflation as an instrument of taxation. Einaudi (e.g. 1944) concurred in this approach, which Baffi (1974) developed in an important analytical and empirical study (with reference to the Italian experience see also Masera, 1979; Cotula and Masera, 1980; Masera, 1987).

8. For an examination of this approach, see Cotula and de' Stefani (1979, ch. xxv), Caranza and Fazio (1983), Vaciago (1983) and Cottarelli *et al.* (1986). In relating equations (9.28) and (9.29), the foreign indebtedness of the public sector has been left out for the sake of simplicity. This can be done in the case of Italy, in view of the relative unimportance of this item so far.

9. In conformity with total domestic credit accounting practices, Table 9.4 and subsequent tables refer to the state-sector deficit and debt.

10. When this calculation is repeated on the basis of the new national accounts, the debt still rises from 90 to 130 per cent of GDP over the same period.

References

ALESINA, A. (1987) 'The End of Large Public Debts', Paper prepared for the conference 'Surviving with High Public Debts: Lessons from the Italian Experience', Castelgandolfo (Italy), June.

ALVARO, G. (1984) 'La finanza pubblica nel sistema economico italiano', in *La finanza pubblica in Italia: stato e prospettive* (Milano: F. Angeli).

ARCELLI, M. and R. VALIANI (1981) 'Il finanziamento del fabbisogno del settore pubblico', *Rivista di politica economica*, December.

BAFFI, P. (1974) 'Il risparmio in Italia, oggi', *Bancaria*, vol. 2, February.

BANCA D'ITALIA (1986) 'Modello trimestrale dell'economia italiana', vols I and II, *Temi di discussione*, 80, December.

BARNETT, W. (1980) 'Economic Monetary Aggregates', *Journal of Econometrics*, 14.

BARRO, R. (1987) *Macroeconomics*, 2nd edn (New York: Wiley).

BLANCHARD, O. (1985) 'Debt, Deficits, and Finite Horizons', *Journal of Political Economy*, April.

BLANCHARD, O., R. DORNBUSCH and W. BUITER (1985) 'Public Debt and Fiscal Responsibility', *Ceps Papers*, 22.

BUITER, W. (1985) 'A Guide to Public Sector Debt and Deficits', *Economic Policy*, November.

CAPRIGLIONE, F. (1987) 'Buoni e certificati di credito del Tesoro', *Enciclopedia Giuridica*.

CARANZA, C. and A. FAZIO (1983) 'L'evoluzione dei metodi di controllo monetario in Italia: 1974–1983', *Bancaria*, vol. 39, pp. 819–33.

CIVIDINI, A., G. GALLI and R. S. MASERA (1987) 'Vincolo di bilancio e sostenibilità del debito: analisi e prospettive', in *Debito pubblico e politica economica in Italia*, a cura di F. Bruni, Collana Giorgio Rota, Ricerca n. 1.

CONFALONIERI, A. and E. GATTI (1986) 'La politica del debito pubblico in Italia' (Cariplo-Laterza).

COTTARELLI, C., G. GALLI, P. R. MARULLO and G. PITTALUGA (1986) 'Monetary Policy Through Ceilings on Bank Lending', *Economic Policy*, 3, October.

COTULA, F. and P. DE' STEFANI (1979) *La politica monetaria in Italia: istituti e strumenti* (Bologna: Il Mulino).

COTULA, F. and R. S. MASERA (1980) 'Private Savings, Public Deficits and the Inflation Tax', *Review of Economic Conditions in Italy*, vol. 3, October.

CUDDINGTON, J. and J. VIÑALS (1986) 'Budget Deficits and the Current Account', *Journal of International Economics*, vol. 21.

DARBY, M. R. (1984) 'Some Pleasant Monetarist Arithmetic', NBER Working Paper no. 1295, March.

DIAMOND, P. (1965) 'National Debt in a Neoclassical Growth of Model', *American Economic Review*, vol. 5, December.

DOMAR, E. (1944) 'The Burden of the Debt and National Income', *American Economic Review*, December.

DORNBUSCH, R. (1986) 'Exchange Rate Economics: 1986', NBER Working Paper no. 2071, November.

EINAUDI, L. (1944) *I problemi economici della Federazione europea* (Lugano: Nuove Edizioni di Capolago).

FEINSTEIN, C. H. (1972) *National Income Expenditure and Output (1855–1965)* (Oxford: OUP).

FRANCO, D. and G. MORCALDO (1986) *Un modello di previsione degli squilibri del sistema previdenziale*, Ministero del Tesoro – Commissione Tecnica per la Spesa Pubblica, Istituto Poligrafico e Zecca dello Stato.

FRENKEL, J. and A. RAZIN (1984) 'Fiscal Policies, Debt and International Independence', NBER Working Paper no. 1266.

FRIEDMAN, M. (1968) 'The Role of Monetary Policy', *American Economic Review*, March.

GALLI, G. (1985) 'Tasso reale, crescita e sostenibilità del debito pubblico', *Banca d'Italia, Contributi all'analisi economica*, no. 1.

GALLI, G. and R. S. MASERA (1983) 'Real Rate of Interest and Public Sector Deficits: an Empirical Investigation', *Economic Notes*, vol. 3.

GEANAKOPLOS, J. D. and H. M. POLEMARCHAKIS (1986) 'Walrasian Indeterminacy and Keynesian Macroeconomics', *Review of Economic Studies*, vol. LIII, pp. 755–79.

IBBOTSON, R. G. and R. A. SINQUEFIELD (1982) *Stock, Bonds, Bills and Inflation: The Past and the Future*, Charlottesville (Va.), The Financial Analysts Research Foundation.

ISTAT (1983) 'I conti della protezione sociale', Supplement to the *Monthly Bulletin of Statistics*, no. 28.

KEYNES, J. M. (1923) *A Tract on Monetary Reform* (London: Macmillan).
KEYNES, J. M. (1936) *The General Theory of Employment, Interest and Money* (London: Macmillan).
KEYNES, J. M. (1963) *Essays in Persuasion* (New York: Norton).
LECALDANO, E., G. MAROTTA and R. S. MASERA (1985) 'Households' Saving and the Real Rate of Interest: The Italian Experience, 1970–1983', *Banca d'Italia, Temi di discussione*, no. 47, May.
LUCAS, R. and N. STOCKEY (1983) 'Optimal Fiscal and Monetary Policy in an Economy without Capital', *Journal of Monetary Economics*, vol. 12.
LUCAS, R. (1986) 'Principles of Fiscal and Monetary Policy', *Journal of Monetary Economics*, January.
MASERA, R. S. (1979) 'Disavanzo pubblico e vincolo di bilancio' (Milano: Edizioni di Comunità).
MASERA, R. S. (1987) 'Four Arguments for Fiscal Recovery in Italy', in M. J. Boskin, J. S. Flemming and S. Gorini (eds), *Private Saving and Public Debt* (London: Blackwell).
MITCHELL, B. R. (1962) *Abstract of British Historical Statistics* (Oxford: OUP).
MITCHELL, B. R. and H. G. Jones (1971) *Second Abstract of British Historical Statistics* (Oxford: OUP).
MODIGLIANI, F. (1961) 'Long-Run Implications of Alternative Fiscal Policies and the Burden of the National Debt', *Economic Journal*, no. 71, Dec.
MODIGLIANI, F. and R. BRUMBERG (1979) 'Utility Analysis and Aggregate Consumption Function: an Attempt at Integration', in A. Abel (ed.), *Collected Papers of Franco Modigliani*, vol. 2 (Cambridge: MIT Press).
MONTI, M., B. SIRACUSANO and P. TARDINI (1983) 'Spesa pubblica, finanziamento del disavanzo e crowding-out', in *Spesa pubblica e sviluppo dell'economia* (Milano: Edizioni di Comunità).
MORCALDO, G. and G. SALVEMINI (1984) 'Il debito pubblico: analisi dell'evoluzione nel periodo 1960–83 e prospettive', *Rivista di politica economica*, vol. 74.
MORCALDO, G. and P. ZANCHI (1984) 'Un modello di previsione del bilancio pubblico per il breve-medio termine', *Proceedings of the Perugia Conference, February 1984*.
SHEEN, J. (1987) 'Inflation, Debt and Fiscal Policy Attitudes', *Oxford Economic Papers*, vol. 39.
SPAVENTA, L. (1984) 'The Growth of Public Debt in Italy: Past Experience, Perspectives and Policy Problems', *Banca Nazionale del Lavoro Quarterly Review*, June.
SPAVENTA, L. (1987) 'The Growth of Public Debt', *IMF Staff Papers*, vol. 34, 2, June.
SPAVENTA, L., R. ARTONI, G. MORCALDO and P. ZANCHI (1984) 'L'indebitamento pubblico in Italia: evoluzione, prospettive e problemi', Report prepared for the Commissione Bilancio of the Camera dei Deputati.
VACIAGO, G. (1983) *La programmazione dei flussi finanziari* (Bologna: Il Mulino).
VAN WIJNBERGEN, S. (1985) 'Oil Price Shocks, Unemployment, Investment and the Current Account: an Intertemporal Disequilibrium Analysis', *Review of Economic Studies*, vol. LII.
VIÑALS, J. (1986) 'Fiscal Policy and the Current Account', *Economic Policy*, vol. 3, October.
ZAUTZIK, E. (1982) 'Base monetaria aggiustata e sue interpretazioni: aspetti teorici e applicazione al caso italiano', *Banca d'Italia, Temi di discussione*, no. 15, December.

10 Measures of Fiscal Stance and Rules for Stabilising the Economy: the Case for Separating Measurement from Policy

Marcus Miller and Alan Sutherland

Address the real issues: do not rely on a summary measure and especially an incorrect summary measure of policy to make your policy arguments for you. (Stanley Fischer.[1])

10.1 INTRODUCTION

There are a number of arguments frequently put forward by economists for adjusting the public sector deficit to get a better measure of the stance of fiscal policy. As the deficit can be affected by short-term fluctuations in income, *cyclical adjustment* has been proposed both to provide a more accurate measure of the discretionary change in fiscal stance and of the sustainability of the deficit. Those advocating *inflation adjustment* argue that inflation acts like a tax on the holders of public debt, the revenue of which is not included in the public sector accounts. But no consensus on the appropriate measurement of fiscal policy has emerged. Indeed, in his discussion of UK fiscal policy Sir Alan Walters (1986) was less than enthusiastic about cyclical adjustment and concluded that '... inflation adjustment is worthless' (p. 73).

It is the contention of this chapter that much of the controversy that surrounds this issue arises because of a failure to distinguish sufficiently the question of how the stance of policy should be *measured* from the question of how the stance of policy should be *set*. Specifically, the merits of a particular adjustment are frequently assessed with regard to the (inflation or output) stabilising properties of a policy of *balancing the budget adjusted in this fashion*. Thus it may be that some of those who call themselves Keynesians

216

advocate cyclical adjustment because of the income stabilising tendencies of balancing the cyclically adjusted budget. It certainly appears true that Monetarists reject inflation adjustment because balancing the budget *without* the adjustment is more anti-inflationary.

To choose adjustments in this way, however, is precisely what Professor Fischer criticises in his remark quoted above: namely to try and achieve a desired policy response by one's choice of how to measure fiscal stance. Such a course of action is likely to produce neither the optimal setting of fiscal policy nor further the understanding of the effects of fiscal policy.

In Section 10.2 of this chapter we, show how different measures of fiscal stance may nevertheless have come to be associated with particular stabilisation rules. We concentrate on cyclical and inflation adjustment; and we provide examples of such adjustments calculated for the UK on an annual basis from 1973 to 1986 in an Annex.

In Section 10.3 we take the argument one step further. First we ask how a policy-maker's choice of fiscal rules might depend on preferences as between output and inflation stabilisation and whether the shocks hitting the economy are output or price shocks. For this purpose we consider two extreme caricatures which we refer to as 'Keynesian' and 'Monetarist' for convenience but without any claim to accuracy. The former is assumed to care *only* about the variance of output (so our Keynesian is not Keynes!) and the latter to be concerned solely with inflation.

What we find, using a relatively orthodox model of output and inflation, is that despite their very different objectives the two policy-makers agree on the choice of stabilisation rule when there are only output (or 'demand') shocks. When it comes to price shocks, however, there is disagreement as each of these straw men shifts to a different policy rule to handle these 'supply-side' disturbances.

At the end of Section 10.3 we spell out what this exercise implies about how these two policy-makers would choose to correct or adjust the fiscal deficit *if they were trying to make the measurement of fiscal policy make their policy arguments for them*. While we find that there is a substantial basis of agreement in face of demand shocks, supply shocks lead to conflict between the policy-makers on how to measure the budget. Moreover, each policy-maker will be faced with a dilemma over whether to adjust the budget as for demand shocks or supply shocks.

In conclusion we suggest instead that a more productive route would be to settle on a consistent measure of fiscal policy and then debate explicitly, in terms of that measure, the way in which the fiscal stance should be varied in response to fluctuations in output and inflation.

Consider, for example, choosing the inflation adjusted deficit on the economic grounds that consumers treat the erosion of the real value of their holdings of government debt due to inflation as a loss of real disposable income; and that such a 'tax' should not be excluded. This is surely consistent with the view that disposable income *should* be squeezed in times of inflation and support for a tightening of the inflation adjusted deficit. So choosing to 'adjust for inflation' in measuring the fiscal stance does *not* imply opting for the 'accommodation of inflation' as an act of policy.

10.2 BALANCING THE BUDGET AND MACROECONOMIC STABILISATION

10.2.1 Dynamics of debt

We start with an equation for the 'dynamics of debt' using terminology from Tobin (1982) – where he discusses the US Federal Debt in history and in prospect.

Using D to denote the time rate of change, this basic dynamic relationship is

$$Dd = x - (n + \pi)d \tag{10.1}$$

where d is the debt/nominal-output ratio, n is the growth of real output, π is the inflation rate and x is the (unadjusted) deficit relative to nominal output. (This will include both the primary deficit and the interest costs of debt service.) That is, the *ratio of debt* to nominal output, d, will only increase when the ratio of the *deficit* to nominal output exceeds the tendency for nominal output growth $(n + \pi)$ to cause d to fall.

All debt is assumed to be 'capital-certain' in nominal terms and to bear a short-term, variable, interest rate. (We ignore non-interest-bearing monetary liabilities and questions of 'seignorage'.) Note that πd measures the effect of inflation in reducing the real value of existing nominal debt.

10.2.2 The Chancellor's target

Let us use this formula to consider why the Chancellor adopted a 1 per cent target for the PSBR/GDP ratio in his evidence to the Treasury Committee in March 1987. The Chancellor said

> Over the medium and longer term the Government's objective is zero inflation. It follows that money GDP will then grow at the rate of growth of the economy, perhaps an underlying 2.5 per cent a year, to be on the safe side. Against that background a 1 per cent PSBR will ensure that public debt does not rise as a share of GDP.

On his bold assumption of no inflation, we see from eqn (10.1) that keeping the debt/income ratio constant ($Dd=0$) implies setting $x=nd$, that is, *to set the deficit* as a percentage of output *at a target which is the product of the growth rate and the current debt/income ratio*. Combining the Chancellor's figure of 2.5 per cent for n with the (approximate) value of 0.4 for d implies that the resulting target for the deficit is 1 per cent of GDP, the Chancellor's target.

Even where inflation is not necessarily zero, however, the same 'target' (nd) will keep the debt/income ratio constant *if it is applied to the inflation-adjusted deficit* ($x-\pi d$) as, clearly,

$$Dd=(x-\pi d)-nd=nd-nd=0. \tag{10.2}$$

Note that adhering to a fixed 1 per cent target for the inflation-adjusted budget deficit means *not* changing the demand pressure of fiscal policy (as measured by $x-\pi d)^2$ when inflation changes.

10.2.3 An automatic inflation stabiliser

But consider applying the same 1 per cent target to the budget *without* adjusting for inflation (which is actually what the Chancellor appears to favour) i.e. setting

$$x=nd=1\% \tag{10.3}$$

Then of course (for the same values of n and d) the inflation adjusted deficit (which is what we are using to measure demand pressure) will be forced to contract with inflation as

$$x-\pi d=(n-\pi)d=1\%-\pi d \tag{10.4}$$

will fall whenever inflation is positive.

This point can be expressed more generally. For any target rate of inflation, denoted μ, one could express a target for the nominal deficit of $(n+\mu)d$ which would imply a real deficit of

$$x-\pi d=(n-(\pi-\mu))d=1\%-(\pi-\mu)d \tag{10.5}$$

Thus the real fiscal stance, on the left-hand side, would be tightened whenever inflation π was above target μ as shown on the right-hand side. (With $\mu=0$ we obtain the earlier result.)

The point we would emphasise is that, *given any fixed borrowing target for the PSBR/GDP ratio, the failure to adjust for inflation imparts a counter-inflation tendency to fiscal policy*: and one may, indeed, be tempted to deny the validity or relevance of inflation adjustment in order to secure this 'inflation stabilisation'. The alternative approach, which we prefer as it avoids the charge of 'mismeasuring things so as to get the right policy conclusion', would be to argue explicitly that the inflation-adjusted deficit be tightened when inflation rises and vice versa.

10.2.4   The automatic income stabiliser

Setting the inflation-adjusted deficit equal to nd not only implies that the demand pressure of fiscal policy is constant in the face of rising inflation it also implies that there is *no* built-in fiscal response to fluctuations in income. But consider setting the inflation and *cyclically* corrected deficit equal to nd

$$x - \pi d + c = nd \tag{10.6}$$

where c is the 'cyclical correction' – the difference between the observed budget deficit and the deficit that would occur if income was at its trend level. (Obviously c depends on the gap between actual income and trend income and will be negative when actual income falls below trend and vice versa.)

Equation (10.6) implies that the following relationship governs the inflation-adjusted deficit

$$x - \pi d = nd - c \tag{10.7}$$

which shows that fiscal policy will automatically loosen at times of recession (i.e. when c is negative) and will automatically tighten when there is a boom (i.e. when c is positive). Thus one may be tempted to support cyclical correction of the deficit in order to secure a degree of automatic income stabilisation.

But if this were the only reason, then cyclical adjustment would also appear as an attempt to mismeasure the budget as a means of achieving a desired setting of policy.[3] (Indeed, it is for this reason that we opt for the inflation but non-cyclically adjusted deficit $(x - \pi d)$ as a more neutral measure of the demand pressure of fiscal policy in Table 10.1.)

10.2.5   Summary

Table A.1 in the Annex presents current estimates of the cyclical and inflation corrections for the UK. These adjustments are designed to measure the 'mechanical' effects of the cycle on the public sector deficit and to allow one to compute the real deficit net of inflationary interest costs: they are not intended to show how the real deficit should be altered for stabilisation purposes. Nevertheless, as we have already suggested, people do seem to use the various measures of the deficit for this purpose – by requiring that the budget on any particular measure be balanced (or, more precisely, set equal to the 'target' *nd*, which is zero when growth is zero, and positive for positive growth).

Table 10.1 Targets for adjusted deficits and stabilisation policy rules: a summary.

| | | *Automatic income stabiliser* | |
		On	Off
		Cyclical adjustment	No adjustment
	On	$x + c = nd$	$x = nd$
Automatic		$x - \pi d = (n - \pi)d - c$	$x - \pi d = (n - \pi)d$
inflation			
stabiliser		Both adjustments	Inflation adjustment
	Off	$x - \pi d + c = nd$	$x - \pi d = nd$
		$x - \pi d = nd - c$	$x - \pi d = nd$

Note: *nd* is the 'target' at which each adjusted budget measure is set.

The link that targeting the deficit creates between measurement and policy is summarised in Table 10.1 using $x - \pi d$, the real deficit, to indicate the demand effect of the deficit. Each cell contains the specific budget measure that is set equal to the target *nd* and then the policy rule that this implies for $x - \pi d$, our 'neutral' real deficit. Thus, in the top right-hand cell is the uncorrected deficit (appearing in line (1) of Table A.1): if this is set equal to the growth term this will (as is shown immediately underneath) help to stabilise inflation by making $x - \pi d$ responsive to inflation. Adding in the cyclical correction as in the top left-hand cell gives the cyclically adjusted deficit, appearing in line (3) of Table A.1. Targeting that makes $x - \pi d$ respond to the cycle in income as well as inflation. Targeting the inflation and cyclically adjusted budget indicated in the bottom left-hand cell (cf. line 6a of Table A.1), however, involves 'switching off' the inflation stabiliser: which, we have argued, explains the hostility it has attracted from the anti-inflation critics.

Inflation correction alone in the bottom right-hand cell defines the real budget deficit (cf line 5a in Table A.1) which we are using as our 'neutral' measure. Targeting this at *nd* provides neither form of stabiliser.

10.3 AUTOMATIC STABILISERS IN A SMALL MACROECONOMIC MODEL

Section 10.3.1 contains a technical assessment of the various possible combinations of automatic stabilisers as set out in Table 10.1. The non-mathematically minded reader may wish to skip to Section 10.3.2 where the main implications of the results are set out.

10.3.1   The model

The model used is described by equations (10.8) to (10.11)

$$y = g + \beta l + \delta \mu + \varepsilon \tag{10.8}$$

$$\pi = \varphi y + \mu + \omega \tag{10.9}$$

$$g = -\theta y - \gamma \pi \tag{10.10}$$

$$Dl = \mu - \pi \tag{10.11}$$

y = log of output (deviation from natural rate)
g = demand pressure of fiscal policy
l = log of real balances
π = price inflation
μ = rate of monetary growth
ε = stochastic demand shock, $\varepsilon \sim N(0, \sigma_\varepsilon^2)$
ω = stochastic inflation shock, $\omega \sim N(0, \sigma_\omega^2)$.

Equation (10.8) is a simple aggregate demand relationship where demand is affected by the demand pressure of fiscal policy, real balances, core inflation and stochastic shocks. Equation (10.9) is a Phillips curve which relates inflation to deviations of output from its natural rate and core inflation. In order to reflect the impact of pre-announced monetary targets core inflation is set equal to the rate of monetary growth. Inflation is also affected by stochastic shocks.

By choosing appropriate values for θ and γ a variety of fiscal rules can be represented. If the government balances the cyclical and inflation corrected deficit it effectively allows the demand pressure of fiscal policy to increase when the level of output falls and decrease when output rises. This can be represented in equation (10.10) by setting θ to some positive value and γ equal to zero.

Alternatively if the government chooses to balance the budget with no adjustment for inflation or income cycles it would allow the demand pressure of fiscal policy to decline when inflation rises and increase when inflation falls. This can be represented in equation (10.10) by setting γ to some positive value and θ equal to zero.

The model is completed by equation (10.11) which determines the evolution of real money balances.

Equations (10.8), (10.9) and (10.10) can be solved to yield the following expressions for income and inflation (we make the simplifying assumption that monetary growth and core inflation are zero)

$$y = \frac{\beta}{\Delta} l + \frac{1}{\Delta} \varepsilon - \frac{\gamma}{\Delta} \omega \tag{10.12}$$

$$\pi = \frac{\varphi\beta}{\Delta}l + \frac{\varphi}{\Delta}\varepsilon + \frac{(1+\theta)}{\Delta}\omega. \tag{10.13}$$

The evolution of real balances is governed by

$$Dl = -\frac{\varphi\beta}{\Delta}l - \frac{\varphi}{\Delta}\varepsilon - \frac{(1+\theta)}{\Delta}\omega. \tag{10.14}$$

With stochastic shocks and dynamic adjustment, the appropriate method of assessing the stabilisation properties of the various fiscal rules is to look at the steady-state (asymptotic) variances of income and inflation for different values of θ and γ. Using equations (10.12), (10.13) and (10.14), it is a simple matter to obtain expressions for the asymptotic variances of real balances, income and inflation and these are shown in Table 10.2.

Table 10.2   Asymptotic variances

Shocks	$\sigma_\varepsilon^2 > 0, \ \sigma_\omega^2 = 0$ (1)	$\sigma_\varepsilon^2 = 0, \ \sigma_\omega^2 > 0$ (2)
Var(l)	$\dfrac{\varphi}{2\beta\Delta}$	$\dfrac{(1+\theta)^2}{2\varphi\beta\Delta}$
Var(y)	$\left(\dfrac{1}{\Delta}\right)^2 \left(\dfrac{\beta\varphi}{2\Delta}+1\right)$	$\left(\dfrac{1}{\Delta}\right)^2 \left(\dfrac{\beta(1+\theta)^2}{2\varphi\Delta}+\gamma^2\right)$
Var(π)	$\left(\dfrac{\varphi}{\Delta}\right)^2 \left(\dfrac{\beta\varphi}{2\Delta}+1\right)$	$\left(\dfrac{1+\theta}{\Delta}\right)^2 \left(\dfrac{\varphi\beta}{2\Delta}+1\right)$

$$\Delta = 1 + \theta + \varphi\gamma$$

Note: The formulae appearing in the table give the steady state variances as a multiple of the instantaneous variances of the shocks.

First consider the case where there are demand shocks but no inflation shocks (i.e. $\sigma_\varepsilon^2 > 0$, $\sigma_\omega^2 = 0$) shown in column (1). The parameters θ and γ enter these expressions only via Δ which is always in the denominator, so it is immediately apparent that, in the presence of only demand shocks, both the automatic income stabiliser and the automatic inflation stabiliser reduce the variance of income and inflation.

Now consider the case where there are inflation shocks, but no demand shocks (i.e. $\sigma_\varepsilon^2 = 0$, $\sigma_\omega^2 > 0$), shown in column (2) in Table 10.2. It remains the case that if the inflation stabiliser is allowed to operate the variance of inflation is reduced. It is also the case that the variance of real balances is reduced. However, the inflation stabiliser has an ambiguous effect on the variance of income. This gives rise to the possibility that allowing both stabilisers to operate would result in a larger variance of income than if the income stabiliser was allowed to operate on its own.

The effect of the automatic income stabiliser depends on whether it is operating on its own or in conjunction with the automatic inflation stabiliser. If the income stabiliser is introduced when the inflation stabiliser is switched off then it will reduce the variance of both income and inflation. If it is introduced when the inflation stabiliser is switched on it is almost certain to decrease the variance of income, however, it could result in a greater variance of inflation than if the inflation stabiliser is allowed to operate on its own. (This last result is particularly likely if β and φ are small.)

10.3.2 Interpretation of results

To aid the interpretation of the results we shall refer to two caricatures who hold extreme and opposing views as regards ouput and inflation stability. We shall assume the first caricature is concerned only with output stabilisation and will be referred to as a 'Keynesian'. (As already indicated, Keynes was not a Keynesian of this type.) The second caricature is assumed to be concerned only with inflation stabilisation and will be referred to as a 'Monetarist' (and a similar caveat doubtless applies). With the help of Figures 10.1 and 10.2 we illustrate graphically the results obtained formally in Section 10.3.1.

Demand shocks

First consider the case of shocks to the demand side which is illustrated in Figure 10.1, with inflation measured on the vertical axis and income measured on the horizontal axis. In each panel of Figure 10.1 S is the short-run Phillips curve and D is the short-run aggregate demand curve. In panels (a) and (b) the demand curve is vertical as, when the inflation stabiliser is switched off, inflation is assumed to have no effect on aggregate demand in the short run. In panel (c) the demand curve is downward sloping which reflects the operation of the inflation stabiliser.

D' is the aggregate demand curve when a temporary shock reduces aggregate demand. When neither stabiliser is working the effect is to shift the demand curve horizontally by the amount of the shock. Panel (a) shows that, in this case, both income and inflation fall. Panel (b) shows the effect of allowing the income stabiliser to work, namely to reduce the horizontal shift of the demand curve and therefore reduce the impact of the shock on

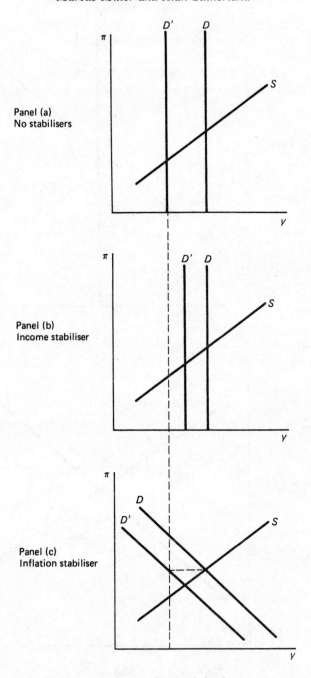

Figure 10.1   Demand shocks.

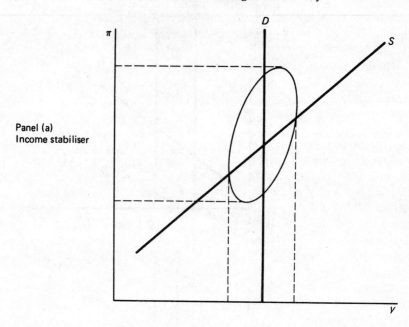

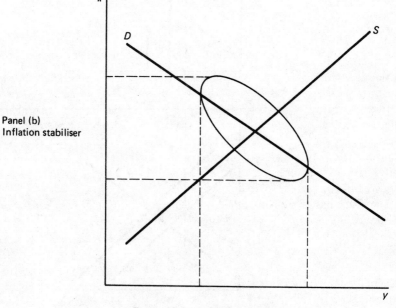

Figure 10.2   Inflation shocks.

inflation and output. This confirms the result of Section 10.3.1 which showed that the automatic income stabiliser reduced the variance of both income and inflation.

The implication of this is that our 'Keynesian', in the face of demand shocks, would be in favour of allowing the automatic income stabiliser to work – which is what we would have expected. What is less obvious, however, is the finding that the Monetarist should also be in favour of the automatic income stabiliser – because it helps stabilise inflation in the face of demand shocks.[4]

Turning now to panel (c) of Figure 10.1 we consider the case where only the inflation stabiliser is allowed to operate. In this case, as in panel (a), the demand curve is shifted horizontally by the amount of the shock. However, with the inflation stabiliser operating, the downward slope of the demand curve implies that both inflation and income fall by less than in panel (a). This is what we observed in Section 10.3.1, namely that the inflation stabiliser reduced the variance of both inflation and income in the face of demand shocks.

Again we have a surprising degree of agreement. Just *as both favour income stabilisation so both favour allowing the inflation stabiliser to operate* in the face of demand shocks.

'Supply' shocks

Figure 10.2 contrasts income and inflation stabilisers in the face of inflation shocks. D and S are defined as in Figure 10.1. However, in this case it is not possible to illustrate the results using simple shifts in these two schedules. Given the complications caused by simultaneous shifts in both S and D, we illustrate the distribution of outcomes by 'probability contours' (the ellipses shown in Figure 10.2) which connect the combinations of income and inflation which have an equal probability of occurring. That the slope of these ellipses should be closely related to the slope of the demand curve is plausible enough, since the main source of fluctuation comes from vertical shifts in S. (This can be confirmed numerically using the algebraic results reported in Section 10.3.1.)

The shape of the ellipses can be used to assess the effects of the stabilisers by projecting the width of the relevant ellipse on to the horizontal and vertical axes. The larger the projected width the greater the variance of the variable measured on that axis. Panel (a) of Figure 10.2 shows that the income stabiliser implies a relatively small variance for income while the variance of inflation is relatively large. This arises because of the vertical demand curve. Panel (b) of Figure 10.2 shows that as the inflation stabiliser imports a negative slope to the demand curve it therefore turns the ellipse in an anticlockwise direction. This increases the variance of income but reduces the variance of inflation. It is for this reason that, as noted in Section 10.3.1, a conflict exists between inflation stabilisation and output stabilisation in the face of inflation shocks.

As compared with what was chosen for 'demand' shocks we now find that, *in the face of inflation shocks*, the caricature Keynesian would like to retain income stabilisation but would prefer to 'switch off' the inflation stabiliser. The Monetarist, on the other hand, would prefer to retain inflation stabilisation but to drop output stabilisation. So each now differs from the other, and each chooses a different policy from what was considered appropriate for demand shocks.

Summary and implications for the measurement of fiscal stance

In the upper panel of Table 10.3 we summarise the way in which this stylised contrast in objectives affects the choice of stabiliser in the face of the different shocks. More important for present purposes is what this implies for how each of the two caricature policy-makers would wish to measure the budget *if they are to pursue their stabilisation objectives by setting a fiscal target for an appropriate adjusted budget*. This is shown in the lower panel of Table 10.3.

Table 10.3   Objectives, rules and deficit corrections

(a) Choice of auto-matic stabiliser	*Keynesian*	*Monetarist*
Demand shocks	Both choose to stabilise both inflation and income	
Supply shocks	Income stabilisation only	Inflation stabilisation only
(b) Choice of fiscal measure	*Keynesian*	*Monetarist*
Demand shocks	Both agree to cyclically adjust deficits	
Supply shocks	Cyclically adjust and inflation adjust	No adjustments

Note: The choice of fiscal measure in panel (b) is based on the need to secure the desired automatic stabiliser by setting the adjusted deficit equal to a constant target. Table 10.1 may therefore be used to define the entries appearing in panel (b) above from those given in panel (a).

It is evident from the table that the prospects for agreeing on a measure of fiscal policy are dim if policy-makers are to advocate policies not explicitly, but implicitly, via the proposed method of measuring the budget.

10.4 CONCLUSION

In the first section of this chapter we have shown that it is possible to make a connection between 'adjustment' of the budget deficit and 'rules' for fiscal policy. In particular, it was noted that balancing the cyclically-corrected deficit introduces an income stabilising element into fiscal policy but *omitting* to inflation-adjust the deficit introduces an inflation stabilising tendency given fixed PSBR/GDP targets. We suggest that much of the disagreement concerning the correct indicator of fiscal stance arises because the opposing sides in the debate tend to argue for their preferred measure precisely on the basis of these 'stabilising' properties.

In the second section of the chapter we investigated how the choice of economic stabiliser would depend on the preferences of the policy-maker and structure of stochastic disturbances. Given *demand* shocks it was found that automatic income and inflation stabilisation was chosen independently of preference. In the face of *supply* shocks, however, the Keynesian policy-maker (keen to stabilise output) chose to switch off the inflation stabiliser, while the (anti-inflation) Monetarist dropped the income stabiliser. Where such stabilisation is sought via targeting an adjusted budget, this implied a possible consensus on cyclical adjustment for demand shocks, but no agreement on budget adjustment for supply shocks (see Table 10.3 panel (b)).

In general, the results of Section 10.3 show that it is unlikely that any consensus will emerge on the correct measure of fiscal stance if the debate on measurement is actually a debate about stabilisation policy. Indeed it was shown that, if measurement and policy are conflated, neither side is likely to have a consistent position on how the budget should be measured as preferred stabilisation policy will depend on the source of the shocks that affect the economy.

It is, of course, hardly surprising to discover that conflicting objectives as between policy-makers and different expectations as to the source of disturbances should lead to different choices of stabilisation policy. Our conclusion is that it is surely more constructive to see such conflict emerging as (predictable) disagreements about how policy should be *set* rather than having it submerged in irreconcilable differences as to how fiscal stance is to be *measured*.

ANNEX: ESTIMATES OF CYCLICAL AND INFLATION ADJUSTMENTS FOR THE UK

In Table A.1 we present current estimates of cyclical and inflation adjustments for the UK from 1973 onwards. (This table brings up to date similar calculations presented in Miller (1985), to which the reader is referred for further discussion.)

Table A.1 Inflation and cyclical adjustment of the public sector financial deficit (all figures as percentage of GDP at current market prices unless otherwise indicated)

		1973	1974	1975	1976	1977	1978	1979	1980	1981	1982	1983	1984	1985	1986
PSFD	(1)	3.8	5.7	7.3	6.8	4.3	5.1	4.4	4.7	3.3	2.7	3.7	4.1	2.7	2.6
Cyclical adjustment*	(2)	−0.3	−1.8	−3.1	−2.4	−1.8	−1.1	−0.6	−2.7	−4.4	−4.7	−4.1	−3.9	−3.5	−3.7
Cyclically adjusted PSFD	(3)	3.5	3.9	4.2	4.3	2.4	4.0	3.9	2.0	−1.1	−2.1	−0.4	0.1	−0.8	−1.0
Inflation adjustment															
Current	(4a)	−3.9	−8.8	−9.9	−5.9	−6.5	−4.0	−6.0	−4.2	−4.0	−3.3	−2.4	−2.6	−2.0	−1.4
Permanent	(4b)	−2.0	−2.6	−2.5	−2.8	−2.9	−2.8	−2.9	−3.1	−3.1	−2.9	−2.6	−2.6	−2.4	−2.3
Inflation-adjusted PSFD															
Current	(5a)	−0.1	−3.1	−2.6	0.9	−2.2	1.0	−1.6	0.6	−0.7	−0.7	1.3	1.4	0.8	1.2
Permanent	(5b)	1.8	3.0	4.7	4.0	1.3	2.3	1.5	1.6	0.2	−0.2	1.1	1.5	0.4	0.3
Inflation and cyclical adjusted PSFD															
Current	(6a)	−0.4	−4.9	−5.7	−1.5	−4.0	−0.1	−2.2	−2.1	−5.1	−5.4	−2.8	−2.5	−2.7	−2.5
Permanent	(6b)	1.4	1.2	1.6	1.5	−0.5	1.2	1.0	−1.1	−4.1	−4.9	−3.0	−2.5	−3.2	−3.3
Memo items																
Public sector debt		50.4	47.8	43.4	43.8	44.1	42.1	39.2	36.8	38.6	34.9	34.6	35.5	34.5	33.7
Gross interest cost		3.1	3.8	3.6	4.0	4.1	3.9	4.0	4.2	4.4	4.2	4.0	4.1	3.9	3.7
GDP at current market prices (£bn)		73	83	105	125	144	165	193	226	248	277	300	322	353	376
GDP at 1980 prices (£bn)		189	185	184	188	193	199	204	200	197	200	207	213	220	225

*Between 1973 and 1979 trend growth is assumed to be 1.4 per cent p.a.; after 1979 trend growth is assumed to be 2.5 per cent p.a.
Calculations of cyclical adjustments are based on the method described in Biswas, Johns and Savage (1985).
Calculations of the inflation adjustments are based on the method described in Miller and Babbs (1985).

The cyclical adjustment in line (2) shows approximately how the deficit would have fallen (as a percentage of GDP) if output had been 'back on trend'. (This trend runs from the 1973 peak of real GDP to the 1979 peak then grows at 2.5 per cent thereafter – the Chancellor's conservative estimate of underlying growth cited above. The figures for actual GDP are shown as a memorandum item.) By construction these adjustments are approximately zero at the two peaks, but average almost 4 per cent since 1980, as the recession of 1979/81 has left the economy below the trend line starting in 1979.

As Sir Alan Walters has argued, these 'adjustments' are not appropriate as a guide to fiscal policy insofar as they are measured from peak-to-peak levels of output (associated in both cases with explicit incomes policies designed to hold down inflation). It may be useful to report that in a similar exercise Price and Muller (1984) found that the shift to a 'mid-cycle' correction involved a reduction of the adjustments by about 2.4 percentage points throughout the period.

Two forms of 'inflation adjustment' are given. The 'current' inflation adjustment involves (approximately) replacing the nominal interest cost by the (net) current real rate of interest. Because *short-run* real interest rates were in fact negative in the late 1970s, the adjustments shown in line (4a) exceed the gross interest cost, shown as a memorandum item. We also show another form of adjustment, where current interest costs are replaced by the *long-term* real interest rate (the latter was put at 2.0 per cent until 1980, after which time it is based on the yield for long-dated indexed stock). As can be seen from line (4b) of the table, this adjustment is much more stable, almost always lying between 2 and 3 per cent of GDP.

Notes

1. See his Discussion reported in *Studies in Banking and Finance*, Supplement to the *Journal of Banking and Finance* (1985).
2. In order to avoid the complications of demand weighted deficits we assume, wherever appropriate, that the government uses discretionary taxes to offset inflation and cyclically induced fluctuations in total tax revenue and discretionary expenditure to offset cyclically induced fluctuations in total expenditure. We also assume that all types of taxes have the same demand effects and all types of expenditure have the same demand effects.
3. Of course, cyclical adjustment is important for reasons not dealt with in this chapter, such as the assessment of sustainability of fiscal policy and of the discretionary element it contains.
4. In practice, however, Monetarists are usually *not* enthusiastic about cyclical correction, cf. Sir Alan Walters's position. This is probably because they are concerned about the difficulty of specifying the centre of the cycle (the 'natural rate' of output and employment) and the inflationary dangers of getting it wrong. Our simple model has assumed away this potential source of error, however, as we freely admit.

References

BISWAS, R., C. JOHNS and D. SAVAGE (1985) 'The Measurement of Fiscal Stance', *National Institute Economic Review*, vol. 113, pp. 50–64.

JAZWINSKY, A. H. (1970) *Stochastic Processes and Filtering Theory*. (London: Academic Press).

MILLER, M. (1982) 'Inflation-adjusting the Public Sector Financial Deficit', in John Kay (ed.), *The 1982 Budget* (Oxford: Blackwell).

MILLER, M. (1982) 'Measuring the Stance of Fiscal Policy', *Oxford Review of Economic Policy*, vol. 1, No. 1.

MILLER, M. and S. BABBS (1985) 'The True Cost of Debt Service and the Public Sector Financial Deficit', in *Studies in Banking and Finance*, Supplement to the *Journal of Banking and Finance*, pp. 79–92.

PRICE, R. W. and P. MULLER (1984) 'Structural Budget Indicators and the Interpretation of Fiscal Policy Stance in OECD Economies', *OECD Economic Studies*, vol. 3, pp. 27–72.

TOBIN, J. (1982) 'Does Fiscal Policy Matter', mimeo, Centre for Research in Economic Policy, Stanford, May.

TREASURY AND CIVIL SERVICE COMMITTEE (1987) *The 1987 Budget*. Session 1986–87 (London: HMSO).

WALTERS, A. A. (1986) *Britain's Economic Renaissance* (New York: Oxford University Press).

Part VI

Policy to Control Interest Rates

11 Interest Rates and Macroeconomic Policy

John S. Flemming

This chapter addresses four themes. The first is the way in which inappropriate monetary policy may cause unemployment. This possibility is not peculiarly Keynesian, indeed Friedman's prescription of steady money supply growth is based on the view that this is the relevant 'appropriate policy' to avoid recession and unemployment. The second theme relates to the relative methodological merits of specifying monetary policy in terms of the quantity of money, as Friedman does (and Keynes is usually thought to have), or in terms of the interest rate itself. Thirdly I look at the same issue in more practical terms of policy design, and finally at the role of the interest rates in achieving an intermediate target for the exchange rate as a way of pursuing a smooth path for nominal GDP.

I

The possibility that inappropriate monetary policy can cause unemployment is most easily demonstrated in the context of a fixed-price Keynesian macro-model of the type developed by Barro and Grossman (1976) and Malinvaud (1977). In such models a disequilibrium price in one market has effects which spill over on to quantities in other markets. Such effects have a particularly strong downward bias, implying a tendency towards unemployment in the labour market, when the quantity transacted at a disequilibrium price in any one market is assumed to be whichever is the smaller of the quantities demanded or supplied at that price, given any quantity rationing in other markets.

Consider such a fix-price economy initially in full Walrasian equilibrium. Now shock its money supply downwards: the equilibrium money price and wage levels should also fall. If their actual levels, and the nominal interest rate, are fixed, aggregate demand falls as consumers' wealth has been reduced by the removal of money. There may also be an accelerator type reduction in firms' demand for investment goods (Malinvaud, 1980; Neary and Stiglitz, 1983). Thus unemployment, with possible multiplier repercussions, ensues even though the real wage is still at its initial, and unchanged, full equilibrium value. If in the process of adjustment prices fall faster than wages the real

235

wage may temporarily rise above this full employment level. In this model unemployment of this kind could also be induced by any shock which raised the equilibrium money stock at the given prices without affecting the equilibrium real wage. A non-accommodated shock to the (conditional) demand for money is equivalent to a reduction in actual money. Whether either is very likely is, of course, an empirical question. Friedman's view is that mistaken policy could generate a money supply shock while any demand shocks are unlikely. It may, of course, also be true that other kinds of shock, real shocks, which cause unemployment could be offset by a suitably responsive monetary policy. Whether failure to respond would then make monetary policy the cause of the unemployment is a philosophical problem.

The framework of the *General Theory* is not consistently one of fixed prices as expounded by Barro and Grossman and Malinvaud. It does, however, have two fix price elements relating respectively to the money wage and the nominal interest rate. Keynes (pp. 172 and 233–4) considered that it might prove very difficult to reduce the nominal interest rate faced by would-be investors below some strictly positive level required to cover the costs of intermediation and irreducible risks. The existence of this 'liquidity trap', at which additional money supply would not reduce nominal interest rates, has been much disputed. The fact remains, however, that as long as cash is readily available (and not subject to a Gesellean 'stamp') there is a non-negativity constraint on the nominal interest rate.

This floor is independent of institutional arrangements. We shall come later to the question of the extent to which the authorities themselves directly control interest rates, but without resorting to a stamp on dated money, or restricting the availability of legal tender, they could not overcome this constraint. The floor itself suffices to imply that periods of relatively rapid downward movement in the price level will be associated with high short-term real interest rates and possibly, therefore, sharp reductions in invest-ment demand and the associated demand for labour. Note, however, that though monetary expansion could not in these circumstances lower the nominal interest rate it might lower longer-term real rates by raising expected future prices and mitigating their immediate fall.

If wages and prices were perfectly flexible a deflationary shock would not initiate a period in which prices were expected to fall rapidly but rather an immediate drop. If they dropped far and fast enough the non-negativity constraint on nominal interest rates would not bind and unemployment need not ensue. Any stickiness in money wages thus increases both the probability of the constraint binding and the unemployment consequences of its doing so.

In what sense Keynes assumed money wages to be sticky is even more widely disputed than the significance of the liquidity trap (see Fender, 1981). My own view is that he chose to make them parametric not as any kind of description, but as a device which would, and did, enable him to analyse the consequences of different degrees of stickiness. Specifically he considered how rigid money wages might cause unemployment and, in Chapter 19, whether making them less sticky would stabilise employment. As I have argued elsewhere (Flemming, 1987a) this last is a complex question involving the assumed conduct of monetary policy too.

Making money wages somewhat more flexible in a world of flexible prices does not necessarily reduce the unemployment consequences of adverse shocks even if perfect flexibility would, by definition, eliminate them. If wages are at all sticky their being less so means that the rate at which they should be expected to fall in response to a deflationary shock increases. If price movements respond to wage movements (as they may even if they can also jump) this implies a more rapid fall in expected prices so that for a given nominal interest rate the real rate is raised and demand depression aggravated. This prospect may make prices fall further on the receipt of the bad news, but money wages will not make a corresponding downward jump unless they are perfectly flexible. In this case the current real wage goes up more, and with it unemployment rises further, in the short run, if wages are more flexible than if they are less.

The consequences of greater flexibility of money wages aggravating the unemployment impact effect of adverse shocks could in principle be mitigated by an appropriate monetary policy which stabilised the price level by expanding the money supply in response to adverse demand shocks. Such a policy is entirely consistent with a programme designed, for instance, to achieve steady growth of nominal GDP since in the circumstances envisaged its absence would lead both the price level and the level of output to fall.

II

Before considering such policies in greater depth it is natural at this point to consider Keynes's conception of monetary policy – its actual and optimal description. In particular I want to suggest that, contrary to most textbooks, Keynes believed that the authorities fixed the nominal interest rate r rather than the quantity of money M.

Given the demand function for money he clearly could not postulate authorities fixing both M and r – he had to make a choice. On p. 245 Keynes lists *the rate of interest* among his 'independent variable(s), *in the first instance*'. On p. 246 he refers to the possibility of explaining the interest rate by reference to the liquidity preference schedule and the quantity of money: 'Thus we can *sometimes* regard our ultimate independent variables as consisting of (1) ... (2) ... and (3) ... the quantity of money as determined by the central bank'. (I have added the emphases throughout).

These passages clearly reflect a reluctance to make a clear choice and an intention to try to have the best of both worlds if possible. I wish to argue that Keynes's second choice, of *M* as exogenous – in which he has been followed by most commentators – was unfortunate and inconsistent. It was unfortunate because it rendered a potentially recursive system simultaneous – and therefore much more difficult to explain (see Appendix). It was inconsistent because an exogenous interest rate is essential to the rationalisation of an aggregate speculative demand for money. This played a key role in Keynes's account of the interest elasticity of the demand for money which was a crucial innovation (see Patinkin, 1976).

An *individual's* speculative demand for money relates simply to his pitting his wits or judgement against that of 'the market'. Thus if I think the market price of bonds 'too high' I will switch more of my wealth into cash than otherwise. This does not, however, mean that a general switch in the representative portfolio towards cash can be explained in these terms. If the supply of money were fixed, as in the 'textbook account', a general feeling that bonds were overpriced would lead to a general attempt to sell and an immediate collapse of the price.

The story would, of course, be very different if the authorities were pegging the price of bonds. In that case a general feeling that the pegged price would not be maintained much longer would indeed lead to net sales by private bond holders, purchases by the authorities, and an increase in money and liquidity.

Speculation is necessarily 'against' someone; in many cases it is 'against the market'. In that case the aggregate of the relevant speculation must sum to zero; the private sector as a whole can only speculate against the authorities and this is only possible if the authorities stand ready to trade at certain prices. In this case the speculation will be driven by expectations about the scale and timing of changes in the pegged price. There is a close analogy with the foreign exchange market; one heard much more about currency speculation as the force driving transactions, and, ultimately, exchange rates, when rates were pegged than since they have floated.

In a free float there must be as much private money backing a rise in the rate (relative to the path implied by interest parity) as a fall. Net private speculation is only possible if the authorities stand ready to buy or sell for, or from, the reserves – just as in the domestic case they must be willing to see the money supply change (which may also be the result of foreign exchange transactions).

Thus Keynes was having it both ways when he relied (uneasily though explicitly) on exogenous money which was subject to interest elastic demand, at the same time as relying (implicitly) on the exogeneity of interest rates, which was also consistent with observed central bank behaviour, to justify that interest elasticity. It can, of course, be rationalised independently of the speculative motive by reference to generalised opportunity costs of cash holding (see, for example, Hicks, 1935).

III

This suggests that we consider the relative merits of active and passive monetary policy in both money supply and interest rate forms. I shall not go here into the problem of finding a satisfactory definition of money or the feasibility of close control of any monetary aggregate (including the monetary base).

We know that the policy of fixing the level, or the growth, of money is, to some extent, self-stabilising in that positive shocks to the economy increase the derived demand for money and thus the interest rate, which is likely to restrain demand. We have also seen that in the case of negative shocks prices might be expected to fall so rapidly as to imply a rise in real interest rates given the inability of nominal rates to go negative. The nominal rate would, however, at least tend to fall – which it would not if it were pegged.

We also know, from the work of Knut Wicksell (1935), that a fixed nominal rate strategy is not stable – being subject to a cumulative process. A shift in the marginal efficiency of investment can raise the natural real rate of interest. If the nominal rate does not respond excess demand occurs, inflation ensues, and real rates fall just when they should be rising. Thus quantity passivity seems to have a clear edge over nominal rate passivity but what of activist policies?

The reason for having an active policy is to be able to respond to shocks – that is to unforeseen developments; there must then exist, at least implicitly, a 'reaction function' prescribing the change in the level of the interest rate (or in the quantity of money) in response to changing circumstances. Note that in the quantity case it is the quantity of money itself rather than its rate of growth that should, apparently, depend on circumstances (Buiter, 1981). This is some distance from even the more pragmatic forms of monetary targetry recently seen. It may be that 'news' on developments comes out in such small pieces that changes in the level and in its growth are not very different. One might, however, imagine discrete shocks calling for stock adjustments which, if rapid, would involve huge swings in the target growth rate of money. To this extent interest smoothing, which would accommodate even sharp shifts in money demand, might seem to have the advantage if a suitable rule could be devised.

Robert Barro (1987) has recently proposed such a rule which involves accommodating contemporaneous disturbances while reducing the money supply in response to lagged shocks in the previous period. This rule is not merely a pegging of the interest rate by authorities standing ready to borrow and lend at that rate – rather it is presented as a money (base) supply rule. The base expands if the current interest rate exceeds its target level and a negative lagged term in the interest rate discrepancy eliminates any inflation expectations effects of the contemporaneous accommodation.

Barro does not address the question of the maturity of the rate which is to be targeted. In fact in his model both the target rate and the actual rate follow random walks which is consistent with the yield curve always shifting up and down by the same amount at all maturities.

This rule is not directed to the achievement of steady growth of nominal GDP. Barro's target nominal interest rate is related to a target inflation rate which varies for fiscal reasons (Barro, 1979; Mankiw, 1986). The inflation tax, like other tax rates, should not be expected to change (Flemming, 1987b) so that it should follow a random walk under certain restrictions on the shocks. Output follows an exogenous stochastic process. Sufficient knowledge of the distributions would, however, enable one to steer a course for nominal GDP provided that responses to the observed shocks were sufficiently fast.

The questions of observability and speed of response are very important and can be used to construct a general argument that active policy too is better done on quantities than prices. This case depends on the plausible proposition that the authorities are always so ponderous that by the time they make a move it will have been anticipated, to a considerable extent, by the market. Thus if the authorities control interest rates directly there will be ample scope for the aggregate private sector speculation discussed above. Such interest rate speculation is liable to destabilise the related quantities. The well-founded belief that bond rates are to be lowered over the next few weeks or months can lead to a sharp movement of shorter rates in the opposite direction as people borrow short to finance speculative bond purchases.

In the case of a predictable adjustment of monetary quantities the details of the authorities' adjustment path are less important. Knowledge that money is to be expanded, albeit fairly slowly, in reponse to a shock, has impact effects on asset prices and interest rates relating to periods longer than the adjustment process similar to those of a step increase. This argument has parallels in counter-cyclical fiscal policy. Suppose that the authorities react to (incipient) recession by fiscal stimulus, this could either affect intertemporal relative prices as with temporary changes in indirect taxes (VAT) or investment incentives, or the instrument could be an apparently blunter one such as public expenditure or personal allowances. If the authorities' actions are likely to be anticipated the blunter instruments are to be preferred (Flemming, 1981).

Consider an economy going into recession. If the authorities are thought likely to cut VAT, or to increase investment incentives, soon, private agents will defer expenditures, thus accelerating the onset of recession and deepening it until the authorities have reacted so fully that no further measures are expected. The expectation of broader measures, however, is, if anything, a reason for trying to get in, for example, private investment first so that the capacity is there to meet the additional demand when it comes.

IV

Though we have seen that there would in principle be advantages in monetary policy being directed to nominal quantities rather than nominal interest rates, in practice, in addition to the problems of defining monetary aggregates mentioned above, the fact that information is available continuously on interest rates means that day-to-day policy is conducted by reference to them: the speculative problems associated with sluggish official responses are reduced, relative to the textbook model where the interest rate is that on consols, by the fact that the controlled rate is very short, less than three months, rather than the bond rate (Flemming, 1988).

We have already seen that there is no conflict of principle in using monetary policy, including an interest rate instrument, to keep nominal GDP on a steady growth path. What would happen if one had a reaction function linking it to some real variable such as unemployment? There are obvious inflationary dangers if the implicit unemployment target is itself for an unsustainable rate – say below the NAIRU. Suppose, however, that danger can be avoided while the counter-cyclic use of the policy is, none the less, vigorous. There is unlikely to be any benefit in taking this policy beyond the point of attaining a steady growth of nominal GDP.

It is, of course, arguable that a little unexpected inflation may be appropriate in response to certain types of real shocks to the economy (Flemming, 1976). This is, up to a point, compatible with adhering to a pre-announced nominal GDP path which implies that any unexpected shortfall in real output is accompanied by some unexpected inflation. To the extent that wages are sticky and mark-ups fixed a smooth path for nominal GDP implies a smooth path for employment.

Since 1981 nominal GDP has grown pretty steadily at between 7 and 10 per cent a year – a narrower range than that of each year's monetary target(s) – but this rate will have to fall at some point as it exceeds the sum of plausible long-run growth and optimal inflation which might add to about 4 per cent.

What interest rate path would be most conducive to steady growth of nominal GDP? This question is not easily answered in the absence of a specification of other objectives and the role and effect of other instruments. James Meade (1987) has proposed that a target of steady nominal GDP growth be combined with a target ratio of national wealth to GDP and has monetary and fiscal instruments, sometimes combined with reformed wage bargaining. He and his colleagues have experimented with a variety of rules for the assignment of instruments to objectives and with different forms of fiscal and monetary policy instrument. Typically monetary policy is represented (if only indirectly) by the (real) interest and exchange rates which play a key role in determining K/Y while the growth of nominal income is driven by fiscal policy.

Meade's model of June 1987 not only gives a monetary interpretation to the real interest and exchange rate but relates nominal wage growth only to two real variables; the unemployment rate and labour's share (post-tax) in national income. This makes me uneasy about the theoretical basis of the suggested assignment. Moreover, Meade and his collaborators (see e.g. Blake and Weale, 1988) have also worked with empirically based macro-models which typically have more nominal variables and allow a variety of roles to fiscal instruments; they are also rather Keynesian. A more optimistic view of market forces might suggest that they could look after both the international and intertemporal allocations of resources provided that the tax and tariff *structures* were suitably neutral. The *level* of tax *rates* would then be set to minimise their long-term deadweight cost – i.e. at a very slow moving level in the absence of wars or other such shocks (Flemming, 1987b).

This would leave monetary policy to stabilise both prices and activity combined, as suggested above, in a smooth target path for nominal GDP. The details of such a policy would obviously depend on the details of one's view of how the economy works – which might be encapsulated by a macro-model. Clearly interest rates should rise, or be higher, if nominal GDP growth is above its target path. The problems are first that data on GDP are not available in a timely fashion, and secondly that it may be appropriate to respond differently to price and quantity (activity) deviations if they themselves respond differently to interest rate changes. As time passes the emerging data on nominal GDP and its split may become available sufficiently rapidly for use in the formation of policy.

Among the most timely data the exchange rate has the property not only of containing information about changes in nominal GDP but is also amenable to influence by interest rates and exerts influence on the path of nominal GDP. The nominal exchange rate does, of course, need to be supplemented by information about foreign prices but these are relatively readily available and, for a group of countries corresponding to an exchange rate basket, can probably even be forecast for a year or so ahead with some accuracy. Moreover it is important that shocks to the equilibrium real exchange rate be suitably accommodated.

What I am suggesting here is not the Artis and Currie (1981) proposition that the exchange rate is likely to be a preferable intermediate target to any measure of the money supply. That role is transferred to nominal GDP ('velocity adjusted money') which is certainly not a final objective. Thus the exchange rate is at best a subordinate intermediate objective.

For our purposes the questions thus become: what exchange rate path is likely to prove conducive to a smooth path of nominal GDP ultimately at 5% per cent p.a. or less, and secondly, what interest rate policy is required to achieve that path?

There are of course other instruments by which the exchange rate could be influenced. Fiscal policy certainly has effects – but I am assuming that that is determined by resource allocation and intertemporal minimisation of dead-weight burdens. Trade taxes and subsidies can influence the exchange rate – but only by distorting both resource allocation and the relationship between the exchange rate and nominal GDP. Intervention may influence the exchange rate for a while both directly, especially if unsterilised, and indirectly, if undertaken openly, by providing information as to the authorities' intentions. This information is relevant even if (sterilised) intervention is not more than transitorily effective if it is indicative of interest rate and money supply changes the authorities would be prepared to undertake if necessary.

The basic rule for interest rates in this case is to set them at the level required to achieve the chosen exchange rate path. Generally an unexpected increase in the short-term interest rate will raise the exchange rate to a level from which it will tend to decline at a rate related to its excess over foreign rates. It is, of course, possible that the markets will have taken an unexpected rate rise as a sign that the authorities have heard some bad news not yet known to the market or that they are behaving erratically so that the £ has become riskier and should, in either case, be marked down. These possibilities do not, however, diminish the scope for conscious use of the interest rate to control the path of the exchange rate within a framework of, for instance, a published path for nominal GDP.

A coherent explicit policy of using an interest rate to control the exchange rate to achieve a published path for nominal GDP would so condition expectations as largely to determine the yield curve of domestic interest rates across various maturities. To this extent policy to modify the yield curve by manipulating the maturity of government debt would be ineffective. An interesting question is whether using any residual scope to twist the yield curve would have any effect on the exchange rate. If, for instance, instruments denominated in different currencies are closer substitutes at short maturities that at long ones a steepening of the yield curve would tend to lower the exchange rate.

If also effects of interest rates on the level and composition of domestic expenditures vary with maturity the assignment of one interest rate to the control of the exchange rate may not preclude the use of debt policy to influence others for other purposes.

The question remains, however, what path the exchange rate should be held to to achieve, for instance, a gradual decline in the growth rate of nominal GDP.

The exchange rate has two effects, over and above those of the interest rate required to achieve it. A higher nominal rate reduces prices directly, though to a degree which varies with the behaviour of profit margins on domestic and imported goods, while a higher real exchange rate reduces competitiveness and output.

Consider an economy in equilibrium with a relatively high inflation rate. A restrictive policy raising the exchange rate will reduce the growth of nominal GDP at the cost of a loss of competitiveness. When and how can this loss be made good (it may need to be more than made good if net foreign assets are run down during the adjustment process)? One possibility is that non-linearities in the system might imply a different price-quantity split of changes in nominal GDP at lower inflation rates so that a looser policy later, designed to restore competitiveness, would do that, and stimulate output growth, rather than nullifying the contribution to the reduction of inflation. Alternatively a sufficiently slow restoration of competitiveness will always work if the level of competitiveness has any effect independently of its rate of change. Note, however, that if the nominal exchange rate is pegged to a low inflation currency after the loss of competitiveness the convergence on the lower foreign inflation rate and equilibrium competitiveness are liable to be non-monotonic.

CONCLUSION

Interest rates remain central to macroeconomic policy. Keynes did not exaggerate their importance, indeed by restricting the argument of the *General Theory* effectively largely to a closed economy he suppressed a key channel of their operation.

APPENDIX

The conventional textbook IS–LM model can be presented schematically as follows:

Identity	$Y = C + I$		(1)
Marginal propensity to consume	$C = C(Y,r)$		(2a)
Marginal efficiency of investment	$I = I(Y,r)$		(3a)
(1)–(3a) imply	$Y = Y(r)$	I–S	(4a)
(Inverse) liquidity preference schedule	$r = r(Y\|M)$	L–M	(5a)
(4a) and (5a) imply	$Y = f(\bar{M})$ $r = g(\bar{M})$		(6a)

The I–S and L–M equations have to be solved simultaneously for Y and r.

The alternative if r is exogenous ($\bar{r}$) is simply:

	$C = C(Y\|\bar{r})$		(2b)
	$I = I(Y\|\bar{r})$		(3b)
(1)–(3b) implies	$Y = Y(\bar{r})$	I–S	(4b/6b)
Liquidity preference	$M = M(Y(\bar{r})g\bar{r}) = h(\bar{r})$	L–M	(5b/6b)

Which is essentially the simplest textbook multiplier model of the chapter before that in which money and interest are introduced.

References

ARTIS, M. J. and D. A. CURRIE (1981) 'Monetary Targets and the Exchange Rate: a Case for Conditional Targets', *Oxford Economic Papers*, vol. 81, Supplement, July.

BARRO, R. J. (1979) 'On the Determination of the Public Debt', *Journal of Political Economy*, vol. 87, no. 5, Pt. I, October.

BARRO, R. J. (1987) 'Monetary policy under Exchange Rate Targeting and Other Arrangements', Mimeo.

BARRO, R. J. and H. I. GROSSMAN (1976) *Money, Employment and Inflation* (New York: Cambridge University Press).

BLAKE, A. and M. WEALE (1988) 'Exchange Rate Targets and Wage Formation', *National Institute Economic Review*, no. 123, February.

BUITER, W. E. H. (1981) 'The Superiority of Contingent Rules over Fixed Rules in Models with Rational Expectations', *Economic Journal*, vol. 91, no. 363, September.

FENDER, J. (1981) *Understanding Keynes: an Analysis of the General Theory* (Brighton: Harvester Press).

FLEMMING, J. S. (1976) *Inflation* (Oxford: Oxford University Press).

FLEMMING, J. S. (1981) 'The Role of Expectations in Fiscal and Monetary Policy', in M. J. Artis and M. H. Miller (eds), *Essays in Fiscal and Monetary Policy* (Oxford: Oxford University Press (for IFS)).

FLEMMING, J. S. (1987a) 'Wage Flexibility and Employment Stability', *Oxford Economic Papers*, vol. 39, no. 1, March.

FLEMMING, J. S. (1987b) 'Debt and Taxes in War and Peace: the Case of a Small Open Economy', in M. J. Boskin, J. S. Flemming and S. Gorini (eds), *Private Saving and Public Debt* (Oxford: Basil Blackwell).

FLEMMING, J. S. (1988) 'Three Points on the Yield Curve', *Money Study Group*, forthcoming.

HICKS, J. R. (1935) 'A Suggestion for Simplifying the Theory of Money', *Economics*, reprinted in J. R. Hicks (1967), *Critical Essays in Monetary Theory* (Oxford: Clarendon Press).

KEYNES, J. M. (1936) *General Theory of Employment, Interest and Money* (London: Macmillan).

MALINVAUD, E. (1977) *The Theory of Unemployment Reconsidered* (Oxford: Basil Blackwell).

MALINVAUD, E. (1980) *Profitability and Unemployment* (Cambridge: Cambridge University Press).

MANKIW, N. G. (1986) 'The Optimal Collection of Seignorage', Mimeo, Harvard.

MEADE, J. E. (1987) 'Monetary and Fiscal Policy: the Assignment of Weapons to Targets', Mimeo, *Department of Applied Economics*, Cambridge.

NEARY, J. P. and J. E. STIGLITZ (1983) 'Towards a Reconstruction of Keynesian Economics: Expectations and Constrained Equilibria', *Quarterly Journal of Economics*, vol. 98, no. 3, Supplement.

PATINKIN, D. (1976) *Keynes' Monetary Thought*, (Durham, North Carolina: Duke University Press).

WICKSELL, K. (1935) *Lectures in Political Economy II* (London: Routledge & Kegan Paul).

12 Interest Rates and the Conduct of Monetary Policy

Terence C. Mills and Geoffrey E. Wood

12.1 INTRODUCTION

The *General Theory* changed how most economists and policy-makers viewed the rate of interest. Before 1936 and the subsequent spread of 'Keynesianism', it had been thought of as a relative price. It was determined by the workings of the economy so as to effect the allocation of currently available resources between the production of goods for current consumption and the production of goods which would allow future consumption. After the *General Theory*, it was thought of as a variable which could, subject to a lower bound set by the liquidity trap, be manipulated by monetary policy so as to affect the level of economic activity and the unemployment rate.

These two views of the rate of interest have rather different implications for how monetary policy should be conducted. Our aim in this chapter is to report the results of some tests which help to discriminate between these two views, and, on the basis of these results, to offer some suggestions for the appropriate conduct of monetary policy.

The plan of the chapter is as follows. First we briefly consider historical discussions of the rate of interest, so as to distinguish between the views we are seeking to compare. Then we develop in some detail the economic analysis which will underlie our tests. After that there is discussion of the periods from which we draw the data for our tests, noting in particular why different periods are used for different tests. The tests are then set out, and their findings reported.[1] The chapter concludes with a discussion of the implications of these results for the conduct of monetary policy.

12.2 HISTORICAL BACKGROUND

The theory which we are contrasting with the 'Keynesian' one is of long standing.[2] It fluctuated in its development, sometimes an earlier author having a clearer and more detailed view of the theory than a later one, and sometimes, too, there being explicit recognition of the existence of a whole term structure of interest rates, while at other times this complication was ignored. Sir Dennis Robertson provides a clear example of a scholar who set out the traditional view in detail. (Earlier examples, differing from Robertson only in the inessential respect of suppressing discussion of the term structure, are Wicksell and Thornton. A very clear summary statement of Wicksell's views can be found in his 1907 *Economic Journal* paper; the work of Thornton on this subject, originally, of course, set out in his 'Paper Credit' of 1802, has recently been discussed in detail by Humphrey (1986).) Robertson provides a very clear statement of his views in his *Lectures on Economic Principles* (first published in three volumes in 1957, 1958, and 1959).

Robertson set out the theory of the rate of interest first of all as a real theory of *the* rate (i.e. neglecting the term structure). He used the word interest, he wrote, not just in Marshall's 'strict sense', that is, 'the payment which anyone receives during a given period in return for a loan'. He used it also in the ' ... wider sense, in which it includes the income, or part of the income, derived by a person or corporation from the investment of his or its own resources – the sense in which Crusoe derived interest from investing his time in making a fishing rod'. He also stressed that there was a demand schedule for funds to invest, demand varying (other things being equal) with the rate of interest.

> There seems to me to be no more objection to speaking of a schedule of demand rates of interest, i.e. of demand prices for the use of investible funds, than to speaking of a schedule of demand prices for tea; and it seems to me to be clearly convenient, and to help to show the unity in the diversity of economic phenomena, to do so.

(All the above quotations are taken from Robertson (1958, p. 51).)

The theory, then, is a *real* theory of the determination of a *relative* price. How was the price determined? Robertson constructs first a demand schedule, ' ... a curve of what some writers have called the marginal efficiency of capital – what I prefer to call the marginal productivity of investible funds' (p. 63).[3] A schedule is drawn up showing the marginal productivity of stocks of capital of various sizes. If the stock is being kept constant at some level, then the marginal product at that point is the rate of interest (in the sense in which Robertson defined the term earlier for Crusoe), and the curve can be interpreted as 'a curve of demand rates of interest indicating, for stationary economies of various sizes, the demand rate of interest on investible funds devoted to the replacement of machines' (p. 65). And if the capital stock is growing, it is because the 'net rate of return on the cost of building a machine (stands) above the hiring price of investible funds' (p. 66). Under such circumstances, what determines how fast the stock of capital is added to? To answer this, it is necessary also to consider supply, and its interaction with a curve of demand rates of interest (i.e. demand prices), showing what rate of interest must prevail if various amounts of resources are to be devoted to investment in a particular period of time. (Period of time both in the sense of, say, a year, and dated so as to take account of technology and the existing stock of capital).

To complete the outline of this part of the theory, it is therefore necessary next to sketch Robertson's analysis of supply. He wished to derive a supply schedule of investible funds to set against the dated demand schedule already derived.[4] We must therefore ' . . . fix our eyes on a float of new waiting which has been in one respect grossed up and in another respect netted down' (p. 69). Grossed up by including funds currently released from fixed capital, netted down by saving brought about by the excess consumption of part of the population.[5]

We have, then, a theory of the rate of interest as determined by the supply of savings and the demand for investment. The rate of interest thus determined is a real rate, which determines the allocation of resources as between consumption now and consumption later, and which would always tend towards the marginal productivity of capital but could only be expected to reach it in the long-run equilibrium of a stationary economy.

How does money enter this story? It does so in two ways. We sketch these only briefly, as there is an extensive discussion in Section 12.3 below. Robertson described the long rate as the rate of interest *par excellence*, and the short rate as being much more variable, but being anchored by the long rate. The short rate is affected by, among other factors, the actions of the monetary authorities in easing or tightening money. The long rate can be affected by such actions, but only when the monetary injection (or contraction) is long lasting. If it *is* then, to quote Wicksell (1907, p. 213)

> if, other things remaining the same, the leading banks of the world were to lower their rate of interest, say 1 per cent below its ordinary level, and keep it so for some years, then the prices of all commodities would rise and rise and rise without any limit whatever; on the contrary, if the leading banks were to *raise* their rate of interest, say 1 per cent above its normal level, and keep it so for some years, then all prices would *fall* and fall and fall without any limit except zero.

To summarise, then, the traditional view of the rate of interest is that it is determined by real forces, so as to equalise savings and investment. Temporary monetary fluctuations can produce temporary fluctuations, particularly in short rates, and long-lasting monetary changes can affect prices, and, as we shall set out in Section 12.3, the nominal but not the real rate.[6] Monetary forces do no more than add disturbances to a basically real phenomenon. In such a world, whatever else monetary policy could do, it could not permanently affect the level of output and employment by permanently changing the rate of interest.

The view we wish to contrast with this has been set out with admirable clarity by Joan Robinson (1952) in her collection *The Rate of Interest and Other Essays*. She does this first by summarising an argument she attributes to the *General Theory*, and then qualifying that argument. In her essay *The Generalisation of the General Theory*, she writes (p. 73)

> When unemployment appears, the argument runs, money wages and prices fall. If the quantity of money is not reduced correspondingly, the existence of cash now redundant to the needs of active circulation causes the rate of interest to fall, and this process continues until the fall in interest rates has stimulated investment (or reduced thriftiness) sufficiently to restore full employment.

That argument plainly implies that a once-for-all change in the supply of money (relative to demand) has a permanent effect on the real rate of interest – a very sharp contrast to the views discussed above. Her main concern with the argument is not that conclusion, but rather the fear that because of 'a confident belief in the normal value of the rate of interest . . . the rate of interest would refuse to fall' (p. 75). She admits that the expectations which produced this stickiness will gradually change, but they will change only slowly, so that, 'the automatic corrective action of the rate of interest is condemned by its very nature to be too little and too late' (p. 76). Her conclusion on the argument is that ' . . . mere monetary management cannot preserve full employment' (p. 77). Note that there is no hint that monetary policy cannot permanently change the interest rate – only the fear that because of sluggish expectations, leading perhaps to the liquidity trap, it cannot do enough.

In her essay entitled *The Rate of Interest*, this model of interest rate determination – liquidity preference – is elaborated.[7] The first generalisation is to recognise that there is a whole range of rates of interest, on different types of asset; these vary with their riskiness as compared to the rate on a risk-free bond, which in turn is determined by liquidity preference. She next analyses an open market operation – but the attention here is on how expectations influence the extent to which such an operation, if carried out at the short end of the yield curve, feeds through to rates at the long end. At the end of her discussion, on page 17, she writes 'to summarise: given the state of expectations, the long and short rates of interest both fall as the quantity of money increases relatively to national income'. The only qualification admitted is the liquidity trap. Finally, there is a brief discussion in the same essay on 'A Cheap Money Policy'. On this she writes '(a) campaign by the monetary authorities to lower interest rates to counter unemployment, if successful, will stimulate activity' (p. 28). The qualification relates, however, not to fears that the effect of money on interest rates is inevitably transitory, but rather to the possibility that either a cartel ('a gentleman's agreement' (p. 29)) or the liquidity trap will prevent rates being driven low enough.

In summary, the theory of the rate of interest she sets out is that it is basically determined in the money market, and can be manipulated by the monetary authorities. Whether or not that was a correct reading of Keynes, it was a popular one. It could scarcely be more different from the more traditional view, although it does have some points of contact so far as short-run analysis goes. As Dennis Robertson put it at the start of his exposition of interest rate theory,

> you mustn't suppose that the glad tidings that the rate of interest depends entirely on the quantity of money and the state of liquidity preference haven't reached my ears – because they *have*, and I regard that as at best an inadequate and at worst a misleading account of the whole matter! (Robertson, 1958, p. 50).[8]

The issue, then, as between these two views on the rate of interest (and the implied role for monetary policy) is whether monetary policy – changes in the quantity of money supplied – permanently affect the rate of interest.[9] It may seem that the obvious way to address this is to go and look for the effects of money on the real rate of interest. We in fact do that, but because the real rate of interest, easy perhaps to define, is not observable, so that even the most careful estimate must be qualified, we also pursue another course. The traditional theory can be elaborated to give a detailed account of the expected impact of money growth on nominal interest rates. We set out this elaboration, and then carry out some tests to see whether it is a satisfactory description of the response. If it is, this provides support, independent of the problem of measuring the real rate, for the traditional view – and, of course, conversely if it does not. We develop this analysis in the next section of the chapter.

12.3 MONEY AND INTEREST RATES

12.3.1 The traditional view elaborated[10]

We set out the effects of a once-for-all shift from one steady rate of money growth to another. The effects of such a shift fall into three groups. There is first an impact effect, which may be a combination of Keynes's liquidity effect and a first-round loanable funds effect. There is then an intermediate effect on real income and the price level, and, finally, there is an effect on price expectations. In setting these out we assume that the monetary change is unanticipated and that prices are sticky.

Consider first the pure liquidity effect. Here the only variable that can change to clear the money market is the nominal rate of interest: both income and prices are assumed to be initially constant. We can thus use a simple money demand curve (Figure 12.1) to illustrate what happens.

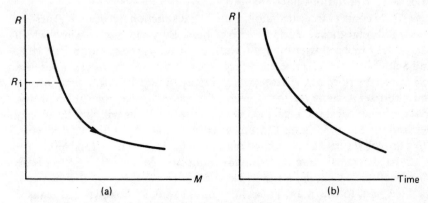

(a)   (b)

Figure 12.1   Time path of the interest rate with both loanable funds and liquidity effects. (a) Money demand function. (b) Movement of the interest rate through time as a result of a pure liquidity effect.

We are initially in equilibrium at R_1. The growth rate of nominal money now rises. The interest rate has to fall; and, as we are having not just a stock increase (in which case a once-for-all drop in interest rates would be sufficient), but an increased rate of change, in this analysis interest rates would decline continually, ending their decline only when the money demand function became infinitely elastic. A second short-run effect, still retaining the rigid price and unchanging income assumptions, may also be important. This is the *loanable funds effect*. This arises because (nowadays) an increased supply of money comes through the banking system. Bank reserves rise as a result of the central bank's actions, there is an increase in supply of loanable funds, and so a *drop* (once-for-all) in the interest rate.[11]

So far, then, two relationships, both short run, one inevitable and one possible but not inevitable, have been identified. The liquidity effect shows a relationship between the level of interest rates and the stock of money; or, alternatively, between the rate of change of the nominal interest rate and that of the quantity of money. From the liquidity effect, so long as the stock of nominal cash balances is growing, the nominal interest rate falls. In contrast, the loanable funds effect relates the level of the nominal interest rate to the change in the quantity of money, or the rate of change of the nominal interest rate to the acceleration in the quantity of money – because acceleration produces increased revenue to the money issuers, and thereby an increase in credit. If both effects operate, an acceleration in the rate of growth of money would produce first a drop in the interest rate, via the loanable funds effect, and then, via the liquidity effect, a falling interest rate for so long as the higher rate of money growth persists. This is set out in Figure 12.2, with the acceleration in money growth being at t_1. So far, nominal and realised real interest rate movements have coincided, because neither the price level nor price level expectations have changed.

Next we come to intermediate effects. The distinction between 'Keynesian' and traditional theory starts to emerge here. By some mechanisms – which can be Keynesian (lower interest rates), or of the type set out in Friedman and Schwartz (1982), where monetary expansion raises the prices of services relative to the price of the assets which supply the services – nominal income starts to rise. Assume for the moment, for the sake of analytical simplicity, that the entire effect is on real income. This rise in income will shift the money demand function of Figure 12.1 upwards, and thus raise interest rates again. How far will it raise them? It must raise them back to their original level – for until that happens, there is a stimulus to income. So the second effect is an income effect, which, via a rise in income, raises rates back to their original level. (Again, to this point prices have not moved, so nominal and realised real rates coincide.)

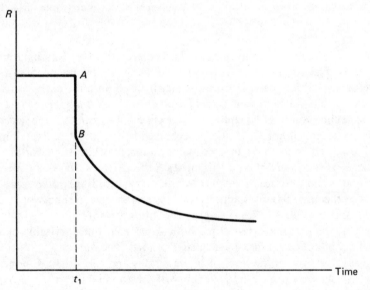

Figure 12.2 Vertical drop in R, from A to B, is the result of the loanable funds effect. Thereafter the liquidity effect operates.

Can one say anything about the path through time of this process, along the rudimentary lines of the path of the impact effects set out in Figure 12.2? One can. Consider Figure 12.3. We have argued that rates would first fall, and then rise to their original level. They need not, however, follow the path *ABCDE* with *AB* the loanable funds effect, *BC* the liquidity effect, and *CD*

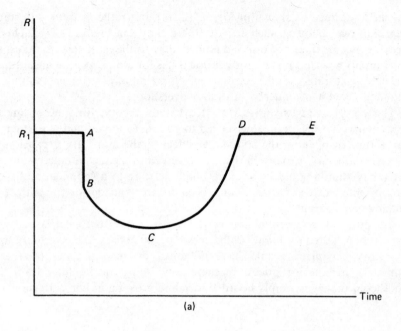

(a)

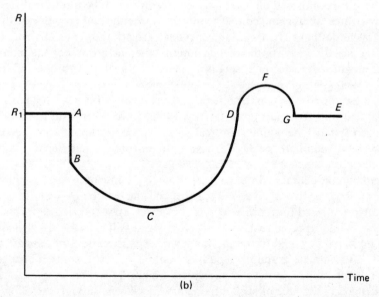

(b)

Figure 12.3   (a) Without interest rate overshooting. (b) With interest rate overshooting.

the income effect, as shown in Figure 12.3(a), but rather a path with some degree of overshooting, such as *ABCDFGE* shown in Figure 12.3(b). This is because income does not respond immediately to the monetary stimulus, so to attain its new and higher growth rate it has for a time to grow faster than the long-run rate – so the income effect is initially stronger than it is ultimately and hence interest rates may overshoot.

This contrasts in two ways with 'Keynesian' theory. First, according to that theory, if a rise in income started to pull up (nominal and real) interest rates, thus dampening the stimulative effect of the monetary expansion, a further monetary expansion would lower rates again. A succession of monetary stimuli could be applied, finally leading to a (nominal and real) rate of interest lower than it had been before, and consistent with 'full employment' output.[12]

Secondly, in 'Keynesian' theory there exists, due to the inelasticity of expectations noted by Joan Robinson (see p. 249 above), the possibility that monetary expansion would have no effect on interest rates (real and nominal), income, or prices. In these conditions, the liquidity trap, the additional money is simply hoarded, demand growing in line with supply.

12.3.2 Price expectations

So far no mention has been made of prices. But a higher growth of money has been superimposed on what must be, according to the traditional view of interest rates, an unchanged real economy. Hence the real growth rate of the system cannot have changed. Higher money growth thus ends up producing a rising price level, with the higher nominal income growth of the intermediate income effect decomposing into unchanged real growth plus inflation, as Wicksell (1907) described.

In these conditions, can the interest rate, as it has so far, stay at its original level? If it did, the real rate of interest would have fallen. But nothing has changed to alter the equilibrium real yield. Hence, as the inflation becomes anticipated, nominal yields will rise until borrowers and lenders are in equilibrium once more.

Initially, the actual real yield will be equal to the rate of interest in nominal terms minus the actual change of prices, and this will be different from the expected real yield until price expectations catch up with price performance. At this point, expected real holding period yields will equal actual real yields and both will be equal to the pre-monetary expansion non-inflationary real yield.[13] A complete graph of the adjustment of interest rates to a change in the rate of money growth is shown as Figure 12.4. (To keep real rates unchanged in the face of such a monetary shock, one should also allow for taxation. This consideration influenced our choice of data period (see below, p. 257).)

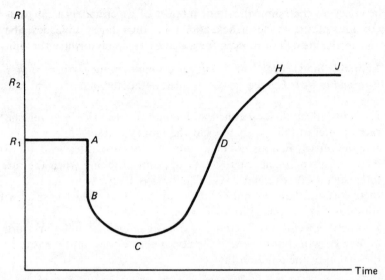

Figure 12.4 $R_2 - R_1$ = expected (and actual) inflation. Hence real rate (nominal rate — expected inflation) is the same at both R_2 and R_1.

We should make clear that we are, for the sake of expository simplicity, setting aside the qualification of the Fisher effect, which was introduced by Mundell (1963) and subsequently discussed by Tobin (1965). These authors showed that, in the presence of a real balance effect, even a fully anticipated inflation reduces the real rate of interest. It does so via its effects on the stock of real cash balances, and thus on wealth. We set this aside in our discussions because, as the effect works only via the stock of outside money, it is likely to be small, and this theoretical preconception is confirmed by most investigations. Studies which do claim to find it significant have generally covered periods of accelerating and highly variable inflation, and the interpretation of their findings is, for that reason, not clear cut.

The behaviour of the real yield on UK indexed gilts cannot be adduced in support of the Mundell–Tobin effect's empirical performance. These securities were introduced at a time of considerable inflation uncertainty, so their subsequent price behaviour is affected by more than subsequent inflation expectations.

12.3.3   Money and interest rates summarised

We first set out some propositions discussed above on the effect of permanent changes in money growth on the nominal interest rate. Having thus summarised the above section, we recast it on the alternative assumption that all money supply changes are transitory.

The effect on the nominal rate of interest of a permanent change in the growth rate of the money stock comes in four stages. (We describe an increase in the growth of money; for a decrease, simply reverse the signs).

1.   Loanable funds effect. The revenue accruing to money issuers, *if they use it to add to their holdings of assets*, lowers the nominal and real rates of interest.
2.   Liquidity effect. So long as neither income nor the price level adjusts, the rate of interest falls, so as to clear the money market.
3.   Income effect. Falling nominal and real interest rates lead to rising income; this pulls the interest rate up, only stopping when the rate of interest is at its original level. This always happens in the traditional theory. It may happen in the 'Keynesian' theory, in which case a further stimulus can be applied to lower rates again.
4.   Inflation expectations. Nothing real has changed, so inflation starts as money growth continues, and the nominal rate rises until it has risen by the extent of the inflation rate.

Now, how are these results affected if all monetary fluctuations are transitory? The word transitory can have two distinct meanings in this context; it is essential to separate them. It can mean that the change in the rate of growth of money is transitory, so that after an upsurge, money growth returns to its previous rate. Alternatively, it can mean that the actual increase in money is temporary, so that after an upsurge there is a subsequent decline, until the money stock is back where it was before.

If money growth returns to its previous (by assumption non-inflationary) rate, then any inflation which results must be transitory. Hence the expected inflation (Fisher) effect is ultimately offset. The monetary increase drives the interest rate through the first three of the phases set out above. Interest rates end at the same level as before. There has been a once-for-all rise in the price level (after temporarily driving output above its natural rate), and as a result the stock of real cash balances is unchanged. In short, the only permanent effect is on the price level.

What if the money stock first rises, and then returns to its previous level? The best way to see what happens here is to analyse it as two separate effects – first a rise in the money stock, and then a fall. A one-off rise would be as above – we would see effects 1–3, and then a once-for-all rise in the price level. There would then be a fall in the money stock, producing effects 1–3, but with their signs opposite to those so far described. Ultimately, the economy would end up as it was before.

12.4   EMPIRICAL WORK

We carry out two different kinds of tests, and we carry them out on two non-overlapping periods. One set of tests explores the effect of monetary fluctuations on nominal interest rates. The other examines the behaviour of the real rate of interest.

It is to avoid running tests of clearly related hypotheses on the same data set that we use non-overlapping data sets. For the 'monetary' tests we used the years 1870–1913, and for the behaviour of the real rate we used 1972–84. By what criteria were these periods chosen?

The period 1870–1913 has two particular advantages for the monetary tests. First, the existence of taxes complicates the Fisher effect; for rates should rise by more than expected inflation, but how much more is hard to evaluate, as the appropriate marginal tax rate is very difficult to calculate. The years between 1870 and 1913 had low and fairly stable taxes (see, for example, Ashworth, 1960, pp. 231–5) and so we can neglect them for this period as they are at most of second order importance. Second, for roughly the first half of the period (1870–86) the general level of prices was falling.[1] This is of particular importance to our tests; for, as Joan Robinson (1952) stressed in her account of 'Keynesian' interest theory, a monetary injection in a period of falling prices should, quite unambiguously, have *no* tendency to raise interest rates. This characteristic of the period thus increases the power of our tests.

Turning to our examination of the real rate of interest we used, as noted above, the period 1972–84. We chose this, rather than the interwar years, for two reasons. First, in a previous paper (Mills and Wood, 1977) we had examined the (closely related) liquidity trap hypothesis for the interwar years. Second, and more pressing, the tests we use in this section of the chapter are better performed on higher frequency data than are available for the interwar years.

We should note that the tests we conduct do not involve the explicit modelling of influences on interest rates which came from outside the UK. If we were aiming to test a fully specified model of interest rate determination this would indeed be a problem. But we are concerned here only with the influence of money on interest rates. The hypothesis that some systematic influence of money could, over the sample periods we examine, be masked by a series of independent events originating overseas strikes us as sufficiently unlikely as not to require qualification of our conclusions.

It is now time to turn to the tests themselves. Although we place greater weight on our direct tests on the real rate, we report the tests in order of the data periods on which they are carried out.

12.4.1 Monetary tests

As discussed above, the 'monetary' tests, investigating the response of interest rates to changes in monetary growth, were carried out on annual data taken from the period 1870–1913. Full discussion of the data series used and the econometric techniques employed may be found in Mills and Wood (1987); attention is centred here on the relationship between monetary growth and interest rates in the following structural model, which was arrived at after extensive modelling and testing of multivariate models of the relationships existing between money, interest rates, output, and prices:

$$\Delta q_t = a_0 + a_{21}\Delta m_{t-1} + a_{31}\Delta p_{t-1} + a_{41}\Delta R_{t-1} + \varepsilon_{1t}$$

$$\Delta m_t = \beta_{10}\Delta q_t + \beta_{11}\Delta q_{t-1} + \beta_{21}\Delta m_{t-1} + \varepsilon_{2t}$$

$$\Delta p_t = \gamma_0 + \gamma_{10}\Delta q_t + \gamma_{11}\Delta q_{t-1} + \gamma_{21}\Delta m_{t-1} + \gamma_{31}\Delta p_{t-1} + \varepsilon_{3t}$$

$$\Delta R_t = \delta_{30}\Delta p_{t-1} + \delta_{41}\Delta R_{t-1} + \varepsilon_{4t} \tag{12.1}$$

The variables are defined in the following way:

Δq_t = annual change in the logarithm of real output (annual output growth),
Δm_t = annual change in the logarithm of the money supply (annual money growth),
Δp_t = annual change in the logarithm of the price level (annual inflation),
ΔR_t = annual change in the *level* of the Consol yield.

In this model all error terms are uncorrelated, zero mean, white noise processes with constant variances. The model is therefore recursive in structure and hence Δm_t is predetermined with respect to ΔR_t. Thus the response of ΔR_t to an exogenous once-for-all shock to Δm_t can be calculated from the implied dynamic multiplier (see on this, Cooley and Leroy, 1985). The estimated coefficients, standard errors and diagnostic statistics of the model, estimated for various definitions of the variables, are detailed in Mills and Wood (1987).

In the empirical exercises, two definitions of the money supply are used, narrow money, M0, and broad money, M3. Note that changes in money growth, although predetermined, do not have a direct effect on the interest rate, rather the effect is indirect through the impact of monetary changes on output growth and inflation (i.e. there appear to be no loanable funds or liquidity effects, just the income and inflation expectation effects). Figure 12.5 presents the response of the interest rate (Consol yield) of a once-for-all (permanent) increase of 1 per cent in money growth for both the M0 and M3 definitions. The patterns of response are qualitatively similar, although the magnitude of the response to an increase in M3 growth is rather larger than that for a similar increase in M0 growth. As stated above, in both cases there are no initial negative loanable funds and liquidity effects. The responses are positive reflecting only income and inflation expectations effects, and they

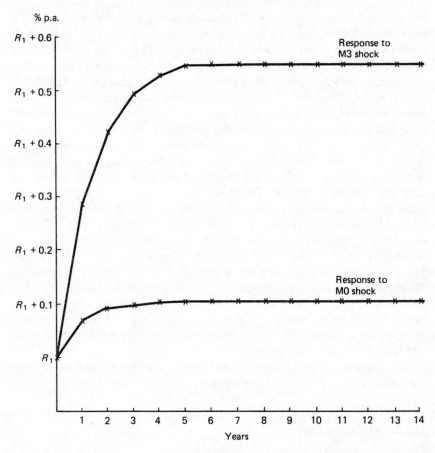

Figure 12.5   Response of nominal interest rate to an increase in money growth.

produce an increase of approximately 0.1 per cent in the Consol yield for a 1 per cent increase in M0 growth, and an increase of approximately 0.55 per cent for a similar increase in M3 growth. These increases are reached in five years, and in both cases there is a very small overshooting of the interest rate. (We would remark here that these responses are found when Greasley's (1986) output and implicit price deflator series are used. When the more traditional output and price series of Feinstein (1972) are employed, M3 is found to have *no effect* on the interest rate, although the response to M0 is essentially unaltered).

Such overall positive responses by the interest rate should occur only if the increased money growth gives rise to an expectation of inflation (or of an increased inflation rate). This means that the above result raises questions for future research. For, if one views the gold standard as a system whereby the money stock bears a fixed (and constant) relation to the stock of gold, increases in the money supply during this period could come about only through gold discoveries. Hence the nominal quantity of money would not change, except as a result of such discoveries. Monetary shocks should thus have been expected to produce once-for-all price level changes, not inflation, and no Fisher effect should be observed. Traditional interest rate theory, in such a money supply regime, would lead one to predict not a positive impact of money growth on interest rates, but *no* impact.

The evidence presented above is not consistent with this. The explanation may lie along one (or possibly both) of two lines. First, the erratic but endogenous nature of gold discoveries (as described by Rockoff, 1984) may have been incorporated into expectations; so that a monetary shock was taken as a signal of more money to come as a new gold-mine or extraction was exploited. Some evidence in favour of this argument is that Mills and Wood (1987) find both the money and price series to be non-stationary. Alternatively, the spread of banking may have produced the belief that bank deposits (part of M3) would grow relative to currency (M0). The appeal of this suggestion is, however, diminished by the fact that the money multiplier was fairly steady for much of this period – for while the currency ratio did indeed fall, the reserve ratio rose (for the relevant time series, see Capie and Webber, 1985, Table I.(3)). Nevertheless, although the results do raise some questions for traditional interest rate theory, they are totally inconsistent with 'Keynesian' theory, because, according to that theory, nominal interest rates should fall, not rise, subsequent to a monetary expansion.

12.4.2   Real rates tests

These tests were carried out on monthly data for the period 1972 to 1984, and so consider only a period of floating exchange rates. They are designed to investigate the effect of money growth on the real rates of return on a variety of financial assets. Crucial here is that the appropriate real rate variable is the expected real rate of return, which is, of course, unobservable. The actual real rate of return can be observed, however, and the important question to consider is under what set of assumptions can these observed real rates of return be used in econometric work in place of their expected counterparts? Mishkin (1981) shows that such a substitution can be made if we are prepared to assume that the expected real rate of return is correlated with a set of observable variables that are part of the available information set and if we are willing to make the assumption that expectations are rational, or equivalently that the asset markets are efficient, so that forecast errors made in predicting expected real returns will be uncorrelated with the available information.

Formally, we denote the expected real return from holding for k periods an asset having n periods to maturity at time t as $\rho_{t,k}(n)$. Assume that $\rho_{t,k}(n)$ is correlated with a vector of observable variables X_t, which are elements of the available information set:

$$\rho_{t,k}(n) = X_t\beta(n) + u_t, \tag{12.2}$$

where u_t is an error uncorrelated with X_t. The relationship between the expected real return, $\rho_{t,k}(n)$, and the observed real return, $r_{t,k}(n)$, can be expressed as

$$r_{t,k}(n) = \rho_{t,k}(n) + \xi_{t,k}(n) - \varepsilon_{t,k}, \tag{12.3}$$

where $\xi_{t,k}(n)$ and $\varepsilon_{t,k}$ are the forecast errors made in predicting *nominal* returns and inflation respectively. Only for the case of a k-period default free asset will $\xi_{t,k}(n) = 0$ and, in general, $\varepsilon_{t,k}$ will be non-zero. Substituting (12.2) into (12.3) yields

$$r_{t,k}(n) = X_t\beta(n) + e_{t,k}(n) \tag{12.4}$$

where

$$e_{t,k}(n) = u_{t,k}(n) + \xi_{t,k}(n) - \varepsilon_{t,k}$$

is a composite error term.

As data on $r_{t,k}(n)$ are available, equation (12.4) can be estimated. Indeed, if we make the assumption of market efficiency, then $\xi_{t,k}(n)$ and $\varepsilon_{t,k}$ will also be uncorrelated with X_t, so that ordinary least squares applied to (12.4) will provide a consistent estimate of $\beta(n)$, i.e. using observed real returns will asymptotically yield the same estimate of $\beta(n)$ as a regression using expected real returns. Some information will be lost through using observed real returns rather than expected real returns, for the presence of the forecast errors $\xi_{t,k}(n)$ and $\varepsilon_{t,k}$ in equation (12.4) mean that the variance of the composite error $e_{t,k}(n)$ will be larger than the error variance of equation (12.2); hence, for example, the standard errors of the estimates of $\beta(n)$ obtained from (12.4) will be larger than those that would be obtained from (12.2) if it were estimable. Additionally, as the maturity of the asset lengthens, the more volatile the price of the asset should be. As a consequence, as the period to maturity, n, increases, so should the variance of $\xi_{t,k}(n)$. Hence estimates of $\beta(n)$ should become less precise as n increases. This approach was utilised on monthly UK data for the period 1972 to 1984 in a series of papers by Mills and Stephenson (1985b, 1986, 1987), in which the formal econometric modelling techniques, data series, and construction of actual real returns for a variety of financial assets, ranging from 91 day Treasury bills to $3\frac{1}{2}$ per cent War Loan, are discussed in considerable detail.

These papers are primarily concerned with using estimates of equation (12.4) to construct measures of expected real returns, to investigate the relationship between real returns and a wide range of macroeconomic variables, and to examine the behaviour of real rates, nominal rates and expected inflation. (A related paper is Mills and Stephenson (1985a), which examines the market efficiency assumption in greater detail.)

We are concerned here, though, with examining the response of real returns to monetary growth, one of the variables included in the X_t vector used in equations (12.2) and (12.4) along with other variables such as growth of industrial production, the rate of unemployment, and exchange rate changes. The results concerning this relationship found in the papers cited above may be summarised as follows. For short-term interest rates (Treasury bills and 3-month bank bills), increased M0 growth is indeed associated with a decline of real rates, a 1 per cent increase in M0 growth being accompanied by approximately a 0.1 per cent decline in real interest rates. For assets of longer maturity (five, ten and twenty year gilts and $3\frac{1}{2}$ per cent War Loan) no association between M0 growth and real rates is found. However, when the sample period is split at May 1979, the later period now reveals a positive association between increased M0 growth and real short-term rates, although the relationship is very weak.[15] Short-term real rates are positively associated with M3 growth over the entire sample period, a permanent 1 per cent increase in M3 growth being accompanied by approximately a 0.1 per cent *increase* in real rates. With longer-term real rates the switch from a negative to a positive association with M3 growth is again found when the sample is split at May 1979; in the early period a 1 per cent increase in M3 growth is accompanied by approximately a 1 per cent decrease in real rates, whereas in the later period the real rate movement is that of an increase of about one-half of 1 per cent.

12.5 SUMMARY AND CONCLUSIONS

In this chapter we have contrasted 'Keynesian' and traditional views of the interest rate. The former view, we have argued, sees the real rate of interest as permanently susceptible to the influence of monetary policy. The latter sees it so only temporarily, rather having it determined by real factors with monetary policy impinging on it to an unpredictable and transitory extent. We have carried out two tests of these propositions. First, we tested the traditional theory's predictions of the effect of money growth on nominal interest rates in the years 1870–1913, and found these predictions substantially confirmed. Second, we examined the behaviour of the real rate of interest from 1972 to 1984 and found no systematic relationship with money growth. We interpret these findings as supporting the traditional, rather than the 'Keynesian', view of interest rates.[16] What does this conclusion mean for policy?

It certainly does *not* mean that monetary policy is unimportant. It tells us, first, that the nominal rate, which monetary policy does affect, is a poor indicator of the real rate; this is confirmation of a well established result. Second, it shows that attempts to manipulate interest rates by monetary policy so as to affect output and employment are misguided; they will have at most transitory effects on interest rates, and these transitory effects are somewhat hard to predict.

Moving from how policy should not be conducted to how it should, do our results have anything to say? In our view they do, albeit indirectly. Some thirty years ago, Phillip Cagan (1958) asked 'Why do we use money in open market operations?' Money, that is to say, rather than some other commodity. His answer was that it is because money impinges directly on the market for every other good, while, to use his examples, this would not be true of open market operations involving use of the stock of copper or the stock of pins. This of course implies that monetary disturbances affect every market. If we cannot produce the beneficial effect of a lower real rate of interest and subsequent higher activity and employment by monetary expansion, all that such expansions do is disturb every market to no particular end. This should surely be avoided.

More recently, Karl Brunner (1986) has argued the same case on somewhat different grounds. Money evolves as a device to economise on information – information about relative prices – and to help the use of that information. The step from a barter economy to a monetary one is enormous. Anything which makes money a less efficient conveyor of information about relative prices imposes great efficiency losses. Hence we should seek to stabilise the value of money. That is the *only* desirable objective of monetary policy. In our view, our results strongly support that conclusion, for we have shown that no price, in terms of an undesirable real interest rate and level of activity, is involved more than transitorily. Furthermore, this transitory period is, on the basis of the results here, very short.

'Keynesian' interest rate theory can provide no justification for attempts to lower the interest rate by monetary policy. The focus of monetary policy should be the price level. Real interest rates are independent of monetary policy, and attempts to manipulate them by monetary policy will serve only to make money less efficient at what it really can do, economise on information.

Notes

1. These tests, we should remark, do not deal with the liquidity trap. We have examined that hypothesis on UK data elsewhere (Mills and Wood, 1977) and it has been examined on US data by Cagan and Schwartz (1975) and Baytes and Marty (1987).

2. Note that 'Keynesian' is in quotation marks. The purpose of this is to avoid our becoming embroiled in a discussion of 'what Keynes really meant'. We shall show below that the view of the rate of interest which we are to contrast with the older one was set out by people who ascribed it to Keynes. Their ascribing it thus is certainly supported by Keynes himself in a short essay (1937) in which he summarised the differences between himself and Irving Fisher on interest rate theory. It is also consistent with Chapter 13 of the *General Theory* (Keynes, 1936). That chapter opens as if it were going to differ from the traditional view only in emphasis. The desire to save is initially (p. 166 of the Royal Economic Society edition) given a part in interest rate determination. But then liquidity preference is introduced, and by page 167 it has been promoted from a determinant of the short-run effect of money on interest rates to the sole determinant, along with the quantity of money, of the level of interest rates. This promotion is effected in a paragraph:

    It should be obvious that the rate of interest cannot be a return to saving or waiting as such. For if a man hoards his savings in cash, he earns no interest, though he saves just as much as before. On the contrary, the mere definition of the rate of interest tells us in so many words that the rate of interest is the reward for parting with liquidity for a specified period. For the rate of interest is, in itself, nothing more than the inverse proportion between a sum of money and what can be obtained for parting with control over the money in exchange for a debt for a stated period of time (Keynes, 1936, p. 167).

3. At this point in his argument Robertson emphasised that ' . . . we must be very careful – much more careful than most writers have been – not to get our dimensions mixed – not to confuse the stock of capital with the flow of new investment, i.e. with the rate at which additions are being made to that stock.' (Robertson, 1958, p. 63)

4. It is worth noting that Robertson does not set out a supply curve of new capital goods as a device for telling us how rapidly the capital stock changes. His analysis is thus either comparative static, or describing different equilibrium growth paths. It does not describe in detail the movement from one such equilibrium to another. This abstinence gives his analysis both great generality – it does not depend on detailed and highly specific assumptions – and considerable simplicity.

5. Robertson defines 'Waiting' as that element of the action of a saver which induces him to wait for the enjoyment of benefits which he has a legal right to enjoy now. It is unnecessary for the present purpose to discuss the determinants of the position and slope of the demand schedule which Robertson examined, for its slope with regard to the rate of interest is for our purpose immaterial. But it is worth noting that at this point in his analysis Robertson wrote as follows. 'There seems to be an odd sort of superstition floating about that this dependence of saving on income is a new discovery, so you must forgive me for asking you to look once more at Marshall's historical survey (IV, 7) of the growth of wealth.' There is then an extensive quotation from Marshall, of which Robertson writes, 'The dependence . . . of present saving,

on immediately past income, could not be more clearly expressed … '
(quotations from Robertson, 1958, pp. 69–70).

6. We set aside the influence of a fully anticipated inflation on the real wage via the real balance effect on the grounds of its well established empirical insignificance. See also the discussion of the Mundell–Tobin effect on pages 254–5.

7. In the course of the elaboration there is a footnote (note 2) where the assumption of a somehow exogenously fixed price level is made. There is, however, no hint that this, far from being a minor simplifying assumption, is of some importance for the analysis.

8. We would emphasise at this juncture that what is at issue is not a revival of the liquidity preference/loanable funds debate: the theories must, of course, be consistent in their equilibrium result. Our concern is whether monetary forces (i.e. liquidity preference) can change the real interest rate in a predictable and permanent way.

9. We take up below the range of margins of substitution between money and other assets. See note 16.

10. A detailed discussion of the material of this section is to be found in Cagan (1972). Friedman and Schwartz (1982) also contain a very full analysis of these effects. They point out that Thornton (1802) produced a full analysis of these effects; Humphrey (1986) provides detailed references to Thornton's work.

11. There are two qualifications to the existence of this second short-run effect. First, if the money growth comes from a gold discovery, the initial effect will be on miners' wages and then on the price of what they buy. Second, none of the revenue which accrues to the issuers of the new money need be used to augment wealth – so the interest rate need not fall. These points were first made by Mill (1848).

12. We do not attempt to define full employment. Robinson (1952) uses the term frequently in her exposition, but provides no definition of it. For our purposes, we could equally well substitute the somewhat more clumsy, but less opaque, phrase 'income produced by a higher level of employment than before the stimulus'.

13. We neglect at this point possible efficiency costs associated with a higher inflation rate. These are discussed below on pages 262–3.

14. Both the length and extent of the fall depend on the price series used, but there is no dispute that there was a fall.

15. May 1979 was chosen as the break point because it is conveniently close to both the mid point of the sample period and the arrival of the MTFS. The positive reaction of very short rates to M0 after that date may reflect the kind of policy anticipation effect which is sometimes found in the US.

16. We would observe at this point that finding money having no significant and persistent effect on the real rate of interest as measured by the adjusted return on financial assets does not mean that we consider changing yields on these to be the only channel of transmission of monetary policy. We regard these yields as indications of all rates of return, far from perfectly correlated with all others, but a convenient indication of movement.

References

ASHWORTH, W. (1960) *An Economic History of England, 1870–1939* (London: Methuen).

BAYTES, J. and A. L. MARTY (1987) 'Interest on Money and the Liquidity Trap', City University of New York Graduate Centre Working Paper, forthcoming.

BRUNNER, K. (1986) 'The Disarray in Macro-Economics', Eighth Henry Thornton Lecture, Centre for Banking and International Finance, The City University.

CAGAN, P. (1958) 'Why Do We Use Money in Open Market Operations?', *Journal of Political Economy*, vol. 66, pp. 34–46.

CAGAN, P. (1972) *The Channels of Monetary Effects on Interest Rates* (New York: NBER).

CAGAN, P. and A. J. SCHWARTZ (1975) 'Has the Growth of Money Substitutes Hindered Monetary Policy?', *Journal of Money, Credit, and Banking*, vol. 7, pp. 137–59.

CAPIE, F. H. and A. WEBBER (1985) *A Monetary History of the United Kingdom 1870–1982, Volume I: Data, Sources, Methods* (London: Allen & Unwin).

COOLEY, T. F. and S. F. LEROY (1985) 'Atheoretical Macroeconometrics: a Critique', *Journal of Monetary Economics*, vol. 16, pp. 283–308.

FEINSTEIN, C. H. (1972) *National Income, Expenditure and Output in the United Kingdom* (Cambridge: Cambridge University Press).

FRIEDMAN, M. and A. J. SCHWARTZ (1982) *Monetary Trends in the United States and the United Kingdom* (Chicago: University of Chicago Press).

GREASLEY, D. (1986) 'British Economic Growth: The Paradox of the 1880s and the Timing of the Climacteric', *Explorations in Economic History*, vol. 23, pp. 416–444.

HUMPHREY, T. (1986) 'Cumulative Process Models from Thornton to Wicksell', *Economic Review, Federal Reserve Bank of Richmond*, May/June.

KEYNES, J. M. (1936) *The General Theory of Employment, Interest, and Money* (London: Macmillan).

KEYNES, J. M. (1937) 'The Theory of the Rate of Interest', in A. D. Gayer (ed.), *The Lessons of Monetary Experience: Essays in Honour of Irving Fisher* (New York: Farrar and Rinehart).

MILL, J. S. (1848) *Principles of Political Economy* (London: Parker, Son and Bourn).

MILLS, T. C. and M. J. STEPHENSON (1985a) 'An Empirical Analysis of the UK Treasury Bill Market', *Applied Economics*, vol. 17, pp. 689–703.

MILLS, T. C. and M. J. STEPHENSON (1985b) 'Short-term Interest Rates in the UK: an Empirical Analysis', Leeds Discussion Paper 142.

MILLS, T. C. and M. J. STEPHENSON (1986) 'Modelling Real Returns on UK Government Stock', *Bulletin of Economic Research*, vol. 38, pp. 237–56.

MILLS, T. C. and M. J. STEPHENSON (1987) 'The Behaviour of Expected Short-term Real Interest Rates in the UK', *Applied Economics*, vol. 19, pp. 331–46.

MILLS, T. C. and G. E. WOOD (1977) 'Money Substitutes and Monetary Policy in the UK, 1922–1974', *European Economic Review*, vol. 10, pp. 19–36.

MILLS, T. C. and G. E. WOOD (1987) 'Money Growth, Interest Rates and Prices Under the Gold Standard: a Re-Examination', Leeds Discussion Paper 87/8.

MISHKIN, F. S. (1981) 'The Real Interest Rate: an Empirical Investigation', in K. Brunner and A. H. Meltzer (eds), *The Costs and Consequences of Inflation*, Carnegie-Rochester Conference Series on Public Policy, vol. 15, pp. 150–200.

MUNDELL, R. A. (1963) 'Inflation and Real Interest', *Journal of Political Economy*, vol. 71, pp. 280–83.

ROBERTSON, Sir D. H. (1958) *Lectures on Economic Principles*, vol. II (London: Staples Press).

ROBINSON, J. (1952) *The Rate of Interest and Other Essays* (London: Macmillan).

ROCKOFF, H. (1984) 'Some Evidence on the Real Price of Gold, Its Costs of Production, and Commodity Prices', in M. D. Bordo and A. J. Schwartz (eds), *A Retrospective on the Classical Gold Standard, 1821–1931*, pp. 613–50 (Chicago: University of Chicago Press).

THORNTON, H. (1802, 1978) *An Enquiry into the Nature and Effects of the Paper Credit of Great Britain* (Fairfield, N. J.: Augustus M. Kelley).

TOBIN, J. (1965) 'Money and Economic Growth', *Econometrica*, vol. 33, pp. 671–84.

WICKSELL, K. (1907) 'The Influence of the Rate of Interest on Prices', *Economic Journal*, vol. 17, pp. 213–220.

Part VII

Should Reflationary Fiscal Policy Have Priority Over Monetary Policy?

13 Monetary and Fiscal Policy in the UK

Alan Walters

13.1 INTRODUCTION

Some twenty-three years ago, a most distinguished group of British econo-mists, all associated with the National Institute of Economic and Social Research, wrote a book, *The British Economy in 1975* (ed. Wilfred Becker-man, London, 1965). A feature of that book, which today may seem most remarkable but in those days was hardly noticed, was that money, monetary policy, and the exchange rate were not mentioned, even *en passant*. Inflation, it was thought, would be controlled by incomes policies, and the co-operative spirit of unions and management. Fiscal policy was the major lever in ensuring that aggregate demand was sufficient to create the full employment level of output and to ensure that there was only an acceptably small percentage of unemployed. Beckerman *et al.* recommended an expansion of government spending to ensure this blissful state.

Monetary policy, to paraphrase the late Lord Kaldor, should be concerned mainly with the maintenance of 'orderly' (financial) markets'; and broadly speaking, the Radcliffe Committee Report (1959) had endorsed Kaldor's view. Liquidity was the important determinant of monetary conditions, but since no one could define it, there seemed to be few constraints on monetary policy.

Some eleven years later, in December 1976, Mr Healey, then Chancellor of the Exchequer, signed the famous, or infamous, letter of intent to the IMF. Monetary restraints had been introduced by the Treasury some time earlier in the April budget, but clearly the IMF commitment implied that they were to be taken much more seriously as a central feature of the economic policy of the UK.

It would be nice to report that between 1965 and 1975 an intellectual revolution caused this change. The arguments of monetarists, and particu-larly of Friedman and his followers, were quite persuasive, but I fear that they would have had little effect on British policy except for the massive macroeconomic errors of the Heath government. 'Competition and Credit Control' (CCC), introduced in 1971, intended to sweep away the controls on credit markets so that the allocation of credit could be determined by cost, but it also swept away the inhibitions those controls exercised over the

271

expansion of the money supply, especially since the authorities were unwilling to tolerate interest rates they thought politically unacceptable. The money supply, on all measures, increased sharply and inflation duly followed. Two major lessons on monetary policy emerged from the turmoil. The first was that rapid increases in monetary growth should be avoided. The second was that monetary policy should be considered in close conjunction with fiscal policy. Possibly a third macroeconomic lesson was that expansionary fiscal and monetary policies did not solve the problem of unemployment.

Such lessons, however, did not penetrate every politician or policy-maker. In the period from the first election of 1974, the Labour government embarked on a very rapid expansion of public spending financed by a large increase in the public sector financial deficit to 7.2 per cent of the GDP in 1975–6, which soon gave rise to the sterling crisis of July 1975. It was undoubtedly this bitter experience of escalating interest rates, depleted reserves, collapsing sterling, inflation at 26 per cent (end of 1975) etc., rather than intellectual conversion of the cabinet, that gave rise to the first commitments to a monetarist constraint in April, 1976.[1] Politicians may be impervious to ideas but not to experience, particularly if it is thought to affect elections.

Of course in 1976 it was not, indeed could never be, the pure stuff of monetarism. The choice of M3 and later sterling M3 as the aggregate to be monitored and contained meant a considerable departure from the 'medium of exchange' definition of money. More than half of M3 consisted of interest bearing deposits which were rarely, if ever, used as a medium of exchange.[2] This, however, did not seem at the time to be a significant issue since, with the exception of the débâcle of CCC, the correlation of all the major monetary aggregates has been very close, and there seemed no obvious reason why such affinity should not continue.[3]

But M3 had two other advantages. The first is that it was closely related to fiscal variables, and particularly the PSBR. If we suppose that there are no changes in the non-deposit liabilities of the banking system, we can decompose the change in (sterling) M3 into:

> PSBR less sales of debt to non-bank domestic sector
> plus   Lending to private sector in sterling
> minus   External financing of public and private deficits.

In effect, the constraint on the expansion of M3 could be, and was, translated, via assumptions about the private sector lending and external finance, to a permissible PSBR and budget deficit. Indeed, John Fforde has suggested that the main effect of monetary objectives was to provide some discipline on the PSBR and other budgetary constraints.[4]

There was another important institutional reason for adopting an M3 target. After its brief and unseemly flirtation with CCC, Britain returned to its system of extensive credit controls and rationing. The constraint on M3 could be translated into the containment of bank lending, external borrowing, etc., and was familiar to officials in the Bank and Treasury. Thus the new targets were not new after all; they were simply new arrangements of old targets. Similarly the mechanisms were not new; they were the old mechanisms (bank rate, after October 1972 minimum lending rate, operations in the bill market, credit controls, exchange controls, etc.) with somewhat different rationalisations. There was clearly no suggestion of a system of monetary base control as in Germany or Switzerland.

One would have imagined that the use of M3 and its association with fiscal policy from 1976 onwards would have ensured that monetary (or more strictly M3) policy and fiscal policy were usually, if not always, in harmony. One should not see, for example, the pattern of loose fiscal and tight monetary policy that was observed in the United States in 1980–83. Such a consistent monetary and fiscal policy would make it difficult to disentangle the effects of each.[5] I shall argue that, fortunately for the analyst, there have been significant divergencies between fiscal and monetary policy, certainly before the 1976 accord and on several key occasions afterwards. These have been largely a consequence of accidents or misinterpretations, which have given grist for the analytical mill.

13.2 NEO-CLASSICISTS AND RATIONAL EXPECTATIONS

It is necessary to review briefly the rival theories of macroeconomic policy so that we know where we are, or should be, according to our beliefs about the efficacy of markets and policy. The Keynesian view of the economy asserted that many markets – particularly the labour market – did not work in the sense that although there was excess supply (of people seeking jobs) the wage rate did not fall – at least it did not fall in the short or even medium term sufficient to clear the market. Unemployment persisted. Similar arguments were applied to the product markets, and it was pointed out that prices, particularly of manufactures, were sticky and did not respond readily to changes in demand. Many Keynesians were content to rest these propositions on general statements about the non-competitive nature of markets, but Keynes himself was concerned to stress the maze of uncertainty and risk within which decisions of great moment were taken. The upshot, however, was that there was no clearly argued case for regarding these markets as failures.

The reactions to this have taken two forms. First the neoclassicists have argued that, in the absence of villains or governments or other parties preventing free contractual arrangements, the microeconomics must require price adjustments and so the markets must clear. There will be no frustrated buyers or sellers, such as the unemployed who would be willing to work at below the market wage (and at or below their marginal productivity) but cannot find jobs. It is alleged that Keynesians cannot justify a theory that has obviously flawed microfoundations.[6] This pure form of the new classical (NC) macroeconomics has markets that clear and where the normal principles of demand and supply are applied. It is, however, a travesty to suggest that the new classicists' thought attributed *all* the massive unemployment in the United States or Great Britain of 1932 to workers' choice for leisure rather than income, or to job-search, or to the cushioning effects of unemployment and welfare benefits.[7] But the new classicists did identify such optimising causes of apparent joblessness which had been thrust aside by Keynesians and largely pooh-poohed by new Keynesians (NKs). Explanations for 'market failures' have been sought from the behaviour of government, the theory of information, which itself was much developed by George Stigler at Chicago, and above all from a new *forward*-looking approach to the formation of expectations (the so-called 'rational expectations' or RE).

RE, in its stark form, simply asserts that people form expectations by taking into account all the information to which they have access, and then with full knowledge of the economic model, including the government's policy rules, they will form expectations that are *consistent* with that model and information set.[8] RE asserted that private sector agents would not make systematic errors (that is to say, reduce their profits or utility) which were avoidable by taking their knowledge of data and model into account. In particular this raised the spectre that monetary and fiscal policy could be ineffective in terms of real output and employment. Where prices respond fully to demand and supply, any counter-cyclical monetary expansion may not be effective because producers will fully anticipate the consequences and raise prices rapidly. All the kick of the monetary expansion will be dissipated in the price rise more or less immediately. Thus known policy rules will have no effect on real output or employment.[9] Only unanticipated or surprise policies will have an effect – and then only until people discern the new government behaviour pattern. This is widely known as the 'policy ineffectiveness' proposition. It applies to interest rate policy rules, such as those which adjust interest rates to eliminate deviations in output and prices, as much as to quantitative monetary growth rules; indeed, unless there is some fix on a *nominal* magnitude, prices will be indeterminate. Anything can happen to inflation.

The combination of rational expectations and new classical market clearing propositions have undermined and at least made ambiguous the expected effects of monetary policy in counter-cyclical operations.[10] Of course one might well argue that, with markets clearing and even without rational expectations, there is little point in pursuing counter-cyclical monetary policy; the 'problem' has been assumed away. But it is not enough to assert that the market clearing model is clearly inappropriate because of, for example, the persistence of high rates of unemployment.

The crucial distinction between the NC and Keynesian approach is that, although the NC allow costs of making adjustments in *real* variables, they do not see any reason why there should be any significant lag in the adjustment of *nominal* variables such as prices. In the Keynesian models also there are costs and lags in adjusting real variables. But the Keynesian models, as distinct from the NC, also have a large role for lags and costs in the adjustment of *nominal* variables – and particularly wages. Indeed, most of the characteristic results of the Keynesian models derive from the differential rate of adjustment of wage rates, prices, etc., through overlapping contract arrangements. The Keynesian argument is that in a crucial sense the price system does not work, and hence the presumption that government should pursue contra-cyclical policies.

Many, perhaps most, RE models have included price and particularly wage adjustment processes, sometimes specified in terms of contracts, which take time to adjust to the final market clearing conditions. In fact such processes are a reflection of our ignorance of the underlying nature of optimisation, including the problems of identification, information and compliance. Nevertheless, such temporary stickiness in prices and wages in the Keynesian models does enable monetary policy to have real effects, and there arises at least the possibility of an effective counter-cyclical policy.[11] Normally it is supposed that different sets of prices react at different speeds with wages the most important laggard. Thus an increase in money first affects prices and so reduces real wages; this accounts for the temporary upturn in output and employment, which is later eliminated and reversed as nominal wages catch up and perhaps even cause an overshoot in real wages. The long-run result is, of course, higher prices.

Another noteworthy contribution of new classicism is to show that under certain pure assumptions – in particular that people live for ever, or that they pursue full-bequest policies to their heirs – different mixtures of bond and tax finance of a given level of public spending have no effect on real output. If an increase in government expenditure is financed by increasing taxes (i.e. the deficit remains the same) then it will have exactly the same effects on output as if the deficit and the borrowing increased by the amount of the spending increase. Whether we finance by deficit or by tax increases is immaterial, at least as far as private consumption is concerned. The rationalisation of this result arises from the fact that people know that, if taxes are not raised this year to pay for increased spending, taxes will certainly be raised in future years in order to service the debt. Thus, with an increased deficit and bond finance, people will save more in order to pay their future tax bills, and so the deficit will not increase aggregate demand or output. The dissaving of the government is offset by the increase in private saving.[12] The NC position on an *expansion* of public expenditure, however financed, is that it will crowd out private spending and thus have little if any effect on permanent demand

and output. However, because of the costs of making real adjustments, there will be a financing effect on the transitory path of output.[13]

13.3　NEW KEYNESIANS[14]

The main elements of New Keynesianism (I think NK, rather than NEWKS) are:

(1) Some propositions about the high costs of information to firms which give rise, in particular, to the argument that increments in wages promote productivity gains, which explain, not the rigidity, but the relative stickiness of wages;

(2) The asymmetry in information in capital markets which are, of course, imperfect, and which implies that there is too little equity and firms are driven to use bank or bond finance with its attendant risks, and this is exacerbated by the fact that production risks cannot be shifted;

(3) The perversity that affects labour markets also is manifest in credit markets, where, because of the asymmetry of information, increasing interest rates may lower the return on capital – due to adverse selection or additional riskiness;

(4) Monetary policy exerts influence but rarely and when it does it is through the availability of credit which affects investment, but this will not be effective in a recession when there is a shortage of willing borrowers.[15]

On the monetary side, the NK view is quite clear. Since credit is a close substitute, money is not required for transactions. And, in any case, the relationship between transactions and income is not one-to-one since most transactions are asset sales and purchases. Although the NK view is that governments can influence market interest rates, it is asserted that this is not 'an important' mechanism by which government controls economic activity. It is through credit availability that monetary policy works – and then only in non-recessionary phases of the trade cycle.[16] Greenwald and Stiglitz do not tell us whether they believe that an increase in the monetary growth rate would lead to inflation in the long run, but the drift of their discussion is clearly against such a conclusion. However, I think most NKs would accept that long-run result, albeit with many reservations and doubts about the definition of money, etc.

13.4　REALITY AND THE NK

Although one may complain about the basis of the NK's process, there is, in the Greenwald Stiglitz account, a considerable description of the pathology of a recession. It would be interesting, but far beyond my present plans, to review all past recessions to see how they shape up to the NK outline. A more modest task is to assess the monetary aspects of the recent recession (or indeed depression) of the early 1980s – clearly the most severe for the United Kingdom in post-war years – in terms of the NK's outline.

There is some correspondence between the NK account of the performance of labour markets and the reality of the 1980s. (But I must leave to others the explanation of why, in the presence of massive unemployment, real wages continue to increase in the United Kingdom and not fall, as they did in the United States.) On the monetary conditions, however, there is no correspondence whatsoever. The NK view that 'banks may be willing to lend to any "good" prospect at the going interest rate, but there is a shortage of willing borrowers' appears to be the opposite of what actually occurred. Of course much depends on the definition of the dates of the recession, but I assume that most NKs would define the recession phase in the United Kingdom to include the period when there was thought to be a considerable amount of excess capacity.[17] Clearly this must cover the years 1980 through to at least 1983. Throughout this period, bank lending to the private sector surged far beyond both government targets and economists' expectations. There was a plethora, not a shortage, of willing borrowers. The banks did not languish with excess reserves for which they could not find suitable borrowers. On the contrary, the banks were bidding vigorously for deposits in order to expand their highly profitable loans.

The increase in the private sector demand for loans was in part explained by the asymmetry of the recession. Corporations, particularly producers of tradeable manufactures, were hard hit by the appreciation of sterling. But, with little adjustment in wages, this appreciation improved both the wealth and liquidity of households, so they increased deposits in the financial sector, made attractive by the high real rates of interest that emerged from the government's effort to contain bank lending, an important item in the sterling M3 aggregate. The financial sector's capacity to lend was also augmented by deregulation – particularly the removal of the corset and of exchange controls.

It has been suggested (by a reviewer) that the NK position would be that 'bank-financed new capital fell somewhat in 1979–81'. Although Greenwald and Stiglitz do not specify that they are concerned only with financing new capital in their article, it would be ungenerous not to consider such an interpretation. There are no data on 'bank-financed new capital'. We can only compare bank lending to industrial and commercial companies with data on capital formation. Fig 13.1 shows how bank lending *rose* from an annual rate of £2 bn in 1978 to an annual rate of £7 bn in current pounds in 1980 and 1981 – a three-and-a-half-fold increase.[18] On the other hand, total private investment *fell* by about £8 bn (at 1980 prices) – divided between £5 bn in stocks and £3 bn fixed.[19] It is, of course, conceivable, but surely most unlikely, that these data are consistent with the NK story. A 250 per cent

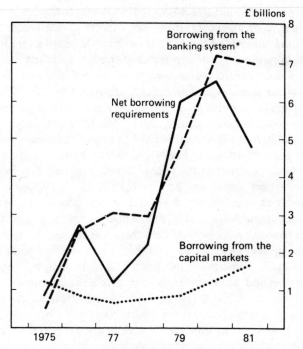

£ billions

Borrowing from the
banking system*

Net borrowing
requirements

Borrowing from the
capital markets

1975   77   79   81

*Including commercial bills held by the Issue Department of the Bank of England.

Figure 13.1   Industrial and commercial companies' finance.

Source: Bank of England Quarterly Bulletin, vol. 23, no. 2 (June 1983) p. 205.

increase in bank lending is very difficult to rationalise in terms of the
moribund lending in activity which NKs suppose is typical of the recession.
The evidence shows that there was a dramatic increase in bank-financed
lending for new capital, particularly in the service and energy industries.[20] All
this requires a more detailed analysis that I can give here. But I believe that
there is sufficient evidence to reject the NK vision of languishing bank
lending being unable to lift investment out of the doldrums.[21]

It is more difficult to establish whether, as NK assert, interest rates were
not '(an important) mechanism by which government controls activity'.[22] We
shall have to defer the examination of interest rate effects in the context of
fiscal as well as monetary policy. Certainly – and a point which does not
discredit the NK view – the high interest rates (and they were very high until
March 1981) did not appear to have an immediate impact on the volume of
loans to the private sector.[23] But changes in interest rates, especially when
most of the loans are at floating rates, have profound effects other than those

on changes in loan demand, on profitability and bankruptcy and so on the level of activity.

I conclude, therefore, that the NK description of the financial characteristics of an economy in recession does not merely lack verisimilitude, but appears to be the antithesis of reality. But it may be objected that verisimilitude is not an appropriate evaluation; one might argue that the real test is whether the NK version gives new and useful insights into the monetary effects on macroeconomic processes. This remains unproven.

13.5 THREE RECESSIONS: MONETARY VERSUS FISCAL POLICY

In much of the discussion of economic policy, the general thrust is to find ways of avoiding, on the one hand, substantial and sustained recessions (depressions) and, on the other hand, persistent inflation. It is unlikely, and probably undesirable, that we can avoid most mild recessions or price changes. But the deep and lasting recessions just like persistent inflation are to be avoided. In this section I review the efficacy of monetary and fiscal policy during the three recessions, 1956–8, 1973–6, and 1979–82.[24] These are the only three post-war recessions in which the annual index of real GNP actually fell, although it must be noted that the fall in the average GDP estimate for the 1957–8 period was very small. (See table 4 of *Economic Trends 1985*.) These three recessions were clearly the most sustained and deepest of the post-war years.

Throughout the discussion of these recessions, the monetary base (M0) or transactions balances (M1) will be used as the basic indicator of monetary policy. The standard argument against the use of M0 is that it is endogenous – in this context it is determined by demand. The Bank of England supplies whatever M0, that is bankers' balances at the Bank and currency, the private sector wants. True – but that does not invalidate M0, suitably interpreted, as a measure of the monetary stance. The main monetary instruments of the Authorities are interest rates and joint open market operations. A monetary squeeze is engineered through raising short-term market interest rates through Bank Rate, MLR and money market operations. The change in interest rates has an effect on M0 (and usually M1) one to two quarters later as people adjust their currency and balances to the new interest rates. In this sense then the Authorities determine a systematic component of M0.

With this chain of causation, it is natural to ask why one uses M0 rather than interest rates as an indicator of monetary policy. The main reason is the difficulty of interpreting *real* rates from the observed nominal counterparts. Quite small changes in inflationary expectations have large proportional changes, magnified by the tax system, on real interest rates: during two of the periods examined here, inflationary expectations were going through dramatic changes and hence measures of real interest rates had very large elements of uncertainty; hence the choice of M0. Another consequence of choosing M0 is that it does lag some three to six months behind monetary policy (i.e. interest rate changes). This contemporaneous movement of M0 and real output is consistent with a *lead* of monetary policy of as long as six months or so. But throughout the discussion the relevant changes in nominal interest rates will be recorded, so the reader who is suspicious of M0 can follow the story with interest rates instead.

13.5.1　1956–8 recession

It is not difficult to demonstrate that there was a substantial monetary squeeze dating from early 1955, as is illustrated in Figure 13.2, panel 3. Bank rate was increased from 3 per cent to 4.5 per cent in February, rising to 5 per cent in February 1956. The annual increase in the money supply had been between £235 and £268 million for the previous three years, and might be thought to be a remarkable manifestation of Friedman's celebrated 'rule'. But then the higher Bank rate in 1955 was associated with a sharp *reduction* of the money stock by £248 million (see Supplement to *Bank of England Quarterly Bulletin*, September 1969). In terms of the narrow money supply, a period of three years in which the expansion had been steady at about 4 to 4.5 per cent a year was reversed in 1955 to a 3.3 per cent *contraction* at the trough and a 1.2 per cent contraction on the average for the year. The reduction in the rate of growth of the *real* money supply was even more sharp. The further reduction of the money supply continued into the first half of 1956, when it started at last to grow again but at a slower rate than in the early 1950s.

During the first three quarters of 1955 fiscal policy was clearly expansionary. Although the budget of 1954 had been more or less neutral, expansionary measures had been introduced in August. And these were followed by the election budget of 1955, with six pence off the standard rate of tax. After the election the give-aways of the election budget were gradually taken back, beginning with increased purchase taxes in October 1955, being later followed in early 1956 by planned reductions in government spending and reductions in investment allowances. But the expansionary effects of the decisions of economic policy included in the budget of spring 1955 were difficult to contain, let alone reverse, and the expansion continued throughout 1956 and into 1957. After a 5 per cent increase in general government spending from 1954 to 1955, there was, in nominal terms, almost a 9 per cent increase from 1955 to 1956 compared with a little more than 4 per cent increase in revenues.[25] Although this is not a neat picture of fiscal management, it undoubtedly demonstrates that the fiscal stance was expansionary

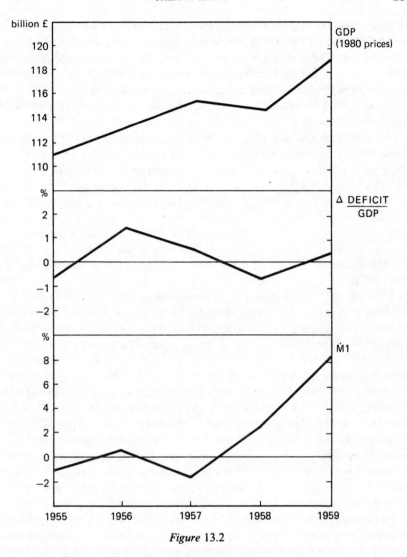

Figure 13.2

between 1955 and 1956. This is confirmed by the annual data representing the change in the budget deficit as a percentage of the GDP at market prices, shown in Figure 13.2, panel 2.

The contrast between the expansionary fiscal policy and the sharply contractionary monetary policy provides almost laboratory conditions for a test of the effects of monetary and fiscal policy on real output. Perhaps the most sensitive indicator of output was the index of industrial production. This showed a sharp and sustained rise during the recovery phase 1952 to

1954; but this slackened off throughout 1955 until there was a sharp decline in the first months of 1956 followed by stagnation until the third quarter of 1958. As for GDP, the rate of growth had averaged 4 per cent for three years 1952–5, then it fell to 1 per cent for two years, 1956–7, finally reaching stagnation in 1958, as shown in Figure 13.2, panel 1. Clearly, in 1955–7, the economy failed to respond to the fiscal stimulus and succumbed to the monetary contraction.

But it is often said stopping booms is no problem for monetary contractions, but that starting a recovery with money is like pushing on a string. But there was very little push exerted on that string until 1957, as illustrated in Figure 13.2, panel 3.[26] Indeed, both in terms of the monetary aggregates and in terms of Bank rate, it is clear that the monetary squeeze continued through virtually to the end of 1957; then throughout 1958 a much easier monetary policy was pursued. This timing accords well with the rise of the industrial production index – which might be dated either in the last quarter of 1958 or the first quarter of 1959. And GDP showed a sharp upturn in 1959 compared with 1958.

Although the upturn in activity is *consistent* with a monetary explanation, we cannot point to a contrary path for fiscal policy. General government spending (in nominal terms) continued to expand at about 8 per cent per annum for 1956 to 1957, that is to say only fractionally less than the expansion in 1955–6. Similarly there was no clear intimation of fiscal squeeze in the figures for the deficit. As shown in Figure 13.2, there was a reduction in the deficit in 1958 and an increase in 1959. Since the upturn in the economy occurred in late 1958 or early 1959, one cannot claim that it was the fiscal expansion of 1959 that ignited the recovery – but nor can one plausibly argue that the relatively mild fiscal contraction of 1958 sparked the recovery. Fiscal policy was much of a muchness, and nothing like the sharp change in monetary policy. We must rest content with the weak conclusion that the case for monetary causation has to be seriously considered, but we cannot demonstrate a clear perverse reaction to fiscal policy.

To summarise this recession and recovery, we have good evidence that the monetary explanation of the 1956 downturn in activity fits the facts rather well. This is reinforced by the evidence that fiscal policy over the critical period of 1955–6 was substantially expansionary and not contractionary. This confirms the power of a contractionary monetary policy to offset an expansionary fiscal stance and to prick the bubble of a boom. For the upturn, however, the results are more equivocal, mainly because although the very sharp monetary expansion was followed, with the usual lag, by the recovery of output, fiscal policy might be construed as at least neutral and even modestly expansionary contemporaneous with the recovery. The recovery, therefore, might also, but more dubiously, be claimed as a consequence of fiscal policy.[27]

13.5.2 1974–6 recession

One may characterise this recession as one of bad luck (with the commodity and oil price rises), compounded by bad policies (those of Heath magnified by Wilson). Fortunately again for the task of separating fiscal from monetary effects, the policies which started in some sort of harmony of rampant expansion in 1971–2, diverged markedly in 1973. Then monetary policy became markedly contractionary, but fiscal policy continued to be strongly expansionist until the first months of 1976. (See Figure 13.3, where the growth rates of M0 and GDP, and the changes in the PSBR as a percent of GDP are illustrated.)

There is some doubt about the exact dates of the monetary squeeze. The M1 series is the first to turn down from its rate of growth of around 15 per cent in 1972. The early months of 1973 was the fairly clear turning point, and in the following year the annual growth rate of *real* M1 fell to zero. (The

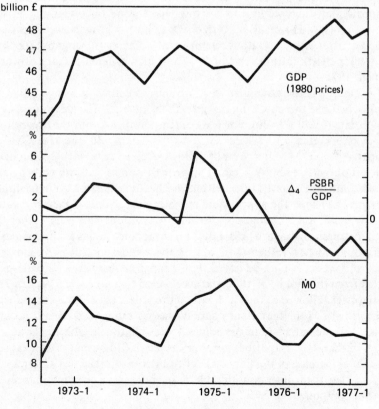

Figure 13.3

turndown in the growth rate of M0 followed approximately one quarter later.) Surely one of the sharpest contractions in M1 on the record. Minimum lending rate, which, at 5 per cent to June 1972, had been at its lowest point since 1964, was raised in stages to 9 per cent by December 1972 – the highest level for more than fifty years.[28] The combination of the evidence on narrow money and interest rate movements suggests that the monetary squeeze began in the last months of 1972 and the first months of 1973. (The growth rate of broad money (M3) did not turn down until approximately one year later, in the first quarter of 1974.)

The picture of fiscal policy over these years to the first months of 1976 is one of unremitting expansion. The PSBR and the public sector financial deficit all increased, not only in money values but also as a percentage of GDP. Even if one makes the adjustment to a 'full-employment' deficit, the fiscal stance remains expansionary through to the middle of 1975.[29] Indeed, it was not until 1976 that Mr Healey brought the public expenditure under some sort of control.

If output had responded to the fiscal stimulus, then, granted the existence of substantial unemployment, it would have gone on increasing at least through to 1976. However, a sharp check to output growth occurred by the second quarter of 1973. Output remained on a plateau (throughout the three-day week period) until the end of 1974 and then suffered a sharp downturn through 1975.

It is clear that the downturn in M1 occurred before – perhaps only three months before – the check to the growth of output. The downturn in the growth rate of M0 was more or less contemporaneous with the downturn in output (see Figure 13.4 where the growth rates of M0 and real GDP are compared). The M1 and output data are consistent with a monetarist explanation with a shortish lag. The growth rate of M3, however, clearly turned some nine months *after* output reached its plateau. As I have argued at length elsewhere, the appropriate monetary magnitude is the aggregate of instruments that are commonly used for transactions purposes, rather than credit instruments that are held, not for transactions, but as a store of wealth. This points to M1 rather than M3 as the critical indicator of monetary conditions. It must also be noted that a rapid increase in wholesale prices started from the middle of 1972 and accelerated to a very rapid pace in 1973. Retail prices followed at only a slightly more sedate pace. Thus the reduction in the growth of the real money supply was far more marked and occurred earlier than the reduction in the nominal rates of growth. The acceleration of prices, particularly (imported) input prices relative to output prices, caused a substantial increase in the financial deficit of corporations in 1973 and, as in 1979–82, led them into considerable bank borrowing which enhanced the non-M1 component of M3.[30]

Notwithstanding the equivocation of timing of the broad money squeeze, the downturn is not dissimilar to that of 1955. The combination of monetary

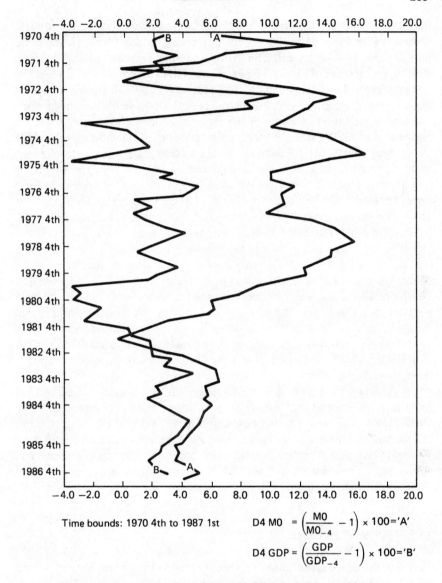

Figure 13.4   Growth rates of M0 and GDP real 1970.4–1986.4

contraction and fiscal expansion resulted in the economy responding to the monetary conditions rather than to the fiscal environment.[31]

Now let us examine the recovery phase of this severe recession. The timing of the lower turning point is, as always, in some doubt, but it is fairly clear that the choice is between the last quarter of 1975 and the first of 1976.[32] Can we therefore attribute this bottoming out to an expansionary fiscal policy? At first sight it appears that there is a good fiscal explanation for the upturn. Over 1974 to 1975 there was a record increase in the PSBR (in nominal terms) from £6.4 bn to £10.2 bn (with a similar increase in the financial deficit), an increase of about 3.6 per cent of GDP. There a fiscalist might be tempted to rest his case, and claim the upturn as his own. But, alas, one must explain why the fiscal stimuli during the previous two years – of about equal magnitude measured in terms of the increase in the deficit (or PSBR) as a percentage of GDP – did not work.[33] Furthermore, if one adjusts to exclude the cyclical effects, the adjusted deficit shows that the fiscal stance was *very sharply contractionary from the first quarter of 1975*.[34] Similarly, weighting and adjusting for inflation gives the same pattern of a sharp squeeze in fiscal policy in the months before the upturn of activity. Clearly there is no case for attributing the recovery to fiscal policy; on the contrary, the recovery took off in spite of the reduction in fiscal stimulus.

The role of monetary policy in the recovery appears to be more convincing. Monetary growth (M1) had stopped in the second quarter of 1974. Monetary expansion started again in the last quarter of 1974 and by the first quarter of 1975 there was a 19 per cent growth and it remained well above 16 per cent for six quarters, that is to say to mid-1976.[35] A money-output causal interpretation would suggest that the lag is at least six months and probably nine to twelve months is the appropriate range. This is broadly consistent with the lag which has emerged from previous studies of the effects of money on output.

On this deep recession of the mid-1970s, the conclusion on the relative roles of monetary and fiscal policy are similar to those of the recession of the 1950s. There is, however, a significant difference. In the 1950s the attribution of recovery to monetary as distinct from fiscal policy was clearly equivocal. In the 1970s, however, we can be more confident that the recovery was stimulated by monetary expansion which dominated the supposed contractionary effects of a reduction in the fiscal deficit.

13.5.3   1979–82 recession

This was the deepest and most persistent recession since the Second World War.[36] Perhaps its most distinctive and painful feature was the rise in unemployment and the persistence of such joblessness at very high levels, until it started to decline from 1986. (Note, however, that *employment* started expanding from late 1982.) Indeed, many left-inclined intellectuals would argue that the recession was really a prolonged slump from 1980 with no foreseeable end in sight. In this chapter I have taken output, not unemployment, as the indicator for the cyclical movements, and this will be used in interpreting this recession. The upturn in output began in mid-1981 (see Figure 13.5) and growth has continued unabated for the period 1981–7.

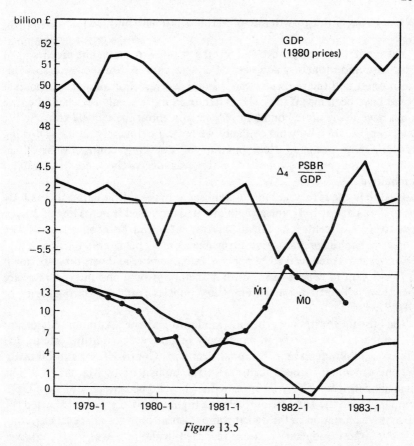

Figure 13.5

First we examine the causes of the downturn in 1979. After a sustained rise for more than three and a half years, the output index surged in the spring and peaked in the second quarter of 1979. If a fiscal squeeze were to be the cause of this relapse, one would expect to find evidence of fiscal tightening during the financial year 1978–9. Yet on all the fiscal measures reported in the NIESR study of David Savage (1982), there was an *expansionary* fiscal policy in operation during FY 1978/9.[37] As far as fiscal policy is concerned, the economy behaved perversely.

Monetary (M1) growth had reached a peak of 25 per cent in the first quarter of 1978. In the subsequent five quarters, that is to the second quarter of 1979, it fell to 12.5 per cent. (The fall in real M1 growth was even steeper.) This monetary squeeze is confirmed by the rise of the Minimum Lending Rate from 6.5 per cent in the first quarter of 1978 to 14 per cent by the first quarter of 1979. All this evidence leads to the conclusion that there was a severe monetary contraction in the course of 1978. And, as can be seen from Figure 13.5, this contraction continued throughout 1979. (As a matter of fact, in terms of the growth rate of M1, it continued until the third quarter of 1980.)

Yet again for the upper cyclical turning point, we observe the precursors of fiscal ease and monetary squeeze. Of course, in this case the fiscal stimulus was modest and the monetary contraction severe.[38] For analytic purposes it would have been nice if the policies had been more evenly matched; then we could have made more confident judgements about the relative efficacy. We have to make do with what evidence we have. Fortunately, in the following recovery there occurred a combination of a severely contractionary fiscal policy with a monetary policy which was decisively (and deliberately) stimulative.

The fall in the rate of growth of M1 ceased in the third quarter of 1980. By the first quarter of 1981, the growth rate had increased from its low of 2.5 per cent to 7.5 per cent. The fall in interest rates had been only slightly less dramatic than the previous rise. From a peak of 17 per cent in the first half of 1980, MLR was reduced to 14 per cent in November and was brought down to 12 per cent in March 1981. Both monetary growth and interest rates are consistent with expansionary monetary policies from the third quarter of 1980.[39]

The fiscal contraction began modestly in the Autumn Statement (November 1980) with both small cuts in public expenditure (about 700 million) and an increase in National Insurance Contributions and oil taxes. But the draconian squeeze came with the budget of 11 March 1981. The financial deficit for FY 1981–2 was reduced by 2.6 percentage points of GDP compared with the 1980–81 outturn (see Figure 13.5). Cyclically adjusted the percentage reduction in the deficit was an astonishing 4.1 per cent. Certainly it is the largest budgetary squeeze recorded in the post-war years and, war years apart, probably the largest ever in the United Kingdom.

In spite of this massive fiscal contraction, the economy turned decisively by the third quarter of 1981 from the precipitous downward plunge of 1980. And to date (September 1987) there has been no cyclical contraction in subsequent years.

The experience of the 1981 recovery is important because, first, it provides some evidence that monetary policy is not 'pushing on a string'; the economy did appear to respond strongly to the easier monetary conditions, contrary to the NK view.[40] Secondly, the effect of fiscal conditions cannot be interpreted in terms such as the change in the public sector deficit or indeed any of the complex variations of that original ·concept, to produce an expansionary fiscal indicator.[41] But our immediate purpose is to point out the domination of a moderate monetary expansion over the draconian budgetary squeeze – surely one of the important examples of the effects of modern macroeconomic management. The failure of the 1981 fiscal contraction to produce the dire effects so confidently predicted by both academic economists and (retired) chief economic advisers appears to have excited little critical re-examination of the phenomenon.[42]

13.6 REFLECTIONS ON THE RECESSIONS

The evidence from the three recessions, although equivocal in some respects, does suggest that monetary conditions were important determinants of activity with results which were consistent with what have come to be called monetarist predictions. As for fiscal policy, one cannot in truth say that it was not important; on the contrary it was on occasion, as in 1981, very important, but not in the way portrayed in the Keynesian or NK framework.[43]

The crucial ingredient which can serve to explain the strange effects of fiscal policy can be summed up in the word 'credibility'. Both 1976 and 1980 were situations where continuation of, let alone expansion of, the large running fiscal deficits and borrowing requirements were simply inconsistent with the rest of the government's policy. And in a real sense the budget is the main instrument over which the government has more or less complete control. (With price and wage controls or guidelines etc., the public has self-justified scepticism. The absurd case of the 'six pounds' (a week) wage increase under Mr Callaghan was a prime example.) A borrowing requirement does have implications for the nexus of interest rates, inflation and foreign borrowings. The point was that, notwithstanding the condition of the real economy in 1980, anything but a tight fiscal squeeze would have destroyed credibility in the feasibility of the Thatcher programme. Scepticism about the political will would have quickly ensued. In my judgement, there would have followed a financial crisis as the markets passed speedy judgement on the borrowing and the implications. Interest rates would have soared instead of sinking. The 1976 period is very similar in its sequence of severe fiscal tightening followed by lower interest rates and monetary expansion and recovery.

This suggests that the tightening of fiscal policy was a necessary, but not sufficient, condition for the easing of monetary policy and the onset of the recovery. This is a very different 'harmony' of fiscal and monetary policy from that which is usually promoted.

Notes

1. In 1968/69, the Labour Chancellor Roy Jenkins promised the IMF that domestic credit expansion (DCE) would be less than £900 million per year. But this was *not* the same as controlling the money stock (see A. A. Walters, *Money in Boom and Slump*, Institute of Economic Affairs, London, 2nd ed., 1969).

2.   It will be noted that only the monetary base is net wealth to the private sector. Commercial bank deposits, on the other hand, are *liabilities* of the bank as well as assets to the depositors, so they net out.

3.   See, for example, David K. Sheppard, *The Growth and Role of UK Financial Institutions, 1880–1962* (Methuen, London, 1971).

4.   John Fforde, 'Setting Monetary Objectives', *Bank of England Quarterly Bulletin*, vol. 23(2) (June 1983) p. 203.

5.   To avoid dispute, it should be noted that I am not discussing the subtleties of assignment theory of Tinbergen, Meade and Mundell. An interesting historical aside, relevant to this issue, was the theory put forward by the New Cambridge School in the early 1970s. The policy consequences of this theory were that the exchange rate should be used to ensure full employment and that the financial deficit of the public sector should determine the deficit on the current balance of payments. I do not think that the New Cambridge School had any discernible effects on policy, largely because the assumption on which their theory was based, namely a constant financial surplus of the private sector, was clearly discredited by the data from 1972 onwards.

6.   See Alan S. Blinder, 'Keynes, Lucas, and Scientific Progress', *American Economic Review*, Papers and Proceedings, vol. 77(2) (May 1987) pp. 130–36. Professor Blinder argues that it is more 'scientific' to base macroeconomics on broad empirical generalisations rather than a fully articulated micro-foundation of the underlying co-operative arrangements through market processes. And if the broad empirical generalisations are inconsistent with the elementary market behaviour, it is best to turn a blind eye to the fundamentals of the markets and rely on the broad brushes of the macro-artist.

7.   This is suggested in B. Greenwald and J. E. Stiglitz, 'Keynesian, New Keynesian and Classical Economics', *Oxford Economic Papers*, vol. (39) (1987) p. 119. The authors discuss New Classical economics as though the NCs meant it to be a description of reality. I doubt whether any NC author thought of the models in such terms. For the most part the NC movement was calling attention to aspects of micro-adjustment which, in terms of the caricature of such models, might serve to explain some of the disappointment with conventional Keynesian models.

8.   I would still at this late day continue to urge that 'consistent' expectations is a much better description than 'rational' expectations. I so described it in what I believe was the first application to macroeconomic phenomena in 'Consistent Expectations, Distributed Lags and the Quantity Theory', *Economic Journal*, 1971, vol. 81, pp. 273–81. Expectations are consistent with both the information set and the model; rationality is another and much more far-reaching matter.

9.   This 'ineffectiveness' result, however, was established only for the Sargent and Wallace Keynesian type of model (with a Phillips adjustment) when RE were substituted for adaptive expectations.

10. Much depends on the speed with which the private sector acquires information. The original formulations (by Sargent and Wallace) assumed that in period t the rate of interest was known only for period $t-1$. If, however, the private sector knows the current rate of interest, *any* optimum rule is very difficult to disentangle and the results become volatile and dependent on the particular values of the model. See M. B. Canzoneri, D. A. Henderson, and K. S. Rogoff, 'The Information Content of the Interest Rate and Optimal Monetary Policy', *Quarterly Journal of Economics*, vol. 98(4) (Nov. 1983) pp. 545–66.

11. One might wonder, however, why monetary policy should be employed in eliminating deviations of output and employment that arise from contractual or informational lacunae. Surely would it not be best to concentrate on the contractual and information nexus as such. Of course this would require that the precise non-price elements be specified and a joint theory of contracts, monitoring, compliance, sanctions, and information be developed. As is well known, excess monetary expansion would generate long-run persistent inflation and much reduce the information content in the price system, which must give rise to further 'stickiness' and costs.

12. The seminal paper is by Robert Barro, 'Are Government Bonds Net Wealth?', *Journal of Political Economy*, vol. 82(6) (Nov.–Dec. 1974) pp. 1095–117. There has been much dispute on the applicability of this 'irrelevance of tax and bond finance' proposition. As I understand it, the evidence does suggest that the form of financing does have real effects, but less than those which arise from simply adding the deficit to aggregate demand. For a survey of the empirical studies on Barro's proposition, see Giancarlo Perasso, 'The Ricardian Equivalence Theorem and the Consumption Function: a Survey of the Literature', *Rivista Internazionale di Scienze Economiche e Commerciali*, forthcoming.

13. See Chapter 2 of my *Britain's Economic Renaissance* (Oxford University Press, 1986).

14. Because I am thought to be unsympathetic to various varieties of Keynesians (though I hope not to Keynes himself), I restrict this review largely to the account of Greenwald and Stiglitz (1987). It may well be argued that their account differs considerably from that of James Tobin, Robert Eisner and many other distinguished Keynesians. Perhaps so, but I doubt if the differences in the effects of monetary and fiscal policy are so large as to limit the critique that follows to this one clique of New Keynesians. Besides, the debate about 'what Keynes really meant' is alive and well among Keynesians and an agreement looks far from being within reach.

15. It must be recognised that Keynes himself was very much aware of the importance of monetary policy in determining real output (via the real rate of interest). On the topic of Keynes and monetary policy, see John F. Brothwell, 'The General Theory After Fifty Years: Why Are We Not All Keynesians Now?', *Journal of Post Keynesian Economics* (Summer 1986) pp. 531–47.

16. It must here be noted that other distinguished NKs would tend to put their trust in variations in tax rates rather than in government spending. Thus they fully reject the 'irrelevance of finance' argument of Robert Barro.

17. The normal NIESR assumption for this period was a trend rate of growth of potential GDP of 2.5 per cent per annum – the same as that actually experienced between the peaks of 1973 and 1979. But if one adopted a definition based on unemployment, then the period would be much longer.

18. *Bank of England Quarterly Bulletin*, vol. 23, no. 2 (June 1983) p. 205.

19. *Economic Trends*, October 1983, pp. 8, 16. These figures are for the whole of the private sector and include houses as well as the investment of non-corporate businesses. The investment of public corporations fell about £500 m, but government investment fell by about £2.5 bn – all over the period 1978/9 to 1981/2.

20. Note also that borrowing from the capital markets also approximately doubled from 1978 to 1981. (*Bank of England Quarterly Bulletin*, vol. 23, no. 2 (June 1983) p. 205).

21. If the NK view is simply that in a recession investment is low – then, of course, that is neither new nor interesting.

22. Bruce Greenwald and Joseph E. Stiglitz, 'Keynesian, New Keynesian and New Classical Economics', Working Paper 2160, *National Bureau of Economic Research* (Cambridge, Mass., Feb. 1987) p. 31.

23. Indeed it was widely thought that, during the depths of the recession, increases in interest rates *increased* rather than decreased the demand for credit, since the corporations were so desperate that they would have to finance the increased interest charge by borrowing more. For obvious reasons this had to be a fleeting transitory phenomenon. Ultimately changes in interest rates do affect the demand for loans in the traditional way.

24. There is the problem that the data will not reveal the *true* underlying relationship. In fact although one may find that the money supply is a prime determinant of real output some six months or so later, this observation could come from a system where the oscillations in activity are due *only* to unexpected monetary variations. See Thomas J. Sargent, 'The Observational Equivalence of Natural and Unnatural Rate Theories of Macroeconomics', *Journal of Political Economy*, vol. 84 (1976) pp. 31–40. In the comparison here I do not need to take issue on the nature of the expectations, but I would concede that, from the circumstantial evidence, in the last two deep recessions, the monetary movements were largely a surprise.

25. *Economic Trends*, 1985, table 153. If one adjusted for cyclical variations in unemployment, there would be virtually no difference to the figures. Unemployment did not start increasing until 1957 (see *ibid.* table 103). Furthermore, it is noteworthy that in an OECD study for the period 1955–65, the UK central government automatic stabilisers were *negative*, that is they were *destabilisers*. See Bent Hansen, *Fiscal Policy in Seven Countries 1955–1965* OECD, Paris 1969) table 2.6, p. 69.

26. The 'net money supply' (roughly M1) reported by Sheppard (*The Growth and Role of UK Financial Institutions, 1880–1962*) was (in billions of pounds sterling):

1951	1952	1953	1954	1955	1956	1957	1958
8.45	8.65	8.98	9.35	9.05	9.19	9.52	9.84

Thus it took three years to restore the nominal stock of money to its 1954 level. Similarly Bank rate peaked at 7 per cent in September 1957 and was brought down sharply in 1958 to 4 per cent.

27. This recession was the backdrop to the deliberations of the Radcliffe Committee (1959) and no doubt had much to do with the general conclusion that quantitative monetary controls were ineffective in managing the economy. But in one sense Radcliffe was correct. The reduction in the money supply had little effect on inflation until the latter half of 1957 – when at last prices stabilised, and the retail price index remained more or less constant through to the first half of 1960. The lag was indeed long – at least two years, perhaps three – before the effect of monetary contraction on prices could conceivably be claimed as a manifestation of a monetarist prediction. The decline of inflation coincided with the decline in interest rates. This period is also worthy of note because it has some claim to being the first (very mild) case of stagflation.

28. Thereafter MLR was relaxed to a low of 7.5 per cent in mid-1973.

29. Note also that 'weighting' items of the government accounts to reflect the degree of 'kick' expected in fiscal stimulus makes little difference to this assessment. Similarly, calculating the 'real' surplus by taking account of the inflationary erosion of public debt will not affect much the *differences* in the public sector deficits or PSBRs. See my *Britain's Economic Renaissance*, Chapter 4.

30. It must also be borne in mind that M3 was much affected by the changes instituted under CCC. The rapid increase in the rate of growth in 1972, especially in interest-bearing assets, was partly a consequence of the new freedom. One might take the point much further and argue that the *acceleration* in the growth rate of M3 ceased in the first quarter of 1973.

31. There remains the question: did the economy simply hit the 'full employment ceiling' as described by Sir John Hicks in his *Contribution to the Theory of the Trade Cycle* (Oxford, 1951), and would not this have occurred, as a consequence of such previous expansionary policies, whether or not there was a monetary squeeze? The ramifications of such a question are many; but it is worth noting that the economy did not expand along a 2 or 3 per cent path marking the 'potential' growth of the economy. Instead, there was a sharp *contraction*.

32. Note, however, that using the production index, *Economic Trends* table 82, one would strictly date it as the third quarter of 1975.

33. The data, representing changes from one calendar year to another in percentages of GDP at market prices, are:

	1971–2	1972–3	1973–4	1974–5	1975–6	1976–7
PSBR	0.8	2.6	1.9	2.2	−2.6	−3.1
PSFD	1.9	1.4	1.9	1.6	−0.7	−2.5

A positive value indicates an expansionary fiscal policy, and a negative value a contractionary policy.

34. See David Savage, 'Fiscal Policy 1974/5–1980/1: Description and Measurement', *National Institute Economic Review*, vol. 99 (Feb. 1982).

35. If one uses the monthly rates of change of M1 and smooths these values with a 12-monthly moving average, the turning point in the smoothed series comes early in 1974. This timing is consistent with the movement of nominal interest rates.

36. I have discussed this recession and the role of monetary and fiscal policy at some length in *Britain's Economic Renaissance*, so the account in this chapter will be brief.

37. The *increase* in the financial deficit as a percentage of GDP at market prices compared with FY 1977/8 was:

Unadjusted	0.81
Cyclically adjusted	1.06
Weighted	0.44
Weighted and cyclically adjusted	0.58

The increase in the PSBR as a percentage of GDP is of a similar order. It will be noted that the financial deficit for 1977/8 decreased, as a percentage of GDP, from that of 1976/7. But the whole thrust of fiscal policy in the Keynesian and NK context is that the economy will react in months not years. So we can dismiss the earlier squeeze as the NK cause of the 1979 downturn.

38. In analysing the downturn, many economists have argued that, with much more fiscal stimulus in 1979, perhaps even late in 1979, the downturn could have been dampened if not reversed. For reasons set out in my *Britain's Economic Renaissance*, I think that such fiscal expansionism would have exacerbated the downturn because it would have created deficits which would be seen by the markets to imply massive retrenchment in the near future. Not the stuff on which to build offsets to a recession or a confident recovery.

39.   Note that the growth rate of M1 continued to rise until it reached a plateau of
       about 15 per cent per annum, where it rested for about four years. The
       monetary expansion was, as it were, a permanent phenomenon – and I think
       was seen to be so by the market.

40.   One important feature of the recovery is the apparent divergence in timing of
       the M1 and M0 indicators. The growth rate of M0 declined to the second
       quarter of 1982, and lagged the change in the growth rate of M1 by about 20
       months. There are many plausible explanations such as deregulation and the
       payment of interest on checking balances – but it does cast doubt on using such
       indicators for short-run purposes.

41.   For additional reflections on the problem, see my *Britain's Economic Renais-
       sance*, Chapters 4 and 5.

42.   So far as I am aware, there have been few considered accounts of the outcome
       by any of the 364 economists who signed the famous 31 March letter to *The
       Times* which predicted that 'present policies will deepen the depression, erode
       the industrial base of our economy and threaten its social and political
       stability'. The reactions might be generally classified into first those who say
       that, since unemployment continued to grow, there was no recovery, and
       second, those who argue that in 1982–3 and in subsequent years fiscal policy
       (particularly in terms of the public sector financial deficit) became modestly
       expansionary and so ensured expansion. A possible sophistication on this latter
       theme is to suggest that the 1981 budget was seen to lay the foundations for
       subsequent expansionary fiscal policy. And it was the *anticipation* of future
       budget relaxation that sparked the recovery in the latter half of 1981. Of course
       such an argument, for which there is much to be said, makes nonsense of
       conventional fiscal policy. It may be thought that the fiscal squeeze in 1981 had
       its main effects on inflation rather than on real output. Certainly inflation fell
       steeply in 1981 and 1982 – but it had been falling since the middle of 1980. And
       what many believe to have been the main ingredient in disinflation, the
       exchange rates, peaked in the first quarter of 1981 and then sterling steadily
       depreciated as monetary policy was eased. The timing of the fall in inflation
       was broadly in line with the monetary contraction of 1978–9 – roughly a two-
       year lag.

43.   An example of Keynesian views in 1985 of the effects of the budget squeeze is
       illuminating. James Tobin wrote of the 1981 policies: 'While Reagan and
       Volcker were converting cyclical deficits into structural deficits, their counter-
       parts in Britain . . . were converting cyclical deficits into structural surpluses.
       Their tax increases and spending cuts hit their economies while they were down
       . . . contractionary fiscal policies prolonged recession and retarded recovery,
       even as spillover of American demands into foreign markets provided some
       relief.' 'The Fiscal Revolution: Disturbing Prospects', *Challenge* (Jan./Feb.
       1985), p. 15. Yet later in that article, Tobin argues for a reduction of the US
       federal deficit because of crowding-out and unnecessarily high interest rates.
       He recommends (in more or less full employment) a combination of lower
       deficits and more expansionary monetary policy – indeed shades of British
       policy in 1980–81, except that there was massive unemployment.

14 Should Fiscal Policy Rule the Roost? The Co-ordination of Monetary and Fiscal Policy

David Currie

14.1 INTRODUCTION

In the *General Theory* and in later writings, Keynes expressed scepticism about the effectiveness of monetary policy in stimulating recovery from the slump of the 1930s, and instead advocated expansionary fiscal measures. For this section of the Keynes Conference the conference organisers posed the question whether this position has continued validity; that is, should expansionary fiscal policy have priority over monetary policy?

The context of the current debate on this question is, of course, very different from that in which Keynes wrote. The slump of the 1930s was associated with falling prices, in total contrast to the 1970s and 1980s where inflationary pressures have been pervasive. High unemployment in the 1930s resulted from a fall in demand, exacerbated if not precipitated by ill-considered government policies (see Kindleberger, 1973), whereas the recession of the 1980s was generated by governments reacting to rising inflation by contractionary policy measures. Keynes's analysis was largely for the closed economy. This may not have been a bad approximation for the 1930s, with import controls, a low degree of openness to trade, limited capital mobility and a conventional though developed financial sector. But now we have a highly open economy, very limited barriers to the international movement of capital, relative freedom in trade (notwithstanding the exception of agriculture and the creeping tendency towards covert protection in other sectors) and a bewildering proliferation of financial instruments. It would be surprising if these contrasts did not modify our views as to whether fiscal policy or monetary policy should have priority.

Moreover, the tools with which we analyse this question have developed over the last half-century since Keynes wrote on the subject. Keynes's analysis was essentially short-run, and although he placed great stress on expectations, particularly in Chapter 18 of the *General Theory*, long-term expectations were exogenous to his analysis. The recent literature embeds short-term analysis in a longer framework, integrating questions of short-run stabilisation with longer-run issues of debt sustainability. It analyses policy initiatives not just as one-off policy changes, but in terms of policy rules, thereby heeding Friedman's warning about the long-run consequences of short-run policy measures (Friedman, 1948). It endogenises expectations, both short and long run, by assuming model-consistent or rational expectations. Moreover, the most recent literature permits the analysis of issues of reputation in macropolicy that, as we shall see, have important consequences for the appropriate relationship between fiscal and monetary policy.

These analytical developments are helpful in examining the respective roles of monetary and fiscal policy. The exchange rate exerts a major influence on the UK economy (as for other OECD countries) through its influence on trade volumes, prices and the valuation of overseas assets and liabilities. In turn, expectations play the major role in determining exchange rate fluctuations under floating exchange rates, or in precipitating pressures on a system of managed rates. Expectations are influenced by the credibility of policy: a major question of credibility concerning expansionary measures is whether they will trigger rising inflation; and with debt-income ratios rising in recent years in many OECD countries (though not the UK), it is not possible to avoid the question of whether expansionary fiscal measures are consistent with long-run debt sustainability.

There is, however, one aspect of these analytical developments which is not helpful. To judge from the various views expressed by present-day economists, the number of divergent (and therefore, the number of erroneous) theories current in debate has not fallen since Keynes's day, indeed if anything it seems to have risen. Yet the assumption of model-consistency does not allow for this divergence of views. It is self-evident that a policy initiative based on a false view of the world is very likely to fail. What is less well recognised is that an otherwise well-conceived policy initiative may fail because market expectations are based on a false view of the world. Thus expectations may precipitate sharp movements in variables, dominated by expectations, and these movements in turn force a reversal of policy.[1] Unfortunately, the literature dealing with the consequences of policy when expectations are erroneous is neither large nor very satisfactory, principally because the problem is a rather intractable one. This is a gap that we make no serious attempt to repair in this chapter.

The plan of the chapter is as follows. In the following section, we discuss the respective roles of monetary and fiscal policy, considering particularly their interrelationship. In Section 14.3, we then focus on the design of policies aimed at expanding overall economic activity, and examine the constraints on such measures. Section 14.4 discusses questions of reputation, rules and credibility. It focuses particularly on the issue of policy co-ordination, both between the central bank and the treasury within a single country, and between policy-makers in different countries.

We shall take fiscal policy to be changes in tax rates, whether direct or indirect, or government spending, whether exhaustive or transfers, carried out either singly or in combination. We shall focus most on fiscal changes that result in changes in the fiscal deficit, so that financial market effects follow directly from the financing of the resulting deficit. However, this is not to downplay the scope for balanced budget changes, and, as we note in certain places, altering the combination of taxes and expenditures may have important effects. We shall follow conventional analysis in taking monetary policy to mean changes in the path of some suitably defined monetary aggregate. However, as we note at the end of Section 14.2, innovation in financial markets may make the definition non-operational, forcing us back to think of monetary policy, as Keynes did, in terms of changes in key asset prices, notably short term interest rates.

Finally, it should be noted that the chapter follows the concerns of this Keynes conference by analysing the respective role of fiscal and monetary policy at the level of broad principle, rather than attempting to assess what specific policy actions are called for in the current conjuncture. (We have already addressed this latter set of questions elsewhere in Currie (1987).)

14.2 FISCAL POLICY AND MONETARY POLICY: SUBSTITUTES OR COMPLEMENTS?

Keynes's advocacy of an activist policy to counter the slump of the 1930s rested on two main propositions: first, that the system left to equilibrate by itself by an adjustment of wages and prices would do so, if at all, very slowly and inefficiently; and that an activist monetary policy would be ineffective in stimulating economic activity.

The first proposition is not the concern of this chapter, being examined in detail in other contributions. However, parts of the argument of this chapter are posited on the basis of its continuing validity. Although strongly challenged by the monetarist school in the 1960s, using the expectations-augmented Phillips curve, and by the monetarist rational expectations school of the 1970s and 1980s, other strands of thought have rightly emphasised a variety of reasons for slowness in price and wage adjustment (including custom markets and insider-outsider distinctions in the labour market). Moreover, some analyses of labour market behaviour suggest lasting effects (termed hysteresis) from demand disturbances that are not offset (see Blanchard and Summers, 1986). Other hysteresis effects may arise elsewhere, for example in international trade (see Baldwin and Krugman, 1986). The inefficiency of pure market adjustments may be argued from these elements alone.

The second proposition concerning the ineffectiveness of monetary policies is the starting point of our discussion. Keynes's argument against the use of monetary policy to stimulate demand has been interpreted in two ways: first, that there may be a floor to interest rates (i.e. the liquidity trap), though Keynes himself appeared to express some scepticism on this point; and second, that expenditures are rather insensitive to interest rates (a low interest sensitivity of the IS curve).

In the conditions of the early 1930s, these arguments, particularly the second, would appear to have had some force. Nominal interest rates were low, and further falls were limited by the lower bound of zero. With the high risk of a fall in the general level of prices, the incentive to invest at these nominal interest rates was small: investors who did so faced the risk of high *ex post* real interest rates and major debt service problems. In any event, for firms facing spare capacity and depressed demand, the incentive to invest was greatly depressed and largely insensitive to interest rates.

In conditions of more buoyant demand, such as the 1950s and 1960s, these arguments had less force. The debates of the 1960s on the relative efficacy of monetary and fiscal policy were generally within the IS/LM framework, and centred on the issue of the relative slopes and stability of the IS and LM curves.[2] (For an admirable survey see Laidler (1971).) Proponents of the powers of monetary policy argued for a steep, stable money demand function and a flattish IS curve, so that the most powerful impulses to aggregate demand come from shifts in monetary policy. A real balance effect on expenditure was also seen as a possible further channel of influence of monetary policy, but was generally regarded as too weak a channel to be relied upon. Advocates of fiscal policy tended to argue the opposite position of a flattish and unstable money demand function and a steep IS curve, so that the impulses to aggregate demand come from autonomous movements in expenditure, giving a role to countercyclical fiscal policy.

In so far as this debate reached a resolution on these empirical matters, it was one of compromise. In broad terms, the evidence suggested that the money demand function was interest sensitive, but that the elasticity was not very high; and that similar conclusions should be drawn concerning the aggregate expenditure function. This conclusion, that the world was characterised by rather steep IS and LM curves, was not particularly convincing, certainly when viewed with hindsight. For it is implied that, if the monetary authorities pursued monetary targets, interest rates would exhibit market volatility in the face of either aggregate demand or money demand disturbances.

However, this debate was rather overtaken by other developments. The first of these was the growing awareness that even if the focus of analysis was the single economy, there was the need to couch the analysis of monetary and fiscal policy firmly in the context of an open economy, not least because of the steady removal of obstacles to capital mobility. With a high degree of capital mobility, the scope for a small open economy to pursue an autonomous monetary policy under fixed exchange rates is clearly rather limited. With a largely passive money supply, adjusting to maintain the fixed exchange rate parity, the LM curve becomes irrelevant,[3] as does the debate about the relative efficacy of monetary and fiscal policy. With floating exchange rates, by contrast, monetary policy becomes crucially important through its effect on the exchange rate. Indeed, the natural extension to the closed economy IS/LM model, namely the Mundell/Fleming model, suggests that, with perfect capital mobility, fiscal policy will be impotent and monetary policy all-powerful in its effects on aggregate demand. This result is largely independent of the interest elasticities of the IS and LM curves, depending instead on the influence of monetary policy on interest rates, thence onto the exchange rate and thence onto aggregate demand. While minor adjustments to the model modify the extreme conclusion concerning the impotence of fiscal policy, the broad conclusion concerning the importance of monetary policy is robust. However, the potency of monetary policy is two-edged: while its effect on the exchange rate amplifies its impact on output, the same effect adds to inflationary pressures from imported prices.

The usefulness of the simple IS/LM model as a framework for analysing monetary and fiscal policy was further cast into doubt by the development of what has come to be known as the buffer stock view of money. (See Laidler (1971) and Goodhart (1984) for an overview.) This emphasises the role of money as a buffer for agents, being run down or built up in response to short-run discrepancies between expenditure and income. As Akerlof (1981) argues, the precise manner in which this buffer is monitored has strong implications for the short-run income and interest elasticities of money demand. He demonstrates that under plausible assumptions both these short-run elasticities will be low, so that a flattish LM curve is entirely consistent with a low short-run interest elasticity. More profoundly, if money is a buffer, the short-run money demand function will be ill-determined.[4] Thus in this view short-run discrepancies between income and expenditure will be reflected in money holdings rather than other financial assets. An implication is that the short-run relationship between real money balances, interest rates and economic activity will be much looser than that suggested by the conventional IS/LM framework. In particular, interest rates will not be unduly volatile in the face of demand or financial market disturbances. A further implication is that, in the short run, the potency of monetary policy will be somewhat diminished, while that of fiscal policy is enhanced.

The third development was that which recognised the linkages between money and fiscal policy through the government budget constraint (see, for example, Blinder and Solow, 1973; Christ, 1979; Feldstein, 1981). The early pre-rational expectations literature (surveyed in Currie, 1978, 1981) emphasised this as a medium to longer-run issue. Expansionary fiscal policy that results in a larger budget deficit will require financing by the issue of additional government liabilities. If monetary policy (defined here in terms of a given path for the money stock) is unchanged, this will imply a greater issue of government bonds. The steadily increasing supply of government bonds relative to money will drive up interest rates, because of considerations of private sector portfolio balance. The process can stabilise only if the initial increment to the budget deficit is closed. This may occur via a rise in net tax revenues if wealth effects on expenditures are large so that aggregate demand rises sufficiently, and if the supply of output is elastic so that output rises. But the more likely outcome is that output will fall because of higher interest rates, or that even if it rises the associated rise in net tax revenues is insufficient to offset the rising cost of servicing an increasing volume of government debt. These effects will be reinforced by the effects of high interest rates on capital accumulation, damaging the supply side of the economy. In this case, the outcome is unstable, unless the initial fiscal stimulus is reversed or monetary policy accommodates.

Similar considerations apply to an exogenous change in the money supply with fiscal policy unchanged. A monetary contraction will generate a fall in output and a budget deficit on unchanged fiscal policy. The financing of this deficit with an unchanged money supply requires additional sales of government bonds, which can have destabilising effects as described in the last papragraph. To avoid instability requires an adjustment to fiscal policy or a reversal of the initial change in monetary policy.

The implication of this analysis is that consistency must be maintained between monetary and fiscal policy in the medium to longer run. This may be done in a variety of ways. Monetary targets may be asserted as having primacy, in which case fiscal policy must be accommodating to avoid undue government borrowing. It is this argument that may be used to rationalise the adherence to PSBR targets within the UK's Medium Term Financial Strategy. Alternatively, fiscal policy may be given primacy, with monetary policy accommodating, perhaps via supporting targets for the exchange rate or interest rates. Or some middle position between these two extremes may be sought.

We return in the following section to this question of how best to maintain consistency between monetary and fiscal policy. But it is worth noting at this stage that this question can only be properly addressed in the context of *rules* for the conduct of monetary and fiscal policy and of issues of policy credibility and reputation (see Section 14.4). This is because of the role of expectations, largely ignored in the earlier literature on the government budget constraint. With forward looking expectations about asset prices and the exchange rate, private agents need assurance that medium-term consistency between monetary and fiscal policy will be maintained. If such assurances are not forthcoming or are not credible, the instability may be brought forward to the present via long-term asset prices and the exchange rate and other forward looking prices.[5] Thus Sargent and Wallace (1981) argue that, in the absence of accompanying fiscal adjustments, a cut in the rate of monetary expansion will fail to lower, and may even raise, the prevailing rate of inflation. This occurs because, in the absence of a supporting cut in the primary fiscal deficit, lower monetary contraction leads to a build-up of debt and a higher debt services burden, which is financed by a more rapid rate of monetary expansion and a higher inflation tax in the future. Anticipations mean that higher future inflation may be brought forward to the present despite the current tightness in monetary policy.

The upshot of this is that policy must not only maintain consistency in the longer run, but must also offer assurances that this will be done. Broad guidelines or rules for the conduct of macropolicy offer one way of accomplishing this. We return to this issue in Section 14.4.

Before moving on, it is appropriate to make a rather fundamental point concerning monetary policy that has important bearing on the analysis of the relative efficacy of monetary and fiscal policy. The predictability of monetary policy (thought of, conventionally, as changes in the stock of some suitably defined monetary aggregate) depends among other factors on the stability of the associated demand for money function. We have grown accustomed to some instability in such relationships. But the recent wave of financial innovation raises rather seriously the possibility that money demand functions may be just too unstable for monetary policy defined in terms of monetary aggregates to have effects that are predictable and usable in policy terms.

The effects of financial innovation may be seen most clearly in the UK. There one has seen a shifting of roles for financial institutions, a blurring, if not total erosion, of institutional boundaries, and the development of a whole new range of swap and futures instruments, all of which weakens the informational content of conventional monetary aggregates. At the international level, the recent Cross report (Bank of International Settlements, 1986) notes the consequences of growing securitisation in banking, which means, for example, that it is largely a matter of choice whether or not banks operating in international markets allow an inflow of funds to register on its balance sheet and therefore in conventional monetary aggregates. Nor is it helpful to aggregate monetary statistics across countries to examine global aggregates, since the growth of new financial instruments has increased the already large problems of consistency between the aggregates of different countries.

These trends invite the speculation that we are now seeing the creation of a world more appropriate to some parts of the 1950s analysis of the Radcliffe Report (HMSO, 1959) than to the monetarist views of the 1960s and 1970s. The Radcliffe Report emphasised, *inter alia*, the enormous opportunities for substitution between alternative assets and liabilities, suggesting that these were sufficiently great to render unhelpful an emphasis on any particular financial aggregate. This representation of the uninnovative, cartelised and regulated financial system of the 1950s and 1960s was widely criticised, so that the influence of the Report's analysis was limited. But today it seems much more pertinent.

These developments raise serious doubts about thinking of monetary policy in terms of monetary aggregates, and therefore about the conventional literature on the relative efficacy of monetary and fiscal policy. It suggests the need to return to the more Keynesian tradition, following Keynes himself, of thinking of monetary policy in terms of policy actions to influence asset prices, particularly the short-term interest rate or the exchange rate. This avoids certain, though not all, of the problems of maintaining consistency between monetary and fiscal policy. One objection to this is that nominal interest rates give a poor indicator of the thrust of monetary policy if inflation expectations are volatile, because the real interest rate may then move in undesirable ways. This is a problem only because the monetary authorities have no adequate measure of the real rate of interest. The obvious answer is for the authorities to encourage the development of a broad market for indexed securities to give a direct measure of the real rate of return on financial assets.[6] Another objection is that interest rate rules give rise to problems of price level indeterminacy or, in a less extreme form, cumulative inflation. But this is not so. Providing that the authorities are concerned about inflation and formulate policy with a view to containing inflationary pressures, the choice of instrument is not crucial. The experience of the UK, where the role of monetary targets has played an ambiguous role, at best, in the containment of inflation is suggestive in this regard. We return to this question in Section 14.4.

14.3   THE ROLE OF FISCAL POLICY IN RECOVERING FROM RECESSION

In this section, we examine policies designed to stimulate the general level of economic activity by a combined package of monetary and fiscal measures. A key policy issue at the current time is the design of policies to bring down the very high levels of unemployment now prevalent in OECD countries as a whole. The feasibility of such policies is, of course, a matter of controversy: some would argue that the equilibrium level of unemployment (or NAIRU) is so high that there is little or no room for non-inflationary demand expansion. This is not the place to assess such arguments, which are discussed by other contributors, and in the following we proceed on the basis that some margin for demand expansion does exist in the OECD as a whole. But to the extent that such arguments have some force, they underline the need for expansionary policies to be friendly to the supply side, acting simultaneously to cut inflationary pressures and expand the economy.[7] An important question which we will consider in what follows is the extent to which expansion in a single country presents greater obstacles than a generalised OECD expansion.

Two principal objections to fiscal expansion centre on the twin dangers of inflation and crowding out. Starting from a position of no deficient demand, such problems are, of course, likely to follow from a fiscal stimulus even if not accompanied by monetary expansion. The excess demand generated by the fiscal deficit will tend to drive up prices; while the issue of debt to finance the resulting deficit drives up real interest rates, as discussed in the previous section. Much of the literature suggests that such a policy, if adhered to, may be totally destabilising.[8] A greater degree of money financing of the deficit will tend to reduce the prospects of total destabilisation, but at the cost of longer-run inflation. But since few of us would advocate a fiscal expansion starting from a position where deficient demand was absent, the interest of this analysis is rather slight.

More pertinent is the analysis that assumes an initial degree of spare capacity in the economy.[9] This literature suggests that any crowding-out that results from fiscal expansion arises essentially from an inappropriate choice of mix between monetary and fiscal policy. To be sure, a fiscal expansion financed solely through bond issues may drive up real interest rates through wealth and portfolio effects operating on asset demands, and may therefore crowd out investment and possibly destabilise the system.[10] But such problems can be avoided by choosing a more accommodating monetary policy, allowing some expansion of the money supply to avoid undue upward pressure on real interest ratess. Monetary accommodation of this kind will add somewhat to the expansionary stimulus, but need not be inflationary unless the overall scale of the policy measures is excessive.

Those who advocate leaving matters to market adjustments tend to argue that our knowledge of the responses of the system is inadequate to design a successful fiscal and monetary expansion of this kind. This argument has some force when applied to short-lived disturbances, but is much less persuasive when demand deficiency is prolonged. Fine-tuning may be dead, but coarse tuning is much needed. Moreover, it is false to assume that the market can operate smoothly while policy actions are necessarily disruptive. Even if agents optimise their own individual adjustment patterns, in so doing they will take the adjustment patterns of others as independently determined. Dynamic adjustment in the aggregate may therefore take the form of a Nash non-cooperative equilibrium in adjustment strategies between agents, with undesirable inefficient characteristics familiar from games of the Prisoners' Dilemma type.[11] An important aspect of dynamic policy design is to mitigate these deficiencies in the process of adjustment to exogenous, non-policy disturbances to the system.

Even if it is the case that policy merely speeds up a process of adjustment that would otherwise have occurred through market mechanisms, it does not follow that it will have to be unwound, with a period of fiscal deficits matched by a subsequent period of surpluses. This could be so if the initial demand deficiency arose from a disturbance which is self-reversing, and therefore temporary in character. Even here, if long periods of demand deficiency have permanent real effects through the accumulation of real capital, technical change and so on, so that hysteresis effects are present, the fiscal expansion may not need to be unwound. But if the system, left to itself, would have equilibrated through the uncertain mechanism of a fall in prices relative to what they would have been, the fiscal expansion, appropriately financed, may simply avoid the fall in prices without undesirably altering the long-run configuration of the system.

The upshot of this is that, were we dealing with a single closed economy, a policy package might be devised to rectify deficient demand. But the individual economy is not closed; and the world economy is made up of many economies, each with its own decision-making mechanisms. It is difficulties raised by these features that we now address.

Consider first the obstacles to a coordinated expansion amongst the major OECD countries. A major difficulty is that of obtaining agreement on the desirability of such an expansion. This is particularly so if the circumstances of individual countries differ somewhat in the market for non-inflationary expansion. There is also the problem of determining and enforcing the appropriate mix of fiscal and monetary policy across countries. With the ratio of government debt to income rising quite sharply in the OECD as a whole, and a real interest rates at very high levels (see Price and Muller, 1984; Atkinson and Chouraqui, 1985; Blanchard and Summers, 1984), there is a strong case for some overall relaxation of monetary policy. Moreover, a different mix of policy action is likely to be appropriate in the US and Europe, in view of existing policy imbalances, notably the large US fiscal deficit.

But even if agreement were found on these issues, there remains the difficulty of creating the incentives for each individual country to participate in a general expansion. This is because of the free rider problem. In a highly integrated world, economic expansion creates considerable externalities between countries. If the rest of the world expands, this stimulates domestic output whilst reducing inflationary pressures at home through an appreciating exchange rate.[12] By contrast, expansion initiated at home will tend to depreciate the exchange rate, adding to inflationary pressures, while the benefits of expansion are generalised by spillovers overseas, and therefore diluted for the initiating country. Countries have strong incentives to free-ride on international expansion, or at best to be followers rather than leaders in the process. The interesting question is whether other benefits or penalties can be devised to be conditioned on expansion, so as to reduce this incentive.

Expansion in the single open economy involves a different set of problems. Domestic expansion in isolation will worsen the current account of the balance of payments both in the short run and the longer run. Unless the country in question is perceived as experiencing an associated improvement in the range of available investment opportunities (as was argued by some rather implausibly to have been the case for the US in the past five years), this deterioration will be unsustainable except for a transitional period. An improvement in competitiveness will therefore be required to offset this deterioration. Some gain in competitiveness might obtain from changes in the structure of taxation, as well as from productivity gains associated with economic expansion. But some fall in real wage costs (relative to trend) will almost certainly be required to achieve the necessary gain in competitiveness. The principal obstacle to expansion in isolation is how to make a rise in demand and a fall in the trend of wage costs mutually consistent. This highlights the need for measures that operate simultaneously on supply as well as demand.[13]

With conventional models of the exchange rate, the need for a gain in competitiveness may only become apparent in the longer run. But with forward-looking expectations in the foreign exchange market, these longer-run considerations are brought forward to the present. The need for a real exchange rate depreciation in the long run as a result of fiscal expansion may well result in an immediate real depreciation. An additional factor is the possibility of higher domestic inflation as the real depreciation puts upward pressure on domestic prices. To the extent that this is anticipated, the nominal exchange rate will be marked down further to reflect future inflation. But with domestic prices sticky in the short run, this nominal depreciation will correspond to a real depreciation. It is easy to see that, if fiscal expansion triggers significant inflationary worries, the exchange rate may fall precipitately, with consequences that validate these concerns. All of this emphasises the need for policy to allay fears that fiscal expansion will lead to higher inflation.

An increasingly popular notion is that potentially inflationary consequences of fiscal expansion can be offset by an associated rise in interest rates to prevent downward pressure on the nominal exchange rate, or, to go further, to induce an appreciation to mitigate any inflationary pressures arising domestically from expansion. This seems to be the policy, intended or otherwise, pursued by the US authorities since 1981. The difficulty with it is that a real exchange rate depreciation is, none the less, required in the long run to restore current account equilibrium (see Giavazzi and Sheen, 1985; Sachs and Wyplosz, 1984). Moreover, as the US experience makes clear, the requirement of current account equilibrium is all the more stringent because of the consequences of transitional external deficits for the net worth of a country and therefore for its debt service needs. Tighter monetary policy now may reduce immediate inflationary pressures, but only by pushing the inflationary pressures into the future (if the expansion is sustained). The danger is that short-run complacency may develop about the feasibility of non-inflationary expansion; and that inflation may emerge just at the time when high real interest rates and a possibly high real exchange rate are curtailing output, so that the end result is stagflation. There is also the worry that the resulting imbalance between monetary and fiscal policy may be destabilising.

The upshot of this argument is that forward-looking expectations in the foreign exchange markets bring forward to the present the policy dilemmas that we have sometimes been tempted to dismiss as longer run concerns. If this is correct, it focuses attention on the question of competitiveness and the possible need for labour market measures to tackle this. Such measures might involve fiscal policy directly, in the form of employment subsidies or in employment taxes, whether temporary or permanent; or may take other forms whether incomes policy of the traditional or tax-based form, reform of wage bargaining (Meade, 1982; Vines, Maciezowski and Meade, 1983), revenue sharing (Weitzman, 1984) or changes in industrial participation or ownership. Discussion of these alternatives is not the subject of this chapter.

To the extent, however, that the policy problem is one of expanding in a world characterised by general depressed demand, there is a real sense in which the resulting emphasis on labour market reform is a second best solution. This is because, despite the obstacles, the first.best solution is general expansion. This may be illustrated by considering a sequence of uncoordinated expansions in different countries. Each country when expanding will need to curtail the trend in unit costs to maintain current account equilibrium in the longer run. But when other countries expand, unit costs may rise again. If the burden of adjustment of competitiveness falls on wages, then wages fall (relative to trend) and rise subsequently. It would not be surprising in those circumstances if wage negotiators were reluctant to ride this roller-coaster. It is the need for adjustments of this kind that enables one to talk sensibly of an external constraint on domestic expansion in the single country, a constraint that may be relaxed by coordinated action. We return to these issues of international coordination in the next section, after first considering the role of reputation in the analysis of fiscal policy.

14.4   POLICY RULES, REPUTATION AND CREDIBILITY

The analysis of reputation in the recent macropolicy literature has facilitated a rigorous consideration of the benefits of policy-makers of having credibility in policy matters. The advantages of reputation arise because of the potential problem of time inconsistency. In the absence of reputation, policy commitments will lack credibility if the private sector perceive that government will have an incentive to renege on these commitments subsequently. A reputation for adhering to policy commitments will give additional influence to policy through its effects on expectations, and may therefore be used to yield an improved policy performance. Such a reputation may be sustained by a variety of mechanisms but if the improvement in policy performance is appreciable and widely perceived, this in itself may be sufficient to sustain the reputation for adhering to policy commitments. This is because it will be seen to be in the interest of government not to renege on its promises.

Thus in the absence of reputation, macropolicy will be generally inferior in its performance. This has two aspects. First, the absence of reputation will impair the ability of policy to respond to macroeconomic disturbances in a stabilising manner; that is, the effectiveness of stabilisation policy will be weakened. But an equally important aspect is that the reputational and non-reputational policy regimes will be characterised by rather different steady states. This may be illustrated by the analysis of Barro and Gordon (1983a, 1983b). In the natural rate model, a government concerned about both inflation and output has a short-run incentive at low inflation rates to spring inflation surprises on the private sector, in order to achieve a temporary gain in output. In the absence of reputation, the private sector will expect the government to do this, and will therefore anticipate higher inflation. Equilibrium will result at that level of inflation at which the marginal costs of higher surprise inflation just equal the marginal benefits of higher output. Since output is then at the natural rate, the non-reputational equilibrium is characterised by a socially inefficient high rate of inflation. A government with credibility will use its reputation to avoid high inflation, leading to a more socially beneficial outcome. Thus the non-reputational regime will be characterised by undue inflation relative to the reputational regime. In the same world or in a more Keynesian one, government will have an incentive to increase government spending, either because of the direct benefits of government spending or because of induced multiplier gains in terms of output. But a government without reputation may be expected to neglect the consequences of a higher debt stock for real interest rates and future sustainable levels of government expenditure and therefore expand current government spending excessively. These expectations will generate high real interest rates now, with adverse consequences for output and investment. The reputational regime, by contrast, would be characterised by lower real interest rates.

This analysis highlights the benefits of reputation in policy. One way in which such a reputation may be established and sustained is by adherence to certain well-specified policy rules that can be easily understood and monitored. This is one rationalisation for the Medium Term Financial Strategy (MTFS) that has provided the framework for UK macropolicy since 1980. However, it is not clear that the MTFS gave great benefits in terms of credibility. Certainly the period since its inception has seen a significant fall in the rate of inflation, but this would seem to have been the result of a sharp rise in unemployment, not necessarily the consequence of credibility effects. This may be because the MTFS contained significant flaws in its design. The central role given initially to monetary aggregates was a serious error (noted at the time), because of the instability of many demand functions, and this error was aggravated by the fact that financial innovation and liberalisation in this period robbed these aggregates of whatever informational content they might otherwise have had. The usefulness of targeting short-term movements in aggregates that play an important buffer role for agents was far from evident. Most seriously, the focus on monetary aggregates left the exchange rate vulnerable to Dornbusch-type overshooting. On the fiscal side, PSBR targets built in a degree of automatic contractionary response to inflation that may have been helpful in controlling inflation (see Begg, 1987). But the implied simultaneous switching-off of automatic fiscal stabilisers (which has been largely, though not completely, carried out in practice) made the real side of the economy much more vulnerable to demand shocks. (This effect was all the greater as fiscal deficit targets were adopted in other countries so that the short-run output effects of aggregate demand distur- bances were accentuated.) It may be argued that this, together with the real exchange rate variation in the early 1980s, was particularly damaging to the real economy.

Of course, policy has adapted in the light of these lessons. Policy has increasingly moved towards covert exchange rate targets that limit the scope for overshooting, and towards a more relaxed fiscal stance (under cover of asset sales). The buoyancy of the UK economy may owe as much to these changes as to the benefits of credibility.

This experience should not, however, prejudice the case for rules for the conduct of macropolicy. Indeed, the need for an alternative set of guidelines for policy is all the more pressing in view of the current absence of clear guidelines for current policy. The alternative is likely to involve a willingness to avoid undue swings in the exchange rate, particularly if they would otherwise lead to prolonged periods of misalignment. This implies maintain- ing consistency between the medium term stance of monetary and fiscal policy. A further implication is that real exchange rate appreciation would not be the main weapon for containing domestic inflationary pressures: this should be tackled by other means, including a balanced contraction of monetary and fiscal policy. In the shorter run, there is much to be said for giving policy greater autonomy, at least to the extent of allowing automatic fiscal stabilisers to operate. This may be done by setting fiscal targets on a medium term basis, averaged over the cycle, with year-by-year targets being monitored on a cyclically adjusted basis. Alternatively fiscal policy may be thought of in terms of a permanent income view of public finances, averaging out swings in taxes and expenditures due to cyclical fluctuations. Monetary policy in the short run could well be directed towards pursuit of an exchange rate target.

So far, we have discussed the benefits of reputation and policy rules in the context of the single economy on the implicit assumption that the various aspects of policy are co-ordinated. Thus we have assumed that monetary and fiscal policy are jointly determined by a single decision-making process, so that we can sensibly talk about government in the singular. This is clearly an approximation, but it is not a bad representation of how policy is determined in the UK and a number of other European countries. But in the US and West Germany, the determination of monetary policy is to an important degree independent of that of fiscal policy.

At first sight, there would appear to be serious disadvantages in failing to coordinate the different aspects of policy, since it may well lead to inconsistencies in policy stance (as suggested, perhaps, by recent US experience). However, in principle, this need not be so. Rogoff (1985) and others have noted that coordination may be undesirable in the international context; while Alesina and Tabellini (1985) show the analogous result that coordination between the monetary and fiscal authorities may not be advantageous. This is because the absence of co-operation may help to limit the inflationary bias noted above that arises in the absence of reputation. For example, in a Barro/Gordon world, in the absence of co-operation, the tendency for the exchange rate to depreciate in response to a monetary expansion will limit the incentive for governments to spring monetary surprises on the private sector, and therefore reduce the inflationary bias of the non-reputational regime. Co-operation may therefore be undesirable in the absence of reputation.

An equally important finding is that reputation may not pay in the absence of cooperation (see Levine and Currie, 1987; Currie, Levine and Vidalis, 1987). Thus, in an open economy, reputational policies to combat inflation may well involve a form of Reaganomics: expansionary policies to lower unemployment combined with a tight monetary stance to contain inflation. Such policies are ineffective if widely adopted to tackle generalised inflationary pressures; but uncoordinated policies may well result in this outcome, and may be destabilising because of the dangers of spiralling interest rates. Currie, Levine and Vidalis (1987) use a reduced version of the OECD Interlink model to investigate these various regimes empirically, and find that the non-cooperative reputational regime is indeed prone to excess deflation in the world economy and an excess level of government spending. It is, in addition, highly unstable. The non-reputational regimes, by contrast, are prone to high steady-state inflation, for reasons analogous to those of the Barro/Gordon model. The results suggest that the benefits of reputation and co-operation are joint goods, and that either reputation without co-operation or reputation without co-operation is not helpful.

These results are suggestive in thinking about the evolution of macropolicy internationally over the past decade or more. A loose and speculative characterisation would be that the international system has moved from a co-operative non-reputational regime at the end of the Bretton Woods era, to a uncooperative non-reputational regime during the early period of floating exchange rates characterised by high inflation, through to a uncooperative reputational regime in the 1980s. The crucial question on the agenda of international policy-makers is whether the further transition to a co-operative reputational regime can now be made, so as to tap the joint advantages of reputation and co-operation.

This is not the place to consider in any detail proposals for the conduct of international macropolicy. However, it is relevant to our theme to note an element of polarisation in the debate on this question between those that emphasise monetary aspects and those that emphasise fiscal policy. The early proposals for coordination focused very much on the use of monetary policy to support a system of target exchange rates; and it is pertinent to note that explicit co-operation within the European Monetary System is almost exclusively confined to monetary policy. IMF thinking, by contrast, has tended to emphasise rather more the need to correct underlying fiscal imbalances (see, for example, Boughton, 1987; Frenkel and Goldstein, 1986).

A theme of this chapter has been the need to maintain consistency between monetary and fiscal policy, and in the international context this would imply a less polarised approach to this issue. Exchange rate targets without supporting fiscal policy will not be viable; fiscal targets with independent monetary targets will not deal with problems of exchange rate over-shooting, misalignments and speculative bubbles in foreign exchange markets.

It is therefore appropriate that the most recent statement by Williamson and Miller of the case for exchange rate zones places at the centre a set of rules for the conduct of fiscal policy as well as monetary policy (see Williamson and Miller, 1987). They envisage the setting of targets for nominal demand growth for each country, together with a set of real exchange rate targets aimed at achieving medium term current account equilibrium. Differences in short-term real interest rates are adjusted so as to target real exchange rates; while fiscal policy is used to target domestic nominal demand. (This assignment stands in contrast to that of the original UK MTFS, though it is closer to current UK policy.) Finally they propose that the average of world short-term real interest rates should be used to target world nominal demand; this is in addition to the stabilising influence on world demand arising from the use of fiscal policy in each country to stabilise domestic demand.

These rules give important roles to both monetary and fiscal policy, though in different respects. The rules are such that only in the setting of monetary policy is acount taken of developments in other countries. This may be over-restrictive. Thus, for example, Currie and Wren-Lewis (1987) find, using the NIESR Global Econometric Model (GEM), that the proposed use of short-term interest rates to control world aggregate demand is not effective, and that fiscal policy needs to be used actively in this role. This is not for the traditional Keynesian reason that monetary policy has limited effects on demand, for the effects of real interest rates in GEM are quite powerful. Rather it is because the effects of monetary policy differ much more across countries than do those of fiscal policy. A general rise in real interest rates to deal with excessive world demand will exert quite strong distribution effects across the world economy. In this role, fiscal policy offers the more reliable instrument.

It would be unwise to place too much weight on these results. They are drawn from a single empirical model and there is the obvious question as to whether they are robust across models. It is also not sensible to propose that the average of short-term real interest rates worldwide should be fixed, not least because this would generate Wicksellian instability problems in the face of shifts in the equilibrium real interest rate. But these results do suggest that over-reliance on monetary policy for stabilising demand at the world level is unwise, and that fiscal policy has a crucial role to play in this. It therefore reinforces the arguments in this chapter that emphasise the importance of fiscal policy, as well as the need to maintain medium-term consistency between fiscal and monetary policy.

Notes

1. This raises the possibility, discussed in the literature, that as a consequence these expectations may be self-confirming.
2. It should be noted, however, that in some writings, the issue became one almost solely concerned with the money demand function, and the IS curve dropped out of sight.
3. It is for this reason that in the macroeconometric models of this vintage, the LM curve was notable by its absence. Under fixed exchange rates, policy is most easily analysed in terms of interest rates and fiscal policy, allowing the money supply to adjust passively as appropriate. The absence of any monetary sectors in these models may well have contributed to the policy errors of the early 1970s, at the time of the move towards generalised floating exchange rates.
4. This may help to explain the very high coefficient on the lagged dependent variable in conventional money demand functions, implying an implausibly slow speed of adjustment of actual money balances towards the desired level. It may also explain at least part of instabilities of empirical money demand functions.
5. Thus if interest rates are expected to rise because of continuing bond issues, the long-term market for government bonds will dry up.
6. The usual non-neutrality of the tax system with respect to inflation means that this measure will be distorted by tax considerations. If this non-neutrality cannot be eliminated these distortions need to be taken into account in interpreting the real interest rate measure.
7. Such measures might be to cut the wedge between the real wage faced by employers and employees, say by cutting NI contributions. Another longer-term measure may be to promote investment. For further discussion see CEPS (1987), Layard and Calmfors (1987).
8. See, for example, Christ (1979); and for a survey of the literature, Currie (1978). It is interesting to note that Tobin (1980) argues that, if policy is stable, the long-run outcome is either crowding-out of investment or higher prices, but not both.
9. See Currie (1978) for a survey.

10. See, for example, Christ (1979). Note that this is not just a problem of escalating interest charges; the effects of bond issues in financial markets may push up real interest rates at the same time as there is deficient demand, causing instability even if taxes or transfers are changed to offset the effect on the budget of rising interest payments on government debt.

11. In developing integrated models of different sectors, each based on explicit optimising behaviour through time, it is very hard to avoid complex eigenvalues. This is despite the fact that the consequent oscillations reduce the welfare of all agents in the system. These oscillations arise from Nash-type interactions between private agents, and leave scope for policy to bring about a welfare-improving change through activist policy.

12. There is a complicated question here of timing and the stance of monetary policy, as the current US example illustrates and we describe below.

13. A difficulty in using the macroeconomic models for analysing this issue is that they frequently do not impose any long-run equilibrium conditions on the balance of payments. This problem becomes particularly acute when exchange rate expectations are forward-looking.

References

AKERLOF, G. (1981) 'Problems and Resolutions of Problems Concerning the Short Run Demand for Money', in D. Currie, R. Nobay and D. Peel (eds), *Macroeconomic Analysis: Essays in Macroeconomics and Econometrics* (London: Croom Helm).

ALESINA, A. and G. TABELLINI (1985) 'Rules and Discretion with Non-Coordinated Monetary and Fiscal Policy'; mimeo, August.

ATKINSON, P. and J.–C. CHORAQUI (1985) 'Real Interest Rates and the Prospects for Durable Growth', OECD Working Paper No. 24.

BALDWIN, R. and R. KRUGMAN (1986) 'Persistent Trade Effects of Large Exchange Rate Shocks', NBER Discussion Paper No. 2017.

BANK FOR INTERNATIONAL SETTLEMENTS (1986) *Recent Innovations in International Banking*, April.

BARRO, R. and D. GORDON (1983a) 'Rules, Discretion and Reputation in a Model of Monetary Policy', *Journal of Monetary Economics*, vol. 12, pp. 101–121.

BARRO, R. and D. GORDON (1983b) 'A Positive Theory of Monetary Policy in a Natural Rate Model', *Journal of Political Economy*, vol. 91, pp. 589–610.

BEGG, D. (1987) 'Recent British Fiscal Policy: Placing the MTFS in Context', in P. Minford (ed.), *Monetarism and Macropolicy* (Institute of Economic Affairs).

BLANCHARD, O. J. and L. J. SUMMERS (1984) 'Perspectives on High World Real Interest Rates', *Booking Papers on Economic Activity*, pp. 273–324.

BLANCHARD, O. J. and L. J. SUMMERS (1986) 'Hysteresis and the European Unemployment', in S. Fischer (ed.), *NBER Macroeconomics Annual 1986*, pp. 15–78.

BLINDER, A. and R. SOLOW (1973) 'Does Fiscal Policy Matter?', *Journal of Public Economics*, vol. 2, pp. 319–37.

BOUGHTON, J. M. (1987) 'Eclectic Approaches to Policy Co-ordination', Paper presented to the CEPR Conference on Exchange Rate Regimes, Money GDP Targets and Macroeconomic Policy, Clare College, Cambridge.

CEPS Macroeconomic Policy Group (1987) 'The Two-handed Growth Strategy for Europe: External Autonomy through Flexible Co-operation', Centre of European Policy Studies.

CHRIST, C. F. (1979) 'On Fiscal and Monetary Policies and the Government Budget Restraint', *American Economic Review*, vol. 69, pp. 526–38.

CURRIE, D. (1978) 'Macroeconomic Policy and Government Financing', in M. J. Artis and A. R. Nobay (eds), *Contemporary Economic Analysis* (London: Croom Helm).

CURRIE, D. (1981) 'Fiscal and Monetary Policy and the Crowding Out Issue', in M. J. Artis and M. H. Miller (eds), *Essays in Fiscal and Monetary Policy* (Oxford: OUP).

CURRIE, D. (1987) 'Options for UK Macroeconomic Policy', *Oxford Review of Economic Policy*, vol. 3, September.

CURRIE, D. and P. LEVINE (1985) 'Simple Macropolicy Rules for the Open Economy', *Economic Journal*, vol. 95, supplement, pp. 60–70.

CURRIE, D. and U. HOFFMEYER (1987) 'Reputation and International Macropolicy Coordination in a Natural Rate World: an Analytical Treatment', Paper presented to the CEPR conference on Exchange Rate Regimes, Money GDP Targets and Macroeconomic Policy. Clare College, Cambridge, July.

CURRIE, D. A., P. LEVINE and N. VIDALIS (1987) 'International Co-operation and Reputation in an Empirical Two-Bloc Model', in R. Bryant and R. Portes (eds), *Global Macroeconomic Policy Conflict and Cooperation*, Macmillan (Proceedings of the International Economics Association London Conference, February 1987).

CURRIE, D. and S. WREN-LEWIS (1987) 'Evaluating the Extended Target Zone Proposal', CEPR Discussion Paper No. 221.

FELDSTEIN, M. (1981) 'Private Pensions and Inflation', *American Economic Review*, Papers and Proceedings, pp. 424–8.

FRIEDMAN, M. (1948) 'A Monetary and Fiscal Framework for Economic Stability', *American Economic Review*, vol. 38, pp. 245–64.

FRENKEL, J. A. and M. GOLDSTEIN (1986) 'A Guide to Target Zones', *IMF Staff Papers*, vol. 33, pp. 633–73.

GIAVAZZI, F. and J. SHEEN (1985) 'Fiscal Policy and the Real Exchange Rate', in David Currie (ed.), *Advances in Monetary Economics* (London: Croom Helm).

GOODHART, C. A. E. (1984) 'Disequilibrium Money: A Note', Chapter 10 of *Monetary Theory and Practice* (London: Macmillan).

HMSO (1959) *Report of the Committee on the Working of the Monetary System.*

KINDLEBERGER, C. (1973) *The World in Depression, 1929–1939* (London: Allen–Lane).

LAIDLER, D. (1971) 'The Influence of Money on Economic Activity: a Survey of Some Current Problems', in G. Clayton, J. C. Gilbert and R. Sedgwick (eds), *Monetary Theory and Policy in the 1970s* (Oxford University Press).

LAYARD, R. and L. CALMFORS (1987) *The Fight against Unemployment* (MIT).

LEVINE, P. and D. CURRIE (1987) 'Does International Macroeconomic Policy Coordination Pay and is it Sustainable? A Two Country Analysis', *Oxford Economic Papers*, vol. 39, pp. 38–74.

MEADE, J. E. (1982) *Stagflation Vol. 1: Wage Fixing* (London: Allen & Unwin).

PRICE, R. W. R. and P. MULLER (1984) 'Structural Budget Indicators and the Interpretation of Fiscal Policy Stance in OECD Economies', *OECD Economic Studies*, no. 3, pp. 27–72.

ROGOFF, K. (1985) 'Can International Monetary Policy Cooperation be Counterproductive?', *Joural of International Economics*, vol. 18, pp. 199–217.

SACHS, J. and C. WYPLOSZ (1984) 'Real Exchange Rate Effects of Fiscal Policy', NEBR Working Paper No. 1255.

SARGENT, T. J. and N. WALLACE (1981) 'Some Unpleasant Monetarist Arithmetic', *Federal Reserve Bank of Minneapolis Quarterly Review*, vol. 5 (Fall) pp. 1–

17; reprinted in Thomas J. Sargent, *Rational Expectations and Inflation* (New York: Harper and Row, 1986).

TOBIN, J. (1980) *Asset Accumulation and Economic Activity* (Oxford: Basil Blackwell).

VINES, D., J. MACIEZOWSKI and J. MEADE (1983) *Stagflation Vol. 2: Demand Management* (London: Allen & Unwin).

WEITZMAN, M. L. (1984) *The Share Economy* (Cambridge, Mass: Harvard University Press).

WILLIAMSON, J. and M. MILLER (1987) *Targets and Indicators: a Blueprint for International Co-ordination of Economic Policy* (Institute for International Economics).

Part VIII

Keynesian Policy in a Historical Context

15 Keynes on Interwar Economic Policy

Nicholas H. Dimsdale

15.1 INTRODUCTION

Keynes's extensive writings on economic policy in the interwar period took the form of newspaper articles, official memoranda, and evidence to government committees in addition to his more academic publications. A good idea of the development of his views on policy questions can be obtained from the volumes of the *Collected Writings* which cover the interwar period. These include his main academic works, *A Tract on Monetary Reform* (1923), *A Treatise on Money* (1930) and the *General Theory* (1936) and his other writings, in particular volumes XIX to XXI of the *Collected Writings*, in addition to *Essays in Persuasion* (1931). The purpose of this chapter is to review his recommendations on policy towards unemployment during the interwar years. This wide field embraces monetary, fiscal and exchange rate policy and so the coverage of each topic must necessarily be brief. More detailed discussion of monetary policy may be found in Moggridge and Howson (1974) and of budgetary policy in Dimsdale (1987).

It is convenient to divide Keynes's discussion of economic policy into three periods which broadly coincide with the application of the ideas of his three major academic works. From the boom and slump of the early 1920s until the return to the gold standard in 1925 Keynes was using the methods of *A Tract on Monetary Reform* (1923), culminating in *The Economic Consequences of Mr. Churchill*. The second period runs from 1925 to 1931 in which Keynes was developing the theory which underlay *A Treatise on Money* (1930) and applied these ideas to the problems of the gold standard and of the world depression. The third period runs from the suspension of the gold standard in 1931 to the outbreak of the Second World War, when Keynes's recommendations on economic policy followed the ideas of *The Means to Prosperity* (1933) and the *General Theory* (1936).

15.2 DEFLATION AND THE RETURN TO THE GOLD STANDARD

In the vigorous boom which followed the First World War Keynes was concerned that restrictive monetary policy was not applied at an earlier stage to moderate the upturn. In a memorandum written in February 1920 he recommended that Bank Rate be raised, if necessary, to 10 per cent to check the boom and, according to the Chancellor of the Exchequer, Austen Chamberlain,[1] he was prepared to hold it at that level for three years. He attributed the severity of the downturn of 1920–21 to 'the loosening influences of war finance on the established regulations of currency'.[2] His recommendations for tightening monetary policy were based on the priority which he gave to the control of inflation rather than the need to appreciate the sterling–dollar exchange rate which had declined sharply since the removal of the peg in March 1919. His arguments for deflation, therefore, differed from those of the Cunliffe Committee (1918) which recommended the return to the gold standard at the pre-1914 exchange rate.

In the post-war world Keynes argued that stability of the price level should be the principal objective of monetary policy rather than stability of the exchange rate. He was critical of the severe deflation which would be necessary to restore pre-1914 exchange rates following the massive inflation of the First World War. In the *Tract* he discussed the problems of adjustment of the Continental economies in addition to the problems of the British economy.[3]

As Britain lapsed into the 'doldrums' of 1922–3, Keynes became increasingly critical of deflation on account of its impact on unemployment. He argued that expectations of a falling price level would make a businessman less willing to incur costs today because of the lower receipts to be expected when output was sold at some time in the future. He would therefore act to protect himself against the risk of falling prices by increasing his holdings of cash and cutting back production, so increasing unemployment. Uncertainty about the price level was a factor increasing unemployment, but it could be aggravated by an announced policy of deflation which created a firm expectation of falling prices.[4,5] Thus when Bank Rate was raised to 4 per cent in July 1923, Keynes criticised the Bank of England for giving greater priority to raising the exchange rate than to encouraging depressed industry.[6] He argued that 'the best way of remedying unemployment would be for those responsible to declare that they would do all they could by means of currency policy to avoid a fall of prices and to promote the confidence of the business world in the existing level of prices.'[7] He suggested that the Treasury Minute limiting the fiduciary issue of currency be amended and that the authorities announce that they will attach more importance to stability of the price level than to the improvement of the sterling–dollar exchange rate.[8]

He examined the reasons for unemployment early in 1923 and suggested that higher real wages in relation to productivity since 1913 might make it difficult to employ the growing working population.[9] He clarified his argument in a letter to *The Times*,[10] claiming that while real wages were approximately the same as before the war, output was about 10 per cent less due largely to the reduction in hours worked per week. As a staunch free trader he rejected the notion that tariffs could contribute toward the reduction of unemployment, when criticising Baldwin's tariff proposals in the same year.[11] Keynes's views on unemployment were set out more fully at a League of Nations conference in 1924.[12] He distinguished between financial factors causing unemployment and other factors. The latter included unemployment benefits which put less pressure on the unemployed to accept offers of jobs, misallocation of labour between expanding and contracting industries, and excessive real wages as a result of the bargaining power of trade unions. These factors could, he claimed, account for 4–5 per cent of unemployment, while the remainder was due to financial factors. Financial forces were more important during the depression of 1921 when unemployment was at 12 per cent than in 1924 when employment had fallen to 8 per cent. Keynes outlined how monetary policy should be conducted using both Bank Rate and open market operations to create expectations of a stable price level. Ruthlessness might be necessary initially in the pursuit of the policy objective, which could become less severe when the public had acquired faith in the declared policy of the authorities.

Concern about unemployment led to Keynes calling for Treasury assistance for the promotion of domestic investment in May 1924. He argued that 'the Treasury should not shrink from promoting expenditure up to (say) £100 000 000 a year on the construction of capital works at home.'[13] The intention should be to prevent repayments of capital by the sinking fund for the national debt from being reinvested overseas by seeking to divert them into home investment. The subsequent controversy over the use of the sinking fund and the alleged bias of the capital market in the favour of foreign investment need not detain us here.[14] What is worth noting is that Keynes was advocating a stimulus to demand because of the difficulty of bringing about adjustments in the labour market due to labour immobility, the activities of trade unions and the disparity of wages between sheltered and unsheltered industries. He argued that labour needed to be drawn into expanding industries by a positive stimulus rather than being forced out of depressed industries by a slow and painful process of adjustment.

Keynes's principal concern in 1924 was exchange rate policy. When giving evidence to the Chamberlain Bradbury Committee in July he explained that his policy was price stability[15] and that this would in due course be likely to lead to an appreciation of the exchange rate to the pre-1914 parity on account of the expected rise in US prices. He told the committee, 'I am against hurrying the day, but I regard it as probable that if we concentrate on a price stability policy we shall probably find ourselves at no very distant date at par.'[16] Inflation in the United States should not be allowed to raise British prices which could be prevented by permitting gold imports only under Treasury licence. In this way the British money supply would be insulated from the outflow of gold from America. Keynes criticised proposals for an immediate return to gold by abolishing the prohibition on gold exports on the grounds that this would lead to severe deflation with adverse affects on business confidence.

He examined the degree of overvaluation of sterling in two articles written in April 1925,[17] arguing that the exchange rate should adjust to the current level of wages and prices rather rising to the old parity by reducing wages and prices. He emphasised that the appreciation of the exchange rate was aggravating unemployment, stating that it was a problem of excessive gold wages rather than excessive real wages. The alternative remedies for the situation were, first, to let the exchange rate fall until gold wages and prices were adjusted (wisdom), second, relying upon a rise in prices in the rest of the world (luck) and, thirdly, forcing down wages and prices to adjust to the exchange rate (misery).[18] On the return to gold in April 1925 he claimed that British wages were too high by 5–10 per cent in relation to the United States and that the excess was larger in relation to some continental economies, including France and Germany.[19]

In *The Economic Consequences of Mr. Churchill* published in July 1925 he argued that the equilibrium of October 1924 had been disturbed by the subsequent appreciation of the exchange rate, which implied an overvaluation of sterling against the dollar of 10 per cent and against European currencies of as much as 30 per cent.[20] Tightening credit to increase unemployment and so force down money wages would create severe difficulties for the export industries, where wages had already been considerably reduced. To remedy the situation Keynes proposed an across the board reduction in money wages in both sheltered and unsheltered industries. The cost of living would fall as a result of the wage cuts to cushion the decline in real wages and Keynes proposed increased taxation of interest on the national debt and other payments, fixed in nominal terms. If agreement could not be reached to reduce money incomes, he suggested that the Bank of England should reverse its monetary policy by seeking to raise prices in the rest of the world. It should reduce interest rates allowing an outflow of capital, while maintaining its reserves through mobilising the gold backing for the currency which was now lying idle. The movement of reserves to the rest of the world would, according to this argument, raise world prices and so increase British competitiveness.

15.3 THE LIBERAL PROPOSALS FOR PUBLIC WORKS AND THE TREASURY RESPONSE

Following the return to the gold standard Keynes examined the possibility of a more expansionary monetary policy to reduce unemployment. Since monetary expansion would be likely to lead to a capital outflow, he proposed the imposition of restrictions on foreign lending. He suggested in October

1926 that the embargo on foreign lending which had been imposed at the time of the return to gold and subsequently relaxed be reintroduced.

He was a contributor to the report of the Liberal Industrial Enquiry *Britain's Industrial Future* (1928) which put forward arguments for a programme of public works. In *How to Organize a Wave of Prosperity*,[21] an article written for the *Evening Standard* in July 1928, he criticised the Bank of England for deflating prices through overvaluation of the exchange rate and credit restriction but failing to reduce costs. He noted that monetary expansion would be likely to lead to a capital outflow and suggested that the Bank of England should encourage foreign central banks to make similar reductions in interest rates. He also proposed that public expenditure on capital account should be increased and criticised 'the timidities and mental confusions of the so-called "sound" finance'.[22] The official response to this and other articles by Keynes supporting the liberal case for public works was the publication of *Memoranda on Certain Proposals Relating to Unemployment* (1929). In this White Paper the Treasury argued that, 'a very large proportion of any additional Government borrowing can only be procured, without inflation, by diverting money which otherwise would be taken soon by home industry. That being so, the prospects of adding largely by the means proposed to the existing volume of employment practically disappear'.[23] The theoretical basis for the Treasury view was set out by R. G. Hawtrey (1925) and his arguments were challenged by A. C. Pigou (1929).

Keynes restated his position on public works in *Can Lloyd George Do It?*, a pamphlet written with Hubert Henderson in support of the Liberal election campaign of 1929.[24] The authors examined a programme of public works of £100 million per annum over three years to be directed towards modernising roads and railways and increasing investment in housing. The cost of the programme would be £18 million per annum at a rate of interest of 6 per cent. Assuming no return from the projects, it was claimed that nearly one half of the cost to the Treasury would be recovered by reduced expenditure on unemployment benefit and increased tax receipts, but the relationship between primary and secondary employment was not fully explained. It was made clear that credit would be expanded and interest rates would not be permitted to rise, since 'it would lie within the power of the Bank, provided it were to pursue a deflationary policy aimed at preventing any expansion in bank credit, to defeat the best-laid plans and to ensure that the expenditure financed by the Treasury *was* at the expense of other business enterprise.'[25] In this way crowding out of private investment would not arise and the constancy of the rate of interest also served to ensure that monetary expansion would not induce a capital outflow. The pamphlet claimed that additional savings would be generated to finance increased investment from saving on unemployment benefits, a reduction in business losses and reduced overseas investment, which would take the form of increased imports. Such an increase could be accommodated in view of the comfortable surplus on the current account in 1929. The discussion of the sources of increased saving rested on the approach of the *Treatise* which had not yet been published.

15.4   THE MACMILLAN COMMITTEE AND THE WORLD DEPRESSION

Keynes became a member of the Committee on Finance and Industry (the Macmillan Committee) which was appointed in November 1929, to review both internal and external aspects of the monetary system. He summarised experience under the restored gold standard when giving evidence to the committee early in 1930, and argued that Britain had not made any progress towards equilibrium since the return to gold in 1925. Despite the use of Bank Rate to deflate the economy and create unemployment, wages and prices had not adjusted sufficiently to improve competitiveness. Although British wholesale prices had fallen by 20% over four years, the decline in prices had been more rapid in the rest of the world. The problem of adjustment had been aggravated by a boom with falling prices in the United States in contrast to the general expectation that American prices would rise after 1925.[26] Keynes suggested that it was still necessary to reduce money wages by 10 per cent to restore equilibrium and he questioned whether adjustment could be achieved by means of the traditional Bank Rate mechanism.[27] Discussion of the return to gold in 1924 had failed to distinguish between an adjustment of prices and an adjustment of costs.[28] While an adjustment of prices might be achieved relatively easily, an adjustment of costs posed much greater difficulties, due to the inflexibility of money wages. The big fall in prices and wages which was achieved in 1921 had been considered to be a good precedent for the relatively smaller adjustment needed in 1925, but, as Ernest Bevin explained to the committee, there were special circumstances which accounted for the flexibility of wages in the post-war slump, which did not apply to wage detemination after 1924.[29] Keynes considered that the only way in which adjustment could have been achieved would have been a general agreement to a reduction in money incomes which he had advocated shortly after the return to gold.[30] In the event adjustment had been impeded by the rigidity of money wages which had remained virtually unchanged since 1924.[31] This was due to the provision of unemployment benefit and widespread public sympathy for working-class resistance to wage reductions.

Keynes's diagnosis of Britain's problems under the gold standard relied upon the analysis of the *Treatise on Money* which was published in October 1930. According to the general case of the *Treatise*, savings and investment were brought into equilibrium through movements in the rate of interest.[32] The rate of interest also worked to adjust overseas lending to the surplus on the trade balance in the short term, while over the longer term changes in competitiveness would adjust the trade balance to foreign lending, through flexibility of money wages. The problem of the British economy lay in the tendency for overseas lending to exceed the trade balance.[33] Foreign lending was high on account of greater prospective returns from foreign than from home investment in a mature economy. The surplus on the trade balance was limited by the lack of competitiveness of the economy which could not readily be adjusted under the gold standard because of the downward inflexibility of money wages. Saving tended to exceed the sum of home investment and the trade balance. Home investment could be encouraged by a reduction in the rate of interest, but this would result in an increased foreign lending, putting pressure on the reserves of the Bank of England and leading, sooner or later, to a rise in Bank Rate. Keynes suggested in Chapter 37 of the *Treatise* that under such circumstances, the 'reserve weapon' of public investment should be used to increase home investment, while the money supply was expanded, keeping the rate of interest constant.

Keynes's argument was similar to that later put forward by Fleming (1962) and Mundell (1963) about the greater effectiveness of fiscal relative to monetary policy for an open economy under a fixed exchange rate with a high degree of capital mobility. Keynes, however, introduced an asymmetry into his argument. He argued that an expansionary monetary policy would lead to a capital outflow, whereas expansionary fiscal policy could not be relied upon to attract a capital inflow and should be financed by domestic credit expansion to prevent the rate of interest from rising.

Keynes examined remedies which would improve the trade balance and those which would promote home investment.[34] The trade balance could be increased by measures to improve competitiveness, such as devaluation, which was agreed to be ruled out by the terms of reference of the committee, but reappeared in the form of a proposal to subsidise exports from the proceeds of a tax on imports. Competitiveness could be increased by improved productivity or by a reduction in money incomes, which Keynes still believed to be 'in some respects the ideal remedy',[35] but was unlikely to be practicable. The trade balance might also be improved by a reduction in imports resulting from a tariff. The departure from free trade could be justified by unemployment combined with the inflexibility of money wages. The balance between saving and investment might be adjusted by reducing saving but this was not emphasised by Keynes, who preferred measures to increase home investment. These might take the form of discrimination against overseas issues, such as tax on interest paid on foreign securities, or by government assistance to domestic investment. Keynes did not consider that the government should undertake such investment itself but rather should give assistance in the form of preferential interest rates to local authorities, public utilities and the private sector generally. The proposals which he put up to the Macmillan Committee for remedying unemployment appeared in its Minority Report. He also discussed them extensively with the Committee of Economists of the Economic Advisory Council set up by the

Labour Government in July 1930, whose activities have been described by Howson and Winch (1977) and in correspondence with the Governor of the Bank of England, Montagu Norman.[36]

Keynes explained in his Harris Foundation lectures given in Chicago in June 1931 that for economies, including the United States, which did not face the special difficulties of the British economy, he favoured a reduction in long-term interest rates as the principal remedy for unemployment.[37] The emphasis on the long-term rate was a change from the *Tract* which had discussed monetary policy in terms of movements of short-term interest rates. Keynes also recognised in these lectures and in his correspondence with Montagu Norman the administrative problems associated with organising large public investment projects which had been put to him persuasively by Sir Richard Hopkins, Permanent Secretary to the Treasury, in his evidence to the Macmillan Committee.[38]

In the Harris Foundation lectures Keynes discussed the causes of the world slump of 1929–31.[39] Using the framework of the *Treatise*, he argued that the slump was the result of the collapse of investment, which he attributed to the persistence of high rates of interest in the 1920s. There had been a willingness among borrowers to pay such high interest rates, but the assessments of projects had in many cases proved over-optimistic leading eventually to a reduction in borrowing. There was also a temporary exhaustion of high yielding projects. The situation had been aggravated by the tightening of credit in the United States and the sharp decline in American foreign lending, which had a major impact on investment in the rest of the world. The remedy for the slump was seen by Keynes as being the restoration of international lending and the reduction in long-term interest rates which would pave the way for a recovery of fixed investment. He did not recommend a general reduction in wages and prices to stimulate recovery. He doubted whether they would be sufficient downward flexibility of money wages, even though money wages might be more pliable in the United States than in Britain. In addition he objected that deflation would aggravate depression by increasing the real burden of debt.[40]

Keynes's discussion with Sir Joseph Stamp in February 1930[41] suggests that he attached considerable importance to the behaviour of money wages. While largely attributing high unemployment in Britain to the severity of recent economic fluctuations, he went on to point to the effect of the dole in making workers more resistant to wage reductions. He told Stamp, 'I cannot help feeling that we must partly attribute to the dole the extraordinary fact ... that, in spite of the fall in prices, and the fall in the cost of living and the heavy unemployment, wages have practically not fallen at all since 1924.'[42] He suggested that the introduction of rent controls might have reduced the mobility of labour and so have contributed to unemployment. He concluded, however, that it was not practicable to reduce money wages, whether they are too high or not, and so preferred to emphasise expansionary policies rather than wage reductions.

The world slump made Keynes more adamant in pressing for public assistance to investment.[43] His advocacy of expansion against a background of depression led to anxiety being expressed by Hubert Henderson in May and June 1930 about Keynes's lack of concern about the balance of the budget. Henderson suggested that a new source of revenue be sought urgently.[44] Keynes agreed that such a new source in the form of a revenue tariff was necessary,[45] but did not come out publicly in favour of protection until March 1931.[46] He then argued that a tariff would raise employment by improving the trade balance and also improve the budgetary position. However, once the gold standard had been suspended he immediately withdrew his support for a tariff.[47] In addition Henderson had raised the question of the relaxation of conditions governing eligibility for unemployment benefit. Keynes agreed that the Insurance Acts should be amended, but did not see this as a way of curing unemployment. He did, however, include in the draft report of the Committee of Economists the recommendation that 'A drastic amendment of the conditions of eligibility for unemployment benefit is, therefore, urgently called for' to promote mobility of labour between sheltered and unsheltered industries.[48]

15.5 MEASURES TO PROMOTE ECONOMIC RECOVERY

Following the suspension of the gold standard in September 1931, Keynes examined three schemes for the management of the exchange rate.[49] These were, first, a managed flexible exchange rate, secondly, a restored gold parity at a lower level than the old exchange rate, and thirdly, a scheme for regulating sterling in terms of a standard for prices. He preferred the third scheme and proposed that sterling be regulated in accordance with an index of the prices of primary commodities. This would imply that the exchange rate would appreciate when prices measured in gold rose and would depreciate when they declined. The mechanism for operating the scheme would be for the Bank of England to vary its buying and selling price for gold in accordance with the behaviour of the price index. The proposal was a development of a scheme for the management of sterling proposed in *A Tract on Monetary Reform*.[50] Keynes now suggested that the scheme would regulate the exchange rate of a bloc of currencies closely linked with sterling against the currencies of countries still adhering to the gold standard. He also considered the initial level at which the exchange rate should be set, outlining the case for a high and a low initial level for sterling, coming down in favour of a relatively low level of about \$3.80. While Keynes's commodity price standard was not adopted, his proposals did have a considerable influence on official thinking about international role of sterling and the level at which the floating rate should be managed. Keynes approved of the decision to manage a flexible exchange rate rather than to devalue to a new fixed rate. He welcomed the setting up of the Exchange Equalisation[51] Account (EEA), having shortly before expressed the view that 'the popular notion that the Bank of England is powerless and cannot fix the exchange at any figure it chooses within reason is in my judgement quite groundless.'[52] However, his suggestion that the managers of the account should not conceal their intervention in the market from the public was not followed by the authorities.[53]

Keynes welcomed the departure from gold as providing an opportunity for following a more expansionary monetary policy. He attached the highest importance to the conversion of War Loan from a 5 per cent to a 3½ per cent basis in July 1932,[54] claiming that 'a reduction of the long-term rate of interest to a low level is probably the most necessary of all measures if we are to escape from the slump and secure a lasting revival of enterprise.'[55] Debt conversion, he argued, should not be regarded as an exercise in bluffing the public, since a reduction in long-term rates was needed by the underlying state of the economy and he suggested that the authorities should aim to secure a falling long-term rate of interest after the conversion operation had been completed. Long-term rates in Britain had been brought down well below those ruling in the United States, even allowing for the general lack of confidence in America. Since there would be likely to be pressure on the sterling–dollar exchange rate, he urged that 'we must stick to our policy and be prepared to sit quietly through a period of exchange weakness without resorting to deflationary measures.'[56] He emphasised the importance of building societies in bringing down the rate of interest charged on mortgages which could have reduced the cost of house room by 25 per cent. In his Harris Foundation lectures he had also argued that the demand for house room was price elastic, pointing to the large component of interest charges in housing costs.[57]

When reviewing the state of the economy in 1933, Keynes pointed out the dangers of being too easily discouraged after the disappointment of early hopes of recovery, since 'slumps carry within themselves the seeds of a reaction – just as booms do'.[58] He was critical of the restrictions imposed by the Ministry of Health on the capital projects of local authorities,[59] arguing that 'when the county council builds houses, the country will be richer even if the houses yield no rent at all. If it does not build houses we shall have nothing to show for it except more men on the dole.'[60] He supported proposals for setting up a National Housing Board to raise funds for the construction of houses at low rents.[61] It would meet the needs of poorer families, while building societies catered for the needs of owner occupiers. Thus lower interest rates and assistance to the investment programmes of public authorities were closely related.

In the period which followed the suspension of the gold standard Keynes concentrated upon the exchange rate and cheap money and did not return to the general case for public works until the publication of *The Means to Prosperity* in March 1933.[62] In this series of articles for *The Times* he used the Kahn (1931) multiplier to quantify the impact of public investment on income, employment and the budget.[63] His exposition of the multiplier is rather confusing since he appears to alter his assumptions in the course of his calculations. According to his central assumptions the income multiplier is 1.32 and not 2, as he claims, but the ratio of total to primary employment is 2 as he states. This point was noted by Professor Giblin in correspondence but was not fully resolved.[64] In Keynes's arithmetical example increased investment of £100 created two-thirds of man year of employment. It reduced expenditure on unemployment benefit by £33 and increased tax receipts by £20, bringing a relief to the budget of £53.[65] He admitted that prices might rise during the multiplier process and argued that this would be a sign that the unemployment problem was being solved, since a given expenditure would produce a larger impact when there were more unutilised resources. As in the earlier proposals for public works, it was recommended that credit be expanded in line with investment expenditure. Long-term interest rates should also be reduced and other countries should be encouraged to follow the British example in this area. Public works were needed to set the ball rolling at a time when business confidence had become depressed. They provided a way of stimulating activity which would gather pace as business profits started to recover.

For Britain Keynes suggested additional loan financed expenditure of £100 million which would on his assumptions raise employment by about 660 000.[66] He admitted that there could be delays in organising capital projects and suggested that part of the stimulus be given in the form of tax relief to private investment which should be quicker acting. Hubert Henderson criticised Keynes's proposals for internal expansion on the grounds that allowance had not been made for publicly assisted programmes merely replacing expenditure which the private sector would have undertaken anyway.[67] He cited as an example investment in housing and suggested that large-scale public works might reduce business confidence and raise interest rates. He pointed out that if a large programme were to be announced, 'you would not get a single order under that programme for at least a year whereas the effects on the gilt-edged market and the like of the announcement of your intention would be immediate.'[68] Keynes did not dismiss this criticism but stated that he was not advocating projects in a gigantic scale and that an expenditure of £60 million per annum would be satisfactory.[69] He supported Pigou's suggestion that when projects were assessed by the Treasury, they should be credited with the saving on unemployment benefit which they could create and added that they should also be credited with additional tax receipts.[70] If projects were not viable on these terms, he would conclude that the rate of interest was too high.

In the final article of *The Means to Prosperity* Keynes proposed international measures to raise prices and output, which should be taken by creditor countries. He argued that prices should be raised by loan financed capital expenditure rather than restriction of output. His advocacy of publicly assisted investment was general and not confined to the special case of the *Treatise*. Keynes was opposed to competitive exchange depreciation, and wage reductions and also to tariffs and other restrictions on trade. Following a scheme suggested by Henderson, he proposed the issue of bonds to Treasuries by the Bank for International Settlements or other international body, which would be equivalent to gold. The issue of gold certificates would provide Treasuries with the reserves needed to underpin expansionary domestic policies. The certificates would bear interest and be reduced should an index of world prices exceed a prescribed level.[71]

These international measures were put forward to relieve 'the state of financial tension', which had increased as the slump persisted. The initial decline in investment had engendered a general lack of financial confidence, which led both individuals and governments to seek to build up their holdings of liquid assets by reducing expenditure and selling other assets. This general defensive shift in desired portfolios aggravated the decline in output and employment. In such circumstances it was unrealistic to expect a revival in foreign lending and widespread default on debt was also undesirable. Raising expenditure through public works, combined with the creation of gold certificates was the means which Keynes recommended to relieve 'the state of financial tension.' The problem was in origin internal for the United States, but external for the rest of the world. Keynes indicated the advantages which had accrued to a country, like Britain, which had abandoned the gold standard, in putting pressure on creditor countries such as France and the United States. Britain should resist pressure to return to gold and seek to gain support for the proposed gold certificates combined with public works. He suggested that these proposals should be discussed at the World Economic Conference.[72]

When the conference was thrown into disarray by President Roosevelt's sudden announcement of the devaluation of the dollar, Keynes supported the American position. He restated his proposals, recommending that other countries should follow the example of Britain and the United States by devaluing their currencies against gold by 20–30 per cent.[73] In this way Treasuries would receive a windfall gain on their gold holdings, a true real balance effect, which could be used to relieve financial tensions by encouraging expansionary policies and the removal of restrictions on trade.

Keynes was generally sympathetic to the New Deal. Although he did not approve of the raising of wages and prices under the National Industrial Recovery Act (NRA), he was enthusiastic about proposals for public works to assist recovery of the private sector.[74] He recommended that long-term interest rates be reduced as in Britain and emphasised the need to encourage the revival of housebuilding, for it was here that public assistance could have maximum leverage on private expenditure. He emphasised that raising employment in a depessed economy required only a rise in spending.[75]

Turning to the British economy, Keynes pressed for further reductions in interest rates in 1934[76] and also, despite difficulties, in 1935.[77] He emphasised the key role of building and electrification in the recovery and their sensitivity to interest rates. He did, however, recognise that further reductions in the yield on gilt-edged might have to await a decline in interest rates in the rest of the world. By 1936 he considered that interest rates might rise since the increase in bank deposits from year end 1932 to 1935 was well below the rise in real output and he argued for more monetary expansion.[78]

15.6 THE *GENERAL THEORY* AND COUNTER-CYCLICAL POLICY

In the *General Theory* (1936) Keynes expressed doubts about the ability of monetary poicy to stabilise the economy since movements in the long-term rate of interest were unlikely to be able to offset the sharp fluctuations of the marginal efficiency of capital and so prevent fluctuations in investment and employment.[79] He recommended greater state intervention in guiding the course of investment to achieve full employment.[80] He also questioned the ability of a wage policy to stabilise the economy.[81] Reductions in money wages in a closed system would have similar effects to an increase in the nominal money supply with constant money wages. They would be open to the same limitations as an expansionary monetary policy. In addition the impact of expectations of a prolonged decline in money wages, prices and interest rates would be depressing, while a lower price level would increase the burden of indebtedness. Keynes admitted that in an open economy reductions in money wages would increase competitiveness, but he favoured a regime of relatively stable money wages with competitiveness being maintained by variations in the exchange rate rather than in money wages.[82] This had also been his advice on the Australian economy in July 1932,[83] but he placed more emphasis on reductions in the rate of interest in his writings on policy in the 1930s than in the *General Theory*.

Keynes's analysis of booms in the *General Theory* was similar to his discussion of 1931. He argued that a boom, which ends in a slump, is the result of the combination of a rate of interest, which on a correct assessment is too high for full employment, with an over-optimistic state of expectation. When over-optimism ceases, the high rate of interest brings about the slump.[84] He discussed the decline in investment in the United States in 1929–31 in similar terms in his Harris Foundation Lectures.[85]

As the British economy revived strongly in the mid-1930s, the question arose of whether restrictive measures were needed to check the boom of

1936–7. Keynes examined the problem of counter-cyclical policy in *How to Avoid a Slump* which appeared as two articles in *The Times* in January 1937.[86] He argued that the economy had reached a point at which a further general stimulus to demand would not raise output. The situation called for selective measures, such as directing expenditure to increase employment in the depressed areas, where high unemployment still persisted. He was strongly opposed to using a higher rate of interest to control the boom, arguing that, if long-term rates were raised in the upswing, it would be difficult to reduce them in the following downturn. He argued that the long-term rate of interest should be held at its optimum level over the trade cycle and that it should not be used as part of counter-cyclical policy. Expenditure should rather be stabilised by varying the rate of capital formation by public and semi-public authorities. Public projects should be postponed in the boom and held in readiness for implementation in the slump. The government should aim to run a budget deficit in the slump and a surplus in the boom. In addition trade policy might be used to stabilise the economy by encouraging imports through tariff reductions in the boom and allowing the trade balance to deteriorate. In terms of Poole's (1970) analysis Keynes was recommending that real disturbances be offset by fiscal and trade measures, keeping the interest rate constant. Shifts in liquidity preference would be accommodated by adjusting the money supply to stabilise the long-term interest rate. Keynes's proposals for the conduct of counter-cyclical policy were discussed by the Committee on Economic Information and embodied in its 22nd Report.[87] They were criticised by D. H. Robertson who argued that interest rates should be permitted to move pro-cyclically to reinforce fiscal policy, in this way both monetary and fiscal measures would act in the same direction over the cycle.[88]

Keynes excluded defence spending from the government expenditure which was to be used to stabilise the economy and he suggested that it be financed largely through taxation. When the government announced a loan financed defence programme of £80 million per annum in March 1937, Keynes considered whether there was sufficient capacity in the economy to meet the resulting additional demand including multiplier effects.[89] He assumed an income multiplier with an upper limit of 3 which would raise expenditure to £240 million at constant prices, representing a rise in output of $5\frac{1}{2}$ per cent. Although unemployment among insured workers stood at $12\frac{1}{2}$ per cent, he pointed out that only half of these were available for employment, the remainder being unemployable, or frictionally or seasonally unemployed. He emphasised the need to direct expenditure towards the depressed areas, where the main reserves of underutilised labour were located, and the need to postpone some public investment. He stated that there was an immediate danger of inflation, which he expected to recede in 1938, when expenditure on rearmament would be useful in warding off prospective recession. He pointed out that, while employing up to 80 to 90 per cent of the economy's resources was a relatively simple problem, there were greater difficulties in keeping the economy operating at 95 to 100 per cent of its capacity.

During the late 1930s there was an inflow of 'hot money' which bolstered the reserves held by the Exchange Equalisation Account. Keynes was critical of the Treasury policy of financing the Account's purchases of gold by sales of bonds rather than by the issue of Treasury bills.[90] He argued that if foreigners wished to hold bank deposits in Britain, the money supply should be expanded, so that the holdings of domestic residents would not be compressed. If, however, the money supply were held constant, the larger money balances of foreigners would necessitate a reduction in domestic money holdings, forcing down bond prices with repercussions on the real economy. Thus disturbances due to movements of 'hot money' should be accommodated and not allowed to alter interest rates.

When advising on government finance in the approach to the Second World War Keynes recommended that expenditure should precede the sale of bonds to prevent the congestion of the capital market and that long-term interest rates should not be allowed to rise. The public should be provided with the assets they wanted to hold within the existing structure of interest rates. As pressure on resources increased Keynes favoured the use of physical controls and higher taxation rather than resort to a tightening of credit.[91]

15.7 SUMMARY AND CONCLUSION

This chapter provides an overall view of Keynes's recommendations on economic policy during the interwar period. It adopts an historical approach to show how his policy presumptions evolved in response to developments in the economy at home and abroad. In this final section the main threads of the discussion are drawn together by summarising Keynes's views on each of the major forms of economic policy and the priority which he attached to them.

Keynes's views on the role of wage policy were subject to a major change of emphasis as the interwar period progressed. In 1924 he argued that excessive real wages were a contributory factor to unemployment in addition to the tightness of financial policy. But even then he did not call for reductions in money wages, preferring a demand stimulus through public assistance to investment, rather than a slow and painful adjustment on the supply side. He adopted a similar attitude in 1930, when he admitted that rigidity of money wages in the face of falling prices both caused unemployment and was aggravated by the general availability of unemployment benefits. His remedy emphasised expansion of demand as in 1924. He did, however, advocate reductions in money wages after the return to the gold standard in 1925, when his preferred policy of allowing the exchange rate to adjust to the level of wages and prices had been rejected. He called for a general reduction in money incomes which would reduce the costs of production in both traded and non-traded goods sectors of the economy and so bring about an improvement in competitiveness under the restored gold standard. In his evidence to the Macmillan Committee in 1930 he still claimed that the adjustment of money wages to an overvalued exchange rate was 'the ideal remedy', although he recognised that it was impractical and would have to be rejected in favour of other measures to improve competitiveness and reduce unemployment.

During the Great Depression Keynes became more critical of wages policy. By 1931 he was arguing that reductions in money wages in response to a deflationary demand stock would not be desirable, even in the United States, where wage flexibility was greater than in Britain. He continued with this line of argument in the *General Theory*, where he emphasised that reduction in money wages and prices would increase the burden of debt and depress business expectations. While interest rates might be reduced by wage cuts, similar results could be achieved by expansionary monetary policy. In an open economy wage reductions would raise competitiveness, but similar results could be achieved by exchange depreciation. In a world of depressed demand and flexible exchange rates, wage reductions, even if practicable, might be harmful rather than beneficial. While Keynes may not have provided an adequate theory to account for wage stickiness, he was surely correct to maintain that there are better ways of correcting a contractionary demand shock than the reduction of money wages.

In 1924 Keynes suggested that 4–5 per cent of unemployment in Britain would be attributed to supply-side factors and the remainder to contractionary monetary policy. He returned to the breakdown of unemployment briefly in his assessment of the state of the economy in 1937. He suggested that about a half of the current unemployment should be remedied by selective measures designed to direct demand to the depressed areas rather than by general expansion of demand and that the remainder arose from seasonal unemployment or unemployment workers. During 1937 unemployment averaged 9.8 per cent for insured employees, and according to Feinstein's (1972) measure of unemployment in the working population as a whole the figure was 7.8 per cent. This would imply that Keynes's irreducible level of unemployment about 4 per cent of the labour force, which is considerably higher than what Keynesian economists came to expect in the 1950s and 1960s but does not seem excessive from the viewpoint of the 1980s.

Keynes's views on monetary policy were also subject to major revision during the interwar period. At the peak of the boom of 1919–20 he urged the use of high short-term interest rates to curb inflationary expectations. In developing his proposals for a policy of price stability which he expounded in the *Tract*, he envisaged that the price expectations of the public would be based on the anticipated behaviour of the monetary authorities. It was for this reason that the central bank should be seen to establish the credibility of its policy in the eyes of the public by taking severe measures in response to price increases, so helping to create a climate in which price stability would come to be generally expected.

During the progress from the *Tract* to the *Treatise* there was a shift of emphasis from the short-term rate of interest to the long-term rate and its impact on fixed investment. Keynes argued that British monetary policy was seriously constrained following the restoration of the gold standard by the threat of an outflow of reserves should interest rates be reduced below those prevailing in other financial centres. The limitations of the special case of the *Treatise* did not apply to the United States and Keynes emphasised that a reduction in the long-term rate of interest was the appropriate response to the US slump in 1931. He argued that the long-term rate was high by historical standards in the 1920s and that its reduction was a precondition for world recovery in 1931.

There is some confusion about real and nominal interest rates in Keynes's discussion of monetary policy. The distinction is clearly drawn in the *Tract*, but it is less clear in his subsequent writings. Since Keynes emphasised the impact of long-term rates on fixed investment, his discussion implies that he is referring to the real rate or equivalently is assuming that prices are expected to remain fairly constant.[92]

During the course of the 1930s and particularly in the *General Theory*, he showed some scepticism about what monetary policy can achieve, which contrasts with his previous enthusiasm. He did not question the impact of lower long-term interest rates on investment in housing and public utilities and in this he differed from some of his Keynesian followers, but he questioned rather the ability of the central bank to vary the long-term rate in response to fluctuations in business confidence. He focused on the inflexibility of long-term interest rates, which made it difficult to reduce interest rates, except under favourable conditions, such as the conversion of War Loan in 1932. He also argued that it was inadvisable to raise interest rates in the boom because of the danger of excessive rates persisting into the next recession. Monetary policy was, he concluded, of limited usefulness in stabilisation policy. This verdict seems to be too harsh. In his discussion of monetary policy in the 1930s Keynes did not develop his notion of 'the fringe of unsatisfied borrowers'[93] in the *Treatise*. This pointed towards the importance of the availability of credit. Variations in short-term interest rates affect the terms under which credit is granted with imperfect capital markets and have an important role to play in monetary policy. Keynes did not discuss these issues in the *General Theory*. He, therefore, understated the flexibility of monetary measures through an excessive concentration upon the behaviour of long-term interest rates.

Fiscal measures played an increasingly important role in Keynes's policy recommendations. Under the restored gold standard publicly assisted investment provided an alternative way of raising demand in an economy, where the potency of monetary policy was reduced by international capital mobility. Keynes developed a special version of the Fleming–Mundell argument that fiscal measures are more powerful than monetary policy in an open economy with a fixed exchange rate and inflexible prices. His argument is acceptable, although there is an asymmetry whereby a reduction in domestic interest rates induces a capital outflow, but a rise in home interest rates does not lead to a capital inflow. In proposing public works Keynes recommended that credit be expanded in line with capital expenditure so that interest rates would not increase and crowding-out could not occur. He suggested that these arguments applied only to the British special case in contrast to the American economy where the *Treatise* prescription of a reduction in long-term interest rates was applicable. In view of the prevalence of open economies with sticky money wages, it could be argued that Britain was in some respects the general case, and it was the United States which was exceptional in approximating to a textbook closed economy.

Keynes made a general case for public works to counter deflation and unemployment in the *Means to Prosperity*. He was surely correct in arguing that expansionary fiscal policy backed up by relaxed credit was the most appropriate way to offset a severe deflationary shock and the subsequent depression of the early 1930s. His proposals for public works were likely to be cumbersome to implement and to involve considerable delays in execution. They are more convincing as a remedy for a severe depression than as the leading element of counter-cyclical policy. He was right to assume that expansionary fiscal policy should be combined with expansion of the money supply keeping the rate of interest constant rather than the money stock, but his proposals for smoothing cyclical fluctuations by varying the pace of public or publicly controlled investment are by no means convincing. It would seem implausible that such a small component of national expenditure could be varied to stabilise the economy effectively. For example, in 1929 fixed investment in Britain was only about 10 per cent of GDP. This problem is compounded by the administrative difficulties associated with varying public investment programmes in accordance with the phase of the trade cycle. Robertson's suggestion that both monetary and fiscal measures should be used over the cycle seems more acceptable.

Keynes was concerned that expansionary fiscal policies should not give rise to mounting budget deficits. He therefore emphasised the importance of the multiplier effects which would raise incomes and tax receipts, so reducing the size of the initial budget deficit arising from loan financed capital projects. He also restricted expansionary policies to the promotion of productive investment which would generate returns, contributing to the finance of any remaining deficit. These ideas were developed more fully in his proposals for a capital budget to be introduced after the Second World War.[94] The discussion of post-war fiscal policy brought out Keynes's aversion to the use of variations in personal taxation as an instrument of counter-cyclical policy.[95] His concept of fiscal policy was closely related to monetary policy in which administrative measures are taken to speed up a process, where delays arise from lack of business confidence in recession and the stickiness of long-term interest rates. Given his restricted view of fiscal policy he seems to have exaggerated what might have been expected from it. While severe slumps might have been avoided, economic stabilisation could hardly have been achieved.

In his recommendations for the management of the exchange rate Keynes showed a remarkable degree of consistency. In the *Tract* he recommended that the price level, measured by an index of primary commodity prices, be stabilised through intervention by the central bank to vary the sterling price of gold. He repeated this proposal both in the *Treatise*[96] and in his advice to the British government upon the management of sterling after the suspension of the gold standard in 1931. When sterling was floated he recommended a policy of exchange management which involved keeping sterling at a relatively low rate against the dollar. Following the devaluation of the dollar in 1933 he suggested that it be allowed to fluctuate within a wide band of ± 5 per cent and suggested a similar degree of flexibility for sterling.[97] His recommendations were intended to avoid the inflexibility of the gold standard and also the wide exchange rate fluctuations which might occur with a floating rate without intervention. This was, however, a second best policy to his first choice of varying the price of gold to stabilise the domestic price level. The adoption of his preferred policy would have led to a degree of stability in domestic prices and would have solved the puzzle, which was noted previously, about the distinction between real and nominal interest rates. Since the price level would have been trendless, real and nominal rates would have coincided so long as financial markets expected that exchange rate policy would continue to be directed towards price stability.

Keynes's views on interwar economic policy evolved in accordance with the development of his main theoretical ideas. He remained a strong supporter of discretionary policies, although the emphasis which he placed on different policy instruments varied during the period. While recommending policy activism, he was less ambitious than his Keynesian successors in the objectives which he set for counter-cyclical policy. He did not envisage 'full employment' as occurring at a particularly low level of unemployment and he was concerned to avoid the problems arising from chronic budget deficits. The fine tuning policies of Keynesian economists, which flourished in the 1950s and 1960s and became discredited in the 1970s, must be distinguished from his own more cautious approach. Now that interest is reviving in less ambitious forms of discretionary policy, reflecting both recent theory and economic experience, there is a need for reappraising Keynes's own recommendations on the conduct of economic policy.

Acknowledgements

I am grateful to participants at the Keynes Conference for their helpful comments and also to an anonymous referee for his suggestions for improving the paper. Financial support from the ESRC is gratefully acknowledged.

Notes

1. Keynes, *The Collected Writings of John Maynard Keynes* (hereafter referred to as JMK), Vol. xvii, p. 183 and p. 181 footnote. See also Howson (1973) (1974).
2. JMK, xvii, p. 430.
3. JMK, iv, pp. 116–40.
4. JMK, xvii, pp. 429–30.
5. JMK, xix, pp. 113–4.
6. Ibid., pp. 100–3.
7. Ibid., p. 115.
8. Ibid., p. 118.
9. Ibid., p. 78.
10. Ibid., p. 79.
11. Ibid., pp. 153–5.
12. Ibid., pp. 182–93.
13. Ibid., pp. 219–23.
14. Ibid., pp. 223–231 and pp. 275–88.
15. Ibid., pp. 250–1.
16. Ibid., p. 250. For an account of Keynes's evidence see Moggridge (1972).
17. Ibid., pp. 349–54.
18. Ibid., p. 353.
19. Ibid., pp. 357–61 and pp. 362–5.
20. JMK, ix, pp. 207 (H) 30.
21. JMK, xix, pp. 761–6.
22. Ibid., p. 766.
23. Cmd 331, pp. 50–1.
24. JMK, ix, pp. 86–125.
25. Ibid., p. 118.
26. JMK, xx, pp. 56–7.
27. Ibid., p. 57.
28. Ibid., pp. 58–9.
29. Ibid., p. 61.
30. Ibid., p. 59.
31. Ibid., p. 64.
32. Ibid., p. 148. Keynes explained that Bank Rate refers to the terms of lending generally and not just to the official discount rate.
33. Ibid., pp. 94–6.
34. Ibid., pp. 99–117 and pp. 119–148.
35. Ibid., pp. 102.
36. Ibid., pp. 350–6.
37. JMK, xiii, pp. 362–7.
38. JMK, xx, pp. 166–79. See Kahn (1984) pp. 77–90.
39. JMK, xiii, pp. 349–52.
40. Ibid., p. 358–67 and pp. 370–1.

41. JMK, xx, pp. 315–35.
42. Ibid., pp. 318–9.
43. Ibid., pp. 345–9.
44. Ibid., pp. 357–60 and pp. 362–4.
45. Ibid., pp. 364–6.
46. JMK, ix, pp. 231–8.
47. Ibid., ix, pp. 243–4.
48. JMK, xx, pp. 431–2.
49. JMK, xxi, pp. 16–28 and see Howson (1975) for an account of official discussions of exchange rate policy.
50. JMK, iv, pp. 141–60.
51. JMK, xxi, pp. 104–5.
52. Ibid., p. 82.
53. Ibid., p. 105.
54. Ibid., pp. 114–25.
55. Ibid., p. 114.
56. Ibid., pp. 120–1.
57. JMK, xiii, p. 365.
58. JMK, xxi, p. 141.
59. Ibid., pp. 155–7.
60. Ibid., p. 114.
61. Ibid., pp. 157–61.
62. JMK, ix, pp. 335–66.
63. Ibid., pp. 340–7.
64. JMK, xiii, pp. 414–9.
65. In *The Means to Prosperity* Keynes assumes an increase in loan financed investment of £100, of which £66 raises domestic incomes, the remainder going into imports and running down of stocks, etc. He assumes a marginal propensity to consume of 0.75. The leakage at each round of the multiplier is $(0.66)(0.75) \simeq 0.5$ and the expenditure series is $66[1 + \frac{1}{2} + \frac{1}{4} \ldots] = 132$, giving an income multiplier of 1.32. Primary employment is the proportion of the initial expenditure of £66 going to wage earners which is assumed to be $\frac{2}{3}$, that is £44. The average wage is taken to be £2.5 per week or £130 per annum, so that primary expenditure gives rise to $44/130 = 0.34$ man year of employment, which Keynes takes as one-third. The total increase in employment is $\frac{2}{3}$ man year and the rise in income is 132.
    The saving to the Treasury is the saving on the payment of the dole of £50 per annum, that is $\frac{2}{3} \times 50 = £33$, Keynes assumes a marginal tax rate of 0.10, so that the rise in tax receipts is £13.2, giving a total saving to the budget of £46.2. Keynes at this stage uses an income multiplier of 2, which makes income rise to 200 and gives increased tax receipts of 20 and a saving to the budget of £53.0. This is not consistent with his previous assumptions which give an income multiplier of 1.32. See JMK, ix, pp. 342–7 for details of the calculations reworked in this note.
66. JMK, ix, p. 365. A reduction in unemployment of 660 000 in 1933 would have reduced the unemployment rate among insured employers from 19.9 to 14.8 per cent. Calculated from Feinstein (1972) Table 58.
67. JMK, xxi, pp. 164–6.
68. Ibid., p. 166.
69. Ibid., p. 181.
70. Ibid., pp. 200–1.
71. JMK, ix, pp. 355–64.
72. JMK, xxi, pp. 210–6 and pp. 229–233.

73. Ibid., pp. 264–8.
74. Ibid., pp. 289–97, pp. 297–304, and pp. 322–32.
75. Ibid., pp. 334–8.
76. Ibid., pp. 316–7.
77. Ibid., pp. 350–2.
78. Ibid., pp. 375–9.
79. JMK, VII, p. 320.
80. Ibid., p. 164.
81. Ibid., p. 262–7.
82. Ibid., p. 270.
83. JMK, XXI, pp. 94–102.
84. JMK, VII, p. 321–3.
85. JMK, XIII, pp. 350–1.
86. JMK, XXI, pp. 384–95.
87. Howson and Winch (1977), pp. 343–53.
88. Ibid., pp. 140–1 and Robertson (1937).
89. JMK, XXI, pp. 404–9.
90. Ibid., pp. 440–4 and pp. 451–3.
91. Ibid., pp. 509–18, pp. 534–46 and pp. 551–64.
92. A similar view is expressed in Greenwald and Stiglitz (1987) p. 129.
93. JMK, VI, pp. 326–9.
94. JMK, XXVII, pp. 396–413 for further discussion see Dimsdale (1987).
95. Ibid., pp. 319–27.
96. JMK, VI, pp. 350–4.
97. JMK, XXI, p. 262 and p. 272.

References

COMMITTEE ON CURRENCY AND FOREIGN EXCHANGES AFTER THE WAR (Cunliffe Committee) *First Interim Report* (1918) Cd 91822, *Final Report* (1919) Cmd 464 (London: HMSO).

COMMITTEE ON FINANCE AND INDUSTRY (Macmillan Committee) (1931) *Report* Cmd 3897 (London: HMSO).

DIMSDALE, N. H. (1987) 'Keynes on British Budgetary Policy 1910–46', in M. J. Boskin, J. S. Flemming and S. Gorini (eds), *Private Saving and Public Debt* (Oxford: Blackwell).

FLEMING, J. M. (1962) 'Domestic Financial Policies under Fixed and Floating Exchange Rates', *International Monetary Fund Staff Papers*, vol. 9, no. 3, pp. 369–79.

FEINSTEIN, C. H. (1972) *National Income, Expenditure and Output of the United Kingdom 1855–1965* (Cambridge: Cambridge University Press).

GREENWALD, B. and J. E. STIGLITZ (1987) 'Keynesian, New Keynesian and New Classical Economics', *Oxford Economic Papers*, vol. 39, pp. 119–132.

HAWTREY, R. G. (1925) 'Public Expenditure and the Demand for Labour', *Economica*, vol. 5, pp. 38–48.

HOWSON, S. (1973) '"A Dear Money Man?", Keynes on Monetary Policy, 1920', *Economic Journal*, vol. 83, pp. 456–64.

HOWSON, S. (1974) 'The Origins of Dear Money, 1919–20', *Economic History Review*, vol. XXVII, pp. 88–107.

HOWSON, S. (1975) *Domestic Monetary Management in Britain 1919–1938* (Cambridge: Cambridge University Press).

HOWSON, S. and D. WINCH (1977) *The Economic Advisory Council 1930–1939* (Cambridge: Cambridge University Press).

KAHN, R. F. (1931) 'The relation of home investment to unemployment', *Economic Journal*, June, vol. 41, pp. 173–98.

KAHN, R. F. (1984) *The Making of Keynes' General Theory* (Cambridge: Raffaele Mattioli Foundation).

KEYNES, J. M. In Sir Austin Robinson and Donald Moggridge (eds), *The Collected Writings of John Maynard Keynes* (Macmillan, London) [JMK].

—— Vol. IV, *A Tract on Monetary Reform* (1923) [1971] London.

—— Vol. V, *A Treatise on Money. The Pure Theory of Money* (1930) [1971] London.

—— Vol. VI, *A Treatise on Money. The Applied Theory of Money* (1930) [1971] London.

—— Vol. VII, *The General Theory of Employment Interest and Money* (1936) [1973] London.

—— Vol. IX, *Essays in Persuasion* (with additional essays) (1931) [1972] London.

—— Vol. XIII, *The General Theory and After: Part I, Preparation* [1973] London.

—— Vol. XVII, *Activities 1920–22: Treaty Revision and Reconstruction* [1977] London.

—— Vol. XIX, *Activities 1922–29: The Return to Gold and Industrial Policy*.

—— Vol. XX, *Activities 1929–31: Rethinking Employment and Unemployment Policies* [1981] London.

—— Vol. XXI, *Activities 1931–9: World Crisis and Policies in Britain and America* [1982] London.

LIBERAL INDUSTRIAL ENQUIRY (1928) *Britain's Industrial Future* (London: Benn).

MINISTRY OF LABOUR (1929) *Memorandum on Certain Proposals Relating to Unemployment*, Cmnd 331 (London: HMSO).

MOGGRIDGE, D. E. (1972) *British Monetary Policy 1924–1931: The Norman Conquest of $4.86* (Cambridge: Cambridge University Press).

MOGGRIDGE, D. E. and S. HOWSON (1974) 'Keynes on Monetary Policy, 1910–1946', *Oxford Economic Papers*, vol. 26, pp. 226–47.

MUNDELL, R. A. (1963) 'Capital Mobility and Stabilisation Policy under Fixed and Flexible Exchange Rates', *Canadian Journal of Economic and Political Science*, vol. 29, pp. 475–85.

PIGOU, A. C. (1929) *Industrial Fluctuations*, 2nd edn (London: Macmillan).

POOLE, W. (1970) 'Optimal Choice of Monetary Instruments in a Simple Stochastic Macro Model', *Quarterly Journal of Economics*, vol. 84, pp. 197–216.

ROBERTSON, D. H. (1937) 'The Trade Cycle: an Academic View', *Lloyds Bank Review*, September.

16 Keynes and the TUC in the 1930s and the 1980s

Bill Callaghan

What, then, divides Mr Keynes from the Labour Movement now? Nothing that I can see. When we come in the end to the sort of society which he envisages, there is no difference that I can detect between it and what is conceived by the Labour Movement. (A. L. Rowse, 1936[1])

16.1 THE RELEVANCE OF KEYNES IN THE 1930s

There is little doubt that the ideas of Keynes had a profound impact on thinking in the labour movement in the interwar years and especially on the thinking of the TUC. A. L. Rowse's pamphlet *Mr Keynes and the Labour Movement* is an enthusiastic summary of the *General Theory*, which he regards as being of the highest importance. His economic judgements may be somewhat uncritical, but his historical judgement seems sound enough. He states that 'it may well prove, when its influence has been fully brought to bear upon economic discussion and policy, to mark a turning-point in both. So much, at least, a historian may say'.[2]

Not many economists get quoted in the annual reports of the TUC, but the report presented by the General Council to the 1931 Congress contains several references to the work of J. M. Keynes. These are set out in a précis of the TUC evidence to the Macmillan Committee on Finance and Industry. Paragraph 281 of the Report states:[3]

Since the fall in wholesale prices, beginning in 1920, was due to the policy of deflation deliberately pursued, it is small wonder that industrialists generally have complained bitterly that monetary policy is decided without adequate consideration of the effects on industry. The inevitable result to industry of the further deflation carried out on the return to the Gold Standard in 1925 has similarly been commented on in trenchant terms by Mr. Keynes in his pamphlet, 'The Economic Consequences of Mr. Churchill'. We are certainly of the opinion that this policy was largely responsible for the coal dispute and the National Strike in 1926. It is a matter for profound regret that the Government entered upon this policy without consultation with organised labour. In view of the close connection between the monetary factor and industrial conditions, we hold the view very strongly that decisions of this kind, which inevitably affect industry, should not be taken without consultation with the Trade Union Movement.

We do not wish, however, to go into the theoretical aspects of this question. We note that the period of a rapidly falling level of wholesale prices has also been the period of acute industrial disputes, lower wages, and unemployment. The general price level is an expression of the relation between the volume of goods and the volume of money, and we therefore ask that two questions may be earnestly considered:

(i) Would stabilisation of the general price level help to avert these evils:

(ii) If so, is such stabilisation of the general price level practicable, without substantial ill-effects in other directions, by deliberately adapting monetary policy to this end?

Our own view is that stabilisation of the general price level is extremely desirable, if it can be attained without resulting in worse evils than those it seeks to rectify. If these great fluctuations in the level of general prices were obviated the entire industrial system would in our view benefit. Whether the general price level can be stabilised or not is a highly technical problem upon which we offer no opinion at this stage. We raise the matter for the Committee to consider because we feel it is one of the most important questions that remain to be determined.

And paragraph 295 is devoted entirely to the views of J. M. Keynes.[4]

(295) Mr. J. M. Keynes's View

"Lastly, we have expressed the view that in the case of certain industries directly affected with a public interest the necessary development and co-ordination can only be achieved if these industries are conducted as public utilities, managed by public or semi-public corporations in the interests of the community as a whole. We would recall the striking words of Mr. J. M. Keynes, "I suggest, therefore, that progress lies in the growth and the recognition of semi-autonomous bodies within the State—bodies whose criterion of action within their own field is solely the public good, as they understand it, and from whose deliberations motives of private advantage are excluded." Again, "It is true that many big undertakings, particularly public utility enterprises and other businesses requiring a large fixed capital, still need to be semi-socialised," and also, "I believe that some co-ordinated act of intelligent judgment is required as to the scale on which it is desirable that the community as a whole should save, the scale on which these savings should go abroad in the form of foreign investments, and whether the present organisation of the investment market distributes savings along the most nationally productive channels. I do not think that these matters should be left entirely to the chances of private judgment and private profits as they are at present."

It will be clear that on some of the points we have raised our attitude is very similar to that of Mr. Keynes, as expressed in the foregoing sentences."

Some of the reaction to Keynes's thinking was less favourable. For example in pamphlets published in 1940 by Emile Burns[5] and the Labour Research Department[6] there are trenchant critiques of *How to Pay for the War* and perhaps it is worth recalling one extract from that work.

And there is the demand of the Trade Unions for some security against the risk that the rise in prices will outstrip the level of wages, even if a scheme for deferred pay or the like is agreed to.

To meet this an important section of opinion, which has received the weighty support of Sir Arthur Salter, Mr R. H. Brand and Prof and Mrs Hicks, recommends that a minimum ration of consumption goods be made available at a low fixed price, even though this might involve subsidies. If I were advising the Treasury, I should look with anxiety on such a proposal taken by itself, since it might in certain circumstances place an almost insupportable burden on the Exchequer. But if it were made part of a comprehensive scheme, including the deferment of a proportion of earnings, agreed with the Trade Unions, I would welcome it.

The minimum ration should not comprise all the articles covered by the cost of living Index, but should be restricted to a limited list of necessaries available in time of war. Nor should any absolute undertaking be given as to future prices. It should be agreed, however, that in the event of any rise in the cost of the minimum ration, the Trade Unions would be free to press for a corresponding increase in wages.

But it should be an absolute condition of such an arrangement that a scheme for deferred pay should be accepted at the same time, and that the Trade Unions should agree, subject to the above safeguard, not to press for any further increases in money wages on the ground of the cost of living.

Without these conditions the weight of purchasing power available in the hands of consumers would render any attempt at price fixation excessively dangerous. The low prices for the minimum ration would merely release more purchasing power for use in other directions, which would drive up other prices to an excessive disparity with that of the fixed ration. To attempt to fix consumption prices whilst allowing an indefinite increase of purchasing power in the hands of consumers would be an obvious error.

For the Trade Unions such a scheme as this offers great and evident advantages compared with progressive inflation or with a wages tax. In spite of the demands of war, the workers would have secured the enjoyment, sooner or later, of a consumption fully commensurate with their increased effort; whilst family allowances and the cheap ration would actually improve, even during the war, the economic position of the poorer families. We should have succeeded in making the war on opportunity for a positive social improvement. How great a benefit in comparison with a futile attempt to evade a reasonable share of the burden of a just war, ending in a progressive inflation![7]

In his autobiography *Men and Work* Walter Citrine describes how Keynes's pamphlet *The Economic Consequences of Mr. Churchill* made a deep impression on him and how it was simply uncanny to see how Keynes's prophecies work out.[8] Later in his autobiography Citrine writes both about Keynes and Ernest Bevin.[9]

The occasions on which Bevin and I discussed policy outside the Council chamber might be counted on one hand, certainly on two. Yet the occasions on which we differed on essentials could, I believe, have been counted within a still smaller compass. Sometimes Bevin would turn up late for a Council meeting. Meantime I had been expounding a certain line of action to the General Council in his absence. Bevin would come in and, without the slightest knowledge of what I had said, would traverse and support the views I had expressed with an uncanny similarity of reasoning. I sometimes wondered whether the rest of the Council members would think he and I had framed the whole policy together in private discussion. I can say with truth, after mature reflection, that I cannot now recall a single issue of first-class importance on which we seriously differed. On tactics, yes, but not on basic policy. So, without external collaboration, we worked together to increase the influence of the T.U.C., to establish its right to consultation in the national sphere, and to make it a centre with power to evolve policy and take decisions on general principles affecting the trade union movement as a whole.

Not long afterwards our policy began to bear fruit. A committee, under the chairmanship of Lord Macmillan, a distinguished lawyer, was appointed to inquire into the working of the finance and credit system. They were not to confine themselves only to the national aspects of the problem, but to several international operations also. Bevin was nominated by the T.U.C., and worthily did he acquit himself. Another member was J. M. Keynes, whom I regarded as Britain's foremost economist. It is true that he was apt to change his mind, but Keynes had courage, knowledge, and insight. Both he and Bevin kept me in touch separately with what was going on. Keynes told me that when the Governor of the Bank of England came to be examined he put up a pitiful exhibition. He didn't seem to know anything about economics or even the principles of banking. When asked how he came to particular decisions he answered, according to Keynes, 'Just nous.' Perhaps he was foxing; and, of course, 'nous' does play quite an important part in the decisions most of us have to make.

One consequence of this inquiry was that since that date few prominent public men ever advocated the cutting of wages as a remedy for a trade depression. Our policy was proved worth while. Our right to be heard on intricate financial questions was fully admitted. I served for years on the National Economic Council, set up by the Government, and later as a member of the Consultative Committee of the Treasury. The war of 1939–45 saw a rapid extension of this policy. The T.U.C. had established its right to consultation. Joint consultation in the individual industries came more slowly. But after the war, with the advent of the nationalized industries, it became an established system.

Citrine wrote that although Bevin had read practically nothing about trade union theory or economics, his native intelligence and flair taught him many things which were not to be found in textbooks or in the dogma of economic theorists. Bevin's interest in economic issues was of course not diminished by his lack of formal training. Alan Bullock in *The Life and Times of Ernest Bevin* describes not just Bevin's work on the Macmillan Committee, but also his work to establish economic policy making in the TUC.

In 1928 addressing Congress and defending the Mond–Turner talks Bevin told the delegates:[10]

I look forward to the time when the General Council will be coming and laying before this great parliament of its own creation annual reports on the discussion of great economic problems, trying to direct your attention on lines of analysis, lines of investigation, and not mere debating points blown by the wind. Thus and thus only will the movement be really intelligently dealing with the real economic problems of our times.

Later in 1929 the TUC Economic Committee was formed and one of its first tasks was to prepare evidence for the Macmillan Committee.

Bevin, along with Citrine, was also a member of the Economic Advisory Council set up by Ramsay MacDonald in 1930. Keynes and Bevin suggested that a small committee be set up to examine the underlying economic situation and report on plans for action. As Bullock records the result was not encouraging and as Keynes wrote to Bevin on 1 May 1930.[11]

Cadman, Balfour, Cole and myself were present. After about half an hour's discussion it appeared that Balfour and Cadman were opposed to recommending any inquiry into the question whether a programme of capital development could help unemployment so . . . we broke up into two groups to prepare two reports.

The paper from Nicholas Dimsdale is an excellent summary of Keynes's writings on interwar policy, the above paragraphs are more partial, but they demonstrate the relevance of Keynes to the economic policies of the TUC and in particular the links between Keynes, Bevin and Citrine. Fifty years on the Economic Committee of the TUC remains and I follow a distinguished line of predecessors as Secretary to that Committee. The Macmillan Committee has been followed by Radcliffe and Wilson and NEDC can trace its intellectual and political roots back to the Economic Advisory Council.

16.2 THE RELEVANCE OF KEYNES TODAY

It seems fruitless to engage in a party game of assessing what, on the basis of the *General Theory*, Keynes would say about economic conditions today if he were alive. Economic conditions have changed and economic theory has developed. It is quite clear that on some key issues Keynes changed his mind, for example whether a cyclical increase in employment requires a reduction in real wages. Minford implies, and Budd *et al.* and Corden explicitly argue, that Keynes believed that higher employment could only be achieved by cutting real wages. For those who want to give such a misleading interpretation an opportunity exists since it was only in 1939, when his 1936 acceptance of the standard neoclassical picture (of a diminishing marginal product of labour combined with a wage equal to the input requiring a negative correlation between employment and the real wage) had been challenged, that Keynes gave serious thought to the question, and came out explicitly rejecting the neoclassical requirement that real wages must fall. Indeed, he wrote that: 'I complain a little that I in particular should be criticised . . . as if I was the first to have entertained the fifty-year-old generalisation that, trend eliminated, increasing output is usually associated with a falling real wage'. (March 1939, *EJ*, pp. 50–1). Keynes would therefore have far greater grounds for complaint that the same interpretation is being made of his *General Theory* almost fifty years after he had explicitly rejected any such intention.

At the risk of great oversimplification it is worth considering the fundamental nature of the Keynesian insight, which Keynes, neo-Keynesians and post-Keynesians might apply today. Joan Robinson[12] has pointed out when Keynes was writing the *General Theory* he thought that the distinction between himself (and Malthus) on the one hand and most other economists from Ricardo to Pigou on the other was that he recognised the concept of effective demand and they did not. However, after the *General Theory* was published Keynes drew the line differently. He recognised, and they ignored, the obvious fact that expectations of the future are necessarily uncertain. It is this recognition of uncertainty which undermines the traditional concept of equilibrium.

Related to the theoretical undermining of Walrasian equilibrium analysis is Keynes's distinctly practical nature. In his panegyric quoted earlier Rowse describes the *General Theory* as a break with that excessive deductivism in economics which has so much prevailed of late and a return to the earlier and sounder tradition of English empiricism. Picking up Keynes's strictures on pretentious and unhelpful symbols Rowse states that 'When it is a question of academic economics ... it does not much matter; it is only when these professors presume to prescribe in the realm of political action that their mental habit is so objectionable'.[13] It is to prescription I now turn.

If the above points are accepted then some of the latter day criticisms of Keynes and the Keynesians appear distinctly trivial or are knocking down only men of straw. In the latter category might come the Chancellor's view that only micro policies can tackle output and employment and that the only effective macro policy is a monetary one. In support of this argument the Chancellor has argued previously that effective demand (Nominal Total Final Expenditure) rose rapidly in the 1970s, but real output did not and unemployment rose. It is certainly true that there were big leakages of demand into inflation and imports but it is a gross parody of Keynes and the Keynesians to state that they were not worried about those leakages then and do not remain worried about them today, when increases in consumption appear to be accompanied by increasing imports and an inflation rate which still remains high by international standards. Concern about the need to control inflation is not confined to the monetarists. Moreover it is a travesty of the Keynesian position to state that the only supply-side policies they have been interested in are incomes policies, and that Keynesians are not interested in improving the supply-side performance of the economy.

In the trivial category are the criticisms of the 'natural rate' modellers. Even if in the long run the output and employment are determined out on the supply side to produce equilibrium, it is patently obvious and agreed by demand and most supply siders alike that the British economy is not at present at an equilibrium state. Whether it ever has been at an equilibrium state is a question I am not competent to answer. So unless the natural rate modellers allow no impact of fiscal policy on the level of output in the short run, the tautological and hence trivial objection to Keynesianism, then for all practical policy purposes there is no difference between the schools of thought. All are interested in how to get more output, employment and increases in living standards with less inflation. The key question is how you do this in a democratic society, given our sort of institutions and social arrangements. Those who want to argue for the weakening of trade unions or public provisions ought to put their cards honestly on the table.

How much the modellers can help in answering actual policy decisions is a moot point. First there is the problem of competing models: as Artis showed in a paper for an ESRC conference on macro-economic models, once the modellers begin to apply judgements, results tend to converge. But even so the modellers cannot easily resolve the 'what-if' questions that policy-makers and those who are interested in policy ask. For example, even if the modellers could resolve their differences on the effects of public spending – they cannot easily tell the policy-maker what the difference is between increasing spending on defence or the NHS, or perhaps more pertinently how to ensure that increases in spending went to create jobs in the public sector rather than pushing up the price of goods and services purchased by the public sector.

Keynes showed himself to be willing to tackle these practical problems including how to deal with inflation as the quotation set out on page 342 above shows. His willingness to allow increased imperfections, which in isolation he might condemn, for the benefit of a greater good, seems to come closer in capturing the nature of policy making and implementation in a free and democratic society, than rigid policy prescriptions from a particular theoretical point of view.

It is the notion of trade-offs between different groups to achieve a number of otherwise competing goals which was at the heart of a report produced in 1979 by the European Trade Union Institute entitled *Keynes Plus – A Participatory Economy*. In that report the ETUI summarised the main elements of a participatory economic strategy as follows:

1. Prices, international or national, are not contained by competition as traditional economic theory postulates.
2. Increased demand is more important for stimulating investment than increased profitability.
3. Productivity and growth are very dependent on sociological factors (work ethics and cultural issues) and are not just related to economic remuneration.
4. Market forces have to be supported, stimulated and directed by democratically-led planning.
5. Income and wealth distribution has fundamental influences on the functioning of the economy.
6. Economic interdependence between nations is increasing and this requires a qualitative change in the policies pursued.
7. The protection of the environment in its broadest sense means that qualitative and not just quantitative growth is required.
8. Wage levels and employment cannot just be looked at as economic factors and cannot be left to be regulated solely by market forces of whatever kind.
9. Workable relationships have to be established between employment and social security, and industrial dynamism and technological change.

10. A workable consensus will not be possible unless the right of trade unions to a say in decisions is recognised and their offer to assume the responsibilities this entails is accepted.[14]

The Chair of the ETUI Working Party was C. E. Odhner, Head of the Research Department, LO Sweden and its members included David Lea of the TUC. The participatory tradition is one that as the quotation from Citrine on page 344 above shows goes back some time in Britain as well as in Sweden.

In his paper Minford recognises that corporatism – his stylised description of the Swedish economy – may bring down the natural rate, though he also argues that it may also increase it. We leave on one side whether one year's comparison, 1987, is sufficient to judge whether corporate economies are more or less successful than non-corporate ones, and turn to Minford's value judgement about 'corporatism' reducing economic and political freedom. I would argue that this is not in fact correct, but for this purpose it is enough to demonstrate that policies of real wage flexibility are equally contentious and equally far from value free. As Keynes pointed out in the *General Theory*:

To suppose that a flexible wage policy is a right and proper adjunct of a system which on the whole is laissez faire, is the opposite of the truth. It is only in a highly authoritarian society, where sudden, substantial, all round changes could be decreed that a flexible wage policy could function with success.[15]

As Nickell has reminded us on a number of occasions when trade unions and employers bargain they agree nominal wages not the real product wage. Whether unions and employers, both individually and collectively, should be bargaining about the real product wage and also the real consumption wage is another matter, but that leads right back into the participatory economy, industrial democracy at the enterprise and tripartite participation at national level.

Flexibility has become one of the vogue words of the 1980s, but, as OECD work has shown, flexibility in one economic sphere, for example real wages, need not be associated with flexibility in another. At its most basic level there has to be some flexibility in the economy to cope with factors such as changes in technology, consumer tastes and the terms of trade. There is more than enough evidence in Keynes's writings to show that he did not believe that the burden of adjustment had to be borne in the labour market.

To return to the Swedish example: inflexibility in some markets is the price that is paid for flexibility elsewhere. In other words the generally co-operative attitude to training, retraining and new technology by Swedish workers is based on explicit employment guarantees and rights to participation.

Obviously there is scope for different value judgements, but as noted above the arguments for greater freedom do not all point one way.

Behind the technical debate is a more fundamental political debate which the ETUI report summarised as follows in dealing with the view that we should as far as possible try to find automatic rules for the economic policy which would tie the hands of the politicians.

> This attitude, of course, has its ultimate roots in a strict conservatism. One of the most fundamental dividing lines between a conservative and a progressive view is the opinion of people's ability, through sensible cooperation and organisation, to create more favourable conditions for societal development. To leave things indiscriminately to market forces is an expression of conservative fatalism: holders of this view cannot always deny that progress has been made in the past, but they always insist that no more progress can be made in the future.[16]

This conservative view is one that is often accompanied by views which are hostile to trade unions and here again the discussion (and the language) is rarely value free as Minford's paper with its references to salami tactics and the French Revolution witnesses. What is remarkable about most of the discussion of the so-called union power models is that it takes place as if employers did not exist and the prime agents were always trade unions. This is surely carrying stylised facts too far. I am not sure what 'debilitation' of the labour market means, but even if it were accepted that the labour market is less efficient than it was, there is no reason why this should be the fault of trade unions (rather than employers) especially given the events of the last eight years.

Indeed, there are good grounds for thinking that improvements in training and retraining and changed attitudes by trade unions reflect not a neoclassical approach but one of bargained corporatism. Apart from the NEDC the other major tripartite body is the Manpower Services Commission and it is worth contrasting the relative success of MSC schemes (at least up to the introduction of the Job Training Schemes) with the DE's Young Workers Scheme, which had explicit neoclassical theoretical backing.

What Keynes would have thought about this, we can only guess. Moreover there have been considerable developments in labour market theory since Keynes's death, in particular the development of labour market segmentation theory by the post-Keynesians, with many other factors determining both money and real wages apart from the demand for and supply of labour.

Most trade union bargainers, who have quite a keen innate sense of the forces of demand and supply, nevertheless find the marginal productivity wage theory difficult to fathom. They know from actual bargaining experience that manning levels do not depend uniquely or mainly on wage levels, but more on the machines and new technology that the management introduce. They and their management counterparts would regard it as not at all surprising that wage increases often promote productivity gains. They know that in many situations the firm is facing increasing rather than diminishing returns to scale.

How do bargainers react to today's circumstances? Because most trade unions operate across a wide range of goods and services they do notice a marked variation in bargaining experience. In one sector of the economy real earnings are increasing fast, and not as a result of trade union push. The CBI report that few wage negotiations are accompanied by strike action or the threat of strike action. In another sector of the economy things are very different. Trade unions find it difficult to organise, indeed for private contractors supplying goods and services previously provided by public authorities there is a shift from union to non-union environment. It is difficult to assess whether productivity is increasing in this predominantly service sector, but pay is not increasing fast, indeed for many contracted out services pay is being cut (and the numbers employed reduced).

Table 16.1 and Figure 16.1 give some information on what has been

Table 16.1   Change in male real earnings 1970–87 (in per cent of the foregoing year)

Year	Average	Lowest decile	Highest decile
1970	—	—	—
1971	0.3	1.2	0.4
1972	4.9	4.5	5.3
1973	4.6	5.4	3.9
1974	− 1.2	0.9	− 2.0
1975	4.8	5.2	5.4
1976	− 0.6	− 0.1	0.0
1977	− 6.9	− 5.8	− 7.6
1978	5.0	3.1	5.2
1979	3.4	2.6	3.4
1970–79	1.6	1.9	1.6
1980	0.8	− 0.9	2.0
1981	0.7	− 0.9	3.4
1982	0.5	− 1.1	0.7
1983	4.3	3.2	4.9
1984	3.0	0.8	3.7
1985	0.6	− 0.3	0.7
1986	4.7	3.0	5.0
1987	3.8	1.8	4.7
1979–87	2.3	0.7	3.1

New Earnings Survey and Retail Price Index.

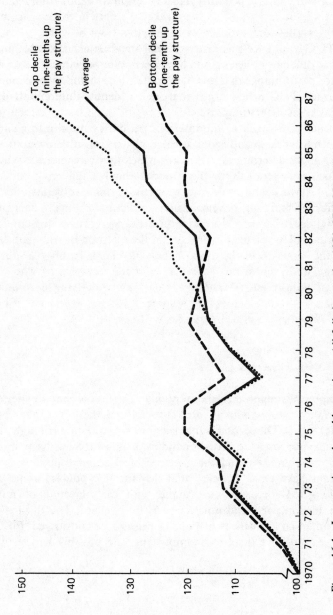

Figure 16.1 Increase in real weekly earnings. All full-time males 1978–87 (1970=100).

Sources: New Earnings Survey and Retail Price Index.

happening to earnings and the change in the distribution of earnings is marked. Whether this was the intended result of policy or a by-product, the policy makers will have to answer, but this change will have implications for many years to come. It is hardly likely to lessen demands for a redistributive policy in the future. Added to the marked changes in earned incomes is the widening gap between those in work and those out of work.

The TUC would see this distributional trend as unacceptable and would argue that different policies could have been followed which would have had a superior performance in terms of output, inflation and employment. In the long run the TUC would argue that such widening differentials will make structural adjustments more difficult.

This leads right back to the interrelationship of the demand and supply sides. Both Keynesian and neoclassical modellers might throw up their hands in horror about determining one factor which they passionately believe to be determined endogenously in their model, but real life may be somewhat different. At any one time the economy faces problems of short-run disequilibrium and long-run problems of structural change. The TUC would argue that securing successful structural change requires the confidence of workers as well as financial markets and the question of who gains and who loses, either in terms of their job or their income, is highly relevant.

For the trade union movement at least the question of who bears the burden of adjustment is central. That is an underlying current of post-Keynesian work, and it does follow some of Keynes's concerns, if not in the *General Theory*, then elsewhere in his writings.

16.3 CONCLUSIONS

This chapter has made three main points. The first is that Keynes certainly had relevance to those with an interest to policy in the 1930s and in particular the trade unions. The second is that leaving aside questions of high theory for all practical purposes the British economy is today and has been in some sort of disequilibrium state and the question of alternative policies does arise. Keynesians have never believed that demand-side policies alone are sufficient. Targeted increases in demand with the objective of minimising leakages into imports and inflation are still relevant. The third is that the distributional consequences of policies need to be considered. Post-Keynesians at least believe these to be important, and possibly Keynes would do too.

Notes

1. A. L. Rowse, *Mr Keynes and the Labour Movement* (Macmillan, 1936) p. 45.
2. Rowse ibid., p. ix.
3. Trades Union Congress, *The General Council's Report to the 63rd Annual Congress*, 1931, p. 275.
4. Ibid., p. 281.
5. Emile Burns, *Mr Keynes Answered* (Lawrence & Wishart, 1940).
6. Labour Research Department, *The Keynes Plan – Its Dangers to Workers* (1940).
7. J. M. Keynes, *How to Pay for the War* (Macmillan, 1940) pp. 33 and 34.
8. Lord Citrine, *Men and Work* (Hutchison, 1960) pp. 136 and 137.
9. Ibid., pp. 239 and 240.
10. TUC Report, 1928, p. 451.
11. Letter from Keynes to Bevin quoted in Alan Bullock, *The Life and Times of Ernest Bevin*, vol. 1. Heinemann, 1960.
12. Joan Robinson in A. Eichner (ed.), *A Guide to Post-Keynesian Economics*. Macmillan, 1979.
13. Rowse, *Mr. Keynes and the Labour Movement*, p. 9.
14. European Trade Union Institute, *Keynes Plus: A Participatory Economy* (Brussels: ETUI, 1979).
15. J. M. Keynes (1936) *The General Theory of Employment, Interest and Money* (Macmillan) Ch. 19, p. 269.
16. ETUI, *Keynes Plus*, p. 20.

17 Keynesian and Other Explanations of Post-war Macroeconomic Trends

Robin C. O. Matthews and Alex Bowen

17.1 INTRODUCTION

Our remit is historical. The question to be considered is how far the Keynesian framework is appropriate for explaining the main macroeconomic events of the post-war period. We could have approached this question by starting from the various components of Keynesian theory and asking how each of these fares when confronted with post-war experience. We have chosen to start from the other end, that is, from the events. As a result, some themes prominent in Keynes will get little or no mention.

We shall ask in particular what were the underlying changes that caused OECD economies to behave so differently before and after 1973. More or less Keynesian and more or less classical answers can be given to that question. There does not exist any established consensus about it within either camp, so it is still a challenge to both. Much less orthodoxy exists than exists on policy questions – not surprisingly, perhaps, because history is messy. The historical question and the policy question are quite distinct. One could interpret historical events in Keynesian, income and expenditure, terms consistently with not attributing a major role to government action in the explanation of those events and consistently, too, with holding that discretionary fiscal and monetary policies are not effective instruments for national governments in a world of small open economies.

The subject of this chapter is the experience of OECD countries as a whole, especially the six largest ones. However, we shall have an eye particularly to issues that are important to the British case.

17.2 THE STYLISED FACTS TO BE EXPLAINED

Events have followed a broadly similar course in the major OECD countries, though with some significant differences, especially in regard to the US. We describe in turn trends in output, in employment and unemployment, and in inflation, comparing three periods, pre-Second World War, 1950–73, and

1973–86, particularly in the UK, France, Germany, Italy, the US, and Japan. Data on those countries for the two parts of the post-war period are shown in Tables 17.1–17.3 and annual movements are shown in Figures 17.1–17.6.[1]

Table 17.1   Output (annual percentage growth rates)

	UK	France	West Germany	Italy	US	Japan
GDP:						
(1) 1950–73	3.0	5.1	5.9	5.5	3.7	9.4
(2) 1973–86	1.5	2.3	1.9	2.3	2.3	3.7
(3) (2)–(1)	− 1.5	− 2.8	− 4.0	− 3.2	− 1.5	− 5.6
(4) 1950–60	2.9	4.6	8.0	5.8	3.4	9.0
(5) 1960–73	3.1	5.6	4.4	5.3	3.9	9.6
(6) 1973–79/80*	1.5	3.1	2.2	2.8	2.4	3.6
(7) 1979/80–86*	1.4	1.6	1.5	1.8	2.2	3.7
Excess of manufacturing over GDP:						
(8) 1950–73	0.2	1.3	1.1	4.2	0.8	5.7
(9) 1973–84	− 2.4	− 1.7	− 1.1	− 0.5	− 0.1	− 1.3
GDP per person hour:						
(10) 1950–73	3.2	5.1	5.9	2.9†	2.5	7.8
(11) 1973–84	2.4	3.5	3.0	1.0†	1.0	3.2

*1979: UK, France, US, Japan; 1980: West Germany, Italy.
†GDP per employee in employment.
Maddison's (1987) data, used in rows (8) to (11), do not incorporate revisions to OECD data which are incorporated in rows (1) to (7).

Sources: GDP and GDP per person-hour 1950–84 (except Italy), A. Maddison, 'Growth and Slowdown in Advanced Capitalist Economies', *Journal of Economic Literature*, vol. xxv, no. 2, June, 1987; GDP 1986, and Italy and manufacturing output, OECD.

17.2.1   Output

(1) In Europe and Japan *the rates of growth of GDP and GDP per person-hour in 1950–73 were higher than in any previous period*, going right back. In the US the same was true of GDP per person-hour, though not of GDP.

(2) In all the countries *the rate of growth of GDP was much lower in 1973–86 than in 1950–73*. So was that of GDP per person-hour. In some countries the growth rate of output fell below its long-term pre-Second World War average. So did the rate of growth of output per person-hour in the US, but not elsewhere. In continental Europe and, to a lesser extent, the US, the 1980s were worse than the 1970s.

Table 17.2 Employment and unemployment (annual percentage growth rates, except row (5))

	UK	France	West Germany	Italy	US	Japan
Labour input (person-hours):						
(1) 1950–73	−0.2	0.0	0.0	2.5*	1.2	1.5
(2) 1973–84	−1.3	−1.3	−1.3	0.9*	1.3	0.6
(3) (2)–(1)	−1.2	−1.2	−1.2	−1.6*	0.1	−1.0
(4) Unemployment's contribution to row (3)†	−0.9	−0.7	−1.0	—	−0.3	−0.2
(5) Increase in unemployment percentage, 1973 to 1984	9.3	7.1	7.0	4.0	2.6	1.4

*Employees in employment.
†Difference between 1973–84 and 1950–73 growth rates in (100–percentage rate of unemployment).

Table 17.3 Inflation (annual percentage growth rates)

	UK	France	West Germany	Italy	US	Japan
Consumer Price Index						
(1) 1951–73	4.4	5.1	2.7	4.0	2.7	5.3
(2) 1973–86	11.3	9.6	4.0	14.4	7.0	6.6
(4) 1951–60	3.5	5.8	1.9	3.0	2.1	4.1
(5) 1960–73	4.7	4.5	3.2	4.5	3.1	6.0
GDP deflator						
(1) 1951–73	4.7	5.7	3.8	4.3	3.0	5.7
(2) 1973–86	11.3	9.6	4.1	15.1	6.4	5.0
(4) 1951–60	4.1	6.8	3.1	2.9	2.5	5.5
(5) 1960–73	4.8	4.8	4.2	5.2	3.3	5.8
Average hourly earnings in manufacturing						
(1) 1951–73	7.7	9.8	8.4	8.6	4.7	12.3
(2) 1973–86	13.5	12.6	5.8	17.5	6.9	9.4
(4) 1951–60	6.7	10.1	7.6	4.8	4.8	9.1
(5) 1960–73	8.1	9.4	9.2	11.1	4.5	14.2

Sources: OECD (various), A. Newell, 'The Revised OECD Data Set', Working Paper No. 781, Centre for Labour Economics (LSE, August, 1985).

(3) *Differences in growth rates between countries were much smaller in 1973–86 than in 1950–73.* This was particularly marked in the 1980s: the four large European countries had practically identical rates of growth of GDP between 1979/80 and 1986.

(4) *Whereas in 1950–73 manufacturing in all countries increased its share of GDP at constant prices, the reverse was the case after 1973.* We shall not have much to say about this feature. We call attention to it here mainly in order to underline the dangers of treating manufacturing as a proxy for the whole economy, as is often done. The changeover was too large to be attributed to increased competition from non-OECD countries and most likely reflects a change in the structure of demand.

17.2.2 Employment and unemployment

(5) *Unemployment in 1950–73 was very low by pre-Second World War standards,* apart from the early 1950s in Germany and Italy.

(6) *There was, after 1973, a steep rise in unemployment* (particularly, outside the US, from 1980) *and in Europe and Japan, a slowdown in labour inputs* (see Figures 17.1 and 17.2). The slowdown in labour input was generally more than is directly accounted for by the rise in unemployment, for various well-known reasons (discouraged worker effects, reduction in overtime, induced migration), to an extent that differed considerably between countries. The slowdown in labour input was smaller than the slowdown in output, implying a slowdown in productivity growth. Throughout the post-war period, labour input in most European countries grew slowly (if at all), both by historical standards and by comparison with North America and Japan.

(7) *The magnitude of the slowdown in labour inputs was rather little related, across countries, to the magnitude of the slowdown in output*; this holds also if a larger number of OECD countries are brought into the reckoning, as well as the six major ones to which we refer. It is therefore a mistake to take for granted, as is sometimes done, that relative success on the unemployment front automatically betokened corresponding success on the output front. The outstanding counter-example is Japan: its low rise in unemployment was accompanied by a far more severe slowdown in output than in any other country. Of course it might be disputed whether slowdown is the best indicator of output performance. One might instead take the actual growth rate of output after 1973 (in which case Japan ceases to be anomalous) or else slowdown compared with growth over a longer past period than 1950–73 (in which case the US *becomes* anomalous). Such alternative procedures would imply different assumptions about the persistence or otherwise after 1973 of the forces making for earlier growth differentials. But anyway employment

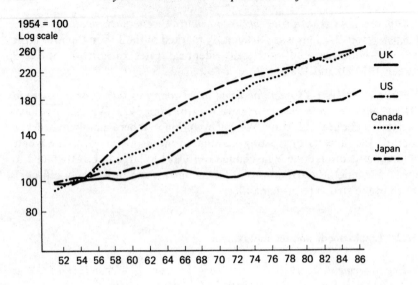

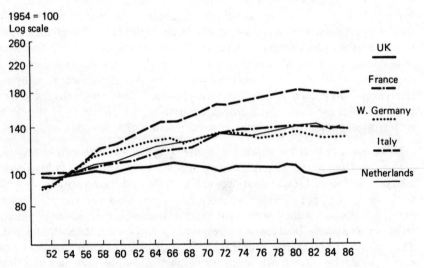

Figure 17.1   Employment in selected OECD countries, 1951 to 1986.

Source: OECD.

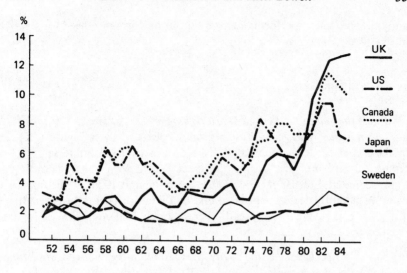

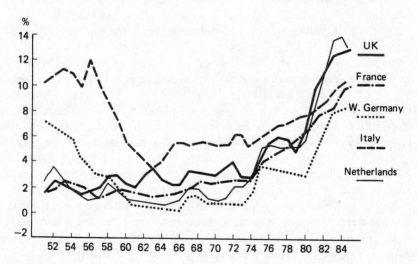

Figure 17.2   Standardised unemployment rates in selected OECD countries, 1951 to 1985.

Source: OECD.

and unemployment performance and output performance need to be looked at separately in comparing countries.

17.2.3 Inflation

(8) *Since the end of the Second World War, the rates of inflation in the OECD have been higher than generally experienced ever before* (see Figure 17.5). The interwar period was punctuated by episodes of hyperinflation in a few countries, and inflation during the First World War reached levels then unprecedented, but the general picture from the mid-1920s to the mid-1930s was one of gently declining prices. Persistent inflation (below levels leading to a flight from currency), spread over virtually all countries, is a novel phenomenon.

(9) *Inflation accelerated in the 1970s, then fell off in the 1980s, with variations between countries in magnitude and timing.* The Korean War, like other wars before it, coincided with rapid price increases, but inflation had subsided to rates near to zero by 1953. There followed a period of gently rising inflation rates (interrrupted by an occasional outlier, such as the 15 per cent p.a. rate in France in 1958), until 1973. Two more serious bouts of inflation then took place, the first peaking in the mid-1970s and the second in the early 1980s. The experience of OECD countries differs in detail. The variability of inflation across countries has been closely related to the average inflation rate. The peak inflation rate came for some countries in 1973–4 (lower part of Figure 17.3), for others around 1980 (upper part of Figure 17.3). West Germany's inflationary bursts have been of much smaller amplitude that those of its competitors. The cross-country variability of inflation has been higher since the demise of the Bretton Woods arrangements in 1971, but the timing of the increase in variability (dating from 1974) does not coincide with the advent of floating exchange rates. The record is similar on a country-by-country basis whether one looks at the rate of change of consumer price indices or at the rate of change of GDP deflators. The same is not the case if one compares increases in earnings because of the differing patterns of real wage growth. Japan, West Germany, and the US had achieved a lower inflation rate by 1986 than the remaining members of the 'Big Six'.

(10) *The level of the prices of primary products relative to manufactures followed (after the early 1960s) much the same path as the general inflation rate* (see Figure 17.4). The prices of primary products increased more rapidly after 1972, but they have been more volatile than those of manufactures during the entire period. Thus up to the late 1960s, variations in the price of manufactures in terms of raw materials were brought about by changes in the prices of the latter. The 'real' price of manufactures peaked around 1962. Its lowest values, in 1974 and 1979, were only a little lower than in the trough of

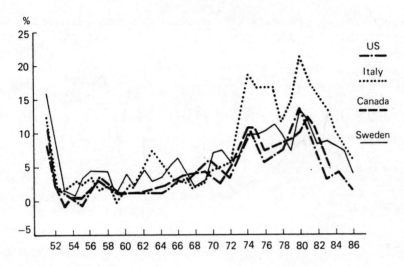

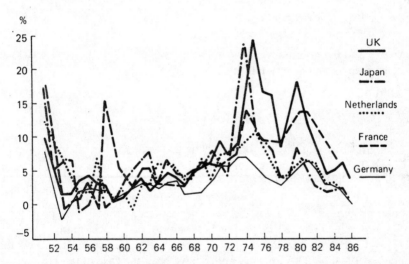

Figure 17.3 Inflation rates in selected OECD countries, (consumer prices), 1951 to 1986.

Source: OECD.

the early 1950s associated with the Korean War commodities boom. Since 1979, the relative world price of manufactures has risen rapidly to levels similar to the very high ones ruling in the early 1960s. This rise coincides with the substantial reduction in inflation rates in the OECD, providing a further instance of the inverse correlation between this real relative price level

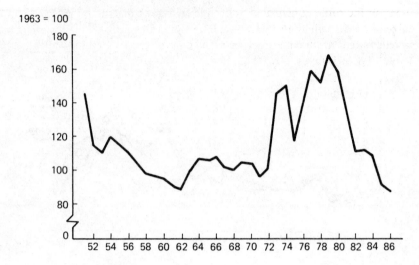

Figure 17.4   World commodity prices relative to the price of manufactured exports.

Sources: IMF, *The Economist*.

variable and the nominal variable inflation. In retrospect, the period 1973–80 can be seen as an exceptional one for relative prices.

17.3   THE TIMING OF THE WATERSHED

In the previous section, we took 1973 as the watershed in the movement of output. This has become the universal practice. It would be wrong, however, to think of the behaviour of output in the post-war period as made up of two plateaux of growth rates, divided by a downward step at 1973. Table 17.4 shows growth rates of GDP between successive national cycle peak years, approximately matched in timing between countries. Germany, Italy, the US, and Japan all had lower growth rates than previously in the cycle that ended in 1973/74. This appears not to have been the case in the UK, but the peak-to-peak measure for the UK is misleading as an indicator of trends in actual output, because output in the year 1973 was sharply above the trend. An alternative measure for the UK is therefore also given, which takes account of all years, not just cyclical peaks. This shows a similar pattern to that of other countries.

   Germany and (less markedly) Italy had consistently declining growth rates, from the 1950s onwards. The other countries, including the UK on the alternative measure, had a long wave in growth rates, first rising, to a peak some time in the 1960s, then falling away, with generally a steeper fall after 1973.

Much the same conclusions follow from regressing the log of GDP on a cubic in time, so yielding a parabola in growth rates. Maximum growth rates, so calculated, are located for the most part even earlier than suggested by Table 17.4, as follows: UK, 1962; France, 1964; Italy, 1959; US, 1965; Japan, 1962.

We shall encounter a similar long wave presently, in connection with capital accumulation.

Table 17.4   Growth of GDP between cycle peaks (annual percentage growth rates)

Dates of UK cycles*	UK	UK (alternative measure)†	France	West Germany	Italy	US	Japan
1951–55	2.8	—	4.7	8.1			
						2.3	8.7
1955–60	2.6	2.5		6.6	5.8		
			5.2				
1960–64	3.4	3.2		5.0			10.2
						4.2	
1964–68	2.8	3.1			5.3		10.2
			5.2	4.1			
1968–73	3.2	2.7			4.3	2.7	7.4
1973–79	1.5	2.2	3.1	2.2	2.8	2.4	3.6
1979–86‡	1.4	1.2	1.6	1.5	1.8	2.2	3.7

*Growth rates are calculated between the following dates: UK as shown; France, 1952–57–65–74–79–86; West Germany, 1952–57–60–65–73–80–86; Italy, 1953–63–68–73–80–86; US, 1953–59–68–73–79–86; Japan, 1952–61–64–70–73–79–86.
†Growth rate between geometric means of annual data for the years comprising respectively the cycles terminating in the years shown (e.g. growth rate between mean of 1952 through 1955 and mean of 1956 through 1960).
‡Latest available date (not necessarily cycle-peak).

17.4   SOME GENERAL CHARACTERISTICS OF ALTERNATIVE APPROACHES

A variety of hypotheses about the post-war period can be devised in the Keynesian spirit, and likewise in the classical spirit. Before becoming more specific, some general characteristics of each may be noted.

Let us first consider the real economy. Keynesian theory, in its textbook $C+I+G+X-M=Y$ version, at one time central in official thinking, is a theory of the *demand* for *output*. It starts from the product market, not the labour market. The demand for labour, being a derived demand, will move more or less closely with the demand for output according to such considerations as the elasticity of short-run supply curves, hiring and firing costs, and expectations of future output; close correspondence is therefore not necessarily to be expected (cf. stylised fact (7)). Keynesian hypotheses are likely to say that 1950–73 was a successful period because demand was strong and 1973 to date has been unsuccessful because demand has been weak (just as some Keynesians used to say, not altogether convincingly, that 1950–73 was *less* successful in the UK than elsewhere because demand was held back by stop-go cycles). Whether valid or not, such hypotheses are incomplete, for in dealing with such long periods as these the supply side can plainly not be disregarded. Most Keynesians would not go as far as to subscribe to the *ultra*-Keynesian theory, that demand wholly determines the long-run rate of growth of output as well as its level, though the effect of demand on capital accumulation and hence on the growth of productive capacity would be more common ground. In this sense a *purely* Keynesian theory of the post-war period is scarcely on: it needs supplementation.

The relation between long-run growth and demand has always been rather troublesome for Keynesian theory (hence Harrod on the natural rate of growth and the warranted rate). One hypothesis holds that in the long run, though only in the long run, demand and supply of labour are kept in line with each other by the real wage, bringing in a classical element, while leaving unspecified the relation between long-run and short-run forces. Another hypothesis, more specific and more fully Keynesian in spirit, is that supply constraints are felt only intermittently, at strong cyclical peaks (the ceiling). Keynesians may cite the convergence of national growth rates since 1973 (stylised fact (3)) as evidence that in 1950–73 output was constrained chiefly by supply limitations, which differed between countries, whereas after 1973 it became predominantly demand-constrained, putting all countries more nearly in the same position. (Similarly, in the days of stop-go it used to be pointed out that it was in boom years, not in recession years, that the UK fell behind other countries.)

With regard to the causes of variations in demand, exports and imports cancel out for the world as a whole, important though they may be for individual countries and sometimes groups of countries (for instance OECD *vis-à-vis* OPEC). Since the macro-trends under discussion have been world-wide, investment and saving, including effects governments may have on them, are likely to lie at the heart of any Keynesian hypothesis.

Investment and saving are conspicuously absent from classical models of events (except in discussion of the US budget deficit). Since those models take output as persistently supply constrained, it becomes a second-order matter how output is allocated between different classes of expenditure – I and S are brought into equality, if need be, by financial markets. Classical models of events since 1973 typically take their start from the labour market, either as an exogenous source of supply contraction or else as the place where the system fails to adapt to shocks (including inflationary shocks caused by wrong monetary policy). The concomitant development of unemployment and of underutilisation of capital that occurred after 1973 are seen not as the joint result of demand deficiency, in the Keynesian manner, but as the result of labour costs making capital unprofitable to use, in the manner of a vintage or other non-malleable capital model. Existing capital equipment is assumed (in the simplest case) to have a zero supply price, hence the apparent asymmetry between labour cost and capital cost as potential supply constraints. At the same time new investment will (a) be discouraged by unprofitability (b) be given a labour-saving bias. Although the classical approach is based on the supply side, classical hypotheses are in practice usually even less explicit than Keynesian hypotheses about the determinants of capital accumulation and productivity growth, typically treating them as exogenous. On this reckoning the slowdown in GDP and the rise in unemployment after 1973 appear as rather separate phenomena, since the latter is too small by itself to account for the former.

Keynesian and classical hypotheses are not in all respects incompatible, so the truth may involve elements of both. Indeed in so far as some consensus about post-1973 is beginning to appear in the literature, as among the contributors to the special 'Unemployment' issue of *Economica* (1986), it does just that, involving both demand deficiency (especially in the 1980s) and a gap between real product wages and the marginal productivity of labour at full employment.

17.5 THE COMPARISON WITH PRE-SECOND WORLD WAR

The rise in growth rates, the fall in unemployment, and the rise in inflation in 1950-73 compared with pre-Second World War constitute a phenomenon that needs explanation at least as much as the far more studied deterioration after 1973. Like most recent authors, we shall have little to say about it, beyond pointing out its importance.[2] Lack of internationally comparable data linking prewar and post-war is an obstacle, and so are the divergent experiences of countries in the 1930s and in 1945–50. Matthews (1968) argued that the fall in unemployment across the Second World War in the UK was not due to Keynesian *policies*. This was taken by some readers as an anti-Keynesian conclusion, but the method of approach remained entirely Keynesian, seeking an explanation in components of expenditure and finding it in investment. The whole question appears to have received very little attention from classical writers, who have given a lot of attention to the interwar period as well as to post-war but have almost always treated the two separately, as belonging to different regimes. As far as the fall in unemployment in the UK is concerned, a classical explanation in terms of the real wage is on the face of it very unpromising, since the product-wage rose considerably *more* than productivity across the war (see Matthews, Feinstein and Odling-Smee, 1982, p. 171). Newell and Symons (1986b, p. 38) refer to the moderating influence on wages of the close links between the unions and the first Labour Government, but they do not pursue this statistically in comparison with the pre-war period.[3] A possible avenue towards a classical interpretation might be sought in the observation that, despite the large fall in unemployment, the rate of increase in labour input across the Second World War in the UK was not in fact particularly great, largely on account of a substantial fall in hours of work. In the US the product wage did rise relatively slowly between 1937 and 1948 (see Kendrick, 1961, pp. 128–9).

17.6   THE POST-WAR PERIOD: EXPLANATIONS OF THE SLOWDOWN

We turn now to trends within the post-war period. We take as the central phenomenon to be explained the decline in the rate of growth of output in the 1970s and 1980s compared with the 1950s and 1960s – the slowdown, for short – along with the associated deterioration on the employment side. Alternative hypotheses will be considered in Sections 17.6.1 to 17.6.4. Sections 17.7 and 17.8 will deal with the associated phenomena: the slowdown in productivity growth and the behaviour of inflation. These phenomena are not only of major importance in themselves but also can point to further hypotheses about the slowdown in output and employment and rule out others.

17.6.1   A long swing in capital accumulation?

Perhaps the simplest though not the most familiar Keynesian type of hypothesis, with some classical overtones, is that the whole post-war period had the character of a grand multiplier-accelerator cycle, overlaid by a variety of contingent events, but in that not so different from other historical cycles.

Such a hypothesis is suggested by the course of capital accumulation, here measured by I/K, the ratio of gross fixed investment to the gross capital stock (see Figure 17.5). The predominant tendency was for the rate of capital accumulation to follow a cycle. It was *not* constant in the 1950s and 1960s, as might be expected if that period had been one of steady state growth, but rose, with a peak rather *before* 1973 (in a few cases considerably before). In the 1960s the capital stock was in all major countries rising faster than GDP, again contrary to the steady state paradigm.

The hypothesis runs as follows. Once the post-war expansion in capital accumulation got under way, it fed on itself in the familiar multiplier-accelerator manner, though with the difference that the feedback was at least as much on the supply side, through increasing productive capacity, as on the demand side. It was strengthened by an increase in the desired capital–output

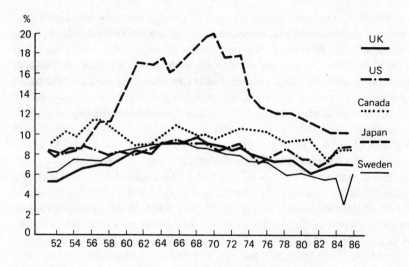

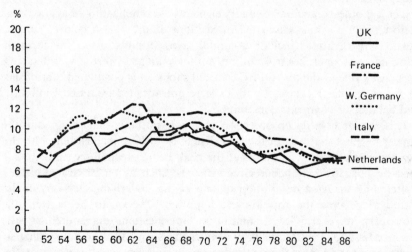

Figure 17.5   Investment–capital ratio in selected OECD countries, 1951 to 1986.

Source: OECD.

ratio, brought about by a progressive increase in the cost and scarcity of labour. The increase in the capital–output ratio called for a reduction in the *required* rate of return (rate of interest) in order for the likely reduction in the *actual* rate of return to be acceptable. This was achieved for a while, with the aid of government subsidies and reductions in capital market imperfections. But that could not continue indefinitely (alternatively: over-optimism on the part of investors, including governments, led to overshooting – 'Chapter-12-

Keynesianism'). The inducement to expand investment therefore tailed off.[4] The general expansion of income continued for longer, fuelled notably from a different source, the monetary expansion of the early 1970s, but that could only be transitory. The contraction once under way acquired cumulative force, making demand the principal constraint on world output, leading to underutilisation even of the now less rapidly expanding capital stock, to the detriment of profitability. At the same time it slowed down the rate of growth of productivity and capacity. A combination of low gross investment and accelerated scrapping (not properly reflected in the capital stock data, the rate of growth of which accordingly understates the contraction) meant that by the end of the period, although there was still a historically large amount of excess capacity, a sufficiently strong expansion of demand to absorb all the unemployed labour would in the short run have come against capacity constraints. Much of the excess capacity was unsuited to the new relative input prices prevailing. Similar hysteresis effects arose from the decline of investment in R&D and in training. The inflation rate followed a cycle similar to the capital cycle, with a lag, and was ultimately caused by it, though with feedback.

The hypothesis can invoke sundry elements as complicating or aggravating factors, such as those discussed in Sections 17.6.2–17.6.4 below. Further possible aggravations include a capital-saving innovation in the form of more efficient stock control and an untimely increase in the world saving propensity due to the first OPEC-induced shock. It is postulated that offsets by governmental Keynesian policies were not adopted because of inflation and balance-of-payments constraints.

It is not necessarily an objection to this hypothesis that things did not appear in quite that way at the time. There is nothing inconsistent with the business cycle analogy in events at the peak being precipitated and aggravated by partially extraneous circumstances, such as temporary monetary overexpansion. As a description of one of the underlying elements in the historical process the capital-cycle hypothesis is not to be written off. Obviously, however, it leaves some important questions unanswered, at best, and needs supplementation. Why were the upswing and the downswing so much larger and longer than in traditional business cycles? It is vague on the relationship between inflation and the real economy and also on the supply price of investment. It is less convincing for North America than for Europe and Japan, since the capital cycle was mild in the US and non-existent in Canada. It does not fully explain the trends in productivity, since these are too large to be accounted for by the rate of capital accumulation. We shall revert to some of these points presently.

17.6.2 Excessive real wages?

This hypothesis takes a different view of the causes of the decline in profitability in the 1970s and the subsequent stagflation. It is often thought of as the most distinctively non-Keynesian, or anti-Keynesian, hypothesis (in relation to the real economy), though, as Bruno and Sachs (1985) have made clear, elements of these two approaches are compatible. It is essentially a theory of stagflation and has not been much developed as a hypothesis about the earlier part of the post-war period.

If the capital stock is rising more than usually rapidly, it is to be expected that the same will be true of the real wage, *ceteris paribus*; moreover, labour's share will rise, if, as usually supposed, the elasticity of substitution between labour and capital is less than one. The rise in the real wage in those circumstances will not have any tendency to cause unemployment. The classical hypothesis, however, is that the real wage rose by more than the appropriate amount, especially in the 1970s, and thereby created unemployment *and* supply constraints, a novel feature. This could have happened because *changes* in the labour market gratuitously pushed up the real wage. Alternatively, it could have happened because labour markets, without necessarily changing from the one period to the other, did not allow real wages to adjust in the necessary way to compensate for other changes in circumstances, such as the productivity slowdown and the rise in raw material prices, those latter changes then being the prime movers.

Between 1973 and 1986, the real product wage grew considerably *less* than it did earlier in the post-war period, in all countries (see Figure 17.6, where the GDP deflator has been used). There is no question, therefore, of gratuitous real wage acceleration having actually occurred through the whole of the post-1973 period. The argument is that the real wage was brought back more nearly on to trend by the pressure of unemployment. Real wages did rise unusually fast in the late 1960s and early 1970s, in most countries continuing to do so into 1974 and in some into 1975. Moreover there is a good deal of independent evidence of wage militancy at that time. The militancy has been interpreted sometimes as an aggressive departure from competitive conditions and sometimes as marking the end of a period when wage increases were artificially kept *below* the competitive level by money illusion or by consent to corporatism or to incomes policy. To the effects of militancy are to be added the effects of the increase in social security payments, payable by employers, that took place in many countries in the late 1960s and 1970s. In some cases the 'wedge' between the take-home pay and the cost of employment to the employer came to approach 100 per cent (Bruno and Sachs, 1985, pp. 192–3, 278).

These are not Keynesian arguments, in the sense that they do not describe what Keynes regarded as the basic causes of unemployment. Traditional Keynesians confronted by the data are inclined to say that in so far as increased wage militancy led to trouble, it did so by producing inflation rather than through raising the real wage. Such people might say that one cannot know whether the real wage was too high, because it is impossible to tell just how large an *equilibrium* increase in the real wage would have been in

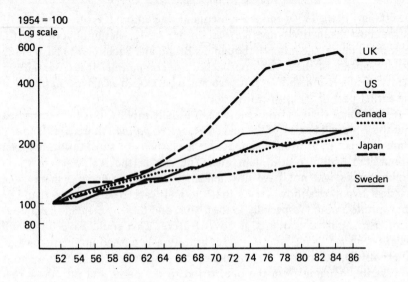

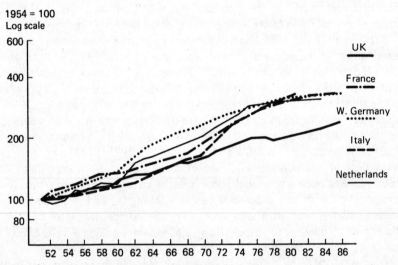

Figure 17.6   Real wage (manufacturing) in selected OECD countries 1951 to 1986.

Source: OECD.

the late 1960s and early 1970s. As to 1974 and 1975, they might say that it is normal in the capitalist system for rises in raw material prices or contractions in demand to impinge first on profits, because profits are the residual claimant on value added; and in so far as the real product wage accelerated, as well as there being a rise in labour's share, that can be attributed to competition in hard times squeezing margins.

Although the real wage argument is un-Keynesian, there is no reason why Keynesians should not accept that a gratuitous tendency for the real wage to rise may have been an element in this situation. In fact people who call themselves Keynesians have been ready to do so, particularly in regard to the wedge. Disputes about the relative magnitudes of such effects are never likely to be settled to the satisfaction of all disputants by econometric means, or indeed by any sort of scrutiny of the data. There are too many unmeasurable variables. The die-hard Keynesian's position just described is an extreme one. But it would also be hard to find people who would maintain that changes originating in the labour market accounted for *all* the stylised facts about the 1970s and 1980s. At the least they have to be held to have been supplemented by multiplier-accelerator effects, since by themselves excessive real wages would tend to bring about proportionately smaller changes in output than in employment, because of the scope for substitution, thus going in the wrong direction to explain the productivity slowdown.

The alternative version of the real wage hypothesis, that real wage movements failed to compensate for other disturbances, is sometimes stated in a tautological counter-factual form; so long as there is high unemployment, real wages *must* be out of equilibrium. Though milder as a historical hypothesis than the hypothesis of exogenous changes in the labour market, this is theoretically even more unKeynesian, in that Keynesians deny that there is ever any presumption that real wages will adjust in that way. It is not at all difficult to think of reasons why labour markets might fail to carry out the requisite compensatory manoeuvres. At least, they appear to have failed to do so over business cycles, going back in the UK to about 1790. Prolonged periods of high unemployment, it is true, go back only about seventy years rather than about 200; and there does exist other evidence of changes in labour market functioning within the post-war period, for instance, adverse shifts in the *UV* curve (the inverse relationship between unemployment and vacancies: see Pissarides (1986)). Only an extreme market optimist could regard full adjustment as the normal state of affairs, but it is possible that adjustment is *slower* than it was at one time, thus accounting for the unusual duration of current unemployment. Testing this hypothesis historically for the UK would require comparative study of the labour market before 1914, since, of course, chronic unemployment began in 1921.

The relevance of real wage considerations to the explanation of differences between countries is perhaps more straightforward and less controversial. Thus the persistence of very rapid real wage increase in Italy right up to 1977 surely reflected peculiarities of their labour market and contributed to their troubles. Among smaller European countries, Belgium and Spain have both had abnormally large increases in unemployment which can reasonably be associated with real wage movements. The comparative literature on this subject has been mainly concerned with the relations between the real wage and unemployment. The existence of such a relation does not necessarily imply the existence of a corresponding relation between the real wage and output (stylised fact (7)). The experience of the UK in the 1980s is noteworthy in this connection: the real wage rose more than in 1973–9, opposite to most European countries, but output performance in the 1980s has not been worse than in the 1970s, whereas on the continent it has.

17.6.3. Excessive real raw materials prices?

The political circumstances accompanying the oil price increases which took place in 1974 and 1979 must lead one to consider the role of supply shocks originating in the markets for raw materials. Exogenous adverse movements in the supply schedules of major inputs into the production process are liable to raise prices and reduce output, and thus become prime candidates to explain the stagflation of the 1970s and early 1980s. They may do this in either or both of two ways: (i) by reducing profit margins or (ii) by leading to the adoption of techniques of production that are less energy-intensive and hence have lower productivity per unit of labour and capital. One or both of these effects of movements in raw material prices may be offset by lower growth in real wages, by acceptance of lower profit margins, or by more rapid productivity growth. The fact that they may not be so offset does not imply that the problem should be redefined *in its origins* as a 'real wages' or 'productivity' problem.

Attention was drawn earlier to the large increase in the relative world price of primary products in the 1970s (stylised fact (10) and Figure 17.4). The prices of primary commodities compared with manufactured goods rose by 91 per cent between 1970 and 1979. However, this is not sufficient evidence to establish that *exogenous* supply shocks were responsible. Raw material prices react to the pressure of world demand, which was growing rapidly in the early 1970s. Unlike the markets for most manufactured goods, most raw materials markets for which prices are quoted are much closer to the ideal of an auction market with flexible prices, even though there is a great deal of government intervention and segmenting of markets. The greater volatility of raw material prices is enhanced by the speculative motive in building up holdings of storable, homogenous, easily traded commodities.

To what extent, then, have there been exogenous shocks to the supply of raw materials? The most striking supply shocks have been the decline in the growth rate of crude oil production after 1974, and the crop failures of the early 1970s, which led to pressure on the international grain market. The price rise administered by OPEC in 1974 was backed up by cuts in supply. Similarly, in 1979, the decline in oil supplies from Iran sustained price increases. OPEC may not have been able to mimic the behaviour of a perfect monopolist exactly, but it did seem to have ensured the existence of a ratchet effect in oil prices: whenever spot prices tended to rise above OPEC posted prices, the latter were raised, but when spot prices tended to fall, OPEC supply was cut back (see Nordhaus, 1980). In the early 1970s, Soviet crop failures were met by substantial Russian imports of grain for the first time, in a period when traditional American regulation of grain prices was vitiated by the rundown in grain stocks (see Bosworth and Lawrence (1982), who also draw attention to some other supply shocks in foodstuffs markets).

Hence, the supply of fuels and food *was* disrupted in such a way as to administer an exogenous real price increase to OECD importers. The prices of non-food agricultural goods and metals and minerals can be explained much more readily by the OECD's level of demand alone.[5]

We can conclude that real raw materials prices in the 1970s did reflect exogenous adverse supply shocks, but that these shocks should not be characterised either as affecting all intermediate inputs on the one hand or just energy on the other. The synchronised expansions of the early 1970s contributed to a temporary demand-side pressure on raw materials prices as well (demand on its own is a much more persuasive explanation of the earlier boom in commodity prices at the time of the Korean War). The resulting terms of trade deterioration for the OECD was particularly severe. As Bruno and Sachs have argued, one consequence of excessive real raw material prices was to reduce the real consumption wage warranted at full employment. The labour markets of OECD countries reacted to this problem differently. It should also be pointed out that the size of this problem differed (even abstracting from the complications raised by flexible exchange rates) amongst countries. Japan and West Germany, for example, were able to mitigate the world food price shocks by reducing the tariffs protecting their agriculture, an excellent example of supply-side economics at work. However, they were more exposed to energy price increases than the USA, because of their greater dependence on imports.

17.6.4 Excessive real interest rates?

Keynes thought that unemployment of labour and (in the short run) underutilisation of capital were more likely to be caused by an excessive supply price of capital (interest rate) than by an excessive supply price of labour (real wage). If interest rates, as determined in Keynes by liquidity preference and the supply of money, are too high, effects will be felt not only on investment, including consumer investment, but also on the inducement to produce output from the existing capital stock. This is because the rate of interest affects the carrying cost of stocks (a variable cost comparable to material prices), the cost of sustaining losses in the hope of better times, the cost of replacing necessary parts in a complementary set of capital equipment, and the cost of using low mark-ups in the interest of the firm's market share in the future (Fitoussi and Phelps, 1986). It is interesting to note that

Newell and Symons (1986b) find significant, negative, real interest rate effects on employment. Their preferred explanation of this finding invokes the investment cost of training workers, but the Keynesian interpretation is obvious.[6]

Public concern about high real interest rates has belonged to the 1980s rather than the 1970s. During most of the 1970s, not only were realised rates in almost all countries low or negative, but so too were *ex ante* real interest rates, as measured by estimates of expected inflation derived from survey data and other sources (see Atkinson and Chouraqui, 1985, pp. 6–7). In the 1980s real interest rates have been much higher than in the 1970s, and high, too, by historical standards. Hence high real interest rates have commonly been seen less as an initiating cause of stagflation than as an aggravation in the 1980s and an obstacle to recovery.

This may well be broadly correct. In so far as it is, it is natural and wholly Keynesian to attribute high real interest rates in the 1980s to tight world monetary policies. We shall not enter here into the debate between this interpretation and the non-Keynesian interpretation that attributes them to the US budget deficit.

However, there is a good deal of doubt about the facts themselves, that is to say about the movement of the supply price of capital. Conventional measures of the real rate of interest are not a good indicator, for several reasons.

In the first place, nominal interest rates matter as well as real interest rates, because of front-loading effects (see below). Nominal interest rates reached their peak in most countries in 1980–81, but there were sharp rises already in the 1970s.

In the second place, *ex ante* real interest rates cannot be measured with any confidence. One of the few market-based indicators that exists, the yield on British government index-linked bonds, does not suggest that the long-term real interest rate in the 1980s has been much above the ordinary (though it has admittedly tended to rise somewhat). Furthermore, tax considerations invalidate the simple Fisher formula used to measure the real interest rate (i.e. nominal interest rate minus expected inflation rate) as illustrated by Feldstein (1982). The exact calculations are complicated and depend on the tax rules, but if interest payments are tax-deductible the Fisher formula can substantially overstate the cost of borrowing, provided that the borrower has enough profit from which to deduct them.

In the third place, account has to be taken of the capital equivalent of the wedge. Here again measurement is complicated, but it has been estimated that in the UK the combination of taxes and subsidies began to turn less favourable as early as the middle or end of the 1960s, or at least then ceased to become more progressively more favourable, which is what it had done previously (see Mellis and Richardson, 1976; Flemming *et al.*, 1976).

In the fourth place, the terms of supply of capital include availability as well as cost; deregulation of financial markets in the 1980s increased availability to some classes of borrowers, though possibly tending to raise cost by bidding up interest rates on deposits.

All things considered, the possibility cannot be ruled out that already in the 1970s, perhaps quite early in the 1970s, there was some rise in the supply price of capital, at a time when a fall would have been more conformable to real trends in the economy. With regard to the 1980s, there is some doubt whether the supply price of capital was really high by historical standards to all borrowers, though it clearly was to some. Possibly whatever trend there was in the latter direction was augmented by greater stringency in requiring activities to attain the stipulated rate of return, without cross-subsidy, on the part of conglomerates and, notably in the UK after the 1978 White Paper, in the public sector.

We have so far focused on the causes of the slowdown in output. We turn now explicitly to the other two major features of the latter part of the postwar period: The productivity slowdown and inflation.

17.7 THE PRODUCTIVITY SLOWDOWN

Already by 1979 the shortfall in productivity growth below its pre-1973 level had been responsible arithmetically for a setback to real GNP of the same order as OPEC1 and OPEC2 combined, in most countries, and much more in some. In the 1980s the gap below the old trend line of productivity continued to widen in most countries, notwithstanding that the effects of the oil-price were going into reverse.

If the productivity slowdown is held to have been exogenous, it ranks as a major primary cause of the difference in the character of events generally between before and after 1973. Apart from the direct effect on the rate of growth of potential output, it would not be surprising that time should have been needed for workers to adjust to the inevitably slower growth of earnings, for firms to adjust to the disappointment in quasi-rents on capital installed before 1973, and for governments to adjust to the changed prospects in the areas for which they had responsibility. The implications are different if the productivity slowdown was endogenous. It then becomes a reinforcing factor for whatever were the prime causes.

The causes of a long-run slowdown in productivity growth, if that is what it was, are not something that a Keynesian theory of demand in the short run can be expected to address. Supply-siders, too, have given this pre-eminently supply-side matter less attention than might have been expected. The literature about it is largely separate from the literature on stabilisation policy. But it seems to us that the case for postulating at least a large endogenous element is overwhelming. Admittedly, some slowdown in some countries may have been inevitable because of diminished scope for catch-up (in the case of Japan that explanation of events would be more convincing if the slowdown had not been so sudden). There were probably also a number of other exogenous or partly exogenous forces (the rise in the energy price, exhaustion of the benefits from freer trade and from changes in industrial structure, and so on). But they are not big enough, on any reasonable estimate, to explain the pervasive movement throughout the OECD.[7] Nor, for that matter, is the slowdown in the rate of capital accumulation, in any case largely an endogenous item, though its effects are quite sizeable.

The exact nature of the endogenous process is not at all clear. Verdoorn effects of some sort have been at work. It is a pity we do not understand them better. At the same time we ought to pay tribute to the intuition of the late Nicholas Kaldor, whose theory of the Verdoorn effect, regarded by him as an extension of Keynesianism, was put forward well before the slowdown occurred. It predicted just what has happened – more than can be said for almost anyone else's theory.

Can anything be learnt about the nature of the productivity slowdown from comparison of the 1970s and the 1980s? Leaving aside longer-term effects of the Verdoorn kind, it is understandable that a contraction in output, or a contraction relative to trend, should have an adverse effect on productivity in the short run, as a result of underutilisation of labour and non-malleability of capital. It is also understandable that, after a rather longer period, there should be some favourable effect, as labour ceases to be hoarded and the less efficient units are withdrawn from production. In the UK something of this sort seems to have happened. Here, and in the US, productivity growth in the 1980s has been markedly better than it was in the 1970s (in continental Europe, by contrast, matters have got worse). In fact in the last few years UK productivity growth has got back to being not much lower than it was in 1950–73. This is not a Verdoorn effect, for output growth has been at about the same rate in the 1970s and 1980s. There is no sign yet of the large arrears of productivity growth accumulated in the meanwhile being made up. All this suggests that the forces behind the productivity slowdown were partly conjunctural and temporary but that these forces have not yet run their course or else, though due initially to temporary causes, have had permanent effects.

17.8 INFLATION: CAUSES

Let us turn now to the issue of inflátion. It is unclear exactly what would constitute a Keynesian theory of inflation and its consequences for the real economy. Keynes considered in *How to Pay for the War* the inflationary consequences of an excess of aggregate demand over aggregate supply at full employment, the so-called inflationary gap. This approach, by stressing the importance of aggregate demand in general, seems to be a precursor of demand-pull theories of inflation, in which a variety of causes (not simply monetary expansion) may lead to a continuing bidding up of prices in product markets. However, at less than full employment, increases in aggregate demand were argued to affect primarily quantities (although Keynes expected real product wages to fall in booms).

In the post-war period, one can distinguish three main approaches to explaining inflation. In the first, the emphasis is on demand-pull: the division of an increase in nominal aggregate demand between quantities and prices increasingly favours the latter as the economy moves towards full employment. This is perhaps the approach traditionally seen as Keynesian. In the second, inflationary pressures from factor markets, operating through a relatively constant mark-up of prices over average unit costs, give rise to cost-push inflation. This approach takes account of imperfect competition and might be called neo-Keynesian. It has much in common with the traditional Keynesian view in so far as demand pull factors are often accorded importance in the relevant factor markets, particularly the labour market (most obviously, through the original Phillips curve). The two views can be reconciled theoretically within the neo-Keynesian synthesis; the questions become, have inflationary shocks arisen historically more often from shifts in the aggregate demand curve or the aggregate supply curve, and do factor markets operate in such a way as to make the aggregate supply curve non-horizontal below full employment. The third approach concentrates on the role of the money supply. Advocates of this monetarist or new classical view agreed that inflation is always and everywhere an essentially monetary phenomenon, there is a close relationship between the money stock and nominal income, but very little between the money stock and real income (especially in the more recent 'new classical' version).

The evidence for the OECD of the post-war period is that aggregate demand affects prices, but through factor markets rather than product markets. Grubb (1985) finds that there is a robust relationship between inflation of average hourly earnings and unemployment in the OECD countries. Most OECD wage equations still contain unemployment effects however much they differ from the original Phillips curve in other respects. Raw material prices tend to vary with nominal demand in the OECD, although other factors have been important in determining the prices of particular commodities such as wheat and, *a fortiori*, oil. The prices of manufactured goods are explained well by a mark-up on factor costs (see, *inter alia*, Gordon (1977), Sawyer (1986), Okun (1981)). Demand effects on the mark-up are very difficult to discern (Layard and Nickell (1986) identify mild demand effects in their work on Britain, however). The relative price change brought about by OPEC shocks, for instance, can be translated by this process into a rise in the general price level. In a market-clearing world, this aggregate price level effect would quickly be removed as producers substituted towards relatively cheaper inputs made cheaper still by the initial fall in derived demand for all factors of production. Induced changes in aggregate demand (e.g. an accommodating increase in the money supply) and non-market clearing factor markets (in particular, the labour market) ensure that this neoclassical model is inappropriate. The evidence is that changes in the general level of prices are not independent of changes in relative prices (see Cukierman, 1984, p. 84).

This is consistent with the work of economists who recast the Phillips curve as a real wage equation, and find that the real product wage tends to vary inversely with unemployment, *ceteris paribus* (Newell and Symons, 1986a). This helps to explain the procyclical behaviour of real wages in many countries, such as the US and UK; real wages seem to adjust more rapidly to changes in unemployment and hence employment, than does employment to changes in real wages (although the negative relationship implied by a neoclassical labour demand may well exist, as argued by, amongst others, Newell and Symons).

The evidence suggests, then, that we examine the behaviour of factor prices to understand the patterns of post-war inflation. Before doing so, let us consider how this evidence reflects upon monetarist explanations of inflation. Brown (1985) points out, first, that in the short run the correlation between real growth and inflation has been negative for the Big Six (except for the US in the 1950s) and, second, that real growth rates have often been more variable over the cycle than has inflation. This does not conform with a picture of increased nominal demand, independent of long-run growth of aggregate supply, leading to increased inflation (with perhaps a temporary positive correlation between inflation and growth). Brown argues that most monetary expansion has simply accommodated the increased transactions demand for money arising from real growth. Only in the early 1980s does he identify an episode where increased money supplies contributed a significant 'monetary impulse' to inflation. Money demand has been too variable, due to business cycle fluctuations and financial innovation, to support the argument that control of the money supply (if possible) was both necessary and sufficient to control inflation on the post-war period.

The sources of inflation in the OECD since 1950, then, seem to be rooted in the labour market and the market for raw materials, although in both cases the term market may be misleading. Up to the late 1960s, a level of demand high relative to full employment output kept unemployment low, leading to higher rates of wage inflation than before. The rate of inflation was not closely related to productivity growth, as wage targets seem to have been related to domestic productivity growth levels. In the later 1960s, exogenous increases in nominal wages contributed to an increase in inflation (see Perry, 1986; Newell and Symons, 1986a); the source of these increases is uncertain (the French students have often been invoked, but the links between them and labour market behaviour are not clear!). Unemployment-vacancy (or

Beveridge) curves also shifted out in several countries to an extent difficult to explain by reference to unemployment benefits. At this stage, the role of spreading expectations of higher inflation became more important. This is one aspect of the story which was emphasised by monetarists (money illusion on the part of workers is not, however, a vital part of Keynesian analyses now that the procyclicality of real wages is acknowledged.)

In the 1970s, increases in the price of raw materials, particularly oil, dominated. To a certain extent the slow rise in their relative prices since the early 1960s can be seen as the commodity market counterpart of the Phillips curve. The administered rise for oil, which OPEC attempted to maintain in real terms (thus contrasting with the Korean War commodity price boom), provided an additional serious shock. Workers tried to maintain their real consumption wages, thereby putting upwards pressure on the real product wage in OECD manufacturing. A cost-push inflationary episode developed, one which contributed to unemployment because of the relative product wage increases and the transfer of income to countries with a relatively low absorptive capacity. Governments chose not to accommodate inflation, especially after the second shock of 1979. Increased unemployment has now brought down wage inflation considerably and slower growth of output has brought down relative commodity prices, which in turn has contributed to lower inflation rates. Some commentors, such as Beckerman and Jenkinson (1986), assign a great deal of importance to the role of primary product prices. Relative world commodity prices do appear to be both a source of exogenous shocks and an important channel through which world demand affects inflation. However we would not dismiss the role of unemployment, including *changes* in unemployment. The relationship between unemployment and wage inflation is such as to suggest that the implied non-accelerating inflation rate of unemployment has now increased substantially in most OECD countries. This has led to further investigation of wage behaviour, in particular. The post-war Keynesian tradition continues to focus on how the price of labour is determined.

17.9 INFLATION: CONSEQUENCES

There is some evidence that investment has been reduced by high inflation. During the high inflation periods of 1970s, *ex post* real interest rates were historically low, but nominal interest rates were abnormally high. This caused problems for the cash flows of many companies as nominal interest payments on given debt increased. The risk of bankruptcy was increased. Wadhwani (1984) estimates that this risk was significant and was reflected in the default premium on shares. He calculates that a permanent reduction of inflation of one percentage point would reduce the number of liquidations by

5.8 per cent of their mean value. The increase in default premia reduced stock market valuation. Thus inflation contributed to reduced investment through the channel of Tobin's q.

There are other reasons to suppose that inflation can have a deleterious effect on stock market valuation and hence on investment. Modigliani and Cohn (1979) believe that the UK stock market was badly undervalued in the 1970s because of systematic valuation errors. First, the current cost accounting convention of deducting the whole of nominal interest payments on debt as a cost removes from the definition of profit the reduction in the real value of outstanding debt. Second, Modigliani and Cohn argued that the stock market capitalises equity earnings using the nominal interest rate, applied to deflated earnings. Wadhwani provides British evidence to complement their empirical results confirming the hypothesis for the US.

One does not have to invoke a stock market valuation theory of investment to conclude from this evidence that high inflation discourages capital formation. The increased risk of default (given an institutional reluctance to index the real value of loans to companies) and the complexities of adjusting accounting (and tax) conventions originally based on the assumption of price stability afflict all corporate economies, regardless of the relative size of their stock markets.

The way in which inflation leads to 'front-loading' interest payments on debt not only reduces the willingness to invest but also increases saving, when, for instance, consumers are tied into long-term loans such as house mortgages. Savings propensities are discussed further below.

Brown presents evidence suggesting that inflation was underestimated more often than it was overestimated. Thus unanticipated inflation has tended to redistribute from lenders to borrowers. At the lower rates of inflation experienced in the 1960s, this may have contributed to rising investment rates through the very Keynesian mechanism of redistributing resources to agents with high propensities to invest. Later in the period, the higher rates of expected inflation probably overwhelmed this effect, as explained below. Inflation itself may have contributed to lower investment directly by increasing the risk of bankruptcy.

Inflation helps to explain subsequent unemployment, perhaps better than the Bruno–Sachs real wage gap (see Perry, 1986). The most obvious channel through which it does this is that of reactive government policy. This is particularly evident after the surge of inflation in 1979, when discretionary changes in fiscal stance in general did not take place in response to the poor employment situation (the US being an exception). A further channel is through an increased savings propensity. Personal sector savings propensities did increase substantially in the 1970s; the relationship with inflation is clear-cut in some countries (e.g. West Germany, UK). The personal sector attempted to maintain real wealth in line with its income; this required additional saving to restore the real value of its nominal assets. The increase in thrift did not lead to increased growth rates in neoclassical fashion, but contributed to recession in the way that the Harrod growth model predicted. The third channel is the Wadhwani effect: firms, given their capital stock, try to improve their cash flow by reducing hiring of variable factors of production when inflation threatens to bankrupt them.

There are thus a number of ways in which inflation has impinged unfavourably on output and employment. Study of the British experience has shown that it has done so systematically in movements from year to year (Britton, 1986). Yet over longer periods the relation between output and inflation has not been uniform. Fast growth in the 1950s and 1960s was accompanied by historically high inflation, seeming to confirm old notions about the Kondratieff cycle; but slower growth accompanied the faster inflation of the 1970s; and further deterioration in the real economy has occurred in most countries in the 1980s as inflation has fallen away. Lags could be invoked in partial explanation. Yet cross-country comparisons also fail to show a negative correlation between a country's average inflation rate and its growth performance: not only Germany and Japan but virtuous Switzerland too have suffered severe slowdowns. Likewise the size of the increase in incremental capital output ratios since the 1970s has not been related to countries' inflation rates (casting doubt on the Friedmanite contention that inflation prejudices the efficiency of investment by creating uncertainty). The combination of well-established short-run effects of inflation on the real economy and non-existent longer-run effects is paradoxical. A natural hypothesis to explain the paradox is that what has proved damaging has been unexpected inflation, rather than high inflation as such. Year-to-year increases in inflation are unforeseen and disturbing, but chronic differences between countries in inflation rates become expected and are adapted to both by individuals in their decision-making and in the development of appropriate institutional arrangements. In this connection it may be noted that in some countries higher inflation has been associated with inflation that is *less* variable from year to year.

The interactions between inflation and trends in the real economy in the comparison of different parts of the post-war period are thus not too difficult to summarise:

(i)   The boom of the period from 1950 to 1973 did lead to inflation, but with the aid of some adjuncts in its last years: militancy, developing relative shortage of primary products, and possibly increasing extrapolation of past inflation, as well as a speeding up in the growth of demand itself.

(ii) The increase in the rate of inflation did contribute to ending the real boom, by its effects on investment, on the propensity to save, and on governments' policies.

(iii) The ending of the boom did bring down inflation, though not so early or so much (yet) as might have been expected. The delay can be attributed partly to the continuing high relative prices of primary products in the 1970s, and partly to features of the labour market that have caused the *level* of unemployment to be a less powerful influence on inflation than was once thought.

Keynesian theory was not properly worked out for an inflationary world, so we should not like to say whether the above summary is compatible with Keynesianism. It must be acknowledged, however, that in focusing, like everyone else, on rises and falls in the inflation rate rather than on rises and falls in the price-level, we are speaking in terms that are more Friedmanite than what used to be thought of as Keynesian.

Why inflation behaved as it did in each phase of the post-war period is perhaps reasonably easy to understand, with the aid of hindsight. What of the reasons why inflation in the post-war period as a whole was so much greater than in earlier peacetime periods? Here perhaps more weight *can* be put on the money supply, seen as accommodation rather than as a propelling agent. Had the world been on a gold standard throughout the post-war period, the rise in prices would surely have been brought to a halt by a shortage of real balances well before 1973, to say nothing of 1979, and well before inflationary expectations took such a firm grip, even allowing for the induced economies that would no doubt have occurred in the use of gold as money.

17.10   SOME CONCLUSIONS AND SOME QUESTIONS

No consensus exists on the question why OECD countries did so outstandingly well, by historical standards, during the 1950s and the 1960s. It remains a major issue. This was the period when Keynesian policies were, broadly speaking, in the ascendant. Was the success *caused* by the policies? Or perhaps by what was *believed* about the policies? At any rate, macro policies adopted by governments did not stand in the way of the historically rapid growth of output, and of prices too, for that matter.

Demand management policies, however enlightened, can hardly be expected to explain such a rapid expansion on the supply side as took place during those decades. So it is natural to look for other causes. Something can be attributed to catch-up with wartime arrears. But growth far outstripped what can be explained directly in that way. Catch-up in a different sense also played a part, namely catch-up with the US's higher level of productivity. The significance of both forms of catch-up is confirmed by the fact that the US surpassed its earlier performance by much less than other countries. But little if any catch-up with the US took place elsewhere *before* the Second World War, though there was already plenty to catch up with. So why did it happen when it did? Other contributory causes can be cited: the growth of world trade, stimulated by relatively stable international monetary arrangements, and the favourable trend in primary product prices. It would be difficult to make much of a case for supply-side policies in the current, political, sense, since taxes were high and controls of one sort or another were still in place in many countries, though both were becoming less severe.

Perhaps it was just a favourable concatenation of circumstances, with mutual reinforcement through capital accumulation and Verdoorn's law. The question that follows from this intellectually unsatisfying conclusion is which of those circumstances are likely to be reproduced in the future. We shall not pursue that question here.

The years between 1968 and 1973 were a transition phase. In retrospect, it is clear that the boom was running out of steam, in almost all OECD countries. The rate of capital accumulation had everywhere passed its peak. Actions by governments contributed to keeping the boom going for the time being, partly by deliberate design and partly as a by-product of supporting the US dollar. In old-fashioned business cycle narratives, 'excesses' by financiers and central bankers at a late stage of the upswing were frequently represented as having prolonged the boom but thereby sharpened the recession. The events of the late 1960s and the early 1970s can be seen in this light.

The steep rise in money wage-rates that occurred during these years had been foreseen as a natural consequence of prolonged full employment by left-wing Keynesians, notably Kalecki, who had never much cared for the reformist conclusion drawn by most Keynesians, that technocratic demand management was all that was needed to enable capitalism to deliver the goods. Was it the resulting rise in *real* wages, and similarly in the *real* incomes of oil producers shortly afterwards, that finally put things into reverse? Or was it their *inflationary* consequences? We suggested that a reasonable case can be made for both, though the effects of the inflation are less open to debate. For the interpretation of history the question is perhaps not too crucial, since the same actions were ultimately responsible either way. The corresponding counter-factual question is whether more resolute and earlier anti-inflationary policy by governments would have altered the distribution of income or just the behaviour of prices and output. In the event, in the 1980s, it appears to have done both. The issue also affects, of course, the meaning to be given to exhortations to wage-moderation. Are they exhortations to make real concessions or are they merely exhortations to avoid getting caught up in a Prisoner's Dilemma?

Future economic historians may be less inclined than contemporaries to give pride of place to spectacular events, whether French students or OPEC or the vagaries of governments' macro policies. A view rather different from the foregoing is that, without any exogenous change in labour markets, pressures would have arisen tending to curtail the boom and also to shift the distribution of income away from capital. These pressures were created by the tendency in the proceeding years for capital accumulation to outstrip the rate of growth of income and reach its peak later. It may be noted, as a digression, that such an interpretation of post-war events as having some of the character of a long swing would permit guarded optimism about the future, since it is the character of swings to swing back. The much-vaunted improvement in the performance of the British economy in the mid-1980s has not featured prominently in this chapter, since it does not show up in the data we have quoted.[8] But at least the flattening out in the growth rate is a movement in the right direction, as is the small improvement in Japan.

The persistence of inflation during the 1970s, and its resumed acceleration at the end of the decade, put paid to naive Keynesianism. They reflected a combination of downward inflexibility of real wages, which was perhaps not such a new phenomenon, and downward rigidity in the real price of the most important primary product, oil, which certainly *was* a novelty. Inflation conditioned government policies in the 1980s. There are both theoretical and empirical reasons for supposing that unexpected inflation, hence (typically) accelerating inflation, is what prejudices real output rather than chronic high inflation. However it is understandable that this academic conclusion did not make much impact on governments' thinking. Accelerating inflation is not as easily distinguishable from high inflation in reality as it is on the blackboard: there were good reasons for supposing that the rate of inflation had been on an upward trend through its cycles in the 1970s and to have accommodated it would have acquiesced in the acceleration.

There is fairly general agreement that the further deterioration on the real side that occurred in most OECD coutries in the 1980s owed a good deal to straightforward demand deficiency: Keynes *redivivus*. We quoted the convergence of national growth rates as a piece of possibly corroborating evidence. Some countries dealt more successfully than others with the tendency for further rises in unemployment, but those countries did not necessarily do particularly well in output.

Comparisons of countries are disorderly. Especially since 1973, different countries get the prizes in the output, employment, and inflation departments. This argues against uni-casual explanations. The case of the US stands on its own. Broadly speaking, trends in the US were like the ones elsewhere but much less marked: less acceleration in output and productivity growth and less reduction in unemployment in 1950–73 compared with the pre-Second World War average, and less slowdown after 1973; a much milder cycle in capital accumulation and a lower rise in capital per unit of labour; and a relatively low rate of inflation. The less marked acceleration in 1950–73 can naturally be attributed to different experiences in the Second World War, during which US output grew rapidly. Trends since 1973, especially the smallness of the rise in unemployment, have suggested greater adaptability to changed circumstances than elsewhere, whether because of a loose fiscal stance or because of flexible real wages (both recommended for imitation, by different commentators). But they have been accompanied by a disturbing feature, unique to the US: labour productivity growth since 1973 has been much slower than the pre-Second World War average. Paradoxically, in the arithmetic of growth accounting, more of the slowdown in labour productivity than in Europe is attributable to slowdown in the growth of capital per unit of labour, because employment kept up better. But even so, total factor productivity in the US, as estimated by Maddison, was practically stationary after 1973. The reasons for this are not understood.

As far as the rest of the OECD world has been concerned, has the long stagflation been in some way a retribution for the long boom of the 1950s and 1960s? Did that boom create inflationary expectations or unfulfillable aspirations and so make inevitable a failure on the output side to match the previous success? One can speculate about whether the long-run *real* economic performance of OECD countries would have been better or worse if the brakes had been applied sharply at some time earlier than they were, say in the 1960s. We have not offered any means of answering that counterfactual question. However, the long-run rate of growth of output and productivity have, save in the US, remained higher since 1973 than they were before the Second World War, and the same is true (just) even of the 1980s. So perhaps the retribution has not been too severe.

Acknowledgements

We are grateful for helpful comments and suggestions to participants in the conference and to an anonymous referee. We are grateful also to the Centre for Labour Economics at the LSE for allowing us to use the OECD data-set compiled there. Responsibility for any errors remains with the authors. The views expressed are not necessarily those of NEDO, though one of us is a member of its staff.

Notes

1. The tables draw heavily on Maddison (1987). Maddison's data go up to 1984 only, and comparable information on employment in person-hours is not available for later years. Maddison's pre-Second World War figures are not reproduced here but are drawn on in the text.
2. The question was a major theme in Ohkawa and Rosovsky (1973), on Japan, and in Matthews, Feinstein and Odling-Smee (1982), on the UK, but neither book sought to deal with the OECD as a whole.
3. It might be argued that the decline in unemployment arose from the decline in replacement ratios across the Second World War. This is the line taken by Benjamin and Kochin (1982) in their riposte to Metcalf, Nickell and Floros (1982), who argued that the level of unemployment compensation relative to

wages was at least as generous in the post-war period as in the interwar years, and was administered more leniently, too. Even if Benjamin and Kochin are correct in suggesting effective replacement ratios fell across the Second World War, they themselves conclude (p. 428) that, 'immediate postwar unemployment rates . . . are too far below interwar unemployment rates for the differences to be explained by our estimates of the effects of the interwar insurance system'. Even if one were to concede a close relationship between replacement ratios and unemployment, this leaves unanswered the question of how higher wages could be sustained without deleterious consequences for employment, given the path of productivity.

4.   The endogenous element in the movement of capital accumulation has been stressed in a number of papers by J. R. Sargent (e.g. Sargent, 1979).

5.   L. Alan Winters (1987) shows that *changes* in OECD industrial production are the most important determinant of the *level* of real commodity prices, but that it takes a long time – perhaps ten years – before prices return to long-run equilibrium after a change in the level of activity.

6.   Other proxies for the exogenous elements of aggregate demand have had mixed success in estimated models of employment determination. This is not surprising considering the difficulty of identifying those exogenous elements.

7.   Maddison (1987, p. 680) finds an unexplained portion of the slowdown in all his six countries, as Denison (1979) had earlier done to a still more marked extent in the case of the US.

8.   GDP grew at about the same rate over the periods 1973–9 and 1979–86 (Table 17.1). However, productivity grew more rapidly over the latter period. Moreover, an extension of that period into 1987 will almost certainly raise the growth rate of GDP from 1979 to rather above that of 1973–9. The exact figures depend on the GDP indicator used, as well as on data revisions. The OECD figures used in Table 17.1 are expenditure based.

References

ATKINSON, P. and J. C. CHORAQUI (1985) 'Real Interest Rates and the Prospects for Durable Growth', OECD Working Paper No. 21, May.

BAUMOL, W. J. and K. McLENNAN (eds) (1985) *Productivity Growth and US Competitiveness* (New York: Oxford University Press).

BECKERMAN, W. and T. JENKINSON (1986) 'What Stopped the Inflation? Unemployment or Commodity Prices?, *Economic Journal*, vol. 96, March.

BENJAMIN, D. K. and L. A. KOCHIN (1982) 'Unemployment and Unemployment Benefits in Twentieth Century Britain: a Reply to Our Critics', *Journal of Political Economy*, vol. 90(2), April.

BOSWORTH, B. P. and R. Z. LAWRENCE (1982) *Commodity Prices and the New Inflation* (Washington DC: The Brookings Institution).

BRITTON, A. (1986) *The Trade Cycle in Britain 1958–1982*, NIESR Cambridge University Press, Cambridge. Occasional Paper xxxix.

BROWN, A. J. (1985) *World Inflation Since 1950: An International Comparative Study* (Cambridge: National Institute of Economic Research, Cambridge University Press).

BRUNO, M. and J. SACHS (1985) *Economics of Worldwide Stagflation* (Oxford: Basil Blackwell).

CUKIERMAN, A. (1984) *Inflation, Stagflation, Relative Prices, and Imperfect Information* (Cambridge: Cambridge University Press).

DENISON, E. F. (1979) *Accounting for Slower Growth* (Washington DC: Brookings Institution).

FELDSTEIN, M. (1982) 'Inflation, Tax Rules, and the Accumulation of Residential and Non-Residential Capital', *Scandinavian Journal of Economics*, vol. 842, pp. 293–311.

FITOUSSI, J. P. and E. S. PHELPS (1986) 'Causes of the 1980s Slump in Europe', *Brookings Papers on Economic Activity* 1986/2.

FLEMMING, J. S. *et al.* (1976) 'The Cost of Capital, Finance, and Investment', *Bank of England Quarterly Bulletin*, vol. 162, pp. 193–205.

GORDON, R. J. (1977) 'Can the Inflation of the 1970s be Explained?'. *Brookings Papers on Economic Activity* 1977/1.

GRUBB, D. (1985) Topics in the OECD Phillips Curve, Discussion Paper No. 231 (Centre for Labour Economics, LSE), October.

KALDOR, N. (1966) *Causes of the Slow Rate of Economic Growth of the United Kingdom* (Cambridge: Cambridge University Press).

KENDRICK, J. W. (1961) *Productivity Trends in the US* (Princeton: Princeton University Press).

LAYARD, P. R. G. and S. J. NICKELL (1986) 'Unemployment in Britain', *Economica*, vol. 53, no. 210(5).

MADDISON, A. (1987) 'Growth and Slowdown in Advanced Capitalist Economies', *Journal of Economic Literature*, vol. xxv, no. 2, June.

MATTHEWS, R. C. .O. (1968) 'Why Has Britain Had Full Employment Since the War?', *Economic Journal*, vol. 78, September.

MATTHEWS, R. C. O., C. H. FEINSTEIN and J. C. ODLING-SMEE (1982) *British Economic Growth 1856–1973* (Oxford: Clarendon Press).

MELLIS, C. L. and P. W. RICHARDSON (1976) 'Value of Investment Incentives for Manufacturing Industry', in A. Whiting (ed.), *The Economics of Industrial Subsidies* (London: HMSO).

METCALF, D., S. J. NICKELL and N. FLOROS (1982) 'Still Searching for an Explanation of Unempoyment in Interwar Britain', *Journal of Political Economy*, vol. 90(2), April.

MODIGLIANI, F. and R. A. COHN (1979) 'Inflation, Rational Valuation and the Market', *Financial Analysts Journal*, vol. 35 (March–April).

NEWELL, A. and J. S. V. SYMONS (1986a) 'The Phillips Curve is a Real Wage Equation' (Centre for Labour Economics, LSE), July.

NEWELL, A. and J. S. V. SYMONS (1986b) 'Corporatism, the Laissez-Faire and the Rise in Unemployment' (Centre for Labour Economics, LSE), November.

NEWELL, A. (1985) 'The Revised OECD Data Set', Working Paper No. 781, (Centre for Labour Economics, LSE), August.

NORDHAUS, W. D. (1980) 'Oil and Economic Performance in Industrial Countries', *Brookings Papers on Economic Activity*, 2.

OHKAWA, K. and H. ROSOVSKY (1973) *Japanese Economic Growth; Trend Acceleration in the Twentieth Century* (Stanford: Stanford University Press).

OKUN, A. M. (1981) *Prices and Quantities: a Macroeconomic Analysis* (Washington DC: Brookings Institution).

PERRY, G. L. (1986) 'Policy Lessons from the Post-war Period'; Chapter 6 in W. Beckerman (ed.), *Wage Rigidity and Unemployment*, (London: Duckworth).

PISSARIDES, C. (1986) 'Unemployment', *Economic Policy*, No. 3, October.

SARGENT, J. R. (1979) 'Productivity and Profits in U.K. Manufacturing', *Midland Bank Review*, Autumn.

SAWYER, M. (1983) *Business Pricing and Inflation* (London: Macmillan).

WADHWANI, S. B. (1984) 'Inflation, Bankruptcy, Default Premia and the Stock Market', Discussion Paper No. 194 (Centre for Labour Economics, LSE), March.

WADHWANI, S. B. (1985) 'The Effects of Aggregate Demand, Inflation, Real Wages and Uncertainty on Manufacturing Employment', Discussion Paper No. 210 (Centre for Labour Economics, LSE), February.

WINTERS, L. A. (1987) 'Models of Primary Price Indices', *Oxford Bulletin of Economics and Statistics*, vol. 49(3).

Part IX

The International Dimension

18 How Valid is International Keynesianism?

W. Max Corden

18.1 INTRODUCTION

It is often argued that US demand expansion and the US current account deficit have been 'supporting' world demand and hence output and employment outside the United States. A country that runs a deficit is said to be making a 'contribution' to the world economy while Japan and Germany, with their surpluses, are failing to do so and deserve some reprimand. More generally, even when current accounts stay constant, it is sometimes argued that economic expansion in one country benefits its trading partners by allowing them to expand, this being the so-called 'locomotive theory'. Similarly, a country that contracts demand is damaging its neighbours. All this is believed to be true even when exchange rates float or are readily adjusted since all the recent discussions have taken place in a floating exchange rate context.

I shall call this line of thought 'international Keynesianism'. It can be decomposed into two elements. First, there is 'domestic Keynesianism', namely the view that management of aggregate nominal demand for domestically produced goods and services is possible, and can affect domestic output and employment over a worthwhile or significant period: a rise in demand raises output while not bringing about an offsetting reduction later. Secondly, there is the international aspect: the benefits of demand expansion spill over abroad. Here I shall focus on the second aspect since the first aspect is discussed in the papers of other contributors. If there is no sound case for domestic Keynesianism then presumably there will be no case for its international extension.[1]

18.2 INTERNATIONAL KEYNESIANISM MARK I

In the 1960s international Keynesianism – what I shall call the Mark I version – seemed obvious. The validity of domestic Keynesianism was of course assumed, as were fixed exchange rates. If there was unemployment and excess capacity the appropriate policy for any one country was to expand aggregate nominal demand. Some of the extra demand would spill over into imports, and also possibly into domestic demand for goods that might otherwise be exported, so that a balance of payments problem might emerge. The argument as it used to be put was that a surplus country did not really have a balance-of-payments constraint and possibly not even a target. It needed to worry only about its 'internal balance' target. Nor, for that matter, did the United States have a constraint even if she was in deficit because of the willingness of other countries to hold dollars. The constraint was faced by countries other than the United States which were below their internal balance targets only because unilateral demand expansion would create a balance-of-payments problem for them. It was certainly the standard British view that Britain was normally in this position.

For a country like Britain a problem of inadequate demand could then be resolved by demand expansion abroad. If her trading partners expanded demand this would raise British exports, bring Britain closer to the internal balance target and put her current account into surplus. If she then supplemented the foreign demand expansion with some domestic demand expansion she could move even closer to the internal balance target while the current account surplus would be eliminated. Hence, concerted demand expansion would allow Britain to move closer to or even attain internal balance while maintaining external balance. The essential point was that any country that expanded aggregate demand would be likely to modify or remove the balance-of-payments constraint for other countries and hence would be doing these other countries a service. This was the essence of international Keynesianism.

If one recalls that the foreign country which British commentators usually had in mind was Germany, the persistent surplus country in the 1960s, one realises how history repeats itself. Now the Americans rather than the British are urging Germany to expand. The present position is not that the United States wishes to engage in domestic demand expansion but rather that she wishes to improve her current account position without having to depart from internal balance. It is worth mentioning the similarity here only to justify the rather thorough exposition of Mark I international Keynesianism.

18.3 A FALSE TRAIL: THE MONETARY-FISCAL POLICY MIX

At one stage there seemed to be a way out of the dilemma, a way out that did not require departing from the fixed exchange rate assumption but that was actually a false trail. This was the Mundellian monetary-fiscal policy mix approach.

A country that wished to expand demand unilaterally without creating a balance-of-payments problem was recommended to combine fiscal and monetary policy so that on balance the interest rate would rise and sufficient capital inflow would be attracted to finance the current account deficit resulting from the net aggregate demand expansion. There were now two instruments – fiscal policy and monetary policy – aimed at the two targets of internal and external balance. External balance was defined now as referring not to the current account but rather to the overall balance, which took into account private capital flows.

This approach implied that only the overall balance mattered – i.e., that external balance required that the reserves did not have to be run down or the government did not have to borrow abroad. A government that started with the situation described above (unemployment and external balance as redefined) and followed this prescription would be borrowing on the domestic market to finance its budget deficit while the private sector would be borrowing abroad to finance the current account deficit. In effect the budget deficit would be financed abroad. In the presence of an international capital market the current account is indeed no longer the absolute constraint it used to be, but this is about as far as one can go in regarding this approach as a solution to the central problem. The Mundellian policy-mix approach ignores the implications of sustained budget and current account deficits.

18.4 THE SOLUTION: FLEXIBLE EXCHANGE RATES

The obvious solution was seen to be to allow the exchange rate to float or at least to allow it to become an instrument of policy. For a given aggregate demand level abroad, a country that wished to expand domestic demand would be free to do so once it could also depreciate the exchange rate so as to maintain the current account at a desired level. A 'switching' policy as well as an expenditure-increasing policy was required. The point seemed obvious and is still obvious. This was the classic argument for flexible exchange rates.

Floating or flexible exchange rates do give countries some independence. Germany may refuse to expand demand either because it believes it has already attained internal balance or because it simply does not believe in domestic Keynesianism. But this need not prevent the United States from expanding demand while maintaining a constant current account. It is necessary only to ensure that the dollar depreciates at the same time. Of course it may not be possible to attain a precise current account outcome in the short run; changing elasticities over time, J-curves and such like, have to be taken into account. But a combination of US monetary and fiscal expansion could bring about both depreciation and the required demand expansion.

It seems to follow that while we may retain a belief in domestic Keynesianism, there is no longer any justification for international Keynesianism when exchange rates can be altered or float.

The present situation is that the United States wishes to see her current account deficit reduced while maintaining internal balance at home. This requires fiscal contraction in the US to reduce aggregate demand and monetary expansion to depreciate the exchange rate. Sufficient depreciation may already have taken place and we may just be waiting for its effects. The decline in demand for US goods and services resulting from the fiscal contraction would be offset by the switching of the pattern of demand away from foreign goods toward domestic goods resulting from the depreciation. Monetary expansion would also affect aggregate demand (through lower interest rates stimulating investment) while fiscal contraction may contribute to the depreciation. In any case, US policy alone, using two instruments of policy, could improve the current account while maintaining internal balance.

If the United States engaged in fiscal contraction so as to reduce or even eliminate the current account deficit German and Japanese export industries would certainly suffer from a decline in demand and, with aggregate demand in Germany and Japan given, the outcome would be deflationary in both countries. But this does not provide support for international Keynesianism. If the German and Japanese authorities believed in domestic Keynesianism and managed their policy instruments flexibly so as to maintain internal balance they could expand domestic demand to compensate for the loss of foreign demand. For example, fiscal expansion in these countries could compensate for fiscal contraction in the United States.

This may sound a little naive since many considerations have clearly been ignored here. Firstly, German and Japanese authorities may not believe in domestic Keynesianism. They may believe that any domestically-generated demand expansion would stimulate inflationary expectations, and hence is to be avoided. Thus they may feel unable to replace foreign with domestic demand. Secondly, even if they do expand domestic demand, the pattern of demand would change from tradables to non-tradables, and the Japanese and German export industries do have reason to be grateful to the United States and other countries that have made it possible for Germany and Japan to run current account surpluses for prolonged periods.

Nevertheless, one conclusion surely stands. Suppose we adhere to the simplest Keynesian approach, namely that in the presence of involuntary unemployment and excess capacity an increase in demand for domestically-produced goods and services would increase domestic output and employment and that this general result is independent of any changes in real wages that might eventuate. Then flexible or floating exchange rates do provide a kind of aggregate-demand policy independence and hence destroy the basis for international Keynesianism Mark I. For any given macroeconomic policies abroad, and allowing for lags and the usual fine-tuning problems, it is open to the monetary and fiscal authorities in any country to manage the level of nominal demand for the goods and services of their own country as they wish. But the qualification about real wages is not minor and provides the clue to the later step in the argument which will provide the foundation for international Keynesianism Mark II.

It has become trite to point out that flexible exchange rates do not insulate countries from their trading and investment partners. There are still links through trade and through the capital market. Demand expansion by Germany and Japan might improve the US terms of trade. Furthermore it might raise or lower world interest rates, and so affect interest rates in the United States. It may affect the relative profitability of tradable and non-tradable industries in the United States. But this does not alter our main conclusion.

When one says that with flexible exchange rates, demand expansion abroad is not necessary to allow demand expansion at home one is not asserting that flexible exchange rates create complete insulation. But for any given terms of trade and given world interest rates, or for any given world reaction functions, they allow the United States or any other country to follow domestic policies of expansion or contraction which (given time for adjustment) could maintain the current account at a desired level. Of course the world reaction functions must not be such as to prevent the desired current account outcome, and this is a matter that I shall come to later.

18.5   AN INTERLUDE: KEYNESIANISM AND REAL WAGES

Before going on to international Keynesianism Mark II an interlude about the relationship between Keynesian policies and real wages is necessary.

In the *General Theory* a nominal demand expansion was assumed to raise prices relative to nominal wages. The neoclassical diminishing returns assumption was built into the model. The increase in employment resulting from demand expansion therefore involved a decline in real wages.[2] It seems indeed a very neoclassical and, in current terms, non-Keynesian conclusion to suggest that employment can only increase if real wages fall. The novelty of Keynes's analysis relative to its neoclassical alternative was that the required decline in real wages was assumed not to be attainable by a decline in nominal wages, either because the latter were rigid downwards or because, for dynamic reasons, a decline in nominal wage would lead to a faster fall in nominal demand. Hence nominal demand expansion was required to increase employment.

This aspect of the model – that extra employment required a fall in real wages – was not given any significance in the *General Theory*. Apart from a brief reference to the Australian policy of wage indexation, the question of real wage rigidity downward did not arise. Furthermore, the model which came to be subsequently accepted as Keynesian and which appeared in most textbooks, assumed constant costs and mark-up pricing. This might be called the 'popular Keynesian model', as distinct from the 'General Theory model'. In this model, which Keynes himself seemed subsequently to accept, real wages might vary during the cycle but not along standard neoclassical lines. In particular, extra employment did not necessarily involve a decline in real wages.

Today we should realise that the General Theory model is far more appropriate than the popular Keynesian model. Normally, demand expansion will raise output and employment only if real wages fall as a result, at least relative to trend and other than in the very short run. The Keynesian policy conclusion that nominal demand expansion can increase employment follows if prices are more flexible upwards than are nominal wages. If nominal wages were sufficiently flexible downwards in response to labour market conditions nominal demand expansion would not be needed to increase employment, while if nominal wages adjusted rapidly upwards to maintain real wages at their initial level, nominal demand expansion would fail to increase employment.

All this is very relevant when we consider the open economy with a flexible exchange rate. Suppose that constant costs and mark-up pricing really did apply to home-produced goods, as was believed – or at least assumed in the popular Keynesian model – for so long. With given nominal wages unilateral demand expansion would lead to increased output and employment. In addition it would have to lead to depreciation of the exchange rate to avoid the current account deterioration that would otherwise result. The depreciation would raise the domestic price level and thus reduce real wages.[3]

While we have made here the popular Keynesian assumption of constant costs and mark-up pricing, for an open economy with a flexible exchange rate we have obtained the important General Theory result that an increase in employment requires a fall in real wages. The reason is that demand expansion leads to depreciation and the depreciation lowers real wages. If the General Theory assumption of diminishing returns actually applied to home-produced goods and services in general (as I believe that it does) the conclusion that unilateral nominal demand expansion has to lower real wages if it is to increase employment is strengthened by introducing the exchange rate effect.[4]

It follows that if there were explicit or implicit wage indexation, so that nominal wages rose sufficiently for real wages to be restored in due course, a general rise in nominal demand would not lead to a sustained rise (or possibly any rise) in employment. Finally the wage and price levels would rise sufficiently to restore the original level of real demand and the real exchange rate.

We have considered two extreme cases of wage behaviour. At one extreme the nominal wage is completely rigid; an expansion of demand will then increase employment and the fact that it happens also to lower real wages is just incidental and, in fact, hardly relevant for macroeconomic policy. At the other extreme, the real wage is rigid; Keynesian demand expansion policy cannot then affect employment. The final step is to introduce the familiar intermediate situation, where a demand expansion successfully causes prices to rise ahead of wages but wages follow with a lag.

Continuous nominal demand expansion can then keep real wages lower than otherwise, at least for some time, until the labour market adjusts. A short-term 'Phillips curve' trade-off between employment and inflation then emerges. (This depends, among other things, on the length of wage contracts and on the 'rationality' of expectations in the labour market.) If the nominal wage increase in any given period is closely related to the gap between actual and desired real wages anything that lowers actual real wages at a given level of employment – such as depreciation of the exchange rate – worsens the trade-off. This last point lays the foundations for international Keynesianism Mark II.

18.6 INTERNATIONAL KEYNESIANISM MARK II

International Keynesianism Mark I applied to a world of fixed exchange rates. Even in that world exchange rates were not absolutely fixed. Britain did devalue twice and France four times. But one could regard the commitment to fixed exchange rates as rather strong. International Keynesianism Mark II applies to a world where exchange rates between major currencies float or are readily adjusted, but where large depreciations are usually regarded as undesirable.

Any country can certainly expand nominal demand unilaterally while maintaining the current account at an initial level. Given capital mobility, this would be brought about by some combination of fiscal and monetary expansion.[5] But this would involve depreciation of its currency and lower real wages and – given some responsiveness of nominal wages to prices and, in turn, prices to wages – would increase inflation. The key point now is that if the country's trading partners expanded demand at the time, the depreciation might be avoided. Thus the authorities of a country where there is a deficiency of demand are likely to welcome demand expansion by its partners. This is subject to some qualifications to be discussed below. But the basic idea of this approach is that the more other countries expand at the same time the less the currency depreciates when the country's own demand is expanded, and thus the less inflation there would be at home for a given increase in employment.

This is the basis for the 'locomotive theory' where expansion in real terms by one large economy makes it easier for others to expand. Demand expansion by Germany and other countries increases demand for US goods and so – given the underlying Keynesian assumption – raises employment in the United States. But this is not a sufficient reason for the United States to welcome German expansion since employment at home could have been increased by expansion of domestic (rather than foreign) demand. There is no need to wait upon Germany. This was the message of the case for flexible rates expounded above. The point of international Keynesianism Mark II is that unilateral US expansion would lead to depreciation of the dollar if the current account is not to deteriorate, hence to a decline in the US terms of trade, to a fall in real wages and thus to 'inflationary pressures' – i.e., increases in nominal wages requiring further expansion of nominal demand to sustain the rise in employment, and so on.

International Keynesianism Mark II welcomes a foreign demand expansion not because it avoids a current account deterioration that might otherwise result from domestic expansion (as with international Keynesianism Mark I) but because it avoids depreciation and hence adverse terms of trade and real wage effects. It results from a situation where depreciation is permitted and indeed happens all the time, but where it is considered to have adverse effects.

Many of the normative arguments that apply to the world of fixed exchange rates thus also apply, though in a much modified form, to the world of floating rates. Countries can engage in unilateral demand expansion – and often do – and since the exchange rate can depreciate they can avoid a balance-of-payments constraint. Hence concerted international expansion is certainly not essential. But unilateral expansion involves some costs to the expanding country – essentially deteriorating terms of trade and real wages – that can be avoided by concerted expansion.

All this is subject to some qualifications and warnings.

Firstly, the government of a country may not wish to engage in domestic nominal demand expansion at all because it may not believe that such nominal expansion would have any worthwhile output-expanding effects, possibly because real wages would be maintained by explicit or implicit indexation. In other words, it may not subscribe to '*General Theory* Keynesianism'. Alternatively, it may believe that any short-run gains would be outweighed by later losses as attempts are made to rein in inflation that was originally stimulated by the demand expansion. It is important not to ignore these potential later losses.

Secondly, a country would not benefit through the terms of trade improvement resulting from nominal demand expansion abroad if this nominal expansion did not have any significant real effects abroad, or if short-term benefits abroad were offset by later losses as inflation is reined in there.

Thirdly, once one allows for more than two countries, real expansion in one country (e.g. Germany) may not improve the terms of trade of a second country (e.g. the United States) because the two countries may be competitive rather than complementary in world markets. The terms of trade of a third country, or a group of countries, may improve, but this may have adverse effects on the United States. In other words, instead of positive transmission, there may be negative transmission. This draws attention to the general point that concerted expansion by industrial countries may improve the terms of trade of commodity exporters relative to industrial countries as a group, while any individual industrial country may be adversely affected by the real expansion of another industrial country.

Finally, even if these three considerations were not thought to be relevant, the foreign country may not wish to engage in domestic demand expansion because it places high weight on the adverse effects of inflation. Hence, concerted expansion may not be desirable from its point of view. But this leads directly to the question of policy co-ordination.

18.7 IS THERE A NEED FOR INTERNATIONAL MACROECONOMIC POLICY CO-ORDINATION?

The popular concept of macroeconomic policy co-ordination can actually be given at least three meanings. First, it can refer to information exchange, secondly it can refer to (what might be called) 'mutual policy modification', and thirdly it can refer to 'current account compatibility'. One particular version of the second meaning rests upon international Keynesianism Mark II, and seems to follow directly from the preceding discussion.

18.7.1 Information exchange

In the first case the aim is to ensure that governments are aware of the policies others intend to embark upon, so that they can make their own adjustments to aggregate demand in good time. For example, the United States may intend to engage in fiscal contraction with the aim of reducing her current account deficit. This is likely to have a contractionary effect in other countries and would then call for monetary or fiscal expansion (or both) there. If other countries were concerned about maintaining internal balance they would need no urging to pursue such policies; they would just require notice that there is a need for the policies, bearing in mind the lags in the fine-tuning process.

The following point with regard to co-ordination is sometimes made. It is argued that the US current account deficit needs to be reduced. Therefore, it is said, in the United States the excess of expenditures over incomes needs to fall and in other countries (i.e. primarily Germany and Japan) expenditures need to increase relative to incomes. Co-ordination is then interpreted to mean that both sides make the appropriate expenditure adjustment, the United States reducing her fiscal deficit and the others increasing theirs. The implicit assumption is that incomes in both countries stay constant –i.e., that internal balance is maintained. The US policy change does then require to be accompanied by an explicit German or Japanese policy change essentially because of the internal balance targets.

On the other hand, no explicit policy changes in the other countries would be needed if they were not concerned with internal balance. A reduction of the US budget deficit would improve the US current account even if fiscal policies and money supplies had stayed constant in the other countries. This assumes that the other countries do not have current account targets of their own but accept the US target. (The case where many or all countries have current account targets will be discussed later.) The reduced interest rate resulting from the US fiscal contraction would lead to some rise in investment in Germany and Japan. In addition the appreciation of their currencies brought about by the US fiscal contraction would have deflationary effects (probably not offset by the effects of higher investment), so that savings would fall. The combination of higher investment and lower savings would produce reductions in German and Japanese current account surpluses. But this would be achieved at the cost of deflation in these countries.[6]

The conclusion is that co-ordination in the form of information exchange is particularly needed when countries have the maintenance of internal balance as an objective of policy. Policy adjustments take time to arrange and to take effect, so that it is certainly desirable that governments get notice of policy shocks coming from abroad. Furthermore, if the United States is to adjust her own monetary policies appropriately to fit in with a given fiscal policy change she needs to know what the German and Japanese monetary and fiscal policy responses will be.[7]

18.7.2   Mutual policy modification

The second interpretation of the concept of international macroeconomic policy co-ordination is the one that is usually given in the theoretical literature on this subject. As there is such an extensive literature it is only discussed briefly here.[8] It is assumed that in the absence of co-ordination governments do have the necessary information but that they follow policies that are in their own narrow interests and neglect adverse or favourable spillover effects (externalities) on other countries. They do take into account the expected effects on themselves of foreign repercussions resulting from the original policy changes, but do not take into account the interests of other countries. There is then scope for countries to strike mutually beneficial bargains: each might modify its policies at least marginally to benefit the other and finally they might all be better off – i.e., there could be a Pareto improvement.

Various examples of this possibility can be given, and can be found in the theoretical literature. The spillover effect might concern exchange rate stability. This case will be discussed separately below. Here the case can be considered which is most relevant for the present discussion, namely the spillover that follows from international Keynesianism Mark II, and which has been the basis for one particular advocacy of macroeconomic policy co-ordination.

In a world of flexible or floating exchange rates, the basic idea, as already discussed, is that any large country that expands its economy while aiming to maintain its current account unchanged will improve the terms of trade of other countries (through appreciation of their exchange rates), hence allows their real wages to rise for given employment, and thus improves their inflation-employment trade-offs. The other countries then feel freer to expand themselves. Thus one country's expansion generates a favourable spillover for other countries. There is positive transmission of economic expansion. If they all expand together real exchange rates and hence terms of trade may not need to change much, if at all. Unless there is co-ordination each country will ignore the benefits that it creates for its neighbours through such expansion, and therefore it will expand less than would be optimal for the world as a whole.

This particular argument for co-ordination rests completely on international Keynesianism Mark II. As expounded more fully in the new literature of international co-ordination theory, in the absence of co-ordination an equilibrium might be attained where each country assumes the others' policies given (a Nash equilibrium). Of course, the assumption that in the absence of co-ordination policy-makers in one country would always assume that policies in another country are given (i.e. that these would be independent of their own actions) is itself rather crude. Game theory suggests complicated dynamic interactions in the absence of co-ordination. In any case, co-ordination can generally lead to an outcome where all participating countries are better off (a Pareto improvement).

These conclusions are subject to various qualifications noted earlier. It is possible that the fundamental assumptions of domestic Keynesianism – that nominal demand expansion would raise real output in the short run – do not apply. The purpose here is only to bring out the international implications of domestic Keynesianism, leaving aside the large question of how appropriate the latter is. Even the assumptions of domestic Keynesianism were appropriate, it does not follow that concerted expansion is necessarily desirable: it all depends on the starting point. A country may have expanded too much – with inflationary consequences – even when favourable effects on other countries are taken into account. In addition, transmission may be negative rather than positive; so that one country's expansion worsens another's terms of trade. Finally, the future adverse effects of inflation resulting from another country's current economic expansion need to be taken into account. For all these reasons, there is no advocacy of concerted expansion here.

With regard to co-ordination, one should really say that co-ordination can lead to an outcome *where all participating governments consider themselves* to be better off as a result. Given that the governments may have the 'wrong' models or social welfare functions (however defined) one cannot be sure that the outcomes would be objectively better.

This qualification takes into account the possibility that there are differences of view – i.e., differences in implicit models or in social welfare functions – among governments or as between governments and the 'objective' independent observer, and also that the interests of governments and their citizens might differ. If political decision-makers were prone to be too expansionary from a national-interest point of view – being held back in their politically-motivated expansionism only by the fear of depreciation of the exchange rate – then the net effect of co-ordination as analysed here might be adverse.

18.7.3 Current account compatibility

A third concept of co-ordination concerns the achievement of current account targets that are mutually compatible. It is worth noting that this concept or objective is not directly connected with the issue of international Keynesianism. Therefore it is only introduced here for completeness. Apart from having their internal balance targets, conceivably all countries could also have current account targets. The discussion so far assumed that only some countries have such targets or constraints. Clearly they cannot all achieve absolute targets independently chosen. This used to be called the $n-1$ problem. It was said that countries other than the United States could and did have targets (though not with regard to bilateral balances) while the United States was the 'nth' country that balanced the system by not having a target. The need for co-ordination rises if there is no 'nth' country willing to accept the current account outcome implicit in other countries' targets, or if some of the targets are bilateral. This issue is of particular interest at present because there is indeed widespread concern in the United States about her current account position and prospects, and some policy proposals imply a degree of 'current account targeting', even of a bilateral character.

To highlight the issue and also relate it to the previous discussion, let us imagine a two-country situation where the United States wishes to eliminate her current account deficit but Japan does not wish to give up her surplus. We assume flexible exchange rates and capital mobility. Both countries have internal balance targets of their own.

Suppose the United States reduced her fiscal deficit and (if necessary) compensated with some monetary expansion to maintain internal balance at home. If there is no policy change in Japan this will depreciate the dollar, reduce the current account imbalance and probably have a deflationary effect in Japan. We can then suppose that Japan uses some combination of expansionary fiscal and monetary policy to restore internal balance. When fiscal policy is used the current account imbalance will be reduced further and when monetary policy is used it is likely to modify the initial effect – i.e., increase the current account imbalance through depreciating the yen.

If the US authorities expected this Japanese policy reaction they could have taken it into account when they initially set their own policies. Alternatively, they might adjust their policies as the Japanese reaction becomes apparent. In any case, there is no compatibility problem provided the Japanese have only an internal balance target but do not have a current account target of their own.

But, suppose the Japanese did have a current account target, and that their target was to avoid any reduction in the current account surplus while still consistently maintaining internal balance. As noted above, the first impact of the US policy change is to reduce the Japanese surplus and produce deflation. To get back to internal balance and their own current account target the Japanese could again use a combination of fiscal and monetary policy. Some monetary expansion combined with fiscal contraction (both depreciating the yen) would probably be needed – in fact the same policies as the United States had engaged in. One could then imagine the United States following with more fiscal contraction and monetary expansion to get the dollar down again, and envisage a process of competitive depreciation through competition in fiscal restraint and monetary expansion. But this is a fanciful story and a natural solution would be to have policy co-ordination or an agreement designed to establish compatible current account targets.

The question really is whether it is sensible for countries to have current account targets which then require to be set by mutual agreement. An alternative view, to which I incline, is that they might have budget deficit targets, depending on various 'structural' or optimal public borrowing considerations (which should not really be independent of world interest rates), and perhaps some kind of internal balance targets, roughly defined. But current accounts and real exchange rates should emerge out of the international general equilibrium system.[9]

This approach is worth spelling out. Let us suppose that there is a reduction in the US fiscal deficit but no change in the fiscal policies of other countries. Exchange rates are flexible and monetary policies aim to maintain domestic demand. The reduced US fiscal deficit would lower world interest rates and stimulate or 'crowd-in' private investment in many countries (supported, if necessary, by some monetary expansion). If the increased investment took place mainly in the United States, the US current account might stay in large deficit. Otherwise the location of the current account deficits or reduced surpluses elsewhere that are needed to make possible a lower US current account deficit would depend on where the new investment opportunities emerged. Countries where investment greatly increased would go into current account deficit. The pattern of current account balances resulting from the US fiscal contraction would thus be determined by the market. It would not be necessary to allocate or co-ordinate changes in current account balances in advance.

18.7.4 Real exchange rate stabilisation

A fourth concept of macroeconomic policy co-ordination has as its objective the stabilisation of exchange rates.[10] There have recently been some well-known agreements between finance ministers of the major industrial countries where this has been the proclaimed objective. Implicitly at least, the aim is to stabilise, or moderate fluctuations in, real and not just nominal exchange rates. The popular objections to large medium-term fluctuations in real exchange rates need hardly be restated here; the concern is, above all, with the adverse effects of real appreciation on the profitability of tradable goods industries and the adverse effects of depreciation on real wages and the inflationary pressures generated as a result.

The basic idea is that countries should adjust their fiscal or monetary policies, or both, to take into account common exchange rate objectives. If fiscal policy is constrained by long-term structural (optimal public borrowing) objectives as in Germany and Japan, or is constrained politically as in the United States, this means that monetary policy in each country has to take into account two objectives: internal balance – itself possibly a compromise between a price stability aim and a short-term Keynesian concern with effects on economic activity – and the common exchange rate objective.

We might imagine a situation where the governments of Germany and the United States agree that the dollar should depreciate more than has resulted from monetary policies in each country that are targeted on internal balance (as this target is conceived by the government concerned). Policy co-ordination in the form of mutual policy modification then requires Germany to tighten its monetary policy somewhat, hence getting more unemployment than it really wants, and the United States to loosen its monetary policy, hence leading to increased domestic inflationary pressures. Both policy modifications will contribute to depreciation of the dollar. If the social welfare function in each country contains both an internal balance objective and the common exchange rate objective, mutual policy modification which causes each country to depart somewhat from its internal balance objective can lead to an outcome where both are better off.

Alternatively, monetary policy in each country might be targeted on internal balance while fiscal policies are modified to take into account the common exchange rate objective.[11] If one took the non-Keynesian view that, other than in the very short run, monetary policies cannot affect real economic variables – and hence cannot affect real exchange rates – fiscal policy co-ordination would be the only possible form of co-ordination when there is a medium-run real exchange rate objective.

In that case, given that dollar depreciation is desired by both countries, Germany would expand its fiscal policy relative to its preferred stance from other (structural or political) points of view, while the United States would have a more contractionary fiscal policy than otherwise. Thus each would somewhat adjust its fiscal policy to take into account the common exchange rate objective. Again, co-ordination in the forms of mutual policy modifications – this time of fiscal policy – could finally make both countries better off. We have thus another possible argument for policy co-ordination which does not rest on domestic or international Keynesianism.

18.8 CONCLUSION

I have simply assumed here the validity or relevance of domestic Keynesianism and taken off from there. For those who believe that Keynesian demand management policies are still relevant or useful for the short run but not the medium or long run the whole discussion should then be interpreted as referring only to this short run. It also means that any co-ordination activities based on Keynesianism Mark I or Mark II have to be speedy since the short-run circumstances which possibly justify them would otherwise change before effects of co-ordination emerge.

The first step was to expound the familiar fixed exchange rate international Keynesianism Mark I, showing that if the current account is a constraint expansion in one country depends on expansion by others. In the prescence of an international capital market, this conclusion has to be modified somewhat since current account imbalances can be financed for a time by the capital market (the Mundellian fiscal-monetary policy mix approach) but budget deficit and current account effects still cannot be ignored. It was then shown that the case for international Keynesianism Mark I seems to disappear once flexible exchange rates are allowed for, since countries could expand unilaterally while keeping their current accounts in balance or at a desired level.

The role of real wages in the *General Theory* and the relevance of real wages for the Keynesian recommendations were then introduced. This led to to international Keynesianism Mark II, applying to a flexible exchange rate world. Unilateral expansion is now possible: there is no balance-of-payments constraint as in the simplest Mark I version. But unilateral expansion involves exchange rate depreciation, and hence a cost, namely deteriorating terms of trade and real wages. This cost can be avoided or modified by other countries expanding at the same time. One country's expansion shifts the inflation-unemployment trade-off of its trading partners in a favourable direction. This then led to one particular version of the international macroeconomic policy co-ordination concept, namely 'mutual policy modification' in the interests of expansion. With positive transmission a large expanding economy is a 'locomotive' for others.

Finally, other versions of the co-ordination concept have been discussed, namely information exchange – which is necessary if countries wish to maintain internal balance when there are policy shocks emanating from other countries – and current account compatibility and real exchange rate stabilisation, both of which raise important issues that arise even when domestic and international Keynesianism do not apply at all.

Notes

1. On the subject of domestic Keynesianism (defined here as a policy approach) I am completely pragmatic. In some circumstances this approach is appropriate for a short-run period that is long enough to be worthwhile to justify some demand management policies. Above all, it depends on labour market conditions.
2. This feature of the *General Theory* has sometimes been forgotten. See pp. 17–18 and many other places, especially Chapter 19. ' . . . in general, an increase in employment can only occur to the accompaniment of a decline in the rate of real wages' (Keynes, 1936, p. 17).
3. With international capital mobility it may not be necessary to avoid a current account deterioration, at least in the short run, since capital inflows can finance a deficit. This is the Mundellian argument discussed above. Demand expansion can take the form of fiscal expansion, which would actually appreciate the exchange rate. The point here is that if the current account is not to deteriorate, there has to be a depreciation.
4. It has to be stressed that the fall in real wages is relative to trend and 'other things equal'. At the conference it was pointed out that in some circumstances an absolute fall in real wages may not be required; moderation in an increase that might otherwise have taken place may be enough.
5. Fiscal expansion on its own would worsen the current account and monetary expansion on its own would normally improve it, in the latter case because of the depreciation induced by lower interest rates. If monetary expansion worsened the current account in spite of the depreciation it induces because a sufficient increase in domestic investment was stimulated by the lower interest rates, then fiscal expansion would need to be accompanied by some monetary contraction. (This simple approach could be complicated by the development of inflationary expectations. Agents in the markets may think that the demand expansion will not be once-and-for-all, or that the starting point is not a Keynesian situation of unemployment and excess capacity.)
6. It is possible that the deflationary effect of appreciation causes German and Japanese investment to decline – in spite of the decline in the interest rate – and this could conceivably be sufficient to offset the decline in savings and so lead, paradoxically, to increases in their surpluses. This is an accelerator effect.
7. The following sceptical argument was made at the conference. What scope is there really for information exchange at international meetings of officials? Likely longer-term changes are widely discussed in each country and could be known in other countries without any explicit co-ordination procedures.

Prospective policy changes are, in any case, uncertain. As for information exchange about firm short-term policy decisions which have not yet been made public at home (for example, the contents of a prospective UK budget), it is surely unlikely that officials will feel free to reveal these to foreign officials before they are revealed, for example, to their own legislators. In my view, this consideration does not rule out a useful comparison or integration of forecasts based on proclaimed or constant policies, and it does not rule out the general values of information interchange, including interchange about broad policy attitudes.

8. See Cooper (1984) and various contributions in Buiter and Marston (1985). The discussion in this section is based mainly on my own contribution in Buiter and Marston (1985).

9. In the discussion in Section 18.3 of the Mundellian fiscal-monetary policy mix approach (applying to a fixed exchange rate regime) it was concluded that sustained budget deficit and current account outcomes could not be ignored. If the argument here is accepted one might argue that the basic problem would be a sustained fiscal deficit, the current account outcome just being a by-product.

10. Strictly, it is one version of the case for co-ordination in the form of 'mutual policy modification', the other version – resting on international Keynesianism Mark II – having been discussed above.

11. This particular co-ordination case is analysed in Corden (1986).

References

BUITER, W. H. and R. C. MARSTON (eds) (1985) *International Economic Policy Coordination*, Centre for Economic Policy Research (Cambridge, England: Cambridge University Presss).

COOPER, R. N. (1984) 'Economic Interdependence and Coordination of Economic Policies', in R. Jones and P. B. Kenen (eds), *Handbook on International Economics*, vol. II (Amsterdam: North-Holland).

CORDEN, W. M. (1986) 'Fiscal Policies, Current Accounts and Real Exchange Rates: in Search of a Logic of International Policy Coordination', *Weltwirtschaftliches Archiv*, Band 122, Heft 3.

KEYNES, J. M. (1936) *The General Theory of Employment, Interest and Money* (London: Macmillan).

Part X

Keynes and UK and German Economic Policy

19 The Irrelevance of Keynes to German Economic Policy and to International Economic Co-operation in the 1980s

Ernst Helmstädter

The West German economy has a very significant impact on the world economy, so the potential international repercussions of all domestic economic measures must be taken into account. Such repercussions may occur at two levels: they may concern the world at large, or they may be restricted to Europe. West Germany produces a relatively small fraction of world output, but a considerable proportion of the output of the European Economic Community. However at the world level the D-Mark has become a key currency with an importance that transcends Germany's relatively modest share of world production, and West Germany has become one of the principal participants in international discussions which seek to arrive at the gradual evolution of new approaches to policy at both the European and the world level.

In the 1980s the European Monetary System has continued to evolve and considerable progress towards monetary stabilisation and fiscal consolidation has been achieved at the European level. This progress would have been impossible without West Germany's lead in the implementation of appropriate domestic measures within the context of its monetary and fiscal policies. There has in contrast been no such progress in the world economy where the tendency has been towards fiscal and exchange rate destabilisation. Owing to fluctuations in exchange rates and in the prices of essential raw materials, payments balances on current account have been in significant disequilibrium for more than a decade; the former international debtors have found it impossible to reduce what they owe, while the United States has added a further dimension to international debt through its enormous borrowings.

The United States is now hoping that the relatively stable European economies will give some stimulus to global trade. It is believed that Germany could lead this move towards expansion and some of our European partners have joined their voices to the international chorus which is requesting that we take this initiative. They believe that the generally high rate of world unemployment calls for new expansionary forces, and the solution is believed to lie in concerted action in favour of economic growth and employment.

What is being asked could in one sense be regarded as what Max Corden calls 'International Keynesianism Mark I' in Chapter 18, namely, concerted action to expand aggregate demand by a number of countries in a financial system where exchange rates are fixed, for this is broadly the situation within the European Monetary System. With regard to the world economy as a whole however, the most significant exchange rates are variable, so Corden's 'International Keynesianism Mark II' appears to provide a more appropriate description of what is being proposed. What would be our chances of success if an economic strategy based on concerted expansion by those of the world's economies which now enjoy payments surpluses were to be adopted? Is such a Keynesian strategy the most appropriate approach to the world's financial imbalances and higher general levels of unemployment, or is it also possible to stimulate growth through a non-Keynesian economic strategy?

An attempt to answer this question is put forward in this chapter on the basis of West German experience. It draws heavily on the accumulated analysis of the German Council of Economic Experts of which I became a Member in 1983. Since 1963 this committee has been appointed to advise West German governments on the development of the economy. There has been a remarkable continuity of thought since the first report in 1964 which was strongly influenced by the analysis of Herbert Giersch, one of the Council's three academic Members when it was set up by Chancellor Adenauer. The views and findings in the Council's most recent report follow naturally from those which have been advocated over a period of years. The Council's advice has occasionally been critical of the policy stance of German Socialist-Liberal coalition governments, while its position has coincided to a considerable extent with those of the present Christian Democrat-Liberal coalition government and of the Bundesbank.

In this chapter the approach to economic policy which has guided the thinking of the Council since Giersch's seminal contribution in 1963–9 will first be set out, because it is an approach to economic policy which is not widely understood outside Germany (although other countries including Britain appear to have begun to adopt a quite similar approach in the 1980s). It will then be explained how Germany is likely to react to international pressures to co-operate in an international Keynesian approach to the world's present economic imbalances, and what the outcome of such co-operation would be likely to be.

19.1 THE APPROACH TO ECONOMIC POLICY OF THE GERMAN COUNCIL OF ECONOMIC EXPERTS

In its annual report for 1976/77 the German Council of Economic Experts deliberately assumed a position which went beyond a Keynesian approach. The Council insisted that 'demand-oriented overall management' should be supplemented by a 'supply-oriented policy'.

> The main purpose of aggregate demand management is to ensure that existing productive potential remains as well-balanced as possible and is utilised sufficiently; and by the same token the aim of a supply-oriented policy is to improve conditions for investment and to modify the structure of production so that adequate growth and a high level of employment appear once more within the realms of possibility. (para. 284)

We can go back to the Council's first reports in Giersch's time to see the origins of our belief that the level of employment depends primarily on supply-side and not demand-side considerations. Giersch has told us that he took advantage of a period of enforced leisure in the United Kingdom in 1944–45 to read the two great English economic classics, Smith's *Wealth of Nations* and Keynes's *General Theory*. His reading of Adam Smith's book became 'crucial for my view of the world' (Giersch, 1986, p. 255), but he responded less favourably to the *General Theory*, and still less favourably to Joan Robinson who came to Munster shortly after the war to 'expound a vulgar Keynesianism . . . It was like Hamlet without the Prince of Denmark: a theory and a policy of full employment without wages' (Giersch, 1986, p. 257). At the same time American Keynesians were visiting Germany and recommending 'expansionist policies, erroneously assuming that we had Keynesian unemployment rather than the classical variety arising from the influx of refugees and the physical destruction of the capital stock' (Giersch, 1986, p. 257).

By the time he became a founder Member of our Council of Economic Experts Giersch had evolved an approach to the assignment problem which was very different from that of the Keynesian Americans who would have created massive inflation in the Germany of the late 1940s if their advice had actually been followed. In this approach which gradually evolved after 1963 it was believed that the prime responsibility for the control of inflation rested with monetary policy, so the Bundesbank had to achieve rates of growth of the money supply which were compatible with a gradual fall in the inflation rate to zero. With the Bretton Woods fixed exchange regime that then prevailed, there was a fixed exchange rate between the D-Mark and the dollar, so in 1960 German inflation could only fall towards zero if United States inflation also fell, and the Americans, influenced from time to time by Keynesian policies, have permitted a persistent upward trend in their price level. It was therefore indispensable to the objective that Germany's inflation rate be reduced towards zero that the D-Mark be decoupled from the dollar and hence be allowed to rise so that Germany's inflation rate could fall below America's. This proved to be the most controversial element in the Council's proposals. German industrialists were appalled by the prospect of revaluations of the D-Mark and even Chancellor Erhard accused the Council of offering 'stones to a public in need of bread' (Giersch, 1986, p. 264). But the policy of freeing the D-Mark from the dollar was adopted and during the 1980s German inflation has indeed fallen towards zero as a result of the prudent monetary policies that the Bundesbank has thereby been free to adopt.

While the role of monetary and exchange rate policies is to control inflation, the German version of the assignment problem attributes the level of employment to how high money wage costs are in relation to the price level (which is determined by the money supply and the exchange rate). In Giersch's words, 'the medium run level of employment was seen to be essentially determined by the level and structure of real wages' (p. 269). The role of fiscal policy was then to determine the growth of potential output through its influence on the supply side of the economy. It exercised such influence via the following transmission mechanisms:

(i) the aggregate supply of savings for (productive) capital formation via the budget surplus or deficit, the tax system and the structure of public expenditures; (ii) the marginal efficiency of autonomous (i.e. not demand induced) private investments via the tax structure and the complementary character of public investments, and (iii) the supply of labour and society's general motivation level via the level and rate and structure of direct taxes. (p. 270)

Giersch took the view that 'In a medium run perspective, the Finance Minister is regarded as responsible for the population's economic mentality and the national economy's dynamism and attractivity on world capital markets.' (p. 270).

Germany has indeed gone on to follow this course of action. We have used fiscal policy to create a supply-side environment that is favourable to growth, monetary policy to control inflation, while for the achievement of high employment we have relied on the moderation and good sense of the German trade unions (which has generally been forthcoming) to hold wages down to a level which is acceptable in relation to the price levels that the Bundesbank's price and exchange rate policies impose on German industry. The countries which have followed Keynesian policies have in contrast assigned to fiscal policy the creation of sufficient demand to permit the attainment of high employment and since this has often involved budget deficits their productive saving has been squeezed with the result that their economic growth has suffered. Their central banks have often been willing to finance whatever wage levels emerged at the employment levels their fiscal demand oriented policies generated, and these countries have then lacked a monetary brake to inhibit inflation. They have therefore been without policies to achieve low inflation and medium term economic growth. Germany would not wish to depart from our quite successful solution to the assignment problem, and there is naturally concern in Germany (which will emerge in the latter part of this article) that pressures to adopt elements of international Keynesianism would implicitly oblige us to go over to a domestic policy mix which has hitherto proved (by the countries which chose it after 1945) considerably less appealing than our own.

The continuity of thought on German economic policy can be demonstrated by showing the extent to which Giersch's solution to the assignment problem is precisely the one set out in the Council of Economic Experts' 1986–87 Report. Thus, we wrote in 1986 that:

Monetary policy's task is to protect the value of money. This necessitates expanding the money supply at a rate which is in line with growth in productive capacity at approximately stable prices. If monetary policy is steady in this sense, it simultaneously contributes to stabilising expectations on the foreign exchange markets. .... Adjustment problems stemming from an abrupt change in the pace of money supply growth can be avoided by making the return to the target path take place gradually. When the actual development surpasses the target, our suggestion to announce a target path for a period of several years is superior to a procedure whereby a monetary target is fixed anew each year and thus contains a discretionary element regarding the starting point. Commitment to a multi-year monetary target requires no more from the central bank than commitment to a promise to keep the value of money stable.

The role of fiscal policy in the offensive strategy against unemployment consists essentially of removing distortions of economic incentives. First of all this applies to the heavy tax burden, and particularly to the high marginal rates of the income tax and the corporation tax, and secondly to the many and varied government subsidies. Both the tax burden and the subsidies impair the willingness to work harder and to assume more risk. The reduction of tax burdens must not however be financed via increased public deficits.

By their wage settlements, employers and employees strongly influence economic performance. It is part of our policy conception for a self-sustained upswing that they reach agreements which keep unit labour costs stable. Otherwise the level of costs would rise again because another fall in import costs cannot be expected. Wage bargaining would then conflict with monetary policy, as the latter would be bound to view the goal of stability as being in danger. The consequence would be that either employment or price stability – if not both – would suffer, and the continuation of the upswing would become uncertain. (English language version: paras 31, 33, 34, 37)

The German Council of Economic Experts sees growth and the medium-term change in employment as depending mainly on supply-side developments, and it is this aspect of our policy analysis that may appear most surprising to those inclined to think along Keynesian lines. The Council is concerned, not merely to utilise existing productive potential, but that present production facilities should be continuously modernised which actually matters far more in the long term. The Council has often pointed to the lessons which can be learned from economic history which underscore the fact that 'the primary impetus for expansion often originates in supply, which automatically creates equivalent demand'.

This wording is reminiscent of Say's Law, a principle which is often misunderstood. What is meant here is that the right kind of supply creates its own demand. Indeed many of the present day problems involving growth and employment can be illuminated by the simple formula of Say's Law provided that this is interpreted qualitatively: 'The right kind of supply invariably creates its own demand'. If producer and consumer goods are supplied which incorporate modern developments in science and technology, which work reliably, and most crucially of all, which fulfil a need that is felt by populations somewhere in the world, then the supplier will be able to obtain a price which more than covers his costs. This kind of supply is created in efficient and well managed factories and workplaces, and these, by designing and producing such goods, create more employment. This is the crux of supply-oriented anti-unemployment therapy.

Economically viable goods must be marketable at prices which more than cover costs, so a cost-cutting strategy is a necessary element in their creation. It is therefore helpful if a country can reduce the costs that stem from taxation, social insurance contributions and above all labour costs, and there is clearly a limit to the extent to which increases in such costs can be tolerated if companies are to continue to sell at prices that cover them.

It is naturally also vital that the firms that make up an economy be flexible, adaptable, and receptive to innovation which are all crucial elements in the improvement of the supply side of the market.

Competitive conditions in industry naturally have much to contribute to bring about this state of affairs, and the Council of Economic Experts considers 'dynamic competition to be the model (*Leitbild*) of a forward-looking economic policy aimed at promoting growth and employment' (Annual Report 1985/86, para. 308). The Council is well aware that economists and governments have only limited means to control developments in the domain of dynamic competition. They can widen the range of markets in which firms have to compete, but they cannot control the extent to which firms subsequently behave more competitively. But the Council has found that something can be achieved by all the time opening up more markets to competitive forces, and by encouraging innovation at every available opportunity.

It is the Council's view that the strength of competitive forces and the pressure to innovate which are vital elements in an economy's *basic* economic drive are the key factors that influence the growth of employment that an economy achieves. Fluctuations will be smoothed out in the course of time, and these long-term considerations will then exercise the dominant impact.

The basic paradigm that guides policy-makers should therefore not be one where the principal object is to spread cyclical stimuli more evenly through time. Stimuli should on the contrary be continuously reinforced so that dynamic forces are created which provide a sustained boost to the economy.

A mature economy can only continue to expand if industries which have become moribund are replaced through the expansion of a sufficient number of new industries, and if out-of-date products which can only be sold at prices which barely cover costs are driven out of the market by a sufficient number of new products which can be sold at prices which satisfactorily cover costs.

In the last resort it is the ratio of value-added to costs of production which is crucial. Imitative competition in which more and more producers enter the market in order to supply older products will gradually force their prices downwards (and so the value-added that these products can earn in the marketplace) towards the level of their unit costs. In an economy with growing competition (and this is something we consistently support), and especially competition which takes the form of a willingness to imitate the products of successful existing producers, the revenues that can be obtained from these in the marketplace will all the time fall in relation to their costs of production. There is only one remedy for this law of rising costs and squeezed margins: innovative competition through the creation of new and superior products to compete with the older ones that are becoming unprofitable. Only new products and the development of new markets can permit the achievement of a more favourable ratio of value-added to costs of production (Helmstädter, 1986).

If an economy has an unfavourable mix of old and new products, too many old models and designs, and too little to offer that is modern and redesigned, costs of production will inevitably be high in relation to the prices that can be obtained for these goods in world markets, so the economy's profits will be low, and it will provide insufficient growth and employment. Such deficiencies cannot be remedied by macroeconomic policy measures because these will be unable to modify the ratio of value-added to costs of production. A government induced rise in prices (via a Keynesian expansion in demand accompanied by devaluation) could of course reduce the real wage for a few months and so temporarily reduce costs of production, but any such advantages to manufactures would be unsustainable. Wages would soon start to chase prices upwards once again and so restore the formerly inadequate ratio of value-added to costs of production. The only solution is the creation of new products which offer a more favourable ratio of value-added to costs of production, and this goal will be best attained via dynamic competition. Governments can assist its operation by removing obstacles to competition through the elimination or simplification of government regulations, and improvement to incentive structures. Every political measure which stimulates innovative activity without inhibiting competition will enhance the process by which new high value-added products are created.

That completes my brief outline of the supply-oriented policies that the German Council of Economic Experts has been advocating since 1963. The present Council and our predecessors have regarded the competitive process itself as the driving force for the achievement of sustained growth and employment. We have argued that Germany should direct its attention in several directions for the achievement of this goal. We have been especially concerned to encourage the development of small and medium sized businesses, and the process of dynamic development through competition may be compared with a millipede. Locomotion is ensured by a large number of small cogs functioning on an all-wheel-drive principle. The concept beloved by international Keynesians of a 'locomotive' as the draught horse of dynamic development is erroneous.

The Council naturally assesses the scope for concerted international action on the basis of this fundamental analysis of the appropriate economic policies for the promotion of economic growth and employment, and this will be the subject of the next section.

19.2   INTERNATIONAL CO-OPERATION AT THE EUROPEAN LEVEL

International co-operation to reduce the degree of fluctuation in exchange rates is pursued with two particular aims in mind: first, so that movements of exchange rates should be to the greatest possible degree predictable, and second to support national efforts to prevent the collapse of particular currencies. Since 1979, these objectives have to a large extent been attained at the European level. At the world level, the system of freely flexible exchange rates, which superseded the Bretton Woods system of fixed exchange rates in 1973 has lagged far behind the European System for the attainment of these objectives. It is an important question why the smaller system should have been successful, while the larger world system has fallen so far short of expectations, and the answer to this question will provide interesting insights into the implications of the two systems for employment (Mattes, 1987b; Schlesinger, 1987).

Although the national currencies represented in the EMS are confined within a system of fixed rates, they can be adjusted up or down, and these modifications have depended on the success of national price stabilisation policies. Divergences between currencies and especially between inflation rates have on several occasions led to corrective adjustments to official EMS exchange rates. Nevertheless, the overall tendency of the European Monetary System has been to reduce inflation in the higher inflation European economies. As Jacques Delors, the French President of the European Commission, has recently remarked, the European Monetary System 'has brought most of the countries concerned back to the path of virtue, the circulus virtuosus where inflation and disequilibria are anathema' (cf. Mattes, 1987a).

The instrument which has made this possible has been the stable D-Mark whose 'absolute postulate of stability' (Mattes) serves like a linkage to gold. The dimensions of the trading area within which the D-Mark functions as an internal currency more or less meet the non-monetary requirements for a key currency. Legally, the European Monetary System has no key currency, but in reality the D-Mark has assumed this role. Its ability to fulfil this function properly depends on the extent to which it can achieve a greater degree of stability than the other currencies in the system, which depends to a considerable extent upon the achievement of a stable price level by Germany.

At present the European Monetary System is still functioning 'asymmetrically' (Mattes): in terms of stability it does not constitute a homogeneous block. In the centre there is the stable D-Mark around which other less stable currencies form a group. By initiating its price stabilisation policy in 1983, France considerably reduced the gap between French and German inflation rates and the Italian inflation rate has also fallen very considerably in the 1980s. There has clearly been a growing tendency for the inflation rates of the countries which participate in the EMS to converge towards Germany's now zero inflation rate. President Delors regards this trend as an indication that the initial phase in the functioning of the European Monetary System has been completed, and suggests that as a next step

the European Monetary System must form the nucleus of an economic system which is more efficient in terms of growth, competitiveness and employment. In view of the spectacular progress that has been made with respect to the liberalisation of capital transactions within the Community, we have no choice but to make further headway by extending the domain of group discussion concerning economic and monetary policy (cf. Mattes, 1987a).

During the initial phase toward's Europe's concerted currency stabilisation process, the D-Mark has tended to be undervalued on a purchasing power parity basis in relation to other European currencies because of Germany's comparatively low inflation rate. This tendency has favoured

West Germany's export trade and had a positive impact on employment: at any rate this is how West Germany's European partners see the situation. Conversely, France and Italy with their faster inflation rates have tended to have overvalued currencies but gained stability advantages which have had favourable supply-side effects. That is the counter-argument put forward by the Germans. The fact is that the corrective exchange rate adjustments which have been needed are becoming less and less significant and they are tending to closely follow relative inflation rates with the result that Europe's relative real exchange rates have been quite stable.

Now that this has been accomplished what is the next phase? Some economic policy-makers believe that the D-Mark may now be too stable and warn against the danger of deflation. In our own discussions about the consolidation of the government budget in the early 1980s some spoke more drastically of the danger of what they described as *Kaputtsparen* (ruinous saving), a form of Keynesian saving that reduces the circular flow of money, goods, etc. Is this to be countered by an expansionist monetary and fiscal policy, or is it possible to devise some other means of pursuing a 'cooperative growth strategy aimed at raising the level of employment' within the institutional framework of the European Community? (Annual Economic Report 1985/86 of the Commission of the European Community).

A proposal has been put forward by the European Commission based on a strategic paper written by a group of experts who want to attain a higher level of growth and employment by means of a so-called 'two-handed approach' (Blanchard *et al.*, 1985). This strategy aims at promoting both supply and demand in order to increase growth and employment.

> Neither supply nor demand will by themselves create and sustain employment growth. This simple point forms the basis of our approach: structural changes on the supply side are required if employment growth is to be sustained, but a boost is needed to start the process. This boost must come from timely supply measures, sustained and validated by demand. (Blanchard *et al.*, 1985, p. 31.)

The strategy envisaged in their paper provides for investment incentives and employment subsidies accompanied by a very slight increase in real wages (1–2 per cent). In the first half of the 1980s businesses hardly expanded plant capacity, they merely adjusted to improvements in input prices. Now they are to be vitalised by a complementary expansion of demand, and monetary policy is to permit this. The group of experts do not say exactly what real growth rate is to be attained by such measures, but they stress that unemployment can only be reduced by a period of accelerated growth.

The European Commission in contrast (1986) ventures to give figures to indicate the dimensions that 'more dynamic growth' might attain. Between 1986 and 1990 the real growth rate in Europe is to average 3–3.5 per cent.

The level of employment is to increase by 1–1.5 per cent per annum. This means that by 1990 the unemployment figure would decrease by 4 percentage points: in the original ten EEC countries unemployment would fall from 11 to 7 per cent, and in all twelve present-day member states it would drop from 12 to 8 per cent.

Without the measures envisaged within the framework of the 'cooperative Community strategy', the Commission estimates that the real growth rate of the ten older member states for the same period would be 2.7 per cent per annum. Thus the growth strategy aimed at promoting employment is supposed to result in an increase in the rate of growth of just under 1 per cent.

In its latest annual report the German Council of Economic Experts unequivocally contests the view that government economic policy can effect a sustained increase in the real growth rate by means of expansionary monetary and fiscal policy measures (Annual Report 1986/87, para. 211). In the meantime, the Commission's proposals for a co-operative Community strategy have been put on ice. They cannot expect any support from West Germany inasmuch as the proposals put forward threaten to trigger an upsurge in inflation. Moreover, the authors of the paper do not indicate how the measures on the supply side are to be put into practice. In this respect the group of experts who have advocated the 'two-handed approach' are just as vague as the Commission.

The underlying explanation of our opposition to the Commission's proposals is of course that a faster rate of expansion of Germany's money supply would be inflationary which runs counter to the principles which have guided German economic policy so successfully since 1963 which I have set out in the previous section of this chapter. At the same time, the proposed use of fiscal expansion to stimulate demand runs counter to our judgement that this should be used to create a fiscal framework to encourage medium-term growth. The larger German budget deficit which the Commission proposes would reduce the aggregate saving that is available to finance productive investment in Germany and so have a long-term tendency to reduce employment.

The Commission's proposal for a concerted economic policy of the member states has some inglorious predecessors, e.g. the 'locomotive or convoy approach', which was taken up at the economic summit in Bonn in 1978, and which was commented on as follows in an IMF staff paper: 'In retrospect, it can probably be said that the Bonn measures placed insufficient emphasis on the medium-term consequences of fiscal expansion, and failed to provide sufficient flexibility for anti-inflationary monetary policies..:' (Horne and Masson, 1987).

The 'hardest and most difficult form of policy coordination: a concerted action as agreed at the Bonn Summit in 1978' (Wegner, 1987b) was doomed to failure from the outset, and most German economists appreciated this: 'The majority of German economists saw in this episode a grave policy error, a verdict which explains also why German policy-makers today are vehemently opposed to a similar concerted effort, this time to ease the adjustment burden of the United States' (Wegner, 1987b). One would think that the 'pitfalls of international fine-tuning' (Horne and Masson) would be generally accepted as a classic example of how not to do things.

19.3   INTERNATIONAL CO-OPERATION AT THE WORLD LEVEL: 1. MANAGED EXCHANGE RATES

The EMS has presented Europe with a stable exchange rate system but global exchange rates have in contrast fluctuated to an excessive degree. In order to lessen the difficulties a number of proposals have been put forward with a view to establishing a system of 'managed' exchange rates. Both monetary and fiscal policy would be geared to assist exchange rate stabilisation within a quite generous fluctuation limit. To this extent exchange rates are not to remain exclusively subject to the whims and vicissitudes of the foreign exchange market and general economic policy. Exchange rate stabilisation is now to rank as an intermediate target in its own right within the framework of the government's economic policy.

Capital movements inspired by economic and political speculation have contributed to the enormous fluctuations in exchange rates which have occurred in recent years. This deplorable state of affairs is to be remedied by the system of 'managed' exchange rates designed to reduce the gains that can be obtained from opportunist international speculation. Within the framework of the new system, fiscal and monetary policies are to be organised so that they will be binding and readily comprehensible, thereby guaranteeing a higher degree of predictability to market operators.

The advocates of this newfangled system are again evoking rosy prospects for the fine-tuning of monetary and fiscal policies via concerted international action.

The proposals threaten to undermine the principles which have guided German economic policy in recent years. Our counterinflation strategy has depended on the selection of monetary growth rates and consequent D-Mark exchange rates which are compatible with a zero inflation rate in Germany. Any modification to this monetary and exchange rate policy would not only damage Germany: it would also undermine the counterinflation strategy of the EMS economies.

In its latest report (Annual Report 1986/87, paras 245–259) the German Council of Economic Experts has expressed strong reservations about 'managed' exchange rates. These reservations are based upon the following considerations:

–In its initial phase the system would have to function with exchange rates negotiated on the basis of political compromises of a kind that could hardly be arrived at on a worldwide scale.

—If such a system were to be established there would be a great danger that all the countries concerned would end up with an averaged inflation rate roughly equivalent to the average of their original inflation rates. In the worldwide co-ordination process it would be virtually impossible to maintain on a longer-term basis a policy of stabilisation such as exists within the framework of the European Monetary System, which has depended upon one major country achieving price stability while the others gradually adjust their inflation rates to the zero rate achieved by that key country.

Under the new scheme the margins of exchange rate fluctuation are to be widened. If this system actually materialised, the probability is that each country's exchange rate would be close to the upper or lower limits of the permitted margins. Two-way movements by individual countries are likely to be exceptional since each state would have a preference for either currency appreciation or depreciation and would allow its exchange rate to drift in that direction to take advantage of the scope for action offered by the widened fluctuation margins. This in turn would trigger constantly renewed speculative flows of capital until the next corrective exchange rate adjustment.

The German Council of Economic Experts believes that there is a direct way of ensuring that the goal of exchange rate stability is attained: consistent and predictable monetary and fiscal policies must be pursued by the leading countries that belong to the world's flexible exchange rate system.

Summing up its conclusions, the Council stresses the following points:

Fixed exchange rates can only be established if all the countries concerned adhere to the same stabilisation policy. This is particularly true in cases where there are no restrictions on foreign trade or capital transactions. At present, however, it is impossible to bring the various national policies into line with each other.

Managed exchange rates can only be established if co-ordinated national stabilisation measures are undertaken on the basis of constantly renegotiated international agreements. Official foreign exchange market interventions will also be necessary and these need to be negotiated between the central banks concerned. But as has been shown above, such conditions cannot be fulfilled at present.

A working system of flexible exchange rates involves a great many presuppositions with regard to the consistency and predictability of national stabilisation policies. The countries concerned need to observe strict disciplinary rules in order to hold to the stabilisation policies they have set out. At the same time – and in this respect a system of flexible exchange rates is quite different from a system of fixed rates – the member states can go their own ways, by for instance pursuing different national inflation targets because the economic goals of the various countries will not be the same. It is essential, however, that each country pursues its own individual targets consistently because it is well known that exchange rates will fluctuate wildly if the inflation prospects of the various countries keep changing.

19.4   INTERNATIONAL CO-OPERATION AT THE WORLD LEVEL: 2. CO-ORDINATION OF FISCAL POLICY

There is something tragicomical about the way in which America's tax-cut-based supply-side economic policy of the early 1980s actually became a classic case of demand boosting policies through its creation of enormous budget deficits. The total government deficit which reached 7 per cent of GNP in 1982 has fallen to 4 per cent in 1987, but it will be years before the American deficit can be reduced to easily financible proportions. The United States government hoped to persuade Congress to agree to cut total public expenditure by limiting the tax revenues available, but these efforts have so far failed to produce significant results.

The American example, like many others, inevitably leads to scepticism about the scope for international economic co-operation to co-ordinate fiscal policies. It would be irresponsible to attempt to remedy national failures through internationally concerted action.

In comparison with monetary policy, fiscal policy is far more deeply rooted in the political process. The internationalisation of fiscal policy can only increase the extent to which it becomes politicised. It is moreover becoming increasingly difficult to achieve the best timing for countercyclical fiscal measures. This timing problem can only become more difficult if there has to be international consultation about any fiscal action.

The current problem is posed by a widespread belief that there should be a concerted international approach to monetary and fiscal policy in an effort to reduce America's trade deficit. Rather than to achieve this by the direct means of reducing America's budget deficit, it is proposed to achieve this indirectly by means of a reduction in the exchange rate of the dollar and through expansionary monetary and fiscal policies by Germany and Japan.

It is most unlikely that this approach to the reduction of the American balance-of-payments deficit will be successful. The devaluation of the dollar should have some effect, but its impact on the trade balance is likely to be insufficient. Despite some recent improvement, the deficit is still running at an annual rate of about $150 billion. America's $264 billion foreign debt is now two and a half times as high as the debt of Brazil, the world's second largest debtor.

The further easing effect on the American deficit of prolonged monetary and fiscal expansion by the German Federal Republic (which would undermine our own medium-term economic strategy where fiscal policy is meant to strengthen the supply side of the economy) would in fact be minimal: 1 per cent extra growth by Germany and Japan for three years would cut it by only $5–$10 billion in view of their quite small fraction of world output. In the opinion of the German Council of Economic Experts, such policies can in any case be ruled out because they would create an immediate risk of a new wave of inflation in Germany where the money supply is already abundant, interest rates are low and the budget deficit is in any case rising. These considerations indicate that the German economy has already made full use of such scope as might have been available for monetary and fiscal expansion. A new wave of inflation in West Germany would be detrimental to the world economy, not least within the framework of the European Monetary System, and it would moreover introduce a further element of exchange rate instability.

19.5 WHAT CAN ACTUALLY BE DONE?

It does not appear that present day employment problems can be resolved by means of international Keynesianism, Mark I or II. There have already been enough post-war experiments to bear witness to the fact that Keynesianism does not really have the sustained impact on unemployment that its advocates expect. These advocates tend to forget that, 'classical unemployment, if fought by Keynesian policies, will merely be transformed into much worse diseases, i.e. capital shortage, unemployment and, eventually, technological unemployment' (Giersch, 1986, p. 272); which explains why these policies so often raise unemployment (the worst cases because they have budget deficits of more than 10 per cent of GNP are Italy and Ireland which also have unemployment rates of well over 10 per cent) instead of reducing it. This means that we can learn little from Keynes in the 1980s.

The unemployment problem with which we are now confronted has little to do with cyclical fluctuations, and cyclical swings in economic activity no longer assume the dimensions for which Keynes and the Keynesians designed their economic and fiscal policies. Our concern today is with sustainable growth rather than with short-term measures designed to foster expansion. Strictly speaking, we are concerned with reinforcing the process of economic evolution, we are interested in innovation and in continuous structural change. Over the past fifteen years a number of economists have been unduly preoccupied with the problems raised by exogenous shocks: but the problem facing us today is not how to adapt to exogenous shocks. Our real problem resides in the need to infuse our economies with a series of endogenous shocks on an ascending evolutionary path. The appropriate model for this was built not by Keynes, but by Joseph Schumpeter. It is Schumpeter therefore who is most appropriate to the domain of economic policy which is most relevant to us.

His model tells us that we must create new products, firms and industries to ensure that there is an increasing degree of competition in our advanced economies. We must offer sufficient opportunities to pioneers in the business world. We must offer more training opportunities for our workers. This is the path that we must follow in order to find a solution to our employment problems. Our need today is not primarily to boost demand or to boost supply. What we have to do is to improve the quality of what we supply so as to create the kind of supply that will open up new prospects for expansion and carry demand along with it. It is not sufficient merely to adapt to existing situations. What we need to do is to evolve so as to transform those situations continually in favour of new products and industries.

It is doubtless true that an economic policy geared to this objective can only claim a comparatively limited degree of feasibility. It must rely on the power of the free market competitive process in the hope that this will itself be able to create the necessary impetus. But such a policy offers more than a reiteration of previous attempts to make Keynesian solutions work. We have decades of Keynesian experimentation behind us and the patient is becoming unfit in consequence. 'The elixir of the economy is dynamic competition' (Annual Report 1984/85, para. 314). Economic policy should be guided by this insight. The principal and indeed sole contribution that stabilisation-oriented monetary and fiscal policies can offer reside in their predictability. Providing those objectives can be fulfilled monetary and fiscal policies can provide a medium-term framework within which firms in individual countries can achieve the development of new products and processes on which the growth of employment in the world economy truly depends.

Acknowledgements

I am grateful to Walter Eltis for his help in the preparation of an English language version of this paper, and for drawing my attention to Herbert Giersch's account of the development of his thinking on economic policy for an English readership.

References

BLANCHARD, O., R. DORNBUSCH, J. DRÈZE, H. GIERSCH, R. LAYARD and M. MONTI (1985) *Employment and Growth in Europe: a Two-Handed Approach* (Brussels: CEPS).

GIERSCH, H. (1986) 'Economics as a Public Good', in *Banca Nationale Del Lavoro Quarterly Review, Roma*, no. 158 (September) pp. 251–73.

HELMSTÄDTER, E. (1986) 'Dynamischer Wettbewerb, Wachstum und Beschäftigung, in G. Bombach, B. Gahlen and A. E. Ott (eds), *Technologischer Wandel – Analyse und Fakten* (Tübingen) pp. 67–82.

HORNE, J. and P. R. MASSON (1987) 'Scope and Limits of International Economic Cooperation and Policy Coordination', IMF Working Paper WP 87/24.

KELLNER, I. L. (1987) 'Commentary on Recent Economic Issues', Hanover Manufacturers Economic Report, July.

KOMMISSION DER EUROPÄISCHEN GEMEINSCHAFTEN (1985) Jahreswirtschaftsbericht 1985–86. Eine kooperative Wachstumsstrategie für mehr Beschäftigung, Brussels.

KOMMISSION DER EUROPÄISCHEN GEMEINSCHAFTEN (1986) Jahreswirtschaftsbericht 1986–87. Abbau der Arbeitslosigkeit in einer dynamischeren europäischen Wirtschaft – Für eine wirksame Anwendung der kooperativen Gemeinschaftsstrategie, Brussels.

MATTES, H. (1987a) Die Geldpolitik der Bundesrepublik Deutschland im Zeichen der Europäischen Integration (mimeographed).

MATTES, H. (1987b) Koordinierung der Wirtschaftspolitik innerhalb der EG, *Wirtschaftsdienst* (May) pp. 247–56.

SACHVERSTÄNDIGENRAT ZUR BEGUTACHTUNG DER GESAMTWIRTSCHAFTLICHEN ENTWICKLUNG:

—Jahresgutachten 1976/77. Zeit zum Investieren.

—Jahresgutachten 1983/84. Ein Schritt voran.

—Jahresgutachten 1984/85. Chancen für einen langen Aufschwung.

—Jahresgutachten 1985/86. Auf dem Weg zu mehr Beschäftigung.

—Jahresgutachten 1986/87. Weiter auf Wachstumskurs.

—Abridged English Language version of Annual Report, 1986/87. Continuing Economic Growth in Germany.

SCHLESINGER, H. (1987) Finanz- und Geldpolitik – Elemente internationaler wirtschaftlicher Kooperation. *Deutsche Bundesbank: Presseauszüge*: No. 63 (September) pp. 1–6.

WEGNER, M. (1987a) 'Problems and Instruments of International Coordination', Munich (mimeographed).

WEGNER, M. (1987b) The Role of the Economist in the EC-Commission, in J. A. Pechman (ed.), *The Role of the Economist in Government: an International Perspective*, Brighton (forthcoming).

20 The UK Government's Financial Strategy

Terence Burns

20.1 INTRODUCTION

For much of the period since the Second World War, United Kingdom governments were influenced by the economics that followed from Keynes's *General Theory*. Monetary and fiscal policies were used with the intention of controlling the level of aggregate demand to achieve an employment rate that governments considered close to 'full employment'. Although apparently successful at first, this strategy increasingly came under question as it became associated with a steady acceleration of inflation after 1961. Table 20.1 shows that the growth of money GDP (GDP expressed in current prices) increased from an average of 7 per cent per annum in the economic cycle from 1961 to 1965 to almost 18 per cent in the cycle from 1973 to 1979. Extra output accounted for almost half the increase in money GDP from 1961 to 1965, but by 1973–79 real output growth accounted for less than one-tenth of the increase.

Table 20.1   Growth of money GDP, output and inflation.
Average annual percentage change

	Money GDP (%)	Output (compromise GDP) (%)	GDP (MP) deflator (%)
1961–65	7.0	3.5	3.6
1965–69	6.9	2.6	4.3
1969–73	11.8	3.3	8.0
1973–79	17.8	1.3	16.0

Source: CSO *Economic Trends Annual Supplement*, 1988 edn (p. 4).

The Medium Term Financial Strategy (MTFS) was introduced in 1980 with the objective of reversing these trends.

Macro policy has been directed explicitly to reducing inflation. This follows from the view that macroeconomic policy is the key determinant of inflation – by contrast with the explanation that it is generated primarily by exogenous forces; for example commodity price shocks, bad harvests or the outcome of a bargaining struggle over incomes.

Similarly, macro policy has been directed less explicitly at economic activity and employment in the short run, not because of a downgrading of these objectives, but because of doubts about the efficacy of policy to stabilise real fluctuations without increasing inflationary pressures. The reduced emphasis on short-term demand management follows from the expectation that the pursuit of a steady nominal macroeconomic framework, avoiding excessive fluctuations in money GDP growth, will deliver steady growth at a rate determined by supply performance. The view is that the longer-term growth of the economy will be promoted by greater micro-efficiency and improved supply performance.

20.2 THE CHARACTERISTICS OF THE MEDIUM TERM FINANCIAL STRATEGY

The essentials of the MTFS have been present since it was first published. These can be summarised as follows:

(a) that macroeconomic policy should be conducted with a medium-term perspective;
(b) that there should be a nominal framework within which the growth of money GDP is gradually reduced and the division of that growth between real output growth and inflation improved;
(c) that the path for money GDP growth should be delivered by monitoring and responding to the evolution of monetary conditions. Initially this was formulated in terms of a target for broad money but quite soon other monetary aggregates and the exchange rate came to play a more dominant role;
(d) that fiscal policy should support monetary policy. Until 1987, when the PSBR had been reduced to 1 per cent of GDP, each version of the MTFS included projections showing a declining medium-term path for the PSBR;
(e) and finally a recognition that macroeconomic policy could only play a part. The underlying growth of the economy and the speed at which it adjusted to shocks would be dictated by success in improving supply performance.

In this chapter I discuss each of these issues: how policy has been conducted in practice, and how it has adapted to changing circumstances and experience.

20.2.1 Medium-term approach

Setting policy within a medium-term perspective has become conventional wisdom. An increasing body of opinion accepts that the concept is correct; debate now centres on the precise nature of the strategy.

Over the past eight years the medium-term perspective has been important. It has ensured that year-by-year decisions have been taken with full regard for medium-term objectives. Public commitment has imposed a discipline on Government. It has played a vital part in conditioning expectations that Government would pursue non-accommodating anti-inflationary policies. And the publication each year of the fiscal arithmetic has meant that full account has been taken of the longer-term fiscal implications before making decisions about taxation or public expenditure.

In practice it is necessary to judge whether departures from the medium-term path require discretionary action or whether they will be self-correcting. There is a bias against fiscal short-term fine tuning and no presumption that policy should respond to every piece of news or hint that the economy may be deviating from expectations. Instead there is a healthy scepticism directed towards short-term forecasts of changes in the pace of activity and an acceptance that it is not feasible to keep the economy on a smooth projected track. The data are unreliable and subject to considerable revision, the errors surrounding short-term forecasts are well documented, and there is considerable uncertainty about the speed and effectiveness of changes in policy instruments. Naturally, this does not rule out action if it appears that a longer-term deviation from the strategy is likely.

20.2.2 The nominal framework

The second essential component of the MTFS has been the nominal framework. The aim – either implicit (1980 and 1981) or explicit (since then) – has been to reduce the growth of money GDP, until it is consistent with the objective for inflation, and to improve its division between real output and inflation.

It is important to stress that the figures for money GDP growth are not precise targets and do not apply to particular years. The ambition relates to the medium-term path. The observed growth rates are bound to fluctuate for a variety of reasons: world conditions; fluctuations in savings ratios; shifts in confidence; and unexpected developments in the pressure of monetary and fiscal policy. It is not possible to offset completely these fluctuations by policy adjustments nor should it always be desirable. And it is no part of the framework to imply that any short-term shock to output has to be matched precisely by an equivalent offsetting movement of inflation; or vice versa.

Moreover, if the unexpected change in output looks likely to persist into the medium term without altering inflation – following, say, a supply-side improvement – it would be right to adjust the money GDP path to accommodate it.

The rate of growth of money GDP fell sharply between 1980 and 1983 much as envisaged in successive editions of the MTFS. The figures are shown in Table 20.2. Money GDP figures were not published in the first two editions; the emphasis was upon monetary targets and there was an unwillingness to be too precise about the speed at which inflation was expected to fall. But the figures were prepared for internal purposes (Burns, 1986). The only inflation forecasts published were those that met the statutory requirements of the Industry Act.

The money GDP figures lying behind the 1980 MTFS implied a reduction from 17½ per cent growth in 1979–80 (having averaged more or less that figure between 1972–73 and 1979–80) to 10½ per cent in 1983–84. As shown in Table 20.2 the outcome for the growth of money GDP in 1982–83 and 1983–84 was broadly in line with those figures, although by 1983–84 it had been reduced to about 8 per cent. Moreover, the pace of deceleration in 1980–81 and 1981–82 was faster than expected and as a result the cumulative growth over the four-year period was less. The implications for the conduct of monetary policy are discussed later.

Real output fell sharply during the period of rapid deceleration of money GDP (Table 20.3). But since 1981–82 money GDP growth has been much less variable; and real output has grown at a fairly steady pace.

Table 20.4 shows some comparative information for the mean and

Table 20.2 MTFS assumptions for the growth of money GDP*
(percentage change)

	Date of publication:									Latest out-turn
	1980	1981	1982	1983	1984	1985	1986	1987	1988	
1979–80	17.5									19.8
1980–81	17.1	13.0								14.1
1981–82	12.0	10.5	10.5							10.2
1982–83	9.6	9.6	9.7	8.3						9.2
1983–84	10.7	9.7	9.7	7.9	8.0					8.1
1984–85			9.6	8.5	7.9	6.8				7.1
1985–86				7.7	6.8	8.4	9.5			9.7
1986–87					6.1	6.6	6.8	6.1		6.9
1986–88						5.7	6.4	7.5		9.8

*Average measure, market prices

Sources: Bums, 1986; successive FSBRs; CSO *Economic Trends Annual Supplement* 1988 edn (pp. 5–7); CSO *Economic Trends,* June 1988 (p. 6).

Table 20.3   GDP data
(percentage changes on year earlier)

	Money GDP (average measure, market prices)	Real GDP (average measure, factor cost)	GDP deflator (market prices)
1979–80	19.8	2.8	16.6
1980–81	14.1	−3.8	18.6
1981–82	10.2	0.5	9.9
1982–83	9.2	1.9	7.1
1983–84	8.1	3.2	4.7
1984–85	7.1	2.5	4.4
1985–86	9.7	3.5	6.0
1986–87	6.9	3.2	3.3
1987–88	9.8	4.3	5.1

Sources: CSO Economic Trends Annual Supplement, 1988 edn (pp. 5–7); CSO Economic Trends, June 1988 (p. 6).

Table 20.4   Growth rates: means and variances (per cent)

	Money GDP		GDP(A) at 1980 prices	
	Mean	Variance	Mean	Variance
1957–62	5.6	0.7	2.6	5.0
1962–67	6.9	2.7	3.3	2.4
1967–72	9.7	3.5	2.5	1.1
1972–77	17.6	25.8	2.1	11.7
1977–82	13.9	14.5	0.8	5.3
1982–87*	8.3	1.6	3.3	0.6

*Figures for the UK for 1987 in this and subsequent tables showing demand components are taken from CSO Economic Trends, March 1988.

Source: CSO Economic Trends Annual Supplement, 1988 edn (p. 4).

variance of money GDP and output growth rates over selected successive five-year periods. (This general pattern is unaffected if comparison is made with other five-year periods.) Over the five years to 1987 the variance of money GDP growth compares well with other post-war periods. In other words, the MTFS has succeeded in its objective of delivering a relatively stable path for money GDP. And this has been accompanied by a steady growth of real output at over 3 per cent per annum. The variance of the growth rate has also been low in comparison with other post-war (and indeed prewar) periods.

20.2.3 Monetary conditions

The third essential component of the MTFS has been the role of monetary policy – particularly interest rates – in delivering the path for money GDP growth. In practice, although the ambition for the path of money GDP (and with it inflation) has been delivered with some success, there have been technical difficulties in monitoring and assessing monetary conditions.

In the early days of the MTFS £M3 was at the centre of the stage – largely for reasons of continuity and simplicity. The practice of monitoring monetary conditions has developed in the light of experience. The essential ingredients have been the same throughout: narrow money, broad money – including the growth of credit – the exchange rate and to some extent other asset prices. But the weight given to these factors has changed from time to time; and a considerable element of judgement has been required.

Of the narrow measures of money, M0 has been the most useful indicator of monetary conditions and it has played an important role since 1983. Over this period, it has had a relatively stable velocity trend of about 3 per cent a year – see Table 20.5 – and although it can be no more than a short leading indicator of money GDP it has a reasonably good record of giving the correct signals about monetary conditions. By contrast the behaviour of broad money has been difficult to interpret. Velocity has been declining since 1980 after increasing throughout the 1970s. This seems to reflect a number of factors. High real interest rates have added to the attractiveness of financial

Table 20.5   Monetary aggregates and their velocity
Average annual percentage change

	M0	M3	Annual change in velocity relative to GDP*	
			M0	M3
1964–73	6.7	11.6	2.7	− 1.1
1973–79	12.6	10.6	4.5	5.5
1979–83	5.1	13.1	5.2	− 2.1
1983–87	4.8	16.5	3.3	− 5.8

*Velocity is defined as

$$\frac{8.\ \text{Money GDP}}{(M + 2(M)_{-1} + 2(M)_{-2} + 2(M)_{-3} + (M)_{-4})}$$

where money GDP is total for year, M is the end-year figure for the relevant definition of money supply and M_{-1} is the preceding end quarter figure.

Sources: Bank of England: *Banking Statistics*; CSO *Financial Statistics*, Table 11.1; HMT estimates.

assets in general. But more importantly, increased competition in financial markets has led to rapid growth in private sector liquidity and borrowing.

The exchange rate has been an important factor in interest rate decisions over the whole life of the MTFS. Figure 20.1 compares the monthly paths for the Sterling Exchange Rate Index and the 3-month interbank rate since mid-1979. The vertical lines indicate the months in which the exchange rate depreciated by more than 2 per cent. It is evident that this almost always coincided with interest rate increases. The most noticeable episodes were the autumn of 1981, the winter of 1982–83, January 1985, and the autumn of 1986. A similar pattern applies in reverse. The periods of sterling strength coincide with interest rate reductions.

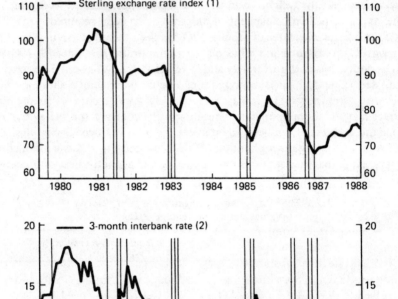

(1) Monthly average.
(2) End of month.
(3) Vertical bars indicate months in which the exchange rate depreciated by more than 2 per cent.

Figure 20.1   The exchange rate and 3-month interbank rate.

Experience during the 1980s suggests that monetary policy does have a substantial effect on money GDP growth. The channel of influence via the exchange rate has probably been the dominant mechanism. However in addition we now estimate rather greater direct effects from interest rates to spending components; not only the housing market, but also stockbuilding and consumer spending.

Many critical accounts of the MTFS focus upon the events of 1980–81. In particular it has been argued that the rise in the sterling exchange rate was caused by an excessive emphasis upon £M3.

There are several weaknesses with this argument. Although the figures for money GDP presented earlier support the view that the stance of policy was tighter than had been expected during 1980–81, the difference between intention and outcome is not large. Given the lack of experience of disinflation in the UK, it was never expected that it would be possible to manage the necessary substantial reduction in money GDP growth on a precise smooth path. The reduction of inflation probably required an initial shock to expectations and it was better to make faster, rather than slower, progress towards lower inflation.

It is also a mistake to conclude that all changes in exchange rates can be explained by monetary policy. The exchange rate is a crucial aspect of monetary policy but over the past ten years exchange rates have been much more volatile than could be predicted by monetary policy alone. Movements away from levels suggested by underlying economic developments have been sustained for long periods.

Finally, the frequent criticism that £M3 was the exclusive focus of policy during 1980–81 does not fit the facts. In the summer of 1980 the strength of the exchange rate, combined with other indicators, was interpreted as demonstrating that policy was indeed sufficiently restrictive to bring inflation down. Despite the substantial overshoot of £M3 from July onwards no action was taken to raise interest rates; and indeed in November 1980 interest rates were reduced by 2 per cent followed by a further 2 per cent cut four months later in the Budget Statement.

It is interesting to note that experience in other major industrial countries in operating monetary policy has been very similar. They have been through many of the same steps, particularly the need to monitor a range of indicators and to take into account changes to the financial system, albeit at different times. But the fact that the major countries have been pursuing anti-inflationary policies together has been helpful. It would have been much harder if the UK had been alone. Inevitably lower commodity prices have been an important part of the transmission process of anti-inflationary monetary conditions for the industrial countries as a whole but that does not belittle the importance of domestic macro-policy in the control of inflation.

To summarise, the combination of change to the financial system and large swings in exchange rates has complicated the conduct of monetary policy.

But despite these difficulties the overall ambition of monetary policy has been achieved with a lower growth of money GDP, made up of declining inflation and steady output growth.

20.2.4 Fiscal policy

The framework of fiscal policy has been retained throughout the history of the MTFS in basically the same form. Projections have been given for government expenditure and revenues for each of the years, combined with an illustrative path for the PSBR and a computation of the scope available for future tax reductions.

A number of objectives have been taken into account in setting the medium-term path for the PSBR each year: in particular that public sector debt should not rise as a percentage of GDP; and that fiscal policy should support monetary policy. The figures for each MTFS are shown in Table 20.6.

Table 20.6   MTFS assumptions for PSBR (percent of money GDP)

| | Date of publication: | | | | | | | | | |
	1980	1981	1982	1983	1984	1985	1986	1987	1988	*Latest out-turn*
1979–80	4.7									4.8
1980–81	3.7	5.9								5.4
1981–82	2.9	4.2	4.2							3.3
1982–83	2.2	3.2	3.4	2.7						3.1
1983–84	1.5	2.0	2.7	2.8	3.3					3.2
1984–85			2.0	2.5	2.2	3.2				3.1
1985–86				2.0	2.0	2.0	1.9			1.6
1986–87					1.9	2.0	1.8	1.1		0.9
1987–88						1.8	1.7	1.0	−0.7	−0.8

Sources: Successive FSBRs, CSO *Economic Trends Annual Supplement*, 1988 edn (pp. 5–7, 162–3); CSO *Economic Trends*, June 1988 (p. 6, 54).

The constraint on the growth of the public sector debt ratio is intended to avoid any escalation of the burden of debt interest payments. This helps to maintain confidence in the sustainability of policy, as a rising debt service burden cannot continue indefinitely. As shown in Table 20.7 this constraint has been met by reducing the PSBR as a percentage of GDP as the growth of money GDP has declined.

The objective of designing a fiscal policy that supports monetary policy is obviously less precise. The PSBR has to be compared with the flow of private sector savings. If the PSBR is high in relation to available domestic savings,

Table 20.7 The PSBR and changes in public sector debt (£ billion)

	1979–80	1980–81	1981–82	1982–83	1983–1984	1984–85	1985–86	1986–87
PSBR	10.0	12.7	8.6	8.8	9.7	10.2	5.8	3.4
Adjustments*	−2.1	+1.6	+1.9	−1.2	+2.7	+3.3	+0.4	+1.0
Change in net public sector debt†	7.9	14.3	10.6	7.6	12.4	13.6	6.1	4.3
Net public sector debt† (end year)	102.8	117.1	127.7	135.3	147.7	161.3	167.4	171.7
Money GDP‡	223.6	248.0	272.1	295.6	317.9	346.5	373.3	403.7
Net debt ratio (%, end year)	46.0	47.2	46.9	45.7	46.5	46.6	44.9	42.5
Memo item:								
Privatisation proceeds (% of GDP)	0.2	0.2	0.2	0.2	0.4	0.6	0.7	1.1

*Adjustments required to reconcile the PSBR with changes in net public sector debt. They comprise discounts and uplift on gilts, revaluations of net foreign currency debt, timing and coverage adjustments.
†Net public sector debt is derived from the consolidated debt of the public sector by deducting the public sector's holdings of liquid assets (*BEQB*, February 1988, pp. 83–5).
‡GDP at current market prices for year centred on 31 March.

Source: CSO, February 1988 *Bank of England Quarterly Bulletin* (net debt figures).

either domestic investment will be squeezed or there will be a need for a capital inflow from overseas. If investment suffers, the growth capacity of the economy will be impaired. Whether a capital inflow is sustainable depends upon the confidence of overseas investors and the available rate of return. If a sustainable inflow is not forthcoming there will be upward pressure on interest rates and/or downward pressure on the exchange rate. At some point both can put undue pressure on monetary policy.

As inflation fell it was expected that the flow of private sector saving would decline. This was an important factor lying behind the desire to reduce the PSBR as a percentage of GDP over the medium term. This view has been vindicated by subsequent events.

Figure 20.2 displays the flow of UK private savings and investment. During the 1970s private sector savings rose as a ratio of GDP. This can be associated partly with the rise in inflation: individuals saved more of their current income to try and make good the erosion of existing savings by inflation. Since the late 1970s the figures suggest that the private sector savings ratio has been on a falling trend. As with the rise in the ratio, we would associate much of the fall with the decline of inflation. In addition there may have been some other temporary factors at work, which may continue to depress savings over the medium term, including the effects of financial liberalisation, unanticipated increases in financial wealth and, as a result, pension contribution 'holidays'.

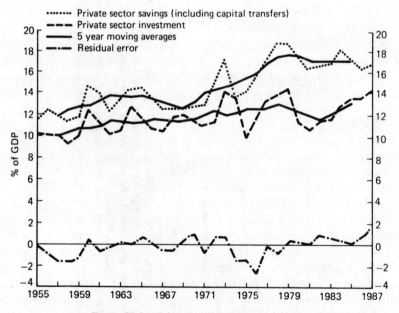

Figure 20.2   Private savings and investment.

At the same time the ratio of private sector investment to GDP has been on a rising trend. Some of this is accounted for by the transfer of investment from the public sector (particularly housing and the privatisation programme). Stockbuilding, which is included in these figures, was negative in the early 1980s but for most of the period since then has been relatively subdued. Fixed investment also fell early in the 1980s but has since risen sharply.

The combination of a declining savings ratio and rising investment ratio has led to a declining private sector financial surplus since the late 1970s. It is difficult to determine the magnitude of the decline since the residual error – the error which remains after summing the private, public and overseas sectors' financial balances – has been increasing in recent years. It is possible that net private saving has fallen by even more than is measured, or that the current account position is better. (Some of the error may also be attributable to the financial deficit of the public sector, but measurement errors are likely to be smaller than for the overseas and private sectors.)

There is now considerable common ground about the need to keep a sensible balance between fiscal and monetary policy; and the idea that at lower rates of inflation and growth of money GDP the ratio of the budget deficit to GDP that meets the objective of balance will be lower. Even so there remain some serious misunderstandings about the operation of the MTFS.

In the early years of the MTFS some argued that steady growth of output would be impossible without fiscal stimulus. The popular question was: 'where will the growth come from?'. We can now see the answer to the question: that the combination of lower inflation, steady growth and lower budget deficits has been accompanied by a steady sustained growth of private sector domestic expenditure and exports. Any real demand that has been withdrawn by the reduced budget deficit has been more than compensated by faster growth of private expenditure as inflation has been reduced, business and consumer confidence have risen and supply performance generally has improved.

It is claimed that the MTFS contains an unconditional profile for the PSBR that will be pursued regardless of the state of the cycle and that this is potentially de-stabilising. This description of policy is incorrect. Figures for the PSBR are given for each year of the MTFS period. But the smoothness of the path is clearly dependent upon the assumed steady path of output. Whilst there is no presumption of the active use of discretionary adjustments this does not rule out accepting some variation if the path of output growth turns out to be cyclical. But even in these circumstances there is no automatic requirement to accept the particular adjustments that are thrown up by the tax and benefit system. As Financial Secretary to the Treasury the present Chancellor delivered a speech dealing with the subject in 1980 when he argued that we were likely to see 'a "stepped" PSBR profile, with the PSBR not changing much as a proportion of GDP in recession years, but falling fairly sharply in non-recession years' (Lawson, 1980). In 1981–82 when output growth was revised down the PSBR target was revised up. Because of steady growth of output since this has been a minor issue.

Further evidence that the PSBR figures in the MTFS have not been rigid targets is shown by examining the pattern of successive revisions. The strictest interpretation of the MTFS would require the PSBR for the year ahead to be set equal to the figure shown in the previous year's MTFS. The Budget measures would have a first-year effect equal to the (theoretical) fiscal adjustment – the difference between the PSBR target set in the previous year and the estimate of the PSBR just prior to the Budget.

Table 20.8 compares the theoretical fiscal adjustment available and the effects of successive Budgets. In general only part of the theoretical fiscal adjustment was used in the Budgets. This gradualist approach to the MTFS is very evident in the successive PSBR figures.

Table 20.8   PSBR for the year ahead (percent of money GDP)

	As published in MTFS	As published in previous year's MTFS	Pre-Budget PSBR	Theoretical fiscal adjustment	Fiscal adjustment proposed in Budget
	(1)	(2)	(3)	(4)	(5)
1981–82	4.2	2.9	5.7	−2.8	−1.5
1982–83	3.4	3.2	2.8	0.4	0.6
1983–84	2.8	2.7	2.3	0.4	0.5
1984–85	2.2	2.5	2.2	0.3	0.0
1985–86	2.0	2.0	1.8	0.2	0.2
1986–87	1.8	2.0	1.5	0.5	0.3
1987–88	1.0	1.7	0.4	1.3	0.6
1988–89	−0.8	1.0	−1.7	2.7	0.9

Column (1): see Table 20.6
Column (2): see Table 20.6
Column (3): column (1) minus column (5)
Column (4): column (2) minus column (3)
Column (5): successive FSBRs

An inspection of Table 20.6 shows that the PSBR figure for the final year in each MTFS was relatively stable and did not change much as the figures for the first year declined. This meant that the steepness of the decline of the PSBR was reduced as the first year PSBR itself fell. This was consistent with gradual progress towards an objective of a low figure for the PSBR ratio.

It is also said that the figures are fudged by the use of asset sales. And yet it has been repeatedly stated that full account is taken of asset sales in determining the path for the PSBR. The published definition of the PSBR has not changed because it has not been necessary. To have constructed an alternative definition could only have directed attention at other income or expenditure components with different characteristics – for example North Sea oil revenues – and provoked even more debate about the best definition. Instead it has become practice to set out figures including and excluding privatisation proceeds.

Finally it is argued on the other hand that over the past two years fiscal policy has been relaxed – explaining the buoyant output growth. Some seem to have reached this conclusion because of the combination of tax cuts and increases in public expenditure totals. But the revisions to original public expenditure planning totals have not prevented a continued decline in public expenditure as a share of money GDP – including or excluding asset sales. The room for tax cuts comes about partly because of the falling share of public expenditure in GDP and partly because at existing tax rates the ratio of tax revenue to money GDP has been rising. The PSBR, including or excluding asset sales, has declined as a share of GDP.

20.2.5 Supply performance

The final component of the MTFS was the acceptance that although the stabilisation of financial conditions was important it could only play a part in improving the growth rate. The key to faster growth was improved supply performance.

This is not the place for a discussion of the details of policies that have been pursued to improve supply performance. But one aspect of fiscal strategy, the balance of public expenditure and taxation, might be briefly mentioned.

It has been an objective of policy to reduce the share of public expenditure in the economy and to lower marginal tax rates. As Figure 20.3 shows, during the 1960s and much of the 1970s the share of expenditure was rising, partly because of underlying demand for public services – health, education, etc.; partly because of the growth of social security expenditure; and partly because of greater State intervention and growth of subsidies. The result was higher tax rates and hence higher wedges between pre- and post-tax returns, with all the accompanying problems of distortions, tax shelters and disincentives. The aim has been to reverse this process: to reduce distortions, to improve incentives and limit the use of tax shelters through lower tax rates and a more neutral tax system; and to improve efficiency by subjecting as much economic activity as possible to the discipline of the private sector.

These effects are typically not captured by model simulation results, except through retention ratios (which are defined as ratios of take-home pay to gross earnings. The Treasury model earnings equation assumes that

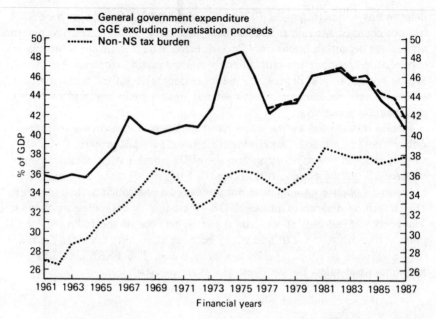

Figure 20.3   General government expenditure and the non-oil tax burden.

employees are more interested in net pay than gross pay. This implies that cuts in income tax should lead to lower nominal earnings growth). Conventional model simulations almost certainly understate the longer-term advantages to output growth of tax reductions compared with higher government spending.

Finally it is worth looking at the evidence for an improved supply performance. Within the money GDP framework we expect improved supply performance to show up as a better split between output and inflation.

Table 20.9 shows the output/inflation split for the UK and the average of the seven largest industrial countries excluding the UK (the G6) from the mid-1950s. In the 1950s and 1960s, UK inflation was a little higher than the G6 average while output growth was well below average. In the 1970s, the output gap continued on a similar scale, but the inflation gap widened sharply.

Since 1983, however, the position has changed markedly. Output growth in the UK has been almost the same as for the average of the G6 countries while the inflation gap has been reduced to 1½ per cent. Compared with the UK's historical performance against the G6 average this represents a distinct improvement with a similar inflation gap to the 1950s and 1960s but without the output growth gap that existed then. In recent years the output/inflation split has been in keeping with that experienced in the 1950s and 1960s – a

Table 20.9*   Output and inflation† in the UK and G6.
Average annual percentage change

	UK		G6	
	GDP	*Inflation*	*GNP*	*Inflation*
1955–64	2.8	2.9	5.2	2.7
1964–68	2.8	3.9	5.1	3.3
1968–73	3.1	7.5	4.7	5.5
1973–79	1.3	15.6	2.8	9.1
1979–83	0.4	10.7	1.6	8.2
1983–87	3.4	4.7	3.5‡	3.1‡

*This and subsequent tables show average values over a number of years. In general, the ranges have been chosen in order that comparisons of period averages are not affected by the cycle in economic activity and are measured between business cycle peaks (as measured by the CSO). However, this is not true of the last two periods (1979–83 and 1983–7) shown in each table as 1983 was not a cyclical peak. These sub-periods have been chosen to (arbitrarily) divide the period since 1979 into two parts.
†Retail prices index for UK; Consumer price index for G6.
‡Includes projections for 1987.

Sources: CSO *Economic Trends Annual Supplement*, 1988 edn; OECD *Main Economic Indicators*.

marked improvement compared with the 1970s. For the G6 average performance has continued to be worse than in the 1950s and 1960s.

A further sign of improved performance comes from a comparison of recent economic forecasts with the out-turn. There has been a persistent bias to the forecasts. The consensus has been that in the absence of policy changes output growth would slow down and inflation pick up. In practice we have experienced the combination of steady growth and a stable or slightly declining inflation rate.

A similar message of improving supply performance comes from examining errors in Treasury forecasts. In the 1970s the outcome for inflation and output tended to be worse than predicted. In the 1980s the pattern has been reversed (see Burns, 1986). Since 1984 money GDP has grown faster than expected relative to successive versions of the MTFS. Both higher output growth and higher inflation have contributed, but the higher growth of output has dominated the higher inflation rate.

One of the driving forces behind this better performance has been the improvement in productivity growth. Although there was a good deal of debate some years ago as to whether manufacturing productivity had quickened or whether it was a one-off phenomenon, there is greater acceptance now that there has been a sustained improvement in productivity growth. In the 1960s and early 1970s, manufacturing output per head rose by 3–4 per cent on average (see Table 20.10) but lagged distinctly behind growth in the G6 as a whole. Performance substantially deteriorated during the 1970s in line with the other major industrial countries but, since then, there has been a marked turnaround. Indeed, between 1979 and 1987, output per head rose on average more quickly than at any time since 1960, and – in marked contrast to that period – more rapidly than the average for the G6.

Industrial competitiveness has benefited from the improved productivity performance, despite the unexpectedly rapid growth of average earnings. Growth of unit labour costs has slowed substantially and, since 1979, unit labour costs for the whole economy have risen less than prices. Company profitability has therefore risen significantly, reversing the downward trend of the 1960s and 1970s.

Table 20.10   Manufacturing productivity: output per head.
Average annual percentage change

	UK	G6
1960–64	3.2	5.5
1964–68	3.6	5.9
1968–73	3.9	5.2
1973–79	0.7	3.0
1979–83	3.6	2.4
1983–87	4.5	3.0*

*Includes projection for 1987.

Sources: CSO *Economic Trends Annual Supplement*, 1988 edn (p. 112), OECD, IMF.

At the same time, there are signs of improvements in export performance. During the 1980s, UK exports of manufactures have maintained their share of world trade growth, putting an end to the trend decline of the 1960s and 1970s. Treasury forecasts have generally underestimated the strength of export growth, for given cost competitiveness and world trade. Table 20.11 compares export growth rates (goods and services) for the UK and G6. Between 1960 and 1980 exports of the G6 countries grew on average by 3 per cent a year faster than UK exports. Between 1983 and 1987 the growth of total UK exports was greater than that for the G6. Even excluding oil exports there has been a much better performance than in the past.

The interpretation of imports is less straightforward as it is necessary to take into account the growth of output and domestic demand. And perform-ance relative to model equations is difficult to judge. Modelling of imports

Table 20.11 Export Volumes (goods and services) of the UK and G6. Average annual percentage change

	UK	G6	UK–G6
1960–64	4.3	7.0	−2.7
1964–68	5.6	8.4	−2.8
1968–73	6.9 (6.8)	9.5	−2.6 (−2.7)
1973–79	4.3 (3.2)	6.0	−1.7 (−2.8)
1979–83	0.5 (−0.9)	3.0	−2.5 (−3.9)
1983–87	5.4 (5.8)	4.6*	0.8 (1.2)*
memo 1979–87	2.9 (2.4)	3.8*	−0.9 (−1.4)*
(Excluding oil in brackets)			

*Includes projection for 1987.

Sources: CSO *Economic Trends Annual Supplement*, 1988 edn. OECD *National Accounts 1953–69, National Accounts 1960–86*, and OECD *Economic Outlook* (December 1987).

has been very imprecise for many years. For example the Treasury model contains important and pronounced time trends in the equations which are necessarily difficult to project.

Table 20.12 compares the growth of the volume of imports of goods and services in the UK and the G6 as a whole. It also shows how the ratio of imports of goods and services to GDP has increased. For most of the period shown UK imports have grown less rapidly than for the G6 as a whole. However this reflected slower growth of output and import penetration

Table 20.12 Imports of goods and services of the UK and G6

| | Import volume | | Value of imports/GDP | |
| | UK | G6 | UK | G6 |
	(average percentage change)		*(average level)*	
1960–64	4.0	7.8	19	8
1964–68	4.6	9.6	19	8
1968–73	7.1	10.6	22	10
1973–79	2.2 (0)	4.4	28 (27)	14
1979–83	1.1 (2.9)	0.1	25 (24)	15
1983–87	6.6 (6.4)	8.1*	27 (27)	14*
1979–87	3.8 (4.6)	4.0*	26 (25)	15*
(Excluding oil in brackets)				

*Includes projection for 1987.

Sources: CSO, *Economic Trends Annual Supplement*, 1988 edn, OECD *National Accounts 1960–86*, OECD, *Economic Outlook* (December 1987).

increased more in the UK than in the G6 as a whole. Between 1979 and 1983 UK imports grew more rapidly in volume terms than for the G6 due in part to the improving terms of trade. In the past four years import volumes in the UK have once again grown less than for the G6 even though growth rates of output have been very similar. Expressed in value terms import penetration is much the same in 1983–87 as in 1973–79 for both the UK and the G6 as a whole.

This suggests that there is no clear message to be drawn about UK performance from import figures. The growth of import volumes and import penetration in value terms is not very different from what might have been expected from past behaviour. What we can conclude is that there has been no tendency for the improved export performance to be offset by worse import performance.

Taking the picture as a whole my own conclusion is that there is clear evidence of improved supply performance although so far it is impossible to quantify. The black spot has been unemployment. Employment has been rising since 1983 but it is only since July 1986 that unemployment has been falling. However, over the two years since then unemployment has fallen by over 750,000.

20.3 CONCLUSIONS

At the end of the 1970s it was decided to put into place a long-term stabilisation programme to defeat inflation. The MTFS was the framework for the commitment to financial discipline. That strategy, as it continues to be pursued today, is identifiably the same as it was at the outset. It has clearly evolved both in presentation and substance, most particularly in the technicalities of the assessment of monetary conditions. It would have been surprising if there had not been changes. But the strategy remains very much intact – the commitment to a nominal framework; the medium-term horizon; elimination of high levels of public sector borrowing; and the prominent role of monetary policy.

As expected the implementation of the strategy has created a favourable climate for economic growth. Measures taken in parallel to improve supply performance appear to have had an increasing effect. This combination of financial discipline and supply measures has led in recent years to vigorous and sustained output growth. It compares well with other G7 countries and the European economies in particular.

Acknowledgement

I am grateful to Stephen King for his assistance during the preparation of this chapter.

References

BURNS, T. (1986) 'The Interpretation and Use of Economic Predictions', *Proceedings of the Royal Society (London)*.

LAWSON, N. (1980) Speech to the Financial Times 1980 Euromarkets Conference (London), 21 January 1980.

Part XI

Conclusion

21 The Continuing Relevance of Keynes to Economic Policy

Walter Eltis

Six years after publication, half the citations there will ever be to an ordinary piece of economics will have appeared. The half life of the average economics article in an academic journal is a mere six years, and very little economics lasts fifty years. The fact that Keynes and Keynesian are part of our language after fifty years and that there is so much interest in present day interpretations of how relevant what he had to say is to our world is a testimonial to his greatness as an economist, and to the importance of his achievement. It is interesting to examine what happens to the economic classics after a long period. In 1826, fifty years after the publication of Adam Smith's *Wealth of Nations* there was a conference to assess its continuing significance and the participants agreed that Smith had been superseded by David Ricardo and that all kinds of errors in his work had been uncovered. But Smith's reputation rose in the 150 years from 1826 to 1976. It is chastening to bear this precedent in mind when we consider the assessments that the participants to this conference have made of the significance of Keynes's *General Theory* to economic policy after its first fifty years.

Unemployment has been far higher in the 1980s than in any previous postwar decade so the economic environment has moved closer to the one that persuaded Keynes to produce a theory to explain chronic underemployment. Because we once again have high unemployment, it is natural that policy makers and professional economists should wish to scrutinise Keynes's work extremely carefully. To the uninitiated it must appear that he was right and that the economic theorists of the 1970s who based powerful economic models on the supposition that markets clear and that governments have no role in the maintenance of high employment were mistaken.

It does not follow from the fact that we again have high unemployment that Keynes's explanation of how this can arise is still the appropriate one. There have been great changes in the world's advanced economies since 1936 so it is rather unlikely that the assumptions about the economic and financial environment on which Keynes based his theory will still be the most appropriate ones. But his theory is clearly a valuable point of departure for our efforts to explain unemployment and to find policies to reduce it today.

451

The distinguished participants to this conference have honoured Keynes by using his 1936 book as a starting point for their own contributions.

But those who are actually concerned with economic policy have moved a long way from him. There is an interesting correspondence between the contributions of Ernst Helmstädter, Member of the West German Council of Economic Experts since 1983, and Sir Terence Burns, Chief Economic Adviser to the United Kingdom government since 1980, and the opening statement by the Rt Hon Nigel Lawson who has been Chancellor of the Exchequer since 1983. All three are immediately responsible for practicalities and they are actually agreed that the principal object of fiscal policy is to create a stable tax structure which will help to produce an economic environment which is helpful to the supply-side of the economy, while excessive unemployment, if it exists, is attributable to macroeconomic considerations, which will often include inappropriately high real wage costs. This latter explanation of unemployment is precisely the one that Keynes was determined to refute in 1936, but fifty years later the British and German Treasuries and Finance Ministries are entirely unconvinced. In view of the success of German economic policy in achieving high growth with an inflation rate that has gradually been reduced to zero, the consistently non-Keynesian approach to economic policy formation that the German Council of Economic Experts has adopted since 1963, which Helmstädter outlines, deserves close attention. The almost identical United Kingdom approach which Burns describes has similarly proved compatible with seven years of uninterrupted growth and some downward pressure on inflation.

Support for a non-Keynesian approach to economic policy is reinforced by the very important article on the Italian economy by Giampaolo Galli and Rainer Masera of the Bank of Italy which outlines and discusses the embarrassments that Italy now suffers from a government debt to GNP ratio of more than 100 per cent which, according to their projections, is likely to double with the most favourable economic assumptions. With Italy's present debt to GNP ratio, almost 10 per cent of the Italian national income is required to pay interest on government debt and this neither promotes economic welfare in the manner of other elements of government expenditure, nor stimulates the supply side of the economy by contributing to the rewards of workers or companies. If Italy's government debt to GNP ratio rises to 200 per cent in the next fifteen years, it is likely that some 20 per cent of the national income will have to be paid to rentiers and therefore become unavailable to assist either production or social welfare. And if some future Italian government does not wish to continue to make this 20 per cent of the national income available to non-producers and non-welfare recipients, it will be driven to destroy the real value of government debt through a hyperinflation with untold social repercussions. That account which Galli and Masera set out brilliantly, describes the trap into which a country can be drawn by a persistent pursuit of Keynesian deficit financing policies. In his very helpful article on what Keynes actually said about economic policy, Nicholas Dimsdale makes it very clear that he would not have lent support to the Italian policy of running persistent budget deficits of more than 10 per cent of GNP. He recommended that the budget should be balanced over the cycle as a whole,[1] but since the Second World· War many Keynesians in contrast to Keynes himself have been · prepared to regard a persistent structural deficit as an acceptable element in Keynesian policies to maintain high employment.

Germany and the UK have avoided that trap by pursuing the policies which Helmstädter and Burns describe, but two of the articles with a UK authorship which are primarily concerned with macroeconomic policy are considerably more sympathetic to the practical use of fiscal expansion to reduce unemployment. Lord Peston, one of the most senior economic advisers to the British Labour Party, has provided a marvellously lucid account of the theory of fiscal policy with strong Keynesian elements. He sets out the case for fiscal reflation when unemployment is judged to be excessive, and explains how difficulties in financing government borrowing should not stand in its way. If a country's GNP can only be raised through spending financed by extra borrowing, either companies will be willing to borrow and spend in which case the momentum for expansion will come from the private sector, or else the market will prefer to lend to the government which will than have to incur the responsibility of borrowing without which there will be insufficient effective demand to permit high employment. He recommends that output and employment be raised, either by private or public borrowing until the Phillips curve begins to slope upwards steeply, at which point further expansion will involve severe inflationary difficulties. But Peston fails to address the consequences of an indefinite continuation of structural government borrowing on which Galli and Masera are so enlightening.

The other policy oriented supporter of a Keynesian approach is Bill Callaghan, the Head of Economic Research of the UK Trades Union Congress, who outlines the close connection between Keynes and the TUC in the 1930s when he and Ernest Bevin both sat on the Macmillan Committee where they were closely allied. Callaghan criticises sharply the view that unemployment depends mainly on the level of real wages, and the articles of those contributors who believe that high employment will be achieved via the operation of market forces without government intervention.

Most of the contributors do not of course have the direct and immediate concern with policy questions of Burns, Callaghan, Helmstädter, Masera and Peston. They are concerned to elucidate, clarify, update and assess the underlying economic theory on which policy decisions are based and they have examined the continuing relevance of Keynes's contribution to some of the issues which are central to modern economics.

The first main theoretical issue which the contributors address is whether market forces can generally be expected to produce high unemployment, or whether, as Keynes believed, there are likely to be persistent market failures which create a general need for macroeconomic intervention. Michael Artis and Bennett McCallum address this question, and Artis provides a powerful account of the Keynesian case that there are significant wage rigidities which preclude a downward adjustment of money wages if that is what is needed to sustain high employment. There are, of course, also various nominal and real price rigidities and Artis sets out the microeconomic reasons for their prevalence, while Robin Matthews and Alex Bowen assess the actual impact on unemployment of real wage rigidities in the 1970s and the 1980s. If as a consequence of these rigidities markets fail to clear or else clear very slowly, there is a case for government intervention of various kinds to arrive at acceptable levels of employment somewhat more quickly. McCallum can find no logical basis for such rigidities (though he acknowledges that they sometimes exist) and he therefore believes that there is no case for piecemeal macroeconomic intervention.

He prefers instead to put macropolicy on to an autopilot aimed to produce a steady rate of growth of nominal GNP, equal to the long-term rate of growth of productive capacity. This would then be compatible with steady expansion at the economy's natural rate of growth with zero inflation. The means he proposes to control nominal GNP is strict control of the rate of growth of the monetary base, and his autopilot will immediately reduce the growth of this if nominal GNP starts to accelerate, and increase it if nominal GNP slows. McCallum's control mechanisms will only permit continuous growth at zero inflation if there truly are no money wage rigidities so that wage increases fall off until the inflation of unit wage costs declines to zero and so becomes compatible with high employment at stable prices. If economic theory says that there are no rigidities, then it must be right to base policy on the supposition that there are none, but as McCallum rightly says, there are difficulties in the way of ascertaining whether his policy rule would actually produce the result he expects because, 'To determine whether this rule would indeed keep nominal GNP close to the desired growth path, one must experiment with the economy or with a model. The former possibility is too expensive and the latter suffers from the absence of any reliable model.' McCallum's rule that the rate of growth of nominal GNP should be held down by means of strict control of a narrow money aggregate resembles extremely closely one of the central features of the UK's Medium-Term Financial Strategy, so Britain may provide some of the evidence that McCallum seeks. It could be held that UK inflation has undoubtedly fallen with reductions in the rate of growth of nominal GNP (and some of the data is presented in Burns's article) but there was also a considerable adjustment cost in the early years because the pace of wage increases only fell when unemployment became very high, so the application of a formula resembling McCallum's to the UK brings out the evidence that here at any rate there are wage rigidities of the kind that Artis describes.

Patrick Minford seeks to explain these rigidities and he reminds us that Keynes stated very clearly in the 1930s that wages will not adjust in the manner required to produce high employment if unemployment benefits are unduly close to the wages that workers receive. There are further passages which Dimsdale quotes which support the contention that this well known position of Minford's was also held by Keynes. Minford provides a clear account of the significance of the influence of unemployment benefits for the equilibrium level of employment. But Stephen Nickell reminds us that there will be circumstances where there will be high unemployment, whatever the level of wages, for these are not the sole determinant of employment. There will be circumstances where lower real or money wages will significantly assist a move towards higher employment and others where they will not, for the interconnection between wages and employment is complex.

We come therefore to the central policy implication of Keynes's analysis, namely that there will be circumstances where changes in wage behaviour will not suffice to produce high employment, and where policy to raise effective demand will also be needed. Whether this is most effectively influenced by fiscal or by monetary expansion has become controversial. John Flemming reminds us that in a good deal of the *General Theory* interest rates are, in effect, fixed, while Dimsdale explains that while Keynes on several occasions regarded a lowering of the long-term rate of interest as the ideal way of expanding the economy, believed that this would be extremely difficult to achieve. Terence Mills and Geoffrey Wood underline how very difficult it is to reduce interest rates by showing that the theoretical *General Theory* means of achieving this, repeated increases in the money supply, appears actually to have the opposite effect: they present evidence that increases in the rate of growth of the money supply have generally been associated with higher rates of interest in the UK. The difficulties in the way of using low interest rates to stimulate economic expansion are underlined further by the strong case that Flemming presents that interest rates are a desirable element in policy to control inflation via their influence on the exchange rate, a policy stance which is not far from David Currie's.

Because he judged that interest rates would be very difficult to reduce to the full extent required, Keynes turned to fiscal expansion via extra public works, etc., as a more practical second best means of expanding effective demand. But even the impact of extra public expenditure upon real aggregate demand – the central Keynesian policy plank – has become controversial. Sir Alan Walters argues powerfully that in the UK after 1956 the real rate of monetary expansion has had far more powerful effects upon aggregate demand than changes in the government's fiscal stance. The precise nature of the fiscal stance and how this may be corrected for inflation and the cycle is carefully examined by Marcus Miller and Alan Sutherland and there is no significant disagreement between them and Walters (on this occasion) about whether fiscal policy in particular years was loose or tight. Walters argues that in the moves into recession and the subsequent recoveries in 1956–8, 1973–5 and 1979–82 the development of narrow money determined the course of the cycle while fiscal policy was often working in the opposite direction. The extreme case for his argument was the huge move into recession in 1979 when real monetary growth was sharply reduced but fiscal expansion continued, and the recovery of output which began in 1981 when the budget was actually tightened by 7 per cent of GNP on a cyclically adjusted basis, but output none the less expanded because real M1 began to grow. Currie agrees with Walters that monetary expansion has powerful effects but questions whether control of any particular monetary aggregate (such as Walters's preferred non-interest bearing M1) would ensure a smooth expansion of demand. He emphasises that monetary policy and the fiscal stance must be compatible, with which Walters is in broad agreement, but Currie would prefer to apply cyclical corrections to the fiscal stance so that the budget would automatically move into larger deficit in recession, while Walters would not wish to adjust the deficit in this way.

The efficacy of fiscal expansion in raising demand is examined anew by Alan Budd and three colleagues from the London Business School. Until recently, the London Business School has taken Walters's view that monetary expansion is far more effective than fiscal reflation, and it aroused considerable interest at the Conference in view of the respect with which the LBS's work is widely regarded, that Budd and his colleagues now agree with Keynes that fiscal policy can have powerful effects. They say that until recently they had taken the view that fiscal reflation would not have a significant impact on output and employment but as a consequence of changing their model slightly they now believe that fiscal reflation can have the quite important effects they set out.

But will the increase in employment last? Since 1968, when Milton Friedman initiated the concept of the natural rate of unemployment, there has been a school in economics which has taken the view that the unemployment rate will tend towards an equilibrium or natural rate which is not significantly influenced by macroeconomic considerations: any attempt to get away from that equilibrium rate would lead to rapidly accelerating wage inflation. Minford is a notable supporter of that point of view, but six of the papers refer to a rather interesting new development in the subject which gives more scope for Keynesian reflationary policies and that is the concept of hysteresis. The suggestion in the hysteresis literature is that a society can become accustomed to any unemployment rate that chance events produce. For instance, if there is a major recession, then as effective demand is reduced, unemployment will rise sharply, and after a time people will become used to being unemployed, and social attitudes will alter so that to be unemployed will become more acceptable, and the economy will reach a temporary equilibrium in which it appears to be locked into far higher unemployment than before. The counter example would be the Second

World War where, because an enormous demand for labour was created and every able bodied person was found something useful to do, there was no belief that a significant number of people needed to be unemployed for twenty years after the war, and there was no social culture which took a significant fraction of unemployment for granted. The unemployment rate averaged 2 per cent from 1945 to 1965.

The hysteresis literature which is at an early stage leaves considerable scope for a Keynesian approach to the creation of employment, because it signifies that whatever high unemployment rate an economy has temporarily settled into as a result of adverse shocks is in principle reducible, for with favourable shocks or stimuli it should be possible for the society to become accustomed to a lower rate of unemployment once again. There is widespread agreement that the hysteresis literature deserves a great deal of careful attention because it gives a society that has high unemployment opportunities to reduce it. If the hysteresis hypothesis is well founded, reflation of the kind the London Business School sets out could have lasting effects on employment.

But would such policies have inflationary effects which could undermine their adoption? If rising demand and employment have a tendency to raise the inflation rate, political judgements would have to be made as to whether the price that had to be paid for cutting unemployment was too high. That fiscal expansion will raise employment is something that has never been doubted by Keynesians but they have been concerned that it might well begin to raise the inflation rate long before the economy reached a high level of employment. It was Keynes's own view that:

> in general, supply price will increase as output from a given equipment is increased. Thus increasing output will be associated with rising prices, apart from any change in the wage-unit (*General Theory*, p. 300)

As it is generally agreed that the wage-unit (i.e. money wage rates) will tend to rise too as employment increases, it is to be feared that fiscal expansion will doubly raise prices, both because it raises wages and in addition because it raises profit margins. This general propensity for fiscal reflation to increase the inflation rate is set out most helpfully in the paper by Christopher Taylor of the Bank of England. Peter Sinclair reminds us however that while we should accept Taylor's presumption and Keynes's own that any expansion of demand will tend to produce a price level which is higher than it otherwise would be, there are further possible effects which might counteract this influence. If fiscal expansion is achieved by lowering taxes, this might well have a favourable impact upon wage behaviour and the price level. If fiscal expansion is combined with tight monetary policy as in the United States in 1980–83, the combined effect of a loose budget and high interest rates might well be to raise the exchange rate, at least for a time, and so produce a lower domestic price level (though this will rise again if the exchange rate subsequently collapses as the dollar has in 1986–8). Fiscal reflation combined with either of those countervailing influences might have a net impact on the price level that is actually favourable.

In the discussion of the paper by Budd and his colleagues at the Conference, it was proposed that if a particular policy mix which can be derived from the information in their paper is followed, then the inflationary effects of fiscal expansion could be rather slight. The combination of policies suggested was a simultaneous increase in public expenditure and in income tax which could then expand the economy with a balanced budget and no increase in borrowing.[2] That would avoid the difficulties with a growing debt to national income ratio from which Italy is so obviously suffering after fifteen years of large structural deficits. The London Business School equations suggest that this particular balanced budget policy mix would reduce unemployment with no significant impact in inflation. If we accept that this line of argument is well founded, the question of political choice again arises, because whether it is worth acquiescing in an increase in income tax in order to cut unemployment is a matter for the electorate to decide.

There is, however, considerable doubt as to whether a balanced increase in public expenditure and income tax would have a zero impact on inflation. It is to be noted that this corresponds to neither of Sinclair's principal cases where fiscal reflation might lead to a lower price level. His countervailing influences include *lower* income tax rates which might reduce money wages, and not higher taxes which can be expected to increase them. Sinclair also attaches weight to the possibility that the higher interest rates associated with fiscal reflation financed by borrowing might raise the exchange rate, but much of this effect would be blunted if higher government spending was accompanied by higher taxation. The LBS authors' belief that these particular reflationary policies should not raise the inflation rate therefore receives little support from Sinclair: rather the contrary, because according to his argument, higher taxation should increase both money wages and inflation. There is also a good deal of published work which finds that increases in personal taxation are associated with faster wage inflation.[3] If there is a tendency for workers to pass on any part of an income tax increase so that their real net of tax incomes fall by less than the full amount of the tax, the money wages that companies have to pay will become higher than they otherwise would be, which will lead to some increase in final product prices. For this reason, income tax increases will raise the price level unless the entire increase in taxation is absorbed by the labour force, and there are no grounds to expect this in view of the statistical evidence from several countries which suggests the contrary.

If this evidence is well founded, the long-term implications of a balanced budget expansion in public expenditure and taxation will be even more discouraging because the adverse effects will not be confined to a higher price level. If the entire income tax increase fails to be absorbed by labour, then the real cost of employing a worker will become higher after taxes are increased, and at that higher cost fewer workers will be employed whenever the economy is actually in long-term equilibrium, so the eventual impact of fiscal reflation financed by an income tax increase could actually be to reduce output and employment.

There is therefore a sharp dichotomy between the short-term impact on demand of a balanced budget expansion in public expenditure and taxation which will be favourable, and its long-term impact on the equilibrium level of output and employment which will be unfavourable. Budd and his co-authors from the London Business School have considered only the short-term effect of these policies so, as with all demand-oriented economic models, they have arrived at a result which is broadly in line with Keynesian theory.

Budd's former colleague at the London Business School (until 1980 when he became Chief Economic Adviser) Burns, is in contrast concerned about the possible adverse effects on supply of higher levels of taxation. Where two economies with similar technological and productive opportunities and an equally skilled labour force are both in long-term macroeconomic equilibrium, and one has a higher level of public expenditure and taxation than the other, its companies will generally have to pay more for labour and its workers will at the same time receive less (for there will be larger tax 'wedge' between the wage costs that companies incur and the wages that remain in workers' paypackets) so with conventional assumptions about the demand and supply curves for labour, equilibrium output and employment will be lower.

In the long term there is therefore a reverse-balanced budget multiplier theorem which states that a balanced expansion in public expenditure and taxation will reduce equilibrium employment and GNP. It is evident from the articles by Burns and Helmstädter that UK economic policy since 1979 and German policy since 1963 has placed more weight on the line of argument that leads to this reverse-balanced budget multiplier, than to the short-term Keynesian balanced budget multiplier which predicts employment benefits from extra public expenditure financed by taxation.

It is an interesting question whether it will be judged right to take advantage of these short-term employment and output benefits if an inflationary price needs to be paid. The economics profession is very much aware of the compensation test that economic changes can be judged worthwhile if the gainers increase their incomes sufficiently to enable them to compensate the losers and still be better off. Any change that raises real GNP must pass this test for with a higher national income there will always be more gainers than losers. This is one reason why until recently most UK economists have viewed with bewilderment any suggestion that the potential output gains which Keynesian reflation can confer when the economy is in recession should be sacrificed because these policies might also raise inflation. If it actually reduces output in the long term, that could be regarded as a good reason for abstaining from reflationary policy, but what if it raises output and also has some tendency to increase the inflation rate? Could this higher inflation rate actually have sufficient adverse effects on economic welfare and efficiency to justify a failure to take advantage of the opportunities to produce more which is offered by Keynesian reflation?

A number of economic issues associated with inflation are very helpfully discussed in the paper by Matthews and Bowen who suggest that if the inflation rate accelerates, each percentage point increase may raise the number of bankruptcies by 6 per cent, Stock Exchange asset valuation ratios will fall and there will be a number of other adverse supply-side effects which will actually reduce employment. This will clearly add to the long-term damage to employment which a decision to benefit from the short-term advantages of Keynesian policies could entail. In addition to these possible adverse long-term effects, it is beginning to appear that there may be a political case against Keynesian reflationary policies if they have a tendency to raise the inflation rate. The Chancellor of the Exchequer makes it very clear in his opening statement that, in his judgement, the electorate does not take kindly to policies which raise the rate of inflation. In fact no British government which has significantly raised the rate of inflation since the Second World war has been re-elected, while four governments which have not raised inflation or have managed to bring it down have achieved re-election; so it may indeed be that the electorate votes out governments which increase the inflation rate.

If that is in fact the case, it would be possible to take the rather simple view that when Keynesian policies were universally adopted in the United Kingdom, politicians had the belief that the achievement of low unemployment was far more important than the containment of inflation. In the 1960s and the 1970s the electorate reacted by voting out a succession of governments which presided over an increase in the inflation rate, while, as Matthews and Bowen explain, the acceleration of inflation in the 1970s discredited the use of Keynesian reflationary policies to limit unemployment in several countries. There is therefore a widespread belief today that the inflation price of fiscal expansion is not worth paying. Perhaps the most damaging scenario is a zig-zag political course in which one government pursues Keynesian policies which raise the rate of inflation and a successor government is then elected to reduce inflation again. Inflation may then end up where it started but there will be an enormous loss of GNP when that sequence takes place because the gain in GNP when effective demand is expanded by the first government in order to raise employment but which also raises inflation is far less than the subsequent loss of GNP when inflation has to be brought down again by the next government. The money wage rigidities which are so helpfully explained in Artis's paper make it very clear that the extra unemployment required to lower inflation is very great. Hence whenever Britain follows a cycle in which one government puts inflation up and the next pulls it down again, there will be a significant loss of national income in the aggregate because unemployment will need to be high for many years to overcome the wage rigidities which stand in the way of slower inflation.

Does that mean that we are locked in and cannot pursue Keynesian policies because these are bound to have an inflationary impact to which the electorate will react unfavourably? It is in fact possible to conclude on a rather more helpful note, for the hysteresis literature suggests that the upward impact on inflation when employment is raised is not inescapable, for a country's 'equilibrium' unemployment rate, or NAIRU, will tend to adjust to any actual unemployment rate which a society becomes accustomed to. The problem is to persuade a society to adjust to a lower unemployment rate. To achieve this, the actual unemployment rate must be reduced which Keynesian reflationary policies can bring about, at least in the short term, and these will then need to be reinforced with micro-policies to bring some of the long-term unemployed who have become accustomed to being unemployed back into the labour market. Such micro policies which include retraining, encouragements to mobility, job counselling, the provision of better information about vacancies, short-term employment opportunities in public schemes and improved administration of the provision of unemployment benefits can get some of the long-term unemployed back into permanent employment. If employment can be raised in a way that brings the long-term unemployed back into the mainstream labour market, which is now very much an objective of UK government policy and of a great deal of academic thinking (and of Taylor's paper) expansion can be achieved without the inflationary pressures that would be experienced in the absence of these microeconomic policies. There is a further consideration which must be borne in mind. It cannot be true that in general all economic expansion which significantly reduces unemployment must raise inflation. In the UK in 1981–8, economic expansion has been accelerating and unemployment has been falling since 1986, but inflation has been broadly stable. The government has been using microeconomic policies of the kinds described to bring the long-term unemployed back into the mainstream labour force, and long-term unemployment has been falling about as fast as total unemployment. There is likely to be a limit to the speed with which such favourable structural changes in the labour force can be achieved, so there will be limits to the rate at which the long-term unemployment associated with hysteresis can be reduced, but within those limits expansion which gradually reduces unemployment need not be inflationary provided that appropriate micropolicies are pursued at the same time.

The UK's non-inflationary expansion in 1981–8 has had a strong supply-side element, and the budget deficit has been reduced from 6 per cent of GNP in 1980–1 to approximate balance (excluding privatisation proceeds) in

1987–8 so the growth of the economy has owed nothing to fiscal reflation. But the real money supply has advanced very fast indeed, by more than 5 per cent per annum according to Walters's preferred measure, so the government has made some use of macroeconomic monetary policy to reflate the economy.

The fact that a sustained non-inflationary expansion which substantially reduced unemployment was possible means that this may also be achievable with the support of fiscal reflation (together with compatible real monetary growth) if appropriate labour market policies are adopted at the same time. A balanced budget expansion may not be the ideal fiscal way to reflate the economy because of the possible impact of rising tax rates upon wage and price inflation, and fiscal reflation financed by borrowing risks adding to inflation because of the difficulties associated with financing persistent deficits and the possibility that these will in due course be monetised.

The scope for Keynesian fiscal reflation may therefore be limited to taking advantage of a small stable cyclically corrected deficit as an element in policies to reduce unemployment in periods of recession, along the lines so helpfully set out by Miller and Sutherland: a tolerance of such deficits was really all that Keynes himself actually recommended, as Dimsdale makes clear. A modest fiscal reinforcement to the economy's natural recovery forces need be no more inflationary than the substantial real monetary expansion that has been so important in the UK since 1981. What we know today that was less clearly understood in 1936 is that such 'Keynesian' reflationary stimuli need to be accompanied by appropriate microeconomic labour market policies, so as to limit the upward pressure on wage inflation.

A problem that remains is that if only a few countries in the world pursue such policies, their imports are liable to expand far faster than their exports, with the result that these governments' reflationary policies may need to be reversed in order to bring their balance of payments under control.

Max Corden, Helmstädter and Currie address some of the problems which must be solved if a co-ordinated expansion which will permit all countries' exports to advance in line with imports is to be achieved. It will be evident from a careful reading of their articles that no more than international discussion to achieve consistency between the exchange rate policies of the various countries is acually to be hoped for in the 1980s. Germany in particular regards Keynesian policies as entirely irrelevant to the amelioration of unemployment and there is no way in which Germany will agree to a faster rate of monetary or fiscal expansion than domestic considerations call for.

The German approach to employment creation is entirely supply oriented and Helmstädter's emphasis on the need for a country's industry to create new products where value-added will be high in relation to wage costs points to an approach to employment creation which individual countries acting alone can adopt without foreign exchange risks. Successful new products perform well enough in world trade to allow an economy which develops them to expand employment and increase exports in line with imports in the same manner as a successful region within a national economy which can prosper, even when its parent economy is in recession.

The UK's post-1981 recovery owes a good deal to successful supply-side developments. For an economy which fails to achieve success in the development of new products, carefully arranged demand corrections with compatible monetary and fiscal expansion in order to ameliorate adverse cyclical influences (which was really all that Keynes advocated) offers the possibility of modest potential gains to economic welfare which a country should surely take advantage of.

Notes

1. See also N. H. Dimsdale, 'Keynes on British Budgetary Policy, 1914–46', in M. J. Boskin, J. S. Flemming and S. Gorini (eds), *Private Saving and Public Debt* (Blackwell, 1987), for a more detailed account of Keynes's approach to deficit financing.
2. The effects that Alan Budd and his colleagues predict from a balanced budget increase in public expenditure and income tax can be derived from Tables 5.3 and 5.4 of their simulations.
3. The UK and international evidence on the impact of personal taxation on wages together with an account of the very large journal literature is summarised in, Anthonie Knoester and Nico van der Windt, 'Real Wages and Taxation in Ten OECD Countries', *Oxford Bulletin of Economics and Statistics*, vol. 49, 1, 1987.

Index